W9-BJZ-208

Homes
Today and Tomorrow

Sixth Edition

Ruth F. Sherwood

**Glencoe
McGraw-Hill**

New York, New York   Columbus, Ohio   Woodland Hills, California   Peoria, Illinois

Teacher Reviewers

Diane DuFour-Wong, M.S.
Family and Consumer Sciences Teacher
G. Holmes Braddock Senior High School
Miami, Florida

Marcia Elizandro, M.Ed.
Family and Consumer Sciences Teacher
Arlington High School
Arlington, Texas

Joyce Courville Hayes, M.S.
Family and Consumer Sciences Teacher
Southeast Raleigh High School
Raleigh, North Carolina

Lori Miller-Goff
Family and Consumer Sciences Instructor
Oak Hill High School
Converse, Indiana

Patricia Shumate, M.Ed.
Family and Consumer Sciences Department Chair
York Community High School
Elmhurst, Illinois

Sarah Stevens, M.S.
Family and Consumer Sciences Teacher
Lufkin High School
Lufkin, Texas

Susan C. Teelin, M.A.
Family and Consumer Sciences Teacher
Camden High School
Camden, New York

Carolyn Blair Wysocki, M.Ed.
Former Interior Design Instructor
Northern Virginia Community College
Manassas, Virginia

Technical Reviewers

Beverly Ujcich
Space Planner
Peoria, Illinois

Susan Winchip, Ph.D.
Associate Professor
Illinois State University
Normal, Illinois

Joseph L. Wysocki, Ph.D.
National Program Leader
Housing and Indoor Environments
USDA
Washington, D.C.

Glencoe/McGraw-Hill

A Division of The **McGraw·Hill** *Companies*

Copyright ©2002, 1997, 1996, 1990 by Glencoe/McGraw-Hill. Previous copyrights by
Ruth F. Sherwood. All rights reserved. Except as permitted under the United States
Copyright Act, no part of this publication may be reproduced or distributed in any
form or by any means, or stored in a database or retrieval system, without prior written
permission of the publisher.

Send all inquiries to:
Glencoe/McGraw-Hill
3008 W. Willow Knolls Drive
Peoria, Illinois 61614-1083

ISBN 0-07-825144-3 (Student Edition)

Printed in the United States of America

9   071   06

Contents in Brief

Chapter	

UNIT 1: HOMES ARE FOR PEOPLE

1   Housing Is a Universal Need.....16
2   Housing and Society.....36
3   The Impact of Technology.....56
4   Careers in Housing and Interior Environments.....78

UNIT 2: ARCHITECTURAL DESIGN

5   Early Homes.....106
6   Homes from the Eighteenth Century to Today.....122
7   Designing Homes for Today and Tomorrow.....148

UNIT 3: MAKING HOUSING DECISIONS

8   Choosing a Place to Live.....172
9   Renting versus Buying.....190
10   Renting a Home.....206
11   Buying a Home.....224

UNIT 4: UNDERSTANDING CONSTRUCTION

12   The Basics of Construction.....250
13   Interior Construction.....278
14   Housing, Landscaping, and the Environment.....304

UNIT 5: USING DESIGN

15   The Elements of Design.....334
16   Color and the Design Process.....350
17   The Principles of Design.....368

UNIT 6: PLANNING INTERIOR ENVIRONMENTS

18   Developing a Design Plan.....388
19   Choosing Backgrounds.....410
20   Recognizing Furniture Styles.....436
21   Selecting Furniture.....458
22   Choosing Lighting and Accessories.....480
23   Completing and Presenting the Design.....500

UNIT 7: DESIGNS FOR LIVING

24   Kitchens, Laundry Areas, and Baths.....526
25   Home Offices and Storage Spaces.....558
26   Home Safety and Security.....576
27   Home Maintenance.....598
28   Remodeling and Renovating.....622

Table of Contents

Unit 1: Homes Are for People

Chapter 1
Housing Is a Universal Need.....16

The Development of Housing.....18
Housing to Fit Human Needs.....22
Housing and Individual Needs.....26
Challenges for Tomorrow.....30
    What Influences Design? Universal Design—
      Versatility for All Abilities.....28
    Career Close-Up Usability Engineer.....32

Chapter 2
Housing and Society.....36

How Culture Influences Housing.....38
Societal Trends that Affect Housing.....42
The Government's Role.....47
    Nonresidential Applications Americans with Disabilities Act—
      Impact on Public Environments.....49
    Career Close-Up Relocation Specialist.....52

Chapter 3
The Impact of Technology.....56

The Technology Revolution.....58
Materials and Construction Technology.....59
Technology in the Home.....68
    Nonresidential Applications Skyscrapers—How High
      Can They Go?.....60
    What Influences Design? These Walls Can Talk.....72
    Career Close-Up Electronic Home Systems Specialist.....74
    *A Visual Guide to...*Systems-Built Homes.....67

Chapter 4
Careers in Housing and Interior Environments.....78

Getting to Know Yourself.....80
Learning about Careers.....82
Developing Your Career Plan.....83
Owning Your Own Business.....86
Finding a Job.....87

On the Job.....92
Careers in Housing and Interiors.....97
   Consumer Sense Judging Post-Secondary
     Training Programs.....85
   Career Close-Up Ergonomic Designer.....100

Unit 2: Architectural Design

Chapter 5
*E*arly Homes.....106

Links from the Past.....108
The Growth of Traditional Styles 109
The Early American Period, 1640-1720....110
   Consumer Sense Living in a Historic District.....111
   Career Close-Up Preservationist.....118

Chapter 6
*H*omes from the Eighteenth Century to Today.....122

Understanding Period Housing Styles.....124
The 18th Century.....125
The 19th Century.....130
The Early 20th Century.....135
The Mid 20th Century to Today.....140
Influences on Housing.....143
   Nonresidential Applications Frank Lloyd Wright
     and Commercial Design.....138
   Career Close-Up Architect.....144

Chapter 7
*D*esigning Homes for Today and Tomorrow.....148

Developing Communities.....150
Housing Reflects Changing Needs.....157
Designing Functional Interiors.....158
What's Happening in Housing Design?.....164
   Nonresidential Applications Planned Communities—More
     Than Just Homes.....156
   Career Close-Up Urban Planner.....166
   A Visual Guide to...Cluster Homes and
     Zero-Lot-Line Homes.....154
   A Visual Guide to...Activity Zones in a Home.....159
   A Visual Guide to...Comparing Floor Plans.....162

Unit 3: Making Housing Decisions

Chapter 8

Choosing a Place to Live.....172

Making Housing Decisions.....174
Influences on Housing Decisions.....175
Choosing a Location.....177
Assessing Community Services.....181
Housing Alternatives.....183
The Choice Is Yours.....185
  What Influences Design? Developers Gauge
    the Market.....177
  Career Close-Up Real Estate Agent.....186

Chapter 9

Renting versus Buying.....190

Renting: Pros and Cons.....192
Buying: Pros and Cons.....193
A Closer Look at Costs.....196
What Can You Spend on Housing?.....200
Deciding to Rent or Buy.....201
  Consumer Sense Condominium and
    Cooperative Ownership.....195
  Career Close-Up Mortgage Loan Officer.....202

Chapter 10

Renting a Home.....206

Selecting Rental Housing.....208
Tenant Rights and Responsibilities.....215
Sharing Housing.....217
Feeling at Home.....219
  Consumer Sense Planning a Move.....211
  Career Close-Up Resident Manager.....220

Chapter 11

Buying a Home.....224

Financial Planning: The First Step.....226
Understanding Financing.....228
Deciding What to Look For.....231
Understanding Resale Value.....234
The Home-Buying Process.....236
  Consumer Sense Special Financing Arrangements.....229
  Career Close-Up Model Home Designer.....244
  *A Visual Guide to...*Finding the Trouble Spots.....240

Unit 4: Understanding Construction

Chapter 12

The Basics of Construction. 250

Understanding Construction. 252
Planning the Housing Site. 253
Architectural Drawings. 256
The Basic Structure. 258
Finishing the Exterior. 263
  What Influences Design? Adapting to the Lay of the Land. 254
  Career Close-Up Roofer. 274
  A Visual Guide to...Basement Construction. 259
  A Visual Guide to...Slab Foundations. 260
  A Visual Guide to...Floor Framing. 262
  A Visual Guide to...Wall Framing. 263
  A Visual Guide to...Ceiling and Roof Framing. 264
  A Visual Guide to...Windows: Parts and Styles. 271

Chapter 13

Interior Construction. 278

The Inner Workings. 280
Electric Wiring. 281
Plumbing. 284
Heating the Home. 287
Cooling and Ventilation. 292
Finishing the Interior. 294
From the Inside Out. 299
  Consumer Sense Checking the Panel Box When
    the Lights Go Out. 282
  Career Close-Up Electrician's Apprentice. 300
  A Visual Guide to...Heating Systems. 288
  A Visual Guide to...Active Ventilation Systems. 293

Chapter 14

Housing, Landscaping, and
  the Environment. 304

Housing and Resources Management. 306
Using Energy Efficiently. 307
Using Water Wisely. 318
Using Building Materials Wisely. 319
Outdoor Living. 321
Landscaping—The Finishing Touch. 323
You and the Environment. 327
  Consumer Sense ENERGY STAR Homes. 314
  Nonresidential Applications Energy Conservation Practices
    in Commercial Buildings. 317
  Career Close-Up Landscape Architect. 328
  A Visual Guide to...Solar Heating Systems. 312
  A Visual Guide to...Landscape Planning. 324

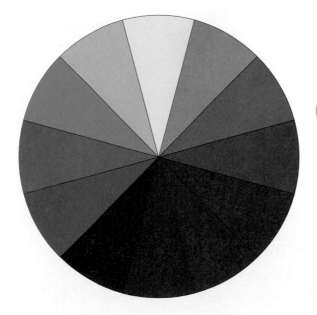

Unit 5: Using Design

Chapter 15

The Elements of Design. 334

Blueprint for Success. 336
Space. 337
Line. 339
Form. 340
Texture. 342
Color. 345
Using Design Elements. 345
　　Consumer Sense Adding Texture to Surfaces. 343
　　Career Close-Up Space Planner. 346
　　A Visual Guide to...How Texture Affects
　　　　Apparent Color. 344

Chapter 16

Color and the Design Process. 350

The Magic of Color. 352
Components of Color. 354
Color Schemes. 358
Color Scheme Success. 362
　　Nonresidential Applications Color Choices—
　　　　More Than Meets the Eye. 356
　　Career Close-Up Color Specialist. 364
　　A Visual Guide to...The Color Wheel. 355
　　A Visual Guide to...Common Color Schemes. 358

Chapter 17

The Principles of Design. 368

Proportion. 370
Scale. 373
Balance. 376
Rhythm. 377
Emphasis. 379
Unity and Variety. 380
Applying Design Principles. 381
　　What Influences Design? From Math to Mozart—
　　　　"Golden Rules" of Proportion. 372
　　Nonresidential Applications Scale—A Principle of Design
　　　　that Can Inspire. 375
　　Career Close-Up Visual Merchandiser. 382

Unit 6: Planning Interior Environments

Chapter 18

Developing a Design Plan.....388

Good Design Requires Planning.....390
Beginning the Design Process......392
Step 1: Identify the Project.....393
Step 2: Assess Client Characteristics.....395
Step 3: Analyze the Environment.....396
Step 4: Develop a Preliminary Budget.....401
Step 5: Compile a Design Resource File.....404
The Next Steps.....405
   Consumer Sense Working with an Interior Designer.....394
   Career Close-Up Interior Designer.....406
   A Visual Guide to...Scale Drawings.....400

Chapter 19

Choosing Backgrounds.....410

The Role Backgrounds Play.....412
Textiles in the Home.....415
Floor Coverings.....419
Wall Coverings.....422
Ceilings.....426
Window Coverings.....427
   Nonresidential Applications Public and
      Private Choices—Backgrounds for Hotels.....414
   Career Close-Up Textile Specialist.....432
   A Visual Guide to...Basic Weaves.....418
   A Visual Guide to...Carpeting Texture.....421
   A Visual Guide to...Window Treatments.....428

Chapter 20

Recognizing Furniture Styles.....436

Changing Styles.....438
Understanding Furniture Styles.....439
Designs that Last.....440
Colonial Period, 1600-1780.....441
Postcolonial Period, 1780-1840.....445
Victorian Period, 1840-1900.....447
Modern Period, 1901-Present.....448
   What Influences Design? Asian Influences on Design.....443
   Career Close-Up Furniture Restorer.....454
   A Visual Guide to...Dining Chairs Through Time.....452

Chapter 21

*S*electing Furniture.....458

Furniture Materials.....460
Basic Furniture Construction.....465
Shopping for Furniture.....473
Caring for Furniture.....475
   Consumer Sense Choosing Fabrics for Furniture.....471
   What Influences Design? People and Furniture on the Move.....474
   Career Close-Up Furniture Showroom Salesperson.....476
   A Visual Guide to...Signs of Quality in Case Goods.....465
   A Visual Guide to...Common Wood Furniture Joints.....466
   A Visual Guide to...Signs of Quality in Upholstered Furniture.....469

Chapter 22

*C*hoosing Lighting and Accessories.....480

Lighten Up.....482
Accessories.....490
   Nonresidential Applications Lighting in Retail Stores—A Means
     to Sell Merchandise.....487
   Career Close-Up Lighting Specialist.....496
   A Visual Guide to...Structural Lighting.....485

Chapter 23

*C*ompleting and Presenting the Design.....500

Step 6: Plan Use of Space.....502
Step 7: Choose a Style and Color Scheme.....509
Step 8: Select Backgrounds, Furniture, Lighting, and Accessories.....511
Step 9: Present the Design.....513
Step 10: Modify and Implement the Design.....518
   Consumer Sense What to Look for in Interior Design Software.....507
   Career Close-Up CAD Specialist for Interior Design.....520
   A Visual Guide to...Elevations and Floor Plans.....506
   A Visual Guide to...Pictorial Drawings.....514
   A Visual Guide to...Renderings.....516

Unit 7: Designs for Living

Chapter 24

*K*itchens, Laundry Areas, and Baths.....526

Planning Kitchens.....528
Choosing Major Appliances.....539
Planning Laundry Areas.....546
Planning Bathrooms.....548
Low-Cost Updates.....553
   Consumer Sense Choosing Energy-Efficient Appliances.....540
   Career Close-Up Kitchen Planner.....554
   A Visual Guide to...Kitchen Layout Options.....532
   A Visual Guide to...Universal Design Features in Kitchens.....538

Chapter 25

Home Offices and Storage Spaces. 558

Home Offices. 560
Designing a Home Office. 562
The Storage Challenge. 566
Planning Storage. 568
Organizing Your Closet. 570
    What Influences Design? The Demand for Storage Space. 567
    Career Close-Up Professional Organizer. 572

Chapter 26

Home Safety and Security. 576

Reducing Health Hazards. 578
Preventing Accidents. 580
Preventing Fires. 584
Promoting Security. 587
Meeting Special Needs. 591
    Nonresidential Applications Design Issues for
        Special Healthcare Facilities. 593
    Career Close-Up Lead Abatement Specialist. 594

Chapter 27

Home Maintenance. 598

Home Cleaning. 600
Outdoor Maintenance. 607
Preventive Maintenance. 607
Home Repairs. 612
Professional Servicing of Appliances. 616
    Consumer Sense Weather Blocking. 608
    Career Close-Up Home Maintenance Advice Columnist. 618
    *A Visual Guide to...*Quick-Clean Routines. 604
    *A Visual Guide to...*Emergency Repairs. 613
    *A Visual Guide to...*A Basic Tool Kit. 615

Chapter 28

Remodeling and Renovating. 622

Reasons for Remodeling. 624
Types of Remodeling Projects. 626
Planning a Project. 629
Hiring Professionals. 635
Doing the Work Yourself. 637
The End Result. 637
    Nonresidential Applications Adaptive Reuse as
        a Means to Historic Preservation. 628
    Career Close-Up Home Remodeling Specialist. 638
    *A Visual Guide to...*Defining Kitchen Remodeling Goals. . . . 631

Glossary. 642

Credits. 652   Index. 655

Special Text Features

A VISUAL GUIDE TO ...

Systems-Built Homes. 67

Cluster Homes and Zero-Lot-Line
Homes. 154

Activity Zones in a Home. 159

Comparing Floor Plans. 162

Finding the Trouble Spots. 240

Basement Construction. 259

Slab Foundations. 260

Floor Framing. 262

Wall Framing. 263

Ceiling and Roof Framing. 264

Windows: Parts and Styles. 271

Heating Systems. 288

Active Ventilation Systems. 293

Solar Heating Systems. 312

Landscape Planning. 324

How Texture Affects Apparent Color. . . .344

The Color Wheel. 355

Common Color Schemes. 358

Scale Drawings. 400

Basic Weaves. 418

Carpeting Texture. 421

Window Treatments. 428

Dining Chairs Through Time. 452

Signs of Quality in
Case Goods. 465

Common Wood Furniture Joints. 466

Signs of Quality in
Upholstered Furniture. 469

Structural Lighting. 485

Elevations and Floor Plans. 506

Pictorial Drawings. 514

Renderings. 516

Kitchen Layout Options. 532

Universal Design Features
in Kitchens. 538

Quick-Clean Routines. 604

Emergency Repairs. 613

A Basic Tool Kit. 615

Defining Kitchen
Remodeling Goals. 631

CAREER CLOSE-UP

Usability Engineer. 32

Relocation Specialist. 52

Electronic Home Systems Specialist. . . .74

Ergonomic Designer. 100

Preservationist. 118

Architect. 144

Urban Planner. 166

Real Estate Agent. 186

Mortgage Loan Officer. 202

Resident Manager. 220

Model Home Designer. 244

Roofer. 274

Electrician's Apprentice. 300

Landscape Architect. 328

Space Planner. 346

Color Specialist. 364

Visual Merchandiser. 382

Interior Designer. 406

Textile Specialist. 432

Furniture Restorer. 454

Furniture Showroom Salesperson. 476

Lighting Specialist. 496

CAD Specialist for Interior Design. 520

Kitchen Planner. 554

Professional Organizer. 572

Lead Abatement Specialist. 594

Home Maintenance
Advice Columnist. 618

Home Remodeling Specialist. 638

Consumer Sense

Judging Post-Secondary
Training Programs. 85
Living in a Historic District. 111
Condominium and Cooperative
Ownership. 195
Planning a Move. 211
Special Financing Arrangements. 229
Checking the Panel Box When the
Lights Go Out. 282

ENERGY STAR Homes. 314
Adding Texture to Surfaces. 343
Working with an Interior Designer. 394
Choosing Fabrics for Furniture. 471
What to Look for in
Interior Design Software. 507
Choosing Energy-Efficient
Appliances. 540
Weather Blocking. 608

Nonresidential Applications

Americans with Disabilities Act—Impact on Public Environments. 49
Skyscrapers—How High Can They Go?. 60
Frank Lloyd Wright and Commercial Design. 138
Planned Communities—More Than Just Homes. 156
Energy Conservation Practices in Commercial Buildings. 317
Color Choices—More Than Meets the Eye. 356
Scale A Principle of Design That Can Inspire. 375
Public and Private Choices—Backgrounds for Hotels. 414
Lighting in Retail Stores—A Means to Sell Merchandise. 487
Design Issues for Special Healthcare Facilities. 593
Adaptive Reuse as a Means to Historic Preservation. 628

What Influences DESIGN?

Universal Design—Versatility for All Abilities. 28
These Walls Can Talk. 72
Developers Gauge the Market. 177
Adapting to the Lay of the Land. 254
From Math to Mozart—"Golden Rules" of Proportion. 372
Asian Influences on Design. 443
People and Furniture on the Move. 474
The Demand for Storage Space. 567

Homes Are For People

Housing Is a Universal Need

CHAPTER OBJECTIVES

- ► Define housing and briefly describe how it has evolved.

- ► Analyze the basic physical and psychological needs that housing satisfies.

- ► Compare and contrast housing needs among people of different ages and life stages.

- ► Assess the importance of building homes that follow the concept of universal design.

TERMS TO LEARN

- adaptable design

- archaeologist

- barrier-free design

- housing

- lifestyles

- nomads

- physical needs

- psychological needs

- universal design

*A*s the late afternoon sun dips into the treetops, you head home for dinner after band practice, stopping to talk with one of your neighbors. Out in the country 30 miles away, Julienne and her grandmother finish weeding their garden and head toward the front porch to enjoy the sunset. On the other side of the world in Shanghai, China, Guofang heats up water for her morning tea. She steps out onto the balcony of their apartment building to join her husband and watch the city waking up around them. While each of these people's surroundings are quite different, they each live in a place they call home.

The Development of Housing

A home is a place of great importance in people's lives. The basic role of a home is to protect people and provide them with a safe environment in which to live. As you will learn, a home meets many other needs as well.

The need for housing is one that people share around the world. **Housing** is any structure built for people to live in. Three basic types of housing that historically have been built are natural shelters, portable shelters, and permanent shelters. Throughout the world, housing has varied greatly from place to place and from one time period to another. Regardless of time or place, people have always tried to create com-fortable shelters for themselves and their families.

NATURAL SHELTERS

Before primitive people created tools, they relied on the landscape for protection and shelter. Early people often camped out in the open and sought shelter from the wind by digging pits. By about 100,000 years ago, people in cold climates were living in caves. In warm climates, trees and thickets gave shelter.

With the invention of simple tools, primitive people were able to improve their shelters. They covered openings with tree limbs. They built ladders to reach caves high on cliffs. They used levers to move rocks in front of the entrances to their caves to close out cold air.

Archaeologists (ahr-kee-AH-luh-jists) are scientists who study history through the relics and remains of old civilizations. By examining bones, charcoal, rock paintings, and pottery chips found in caves, they know that humans occupied some caves thousands of years ago. Archaeologists have also found the remains of elaborate underground dwellings. These shelters had sturdy roofs, fireplaces for cooking, places to store food, and mounds that were covered with animal skins and used as beds.

The Mongolian herders periodically move their families and animals to new grazing areas. The family's portable home is a wooden framework covered by felt made from the wool of their animals.

PORTABLE SHELTERS

Primitive people survived by hunting, fishing, and gathering wild fruits and seeds. In some parts of the world, the hunters and food gatherers had to move frequently to be near new sources of food. These people learned to devise shelters that could be taken apart, moved, and reassembled at the next location. Such shelters were usually built around a collapsible framework of wood or other materials. The framework was then covered with animal skins, branches, or grasses. Chapter 5 gives more information on the development of Native American housing.

Today, portable shelters are still used by **nomads**, people who wander from place to place in search of food for their grazing herds. For example, some Bedouins of the Sahara Desert region of North Africa live in tents made from camel hides or palm branches. Nomads in Kenya, a country in East Africa, live in portable huts. The huts can be easily taken apart, put on an animal's back, and set up in a new location. In Turkey and Mongolia, shepherds often live in *yerts*—transportable circular dwellings made of thick wool felt covering a wooden frame.

PERMANENT SHELTERS

With the development of farming and keeping herd animals, early people no longer had to move continually to find food. They could stay in one place as they planted and harvested their crops and tended their herds. They began to select locations for permanent shelters and chose areas with good soil and water supply. Two of the earliest known villages have been found in present-day Israel and Syria. These villages date back to 8000 and 7500 B.C.

The kinds of shelters that were built depended on usable materials in the area. In Southwest Asia, for instance, farmers in the region of Tigris and Euphrates Rivers used giant reeds that grew along the riverbanks. The tall grasses were bound together to make a cone-shaped hut. Today, in New Guinea, an island in the Pacific Ocean, people follow a similar construction method using native bamboo.

As agriculture methods improved, farmers began producing surplus grain. They needed a place to store and preserve the grain until it was needed. A new type of shelter, called a *granary*, was devised to meet this need. The granary established the idea of building shelters for possessions.

As the centuries passed, people improved their methods of constructing housing, but using readily available materials remained a basic principle. For example, in areas where building materials were scarce, mud bricks were made, dried in the sun, and used to build shelters. European peasants used the stones they had dug out of their fields to construct stone cottages. Natives of the Arctic learned that ice blocks, with their insulating properties, could serve well as a building material for temporary or permanent shelters.

DISTINCTIONS WITHIN COMMUNITIES

In primitive societies, individual shelters were very much alike. As communities began to form, however, distinctions in housing developed. These differences were largely based on an individual's standing in the community. A good example of this gradual change can be found in ancient Mesopotamia.

As early as 3500 B.C., a people known as Sumerians settled between the Tigris and Euphrates rivers in an area now known as part of Iraq. Their farming flourished because they learned how to control the rivers to irrigate their fields and food supplies increased. Fewer people were needed to produce food, so they began to do other jobs such as making pottery and cloth. In time, they became more organized and set

up governments. As the population grew, they built cities.

In the center of a city were the two-story houses of the upper class—the priests and merchants. Their homes were symbols of their wealth. Behind these houses were the one-story homes of the middle class—government officials, shopkeepers, and skilled workers. On the outskirts of the city were the crude mud-brick homes of the farmers, unskilled workers, and people who made their living from fishing.

Other civilizations, including the ancient Greeks and Romans, developed in a similar way. Even in China, which was cut off from Western civilizations, archeologists have found evidence of the same type of community development. The wealthy and the powerful Chinese lived in cities in stately wooden houses. The poor people lived in the countryside in mud huts or caves scooped out of the ground.

As rich people gained more possessions, they became interested in protecting their increased wealth. They wanted housing that would protect them from robbers and enemy attacks. They chose building sites that could be protected from intruders, such as a cliff, a mountainside, or a river or lake. There

The Native Americans in the Southwest built pueblos from native clay. These multifamily dwellings provided permanent shelter for generations of families. Some are still in use today.

In the late Middle Ages, the nobility built castles to protect their family and possessions. What security features can you see in the castle in this photo?

was a time of increased interest in art and great advances in technology. Applied to housing, the new technology made homes brighter, better ventilated, and more sanitary.

The growth of a prosperous middle class during the Renaissance also influenced people's expectations of housing. With more leisure time, people began to use their homes for relaxation, entertainment, and privacy.

By the 19th century, many homes—particularly in industrialized nations—had become centers of social activity. For instance, in England, families, neighbors, and friends would frequently be entertained in the elaborate homes of the rich and the middle class. Guests would often stay for months at a time.

they would build their homes of sturdy materials. For example, in medieval times in Europe, a castle was constructed of thick stone walls to withstand battering rams. A moat and high battlements were additional security features.

The large Italian villas of the 19th century were ideal for entertaining guests.

COMFORTABLE SHELTERS

In earlier times, even the homes of the rich were not especially comfortable. Medieval castles, for example, appeared imposing but offered little more comfort than a primitive cave. Cold wind blew through the rooms and passageways. Stone floors were cold. Light came dimly through narrow windows fitted with small bits of thick glass.

It was not until the Renaissance that housing generally became more comfortable. The Renaissance, which began in Italy in the 1300s,

Housing to Fit Human Needs

People's needs throughout the centuries have determined what their housing has looked like. As their needs have changed, their housing has kept pace. Individuals may vary from place to place, but there are fundamental types of needs that are universal—the basic needs of human beings that help determine the housing they require.

Housing is designed to fulfill both physical and psychological needs. Some needs may fit into more than one category for some people. In addition, some needs are more complex than others.

PHYSICAL NEEDS

When you eat a hamburger or take a nap, you are helping to satisfy your physical needs. **Physical needs** include all the things the body needs to survive: air, sunlight, shelter, sleep, and food. Housing helps meet physical needs by protecting people from the weather. It also provides a place to eat, sleep, and be safe.

Shelter

Protection from nature is the most obvious physical need that housing fulfills. Throughout the world, the elements of nature—temperature, humidity, rain, snow, wind, and sunlight—have influenced how people build their housing.

In the United States, the climate varies widely, creating a need for many housing styles across the nation. For example, the North has

The natural environment influences housing styles across the country. This house has a steep roof to shed heavy winter snows.

cold, snowy winters, so homes in that region tend to have low ceilings to contain the heat. Steep roofs help shed snow. The hot, dry air of the Southwest has led to a different style. One type of southwestern house has thick clay walls and a flat roof of timber and clay tiles. This construction helps keep the interior cool.

Sometimes people can take advantages of natural features, such as a hillside or a grove of trees, to help meet the need for shelter. High in the mountains of Switzerland, villages are built on the sunniest slopes, and the main living areas of homes face southward. The sun's warmth helps heat the homes.

Sleep

Regular sleep is another need that housing helps to fulfill. Without a safe, comfortable place to sleep, people may not get the rest that they need to function or to perform well at their jobs. In North America, most people are fortunate to have their own homes in which to sleep.

In North American homes, specific rooms often are set aside for

sleeping. In other countries, sleeping arrangements vary. In Japanese homes, for instance, sliding paper screens separate rooms. People sleep on the floor on padded quilts that are taken out at night and put away during the day. This practice enables rooms to be used as living rooms during the day and as sleeping areas at night. It is similar to our idea of sofabeds and futons that convert living space into sleeping areas.

Food

Most housing provides a place for food preparation and eating. In some countries, homes have a separate room—a kitchen—for cooking. In other countries this is not the case. In Indonesian homes, for instance, living rooms also serve as kitchens.

People can eat almost anywhere in a typical home, but usually a specific space is reserved for this activity. Americans usually have their main meals in a kitchen or dining area. For a special occasion, people often gather to share a more formal meal. In fact, many social occasions and holidays are built around eating together.

Safety and Security

Early homes helped keep their occupants safe from animals and people who might harm them or steal their belongings. Safety was one of the reasons people grouped homes together and formed the first towns and villages. By living together, they could help protect one another. The Pueblo people of the American Southwest built their homes in the sides of cliffs so that hostile tribes could not attack them easily. On the American frontier, early pioneers built homes in settlements, but they moved inside the nearby *stockade* for safety during attacks. The stockade had walls of logs, and inside were small sheds or cabins to house new arrivals or to shelter pioneers from danger.

Today, people still look to housing to provide a place of safety for their family and their possessions. People may increase their sense of security by building fences or installing special locks. However, communities also must take action to increase everyone's safety. When neighbors work together, they send a message to criminals that their neighborhood is organized and people look out for one another. Home security and crime prevention each plays a part.

PSYCHOLOGICAL NEEDS

There is more to life than eating, sleeping, and staying safe. Human beings also have psychological needs. **Psychological** (sy-kuh-LAH-jih-kuhl) **needs** are needs related to thoughts and emotions. They include the need for love and belonging, fun and relaxation, and comfort. They also include the need to feel a sense of identity and to express oneself. Housing that provides opportunities to meet psychological needs is more than just a structure—it becomes a home.

Preparing meals together is an opportunity for families with busy schedules to spend time together. How is this family meeting both physical and psychological needs?

Love and Belonging

The need for love and belonging to a group is satisfied by family, friends, and coworkers. In addition, this need also includes wanting to be a part of a larger community, perhaps as a volunteer. The need to feel connected is often considered a social need. Depending on its type and location, housing can play an important role in providing people with a sense of belonging.

Housing is, of course, the primary setting for the family. In most cultures, the family home is where children first learn how to interact with other people. Children learn skills and cultural behavior by observing their parents and other family members. Homes give family members space to live, work, and play together—sharing experiences that help build affection and closeness. Central areas—such as a living room, family room, or the kitchen table—are favorite places for people to be together.

Housing also provides opportunities for interaction with friends. You might invite a friend home to watch a video or work on a school project. When you do, you are using housing to meet your need to be with other people. Human interaction provides fun and relaxation, mental stimulation, and emotional security.

Many people also feel the need for some time alone in a personal space, though this varies with culture. Privacy allows people the opportunity to think, daydream, or work without interruption. In some homes, bedrooms are viewed as personal space for privacy. Privacy can also be achieved through furniture arrangement. For example, tall bookcases can divide a living room into a gathering space and a more private area.

When choosing a place to live, people often consider their need to be a member of a group. Some may decide to live in a large city because it offers many social and cultural activities and opportunities to meet people. Others prefer to live in a small town where they can get to know everyone personally. Some want to live in a particular neighborhood because they feel welcome and comfortable there.

Not all people experience a sense of community in their daily lives. There is actually a growing trend toward isolation in North America. Studies show that people within neighborhoods don't interact as much as they did in the past.

Some housing designers are creating planned communities intended to provide a sense of neighborhood that many areas have lost. These communities often resemble older city neighborhoods because all of the homes are close to one another. Features may include attached homes, roomy front steps or stoops, and front porches designed to encourage people to get together with neighbors. You will read more about planned communities in Chapter 7.

Identity

Imagine a neighborhood where all the houses are white with black roofs and each house has exactly the same kinds of trees planted in exactly the same location. Wouldn't this sameness be uninteresting? Could a person accidentally walk into the wrong house?

A neighborhood party is a great way to develop a sense of community. Think of three ways you could make a positive difference in the lives of your neighbors.

Even though these homes are similar, residents have personalized them with distinctive touches. Why would this be important for the people who live in these homes?

Most people like to personalize their homes. Even people living in rental units can add individual touches. Putting out a decorative welcome mat or hanging a door wreath personalizes the exterior. Creative arrangements of potted plants and outdoor furniture on balconies also express individuality. Inside their homes, people use many creative decorating ideas to express their personal identities.

People's tastes, values, attitudes, and personalities show others who they are and determine how they live their lives. These qualities help form the lifestyle that people choose. **Lifestyles**, or ways of living, influence people's choice of housing.

Housing meets the need to express personality in several ways. First, people choose housing styles and furnishings based on their likes and dislikes. They select housing that reflects their image of themselves. One person may choose an ultramodern style, while another wants a more traditional look. People also choose housing that reflects their values. A family that values a simple, natural lifestyle might live in a rustic cabin in the mountains—or at least decorate their city apartment to resemble one.

Housing can also be a symbol of achievement. A young adult's first apartment represents independence. As people achieve financial success,

they might choose larger, more expensive housing. Some people select housing to convey a certain image. They choose a home that they feel others will recognize and admire. Most people, however, are more interested in choosing a home that suits their needs and lifestyle than one that will impress others.

Creativity

Another psychological need is the need to be creative, which lets people use their imagination and skills to express themselves. With a little imagination, people can add a unique look to their homes. Even pioneers on the American frontier were creative when building housing. Although materials and supplies were limited, they built their own log cabins and made many of the furnishings.

You don't have to build a house to express your creativity. Deciding what color to paint the walls and how to coordinate the furnishings requires imagination. Rearranging furniture and adding accessories can be a creative outlet. Making art to hang on the walls or even the refrigerator is a good way to exercise creativity. Housing also provides space for hobbies and other creative outlets.

Housing and Individual Needs

While people may have the same basic physical and psychological needs, they also have unique needs individual to them. For example, an artist may want a home with plenty of northern light. A big family may choose a home with a large dining area so they can enjoy meals together. People's housing needs are also influenced by their stage of life, their family situation, and their personal or special needs. Some people list among their top priorities having one home they can live in through all the stages of their life. Others look forward to the mobility of moving around from place to place.

The early years of marriage for a couple are called the *beginning stage*. At this point, the two people are getting to know each other better and are learning to act as a team. They may be actively making career plans. One important choice they need to make together is where to live.

The next stage for many families is the *parenting stage*. During this stage, the family expands. Children are born and develop. While raising children, the parents' focus is on home and family life. The end of the parenting stage is marked by the grown children leaving the family home. This process is often called the *launching stage*.

Many young adults share housing as they become established in their careers. What are the economic advantages of doing so?

HOUSING NEEDS THROUGH THE LIFE SPAN

It is not uncommon for people to move a number of times and live in different types of housing during their lives. They may move to different cities or just change residences within an area. Changes in housing often correspond to situations that occur during a person's life span. Sometimes the life span is referred to as the *life cycle*—the stages of life from infancy to old age. Individuals move through their own life cycle as they grow through infancy to childhood to young adulthood to adulthood. Many adults make the choice to marry, and they then enter into a *family life cycle*. These are the stages many families go through during their lifetime together.

In the parenting stage of the family life cycle, parents are involved with raising their children. How might a parenting family's housing needs differ from a family in the aging stage?

With the children grown and on their own, parents become a couple again. They move into the *aging stage,* also called "middle age." During this time, many couples find new interests they enjoy together. Their careers may reach an all-time high. Sometimes grown children return home due to economic conditions or a change in the child's life, such as divorce. Often parents become grandparents during this stage. In some cases, the parents care for their grandchildren on a regular basis.

The family life cycle is completed with the *retirement stage.* Changes in income and health as well as lifestyle interests often bring about new housing needs during this stage.

Of course, every person and family does not follow this cycle exactly. For example, not everyone marries or has children. Not every family goes through the stages of the family life cycle in the same way. Remember, everyone and every family is unique.

Let's look at a few examples of how housing needs tend to change as family members age and move into new life situations.

- Michael and Rose just got married and are moving into their first apartment. They chose an affordable, small place close to their jobs. They are interested in saving money for a place of their own.
- Marie and Antonio have been married for a five years and have a two-year-old son. They are buying a home in a neighborhood with other families with young children.
- Estella has a two-bedroom apartment next to a community park. Her two grandchildren live with her.
- Kunal has moved back home with his parents after his divorce.
- Andre and Diana, whose children are grown and living in different cities, plan to sell their large two-story home and move into a one-story home with a small yard.
- Sam is retired and thinking about selling his house and moving to a retirement community.

As you can see from these examples, each family managed to select a home that fits its needs.

SPECIAL HOUSING NEEDS

Many people have special needs that affect their housing choices. For example, some older people have difficulty living alone and need help with such things as preparing meals or cleaning a home. In the first decade of the 21st century, the over-85 population will grow to 5.7 million. That's a 1.5 million increase from the end of the 20th century. One impact of this growth is an increased demand for housing that's suited to the health-related needs of these people. Senior housing choices used to be limited to nursing homes and care facilities. Today, a broader range of options is available. Re-

tirement housing in which elderly people maintain an apartment, yet are assisted, is one solution. In many such arrangements, senior citizens are served meals, can socialize with others, and can enjoy transportation and shopping services.

People with disabilities also have special housing needs. They want comfortable, efficient housing that meets their requirements. Technological innovations have assisted them in this goal. A person with a hearing impairment can be warned of a fire by a smoke detector that lights up rather than just sounding an alarm. A visually impaired person may have a microwave with a braille control panel. A person in a wheelchair can conveniently use a kitchen sink with an open area underneath instead of an enclosed cabinet. Some people with mental disabilities reside in group living centers. The living situation provides them assistance with meals, supervision, meeting daily care needs, and employment.

UNIVERSAL DESIGN

Older people and those with permanent disabilities are not the only ones with special housing needs. Many other people find their housing unsuitable at one time or another. A toddler may be in danger of bumping against the sharp corner of a kitchen cabinet. A young child may have difficulty reaching clothes hanging in a bedroom closet. A teen with a broken leg may have difficulty going up stairs. A short adult may not be able to reach upper shelves easily. A parent pushing a stroller may have difficulty getting up the front steps.

What Influences DESIGN ?

Universal Design—Versatility for All Abilities

Imagine walking through a home and seeing that each room used a different type of flooring: pale blue carpet in one room, vinyl tiles in the next, hardwood in another. Is this a new trend in home design?

In a way, it is. Using contrasting floor coverings is an example of a simple way to apply principles of universal design—creating living spaces that accommodate a range of needs and abilities. The differing colors and textures serve as cues to help a person with impaired vision navigate the home. More homes will be designed with such diverse needs in mind, if housing trends follow societal trends that may spur the demand:

- Advances in medicine allow people to live not only longer, but healthier, lives. Most older people want to continue to live independently. They will be increasingly able to do so, with some modifications in home design. You may see more single-level homes. Easy-to-grasp, lever door handles may become commonplace.

- Similarly, the number of people with disabilities is rising, as medical science saves lives that once were lost to accident and illness. Wider doorways that can accommodate wheelchairs may become the industry standard, and electrical outlets may be routinely mounted at higher levels.

- Rapidly rising costs will make professional care less available. Fewer people will be able to afford assisted living facilities or in-home care. Remaining in their own homes or moving in with family members will be their only options. Either way, homes with universal access will be in demand.

THINKING IT THROUGH

1. Imagine that an illness has left you or a family member with a serious hearing loss. What aspects of your home's design would make it hard for you to function? What modifications would provide a remedy?
2. How might older people and those with disabilities use their growing numbers to push for more accessible housing?

This bathroom is an attractive example of how universal design can be incorporated into new homes. How many universal design features can you identify?

Exterior

- Rather than steps, use a ground-level entrance or a ramp with non-skid surface. The ramp should be wide enough to accommodate a wheelchair or baby stroller easily with turn-around space.
- Provide secure handrails for both ramps and stairways.

Interior

- Wide doorways, hallways, and space within each room accommodate someone who uses a wheelchair, walker, or crutches. Thresholds should be flush with the floor.
- Light switches and electrical outlets should be mounted at levels easily accessed from a wheelchair. These might benefit people of different heights, too. For better visibility, outlets should contrast with the wall.
- Lever-type doorknobs are easier for children and people with arthritis to use than round ones, yet they cause no inconvenience for others.
- Built-in flexibility is another way to achieve universal design. Instead of having a fixed shelf and rod, a closet can include adjustable shelving units that are easy to adapt to the individual.

Until recently, most homes were designed and built for "average" users—able-bodied adults of average height. People with different needs had to endure the inconvenience, make changes to their homes, or move to more accommodating quarters. Today, many home designers and builders are taking a different approach. They have adopted a philosophy called **universal design**— designing interiors and products to accommodate all people with a variety of requirements, needs, and abilities. Universal design acknowledges that people come in different sizes, ages, and abilities. When homes are built to suit many different people, residents are less likely to require special adaptations, even if their needs change.

One aspect of universal design is **barrier-free design**. This means that living spaces are designed without structures that would prevent access by people with special needs. Some owners choose to include **adaptable design** features—design features that are temporary and can be easily changed. For example, a landlord may install a wheelchair ramp or special cabinets for a tenant with special needs. The ramp or cabinets can be removed when the tenant moves out.

Since needs are individual, how can homes be built to accommodate many different needs? Here are some common approaches.

Bathrooms

- Enough open space should be allowed for people in wheelchairs to turn around easily and for parents to help children with needs such as bathing.
- Single lever controls for sinks and tub faucets are easiest to operate.
- Grab bars in the tub or shower may be built in, or walls may be reinforced for adding grab bars later.

Kitchen

- Vary the heights of the counters. Some counters can be higher, allowing tall users to work without bending over. Other countertops can be lower, making them convenient for children, short adults, and people who are seated.
- Knee space under the kitchen sink or cook top allows wheelchair use. The space can be temporarily concealed with removable cabinets.
- Appliance controls and water faucets should be easy to use. This could include front-mounted controls on cooktops.
- Space should be sufficient for turning in a wheelchair.
- Cabinets with pull-out shelves are easiest to use. Cabinet knobs should contrast with the cabinet color for clear visibility.

People have many reasons for choosing homes with universal design features. For some, it is the only housing that suits their present needs. Others may not have physical challenges themselves but want their homes to be usable for visitors who do. Many people who choose universal design are planning for their possible future needs. They want to avoid the disruption of moving or remodeling in later years. Cost is also a consideration. Although some universal design features add to the cost of building a home, savings are realized in the long run. Designing wide doorways when a home is built, for example, is less costly than replacing narrow doorways with wide ones later.

Universal design proves that homes can be attractive, pleasant, and functional at the same time. By designing homes to better accommodate individual needs, universal design benefits everyone.

Challenges for Tomorrow

There are significant issues in housing for the future. One is to create housing that is useful to the greatest number of people. Universal design can help meet that need. Architects, planners, and builders must make sure that they meet the challenges of designing and building usable housing to meet a variety of needs. In the future, universal design features may be included in every new home. Housing designers and builders must keep looking for ways to accommodate the needs of people regardless of age, height, physical disability, or other physical factors.

A second challenge is to find ways to make better housing available to low- and middle-income people and to improve the social environment. For example, there is a desperate need for good housing in the older, low-income areas of many cities. Housing problems are closely related to other social problems, such as delinquency and crime. Some experts believe that providing good housing is a key to solving these problems. To foster a better social environment, homes need to be in locations where residents will be close to such conveniences as schools, parks, and shopping.

Using solar energy is one way to conserve resources.

A third challenge is to conserve energy and natural resources. Builders and housing designers need to create living spaces that better relate to the natural environment. This means making careful use of land and natural resources. Every year in the U.S., homes account for more than 30 percent of the total energy consumption and produce nearly 20 percent of all air pollution emissions. Designing, building, and operating homes to use materials, energy, and water efficiently is essential to ensure adequate housing in the future.

Throughout history, housing has been designed to fulfill basic human needs. With the spread of civilization and technological advances, other considerations have become important. As you will learn in the next two chapters, housing design is influenced by a culture's customs, by current trends in society, and by available technology. Basic needs are still being met, but comforts and wants are also a significant part of modern home design.

Usability Engineer

Pearl Biden

While I was in high school, my brother was severly injured in a car accident. He needed a wheelchair to get around. Unfortunately, our home had two stories with steep steps between floors. The bedrooms and bathroom were upstairs and had narrow doorways. That's when I learned the meaning of the terms *barrier-free* and *accessible*.

Today, I'm a usability engineer, someone who makes homes truly accessible for those living in them. Whether it's new housing being designed or existing homes being modified, I help make them "user friendly." It's a job that gives me much satisfaction.

When my company is hired to modify a home, the first step is to meet with the family members. I listen to their needs and concerns, discuss possible options, and help them plan their choices. I may also meet with the people who will perform the construction work to make sure they understand the family's desires and needs. I, or someone from our firm, will suggest architectural features that need to be included to make a home fully accessible.

> **"Whether it's new housing being designed or existing homes being modified, I help make them 'user friendly'."**

Sometimes a usability engineer is hired by the owner of rental housing. The owner may want to make a unit temporarily accessible to a tenant who requires a wheelchair ramp. You might call it "flexible design"—the ability to go from a specialty design to an ordinary one within hours. Other owners are converting their rental units to be fully accessible to accommodate people with a variety of disabilities.

While the unique needs of an individual determine some design fea-

"It is very important to stay current with the latest advances in accessible home design."

tures, there are some elements common to all accessible homes. Features useful for all people include wide doorways; smooth, hard flooring; maneuvering space in bathrooms; and kitchens with an open central floor area and pullout storage shelves. Other universal features include remote control units at the bedside; also light switches, thermostats, and appliance controls at lower heights that are accessible to all.

The courses in architecture I took in college help me to understand what accessible features are suited to particular kinds of home construction. I have also learned about the characteristics and needs associated with various disabilities. My design training and creative skills help me to visualize and plan a home to meet the needs of individuals. It is very important to stay current with the latest advances in accessible home design; ongoing research is continuously showing usability engineers how to their job better.

Career Profile

Usability engineers, sometimes called accessibility designers, make sure that a home or building is fully accessible to the occupants. These professionals may work with an already existing building to make it more accessible, such as adding in wheelchair ramps or lowering cabinets. Usability engineers may also work with construction companies at the beginning stages of development to ensure that the building will be fully accessible and within building regulations.

Education
▸ Courses in design and architecture are necessary.
▸ A bachelor's degree is required.
▸ A master's degree is required if working in the special needs design field.

Skills Needed
▸ One to three years of on-the-job training is generally needed for advancement.
▸ Good written and oral communication skills.
▸ Must have good problem-solving skills.

Career Outlook
▸ Employment opportunities are expected to grow faster than average.
▸ With the population of older adults growing, the demand for accessible housing is expected to increase.

Career Activities
1. List design ideas that would make a home fully accessible for an individual in a wheelchair.
2. Identify design ideas that would make a retirement home fully accessible.

CHAPTER 1

Review & Activities

Chapter Summary

➤ Housing has evolved from natural shelters to permanent, comfortable shelters.

➤ Housing should satisfy people's basic physical needs.

➤ Housing that satisfies basic psychological needs can encourage interaction with family and friends and help people's feeling of well-being.

➤ As people move through the family life cycle, their housing requirements change.

➤ The goal of universal design is to make housing useful for people of all ages, sizes, and physical abilities.

➤ The challenge for the future is to create affordable, comfortable housing for all people and to conserve our natural resources.

Checking Your Understanding

1. How would you define housing?

2. What caused people in ancient times to change from portable to permanent shelters?

3. Give two examples of how housing changed during the Renaissance.

4. How does the physical need for shelter affect housing styles?

5. Identify three psychological needs that housing can satisfy.

6. How can housing encourage interaction with others?

7. Explain how housing can reflect personal identity.

8. Compare and contrast possible housing needs at three stages of the family life cycle.

9. What challenges do housing designers face in making homes adaptable to all people?

Thinking Critically

1. Do you think that people in North America take comfortable housing for granted? How might they feel if they lived in a developing nation?

2. List three types of housing that you would consider inadequate. For each type, identify the physical or psychological needs that this housing does not satisfy.

3. How can the look of a home reflect a person's personality? Describe three examples.

4. What would be the advantages and disadvantages of having all new homes incorporate the principles and guidelines of universal design?

5. Do you think that the housing industry has a responsibility to build houses that conserve natural resources? Why or why not?

Review & Activities   CHAPTER 1

Applications

1. **Uncovering History.** Reread the description in the chapter about the caves archaeologists have found. Then do research on the Internet or check references in your school's media center to find information about the Lascaux caves in France. Write a short description of this important archaeological finding.

2. **Renaissance Home.** Imagine that you are living during the Renaissance. A friend has asked you for advice about the type of home she should build to reflect the new Renaissance values. Describe your innovative ideas.

3. **Matching Lifestyles.** Write a description of a home that would ideally suit your present lifestyle. Use your imagination to make your description as complete as possible.

4. **Housing Ages and Stages.** What kind of housing do you imagine you will live in when you are 21, 41, and 71? Find two interior and exterior pictures that show the kind of home you think you will want to live in at each age. Use magazines, newspaper real estate ads, travel brochures, and other sources. Briefly explain how these pictures reflect your goals at each of these stages of life.

5. **Applying Universal Design.** Draw a simple sketch of a room that includes at least five universal design features. Label the features, and explain why they make the room universally usable by adults, children, elderly people, and people with disabilities.

6. **Building a Better Future.** Using Internet or print resources, find examples of innovative green building techniques designed to use materials, energy, and water efficiently. Working with three or four other students, combine your findings and prepare a poster or a website article to share with others.

BUILDING YOUR PORTFOLIO

You are the assistant curator for a design and housing museum. The museum is planning an exhibit on primitive housing. The curator has asked you to write a plan for the exhibit. Think about the materials that you will include. Should the museum display photographs, drawings, or scale models? How will the exhibit be organized? How much space will you need? Will you include an interactive computer display? Will you include a virtual tour of the exhibit on the museum's web site? Answer each of these questions in your plan. You may include sketches or pictures to illustrate your ideas.

Housing and Society

CHAPTER OBJECTIVES

- ► Describe how housing reflects cultural views and values.

- ► Point out ways in which cultures influence each other.

- ► Identify social trends that affect housing.

- ► Explain the major ways in which government influences housing.

TERMS TO LEARN

- baby boomers

- culture

- demographics

- extended family

- household

- nuclear family

- single-parent family

- status

- telecommute

*I*n your mind, take a snapshot of your home. Imagine three people on various parts of the globe doing the same thing. If the snapshots were put together in a scrapbook, your home might look quite different from the other three. What similarities might you expect to see? What would account for the differences?

*H*ow Culture Influences Housing

Traveling around the world, you would see a vast array of types of housing—from houseboats to apartment blocks to palm-covered huts. What accounts for these vast differences in housing styles? Of course, the physical environment has an important impact. As you learned in Chapter 1, geographic characteristics—such as altitude, climate, and terrain—greatly influence housing design. In addition, the building materials available play an important role.

Culture is another major influence. **Culture** is a combination of all the customs, beliefs, and ideas of a group of people. It includes people's values, traditions, and social habits, as well as their arts and religion. Culture affects every aspect of life, including housing. It affects the types of homes people build, the style of individual homes, and the arrangement of the rooms and furnishings within the home.

CULTURAL VIEWS AND VALUES

Because different parts of the world have different cultures, home design varies from place to place. In addition, cultures often change over time. As they do, people's housing needs and preferences may also change.

For thousands of years most of the people in Saudi Arabia lived as nomads in the desert, using tents for shelter. Some still live that way, but many Saudis have adopted a different lifestyle.

A typical new house owned by an upper- or middle-class Saudi Arabian family has central air conditioning and electric appliances. However, these homes, though modern, have been designed to preserve Middle Eastern cultural traditions. For instance, many Saudi homes have two living rooms. This feature makes it possible for women and children in the family to remain separate from male visitors, according to Saudi custom. A visitor to some homes would also find a dining room without furniture, and instead find a rug on the floor on which to sit and eat a meal.

Different Kinds of Households

When discussing housing features, not only homes but also households must be considered. A **household** is made up of all the people who live together in one housing unit. The size and makeup of households vary from culture to culture.

One type of household is the **nuclear family**. The traditional nuclear family has a father, a mother, and one or more children. There are fewer nuclear families today than in the past.

In many cultures, households more typically consist of extended families. An **extended family** includes other relatives in addition to parents and children. For example, a mother, a father, children, perhaps an aunt or an uncle, and grandparents may all live together. On the island of Sumatra, housing is built to accommodate very large extended families. As many as 100 people, all related, share a long, rectangular house. The house is on stilts with space underneath for cattle stalls, chicken coops, and storage. In rural Nigeria, members of an extended family build their huts next to each other inside a compound or walled area. The women and children tend the gardens, and the men herd livestock.

. In North America, households made up of extended families are becoming increasingly common for several reasons:

- Many people who come to North America from other countries continue the extended family tradition of their native culture. This is often true of people from countries of Southeast Asia, for example.
- Aging parents who need assistance because of poor health or physical limitations may move in with their children. Research reveals that more than 22 million households include an aging family member.
- Adult children may move into their parents' homes for financial reasons.

Situations like these affect people's housing choices. For example, the Diaz family purchased a large older home. They converted part of the space into a small apartment for Mr. Diaz's mother. This arrangement provides the elder Mrs. Diaz with privacy and independence, yet it retains the benefits of shared housing.

The living arrangements in a typical household in some countries would seem crowded to most people in North America.

A growing number of American children live in a home where three generations are present.

Still other household patterns are increasingly common in Western societies. There are many couples who postpone having children or don't become parents. Other families, called **single-parent families**, have only *one parent living with one or more children*. As a result of these patterns, the demand for smaller homes, or those with fewer bedrooms and more living space, may increase.

Another change, especially in North America, is the increase in the number of people who live alone. Some are young people who have recently graduated from high school or college. Others are people of any age who have never married or are widowed or divorced. Many of these people like the independence that living alone offers. Some single people, especially in large cities, like the economy and simplicity of small apartments. Other single people choose larger living quarters that provide space for hobbies and entertaining.

Many people today share houses or apartments. By doing so, they may reduce their housing expenses or live in better housing than each person could afford individually. Other advantages include companionship and shared household responsibilities.

Whatever the makeup of the household, one of the main goals of its members is to have satisfactory housing. While individual priorities vary, satisfactory housing usually means a home that helps people meet their physical and psychological needs, is affordable, is economical to maintain, and provides the space and surroundings in which they feel safe and comfortable. Unsatisfactory housing can lead to stress, conflict, and social problems among the household members.

A Varied Concern for Privacy and Individualism

The design of housing in particular places is often determined by the attitude of the society toward privacy and individualism. Most people in North America value privacy. Walls and separate rooms provide household members with a chance to be alone when they choose. Individualism is also valued. Family members often personalize their areas of the home, decorating these areas to suit their tastes and lifestyle.

In some Asian countries, more emphasis is placed on working together to accomplish group goals rather than on privacy. For example, at one time people living in cities in China used public bathing facilities. Cultural changes have occurred, however, and now city residents live in homes with private bathrooms.

Some people in Israel also value group goals, but in a different way. Some Israelis live in farming communities called *kibbutzim*. People in a kibbutz all work to support the group. They live in separate homes, but all the homes are owned by the group, not by the individuals.

Most adults, teens, and children value personal space in their homes.

Housing and Status

The way a person's importance in society is perceived by others is called **status**. A person's job, income, dress, and social position are main factors that influence his or her status. The size of the person's home and its location, design, and furnishings can also be symbols of status. For example, status can be reflected in such housing characteristics as:

BUILDING MATERIALS. In India, for example, there are two types of houses, called *pucca* (superior) and *kacha* (inferior). Pucca homes are generally made of birch or stone held together with mortar, and they have wood, tile, or cement roofs. Kacha homes are usually made of brick or stone held together with mud, and they have straw-covered roofs.

TYPES AND NUMBERS OF ROOMS. New houses for the middle and upper classes in India generally have a separate kitchen and a modern bathroom. In the houses of poorer people, however, cooking is usually done in the central living room, and there is rarely a bathroom with plumbing.

THE AMOUNT OF LAND SURROUNDING A HOUSE. In many cultures, people perceive the quantity of land around their house as a symbol of status. For example, in England many people live in one of a series of identical

Large homes in prestigious neighborhoods have been American status symbols for many years.

houses situated side by side and joined by common walls. These structures, called terrace houses, were originally built for factory workers. They have small rooms and usually a small garden in front. People with more money often live in two-family houses. These houses have bigger rooms, open land on one side, and a larger garden or lawn in front. Some people live in detached houses, which stand alone on a plot of land. These houses are usually much more expensive and therefore regarded as status symbols.

INFLUENCING OTHER CULTURES

What people learn from other cultures influences their own homes, both in terms of building designs and methods of construction. When one group's habits and beliefs spread to another group in this way, cultural influences occur. For instance, whitewashed walls and red-tiled roofs are characteristic of Spanish architecture. Early Spanish settlers brought this style to the New World, where it became popular in the southern and southwestern areas of what is now the United States. Similarly, other European settlers brought their European styles to North America. These styles were gradually adapted all over the country.

Cultural exchange from countries around the world has influenced housing styles in the U.S. What part of the world do you think influenced this housing style?

cern about the environment, builders in North America are studying energy conservation techniques used in countries with limited natural resources. For example, North American homes traditionally have a hot water heater that keeps hot many gallons of water. Today's energy-conscious builders are more often using on-demand water heaters that heat water at the point it is needed. This technology has been used in other parts of the world for decades.

Cultural change happens most rapidly in large cities, where many people from different parts of the world meet and share ideas. Since rural areas usually have a smaller influx of people from other cultures, the traditional local culture tends to be preserved.

Modern high-rise apartments in Dallas, Paris, and Cairo may all be built of the same materials (steel and concrete) in a similar style. On the other hand, houses in rural areas tend to be built in traditional local styles. For example, you might find a log cabin in the north woods of Minnesota while you would see a house made of stone and cement in the countryside of Guatemala.

Because of advanced communications and increased trade and travel, cultures are influencing each other far more rapidly today than at any time in the past. Although this process can add to the variety and richness of cultures, it doesn't always have positive results. At one time, the natives of a tropical region of Peru decided to replace the straw roofs of their huts with metal roofing. They believed that the metal roofs symbolized a more modern way of life. However, the high humidity in the region made the metal rust. Moreover, the metal roofs made the huts unbearably hot. The Peruvians realized that the environment, not status, is most important in choosing building materials.

On the other hand, there are positive influences. In this time of con-

Societal Trends that Affect Housing

Societal trends that influence housing vary from culture to culture throughout the world. The history of the kitchen in North American homes provides a good example of the influence of social change on housing.

In the homes built by English settlers during the colonial era, the kitchen was the only room in most houses that was continually heated. Consequently, it was used as the main room for many indoor activities. It was the place where family members ate meals, did their work, and socialized. The kitchen was an important gathering place for friends and neighbors, since there were few forms of entertainment outside the home. Because so many activities took place there, the kitchen was often the largest room in the house.

Compared to the colonial kitchen, a typical kitchen of the 1940s occupied a much smaller portion of the home. It also had a much more specific purpose—meal preparation—reflecting society's emphasis on efficient work methods. Other former functions of the kitchen were taken over by other rooms. Socializing took place in the living room. Families ate meals together in a separate dining room.

Today, jobs, sports, and school activities often take family members away from home. Because families eat fewer meals together, separate dining rooms have become less popular. Often the kitchen is a place where family members cross paths, preparing and eating informal meals and snacks as they follow their own schedules. Some kitchens are now designed to allow more than one person to cook, making meal preparation a family activity. The kitchen is often now the social gathering and entertainment area in the home.

Interestingly, many modern kitchens are open to an adjoining family room, bringing to mind the multi-purpose kitchen of colonial times.

As the history of the kitchen shows, many different societal trends can affect housing. Some of the trends affecting housing today, discussed on the next few pages, include:

- Changing family structures and roles.
- Changing fashions and personal tastes.
- Longer life spans.
- Changing economic conditions.
- Increasing environmental awareness.
- Working at home.
- Mobility and diverse communities.

As family roles have changed, all family members often share in preparing the evening meal. **How do today's kitchens reflect this social change?**

FAMILY STRUCTURES AND ROLES

Family structures and roles within the family continue to change. In a large percentage of nuclear families, both husband and wife have full-time jobs outside the home. Meanwhile, the number of single-parent families is increasing. Because of the time demands faced by most working parents, children often help with household duties.

Many home designers and builders are looking at these trends and planning housing to fit present and future needs. As you read in Chapter 1, the concept of meeting all family members' needs through universal design is influencing housing today. For example, kitchens in many homes are being designed with children in mind. A work area with lower cabinets and counters and a microwave oven allows children to prepare their own snacks or to help with family meals.

FASHION AND PERSONAL TASTE

Fads and fashions affect housing design, just as they influence clothing styles. Certain colors or themes are popular for a few years and then the styles change. For example, during one period, bright colors were very popular in interior design. Later, subtle tones became more common. You can usually spot these trends by observing the furnishings that are currently featured in magazines and newspaper articles.

Another current trend is that people are spending more time at home, and entertainment is an increasing function of the home. Consequently, home entertainment centers and computers are popular additions in homes.

Although styles change as fads and fashions come and go, certain elements in American design remain constant. Many Americans seem to prefer simplicity and comfort in their homes. They tend to like informal settings, light interiors, and open spaces. Others like traditional touches in their home design. Housing and design choices will always be determined by people's personal tastes.

Baby boomers' desire for new housing brought about a surge in construction. What impact will this large segment of the population have on American housing in the future?

POPULATION TRENDS

Demographics—the statistical characteristics of a population—have a great impact on housing. Demographic information comes from the U.S. Census Bureau and many other public and private surveys. Such information is used both to learn about people today, and also to predict future trends. The number of people in various age groups affects the type of housing built, where it is built, and specific design features. In general, the average age of Americans is rising. People age 65 and older now outnumber teens. The U.S. Census Bureau estimates that the population of older Americans will increase by about 75 percent by the year 2030. That's compared to a growth of about 6 percent for people 18 years and under.

The fact that Americans are now living longer has created special housing needs. The majority of older adults continue to live independently, alone or with a spouse. Many retired Americans move to the warm regions of the southern United States. This has resulted in a housing boom in these regions. Even if they do not relocate to new areas, many retired people move to smaller, more manageable housing units. Older adults may require homes that accommodate physical disabilities, such as poor vision, arthritis, or hearing impairments. Some older adults move to retirement homes or other buildings that offer a higher level of assistance. Others move in with family members.

People born in the 20-year period immediately following World War II, the **baby boomers**, form the largest group of Americans. As the baby boomers age, a larger number of Americans will be over age 65 than ever before. In 2000, nearly 35 million people were age 65 and older. In 2050, the number is projected to be nearly 80 million. Baby boomers have also affected housing design. As they grow older and become "empty nesters" (families whose children have grown and left home), they are looking for smaller homes with fewer stairs and less maintenance. These houses are sometimes called "patio" homes because they feature low-maintenance patios and relatively small yards.

In contrast to the large number of baby boomers, your generation is much smaller. Although it is uncertain exactly how your generation will affect housing design, you may have an easier time buying a home than did the generation before you. As baby boomers move out of the housing market, a surplus of homes may be available. Noting that there may be fewer first-time buyers, some experts predict that the price of housing may decrease sharply in some areas of North America.

ECONOMIC CONDITIONS

The economy affects people's choices of housing and the value they receive when they buy a home. These economic conditions include the level of interest rates for home loans, unemployment, inflation, and the cost of living. One or more of these can determine if people choose to delay home purchases and what type of home they choose to buy.

For example, the state of the economy affects interest rates for home loans. Depending on the amount of money available for home loans, interest rates vary. *Interest* is money paid for using borrowed money. Interest rates are usually given in percentages. Interest rates may go up when loan money is scarce or go down when loan money is plentiful.

Prices of homes also affect affordability. Housing prices have risen drastically during the last 50 years.

On the average, 32 percent of people's income is now spent on their monthly home payments. In the 1970s, it was only 24 percent. In some parts of the country, population increases are outpacing available housing. In those locations, people are bidding for homes and sometimes offering more than the sellers' asking price. The same holds true for renters in areas of the country where rental property is scarce.

In some cases, the cost of housing has risen faster than people's incomes. One result is that some people must live in substandard housing. Problems with substandard housing include overcrowding, unhealthy and unsanitary conditions, unsafe situations, and lack of contact with any natural environment such as parks. Substandard buildings and homes can have poor plumbing, dangerous electrical wiring, rats and insects, fire hazards,

When living conditions are undesirable, the result can be destruction of property and increased crime. How can a sense of community help lessen these problems?

and deteriorating structures. Housing problems are linked to violence, vandalism and destruction of property, verbal abuse to family members and neighbors, and theft and crime. Substandard housing has an impact on us all.

ENVIRONMENTAL AWARENESS

Rising fuel costs, concern over pollution, and an interest in recycling are some of the environmental concerns that impact housing today. For example, insulation in homes was not used in the early 1900s. Today, builders wouldn't think of constructing a home without it. Proper insulation cuts down on the cost of heating and cooling a home and conserves resources. Materials that once collected in landfills are being used in a variety of home products. For example, recycled plastic is used for many home products such as porch decking and roofing.

Solar panels are no longer an oddity found on just a few homes. Future projections promise more innovative heating and cooling concepts. In Chapter 3, you'll learn other techniques builders and homeowners use to conserve our resources.

WORKING AT HOME

Many of today's homes do double duty as offices. Studies reveal that more than 55 million people work from their homes every day. Some people start their own home-based businesses, such as writing or consulting. Others **telecommute**, or work from home while keeping in touch with an employer's office. A telecommuter might attend a meeting with a conference telephone call, access the company's sales data using a home computer and a cable modem or satellite connection, and use e-mail to send a report to a colleague hundreds of miles away. Technological advances have made working from home easier and more efficient.

Some people feel that there are tradeoffs in working at home. Although people who work at home gain a quiet, independent place to work, some may feel isolated. In addition, some people find it more difficult to separate their work and personal life when living and working in the same environment.

Today, many people adapt existing spaces—such as a dining room, an unused bedroom, or part of a basement—to incorporate home offices. More homes being built today may be designed and built with space for a home office.

MOBILITY CREATES DIVERSE COMMUNITIES

If you had a bird's eye view of the country, you would see heavily populated cities, suburban areas, small towns, and homes out in the country. Our nation offers people the opportunity to choose from a variety

Many people relocate because of job opportunities. What do you think are other common reasons?

of lifestyles. Many people choose to live in a city to be near their work and cultural activities. They enjoy being at the center of city activity. Some people prefer small towns because of the neighborliness and feeling of safety. You'll find many families in suburban areas enjoying pleasant yards and more spacious surroundings. In rural areas, you'll find families living on farms, but also many families simply choose to live in a rural environment. Nationally, non-metro areas are growing three times faster than they did 20 years ago. Many people want to live outside of congested cities and are choosing small towns and rural areas.

Each year, approximately one out of every five people in the United States moves. The average American will have 12 to 13 homes in his or her lifetime. Often, people move because of a job or because they desire a different lifestyle.

People in their mid-20s move more than any other group. In fact, each year one-third of all people in their 20s move. What are the reasons you think young adults move so often?

People aged 45 and older are less likely to move. In fact, fewer than one tenth do. Therefore, as the population ages, experts predict that people will tend to stay in their homes longer. This decrease in mobility may have an impact on new housing in the future.

The trend toward working at home is another factor that may decrease mobility. Instead of relocating to take a new job, more people may telecommute or start their own businesses.

Moving to rural areas has become increasingly common. Why would some people prefer country living?

The Government's Role

In the United States and Canada, as in most countries, government bodies are involved in many aspects of housing. For example, governments provide a legal system for the buying and selling of property, impose taxes on homeowners to pay for community services, and are involved in funding new housing

STATE AND LOCAL GOVERNMENTS

In the earliest North American settlements, few regulations affected housing. Towns simply expanded as more people needed homes. Laws did not restrict where houses could be built. No one checked to see whether the homes were safe.

State and community officials now take a much more active role in controlling development by adopting comprehensive plans for future growth. Officials look at how available space can best be used for housing, business, and industry in the future. By setting aside certain areas for particular uses, the planners attempt to provide the best living and working environments possible. Space is set aside for parks. Plans are made for schools and shopping areas. Public transportation is made accessible.

Local government officials also play a role in ensuring that housing meets minimum standards for safety, sanitation, and space. Every unit, for example, must have a bathroom. Local codes require fire exits for multiunit buildings.

Many state and city governments have enacted laws that control expansion of housing developments in certain areas. These "open space" laws, in most cases, are designed to limit development so that overbuilding does not occur. This strategy aims to prevent such problems as water shortages and traffic congestion. Other laws have been passed to revitalize inner cities. As a result, many cities such as Chicago, Illinois, have seen their inner-city neighborhoods revive.

FEDERAL GOVERNMENT ACTIONS

Prior to the 1930s, the U.S. government provided little help in solving housing problems. People who could not find or afford housing turned to their families, charitable organizations, or sometimes local government. The economic hardship of the Great Depression of the 1930s, though, left millions without adequate housing. Poverty and homelessness are still intertwined today. The U.S. government has stepped in to help.

Public Housing

The U.S. government works with local housing agencies to help provide housing for those in need. The local agency identifies the need for low-income housing and determines how it can best be met.

In the past, the most common solution was to build large buildings with many apartments. The local housing agency managed the building and determined who was eligible to live there. Residents usually paid a set percentage of their income for rent, and the government paid the rest. However, that type of housing project has been criticized for isolating low-income families from the rest of the community. In many communities, the deteriorated public housing is being demolished.

Most new developments have plans that outline where houses can be built, along with other features such as parks. What is the importance of green space?

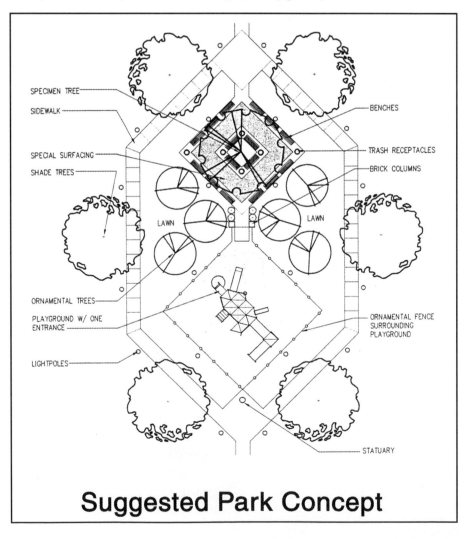

Suggested Park Concept

Americans with Disabilities Act—Impact on Public Environments

The American with Disabilities Act became law in 1990. Since then the ADA has improved access for individuals with disabilities so that they can participate in community life without unnecessary barriers.

The Americans with Disabilities Act bans discrimination against Americans with disabilities in employment, transportation, public accommodations, public services, and telecommunications. All people must be considered equally when it comes to new construction and changes in public accommodations and commercial facilities. This means that builders must take into account the needs of all Americans when designing or adapting public or commercial buildings.

The 1988 Fair Housing Amendments Act protects persons with disabilities from unfair and discriminatory housing practices. It also provides for architectural accessibility and adaptable design requirements in new multiple-family housing built for first occupants after March 13, 1991.

Here are some examples of how architects and designers work to create accessibility:

- **Involvement in civic life.** Every citizen has a right to participate in the civic life of our country. To address problems associated with hearing losses, a New York community purchased a public address system for town board meetings. To make town halls and courtrooms accessible many communities have installed entrance ramps and renovated restrooms.

- **Educational opportunities.** To provide accessibility to persons with disabilities numerous universities and colleges across the nation have developed a broad range of facilities and programs. This has included modifying elevators, entrances, restrooms, telephones, and classrooms. Distance education programs have allowed individuals who are not able to live on campus access to educational opportunities.

- **Living the American style.** Living the American style includes having accessibility to shopping, dining, recreation, and travel. To provide accessibility to persons with disabilities stores, hotels, stadiums, theaters, restaurants, and transportation systems have removed barriers to entrances, restrooms, ticket counters, and cashier stations.

- **Accessible health care.** Providing access to health care in the public and private sector includes hospitals, long-term care programs, and offices of physicians. Modifications to these facilities included providing accessible parking, restroom facilities, installing ramps, widening doors, and lowering information counters. These facilities also have effective communication for individuals with hearing, speech, and vision impairments.

You, the *Designer*

Imagine you are part of a design team responsible for providing accessibility for people with disabilities in a remodeled museum. Decide what accessible features you would recommend for the entrance of the museum. What accessibility features would you use in exhibit spaces? Give rationales for your choices.

In the place of those large buildings, new public housing programs are incorporating low-income housing throughout communities. Residents are encouraged to become part of their new neighborhoods. In some programs, new buildings contain no more than 20 apartments. In other programs, housing agencies work with private owners to rent to low-income families. The government guarantees the owner fair rent and may help pay part of it. In other instances, those in need are given housing vouchers that they may use to move closer to job opportunities.

In Canada, the government provides funds to build accessible housing for elderly people, low-income families, and people with special needs. In addition, the government provides funding for personal support and homemaking services for these people and for those with specific medical conditions.

Urban Renewal

Urban renewal programs attempt to redevelop run-down urban areas. The U.S. government has provided much of the money needed to make major improvements in large inner-city areas. In some cases in the past this meant clearing and rebuilding whole neighborhoods. Families and businesses had no choice but to move. Since the 1960s, more emphasis has been placed on saving and repairing existing buildings whenever possible. For example, the federal government has bought homes that were in poor condition and given them to a local housing agency for repair. The homes can then be sold to needy families at affordable prices.

Most American cities have implemented programs to help the homeless, but unfortunately the problem has not been erased.

Providing for the Elderly and the Disabled

The U.S. Department of Housing and Urban Development (HUD) provides funding for housing the elderly and the disabled. This funding is available for rent assistance, group housing, adapting an existing home for all needs, and new construction of *barrier-free* homes, or those homes without structures that would prevent access to people with special needs. HUD often funds programs that help aging adults and people with disabilities live on their own in independent facilities.

Emergency Shelter Grants for the Homeless

Many people, either briefly or for the long term, are without adequate housing. Estimates reveal that 3.5 million people will experience homelessness in one year. Families make up 43 percent of the homeless in the United States, with children accounting for almost one-third of all homeless people. That is over 1 million children. Homelessness is not directly related to not having a job. A recent study found that one out of five homeless people has a job. The number of homeless people in North America seems to be growing. Because of this, greater emphasis is being placed on developing housing for the homeless.

Poverty and the lack of decent affordable housing underlies the problem of homelessness. HUD, through Special Needs Assistance Programs, grants states and communities funds for housing the homeless. These funds can be used to renovate or convert buildings to be used as homeless shelters.

HABITAT FOR HUMANITY

Partnership is empowering. That is the simple philosophy behind Habitat for Humanity International. Habitat for Humanity is a nonprofit housing ministry dedicated to eliminating poverty housing and homelessness around the world.

Habitat houses are built through partnership. Volunteers from all walks of life contribute their time and skills to build or renovate homes. For example, former U.S. President Jimmy Carter is an active Habitat volunteer. The family that will become the homeowners are also partners in the process. They contribute hundreds of hours of

Since Habitat for Humanity began in 1976, more than 100,000 homes have been built in more than 60 countries.

"sweat equity" to help construct their own homes. By investing themselves in the building process, homeowners gain self-esteem and new skills. In addition, the new homeowners make a down payment and modest monthly payments that are used to build more housing through a revolving Fund for Humanity.

By bringing people together to work on a project, Habitat builds new relationships and a sense of community as well as new housing. Thanks to Habitat for Humanity, thousands of American families are able to own their own homes.

Relocation Specialist

Matthew Kingfisher

The corporation I work for has offices and manufacturing plants around the world. That's why we have our own relocation department. Smaller employers hire companies that specialize in relocation to help move their employees.

Eighteen months ago I was working in the purchasing department when a job as a relocation specialist was posted. A few years back in another

"I know firsthand how tough moving can be. Changing jobs is stressful and when someone has to find a new home, too, there's even more stress."

city, I had worked in real estate, so I thought I might have a shot at the job. The interviewer seemed interested in the fact that I had moved a number of times myself. I know firsthand how tough moving can be. Changing jobs is stressful and when someone has to find a new home, too, there's even more stress.

When I'm notified that an employee is being transferred to another city, I arrange an orientation. Most of the time that's a meeting with the employee and his or her spouse. Sometimes when several people are moving to the same location, I schedule a group orientation to save time. That might involve as many as 25 people meeting over the phone lines!

First I cover our employer's rules and regulations for moving. I explain how expense books should be filled out. It's extremely important that this be done correctly. We talk about trips they will be allowed to take for house-hunting purposes. I assign them a moving company. Then it's their job to contact the movers and meet with them.

Our employees have the option of selling their home themselves or having us help. They are given a guarantee of a minimum selling price for their home. If it sells for less, we make up the difference. Sometimes I

last all day. They all would need to visit the company doctor for shots and talk to our staff psychologist. I would also help arrange for passports, tax advice, pets, and language tutoring. Some families choose to study the language before they leave and also once they arrive at their destination. Most of our employees stay abroad for 3 to 5 years. My plan would be to be around to help with their return move to the United States.

help with financing a home in their new location. If the employee doesn't have a 20 percent down payment, I arrange for financing to allow him or her to put 20 percent down.

Some employers pay moving bonuses to their employees. Our company typically pays an extra month's salary that the employee uses to pay relocation expenses. If their move is to what we classify as a high-cost area, they receive more money. Currently we have offices in five areas of the U.S. that have a higher cost of living. It's possible that we'll be adding to the list.

My next challenge may be helping with international moves. This position would be even more demanding. My orientations with families would

"When I'm notified that an employee is being transferred to another city, I arrange an orientation."

Career Profile

Relocation specialists provide services to individuals and to corporate clients and their employees throughout the world. They use knowledge of housing and real estate industries, as well as new computer technology to explore options and ensure a cost-effective move. Effective teamwork is necessary. Customer satisfaction is the ultimate goal of relocation services.

Education
▶ Classes and work experience within the real estate industry are desirable. A real estate license is sometimes required. Proficiency with applicable computer programs is necessary.
▶ Knowledge of the housing industry, real estate-related documents, sale and re-sale contract negotiations, the mortgage process, and relocation tax law are important.

Skills Needed
▶ The detail person who can multi-task while utilizing strong verbal and written communication skills will be an effective relocation specialist.
▶ An ability to use real estate and service-related Internet searches on the client's behalf, as well as proficiency with software programs proves invaluable.
▶ An ability to track and analyze financial data, coupled with a problem-solving approach.

Career Outlook
▶ Prospects are brightening for this career. Demand for varied relocation services is growing rapidly, especially in areas dominated by high-tech growth.

Career Activities
1. Research the cost of housing in various regions of the United States. Where are housing costs highest? Lowest?
2. Imagine that you're helping a family with two teens relocate in Madison, Wisconsin. Use the Internet to learn facts about the area that would be helpful to the family.

*R*eview & Activities

Chapter Summary

➤ A group's culture affects the type, style, arrangement, and furnishings of its homes.

➤ The housing of a cultural group reflects that group's values, including attitudes toward households, privacy, and status.

➤ Because of increased travel, trade, and communication, cultures today often share housing styles and concepts.

➤ Societal changes can create a demand for new styles of housing within a culture.

➤ Changing family roles and structures, changing economic conditions, and increasing environmental awareness affect housing choices.

➤ State and local governments can develop and enforce regulations for controlling the growth and quality of housing in an area.

➤ Government programs can help people with a wide variety of housing needs obtain safe, secure, and affordable homes.

Checking Your Understanding

1. What is meant by the term *household*? Give examples of three different types.

2. Describe a type of living arrangement that shows how some Israelis value group goals.

3. Explain how the land surrounding a house reflects status in England.

4. Give an example of how one culture's housing traditions have spread to another culture.

5. Identify four societal changes that have affected housing in America. Give an example of each.

6. By the year 2050, will there be more or fewer Americans over age 65 than today? How might this affect the housing market?

7. How might the trend toward home offices affect housing needs?

8. Describe three kinds of federal housing programs.

9. If a family wants to own a Habitat for Humanity home, what must they do?

Thinking Critically

1. You have read that the result of one culture's influence on another is not always positive. How might it be possible to protect cultures from damaging influences? What are the dangers of limiting outside influences?

2. What cultural views and values are reflected by the housing in your school district? Discuss differences and similarities between neighborhoods in your district as well.

3. What local government housing regulations would you want enacted to protect the quality of life in your neighborhood?

4. What type of housing might you develop for the homeless? Explain your reasoning.

Review & Activities

Applications

1. **Analyzing Housing Needs.** In the classified section of your local newspaper, find description of homes that would be suitable for each of the following households: a young single person, an extended family, a couple without children, and a single-parent family. Explain why each home might suit the needs of that household.

2. **Journal Writing.** Write a journal entry describing your own feelings about privacy and individualism as they relate to housing.

3. **Refit a Home for the Environment.** Working in groups of three to five students, research innovations in new or existing housing that help preserve our natural resources. You could use the Internet and interview local contractors about new techniques. Compare your group's work with your classmates' findings and assemble all the guidelines into an illustrated booklet or website for homeowners.

4. **Balance Work and Personal Life.** Write a short magazine article giving tips for people who work at home. Focus on how they can keep their work life separate from their personal life.

5. **Community Living Conditions.** During the early years of the 20th century many immigrants moved to the United States in search of better lives. Most lived in large cities in crowded apartment buildings known as tenements. Research tenement living and explain the harsh conditions under which these immigrants lived. Does this still occur in today's society?

6. **People on the Move.** In the last 20 years, the number of existing one-family homes sold in the South rose from 1,092,000 to 1,868,000. In the Midwest, the number of homes rose from 806,000 to 1,130,000. Which area had greater percentage increase in sales? By what amount?

BUILDING YOUR PORTFOLIO

You have decided to enter a contest sponsored by the Advanced Housing Study Committee. The committee is interested in finding new ideas for housing. The theme of the contest is "Designing the Ideal House." To enter the contest:

➤ Describe in 150 words or less a new home that would be ideally suited for the 21st century.

➤ Try to describe a home that could be used by many types of families or that could be changed to adapt to a family's needs.

➤ Include facts about societal changes that support your design.

➤ Create a drawing of your home, if you choose.

Entries will be judged on practicality and originality.

The Impact of Technology

CHAPTER OBJECTIVES

► Analyze the role of technology in home construction.

► Evaluate the benefits and drawbacks of different natural and manufactured materials used in home construction.

► Describe the three basic methods of home construction.

► Evaluate the role of high technology in homes today.

TERMS TO LEARN

- automated management systems
- biomaterials
- biometrics
- computer-aided design (CAD)
- conventional construction
- engineered wood products
- green building
- manufactured homes
- modular homes
- site
- systems-built homes
- technology

$\mathscr{I}$t's hard to realize all the planning, hard labor, skills, and time it took to construct a home in the 1700s. Families and friends often combined their skills and resources to make the task of building a home less difficult. Even a one-room house presented many challenges. Today's builders utilize new materials, specialized tools, and state-of-the-art construction methods to assemble homes in record time.

$\mathscr{T}$he Technology Revolution

Since the Stone Age and the dawn of tool making, people have worked to improve the quality of life. State-of-the-art tools advanced from axes with stone blades to hardened iron and steel machinery. The Industrial Revolution, which began about 1750 and lasted until about 1900, spurred on many technological advancements that benefited the building industry. In 1885, for example, builders in Chicago completed construction of the first metal-framed skyscraper. Today major advances in technology continually change building materials, tools, and techniques of housing construction. In the past, *technology* was often described as "the study of making and doing things." It focused on tools and machines. Today, **technology** is defined as the practical application of knowledge—people using what they know to change their environment.

$\mathcal{M}$aterials and Construction Technology

For centuries, people were forced to build with locally available materials. Today, builders can import materials from other locations and even create new materials. Builders have access to the broadest range of both natural and manufactured materials. In addition, advances in technology have led to the development of more effective and efficient tools and building methods for use in home construction.

NATURAL MATERIALS

Natural building materials are resources provided by nature that have been adapted for use in construction. The three most commonly used natural building materials in home construction are wood, stone, and brick.

Wood

Almost every home contains some wood in its construction. Lumber—boards and large pieces of wood cut from logs—is the basis for many interior house frames, floors, woodwork, doors, and other building parts. The construction industry uses approximately one-half of all the lumber produced from trees in the United States. About one quarter of all lumber is used in the repair and remodeling of homes.

Wood is divided into two classes: *softwood* and *hardwood*. Although these terms sound as if they relate to the hardness of the lumber, they actually refer to the type of tree the lumber comes from. In fact, some softwood lumber is actually heavier and harder than hardwood.

Softwood lumber comes from trees of the conifer family. These trees, more commonly known as evergreens, include various pines, cedars, redwood, and spruce. The wood from these trees is used for flooring, walls, and roof supports as well as for door frames and window frames.

Hardwood lumber is the product of broad-leafed trees. These trees, which generally lose their leaves in autumn, include oak, walnut, maple, and birch. Hardwoods are used mainly in furniture making, although they are also found in flooring, paneling, and trim.

Even though the United States is one of the major producers of lumber in the world, it imports more lumber and wood products than it exports. Imported wood products include teak, mahogany, bamboo, and cork. The United States and Canada together supply one-third of the world's logs.

Wood adds to the beauty of a home's interior. Whether using wood to surround a sunroom hot tub or panel a family room wall, the choice of grain and color affect the feel of the room.

Skyscrapers—How High Can They Go?

Since the pyramids in Egypt were constructed, people have been designing ways to build tall structures. The invention of steel allowed skyscrapers, the first modern tall buildings, to be constructed. In 1857 the invention of the elevator made it practical to construct buildings taller than four to five stories high.

As buildings became taller, technological improvements focused on dealing with high winds. To prevent a building from falling over, tall buildings are engineered to bend like a tall blade of grass. Today, technological improvements in materials and computer analyses allow architects and engineers to design buildings in a variety of forms, shapes, and heights. Predictions call for skyscrapers that house entire communities in the future.

Architects and engineers base new techniques on an understanding of the technological advances in tall buildings of the past. Here are some famous examples:

- *Chrysler building.* In 1930, at a height of 1,046 feet including 77 stories, the Chrysler building was the world's tallest building for four months. Walter Chrysler, president of the Chrysler automobile company, had the building designed in the motif of the automobile, including hubcaps, mudguards, and hood ornaments. This New York City landmark is internationally known for its Art Deco style, which is characterized by Z-shaped ornamentation.

- *Empire State building.* The Chrysler building's short period of fame as the world's tallest building was due to the construction of the Empire State building in New York City in 1931. It surpassed the Chrysler building by 204 feet and 25 stories. A steel frame weighing 60,000 tons supports the building. The building was finished with 10 million bricks, 200,000 cubic feet of Indiana limestone, and 730 tons of aluminum and stainless steel. The building is so strong it survived an airplane crashing into the building.

- *Sears tower.* Chicago is the birthplace of the skyscraper. Thus, it is appropriate that the Sears tower located in Chicago became the world's tallest building in 1974. At 1,454 feet the Sears tower was built of nine huge steel framed tubes bundled together. This created a light but extremely strong, tall building.

- *Petronas towers.* The Sears tower was surpassed as the world's tallest building in 1998 by the construction of the Petronas towers in Malaysia. Including the spires that top the Petronas towers, the height of the building is 1,483 feet. The floor plans of the Petronas towers are in the form of an eight-pointed star, a design traditionally used in Malaysian Islamic patterns. The Towers are very well known for the technologically complicated skybridge that connects the two towers on the 42nd floor.

You, the *Designer*

Imagine you are part of a design team responsible for designing a skyscraper that houses an entire community near Seattle, Washington. What shape would you recommend for the building? What materials would you use on the outside of the building? Give rationales for your choices.

Stone

Although wood is perhaps the most commonly used natural material for building homes, it is not always available. People who live in rocky, treeless areas, such as southern Italy and western Ireland, traditionally build their homes from local stone. Homes built hundreds of years ago are still standing today, as evidence of the strength and durability of this natural building material.

Stone is taken from natural deposits in the earth. It is mined through *quarrying*, the excavation of a large stone deposit. Quarried stone used for building construction is called *dimension stone*. This stone is cut, often at the quarry site, into large blocks or slabs of different sizes and shapes. The most common types of dimension stone used for residential construction are limestone, sandstone, marble, and slate. Limestone and sandstone are used primarily in heavy construction, such as exterior walls. Marble, which is often polished to a high luster, is used to decorate stairways, fireplaces, and floors. Slate, a fine-grained rock, appears most commonly in roofing shingles and flagstone flooring.

In many countries, housing styles vary from region to region, depending on the type of stone quarried. In the Cotswold Hills of central England, for example, houses are typically made of cream-colored limestone, while in southwestern England, whitewashed stone cottages are common. In other areas of the country, houses are built of red sandstone.

Brick

Still another natural material widely used in home building today is clay. In primitive times, clay was applied wet, like plaster, and allowed to harden. Today, clay used for construction is made into bricks.

The first bricks, used more than 5,000 years ago, were made of molded clay that was permitted to bake hard in the sun. Today, bricks are baked—or "burned"—in ovens that reach temperatures of 2200°F (approximately 1200°C). The heating process gives the bricks their characteristic color.

Bricks are used in the construction of many types of homes, from large buildings to single-family homes. They can form a building's structure or be used for fireplaces, chimneys, and decorative facings for interior or exterior walls. Bricks are a strong, versatile, and durable building material.

When choosing brick for their home, buyers often look for patterns and colors they like on actual homes. With this information, the supplier can identify the same or similar styles in the samples.

About 30 friends and neighbors helped form the walls of this unique Illinois home. Walls were made from straw bales and held in place by bamboo. Three coats of stucco were then applied. What would be the environmental benefits of the house?

MANUFACTURED MATERIALS

Although wood, stone, and brick are widely used in home construction today, natural materials have their limitations. Some natural materials are not suitable for particular uses. Another limitation of natural resources is that their supply is limited. The massive cutting of trees in the 20th century has led to a scarcity of lumber. This shortage has, in turn, led to yet another problem: higher cost. When resources, such as lumber, are in short supply, the price goes up. Concerns such as these have led to the development of manufactured building materials.

Engineered Wood Products

In addition to dwindling resources, builders have been concerned with the low quality of lumber being produced. To conserve resources, keep prices down, and develop more reliable products, technology has provided home builders with **engineered wood products**, or manufactured materials formed from wood. One type, called composite lumber, is made by applying high pressure to paper-thin strips of wood that have been sprayed with glue. Composite lumber is made from trees such as the aspen, which have trunks too slender to make good conventional lumber. Because these trees are fast growing and short-lived, their use does not interfere with conservation efforts.

Building components made from engineered wood products for use in home construction include joists and beams. According to experts, the uses for engineered wood products will not change in the near future, but the materials and technology used to produce them probably will.

Concrete and Cement

Of all manufactured building materials, concrete—a mixture of gravel, cement, and water—is the oldest. It is also one of the most durable. In fact, concrete columns built by the Egyptians 3,600 years ago are still standing.

Concrete used in home construction today is often delivered in the form of blocks. These blocks have a wide range of uses. Liquid concrete is also used. It can be poured to form the foundation, or underlying support, of homes as well as exterior elements, such as porches, patios, and steps. Precast concrete is used to provide energy-efficient walls to frame homes.

Concrete provides builders with many advantages over wood and brick. It is twice as strong as brick. It is also relatively inexpensive to produce, slow to disintegrate, and fire-resistant.

A new type of siding for exterior walls is called fiber-cement siding. Fiber-cement siding is a mixture of cement, sand, and cellulose fiber. It looks like wood siding but it is more durable, termite resistant, won't catch fire, and is warranted to last for 50 years.

Using steel in homes has many advantages. Steel is lighter than wood, is economical, and has high strength. A steel-framed home will also resist termites and withstand rugged environmental conditions.

Steel

More and more homes are being built with steel. Steel is often used as the internal frame of a house because it can withstand severe weather, insect attacks, and fire. Steel framing is longer lasting than other materials. It won't crack, warp, twist, rot, split, or settle like wood framing might. Steel-framed houses are strong. For example, steel provides outstanding resistance against earthquakes and hurricane winds up to 110 mph. Since steel is stronger than wood, fewer building materials are required. Steel can benefit indoor air quality because it does not need to be treated with chemicals or resins.

Other Manufactured Metals

Aluminum, another manufactured metal, is commonly used in North America in the form of siding to cover frame houses. This metal provides insulation, prevents rotting,

and eliminates the need for repainting. In addition, many modern homes have metal window frames, which require less maintenance than wooden frames.

Foam

Home builders only a few years ago would never have thought of using foam, but today rigid plastic foam products as well as spray foam are finding their way into many homes. One new technology features snap-together rigid foam blocks and concrete. Interlocking blocks are snapped together to form the foundation and walls of a house. Then steel rods are passed through the blocks to reinforce the walls and concrete is poured into the block cavities. The result is a very strong and energy-efficient house that uses 50 percent less energy than similar-sized houses.

Some homes are being built with structural insulated panels (SIPs). Structural insulated panels consist of two exterior panels adhered to a rigid foam core. The SIPs provide excellent insulation and sound proofing.

Spray foam is another energy-efficient way to insulate a home. It's sprayed into place and expands to fill even small cavities. Spray foam is safe for the environment, too.

Plastic

Because plastic is light and flexible and can be formed into nearly any desired shape, it has been gaining acceptance in recent years as a building material. In fact, the United States building industry is now the world's second largest user of plastics. The disadvantage of using such materials as plastic and metal is that they are not *biodegradable*—they will not break down over time if they become refuse, so they are not kind to the environment.

Plastic is used in many ways and forms in home construction. For plumbing, it is lighter in weight and less expensive than copper, the metal traditionally used for pipes. Plastic is also being used in sheets for siding and roofing. It's used as insulation for cables and wires. There is even plastic "lumber" from recycled plastic. Builders find it provides a low-maintenance option for residential decking and other outdoor uses. Durable plastic lumber can also be used for interior framework on homes.

Recycled Materials

Today, people consider recycling such products as newspapers, plastic, and glass an essential part of their daily lives. Recycling has also found its way into the home-building industry. **Biomaterials**, organically-based building materials manufactured from recycled matter, are being used in construction in a number of ways. Construction experts have found that, like plastic, biomaterials can be molded into a variety of shapes and forms. One type of high-strength biomaterial is made from wheat straw, wood shavings, recycled newspaper, and recycled plastic. This material has been used to build interior walls and outdoor decks. Floor tile made from recycled car windshields is another example.

Biomaterials offer several advantages over wood. These new materials typically last much longer and do not warp or split. Biomaterials are also less costly than lumber yet they can be drilled, nailed, and screwed.

Yet another advantage of biomaterials over conventional building materials is that they can be customized to meet specific uses and climate conditions. For example, if a more flexible material is needed for a particular use, more fiber in the form of extra newspaper or straw can be added.

When biomaterials were first introduced, there were some disadvantages. They often didn't look like wood, and glues used in their manufacture produced dangerous fumes. Strict regulatory controls helped eliminate most problems.

For the homeowner who doesn't want to repaint a deck every few years, vinyl is an option. This product maintains its color, holds up well in harsh climates, and is completely recyclable.

Green Building

Every year, housing in North America accounts for more than 20 percent of the total energy consumption and contributes to the problem of pollution. The average home produces more air pollution than the average car. Housing construction, renovation, and demolition create about 58 million tons of waste a year. In response to these problems, more and more builders and home buyers are looking toward green building. **Green building** is designing, building, and operating homes to use materials, energy, and water efficiently. Green building results in lower heating and cooling costs, less maintenance, and healthier indoor environments. Some green-building techniques include:

- Using alternative energy technologies such as solar energy and geothermal heat pumps.
- Using more insulation and insulating properly.
- Using energy-efficient heating and cooling systems as well as lighting, windows, and appliances.
- Choosing recycled and recyclable building materials. For example, steel-framed houses can be made from recycled steel. A typical 2,000 square foot wood house requires about 40 to 50 trees, while a steel-framed house can be made from 8 recycled cars. In the last decade, more than one trillion pounds of steel scrap has been recycled and kept out of landfills.
- Designing homes to use less material. Steel provides advantages in this area, too. Because steel is stronger than wood, less material is needed.

One organization leading the way in green building is the Partnership for Advanced Technology in Housing (PATH). PATH is a public/private partnership that works with industry leaders to advance the home building industry. PATH provides the latest information on innovative building materials and methods. Through the use of PATH-evaluated technologies, annual carbon emissions from homes in the next few years could be reduced by 13 million tons. That's equivalent to the amount of carbon emissions produced each year by more than 10 million cars.

TOOLS AND METHODS OF CONSTRUCTION

As you have seen, technology has changed the types of materials used within the construction industry. There have also been changes in the tools and methods used to build homes.

Tools

For centuries, the only tools available to construction workers were simple ones, such as the hammer and the handsaw. Labor by hand was the only construction method used. Homes were built slowly and one at a time.

A skilled crane operator can move building materials into place with speed and ease. There are different sizes of cranes to match the weight of the material and the height of the structure.

Today, although hand labor continues to play a vital role in construction, new tools and methods are making the process more efficient. Heavy equipment, such as cranes and bulldozers, is commonplace at construction sites. This equipment saves time and cuts down on the number of workers needed for a job.

Even hand tools have changed. For example, on a construction site you'll find that power nailers are taking over the work of hammers. The handheld tools used today for home building are more powerful and efficient than their predecessors. They are also far more specialized, with each tool designed to perform a particular task.

Many companies making new tools are designing them to be light and portable, eliminating the need for attached cords or hoses. Lighter tools also cause fewer injuries than heavy ones do. New batteries have been developed to boost power for power tools so that they can perform for longer periods of time. Some new tools have been designed to work together, with one tool capable of attaching to another to perform a specific task.

Methods

Many of the labor-intensive tasks were once painstakingly done by hand at the housing **site**—the land and surrounding environment on which the home will be built. Now many tasks are accomplished by machines more quickly and less expensively at the factory. For example, kitchen cabinets and other fixtures are precut, and bathroom fixtures can be molded in one piece. Workers in factories can even produce entire homes in sections and transport them to the housing site. In some cases, robots handle much of the labor.

Imagine building your dream house or seeing remodeling plans before a worker ever picks up a saw. Computers make it possible and are becoming increasingly important in planning home building.

Computer-aided design (CAD) programs—software that enables designers, architects, and drafters to make construction drawings, interior designs, and other drawings using a computer—are very useful. Designers can complete their plans more quickly and efficiently than ever before. These programs help builders in many tasks, including identifying design flaws and correcting them before construction begins. Home buyers can log onto the Internet to find home plans they like—and shop for existing homes.

Regardless of technological advances, human skills will always be required in home building. Skilled workers must operate the tools and make sure that the methods and materials used are the best ones available for the jobs to be done. Skilled workers also must make sure that the finished homes meet high quality standards.

TYPES OF CONSTRUCTION

As mentioned previously, some homes are made from assembled sections built in a factory. That method is just one of the options available for building homes today. In general, newly built homes fall into three categories, based on their method of construction: conventional construction, systems-built homes, and manufactured homes.

Conventional Construction

The most common way of building a house, which for centuries was the only way, is through conventional construction. **Conventional construction** is a building method in which materials are cut and assembled piece by piece at the home site. Houses constructed in this fashion are sometimes referred to as *stick built* or *site built*.

In conventional construction, lumber or steel and other materials are brought to the building site. There they are measured, cut, and assembled piece by piece. While this method can produce a well-built home, it has some disadvantages. Usually there are excess materials that go to waste. In addition, bad weather can delay construction for days or even weeks.

When a house is built conventionally, the homebuyer can closely observe each step in the process.

Systems-Built Homes

Here are three types of systems-built homes:

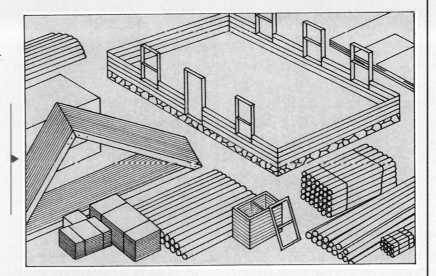

PRECUT PACKAGE
The parts of this type of home are cut to specific dimensions at a factory, and some components are preassembled. Most of the assembly, however, is done at the site.

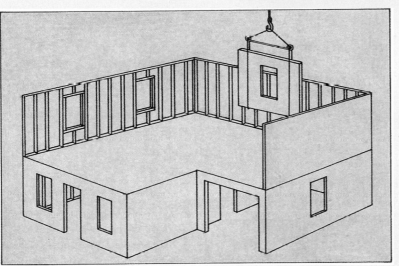

PANELS
Panels that will eventually become the walls, roof, and floor of a home are assembled in the factory. They are attached to one another at the building site. In panel construction, labor costs are reduced.

MODULAR
Modular homes are built from a set of coordinated boxlike sections, or modules. Many factories make modules according to the buyer's specifications. The various modules contain separate sections of the home, such as the master bedroom and bath in one module and the kitchen and dining room in another. While the modules and roof panels are built at the factory, the foundation is constructed at the building site. A crane sets the modules in place, one at a time, and then they are fastened together.

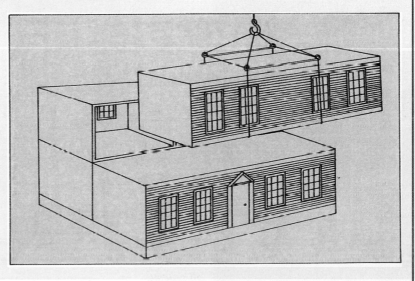

Systems-Built Homes

A **systems-built home** is a dwelling whose parts are manufactured in a factory, with the building completed at the site. In a systems-built home, quality is tightly controlled and waste is kept to a minimum. These homes are well built and usually cost less than conventionally built homes. They are ready to be occupied in much less time than a home built on-site. The three major types of systems-built homes are built from precut packages, series of panels, and coordinated modules. **Modular homes** are homes made up of separate boxlike sections, or modules. Figure 3-1 illustrates these three types of systems-built homes.

Manufactured Homes

A **manufactured home** is a dwelling completely assembled at a factory and transported to the site. Another term for this type of housing is *mobile home*. The majority of these homes, however, are never moved once they have been installed at a site. Manufactured housing is the fastest growing type of housing in North America.

Manufactured homes are generally less expensive than conventionally built ones, but the cost varies, depending on size and features. Manufactured homes are fully equipped with major appliances, draperies, lighting fixtures, and car-peting. Homeowners may add such extras as cathedral ceilings, skylights, carpet, and tile.

Although manufactured homes can, in theory, be placed almost anywhere, in certain areas they are restricted to designated parks. This situation, however, is changing. In the future, it may become common to find manufactured homes in almost any neighborhood.

The United States Department of Housing and Development (HUD) has strict requirements for manufactured homes. These standards cover all equipment and installations, including plumbing, heating, electrical systems, and fire safety.

Technology in the Home

Through technology, web-based operation of all the appliances in a home is now possible. A simple palm pilot may eventually be the only device you need to control all systems.

Technological advances in construction have created homes that are assembled quickly and efficiently in factories. Technology has also expanded inside the home, changing the way people live.

ADVANCES IN HOME TECHNOLOGY

The term *high technology* or *high tech*, describes advanced developments in such areas as electronics and computers. High technology has introduced the use of the integrated circuit, or computer microchip, into the home. These microchips are small enough to fit on the fingertip, yet can control many important functions in home entertainment, lighting, communication, and security systems. Other technological advances have improved appliances and heating and cooling systems, making them more convenient and more energy efficient.

Appliances

Today's appliances are more automated, provide more convenience, and save more energy than past models. For example, some refrigerators can alert you if a door is left ajar or if maintenance is needed. Dishwashers can sense how dirty the dishes are and provide the appropriate level of cleaning. What other types of "smart" appliances would you like to see developed?

Lighting

Home lighting has been improved in recent years. Fluorescent lighting is more energy efficient than regular incandescent lightbulbs. Solar lighting, which captures and uses the sun's energy, is often used outdoors. Now there are LED (light emitting diode) lamps that consume less than a quarter of the electricity a fluorescent lamp does. LED lamps last about 10 times as long, too.

Programmable Heating and Cooling

Guidelines for conserving energy in the home suggest turning down the heat or air conditioning at bedtime and when no one is home during the day. To handle these temperature changes, some people install a programmable thermostat. With this device, people can have the computer in the thermostat turn down the temperature after everyone is in bed and then turn up the heat in the morning before people wake up. The heating temperature can then drop again if everyone is out for the day and return to a more comfortable temperature as people start to arrive home. Programmable thermostats can even allow for variations between weekdays and weekends.

Another energy-saving technique divides a house or building into zones or areas in which heating and cooling are controlled independently. That means when the temperature drops in the kitchen and family room, more heat is directed there instead of the whole house. Separate thermostats monitor each zone. When this method is combined with programmable thermostats, significant reduction in energy use is possible.

Solar energy is used to power this light. What other ways can solar energy be used in the home?

Entertainment

High technology has redefined people's idea of entertainment. Home entertainment systems—including digital TVs, DVD players, videocassette recorders, video game systems, and computer game software—change frequently in response to innovations in technology. Digital cameras and digital movie cameras offer many people the opportunity to create their own electronic entertainment. Satellite dishes and digital cable systems offer more channels and better reception to television viewers at increasingly lower costs.

The computer has quickly become a fix-ture in many homes, especially because of the widespread acceptance of the Internet.

Computers also offer people a wealth of information about hous-ing. On the Internet a person can take a virtual tour of houses for sale, find a place to rent, or learn about new building techniques. People needing information about housing programs can visit the government's various websites. People in the mar-ket to buy new furniture can visit an electronic furniture store where they can look over a selection of couches, visually try out different fabric cov-erings, and finally make their pur-chase online.

Security

Electronic door locks are a very reli-able method of securing a home. They allow doors to be locked or unlocked with the push of a button or by entering a combination on a keypad. Locks can even be hooked up to a timer for automatic locking at night, or they can be activated from a remote location. If a person doesn't want to use keys to lock a door, a lock that is powered by a bat-tery and an infrared light is avail-able. When the user touches the doorknob, a small light appears just above it. Then, to lock the door, the person enters an access code.

Communication

Personal computers offer many ways for people to share information. Electronic communication has made the world accessible. E-mail is a pop-ular means for long-distance family members and friends to stay in touch. Parents can share new photos of their children with far-away grandparents in only moments. It's even possible to form friendships with people around the world and share events of daily life.

Computer users can log on to the Internet to read the latest news sto-ries and sports scores, listen to music, or shop for everything from books to clothing to food from a local grocery store. People with com-mon interests can "chat" online or post messages for help about hob-bies, computer problems, and many other topics.

Electronic communication in the home can extend beyond the per-sonal computer. For example, there are electronic picture frames that hook up to a phone line and family and friends can download new pho-tos to each other. Memos and notes to other household members can be left in an electronic organizer rather than posted on the refrigerator.

A recent development in security systems operates on the principle that the iris of the human eye is unique. If this iris scanner recognizes you, you'll be allowed to enter the building.

Heating or cooling your home while you're away wastes energy and costs money. With a programmable thermostat, you can set temperature settings to change automatically according to your schedule.

An even more high-tech method uses **biometrics**—reading the physical characteristics of a person—to allow entry. One system scans the iris of a person's eye and matches it by computer to a list of people authorized entry. Fingerprints, palmprints, and voice can also be used. So far this technology is used primarily in business and industry. What advantages would it have in a home?

Motion-sensitive lights can be installed outdoors and inside a home. When a sensor detects movement, the light turns on. Motion-sensitive lights can deter intruders. They are also helpful to people who arrive home in the dark. Motion-sensitive lights inside the home are also an energy-efficient way to light less frequently used rooms.

Closed-circuit television (CCTV) is a system gaining popularity for use in those areas of a home that owners would like to keep secure. They might want to view children playing in a backyard, a baby asleep in a nursery, or unexpected guests approaching the front door. The system installs in a television set, and separate cameras are placed in the areas to be observed. With a remote control, a homeowner can check each site and view the home area on the television screen. The homeowner can also speak through a telephone hooked up to an intercom in the area being observed.

THE AUTOMATED HOME

The advances described on the preceding pages are only a small part of home technology. Some homes are equipped with **automated management systems**, central control units that oversee daily functions in a home. Such automated systems are designed to maximize comfort, convenience, and safety while minimizing energy use.

These Walls Can Talk

Think about the ways housing design was changed by indoor plumbing. Space for pipes, sinks—not to mention a bathroom—had to be included when a home was built. Today, rapid advances in computer technology promise another "revolution" in housing: home automation.

You've probably heard of "smart" homes that are programmed to actively influence their environment. Window blinds draw at a certain evening hour, for example, and the thermostat resets to a more comfortable temperature. Experimental versions of this technology are being further refined. Imagine walls with embedded sensors that "beep" the relative of a sick or elderly person if they don't detect movement for a certain time period, then notify paramedics and even relay the person's health background.

Getting all components to work together could be like directing six-year-olds in a school play. The key is systems integration technology, which allows different systems to "talk" to one another in a common language. Two methods of providing this exchange are finding their way into the home:

- A networking microchip in a device turns a home's wiring system into a communication system by plugging into an outlet. No change or addition to the current wiring is needed. The chip allows wires to carry both electric impulses and digital data. Just as Internet access comes over a phone line, electronic devices are managed through the same slender wires that power the appliances themselves. You could turn on the VCR and play the recording over several TV sets by typing a command into your home computer.

- Integrated electronic systems are included in the home design. This approach allows the more complex task of coordinating different systems. An architect, after learning the client's needs, consults a systems integrator or integration team. That firm customizes software that, for example, lets the security system turn on and off lights and the television when the family is on vacation. Wiring for this technology runs from a single utility room, which houses the needed equipment, to each integrated component, and to a keypad control that accesses the centralized system from each room.

THINKING IT THROUGH

1. Explain what elements of the systems in your home—including lighting, heating and air conditioning, food preparation, and entertainment—you would integrate to make them more useful.

2. Investigate fiberoptic and wireless technology. How are these technologies used in homes today? How might their increased use affect housing design?

In one system, wall outlets are provided throughout the house not only for electrical appliances but also for gas appliances, telephones, central vacuum, and audio and video equipment. These outlets are linked to a central computer "brain." When plugged into the outlets, devices that are compatible with the system can be operated automatically through programmed instructions or remote commands. When away from home, the homeowner can even enter commands over the telephone. Here are some examples of what an automated management system can do.

- Sensors can automatically turn lights on when someone enters a room and off when the room is unoccupied.
- The water heater can be set to turn itself off when it is not needed and to have hot water ready when it is required.
- Baths and showers can be programmed to deliver water at a preset temperature.
- A single home entertainment center can send signals to any audio or video outlet in the home.
- People can awaken each morning to find the room temperature automatically adjusted, the motorized blinds opened to let the sun in, and coffee brewing.

- The system can monitor the efficiency and performance of appliances and alert occupants to any problems.
- If a sensor detects smoke, the system's "brain" can sound an alarm, light a safe exit path, turn off unneeded electricity, and call for help.

Installing an automated home system adds considerably to the cost of building a home. In the long run, however, the system may reduce energy bills and insurance costs.

The demand for the most up-to-date housing features continues to grow. In response to this demand, the building industry will increasingly turn to new technology. People will create more advanced tools and methods of construction and invent new materials to make home building even faster and more efficient. As technological knowledge grows, people who rent or buy housing will benefit.

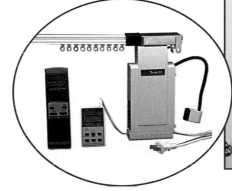

Technology has made thousands of new products available. This system opens and closes drapes by remote control or at preset times. Besides adding convenience, such a system can save energy or help someone with a disability live more independently.

Electronic Home Systems Specialist

Ebony Pines

Although many devices described in science fiction fifty years ago seemed impossible then, they're now state-of-the-art features in some modern homes. Today, an electronic home-management system can use computers to track changing sunrise and sunset times and then adjust home heating and lighting to match. Lights and appliances can be programmed to react automatically to the month, the season, or to other conditions. The system can even turn off a television set when children are supposed to do homework.

Homeowners like the advantages of these systems. Controlling temperature saves energy. Having an intercom is convenient, and people feel safer with security and fire alarm systems.

As a self-employed electronic home systems specialist, I guide homebuilders and buyers to the right system for them. I make sure the installation is handled correctly. Once the software is set up, the homeowner can access up to 300 different devices with one computer.

Since I've been interested in electronics for as long as I can remember, this profession is a natural fit for me. My friends always came to me when they had problems with their VCRs and stereos. For me, playing around with computers and figuring out how they "think" is fun.

No one was surprised that my first job after graduating from college was with a security systems company, installing different systems in homes and businesses. When I started hearing about automated home-management systems, I thought I might like to specialize in that area. I got the training I needed and eventually

"Once I set up the software, the homeowner can access up to 300 different devices with one computer."

ten carefully to what they want. At our first meeting, I bring brochures and photographs that show equipment. While we discuss all the latest options, I answer a lot of questions and ask them too.

It's exciting to see how advances in technology are transforming the science fiction of the past into the "thinking" homes of today. It makes you wonder what's ahead in the coming decades.

worked my way from installing systems to designing them.

The best time for clients to choose an electronic system for the home they're building is during the planning stage. That's when I use what I've learned from my father, who works in the construction field. With the builder's help, I decide where wiring and receptacles will go and the best location for the computer terminals. I also identify what doors and windows will work best with a security system. After pinpointing the client's needs and discussing the budget, I estimate costs for materials and labor and figure my own fees for designing and installation.

Math skills are very useful, but so are good communication skills. I have to talk to clients about equipment in terms they'll understand and also lis-

"With the builder's help, I decide where wiring and receptacles will go and the best location for the computer terminals."

Career Profile

Electronic home systems specialists design computerized home-management systems for existing homes, as well as new ones. As part of their job, they make sure that proper wires and cables are in place for telephones and computer equipment. In an older home, they might have old fuse boxes replaced with new circuit breakers. Electronic home systems specialists keep track of technological advances so they can supply clients with the most up-to-date information.

Education
▸ High school diploma is required, college recommended.
▸ Formal apprenticeship programs are offered; some workers learn skills informally on the job.
▸ Specialized training can be provided at technical institutes.
▸ Courses in math, mechanical drawing, science, and technology education are very helpful; courses in electricity and electronics are needed.

Skills Needed
▸ Good communication skills are used to present ideas to clients.
▸ Math skills are necessary for figuring costs.
▸ Good color vision for distinguishing different colored electrical wires is needed for any hands-on work.
▸ Knowledge of construction is very valuable.

Career Outlook
▸ Employment outlook is good but varies with the economy.

Career Activities
1. Explain in writing what you think would be the most useful feature to have in an electronic home-management system and why.
2. As an electronic home systems specialist, you have a client who wants more system features than the budget will allow. What do you suggest?

Review & Activities

Chapter Summary

➤ Technology will continue to play an increasing role in improving home construction.

➤ Both natural and manufactured materials are used to build homes.

➤ Green building techniques conserve natural resources and protect the environment.

➤ Technology continues to improve the tools and methods used in the construction industry.

➤ Three main types of construction are used by the housing industry today.

➤ High technology is helping to create more useful and efficient features and systems in homes, often while lowering energy use.

Checking Your Understanding

1. Define technology and explain the role it plays in housing construction.

2. Identify two natural building materials and describe the uses of each in home construction.

3. Discuss a disadvantage of using wood in building homes.

4. Identify two advantages of using brick and stone in building.

5. Discuss how plastic and recycled materials can replace wood and other materials in housing construction.

6. What improvements have been made in hand tools?

7. Name and describe the three types of home construction detailed in the chapter.

8. What are three ways in which high technology has improved daily life in the home?

9. What is an automated management system? What are some of the advantages and disadvantages of building a house equipped with such a system?

Thinking Critically

1. Although homes built today utilize technology extensively, there is also greater use of natural materials (or high-tech imitations) in interiors. Why do you think this is happening?

2. Explain why you agree or disagree with this statement: High technology is causing people to lose touch with simpler things in life.

3. Do you think that architects and builders have an obligation to use more recycled materials in building homes? Discuss your views.

4. How do you think that technology will change people's homes in the future? Explain your ideas.

Applications

1. **Surviving Earthquakes.** After the San Francisco earthquake of 1906, builders reevaluated the building materials that had been used. Find out about the differences between building materials and construction methods used before and after the catastrophe. Then, research the 1989 earthquake in San Francisco and how the buildings held up that were constructed to withstand earthquakes.

2. **Marketing Your Miracle Material.** Imagine that you have developed the perfect building material. Based on the information provided in the chapter about current trends in home construction technology, write an article to be published on the Internet in which you give as many details as you can about this miracle product.

3. **What's New?** Using print resources and the Internet, identify a tool, building material, construction method, or technology for the home that is beyond those mentioned in the chapter. Share your findings with the class in an oral report.

4. **Inventing a Computerized System.** Think about some of the tasks you perform during the average day. Choose one task and invent a computerized system that would save time or energy, or make the job more fun.

BUILDING YOUR PORTFOLIO

Imagine that you run a home-building company that uses only the latest building methods, tools, and materials. Prepare a brochure or web page promoting your company to potential home buyers. In your brochure or web page, provide details about the following:

➤ The building materials your company uses.

➤ The tools and methods you use in home construction.

➤ The types and styles of home construction you specialize in.

➤ The ways in which your company uses the latest technology to create advanced interior systems.

If possible, design and print your brochure or web page.

Careers in Housing and Interior Environments

TERMS TO LEARN

- ability
- apprenticeship
- aptitude
- employability skills
- entrepreneurs
- entry-level job
- interview
- job application
- job shadowing
- mentors
- networking
- portfolio
- résumé
- references

CHAPTER OBJECTIVES

► Determine how personal characteristics relate to career decisions.

► Identify resources for career information.

► Develop a career plan.

► Identify the steps in getting a job.

► Identify the skills necessary for keeping a job.

The future is now—at least when it comes to planning your career. Thinking ahead to your future work life can be both exciting and scary. Having a job and earning an income are exhilarating prospects. Figuring out your career interests and then finding and keeping a job in a competitive market can be more difficult. That's where this chapter will help you. The best way to avoid worrying about your future prospects is to plan ahead and prepare for the career you want.

Getting to Know Yourself

With hundreds of different jobs in the areas of housing and design, you have a lot to consider. Where do you start? The best place is to think about your hopes and dreams for the future. Where do you want to live? Do you want to travel or work from your home? How much time and energy do you want to devote to a job? What do you want from a career? A high salary? Personal satisfaction? Plenty of free time? Only you can answer those questions, but with a career search you don't stop with your dreams. There are other factors to consider.

YOUR VALUES

Becoming aware of your values is an important way of getting to know yourself better. Your values are the principles that you want to live by and the beliefs that are important to you. For example, if you spend time mastering new computer software programs, you may value learning and challenging yourself to acquire new skills. You might be interested in a career involving technology, such as designing new building materials. You need to keep your values in mind as you think of your career options.

Many people never stop to consider how their career and their personal and family life are related. A person who values time with her or his family but chooses a job requiring extensive overtime, won't be happy. Someone who likes independence and flexible work hours won't like a highly structured nine-to-five job. Career choice has a tremendous impact on family life.

A real estate agent shows homes according to the prospective buyers' schedules. That may mean being away from family on nights and weekends.

YOUR PERSONALITY AND INTERESTS

Next consider how your personal characteristics pertain to a career. Are you enthusiastic? This is a requirement for most sales positions. Are you in good physical condition? Construction workers must spend many hours doing physical labor. If you like working with people, information, or data, there are housing and interior environment careers for you, too.

Now think about your interests. What are your favorite activities? Make a list of the top ten activities you enjoy. Try out new activities, too.

Another helpful way to identify interests is to take an interest survey. You simply choose from a long list of activities those you might most enjoy. The survey results identify types of careers that might suit you. A vocational counselor can help you find an interest survey.

YOUR APTITUDES AND ABILITIES

Next consider your aptitudes and your abilities. An **aptitude** is a natural talent or your potential for learning a skill. An **ability** is a skill you already have developed. For example, you may have an aptitude for design. This is demonstrated in your ability to arrange and decorate your room attractively.

Think about the school subjects you enjoy the most and in which you do best. If you do well in graphic arts classes, you could think about a career as a drafter or architect.

To get a clear picture of your aptitudes and abilities, make a chart with the headings *Intellectual*, *Physical*, and *Social*. List your aptitudes and abilities in each category. Share your chart with others you trust. What can they add?

If you enjoy working with others more than you like working alone, you might be a "people" person. The career you choose should fit this characteristic.

Learning about Careers

With your personal characteristics in mind, start investigating careers. To make the best career choice, you must know the responsibilities, skills, and knowledge required for the job. You can learn more about careers in several different ways. This chapter and the *Career Close-Up* features throughout this book highlight a variety of related careers. The object is to find the careers that match you—your interests, aptitudes, values, and personality.

RESEARCHING CAREERS

Don't stop your investigation here. Talk with people who are working in jobs you think you might enjoy. Ask what they like and dislike about their jobs. School counselors and teachers can recommend courses that will be helpful and suggest sources of information about jobs.

The Internet is another valuable resource. You can find websites for companies in the housing and interior environment industry, newsgroups, and bulletin boards created by trade organizations, companies, and individuals—all helpful for career research. You can search for everything from job descriptions to company profiles. Newspaper classified ads from other cities and online versions of trade publications are also available.

The *Dictionary of Occupational Titles*, *Occupational Outlook Handbook*, and *Occupational Outlook Quarterly* are good references that you can find in a library or on the Internet at the U.S. Department of Labor site.

The Internet is a valuable tool for researching careers. Check your school's media center and the public library for other helpful resources.

This remodeling specialist plans how to modernize homes. After meeting with clients to talk about their ideas, she spends time creating designs and preparing cost estimates. Such varied activities help make her days interesting.

JOB SHADOWING

The more firsthand knowledge you have before you make a decision, the better the chance of a positive outcome. One of the best ways to learn about a job firsthand is job shadowing. **Job shadowing** means spending time with a person at work and learning by watching as he or she performs the functions of the job. The person you are observing follows a regular workday while you stay quietly nearby—like a "shadow."

How do you arrange for job shadowing? Sometimes your teacher or counselor can help. You can also make your own arrangements by contacting companies and asking to job shadow a person with a specific position. You can then evaluate whether you are interested in that career and seek advice on how to prepare to enter that field.

WORK EXPERIENCE

On-the-job experience can be very helpful in learning more about various career areas. If you can, take advantage of a work-study program while you are in school. This may help you explore your interests and skills. There are also many part-time and summer jobs in the housing and interior environments fields. You can also gain helpful general knowledge and skills from other jobs. For example, you gain experience working with people when you do volunteer work in a hospital.

Job shadowing is a great way to find out more about a career. By spending time with a person on the job, you learn firsthand what a typical workday is like.

$\mathcal{D}$eveloping Your Career Plan

If you do your research well, you'll turn up several career choices that interest you. Now you can narrow the field by comparing your personal data with the career information you've gathered. A good tool to use is the personal Career Profile Form shown in Figure 4-1. Complete a career profile for each career choice you have identified. Rate each row across from 1 to 10 according to how well they match. See which career choice has the best overall match. Based on your information, what career do you want to pursue?

Keep in mind that your choice is flexible. As you grow and change, your choice may change, too.

SETTING GOALS

You have already accomplished goals in your life. You achieved them, step-by-step. You reach a long-term goal by accomplishing a series of short- and medium-term goals. Use the same strategy when working toward your ultimate career goal. To get started, set some short-term goals. For example, your long-term goal might be a career as a public relations specialist who handles consumer, community, and media relations for a company. You will need excellent communication skills. A short-term goal might be to improve your communication skills

FIGURE 4-1

Career Profile Form

NAME: **Jack Wu**   CAREER: **Landscape Architect**

Personal Information	Career Information	Match
YOUR VALUES I believe in helping to preserve the environment. I also want the chance to express my creativity.	**CAREER VALUES** Landscape architects design areas that are both beautiful and compatible with the natural environment. I would be able to use my creativity as well as work with other creative people.	9
YOUR INTERESTS My hobbies include gardening, art, and reading historic novels.	**CAREER DUTIES AND RESPONSIBILITIES** As a landscape architect, I would need a good knowledge of plants. Artistic talents are needed to complete the drawings.	8
APTITUDES AND ABILITIES My best subject is English. My teacher says I'm excellent at reading comprehension. I have a natural sense of design, but I'm about average at actually drawing.	**APTITUDES AND ABILITIES REQUIRED** Good verbal and writing skills are essential since landscape architects must communicate with other professionals involved in the project and prepare written reports with their detailed plans. Computer-aided design is an essential tool for landscape architects, so excellent drawing skills are not necessary.	8
EDUCATION/ TRAINING INTERESTS I'm interested in going on to college to achieve my career goals.	**EDUCATION/ TRAINING REQUIRED** A bachelor's degree and sometimes even a master's degree are required.	8

by getting a position on the school newspaper. Another might include a summer job working with consumers. You also know from your research that you will need a college degree. You set a medium-term goal of attending a college with a good public relations or journalism program.

People who are happy in their work have found careers that suit them well. Making a conscious effort to figure out what's best for you is far better than leaving the process to chance.

Develop a career plan by creating short-, medium-, and long-term goals. This will also allow you to make "course corrections" if you change your mind about your ultimate career choice. At any point along the way you can head off in a different direction.

EDUCATION AND TRAINING

To reach your long-term career goal, you need the necessary education and training. Almost every job requires some special training and having advanced education and training means you'll have more career opportunities to choose from.

You may get your start with an **entry-level job**—one that requires little training, though often a high school diploma. For entry-level jobs, many companies offer on-the-job training. This may consist of a few days of orientation or more formal long-term instruction. If a higher level job interests you, you will have to gain experience and often get further education to increase your skills.

Consumer Sense

Judging Post-Secondary Training Programs

After high school, you can get ready for many careers by completing a technical training program. These are available from both public and private schools. How do you judge quality? Learn the answers to these questions:

- **HOW LONG HAS THE PROGRAM OPERATED?** A long history offers some assurance of quality. Newer programs may provide a good education, but they don't have a "track record" to demonstrate their success.
- **WHAT IS THE PROGRAM'S REPUTATION?** Ask professionals in the field how they view the program. Would they hire one of its graduates? Is the program known for success in the field that you want to specialize in?
- **WHAT PERCENTAGE OF STUDENTS GRADUATE?** If the numbers are low compared to other programs, try to discover why. Is it cost? Difficult or poorly designed courses?
- **WHAT IS THE RATE OF EMPLOYMENT OF GRADUATES? ALSO ASK ABOUT THEIR AVERAGE SALARY.** A large percentage of graduates working in advanced positions speaks favorably of a program. The skills they learned apparently serve them well in the "real world." A quality program will share the "success stories" of its graduates.
- **WHAT IS THE INSTRUCTOR-TO-STUDENT RATIO?** Smaller classes allow for more individualized instruction.

- **WHAT IS THE COST?** The most expensive education is not necessarily the most useful. On the other hand, knowledgeable instructors, up-to-date materials, and valuable learning experiences often carry a substantial price tag. A "cheap" education may be just that. Treat your education as an investment.
- **IS THE PROGRAM ACCREDITED, AND BY WHOM?** Accreditation means the program meets the standards, including some of the points listed above, of the accrediting organization. For example, accreditation by a reputable organization confirms a program's quality.

YOU THE CONSUMER . . .

After a careful search, you've found a training program that promises to give you the education you need and a price you can manage. You're excited to start—until you talk to one of its graduates. This person cannot find a job, and blames it on the program's poor preparation. How do you follow up this person's claim? How do you decide how much weight to give it?

For some careers, you learn on the job and are trained by a master in the profession.

At the next level, are jobs that require specialized training. Workers may need vocational-technical or trade school training or a two-year college degree. Some careers require an apprenticeship. An **apprenticeship** program combines on-the-job training by a skilled worker and classroom instruction. Completion may take from several months to several years, depending on the craft. In some cases, workers must pass a state licensing exam.

Still other jobs require advanced education. A training period of several years after college may also be required. In some instances, the worker must take an examination to become licensed in his or her field. The research you have completed for your career choices will tell you how much education and training you need.

BASIC JOB SKILLS

What does every employer want in an employee, no matter what the job is? The answer is employability skills. **Employability skills** are those general skills required to acquire and retain a job. Many employers put dependability, responsibility, and a positive attitude at the top of the list. Along with those, the following skills are essential for most jobs:

- The basics—reading, mathematics, writing, speaking, and listening. You also need to understand and appropriately use nonverbal communication.
- Thinking skills—problem solving, decision making, creative thinking, visualizing how to accomplish a task, and reasoning.
- Personal qualities—integrity, honesty, self-esteem, sociability, and self-management.

Employability skills are valuable for any future in which you picture yourself.

*O*wning Your Own Business

Do you dream of running your own business? The housing and interior environments industry offers many opportunities for entrepreneurs. **Entrepreneurs** are people who start their own business. An entrepreneur's life is challenging.

Most entrepreneurs share certain traits, such as the following:

- Motivation. Successful entrepreneurs are self-motivated. They know how to set and achieve goals.

Doing careful research and planning before starting a business makes success more likely.

- Foresight. Entrepreneurs see problems and find ways to solve them successfully.
- Decision making. Those who make sound decisions stand the chance of being more successful.
- Relationship skills. Being able to get along with others, negotiate, and resolve conflicts are vital skills.

Many people start their own business as a second job. When the business becomes more established, they become self-employed.

Are you cut out to be an entrepreneur? Consider the advantages and disadvantages. Some aspects of working for yourself are appealing. You make the rules, set the schedule, and make the decisions. The potential for financial gain depends on how hard and wisely you work. You receive all the profits. Entrepreneurs generally feel a lot of personal satisfaction.

On the downside, managing your own time requires that you be self-disciplined and a self-starter. Many entrepreneurs work alone and are on the job long hours. You'll also need to wear many hats. You'll probably be the manager, the worker, the advertiser, the accountant, and the one in charge of maintenance. Most entrepreneurs have variable incomes, and without a steady income you must be an excellent money manager.

Finding a Job

Congratulations! You've done your personal evaluations and your research. You've gotten the education or training you need. Now you are ready to make the move into the world of work. You might think that life would be ideal if you could go from school and step into your ultimate career goal, but there is still a lot to learn. Most people start at a lower-level position and work their way up.

Getting a job opens the door to a whole new way of life. You'll have new responsibilities, new surroundings, new friends, and a paycheck.

Finding the right job begins with a job lead. This can be a tip from a friend, a help-wanted ad in a newspaper, information from a counselor or teacher, or by networking.

NETWORKING

Networking is communicating with people you know or can get to know to share information and advice. Networking is not as difficult as you might think. Start by making a list of all the people you know, even casual acquaintances. Then contact the people on your list, let them know you are looking for a job, and ask for any information that may lead to a job. Some won't be able to help you at this time, but others will be able to direct you to another person who can help. Eventually networking can lead to a job. Research shows that more than one-third of the jobs people get happen because of networking.

Networking is one way to find out about job openings. When you're alert to the possibilities, you'll start noticing the people around you who might have information to share.

JOB ADVERTISEMENTS

Job ads are another way to find a job. Look in the classified ads in newspapers or in magazines that cover your field of interest. Study an ad carefully to determine the necessary skills and qualifications. How will this job help you meet your long-term career goal? Not every job will have a direct application to your career goal, but you can still learn valuable skills.

THE INTERNET

Don't forget about the Internet as you look for a job. When you are online, hundreds of job-listing sites are just a few keystrokes away. Type in any of these search words to access worldwide opportunities: *employment opportunities, jobs, job listings,* or *careers.* You can also check to see if there are any job openings at companies where you would like to work.

EMPLOYMENT AGENCIES

Employment agencies match job seekers and companies with job openings. Job seekers fill out applications at the agency. Businesses call the agency when they have openings. The agency then matches qualified applicants to the positions available. There is normally a fee for jobs found through an employment agency. Sometimes the applicant pays the fee; other times the employer pays. Be sure to ask.

PREPARING A JOB-WINNING RÉSUMÉ

Developing a résumé and keeping it up-to-date will make it easier for you to land the housing job of your choice. A **résumé** is a brief summary of your personal information, education, skills, work experience, activities, and interests. You will send your résumé to an employer when applying for a job or you may post it

on the Internet. Think of your résumé as an advertisement about yourself. In it you cover the facts of your experience and education in a positive way that will tell an employer at a glance how you can contribute to the workplace. A well-written résumé helps convince the employer that you are the right person for the job. Don't be shy. Be honest, but make yourself look good.

The best résumés are brief, usually only one or two pages. Carefully choose what to include and what to emphasize. If you don't have any work experience, focus instead on your skills and education. Be sure to include any volunteer work you have done. That can let an employer know you are reliable and have a good attitude toward work.

With your résumé, you'll also send a cover letter. This is a one-page letter telling the employer who you are and why you are sending your résumé. If you learned about the company from someone, say so. In the body of the letter highlight why you are right for the job. Conclude by asking for an interview. Be sure to include your phone number and e-mail address. See Figure 4-2 for an example of a résumé written by a recent high school graduate. Effective résumés and cover letters can get you an interview.

FIGURE 4-2

State the job you are applying for. Be sure to change this for each job.

List the schools you have attended and diplomas or degrees you've received. Also include any subjects or programs that pertain.

List your work experience beginning with your most recent job. Include volunteer work if it applies to the job you are seeking.

Include any honors or awards you have received in school or your community.

Identify any business or other skills and abilities that will be useful on the job.

You may include references on your résumé or prepare a separate sheet.

Chad Williams
900 Federal Way
Seattle, WA 98000

Job Objective
Seeking a position as an assistant in a real estate office. Desire position with opportunity for career growth.

Education and Training
High School Diploma, Seattle North High School. Graduated in top ten percent of class. Ten credit hours from Rockway Community College.

Relevant Courses Taken: Housing and Interior Environments, Keyboarding, Word Processing, Marketing, General Business.

Work Experience

June 2001-Present   Office Clerk. Patriot's Landing Retirement Center. Assist office manager with mailings, answering the phone, planning promotional events, word processing correspondence, and updating database. Maintain the photocopy machine. Create the "What's Happening" community event calendar on the center's webpage.

June 1998-May 2001   Newspaper Carrier. *Seattle Times.* Managed my own paper route for two years. Responsible for delivering the morning edition to 100 residents, collecting subscription fees, filling in for other carriers as needed. Recognized as Best Carrier in 2000.

Honors and Activities
Dean's Honor List, Student Council Member, Orchestra and Band Member, Chairman of Fundraising Campaign for Seattle North Band

Skills and Abilities
Skilled on both IBM-compatible and Macintosh computers. Accomplished in desktop publishing, spreadsheet, and word processing software.

References
Available upon request.

BUILDING YOUR PORTFOLIO

You can use a **portfolio**—a collection of examples of your best work—to share with others what you are capable of doing. What could you put in a portfolio to show on your first interviews? Each chapter in this textbook concludes with a portfolio activity that can be included. You could include assignments from your other courses as well. Review your work and choose your best examples to show a prospective employer what you have achieved. You may ask teachers or employers from part-time jobs to write a letter of recommendation. Writings, drawings, computer-generated art, and photographs of work you have created or built can be added to demonstrate your abilities.

JOB APPLICATIONS

A **job application** is a form employers use to ask questions about an applicant's skills, work experience, education, and interests. Employers do not have the right to ask about your race, religion, gender, children, or marital status. Always fill out an application completely and accurately. Follow these job application tips:

- Follow directions exactly.
- Print neatly. Answer all the questions. If you have nothing to write, draw a line or print "Not Applicable" or "NA" in the space provided.
- Make your statements positive.
- Keep your options open. If asked to state the salary you want, write "Negotiable." If asked if you will work nights, write "Will consider."

- Prepare lists of information you will need in advance. This includes schools you have attended and jobs you have held along with addresses.
- Prepare your references in advance. **References** are people, such as teachers and former employers, who will recommend you to an employer. Ask permission of the people before you use their names as references. Take along their addresses and phone numbers to complete the application.
- Never lie or exaggerate on the application.

THE INTERVIEW

All your hard work has paid off! You've been asked to come in for an **interview**—a formal meeting between an employer and a job applicant. This is the employer's chance to meet you in person and learn more about your qualifications. It is your chance to show how your career research can pay off.

Before the Interview

Before you go on the interview:

- Find out everything you can about the company. Visit the company's Internet site. Talk to anyone you know who works for the company.

- Practice your interviewing skills. Have a friend ask you typical questions and comment on your answers.
- Plan what you will wear. The first impression you make when you walk in the door is based on your smile and your clothes. Being well-groomed and dressing appropriately are important. Match your clothes to the job.
- Make sure your portfolio is in order. Take along an extra copy of your résumé, cover letter, and list of references.
- Plan to arrive a little early. You may need to make a trial run the day before so you are certain how long it will take you to get to the interview. Make sure you add extra travel time for unexpected conditions.

People tend to feel more confident when they look their best. It's a great way to help get an interview off to a good start.

During the Interview

When you meet the employer for the interview, project a positive attitude. Remember the employability skills employers are most interested in and convey those. A firm handshake will show you have confidence. Maintaining eye contact lets the employer know that you are paying close attention. Speak clearly and avoid using slang. Give specific answers. Always be honest, but don't undersell yourself. Stress school activities and volunteer work that show you are dependable, able to work as part of a team, and are responsible. Some questions may be asked to assess your problem-solving skills or you may be asked to role-play a situation. Keep in mind that the employer is not looking for one right answer but is evaluating your thinking skills.

Be prepared to ask your own questions, too. This is one of the reasons you did research on the company. You may ask questions about the business, such as "What plans do you have for selling your new line of furniture over the Internet?". You may also ask questions about employee benefits, such as "What does the health plan cover?".

Interviews can be stressful, but don't let yourself be overwhelmed. Hang on to your positive attitude. Relax and be yourself. The worst thing that can happen is that you don't get the job. There are other jobs. The most important point is to be certain that you and the company will be right for each other.

At the end of the interview, you may be offered the job then and there. If not, thank the interviewer and ask when the decision will be made. Ask when would be a good time to check back.

Interviewing can be stressful. If you arrive prepared, you're more likely to feel calm. As you begin an interview, take a few deep breaths, smile, and let the interviewer take the lead.

Follow Up

The interview process doesn't end when you leave. You need to follow up. Ask yourself, What went well? How could I improve for the next time? Did I forget anything important? Is there additional information about me that might be beneficial to give to the employer? Also, send a follow-up letter to the employer. Thank the interviewer for the time, reinforce how your skills could help the company, and restate your interest in the job. Don't forget to check back.

The Offer

You've done it! You've been offered a job. Believe it or not, you don't have to rush into saying yes. If you want to think about it, ask for a day to make your decision. List the job's pros and cons before calling back to accept. If you are offered the job but at a lower salary than you were looking for, think it over. You might change your mind or be able to negotiate the salary.

Remember, though, just because you have been offered a job, you don't have to take it. You may decide that the job isn't for you, or you have been offered a better position in the meantime. If you decide not to take the position, let the employer know. You don't have to give reasons for turning the job down. Just say, "Thank you for considering me, but I am not interested in taking the position."

If an employer doesn't offer you the job, consider it a learning experience. Ask why you weren't hired. Do you need more training? How did you come across in the interview? Any feedback you get will help you in future interviews.

On the Job

You've got the job, and now the work starts of keeping and advancing in the job. No doubt your employability skills impressed the employer during your interview and now is the time to show how you can apply those to your job.

Always arrive to work on time. While you are on the job, produce quality work and maintain productive work habits. Manage your time wisely. Identify the goal of the job you are given and try to visualize the steps to reaching it. Some jobs require handling more than one task at a time. Set priorities or ask your supervisor for help in determining which assignments are the most important. Be cooperative, no matter how unimportant a task may seem to you. Entry-level jobs often involve the worst tasks and little responsibility. If you find yourself in such a position, smile and do the job well. When you really demonstrate your employability skills, you will advance in the job.

Show willingness to learn and to follow directions. Listen carefully to your instructions and take notes if possible. Use good communication skills. Speak clearly. If you must write reports, always proofread your work to catch any errors.

TEAMWORK

Getting along with your coworkers as well as your manager is an important part of any job. Treat others fairly. Be courteous and kind. Remember, though, you are on the job to work, not to socialize. Do your fair share, and pitch in to help someone who is behind. Teamwork is essential on many jobs. Be a positive and productive part of the team. Don't be afraid to take on more responsibility.

When you're on the job, listen carefully as your responsibilities are explained. If you don't understand the instructions, ask for more information. Most supervisors are happy to give you the help you need to do the job correctly.

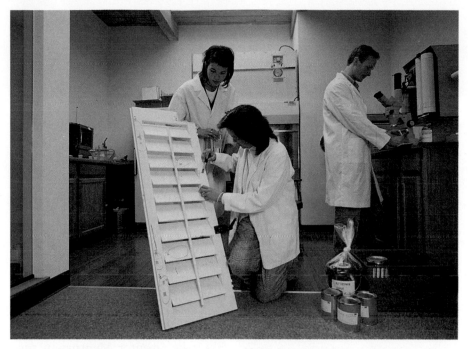

Teamwork is part of many jobs. What do you think might cause a team to have problems working together? What would help them work well together?

LEADERSHIP

If you are asked to take the leadership role, you will want to foster these qualities:

- Generate a plan based on the tasks needed to be done, the resources your team has, and the alternatives. Communicate the plan clearly to the team and make sure all members understand their role.
- Promote teamwork. Keep the door to communication going both ways. Include the team in decision making. Ask for feedback and listen carefully when it is given. Understand the needs of your team and adjust your plans to accommodate the team's goals.
- Keep the team on track. Provide guidance when team members need it, watch to make sure goals are being met, reevaluate the plan

as necessary, and help everyone achieve her or his full potential.
- The best leadership skill is to set the example. If you want others to give their best, demonstrate this by giving your best. Show initiative, help others, act with maturity, keep a positive attitude, and always act ethically.
- Be a team player yourself. Respect others' ideas and show their input is valued. Praise good work and thoughtfully offer constructive criticism when necessary.
- Use your problem-solving and decision-making skills to develop creative solutions.

One way you can gain leadership skills now is by participating in a Family, Career, and Community Leaders of America (FCCLA) program. FCCLA is a national organization of high school students

enrolled in Family and Consumer Sciences courses. FCCLA activities and skill events provide opportunities for leadership development. Membership will also help you gain invaluable experience and help you develop job skills.

ETHICAL BEHAVIOR

Ethical behavior is crucial to success. Two important aspects of ethical behavior are being trustworthy and honest. One of the most common ways employees demonstrate honesty concerns work hours. For example, if a worker takes an extra 15 minutes at lunch every day, the employer is being cheated. Those 15 minutes a day add up to over 5 hours in a month.

What about honesty over money? Obviously stealing money from a company is dishonest. Realize, too, that it is also dishonest for employees to overcharge employers on expenses for which they are reimbursed.

When employees lie to their supervisors or coworkers about work they haven't done or don't admit when they have made a mistake, they are not being trustworthy. Would you want to work with someone you couldn't trust?

Remember, too, to respect the property of others and be fair. Don't go along with the wishes of other people because they pressure you. If the company ethics don't match yours, don't hesitate leaving the job. Always treat your employer with the same respect and trust as you would like to receive.

RESOLVING CONFLICTS

There will be times on the job when conflicts will arise. You may disagree with your team on how to accomplish a task or you may have a personality conflict. Don't assume you know the other person's point of view. Ask and give the other side time to talk. Respect the opinions of others. Try to understand their needs. Keep any discussions professional. Keep your body language such as gestures nonthreatening. Don't make personal remarks. Treat others fairly and ethically. Be open to creative solutions and be willing to compromise. Sometimes both sides have to give a little to reach a solution that pleases everyone.

MANAGING MULTIPLE ROLES

Everyone has multiple roles in life, each with specific responsibilities. You may juggle work, family, community and social obligations. Sometimes you may feel that there isn't enough time to do everything that is important to you. For example, if your job requires frequent travel or you work two jobs, family time may be limited.

Pressure from multiple roles can make a person less effective in each of them. A frustrating situation at home may cause you to have trouble concentrating at work. A problem at work can interfere with enjoyment of social activities.

What's the solution? Unfortunately, there's not one that fits every situation. Learning how to prioritize, effectively manage time and energy, and handle stress all help. However, sometimes it's necessary to cut out some activity or even find a different job. The way you balance your work with the other roles you have in life will influence your satisfaction with your career.

MENTORS

Have you ever been in a position to help someone learn how to do a task? If so, you have a glimpse of what it is like to be a mentor. **Mentors** are successful workers who share their expert knowledge and demonstrate correct work behaviors. Some companies assign mentors to new employees. They introduce employees to their coworkers and help them learn the procedures for their new jobs. They may help them develop key skills such as conflict resolution, negotiation, teamwork, and leadership. Sometimes these programs are called corporate coaching.

Although handling criticism on the job can be difficult, avoid becoming defensive. Your supervisor's comments can be helpful if you view them as an opportunity to learn how to do a better job.

A mentor can both provide helpful advice and suggest ways to improve your skills.

If you join a company that doesn't have a formal mentoring program, you may want to work at developing a mentor relationship. With a trusted mentor, you can show your ignorance and ask "dumb" questions without feeling judged or embarrassed. You will learn from the mentor's experience, advice, and wisdom. Your mentor's guidance can help you advance in your career. The mentor can gain from the relationship, too, by having the opportunity to strengthen his or her leadership skills. Your mentor may also get recognition from the company when you succeed.

MAINTAINING YOUR PORTFOLIO

As you gain work experience, keep your portfolio up-to-date. Include your best work. Some examples of what to include in a portfolio are:

- Photographs of projects. A builder could display homes in the process of being built as well as completed houses.
- Letters of recommendation. An interior designer may include letters from satisfied clients.
- Awards and certificates. A researcher could have an industry award for outstanding work.
- Certificates of completion. Workers who attend training seminars or take continuing education classes could add certificates or diplomas to their portfolio.

LEAVING A JOB

With so much change in the world today, it is no surprise that employees choose to explore new job opportunities. Be certain, though, to leave your present job on good terms. You never know when you may need this employer as a reference for a future job, or when you may be working with a coworker or manager again. Also, you may want the option of returning to this company if your next job doesn't work out. Follow these guidelines:

- Leave your work in order and as completed as possible. Explain to your replacement or your manager the status of any work in progress.
- Give a reasonable amount of notice. Two weeks notice is standard.
- Offer to answer questions from your replacement. This gesture is appreciated by managers

- Be tactful about why you are choosing to leave. Even if you did not get along with your boss or disagreed with the ethics of the company, don't air that news. You can merely state that you were given an offer "too good to pass up."
- Sometimes your present employer will make a counteroffer of a bigger salary to encourage you to stay. If money was your reason for leaving, you may choose to accept the offer. If other reasons have affected your decision, know what your requirements are for staying around. If you have definitely made up your mind to leave, let your employer know up front that your decision is non-negotiable.

STAYING ON THE CUTTING EDGE

Change is a constant in our technological world. Less than 20 years ago, computers weren't commonplace and many jobs did not involve high technology at all. Today, it is difficult to find a job that doesn't involve computers in one form or another. Salespeople use computers to track accounts, demonstrate new products, and keep records of sales. Bricklayers may use handheld computers to help them determine how much material to purchase. All employees may use the Internet to research new advances in their field.

Employees need to keep up-to-date on changes in their industry and advances in technology. Some employers help pay for continuing education classes for employees or send personnel to training seminars. Other times it is up to the employee to shoulder the responsibility. Community colleges offer classes that will benefit many employees. Check magazines related to your industry to find out about seminars teaching new techniques. Not all learning has to be formal. Whenever you learn how to operate new software or read a book to develop a new skill, you are advancing your education and training. Open your mind and keep learning about the world around you.

Continuing education helps employees stay knowledgeable about new trends and technologies in the world of work.

Careers in Housing and Interiors

On the following pages you will read about just a few of the choices you could make at various job levels within various career areas. Keep in mind that these charts represent only a sampling of careers in each area. Many more opportunities exist in the housing and interior environments field.

FIGURE 4-3

Careers in Communications

JOB TITLE	Description	Skills and Aptitudes	Education and Training
RESEARCHER	Helps writers for magazines and newspapers find information, graphics, and photography for articles.	Computer expertise; online database knowledge; familiarity with the Internet; communication skills.	College education is preferred.
DEPARTMENT STORE ADVERTISING WORKER	Assists photographers, designers, artists, and writers; proofreads material; gathers samples; and helps plan special projects.	Good writing and communication skills; ability in the areas of design and art.	High school diploma.
CONSUMER ADVOCATE	Provides a link between consumers and companies that manufacture, sell, and repair products; writes publications and answers questions.	Good writing and speaking skills; ability to work well with others; ability to remain calm under pressure.	High school diploma; some college education in communications, law, and community education preferred.
PUBLIC RELATIONS SPECIALIST	Presents positive information about the people or organizations represented; writes reports, news releases, booklets, and speeches.	Good speaking and writing skills; ability to work well with others; organizational skills.	College degree in public relations, journalism, or communications is desirable.
CONSUMER SCIENCE WRITER	Covers developments in housing and interior environments for magazines, newspapers, and radio and television stations.	Good writing skills; organizational skills.	College education in English, journalism, or consumer education; courses in marketing and business are useful.

FIGURE 4-4

Careers in Construction and Home Design

JOB TITLE	Description	Skills and Aptitudes	Education and Training
SURVEYOR'S ASSISTANT	Helps measure distances, directions, and angles of a piece of land.	Must be in good physical condition; aptitude in math and physics helpful.	High school education; can advance with further training and education.
BRICKLAYER	Builds and repairs walls, fireplaces, and chimneys.	Good physical condition; works well with others.	Three-year apprenticeship program.
HEAVY-EQUIPMENT OPERATOR	Drives bulldozers, cranes, and other large construction equipment.	Ability to judge spaces correctly and handle many controls; aptitude in physics helpful.	Apprenticeship program or certified operator training by manufacturers.
CONSTRUCTION TECHNOLOGIST	Supervises construction workers; performs technical work; may specialize in estimating, quality control, specifications, or purchasing.	Technical knowledge of construction; aptitude in science; communication and leadership skills.	College degree in construction technology; experience in construction is helpful.

FIGURE 4-5

Careers in Home Furnishings and Interior Design

JOB TITLE	Description	Skills and Aptitudes	Education and Training
ADVERTISING ARTIST	Produces the advertising artwork; works in ad agencies, stores, or graphic design firms.	Artistic talent; expertise in illustration and page-layout software.	Graphic design training at a two- or four-year school.
INTERIOR DESIGNER	Plans and furnishes interiors; prepares and presents design ideas; develops clients' ideas into design concepts.	Creativity and knowledge of color, design, and furnishings; flexible; good communication and selling skills.	Interior design training at a two- to four-year school; work experience; state licensing may be required.
BUYER	Determines which merchandise a store will carry; chooses the suppliers; negotiates prices; awards contracts.	Creative thinking and problem solving; trend forecasting; time-management, communication, and computer skills.	College degree in business or merchandising.
FURNITURE DESIGNER	Designs functional and appealing furniture for manufacturers, design firms, and furniture shops.	Artistic ability; uses design software; ability to visualize; good problem-solving skills.	College degree in art and design; computer-aided design courses.

FIGURE 4-6

Careers in Home Maintenance and Remodeling

JOB TITLE	Description	Skills and Aptitudes	Education and Training
ENTRY-LEVEL MAINTENANCE WORKER	Cleans homes and offices; pool maintenance workers clean and repair pools.	Good physical condition; ability to work well with others.	No special schooling needed; education and training may lead to higher wages.
PEST-CONTROL WORKER	Eliminates undesirable insects and animals such as cockroaches, termites, and rodents from homes.	Good physical condition; good communication skills; basic skills in math, chemistry, and biology.	High school graduate; federal and state certification and licensing that requires instruction and job training.
HOME REMODELING SPECIALIST	Plans and estimates the cost of remodeling projects; carries out the job.	Math, communication, and people skills; uses design software; ability to visualize; problem-solving and construction skills.	College degree in construction technology. Some specialists have experience as carpenters, plumbers, or electricians.
INDUSTRIAL DESIGNER	Develops products such as home appliances, garden tools, computer equipment, tools, and office equipment.	Artistic talent; research skills; knowledge of design software; ability to visualize; knowledge of current trends; good problem-solving skills.	College degree in industrial design, engineering, or architecture.

FIGURE 4-7

Careers in Real Estate

JOB TITLE	Description	Skills and Aptitudes	Education and Training
REAL ESTATE CLERK	Assists in office; compiles lists of homes for sale; copies contracts; answers the phone.	Computer, time-management, and communication skills; work well with others.	High school diploma.
APPRAISER	Determines the value of a piece of property and writes a report detailing its worth.	Good organizational skills; ability to pay close attention to detail; good writing and math skills.	College degree in business administration, math, or accounting; technical education in appraising.
LAND DEVELOPER	Creates neighborhoods from undeveloped land; may also develop shopping and industrial areas.	Knowledge of construction methods; good money-management and communication skills.	College degree in business administration, engineering, or architecture is desirable.
REAL ESTATE OFFICE MANAGER	Keeps office running smoothly; tracks sales; keeps records; manages sales and office staff.	Work well with others; organizational, computer, and communication skills.	College degree in business administration is desirable.

Shane Dillard

Ergonomic Designer

The day you realize that one size does not fit all is the day you start to appreciate ergonomics. Also called human factors engineering, *ergonomics* is the study of designing space and products to meet people's needs. Ergonomic designers adapt tools, appliances, and furniture to accommodate differences in people's size and shape, and in their physical and mental strengths and limitations.

"Ergonomics combines analytical skills with creativity, and technology with human contact."

I'd always been interested in engineering and design. I was working for a manufacturer as an industrial designer, adapting offices and assembly lines to help workers be more productive and happier with their jobs. I found this work very rewarding. It gave me the chance to combine my analytical skills with my creativity, and technology with human contact. I was getting paid to improve the quality of life for many other people.

My focus changed when my grandfather's health became a problem. He was having trouble doing everyday tasks for himself but was determined to live independently. As we worked to break down the types of problems he was having, I began to see that they could be solved by simple ergonomics. He had trouble turning the round, knob-like faucets in the bathroom. We replaced them with faucets that had handles that he could grasp more easily. Sometimes he felt unsteady stepping in and out of the tub. We mounted a grab bar on the wall.

While trying to help my grandfather overcome some of his physical limitations, I sometimes felt frustrated at the lack of flexibility in modern design. I knew the technology existed; why wasn't it being

an eye out for new technology that I can incorporate into a design; however, I prefer simple, standard modifications whenever it's possible. A refrigerator door that's difficult to open, for instance, might need only a slightly less powerful vacuum seal. I always try to remember the exact needs of the client. As I see it, ergonomics is a continuation of our attempts to conform the environment to our needs.

applied? I investigated and found work with a firm that designs consumer products, specializing in universal design. Our goal is to make products accessible to as many people as possible. We've designed a convection oven with legroom so people in wheelchairs can do their own cooking. We've developed visual cues to tell people with hearing impairments when someone is at the door.

People without disabilities also hire us. We work with their architect or interior designer to arrange their space—usually a kitchen, bathroom, or home office—more efficiently and comfortably.

I start a project by talking with the clients to identify the particular—or potential—problem: what isn't working in the environment? What improvements do they envision? How much money have they budgeted for the changes? I like to see the product or space myself for a hands-on assessment. Then on my computer, I experiment with different designs. I keep

> *"Our goal is to make products accessible to as many people as possible."*

Career Profile

Ergonomic designers create products that are shaped to the people who use them every day. They link technology and design with how people function at work and at home. This specialized designer can work in a wide range of industries, such as furniture and environmental design, computer animation and special effects, medical products, consumer electronics, and building and transportation design.

Education
▸ At least a Bachelor of Arts degree is required. Advanced degrees are becoming more desired as employment opportunities increase.
▸ Courses in ergonomics, biomechanics, engineering principles, the physical sciences, psychology, sociology, photography, electronic media, and interior design are helpful.

Skills Needed
▸ Creative problem-solving skills and excellent communication and presentation skills are required.
▸ A mechanical aptitude and the ability to convey concepts with quick sketches, as well as computer proficiency in CAD programs, are also necessary.
▸ Self-motivated people who have strong analytical skills and enjoy creating solutions to everyday challenges may like ergonomic and industrial design.

Career Outlook
▸ Ergonomic and industrial designers are in high demand this decade. Due to this high demand, the compensation packages are attractive. More information can be obtained from the Industrial Designers Society of America.

Career Activities
1. Study how students at your school use their backpacks. Sketch a design for a new backpack that would help improve students' posture.
2. Create a prototype of the new backpack and explain why you think it would be a better option for students.

Chapter Summary

➤ Knowing your abilities, aptitudes, values, and interests is an important first step in choosing a rewarding career.

➤ When you are ready to learn about specific jobs and careers, many resources are available, including vocational counselors, libraries, the Internet, and job shadowing.

➤ Setting short- and medium-term career goals will help you accomplish your ultimate career goal.

➤ Jobs can be classified as three types: entry-level, those requiring some training and education, and those requiring advanced education and training.

➤ Many people choose to start their own business in the housing and interior environment fields.

➤ When looking for a job, explore job leads, write a top-notch résumé, research prospective employers before going in for an interview, and use the interview as an opportunity to show how your qualifications match the needs of the employer.

➤ To be successful on the job, maintain productive work habits, be a team player, always be ethical, and learn to manage your multiple roles.

Checking Your Understanding

1. What is the difference between aptitude and ability?

2. What are three ways you could learn about different careers?

3. Why is it important to set short-, medium-, and long-term goals on the path to an ultimate career goal?

4. What is an apprenticeship program?

5. What are the advantages and disadvantages of being an entrepreneur?

6. Name four ways of finding out about job leads.

7. What should you cover in a résumé?

8. What is the difference between a reference and a mentor?

9. Name three leadership qualities.

10. Why is it important to leave a job on good terms?

Thinking Critically

1. You will job shadow next week. Identify what you might do before, during, and after the experience to get the most from it.

2. Do you think a college education is important for most jobs? Is college helpful even for jobs that don't require it? Explain.

3. Why do you think employers rank dependability and having a positive attitude as top employability skills? Describe specific ways in which employees having or not having these characteristics could affect a company.

4. In what ways can you stand out positively in an interview?

5. Suppose that you enjoy working with people. Identify at least ten careers in the housing and interior environment field you could pursue.

Review & Activities

Applications

1. **Presenting Yourself.** Make a chart listing your aptitudes and abilities, as described on page 81. Then using this self-analysis, write a 30-second "commercial" summarizing your abilities. Present your commercial to the class either on videotape or live. As a class, evaluate the presentations to help classmates recognize abilities they have that they did not cover.

2. **Write a Cover Letter.** Look through the want ads in the local newspaper or at a job website on the Internet to find an interesting position. Write a cover letter, using standard business style, that you could send with your résumé. Highlight how your qualifications make you the right person for the job. Trade letters and a copy of the ad with a classmate. Evaluate the work you are given and give your partner constructive feedback.

3. **Interviewing Skills.** In groups of three, identify a job that interests you. Separately develop interview questions. Have two members act as the interviewer and applicant, while the third member evaluates the applicant. After each person has served in each role, comment on each other's interview style.

4. **Teamwork and Leadership.** Divide into teams of four or five students. Decide what type of company you work for and then develop a handbook on the employees' code of ethics. Include examples of acceptable as well as unacceptable behavior on the job and determine what actions the company will take if an employee breaks the rules. After your handbook is completed, choose one topic to present to the class.

BUILDING YOUR PORTFOLIO

Choose three careers in the housing and interior environment field that interest you. Make a chart that lists the following for each career:

- ➤ **Nature of the Work.** Three to five points that describe what a typical workday is like on this job.

- ➤ **Work Environment.** Where does the work take place? Are there opportunities for self-employment?

- ➤ **Training/Education.** What initial training and education are required? Are more education and training required to advance on the job?

- ➤ **Salary Range.** What are the potential earnings from the lowest to the highest?

- ➤ **Related Occupations.** What careers require similar skills or have a similar nature of work?

- ➤ **Future Outlook.** Are employment opportunities in this career area expected to increase, decrease, or stay the same in the future? What is the international outlook?

Using print or Internet resources, including the *Occupational Outlook Handbook,* find the information you need. Document your sources. Then identify short-, medium-, and long-term goals to reach that career goal.

Architectural Design

*E*arly Homes

CHAPTER OBJECTIVES

► Describe how Native American housing was influenced by culture and environment.

► Identify primitive dwellings used by the early colonists.

► Analyze the characteristics of early English, German and Dutch, Swedish, Spanish, and French homes in North America.

TERMS TO LEARN

• adobe

• Cape Cod house

• clapboard

• coquina

• dormer

• ell

• gable roof

• gables

• gambrel roof

• garrison house

• half-timbered house

• pitched roof

• pueblo

• saltbox house

• shingle

• stucco

• thatch

*L*ooking at pictures of early homes, it's sometimes difficult to remember that they were "home" to real families. Our country began in Native American lodges, log cabins, and quaint New England farmhouses. These homes also form the roots of today's architectural styles.

*L*inks from the Past

Stroll down a street in an older part of town and you likely will see a wide variety of housing styles. You might see many of the same designs in a number of cities. If you were to examine these styles closely, you might find traces of homes designed hundreds of years ago.

Although some homes are truly modern creations, many are modifications of early American styles. As the country has grown, regional styles spread across the continent. These styles were modified to suit the weather conditions and terrain of the colonists' new land.

The modifications made today are different from those made by the colonists. Technological advances have made it possible to adapt many designs. In the past, some designs would have been restricted by climate, terrain, and the building materials available. Most climate conditions can now be offset by central heating and cooling systems and by insulation. Building materials can be transported to almost any location. However, some regional differences in housing still exist. Homes in New England, for example, often show links to that area's Cape Cod, Georgian, and Federal styles of the past. Features such as pitched roofs fit well with the climate.

To examine the influence of Early American housing on the styles of today, this chapter describes the housing of Native Americans and of settlers from the major countries that established colonies in North America. Knowledge of the characteristics of each style will help you understand the origins of today's homes and furnishings.

The Growth of Traditional Styles

American architecture traditionally dates from colonial times. The actual history of housing in North America, however, starts much earlier. Before colonists arrived from Europe, Native Americans lived on the continent in a variety of types of dwellings, each suited to their particular tribe's needs. Eventually the colonists began to build their own structures. Learning about these early homes is a good place to begin your study of the history of homes in America.

NATIVE AMERICAN HOMES

Native Americans lived throughout the North American continent, from the forests of the eastern shore to the deserts of the Southwest. Each group or tribe developed a distinct way of life. Many depended on hunting or fishing for their survival. Some raised crops and domestic animals.

Environment and culture were the two main influences on the type of housing developed by each tribe. Environment determined which building materials were available and the type of protection from the elements that was needed. Some of the cultural considerations were social organization; religious beliefs; methods of obtaining food; and size of the group, family, or organization. Hunters of the Great Plains developed dwellings different from those of the farming tribes of the Northeast and the Inuit people of the Arctic.

Native American homes did, however, have some common characteristics. They were simple structures with dirt floors and no windows or chimneys. They tended to be dark and crowded. Cooking was done over an open fire. There was little furniture. Weapons, tools, and other possessions were stored on shelves or hung from walls.

Tribes that depended on hunting or on gathering food had to move from place to place. Therefore, they developed dwellings that could be easily constructed at the new site or carried from place to place. The tribes of the eastern woodlands carried reed mats which were wrapped around rounded wood frames to create a domelike structure called a "wigwam." A wigwam could house one or two families. The tepee was

The tepee is one of the most familiar styles of early Native American homes. What were some reasons for building this type of shelter?

the invention of the tribes of the central and western plains who roamed in search of game. It was a cone-shaped tent covered with buffalo hides. This tent could be put up and taken down rapidly. It was perfectly suited to the nomadic life of the people who developed it.

Farming tribes established more permanent villages. They constructed homes intended to last for many seasons. The Iroquois tribes of the Northeast, for example, developed the *longhouse,* built from young trees that were bent to form a long, rectangular frame with a barrel-shaped roof. The frame was covered by overlapping strips of bark. The longhouse was designed to house several families. The public buildings of the Iroquois were also built this way. Some reached lengths of 100 feet (30 m).

The tribes of the Southwest also built more permanent structures. The Spanish people called these structures pueblos (PWAY-blohz), meaning "villages." **Pueblos** were houses built on top of each other into cliffs and caves and on the level ground. Pueblos were built of the only material available to these tribes, clay. The clay was formed into sun-dried bricks called **adobe** (uh-DOH-bee).

Climate was a major consideration for the Inuit people of the cold North. They lived in houses built partially underground and covered with sod. These homes had long, downward-sloping entrances. This construction kept the Inuit people well insulated from freezing temperatures and served as protection against the wind. In the snowiest regions, Inuit tribes built their dwellings from blocks of ice, lightly covered with snow. Very often, ice was the only building material available. However, when constructed properly, these ice houses served the Inuits as well as sod homes.

THE FIRST COLONISTS

The colonists who came to the New World represented many groups. Some came seeking religious freedom; others were adventurers determined to find wealth. A few were powerful aristocrats with vast land holdings. There were also individuals who had been exiled as punishment for a crime.

Upon landing in the New World, the first settlers were faced with the immediate problem of finding sources of food and building shelters. They had few tools and materials with which to accomplish these tasks. Some of them weren't able to make a home in the wilderness. In 1585, for instance, the first English settlement in North America was established on the island of Roanoke, North Carolina. This first group of settlers soon gave up and returned to England; a second group disappeared without a trace.

Those who did survive followed the example of the Native Americans. They saw how the native people adapted their dwellings to the surrounding environment and tried to do the same. Little is known of the earliest temporary shelters. Their owners usually destroyed them as soon as permanent dwellings were built. It is known, however, that huts of bark and branches, held together with clay, were used as crude shelters. Other types of early dwellings included a triangular, tentlike structure made up of logs propped up against each other, as well as a shed-like roofed house built into the side of a hill. As the new colonists grew more prosperous, they replaced their primitive one-room dwellings with larger, more permanent structures.

The Early American Period, 1640-1720

To feel more at home in a strange land, the colonists wanted to create an environment that was familiar to them. When they built their permanent houses, they patterned them as much as possible after the ones they had left behind. Modifications were made to suit the weather conditions and terrain.

Living in a Historic District

The stately homes in a historic district can be an impressive sight. Compared to some subdivision housing, many of these structures are large and rambling with distinctive features and real personality. Do you wonder about the responsibilities of living on the other side of the wrought-iron gates?

Your first response may be, "I wonder what it takes to keep up the place." Indeed, the cost of maintaining a home in a historic district is beyond many families. Any big space takes more energy to warm and cool, and more resources to paint and keep clean. Plus, even a well-preserved older home can't escape the effects of aging. Original woods and roofing may not be as durable as modern materials.

At the same time, homeowners may be restricted in the changes they can make. Preservation districts are created to save the style and architecture of a certain region or period. In many areas, a district commission must approve any major change affecting the home's outside appearance. That includes adding a porch, painting a different color, or removing a large tree. Approval is also needed for major interior renovations if the home has landmark status.

Even where a commission has only advisory powers, homeowners are expected to live up to the spirit of preservation. Putting solar panels on a Victorian home won't win a homeowner many friends among preservationists—or neighbors.

Fortunately, other money-saving updates have little or no effect on a home's appearance. Insulation can be added. Newer doors and windows which duplicate the originals are generally permitted. Some vinyl siding that is colored, sized, and finished specifically to replicate the original wood exterior may be acceptable. Likewise, interior details, such as moldings and wallpaper, are more available as reproductions.

For those who are willing and able to follow the neighborhood standards, owning a home in a historic district certainly has its rewards. Living in a beautiful home can be one of life's pleasures. Beautifying the area, thus fostering civic pride, is a way to give back to the community. If the district is promoted as a point of interest for tourists, you may even help the local economy.

YOU THE CONSUMER . . .

You're a member of your town's zoning board. A husband and wife are interested in buying and restoring a home in a preservation district. After making much-needed repairs, they would run the home as a bed-and-breakfast, which would also qualify them for federal tax breaks that they need to make the improvements. They are petitioning the board for a zoning exemption to bring a business into a residential area. The couple argues that their business would publicize the district to tourists and add to the town's tax revenues. However, some of the neighbors are concerned about the impact on safety and property values. What more information do you need before voting in this matter? What facts would incline you toward or against approving the couple's request?

Early colonists learned to survive in the New World through perseverance and by adapting building methods from their homelands.

As more people emigrated to North America, the workforce become more specialized. Records show that numerous experienced stonemasons and carpenters were among the first arrivals. They came with their *apprentices*—individuals who had entered into a legal agreement to work, usually for seven years, with a skilled master to learn a trade. Construction techniques began to be refined.

Local materials were used as a basis for construction in the New World. Wood from New England forests was made into lumber. Local stone was quarried. Settlers in Virginia, southern New Jersey, and Philadelphia found a good supply of brickmaking clay there. Handmade brick quickly became a popular building material in those areas. Lime for mortar between the bricks came from seashells.

ENGLISH SETTLEMENTS

The first two successful English colonies were started at Jamestown, Virginia, in 1607, and in Plymouth, Massachusetts, in 1620. By 1640, a sprinkling of tiny English settlements dotted the eastern edge of North America. Between 1640 and 1720, small, isolated settlements grew into bustling towns with larger and more comfortable houses. Some roads were constructed. Trade by land and sea grew.

Many of the first permanent dwellings constructed by the English colonists were patterned closely on half-timbered houses found in England. In the **half-timbered house**, the wood frame of the house formed part of the outside wall. The spaces between beams were filled in with brick or plaster. The roof was constructed of **thatch**—bundles of reeds or straw.

Some of these early houses were covered with shingles or clapboards. **Shingles** are thin, oblong pieces of material, usually wood, that are laid in overlapping rows to cover the roof and sides of a structure. **Clapboards** are boards with one edge thicker than the other laid in overlapping rows to protect the walls from the elements. A huge chimney served one or several fireplaces, which were used for cooking and for heat in the cold winters. Windows were generally small in order to reduce heat loss and minimize the use of expensive glass.

This re-creation of an early English colonial home in Jamestown shows half-timbered construction and a thatched roof. This home gave much more protection from the weather than earlier colonial homes.

This two-story, Cape-Cod-style house includes the traditional rectangular form, central chimney, and pitched or gable roof. Note the wood shingled exterior.

right angles to the length of the structure, was sometimes added. The original house was frequently built with a chimney at the end of the structure. These were called "half-houses" because when an addition to the house was made, it was placed so the fireplace and chimney would be in the center and could heat every room.

One drawback of the Cape Cod style was that the simple pitched room left little usable space on the second floor. The slope of the roof restricted the size of the rooms, door locations, and furniture placement. To overcome these problems, a new type of roof was developed. The **gambrel roof** has two slopes on each side, the upper slope being flatter than the lower slope. This allowed interior space for full-sized upstairs rooms.

Many English settlers in the northeastern colonies built a style of home called a **Cape Cod house**—a house with a simple rectangular design, a central chimney, and a **pitched roof**. This is a two-sided roof with a steep angle. A pitched roof is often called a **gable roof** because it forms triangular end walls, known as **gables**, on the house. The Cape Cod remains a model for many American homes

The interior of the Cape Cod was divided in to one large room, called the "great room," and one or two small rooms. The great room functioned as the center of family life. The large fireplace, used for cooking, usually furnished the only light in the dwelling. Almost all indoor tasks were performed at or near the fireplace—weaving, sewing, and furniture making. Some family members even slept there.

Although small, the Cape Cod house was built for expansion. As families grew, an **ell**, or extension built at

While homes in settlements along the Atlantic coast began to include more style and comfort, those who made their way inland still built rough shelters from available materials.

When time and material permitted, some colonists built houses that had two full stories. The **saltbox house** began as a two-story, pitched-roof house. The need for extra space prompted some owners to build an additional set of rooms along the back of the house on the first floor. They brought the roof line down to cover the addition. The long slope of the roof is similar to the sloping cover on the wooden saltboxes common in colonial kitchens.

The **garrison house** can be recognized by a second story that overhangs or projects from the first story. This style was copied from the Elizabethan houses (houses built during the reign of Queen Elizabeth I, 1558-1603) found in England at that time. Such an overhang was first used on forts, or garrisons, to prevent attackers from scaling the walls.

Today, if you visit the restored town of Williamsburg, Virginia, you will see many of the English dwellings just discussed. Since Williamsburg was the colonial capital, however, the homes there are more stylish and sophisticated than the average colonial home of this period.

GERMAN AND DUTCH SETTLEMENTS

The majority of German settlers who came to North America in the late 17th century settled in southeastern Pennsylvania. The Germans built large, durable houses of wood and quarry stone. The typical German house provided entry into a first-floor kitchen. The fireplace was located in the center of the first floor. On the opposite side of the fireplace was a large family room for entertaining. Some of the larger houses had small bedrooms behind the family room. In some German houses, an abbreviated roof, or "hood," was built between the first and second stories.

The Dutch came to the New World more than a century earlier than the Germans. Their first settlements were in New Amsterdam (now New York City) and in the Hudson Valley to the north. The Dutch used stone and brick to build houses considered large by colonial standards. Some houses were four or five stories high. The Dutch homes were noted for their decorative brickwork and intricate stepped gables. The gambrel roof design in Dutch Colonial homes gave more usuable space beneath the roof. To add light, these roofs often contained **dormers**—structures projecting through a steeply sloping roof. The window set in this structure is called a "dormer window." This feature shows up in later architectural styles. Also characteristic of Dutch styles were metal gutters, small windows with sliding shutters, and the "Dutch door"—a door divided in half horizontally. This design allowed the top half to stand open like a window while the bottom half remained closed.

The saltbox house characteristically has a long, sloping back roof and a central chimney.

What might be the functional purpose of the hood on this German home?

This modern home shows the influences of Dutch country architecture. The gambrel roof and dormers give the second floor more usable living space.

SWEDISH SETTLEMENTS

As settlers moved westward into dense, unexplored forest, the log cabin was their most common and practical shelter. These early settlers had to clear the land for farming, so they used the trees they felled to build their dwellings. This system was used by pioneers for many years as they pushed their way across the continent. The log cabin was so common that it has become a part of American folklore and is looked upon as a truly American building style. The fact that its origins were Swedish has almost been forgotten.

In Sweden, houses were traditionally made of wood. Swedes who came to the New World called on their knowledge of log construction. They felled the trees, cut them into logs, and laid them on one another horizontally. The logs were joined with notched corners and the joints were filled with clay, bark, or moss.

The log cabin was a primitive, small building. Its length rarely exceeded that of a single log. Sometimes a cabin was divided into two rooms with an attic above, but more often there was only one room. Originally, the roof was of bark or thatch. Later, wood shingles were used.

SPANISH SETTLEMENTS

The Spaniards were the first Europeans to establish colonies in the New World, mostly in Florida and the Southwest, in the early 1500s. The oldest Spanish house still existing in the United States is located in St. Augustine, Florida. Built about 1565, it is made of **coquina** (co-KEE-nuh), a soft porous limestone composed of shell and coral. Many of the Spanish houses in the South were rectangular, with balconies that faced the street. Kitchens were often separate so that the heat from cooking fires would not affect the rest of the house. The interior was usually simple, with whitewashed plaster walls, beamed ceilings, and earthen floors. The more elaborate houses used tile on the floor or roof.

In the Southwest, the Spanish settlers at first adopted some of the features of the natives' housing. These early Spanish houses had thick adobe walls, flat roofs, rough-hewn beams projecting through the outside walls, and deep-set windows.

In the 17th century, a more elaborate style was created by Spanish settlers in California and other parts of the Southwest. These houses were covered with adobe, brick, or stucco. **Stucco** is a plaster material made with cement, sand, and lime. These homes featured rounded archways and windows and red tile roofs. Porches and balconies often went around the outside of the dwelling. Some homes of this type had inner courtyards.

This home is modeled after early Spanish architecture in the Southwest. How does it compare with the pueblos built by Native Americans in the region?

Pierre Menard built this French colonial home in 1803 along the Mississippi River in what is now Illinois. How was the French style adapted for its location?

FRENCH SETTLEMENTS

The early French colonists who settled along the St. Lawrence River built houses of stone or wood, with the high, steep roofs common in French country cottages, particularly in Normandy, France. The typical home had small windows and heavy wooden shutters that could be closed to protect the occupants from cold weather. Original buildings in this style are found today in New York State and Canada.

The French cottage style had to be adapted when built by settlers in the hot and humid southern Mississippi Valley. A porch was added that was covered by a broad roof extending around the house. It helped keep the house cool and protected it from the rain. Often the houses were raised on posts a full story above the

ground. This was done to improve air circulation and protect the house from floods. The houses were usually painted white. The rooms had many doors and windows, which allowed for the flow of air.

In later versions of this style, galleries, or roofed balconies, were added, which provided shade and outdoor living space. The galleries could be reached from inside the house as well as by outside stairs. Posts supporting the balconies were made of wood or ornamental iron. Many such houses can still be seen in the French Quarter of New Orleans.

As you can see, the houses of the colonial era of North America were as different and varied as the people who built them. Each culture made its distinctive contribution to the Early American period. While attempting to recreate the homes they had left behind, the colonists had to adapt their building practices to their new lifestyles and living environments. This meant their houses were similar to, but smaller and less elaborate than, those of their European counterparts. Such adaptations made these homes distinctly American.

Tom Chaney

Preservationist

Sometimes, a person who buys an old house decides to restore it to the way it looked when it was first built. That's when I'm called in. As a preservationist, I must find out how the house once looked and then organize and carry out the restoration work.

"A town with an active historical society may be able to furnish photographs showing how the house looked during different periods."

I start by doing research, first with resources in the local community. Municipal records supply me with the year the house was built, details about any additions made to it over the years—perhaps even the number of times the roof was replaced. A town with an active historical society may be able to furnish photographs showing how the house looked during different periods. Even a black-and-white picture gives an idea of color values by showing which areas of the house were dark, medium, or light.

I then check this information against what I can find in books about old homes and architecture. I also use my knowledge about the color schemes that were popular in various eras. Like clothing fashions, house painting has changed with the times, and a good preservationist is aware of these trends. Only after about 1915 did it become fashionable to paint houses white and use only one accent color for the trim.

Next I determine the house's original paint color. On the outside of the house, I choose areas least affected by the weather—behind shutters, for example. Holding a small knife, I turn the blade to carve a circle in the layers of paint. The result should look like the annual rings of a tree, with

each ring indicating a new paint job. A similar technique is used inside. I check paint layers inside the closets, under moldings, and behind doorbell chimes.

Reproducing the original paint colors comes next. Most paint stores can custom mix thousands of different colors, and sometimes they can supply the exact shades I need. Many use a computer to analyze a scrap of the original paint color and determine its pigment formula in modern paint.

Once the colors are supplied, I can move on to wallpaper patterns, flooring, woodwork, and accent pieces. I keep a list of manufacturers, architectural dealers, and craftspeople who can furnish the items I need. The ability to establish and maintain these contacts is invaluable. A preser-

vationist is usually responsible for making all these arrangements and seeing the project through to its completion.

Of all the parts of my job as a preservationist, it's the research I like the most. Yes, I do take pride and sat-isfaction in seeing the final product emerge from the hands of the builders and skilled craftsmen. But it's the initial "detective work" that excites me the most. The evidence lies all around me, and the fun is in the pursuit.

> "It's the initial 'detective work' that excites me the most. The evidence lies all around me, and the fun is in the pursuit."

Career Profile

Preservationists restore houses to the way they looked when they were first built. They spend a lot of time researching what the house originally looked like: from what color of paint was used to what the wallpaper was used. They also look for pictures or records of the house. Once the research is complete, the preservationist makes sure that the restoration work is completed correctly.

Education
▶ A bachelor's degree in historic preservation, architecture, anthropology, architectural history, history, anthropology, or American studies is required.
▶ A master's degree in history, museum studies, or interior design with concentration in historic preservation is helpful.

Skills Needed
▶ Must be able to complete detailed investigations of historic structures.
▶ Good written and oral communication skills.

Career Outlook
▶ Preservationists will be able to find jobs as long as older buildings are valued.

Career Activities
1. Make a list of the places in your community you might find information about a building that you want to restore. What types of information might each source have?
2. Debate whether preserving historic buildings is worthwhile.

Review & Activities

Chapter Summary

➤ Native American tribes' culture and environment determined the type of housing they developed.

➤ The earliest colonists built simple, primitive homes often based on Native American homes. Later they built sturdier one-room dwellings and larger permanent homes.

➤ European colonists often built their American homes in the style of housing from their country of origin.

➤ Foreign styles were adapted to the climates and culture of the New World, creating a wide range of American housing styles.

Checking Your Understanding

1. How did the shelters of Native American hunters and food gatherers differ from the shelters of Native American farmers?

2. How did climate influence the design of Inuit homes?

3. Identify three types of temporary shelters built by the first colonists who came to the New World.

4. Discuss the difference between shingles and clapboards, and tell how each is used in house construction.

5. What simple, early English style is still a popular model for American homes? Briefly describe this style house.

6. Explain how the saltbox style evolved from a house with a normal pitched roof.

7. Describe three characteristics of the Dutch homes in New York State.

8. What group was responsible for bringing the log cabin design to North America?

9. How did Spanish settlers in the Southwest adapt native building styles?

10. Describe a typical French-style house in New Orleans.

Thinking Critically

1. Consider the early settlers in Jamestown who came to a strange new land not knowing what awaited them. What does this say about the settlers' character and the kind of people they were? How might these qualities have influenced their housing decisions?

2. What room in a modern home would you consider most similar to the great room of an original Cape Cod house? Why? How might the needs of people today and those of the past be similar?

3. Compare and contrast Early American housing styles. How were they similar? How were they different?

4. Which historical housing design would you choose for a large family? Explain your answer.

Applications

1. **Native American Homes.** Research one variety of Native American housing. Write a paper explaining how these homes were made, what materials were used, and how the homes met cultural needs.

2. **Environmental Influences.** Write a brief description of the climate and environmental conditions in your area. Then think about how these conditions have influenced construction materials, style, and location of housing. Is this influence greater on older or new homes? Summarize your thoughts for the class, using specific examples of homes in your town.

3. **Writing an Advertisement.** Choose an early home style discussed in the chapter. Then write an advertisement for the *Colonial Times Gazette* to offer the house for sale. Write the advertisement so that it reflects the historical period and addresses the people who would be living at that time.

4. **Styles in Town.** Take a walk down a street in your town or city. Take notes on and keep track of the number of different housing types you see in a one-block area. Note whether they are mostly multifamily dwellings or single-family, their styles, and their architectural details. How are they similar or different to the designs of early settlers?

5. **Modern Versions.** Using illustrated ads for houses for sale or a real estate company's website, find a modern version of the early home styles found in this chapter. Mount or print out at least three of these ads. Identify features that are similar to the original styles.

BUILDING YOUR PORTFOLIO

In 1587, a second group of English settlers tried to colonize Roanoke Island, off the coast of North Carolina. Three years later, the settlers had vanished. You are a historical investigator hired by a relative of one of the lost settlers to find some clues about the living conditions for those who lived there. Using reference materials and the Internet, research the type of housing these people set up on Roanoke Island. Write a report for your client.

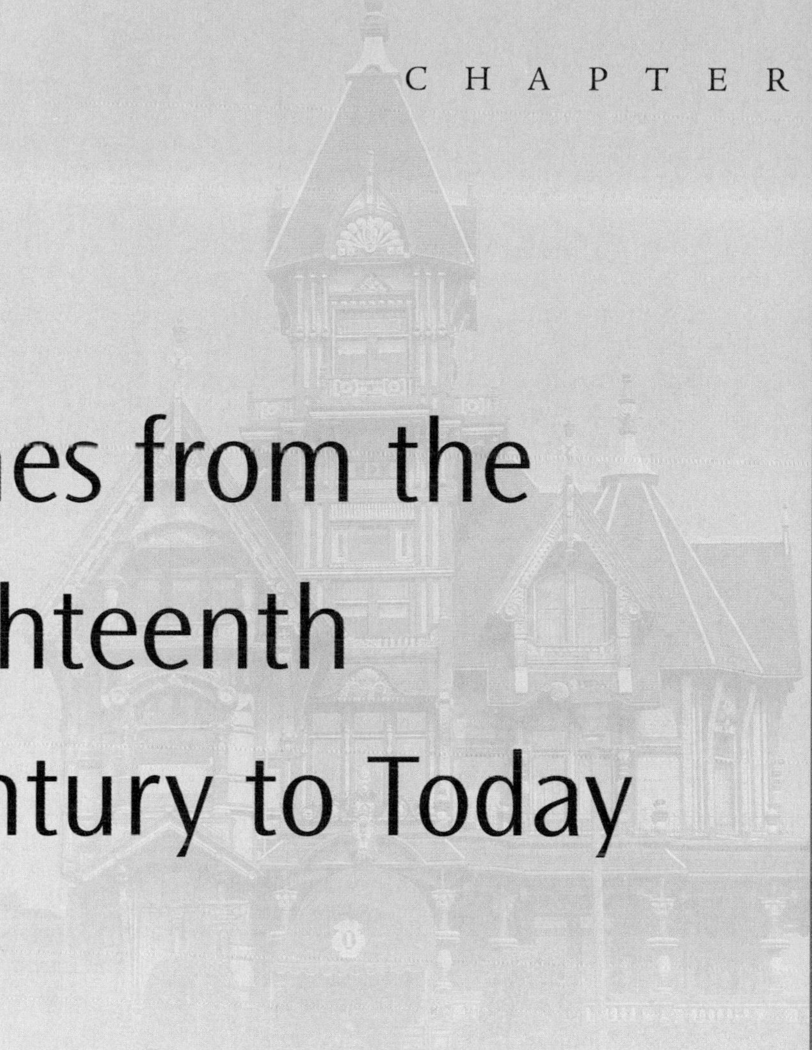

Homes from the Eighteenth Century to Today

CHAPTER OBJECTIVES

► Evaluate how events in America's history have affected housing design.

► Compare and contrast housing styles in the 18th century.

► Compare and contrast housing styles in the 19th century.

► Evaluate historical housing elements that influenced 20th century designs.

► Analyze the uniqueness of housing designs in the late 20th and early 21st centuries.

TERMS TO LEARN

- bungalow

- cornice

- fanlight

- gingerbread

- hip roof

- mansard roof

- pediment

- pilasters

- portico

- tenement

America in the 18th century was still undergoing enormous change. Waves of new immigrants continued to arrive, bringing with them rich heritages and traditions, including native home-building styles. At the same time, architects were emerging as the creators of a new housing revolution—and a new discipline that would keep the face of American housing changing and evolving. That evolution continued through the 19th and 20th centuries and into the 21st.

Understanding Period Housing Styles

Architectural history traditionally is divided into various periods. Each period is influenced by the historical events of its time and is characterized by distinctive housing styles. However, it's important to understand the one period flows into another, often overlapping; so dates can only be approximate. Several design movements can exist at the same time in different areas of the country. In addition, all houses of a certain style do not look identical. Architects and builders often add their personal stamp to each house they create. Variations can be seen from town to town and region to region.

Compare this old stone home to the highly decorative one above. Learning more about architectural styles will help you better understand and appreciate our country's history.

The design characteristics discussed in this chapter are the most common ones for each style or period. In identifying the style of a specific house, look for the overall "feeling" of a style, as well as for particular design details. However, keep in mind that many homes—especially more recent styles—break the traditional rules, creating new, individual designs.

The historical homes you see today don't represent all the housing of a particular period. The homes that remain as examples of early architectural styles tend to be those of the middle or upper classes. Built of more durable materials, they often stayed in one family for many generations. It is important to remember that, in any period, a large number of people lived in very simple homes. Most of these homes did not last, since they typically were not built as solidly or expensively as middle- and upper-class homes.

The 18ᵗʰ Century

Eighteenth-century life in America was filled with contrast. On the frontier, people lived in the roughest shelters. Along the East Coast, businesses and plantations grew steadily; elegant houses and furniture were in demand. Modest homes continued to be built by new arrivals to America.

IMMIGRANT STYLES

These new immigrants, like earlier ones, brought their styles of homes to the colonies or they created new styles adapted to the new land. They built homes in sturdy, distinctive styles that added to the variety and richness of America's housing. Materials and styles of building were then passed on to other immigrant groups, who, in turn, took them to other areas.

The English used timber sawed into boards to build their homes. The Dutch used stone and brick, Germans used wood and quarry stone, while Swedes used squared logs. Log cabins were erected from the Carolinas westward to Texas. This type of cabin was modified from the original one-room style to a larger version with two rooms side-by-side, often with a breezeway between them.

Spanish immigrants, who began to settle in the southwestern United States, brought the Spanish influence of cut stone and adobe brick for home building. In addition, a new American technique was born—building homes with sun-baked adobe clay.

FIGURE 6-1

18ᵗʰ Century Architectural Styles and Periods

Periods and Styles	Approximate Dates
Immigrant Styles	continuous
Georgian Period	1700-1780
Georgian Style	1700-1780
Federal Period	1770-1830
Adam Style	1780-1820
Early Classical Revival	1770-1830

Give some reasons why you, as an early settler in the eastern wilderness, might have chosen to construct a log cabin for your home.

In England, Georgian-style buildings were constructed of brick and stone. American builders used these materials when available but had to adapt the style when they weren't. The walls of George Washington's Mount Vernon home in Virginia, for example, are actually made of wood. They were carved and painted to look like stone.

The main characteristics of typical Georgian houses in America include:

- A formal, balanced design. Houses are often two or three stories high.
- A gable roof, which is a pitched roof with two sloped sides, or a **hip roof**, a roof with four sloped sides.

THE GEORGIAN PERIOD

For many, life in colonial America was comfortable. Americans, like Europeans, were becoming more prosperous, better educated, scientifically curious, and interested in history and the arts. The link to England was still there. This factor, combined with the new prosperity, turned people to the formal Georgian style of home that was then fashionable in England. This style was very popular in America throughout most of the century.

Georgian Style

The Georgian style was named for the kings of England who ruled during that time: George I, George II, and George III. The colonists copied design details that had long been popular in England.

How many characteristics of the Georgian style can you identify in this house? Compare its broken pediment to the triangular pediment on the next page.

- Large windows symmetrically placed. The windows consist of many small panes.
- Doorway details. The front door is the focal point of the house. Typically, the door is framed by **pilasters**, which are decorative flattened columns. The doorway is often topped by a **pediment** (PED-uh-munt)—a triangular or arched decoration. The door itself has decorative panels.
- A distinctive cornice. A **cornice** (KOR-nuhs) is a decorative strip at the area where the roof and the walls meet. Georgian houses often have a cornice of toothlike molding.
- A central chimney or a chimney at each end of the house.
- Contrasting materials. Red brick is often used with white wood trim, but other materials are also common.

Inside the typical Georgian house, molded plaster ceilings conceal the beams of the second floor. Wood paneling or wallpaper covers the walls. An ornate rectangular fireplace, topped by a mantel, is often the center of interest.

Many Georgian houses are square or rectangular. Larger Georgian-style houses often have a central section with a wing on each side to accommodate the kitchen and offices or guest rooms. Georgian homes are generally built around a central hall with a wide staircase. These homes reflect the gracious, somewhat formal style of living that had become popular among upper-middle-class and wealthy colonists.

The upper classes, with much leisure time to enjoy, turned their attention to the arts. Men and women had their portraits painted. In the evenings, they entertained family and friends by playing the harpsichord or the newly invented "pianoforte" (today's piano). The formal Georgian home provided the perfect backdrop to display portraits, as well as affording ample space for entertaining.

Decorative characteristics of the Georgian style were applied to "row houses," sometimes called "town houses." *Row houses* are a continuous line of two- or three-story houses that share a common wall with houses on either side. This kind of hous-

The Georgian style was the first in this country with major emphasis on decorative elements. What do you think brought about this change?

Pediment

Paneled Door

Pilasters

ing first appeared in such American cities as Boston and Philadelphia during the 18th century.

Achieving the decorative look of the Georgian style required the work of craftsmen and artisans. Many European immigrants supplied the labor to build these houses and row houses. Their skills as woodworkers, brickmakers, glassmakers, and plasterers can still be seen today.

THE FEDERAL PERIOD

In the 1770s, American attitudes toward England changed. From 1775 to 1783, the colonists fought and won the American Revolution. This war brought to an end many of the old political and social patterns. People who had been leaders because of their ties with England died in the fighting or had been forced to emigrate. New trend-setting leaders emerged, many of them traders and merchants. Cities with busy ports grew in importance; the expanding frontier opened up new possibilities in the west; and the tide of immigration from Europe continued.

With a sense of renewed patriotism after winning the American Revolution, Americans turned away from the English Georgian style. They sought architectural styles that expressed America's newly won freedom and independence. These styles make up what is known as the "Federal period," named in honor of the new federal government of the United States. They were popular at the end of the century as the young country looked for ways to express its new identity.

These Adam-style row houses, when compared with the Georgian style on the previous page, show how the new style evolved from the old. The fanlight above the doorway replaces the triangular pediment. Decorative glass sidelights replace the pilasters beside the doors.

During the Federal period, two distinct architectural styles developed. The more popular, often called the "Adam style," borrowed from English architects but was "Americanized" to be different from European architecture. Although Early Classical Revival style is a thoroughly American innovation, the two styles share many characteristics.

Adam Style

The Adam style was named in honor of the English architects Robert and James Adam. These two brothers took the Georgian features and combined them with elements from classical Greece and Rome. They paid particular attention to decorative interior details. The style made its mark in America from about 1780 to 1820.

Some of the features of the Adam style are:

- A rectangular design with one or more stories. Some homes have a center section with a wing on each side.
- Gable roofs. The slopes of the roof generally face the front and back of the house. A decorative cornice often extends across the front and back of the house at the roofline.
- Symmetrically placed windows. As in the Georgian period, the windows have many panes. A **fanlight**—a semicircular, round, or oval window with fan-shaped panes of glass—is often above the door or in the pediment.

- Decorative interiors. Plaster and wood carvings in classical design are used on walls and ceilings. The mantels around fireplaces are especially decorative.

Early Classical Revival Style

Between 1770 and 1830, many architects turned to ancient Rome to find new ways of expressing American independence. They were led by Thomas Jefferson, who was an architect as well as President, statesman, and inventor. Jefferson's home, Monticello, and the buildings he designed for the University of Virginia include features from the buildings of antiquity.

The style Jefferson helped develop became known as "Early Classical Revival." It was used for many government buildings, as well as row houses and other residences. These included many of the buildings in the new federal capital of Washington, D.C. The Early Classical Revival style also extended beyond the eastern United States to new states being settled, such as Texas, Iowa, Kansas, and Minnesota.

The Early Classical Revival style is similar to the Adam style in several ways. The rectangular shape of the buildings, with windows symmetrically placed, is common in both types. The fanlight window is another feature found in both styles. The feature that distinguishes Early Classical Revival style structures, however, is the **portico** (POR-tih-koh). This is a tall, open porch, supported by columns, over the front entrance. The portico is topped by a triangular pediment. Sometimes the porch is built up on a foundation and extends to the roof of the house or building. This revival of the classic design of the past paved the way for greater interest in classic styles as America moved from the 18th into the 19th century.

This Early Classical Revival home has timeless appeal. It shows that the style can be adapted to small, as well as large, buildings.

The 19th Century

In the early 1800s, the Industrial Revolution was sweeping America. Throughout the 19th century, manufacturing grew steadily. The results of industrialization changed America forever.

Along with the growth of factories came new demands. Because more workers were needed, immigrants began pouring into the country in greater numbers to provide cheap labor. Railroads were built to ship the new products to the expanding population. What effect did all this have on housing in America?

First of all, the construction industry was one of many developing at a rapid pace. With mass production, factories could make in quantity the products needed to build and furnish homes and businesses. As prices for homes dropped, more people could afford to buy them. This raised the standard of living for many people.

Not everyone was so fortunate, though. Because of low wages, many factory workers could not afford decent housing. Factory owners built row houses, which they rented to their employees. However, many more poor quality houses were built near the factories. Apartments and other multiunit dwellings also became common in cities. **Tenements**—apartment complexes with minimum standards of sanitation, safety, and comfort—were built. Workers and their families crowded into them.

FIGURE 6-2

19th Century Architectural Periods and Styles

Periods and Styles	Approximate Dates
The Romantic Revival Period	1820-1880
Greek Revival Style	1825-1860
Gothic Revival Style	1840-1880
Italianate Style	1840-1885
Victorian Period	1860-1900
Mansard Style	1860-1880
Queen Anne Style	1870-1890

Multifamily homes in the late 1800s were often crowded and unsanitary. To save money, several families, or a large extended family, would live together in a small apartment.

At the same time, a considerable number of Americans became wealthy from the profits of industrialization. They spent their money on travel and newer and larger homes. From their travels to Europe, they returned with ideas that they incorporated in their own homes.

While all of this was going on, housing styles in America were also changing. During the 18th century, one style had dominated—the Georgian. During the 19th century, there were many styles, from those that imitated the classic styles of the past to the fancy designs of Victorian homes. Housing during this century reflected a mixture of ideas and a spirit of fantasy and excitement. The American housing scene was as varied as the people who came together to create it. It mirrored the many changes in the economy and in society.

THE ROMANTIC REVIVAL PERIOD

During the first half of the 19th century, many writers and artists found inspiration in the European past. They were especially drawn to ancient Greece, medieval Europe, and Renaissance Italy as sources of inspiration. Nineteenth-century architects expressed these patterns of the past in the Greek Revival, Gothic Revival, and Italianate styles.

Many mansions in the South were built in the Greek Revival style.

Greek Revival Style

The Greek Revival style flourished from about 1825 to 1860, ending around the time of the Civil War. Its features were linked to the temples of ancient Greece. One of the most famous variations of Greek Revival architecture is the Southern plantation style. Such homes had a two-story porch supported by columns across the entire front of the house.

Typical characteristics of the Greek Revival style include:

- A two-story rectangular house with symmetrically placed windows.
- A gable roof emphasized by wide trim at the cornice.
- Pilasters on the corners of frame houses or across the whole front.
- An elaborate entrance. The door is usually surrounded by small windows and may also have additional wood or masonry (stone or brick) framework.
- Columns supporting a small or large porch. Sometimes the columns are simply set into the entrance. Greek columns are most common.

Gothic Revival Style

One of the styles that became popular all over America during the 19th century was the Gothic Revival style (1840-1880). Designers used such European features as pointed arches and circular windows with ornamental carved stone. Many Gothic Revival homes were built of wood because stone was very expensive in many parts of America and because there was a shortage of stonemasons. Countless houses were built with high-peaked Gothic gables decorated with **gingerbread**, lacy-looking, cutout wood trim.

The pointed arches and gingerbread trim of this house are characteristic of the Gothic Revival style. Many middle-class families lived in Gothic Revival homes. Some even included the new technology of indoor plumbing and gas lights.

Victorian styles are often very elaborate. Their detail was largely, and loosely, taken from medieval and Renaissance European styles. Because of the new technology in America at the time, the use of complicated details and shapes in housing design was possible. The Mansard and Queen Anne are two of several styles that were popular during the Victorian period.

Mansard Style

The Mansard style (sometimes called the *Second Empire style*) showed the French influence during the Victorian period. It was most popular between 1860 and 1880. The most notable feature of this style is

Italianate Style

Architectural features of Italian villas, or estates, were also reproduced in houses in America during the 19th century. Homes built in the Italianate style (about 1840-1885) were often square and two stories high. They featured wide, overhanging hip roofs with decorative brackets, or supports, at the cornices. Their long, narrow windows were commonly arched and crowned with an inverted, U-shaped structure.

THE VICTORIAN PERIOD

The Victorian period takes its name from Queen Victoria, who reigned in England from 1837 to 1901. The entire time of her reign is often described as the Victorian period. In America, however, Victorian housing styles were most popular from about 1860 until the end of the century.

In what ways is the Italianate style different from the Gothic Revival style which preceded it? Are there any similarities?

What would be the main advantage of the mansard roof? How would the dormers add to that advantage?

wraparound porches with railings and columns. Many Queen Anne houses have a circular tower that extends the entire height of the building. A variety of decorative woodwork was used on Queen Anne homes, from spindlework to brackets and half-timbering.

The End of the Victorian Period

In general, houses built at the end of the Victorian era were less elaborate than those built earlier in the period. Their architectural lines were cleaner and simpler. Homes for the wealthy, however, were built on an even larger scale. Some common Victorian features—such as irregular gables and

the boxlike mansard roof. A **mansard roof** is a roof that has two slopes on all sides, with the lower slope being steep and the upper slope almost flat. (See Figure 6-3.) Other features of the Mansard style are decorated cornices and French windows, which are long windows that open lengthwise at the middle. Dormer windows for the top story project from the lower slope of the roof.

Queen Anne Style

In the 1870s and 1880s, the most fanciful of the Victorian styles, the Queen Anne style, became popular.

Some typical details of this style are an irregular steep roof with ornamental gables, overlapping decorative wood shingles for siding, and

The ornamentation of the Queen Anne style showed off the greater wealth of the industrial age. Decorative details were highlighted by different colors of paint. Can you identify the style of the white house in the background?

FIGURE 6-3

Roof Styles

These five basic roof designs are those used most often in the 18th to 21st centuries. Roof styles were sometimes modified to blend with the character of a particular housing style.

CENTURY	Gable	Hip	Gambrel	Mansard	Flat
18TH CENTURY	Immigrant Styles Georgian Adam	Georgian Early Classical Revival	Immigrant Styles Adam (rare)		Immigrant Styles
19TH CENTURY	Greek Revival Gothic Revival Queen Anne	Italianate	Dutch Colonial	Mansard Style (Second Empire)	Italian Renaissance
20TH-21ST CENTURIES	Tudor Chateauesque Craftsman Ranch Contemporary	Colonial Revival Mission Prairie Craftsman Ranch	Colonial Revival		International Contemporary

windows, wooden wraparound porches, and patterned wood shingles—were easily adapted to the smaller middle-class homes being built at the end of the century.

In addition, by the late 1800s, multifamily housing was changing. In this type of housing, many families live in individual units within a larger structure such as an apartment building. The invention of the safety elevator in the 1850s and the use of steel-frame construction meant that apartment buildings could safely have many stories.

These tall apartment houses offered several individual homes on each floor. Residents reached their homes not by endless flights of stairs but by elevators.

As was true of single-family homes at the end of the Victorian period, architects and designers of multifamily housing also started to build as simply as possible. Their designs stripped away the overwhelming amount of ornamentation and details found in the earlier Victorian period. An entire world of architectural possibilities opened up.

The Early 20th Century

Early in the 20th century, America experienced one of the most creative and productive times in the history of home design. Traditional styles from various cultures and countries were being adapted to new ways of living. Architects also took bold steps in new directions. In general, two architectural movements took hold in the 20th century. One was based on traditional styles. The other, based on new ideas, was called *modern*.

FIGURE 6-4

Early 20th Century Architectural Styles

Styles	Approximate Dates
Period Revival Styles	
Colonial Revival Style	1880-1955
Tudor Style	1890-1940
Chateauesque Style	1880-1910
Mission Style	1890-1920
Modern Styles	
Prairie Style	1900-1920
Craftsman Style	1905-1930
International Style	1925-present

PERIOD REVIVAL STYLES

Included in 20th-century housing designs are those that copy past styles. When Victorian architects copied the past, they mixed styles freely. Twentieth-century architects, however, wanted to copy styles in more pure form. The resulting styles came from European and American history.

Colonial Revival Style

From 1880 to approximately 1955, many middle-class Americans duplicated house styles from their own country's past. The Colonial Revival brought back such styles as the Georgian, saltbox, and Cape Cod.

The door and windows of a Colonial Revival home have distinctive features. The door is prominent, usually with a decorative pediment supported by pilasters. In some homes, the pediment extends forward, supported by slender columns, to form an entry porch. Windows appear in symmetrically balanced pairs, with double-hung sashes.

Where in your area can you find an example of Colonial Revival architecture?

Compare this Tudor-style home with the 17th century English colonial home on page 112. Why do you think the Tudor style again became popular during this later time period?

Tudor Style

During the period 1890-1940, the Tudor-style home was also popular. Its half-timbered look (resembling homes from very early England) is probably its most dominant characteristic.

Many Tudor-style homes feature steeply pitched gables at the front and sides; tall, narrow windows, usually placed in groups, with many small panes; and massive chimneys with decorative *chimney pots* (earthenware pipes placed at the tops of chimneys). Stucco, brick, and stone are among the most commonly used exterior wall surfaces.

Chateauesque Style

French palaces provided the model for another housing style. Chateauesque homes often featured towers, turrets, ornamental metal cresting, elaborate moldings, relief carvings, and arched windows and doorways. These castlelike details give Chateauesque homes a grand look.

Wealthy Americans hired European-trained architects to build these large, impressive homes. Many descendants of the original owners, however, could not afford to keep up the grandest of these ornate buildings. Some are used today as schools or museums.

Mission Style

The Mission style was born in California and spread eastward from 1890 to 1920. Although the Mission style is most commonly found in the southwestern United States, examples can be found throughout the country.

Inspired by California's Hispanic heritage, its unique characteristics were fashioned after the old mission churches and houses in southern California. The Mission style includes such design details as arched doorways and windows; tile roofs often hidden by *parapets* (low walls or railings along balconies);

The Mission style gained popularity after the Panama-California exposition in 1915.

FIGURE 6-5

Architectural Styles—Mid 20th Century to Today

Styles	Approximate Dates
Postwar Modern Styles	
Ranch Style	1935-present
Contemporary Style	1950s-early 1970s
Split-Level Style	1950s-present
Shed Style	1960s-1970s
Traditional Styles	1900-present
Innovative Designs	
A-Frame	1940-present
Geodesic Dome	1940-present

and exterior walls made of stucco. In addition, bell towers and turrets with pyramid-shaped roofs often added charm to the Mission style's traditional shapes.

MODERN STYLES

While some architects were looking to the past, others wanted to create something different. Modern styles have been developing throughout the 20th century. They began with the Prairie and Craftsman styles early in the century and picked up again later with other designs such as the International style.

Prairie Style

At the beginning of the 20th century an American architect named Frank Lloyd Wright began designing homes in the Prairie style. These were very different from the homes of the Victorian era. Most Prairie-style homes were built until about 1920.

Wright's homes are characterized by their emphasis on horizontal lines, low-pitched roofs with overhanging eaves, wide porches, and such details as rows of leaded-glass windows. In the interior of these homes, rooms flow into one another, giving a feeling of spaciousness. The rooms are open and designed to connect with the outdoors. Porches, terraces, and rows of windows help draw the outside environment in. Wright custom-designed furniture and carpets to fit each home that he designed.

The Prairie style is not limited to the homes designed by Wright or the young architects he trained. Its influence can be seen in homes built throughout the United States in the first quarter of this century. One of the most common forms is the square, two-story house with a hip roof and wide front porch. This form is sometimes called "American Foursquare."

Craftsman Style

The Craftsman style originated in southern California, developing at the same time as the Prairie style and sharing many of its characteris-

The Craftsman style started as a reaction against the machine age. Its original English architects built their Craftsman bungalows with hand tools. While this proved impractical for widespread use, the "handcrafted" look remained.

Frank Lloyd Wright and Commercial Design

Frank Lloyd Wright is internationally known for his residential designs of the early 20th century. However, Wright also designed commercial and industrial projects. One such prominent design is the S.C. Johnson Wax and Sons Inc. Administration Building and Research Tower located in Racine, Wisconsin.

In 1936 Herbert Johnson commissioned Wright to design a building for the Johnson Wax corporate offices. The building was completed in 1939 and is famous for office furniture designed by Wright and the "Great Workroom"—an open office area. Wright uniquely designed the support columns in the form of lily pads and included many of the elements of the Prairie style that made his residential designs successful.

Identifying the characteristics of the Prairie style in a variety of settings helps designers to evaluate historical architecture and suggest solutions to clients. Wright applied elements of the Prairie style to the Johnson Wax building, including:

- **Emphasis on horizontal lines.** Brick was used extensively for the interior and exterior of the building to emphasize the horizontal line. Even the vertical joints of the mortar between the bricks were about the same color as the bricks to create the illusion that the bricks were seamless. To reinforce a continuous horizontal line, Wright designed special windows in the shape of glass tubing. The horizontal line was also evident in the mezzanine area surrounding the "Great Workroom."

- **Rows of windows.** The use of natural light in interiors of the Prairie style was critical to Wright as a means to see colors in their true state and to create a pleasant environment. To accommodate natural light, Wright designed rows of beautiful leaded-glass windows that were placed close to the ceiling of a room. This allowed the natural light to "bounce" off of the ceiling and produce a soft diffused light source to the interior. The concept of soft light was also used in the skylight of the "Great Workroom."

- **Unity in materials.** To create overall unity of structure brick was used on the interior and exterior of the building. Oak was used for furniture, floors, and trim around doors and windows. To assure unity in all objects used in a building, Wright designed the furniture, light fixtures, flooring, murals, and fabrics. Decorative accessories and leaded-glass windows were often designed with motifs associated with the prairie, such as butterflies and the sumac, a native tree of North America.

- **Colors of the prairie.** In custom designing all elements of a building Wright was able to be very selective in the color choices. Wright primarily used the colors of the prairie—goldenrod, brown, yellow, muted green, rust, gray, and red.

You, the *Designer*

Imagine you are part of a design team responsible for designing a building in the Prairie style. Decide which characteristics you would recommend for the interior and exterior of the building. Give rationales for your choices.

tics. The Craftsman style, however, is distinguished by the development of the **bungalow**. This is a small, one-story house with an overhanging roof and a covered porch. A variation of this style is the one-and-a-half-story type. The bungalow met the need for smaller, less expensive homes. The Craftsman style was adapted for use across the United States until the early 1930s.

The Craftsman style has distinctive features, such as:

- A low-pitched gable roof (although some examples have hip roofs).
- Decorative beams or braces under the eaves.
- Full- or partial-width porches with the roof supported by columns or pedestals extending to the ground.

International Style

After the end of World War I, European architects began to experiment with new materials and new building methods. The result was the International style, also called Modernism or Functionalism. The International style used design elements in ways that departed drastically from tradition. Among its best-known originators were the architects Le Corbusier (luh kawr-byooz-YAY) (Charles E. Jeanneret) of Switzerland, and Walter Gropius (GROH-pee-uhs) and Ludwig Mies van der Rohe (meez VAN-duh-ROW) of Germany. In the late 1930s, the immigration of Gropius and Mies van der Rohe to the United States helped introduce the style here.

Houses built in the International style emphasize function, or usefulness. Thus, elements that are purely decorative or ornamental are avoided. A typical International-style house combines simple geometric shapes to create an asymmetrical design that resembles a piece of sculpture. The innovative design was made possible by the use of a steel skeleton, which gave architects more freedom than traditional methods of building. The roof is usually flat. The exterior walls feature smooth, blank surfaces and large expanses of windows. Although it is not commonly used for residences, the International style is important because of its influence on later housing designs.

While the Prairie style was a distinct departure from previous architectural forms, the International style, shown here, was even more radical. Phillip C. Johnson brought the International style to the U.S.

The Mid 20ᵗʰ Century to Today

The United States was in the midst of World War II until 1945, so home building was at a standstill. When it started up again, people wanted *modern* styles. During this time, several new styles emerged that changed the face of home building.

POSTWAR MODERN STYLES

The styles after World War II ignored historical styles in favor of new, innovative ones. These styles include ranch, contemporary, split-level, and shed.

Ranch Style

A ranch house is a long, low, one-story house. It resembles the rambling one-story houses built by the early settlers of the West. The

Craftsman and Prairie styles also influenced the ranch house design.

The ranch-style home features a low-pitched gable or hip roof. Most have decorative shutters, decorative iron or wooden porch-roof supports, and picture windows. Some have partially enclosed patios or court-yards based on the Spanish influence. Private outdoor living areas are generally in the rear, in contrast to the front porches of the 19ᵗʰ and the early 20ᵗʰ centuries.

Although ranch-style homes appeared as early as the mid-1930s, this style dominated American home building from the early 1950s through the 1960s. It became popular as people moved to the suburbs. Because suburban lots were larger than city lots, it became possible to utilize the spread-out floor plan of the ranch. In many parts of North America, ranch homes are still popular. With the importance of universal design, the one-story ranch is often preferred by people who want to make their homes accessible to all.

Contemporary Style

The contemporary style was popular among architects in the 1950s, 60s, and early 70s. It features wide eave overhangs, flat or low-pitched roofs with low gables, exposed supporting beams, contrasting wall materials and textures, and unusual placement and shapes of windows. This style is designed to integrate into the landscape around it. (This style is very different from the International style, which is meant to stand out

The ranch-style home typically had a patio in back instead of a porch in front. What other changes during the 1950s and 1960s also separated families from their neighbors?

The Shed style is very angular with a variety of geometric shapes. How might this affect the usability of the space within?

from its surroundings like a piece of sculpture.) Some contemporary homes appear to be strongly influenced by the Craftsman and Prairie styles. The contemporary style is sometimes called American International.

Split-Level Style

The split-level home became popular during the 1950s as a modification of the ranch-style home. The split-level has the horizontal lines, low-pitched roof, and overhanging eaves of the ranch style—but the similarity stops there. A split-level house has three levels of living space, each connected by short flights of stairs. Some split-levels have a basement, which adds a fourth level. The split-level often has some traditional decorative details, but it is clearly a modern home.

The split-level house was originally designed to take advantage of a sloping lot. Because of the interior advantages of this house, however, it is also built on level lots. It provides the space of a ranch home without requiring as large a lot.

Shed Style

The shed style appeared during the 1960s. It grew out of the teachings of several famous architects, including Charles Moore and Robert Venturi. The roofline of a shed-style home is made up of a combination of steeply pitched *shed roofs*, each of which may slope at a different angle and face in a different direction. There is little or no traditional ornamentation. The exterior is usually wood shingle; but many of these homes feature board siding applied horizontally, vertically, or diagonally. The entrance is not obvious, and is usually set back. The windows are usually small and placed asymmetrically.

Identify as many traditional elements as possible in this modern house. Would you prefer a home with some traditional features or an International-style home?

INNOVATIVE DESIGNS

New designs often break all the existing rules of accepted housing designs that came before them. Two of these innovative designs that redefine housing are the A-frame and the geodesic dome.

A-Frame

The A-frame is a design in which the gabled roof continues to ground level on two sides. This eliminates the need for separate side walls. The A-frame usually is used for vacation homes. Ease in building and the broad range of building materials that can be used during construction are the main advantages of the A-frame. The biggest disadvantage of the A-frame style is the odd interior space created by its design.

TRADITIONAL INFLUENCES

Many people are drawn to homes that reflect the traditions of the past. Unlike architects of the 1920s and the 1930s, most designers and builders today are not as concerned with constructing replicas of historical styles. They do, however, borrow some of the elements of one or more styles to create homes with traditional appeal. Yet, the traditional styles are adapted to suit today's more casual tastes and lifestyles.

Traditional elements of style are often used for the exterior design on both single-family and multifamily housing. For example, an apartment building with an entrance featuring elaborate masonry framework might hint at the Greek Revival style. Row houses with pediments over each entrance may remind you of the Georgian style. Red tile roof can give a group of town houses a Spanish flavor, while gingerbread trim brings to mind Victorian farmhouses.

This A-frame home has three floors. What rooms might be located on each?

Geodesic Dome

In 1947 the American architect R. Buckminster Fuller invented the geodesic dome (JEE-uh-DE-sik), an efficient home built of triangular frames that are joined to form a self-supporting roof and walls. The frame is metal or plastic covered by either a flexible skin or rigid panels. Because the dome is structurally self-supporting, interior walls are not needed. As a result, great flexibility is possible for interior floor plans.

The geodesic dome also provides low-cost, energy-saving housing. Less building material is needed than in traditional housing. Heat loss is minimized by the decrease in exposed surface area. However, many people consider this dome house to be unattractive. As a result, few have been built.

These Puerto Rican condominiums use bright colors and bold shapes. How well would this style fit into your neighborhood?

Influences on Housing

As you can see, many factors have influenced the development of home design in North America. Not only the environment but also the history and the political, economic, and social conditions of the country have played a role. At many times, architects and builders have looked to the past for inspiration. They have combined elements of more than one style to create new styles. In recent years, they have designed new forms and shapes of housing. Changes will continue as architects adapt housing styles to fit American lifestyles.

Chris Harrison

Architect

There are two things that every successful architect has to have—artistic sensitivity and engineering knowledge. Any building I design has to be structurally sound and able to support the ways it will be used—that's the engineering side. It must also be pleasing to the eye so that the people who live or work there will feel comfortable—that's the artistic side.

"When I'm designing a residence, I first sit down with the clients to listen to what they want in their home."

When I'm designing a residence, I first sit down with the clients to listen to what they want in their home. Sometimes they come with photos of homes they like and lists of features they want incorporated in the design. I add some realistic touches—what is structurally possible and the probable costs involved. This is an important part of my work. Gaining client satisfaction at this early stage is essential if they're going to be pleased with the final product.

Making the sketches and final drawings has been greatly simplified by a computer-aided design (CAD) system. Besides speeding up my work, the CAD system has a number of special features that are great for architects. I can "sketch" a building on the computer screen—or call up one of the many basic designs stored on computer disks and adapt it for a new project. With a few keystrokes I can turn the design for one town house into a design for a 12-unit development. In seconds I can relocate the garage of a ranch house from the right side to the left.

Architects have to create many separate drawings of the same structure. With the CAD system, the information in various drawings is linked. For example, the computer can use the information in two-dimensional draw-

ings to automatically generate a three-dimensional view of a home. I can then use software to add realistic details and rotate the drawing on the computer screen. This really helps my clients see what their new home will look like from all angles—almost as if they had seen a video of the finished structure. I can take them on a virtual "walk-through" of the house.

CAD also gives me the flexibility to update a design as new ideas and difficulties occur to me. It can even alert me to potential mistakes. Best of all, the system supplies me with excellent drawings in a fraction of the time it would take to do them by hand. Students shouldn't be fooled into thinking that CAD skills are all they'd need to become a good architect though.

Once the design of the structure is complete and approved, I turn to supervising its construction. I make

sure that the proper materials are ordered and used, and that costs are kept within the approved budget. I have to ensure that all national and local zoning laws and building codes are followed. If physically challenged people will be living or working there, additional requirements must be met. It's an important part of my job to see that the various contractors who do the actual construction comply with these guidelines.

"Once the design of the structure is complete and approved, I turn to supervising its construction."

Career Profile

Architects design and oversee the construction of buildings and other structures. Most architects now use CAD (computer-assisted design) programs to develop building plans instead of drawing them by hand. Once the design is complete, the architect will supervise its construction. An architect's job isn't finished until construction is complete and the building passes all inspections.

Education
▶ A bachelor's or master's degree in architecture is needed from a school that is accredited by the National Architectural Accrediting Board (NAAB).
▶ A 5-year program leads to a bachelor's degree and a 6-year program leads to a master's degree.
▶ Most states require a 3-year apprenticeship program with an accredited sponsor before being eligible for accreditation.
▶ Candidates must be able to pass all sections of the Architect Registration Exam (ARE) before becoming licensed.

Skills Needed
▶ The ability to communicate effectively and work well within a team.
▶ Computer skills, especially in CAD programs.
▶ Design and engineering skills.
▶ The ability to focus both on small details and the big picture.

Career Outlook
▶ Average growth is expected in the near future.
▶ The growth prospect is directly related to the level of activity within the construction industry.

Career Activities
1. In teams, conduct an environmental study within your classroom. Determine how effectively space is being used and what changes might be made to improve the area.
2. Develop a floor plan for your classroom based on your findings. Share your findings with the rest of the class.

$\mathcal{R}$eview & Activities

Chapter Summary

- Historical events, such as immigration and wars, affected housing in the 18th, 19th, and 20th centuries, and still do today.
- In the 18th century, immigrant groups adapted their native styles to America.
- During the 19th century, architects copied styles from Europe's past. The Victorian period combined features from those styles.
- During the first half of the 20th century, some American architects copied traditional styles from England, France, and colonial America, while others developed Modern styles with simple, clean lines.
- During recent years, architects have adapted traditional housing styles to today's lifestyles and have developed new housing forms.

Checking Your Understanding

1. What are three distinct features of the Georgian style?

2. What style is characteristic of early government buildings in Washington D.C.?

3. How is the Early Classical Revival style similar to the Adam style? How is it different?

4. What is the main feature of a Greek Revival house? a Gothic Revival House? an Italianate house?

5. What are the main features of the Mansard and Queen Anne styles?

6. How did some buildings from the end of the Victorian period form a link to the Modern style?

7. Discuss some characteristics of Frank Lloyd Wright's Prairie-style homes.

8. How was the International style introduced to the U.S.?

9. Describe three advantages of a ranch home.

10. How do innovative designs break architectural rules?

Thinking Critically

1. Explain why you think George Washington and Thomas Jefferson wanted the newly established United States to adopt Greek and Roman architectural styles for its public buildings?

2. Using your knowledge of the Industrial Revolution in the late 1800s, speculate how technological and social changes influenced housing of the time.

3. Think about the mood of America following World War II. Why do you think many people wanted to abandon the past and look for fresh new housing designs?

4. What values of society are emphasized by the following styles: Georgian, Early Classical Revival, Prairie, and geodesic dome? Which housing style most closely fits your values?

5. Describe the main styles or forms of housing in your area. Explain why you think these styles or forms have become popular.

Review & Activities

Applications

1. **Making Connections.** Make a horizontal time line for the years 1720 to the present. Above the time line, indicate major events in American history and in your area's local history. Below the time line, indicate the periods and characteristics of American architecture.

2. **Improve on a Design.** Select a housing design from the chapter. Then make a chart with the following headings:

   · Characteristics
   · Advantages
   · Disadvantages
   · How It Can Be Improved

   Evaluate the design and fill in the chart.

3. **Persuading Others.** The year is 1940. You are an architect who advocates a break with the past and a new era of housing design. You want to persuade prospective homeowners to let you and your partners design modern housing for them. Using the information you have learned from the chapter and any outside source, write a persuasive speech about the new world of modern house design.

4. **Create a New Design.** Imagine that you are creating a new housing design. You can use only one characteristic from each of six different housing styles discussed in the chapter. (For example, select a Mansard roof and a half-timbered exterior.) Name your style, draw a sketch, and give reasons for your choices. Describe how your new style makes good design sense.

BUILDING YOUR PORTFOLIO

You have been hired to create a brochure to be given to visitors to a historic home. (Choose a home in your area or work from an Internet site.) The brochure should include information on life when the house was built, its architectural details, and any modifications later made to the building. Include photos or drawings to enhance the brochure.

Designing Homes for Today and Tomorrow

CHAPTER OBJECTIVES

▶ Explain how planning and regulation are used to assure quality of life in new housing developments.

▶ Describe how lifestyle changes are reflected in housing.

▶ Describe the various activity zones in a home and evaluate their importance.

▶ Distinguish between open and closed floor plans.

▶ Identify factors to consider when evaluating a floor plan.

▶ Analyze the advantages and drawbacks of various floor plan options.

▶ Identify recent developments in housing design.

TERMS TO LEARN

- aesthetic codes
- building codes
- closed plan
- floor plan
- open plan
- private zone
- service zone
- social zone
- traffic pattern
- zoning laws

$\mathcal{T}$ry to imagine what homes of the future might look like. It's hard to predict the future, but housing designers and developers must try to do just that! When considering futuristic housing designs, what aspects of today's home would you like to keep? What would you like to change? This chapter explores the factors considered in designing homes and communities.

$\mathcal{D}$eveloping Communities

People have been planning communities for hundreds of years. During colonial times, villages often grew up around a *village green,* an open grassy area that became a common gathering place. Government buildings, churches, and shops were centrally located around the green. Houses were constructed near the public buildings, with farmland developed just beyond.

Some community plans were devised by the immigrant groups that settled areas. For example, the Dutch built a wall on Manhattan Island to protect them from invasion. The large estates and plantations of the South, reflecting the French influence, were located far apart.

Another type of community plan was devised for the city of Philadelphia by William Penn, an Englishman who founded the colony of Pennsylvania in 1681. Penn brought to the colonies a *grid-iron* design—straight streets crossing one another at right angles. Many communities later adopted Penn's plan.

As society became less agricultural and more industrial after 1900, cities grew as people sought jobs there. As an alternative to living in the crowded tenements that sprang up in the cities, people wanted homes of their own. Because city lots were expensive, developers began building small houses on the outskirts where land cost less. Gradually, residential districts, called "suburbs," surrounded most cities. Suburban residents who worked in the city, commuted to their jobs by car or public transportation.

Today, development continues at a fast pace. Entire neighborhoods can spring up within a year or two, complete with shopping malls. However, lessons have been learned from unregulated growth in the past. Haphazard building results in traffic congestion, pollution, loss of natural habitat, and an unending

Computer-generated models communicate the final look of a proposed development during the planning stage.

sprawl of homes, businesses, and industry. Managing rapid growth without these drawbacks is a result of deliberate planning, often referred to as *smart growth*.

BUILDING LAWS AND REGULATIONS

To make sure that growth is orderly and neighborhoods are attractive, most towns and cities have passed laws and regulations governing the use of land. Usually, these laws and regulations are created and enforced by a city council or another local government body. Most regulations include zoning laws, building codes, and aesthetic codes.

Zoning Laws

In many communities today, factories and businesses tend to be located in one area, while houses and small apartment buildings are in another. This is the result of zoning. **Zoning laws** are laws that determine the type of building that may be constructed in a particular zone, or section, of a community.

For example, some areas are set aside as residential zones. *Restricted residential zoning* means that only single-family homes may be built in the area. *General residential zoning* typically allows apartment houses, town houses, two-family dwellings, and some businesses or stores.

Commercial zoning is another type of regulation. Stores and office buildings may be located in commercial zones. Few homes are built in a zone set aside for businesses. Districts zoned as *industrial* consist of factories and warehouses. Some zoning laws set aside other areas as *greenbelts*—parklands and farmlands where no building is permitted. Many states are making efforts to preserve open space. For example, New Jersey has a goal of preserving 1 million acres of farmland and open spaces from development.

In addition to land use, zoning regulations may specify:

- Minimum lot size.
- The distance a building may be from property lines and other buildings.
- Maximum heights of buildings.

This former farmland is zoned for commercial development. Do you live in an area where there's concern about new development taking over undeveloped land? If so, what are your thoughts?

Zoning laws are important because they can prevent a company from tearing down houses in a neighborhood and constructing a factory next door to other homes. Zoning must make sense for the community's needs. Also, in order to be effective, it must be enforced. Most communities have maps indicating zoning. These maps are usually on display in the city hall. Real estate agents and salespeople often provide copies to home buyers.

Building Codes

Usually, before construction can start, the builder must apply for a building permit. During and after construction, building inspectors visit the site to determine whether all building codes have been met. **Building codes** are rules that regulate the quality of building materials and set standards of quality and safety for construction.

Building codes can vary from area to area, since they are developed by each community to match local soil, weather, and other conditions. However, most areas have adopted some standard codes, such as the Uniform Building Code (UBC) in the United States. Other regulations include federal standards for public buildings to accommodate people with disabilities, such as the Americans with Disabilities Act.

Building codes regulate several areas of construction, including:

- Type and quality of building materials.
- Form of construction.
- Provisions for health, safety, and sanitation.
- Use of flammable materials.
- Installation of fire exits, where necessary.
- Electrical work.
- Type and installation of plumbing, heating, and ventilating systems.

Aesthetic Codes

In addition to zoning laws and building codes, some communities have **aesthetic** (es-THE-tik) **codes**, codes that regulate the appearance of buildings in order to maintain the beauty and the desired look of an area. In some condominium developments, for instance, the homeowners' association strictly controls the exterior appearance of individual units. For example, perhaps all doors must be of the same design, and they may be painted only in certain colors. In some developments, the style of patio furniture is also controlled. An aesthetic code may even regulate such practices as hanging towels or clothing over outside patio or balcony railings.

In designated historic areas, homes often must conform to standards set according to the time period in which the homes were constructed. For example, in a historic area featuring ornate Victorian homes, owners may be required to paint homes only in colors that were commonly used in the Victorian period. Owners often must have remodeling or home improvement plans approved by a neighborhood association to be sure that the proper "period look" of the home is preserved.

Building inspectors are responsible for making sure buildings meet building codes. Such codes protect the people who live and work in the buildings.

From looking at this planned neighborhood, what do you think the goals and concerns of the developers were?

PLANNED NEIGHBORHOODS. Many housing developments can be referred to as "planned neighborhoods." The layout of the development, the type and appearance of housing units, and the use of surrounding land are all carefully planned before construction begins. Roads are designed to cut down on traffic. Grassy open areas, resembling private parks, may be set aside. The locations of neighborhood schools, recreation, and shopping are also determined in advance.

Some planned neighborhoods use innovative layouts to make the most of available land. Two of these innovations, *cluster homes* and *zero-lot-line homes*, are described in Figure 7-1 on page 154.

Some planned neighborhoods are designed for specific groups of people of similar ages or interests. Retirement housing developments are an example. They frequently offer planned recreational activities for older residents.

Planned neighborhoods are popular in North America today. The idea of smart land use and a ready-made neighborhood appeals to many people.

Many resort communities, whether near the ocean or in the mountains, have codes to protect the natural beauty of the area. One community might, for example, prohibit storing garbage containers in the open; another might restrict the use of certain materials and colors on building exteriors. Many communities have citizens participation in review boards that approve plans before a building can be constructed or the exterior remodeled.

PLANNING NEW COMMUNITIES

In order to manage growth and development within their communities, most towns and cities agree on a plan. Local city councils usually appoint a group, such as a *planning commission,* to make sure that land is developed appropriately. These commissions consist of local residents who may then hire a professional planner or other experts to make recommendations about present and future changes.

Rather than develop farmland or open space, many city planning commissions are now promoting infilling. *Infilling* is the redevelopment of rundown homes and construction on vacant lots within cities and mature neighborhoods. For example, in Mountain View, California, an unused shopping mall was replaced with a neighborhood that features a mix of shops, offices, and homes.

Planning commissions usually offer general recommendations about land development within a community. In contrast, some neighborhoods and communities are planned in detail from the outset. Such planned housing developments include planned neighborhoods, master planned communities, and cooperative housing communities.

Cluster Homes and Zero-Lot-Line Homes

These innovative housing layouts are designed to allow more homes to be placed in a given area of land without seeming crowded.

CLUSTER HOMES

Clustering, also called *open space development*, groups homes into areas in the development site while preserving open spaces, forested land, wetlands, or other ecologically valuable land. All residents of the area can then enjoy the beauty of the natural surroundings. In some cluster development sites, homes are clustered in groups of 5 to 30 around a central green. The green functions as a gathering and recreation space. The dwellings face in different directions, adding variety. Both single-family and multifamily homes can be built as cluster housing.

A. Common landscaped area.

B. Homes grouped around common court.

C. Small private yards.

D. Parking grouped away from homes.

E. Small private yards.

F. Home sits on lot line, acting as tall fence; no windows overlooking neighbor's yard.

G. Some homes may be backed against each other.

H. Common open space.

ZERO-LOT-LINE HOMES

Zero-lot-line homes—sometimes called *patio homes*—sit on relatively small lots. Each home is placed on a lot line rather than in the center of the lot. That gives each house more useable yard space. Each home acts as a tall fence and has no windows overlooking a neighbor's yard. Some homes may be backed against each other. Many zero-lot developments have open common spaces for all residents to enjoy.

MASTER PLANNED COMMUNITIES.

Master planned communities take the planned neighborhood concept one step further, creating developments that are virtually self-contained towns. The earliest and most successful experiment in a master planned community began in New York in 1946. William Levitt built "Levittown," a community of 17,450 identical houses plus community swimming pools, recreation centers, and schools. Built on the site of former potato fields on Long Island, the small, one-story, single-family homes represented affordable housing for young families at the end of World War II. Although this community exists today, most of the homes now have second stories or other additions.

New master planned communities, sometimes referred to as *new urbanism*, follow the same concept. These communities feature housing, shops, public spaces such as parks, and public buildings such as a library and community center. The emphasis is on community. Rather than the suburbs of the past that were built for the automobile, new master planned communities are "walkable" neighborhoods where residents can walk down the street to mail a letter, buy groceries, or go to a movie. Both multifamily and single-family housing are included in master planned communities. The homes are designed to meet a variety of needs. Gone are the developments in which every house looks just like the one next door. Master planned communities today also are designed to conserve energy and land. Unlike many housing tracts of the past, the new communities place a high value on preserving the environment.

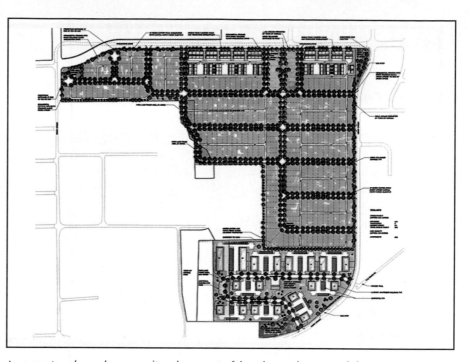

In a master planned community, placement of housing and commercial space are preplanned.

One such community is Owings Mills New Town in Baltimore. Here, the community has home dwellers with different housing needs and who were at different stages of life. The housing options include single-family homes, town houses, and apartment units. Some housing is designed especially for senior citizens. Residents have the option of either renting or buying a home.

In Owings Mills New Town, housing is organized into neighborhoods that are linked to one another by landscaped walking and jogging paths. Sports facilities—such as tennis courts and swimming pools—a day-care center, shopping, and a bordering forest preserve are within easy access.

COOPERATIVE HOUSING COMMUNITIES.

Another form of planned communities—cooperative housing—is on the rise. These communities balance the traditional advantages of home ownership with the benefits of shared common facilities such as a large dining room, meeting rooms, recreational areas, workshops, and child care. The people in cooperative housing are committed to living as a community where people build friendships and trust among neighbors. Cooperative housing has its roots in Europe.

Planned Communities—More Than Just Homes

Frederick Law Olmstead (1822-1903) is one of the individuals responsible for developing the concept of planned communities. As a landscape architect, Olmstead developed plans that combined the best aspects of city and country life. His most famous plan is the magnificent Central Park in New York City. Olmstead designed Central Park to integrate recreation, densely forested areas, gardens, lakes, commerce, and residences with a large city.

Many planned communities are located in or near urban cities. Developers are concerned with creating an environment that promotes a sense of place and community. The goal is to create a community that provides opportunities for people to live, work, and participate in social activities.

To create prosperous and livable planned communities designers and architects apply several principles. Here are some examples of how this works:

- *Integration.* Planning a complete and integrated community involves developing a setting that creates a balance between public and private areas. In the public areas, communities develop compact, multiuse land patterns that integrate commercial, civic, educational, cultural, entertainment, religious, and recreational facilities. Scenic transitional areas are developed between the public and private sections of the community. These areas are large open spaces for parks, wildlife refuges, and gardens. Whenever possible natural terrain and vegetation is preserved.

- *Conservation.* To protect the environment planned communities focus on minimizing the impact of cars and promote exercise. The size of the community is limited to encourage walking and bicycling to housing, jobs, and daily activities. Pedestrian walkways, bicycle paths, and transit stops are within easy walking distance to work and community activities. Planned communities conserve resources and minimize waste by efficiently using water, incorporating natural drainage, and recycling.

You, the *Designer*

Imagine you are part of a design team developing a planned community. What considerations would be important in blending commercial and residential areas? What would you include in the community? Would you include industry in the plan? Give rationales for your answers.

Housing Reflects Changing Needs

Just as our communities have changed over the years, housing styles have changed, too. Social trends help shape people's housing needs. Economic conditions, lifestyle changes, physical needs, and advances in technology are just some of the factors that influence housing design. Changes in housing and home design take place more gradually than do some other changes, such as clothing styles. A look at homes through the 20th century, however, shows that just as the outward appearance of a home often reflects its era, so does the way in which space within a home is designed and used. For example, some of the rooms featured in yesterday's homes are no longer used for the same purposes. Years ago, many people used cellars to store food; now they use refrigerators and freezers. Few homes today have a formal parlor for people to gather in, but many have a casual family room.

Large Victorian homes were divided into such specialized rooms as a dining room, kitchen, parlor, library, and music room. Today's houses are more likely to have open space and multipurpose rooms. The dining area, living area, and kitchen, for example, may be included in one large open area, often called a "great room."

Many homes in the 18th and 19th centuries were two or more stories high, which kept family activities separated. The bedrooms were all upstairs. Many of today's homes are on one level or have split levels. If two-storied, the home may have some sleeping space and a bathroom on the first floor, as well as on the second.

A room you would not have found in most homes just 20 years ago is a home office. Today, with over half a billion people working from their homes, there is an increased need for home office space. In some homes, an extra bedroom or finished area in the basement serves as an office. Many new homes are being designed with room specially designated as a home office.

Designing and building functional homes to meet the needs of all people—regardless of age, type of family, or physical need—has become more of a challenge than ever. Home designers and builders must think through numerous situations that could have an impact on universal design. For example, how might a home with an open kitchen and family room design benefit a single-parent family or a household in

At the end of the last century in the Victorian era, the parlor was set aside for entertaining guests and not used by the family on a regular basis.

which older people live independently? That's right, a single parent might want to be near the children while preparing meals. An older person would find it easier to move around in a home with a more open design. In addition to such factors as these, designers and builders must consider the cost factor and environmental concerns in order to develop affordable, functional housing.

As you read through the following pages, you will discover a number of elements essential to making homes functional, livable, and comfortable for those who inhabit them.

The floor plan for this home allows someone working in the kitchen to interact with those in the next room.

$\mathcal{D}$esigning Functional Interiors

Most of the changes just discussed have to do with the way space within the home is organized. Although Chapters 5 and 6 focus on exterior style details, the fact is, well-designed homes are planned from the inside out. That is, successful architects begin by thinking about how a home will be used. They carefully consider the needs and lifestyle of the home's potential occupants in order to decide on the number and types of rooms, their size and shape, and how they should be arranged.

The end result is a **floor plan**, a diagram of a home or other structure that shows the arrangement of rooms.

Homes can be as varied as the people who live in them. However, well-designed floor plans have some characteristics in common.

ZONES FOR DIFFERENT ACTIVITIES

Today's homes must fulfill numerous functions in a limited space. When several activities are going on at the same time, as often happens, there may be a conflict. For example, some activities are noisy, while others require quiet and privacy. The need to take different activities into account adds to the challenge of designing a home.

Well-designed homes divide the space into zones. The three most common zones are private, service, and social. Each zone contains rooms or areas with similar functions. By keeping the three zones distinct, as shown in Figure 7-2, activities are less likely to cause conflict.

The **private zone** provides quiet, comfortable areas for sleeping and relaxing, as well as privacy for bathing and dressing. In most homes, the bedrooms and bathrooms are the core of the private zone.

The **service zone** is where household work is done. It includes the kitchen, one of the busiest and sometimes noisiest areas of the home. A laundry room, workshop, or garage may also be part of the service zone.

The **social zone** is the part of the home used for activities and entertainment. A living room, for example, would be considered part of the social zone, as would a dining room, family room, recreation room, or entrance hall. Patios, decks, and other outdoor living spaces can also be considered social areas.

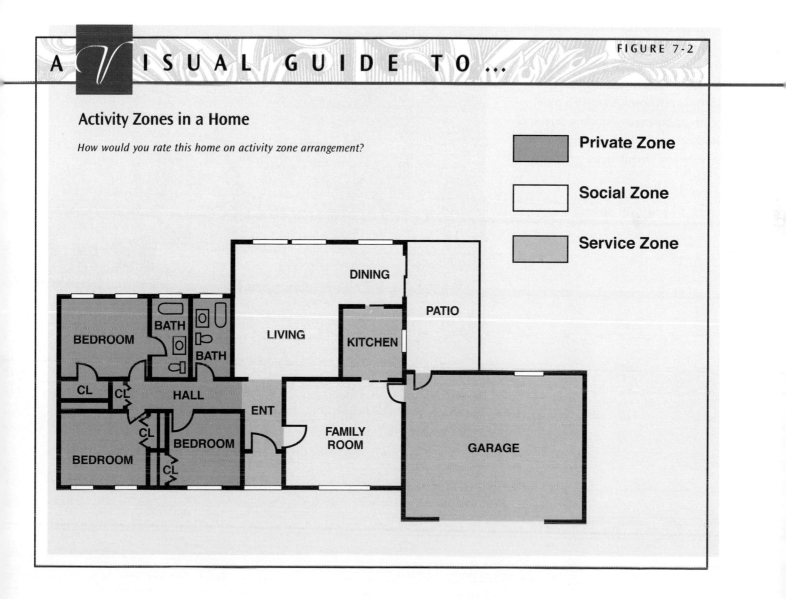

FIGURE 7-2

A VISUAL GUIDE TO...

Activity Zones in a Home

How would you rate this home on activity zone arrangement?

Private Zone

Social Zone

Service Zone

DINING

PATIO

BATH

BEDROOM

LIVING

KITCHEN

BATH

CL   CL

HALL

ENT

CL

BEDROOM

FAMILY ROOM

GARAGE

BEDROOM

CL

Setting aside separate zones for privacy, service, and socialization has advantages for daily living. For example, in the later evening, television noise or kitchen clatter is less likely to disturb a young child sleeping in a bedroom. Furthermore, zones enhance the convenience of the home because they allow similar activities to take place near one another.

There are many variations on the zone concept. In a home with two or more levels, some zones may be repeated. For example, there may be one private zone on the main floor, where the master bedroom is located, and another for the second-floor bedrooms.

In small homes, there may be little physical separation between zones. Still, a thoughtful design can establish clearly defined spaces for specific purposes. Even in a one-room apartment, a folding screen or bookcase can divide the space into private and social areas.

OPEN AND CLOSED FLOOR PLANS

As you read earlier, today's homes often include a multipurpose area. The living room and dining room may be combined into one L-shaped room. The kitchen and family room may be separated by a low divider instead of a full wall, or they may be completely open. When few dividing walls separate rooms, that part of the home is said to have an **open plan**. In a **closed plan**, rooms are separated and self-contained.

Each type of plan has advantages and drawbacks. Open plans seem more spacious. Lifestyles today tend to be more informal and many homeowners favor an open plan that offers flexibility for entertaining. Closed plans allow for greater privacy and better separation between zones. Many homes combine the two, with an open plan in the social zone and a closed plan in the private zone.

In this open-plan home, the living room, dining room, and kitchen all flow together. Would you like this openness?

EVALUATING A FLOOR PLAN

Because the space in any home is limited, it's important that it be used wisely. The easiest way to evaluate how space is used in a home is to look at the floor plan. A floor plan is drawn as if the roof has been taken off, providing a downward view into the house. One-level floor plans show a single view. For a two-level home, there are two views of the floor plan, one of the lower level and a second of the upper level. By studying the floor plan, an evaluation can be made about whether the layout of a home is functional and well suited to the needs of those who will live there.

One of the most important considerations when evaluating a floor plan is the **traffic pattern**, the paths people take as they walk from room to room during everyday activities. A well-designed floor plan provides convenient pathways to all areas of the home. At the same time, hallways should be as short as possible to avoid wasted space. Easy access should be provided between closely related areas. It should be easy to get from the kitchen to the dining area, for instance, and from each bedroom to a bathroom.

Economy of construction is another consideration. For example, having to install long runs of plumbing pipe adds to the expense of building a house. Costs can be reduced if two areas that require plumbing, such as kitchen and laundry areas, are placed back-to-back or, in a two-story home, if one bathroom is above the other. That way, the plumbing pipes for both rooms can be located in the same wall.

Figure 7-3 on page 162 shows two floor plans. One floor plan is a less efficient, poor design, while the other is a functional, more effective design. Compare the two plans and evaluate the differences.

FLOOR PLAN OPTIONS

Another consideration when designing or choosing housing is the number of levels in the home. Each option has its advantages and disadvantages. The choice depends on who will live in the home and their needs and preferences.

One-Level Home

Many people prefer a home that is all on one level. Many apartments fit in this category, as do manufactured homes and ranch-style houses. All parts of the living area are easily accessible without going up or down stairs. Eliminating stairways also increases the usable space in the home. In a ranch house or ground-floor apartment, the architect can plan for any number of rooms to have direct access to outdoor patios. Exterior maintenance of a one-story house, such as painting, cleaning gutters, and changing window screens, is simpler than with a two-story house. A one-level home generally has more universal design appeal. Older people who do not want to contend with stairs or middle-aged people who want a home that can be adapted to their needs as they age often choose one-level homes.

On the negative side, the sprawling design of large ranch houses can be a problem in areas where land is scarce. It also increases the cost of the lot, foundation, and roof construction. Compact homes require less material to build and therefore reduce the impact on the environment, as well as the budget.

Two-Level Home

Many single-family homes and multifamily units have two levels of living space. The traditional approach has been to place the social and service zones on the first floor and the bedrooms on the second floor. This floor plan option is a popular one because it maintains privacy. However, stairs must be climbed to reach any of the bedrooms. A universal design approach includes at least one bedroom on the first floor.

A different kind of design that is a variation of a two-story home is a home with a "loft." A loft is the space just below the roof of a house that can be made into an open living area. A builder can create a bedroom or another type of room and enclose it with a railing. The appearance from the lower level is similar to that of a balcony. Instead of simply a hallway, however, there is a room extending back from the railing. This plan can open up a small room, creating a feeling of space. A drawback is that, without a fourth wall, the open area lacks privacy.

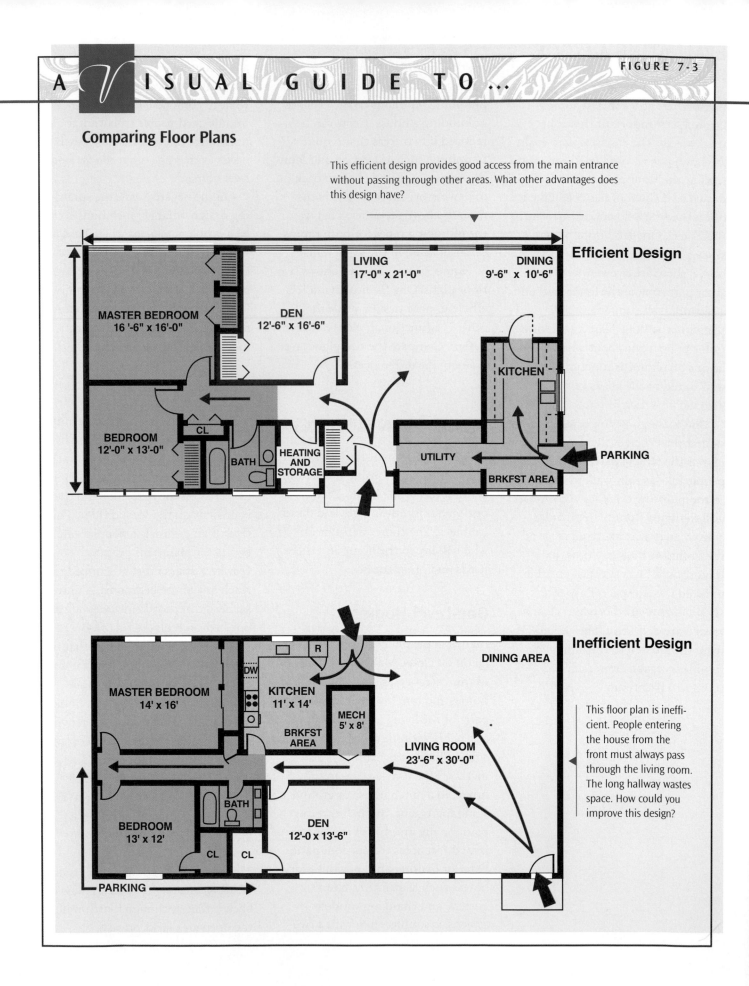

FIGURE 7-3

A *V* I S U A L   G U I D E   T O ...

Comparing Floor Plans

This efficient design provides good access from the main entrance without passing through other areas. What other advantages does this design have?

Efficient Design

LIVING
17'-0" x 21'-0"

DINING
9'-6" x 10'-6"

MASTER BEDROOM
16 '-6" x 16'-0"

DEN
12'-6" x 16'-6"

KITCHEN

BEDROOM
12'-0" x 13'-0"

CL

BATH

HEATING
AND
STORAGE

UTILITY

BRKFST AREA

PARKING

Inefficient Design

MASTER BEDROOM
14' x 16'

DINING AREA

DW

KITCHEN
11' x 14'

MECH
5' x 8'

BRKFST
AREA

LIVING ROOM
23'-6" x 30'-0"

R

This floor plan is ineffi-cient. People entering the house from the front must always pass through the living room. The long hallway wastes space. How could you improve this design?

BATH

BEDROOM
13' x 12'

DEN
12'-0 x 13'-6"

CL   CL

PARKING

If you were married with young children and buying your first home, would you be willing to give up other living space for a home office? Why or why not?

Split-Level Home

As you read in Chapter 6, a split-level home has three or more levels of living space, each separated by a short flight of stairs. The split-level design uses space very efficiently. In a typical split-level home, the entrance, living room, dining area, and kitchen are at ground level. The bedrooms are a short flight above. The garage, laundry room, utility area, family room, and perhaps another bedroom and bath, are a short flight below. Multiple levels allow for good separation between zones, yet only a few steps are required to go from one level to another. These advantages have helped make the split-level home popular.

Split-Entry Home

A split-entry home has two levels of living space, with the lower level partially below the ground. The design is so named because the entrance to the home is located midway between the two main levels.

Persons entering a foyer area must go either up or down a short flight of stairs to reach one of the main levels. This arrangement has the advantage of keeping the entry separate from the living room. The upper level usually contains the living room, kitchen, dining area, and bedrooms, while the lower level contains the laundry and utility area, family room, perhaps a bathroom, and often another bedroom. However, no part of the home is accessible to someone who cannot climb stairs.

What's Happening in Housing Design?

Demand often creates change. In Chapter 3 you read how innovations in building materials have been developed because of the demand to protect the environment and make better use of our dwindling resources. More energy-efficient and environmentally friendly homes are already part of the future of housing. Other innovations in housing design are sparked by the interests of home buyers. Homebuilders and designers answer that demand by incorporating many of these features into new homes.

An increasingly popular design feature in two-level homes is a laundry area on the second floor. This is a sensible option since much of the household's laundry originates in or near the bedrooms and baths. A laundry area nearby eliminates carrying heavy loads of laundry down flights of stairs, then back up.

Another feature that has been received enthusiastically is the media room. Now that personal computers have become so common, what was the family room may now be the start of a media room. Other high-tech equipment that may be in a media room include a home entertainment center with a video or DVD player, HDTV, and surround sound.

In keeping with the interest in making communities more neighborly, garages are often placed around the side or in the back of the house. Front porches are becoming popular again so that the house and sidewalk are more inviting and the neighborhood is more pedestrian friendly.

For years, homeowners have tried to find ways to bring the outdoors inside. Builders have responded by adding sunrooms to homes and creating attractive outdoor living spaces such as patios and decks. In some homes, living rooms, family rooms, media rooms, and even bedrooms open up to an outdoor living space. In some parts of the country, homes are being built around an interior courtyard where family members can enjoy privacy and good weather.

According to the American Institute of Architects, an interesting trend for the future is single homes designed for more than one family. For example, a home with two separate living areas and shared common spaces might be desirable for a large extended family that includes two or more nuclear families. Each family would have its own private living area, while a large common area would serve as a place where the families can get together for meals and socializing.

A sunroom can expand usable living space during part or all of the year. Are sunrooms popular in your area? Why or why not?

Some people are concerned that many homes being built today are too big. They advocate building homes tailored more to actual space needs. Land and material usage and the costs and availability of energy are some of their concerns.

When evaluating new design elements, keep in mind that they must be compatible with the home design to function properly. People want a desirable floor plan that conforms to their lifestyle. They may want rooms that can be adapted to certain uses—a desire that varies from person to person. One person's main requirement may be a large office, while for another, it might be a second-floor laundry room. All people in the market for a home likely want comfort and an efficient use of space. Architects may always be searching for new designs that improve interior spaces of homes.

Urban Planner

Eric Musseli

As an urban planner, I help the public officials and civic leaders in my city visualize and plan development projects. We want to make sure that such development will improve the quality of life here, not decrease it. As you might expect, though, everyone has different ideas and concerns. Each person's needs, as well as the benefit of the program to the majority, must be evaluated.

I can't point to any one person or event that prompted me to become an urban planner. It was really a

"I help the public officials and civic leaders in my city visualize and plan development projects. "

whole series of things. In high school I learned about the differences in the way people live in different parts of the country and in other cultures. That got me thinking about how the buildings and houses, shops, and the park in my own neighborhood influenced how neighbors felt about themselves and each other. Most people have concerns about the safety of their neighborhoods or schools. They grumble about the state of roads or the problems of traffic and pollution. They want good jobs, good healthcare, or a few trees planted here and there.

By the time I entered college, I was beginning to realize that community planning is a two-way street. I began to be interested in how local government worked. A college internship in a nearby town opened my eyes to the responsibility elected officials and business leaders often feel to provide ample housing and building space, an educated work force and secure employment, and access to recreational and healthcare facilities. However, other community members may worry that the homeless will be overlooked as apartment buildings spring up. A parents' group may want a crosswalk provided so their children can walk safely to school.

My first job as an urban planner was for a small city wishing to expand

An urban planner must listen to the dreams of developers but also take into account the concerns of residents who may fear their neighborhoods will be disturbed by a new building or an intersection. I had to answer questions such as: Would public roads crumble under heavy traffic? Would there be ample parking? Is "green space" to be included in a community's plans to build? Are there wetlands to be preserved? Will enough farmland be left to feed all our people? Today's urban planner must take a regional—even a world—view.

and yet maintain its historic neighborhoods and downtown area. It certainly meant I had to work with varying points-of-view. I listened and learned about building and zoning codes, and how the inspection of government offices, schools, and hospitals guarantees the safety and accessibility of public facilities. I met with elected officials and civic leaders to discuss their concerns and hopes for their city and area. Many people wanted to save the abandoned downtown and see older neighborhoods rejuvenated, but I had to determine if that could be done economically and to the long-range advantage of the whole city. Meanwhile, another neighborhood group wanted to know if our public infrastructure could support another civic leader's suggestion to build a new mall on the outskirts of town. With the help of staff, I suggested projects, designed plans, gathered pertinent data via computer, and proposed budgets.

"An urban planner must listen to the dreams of developers, but also take into account the concerns of residents."

Career Profile

Urban planners, sometimes called community or regional planners, develop programs that help promote growth and the best use of a community's land and resources. They help a wide range of public officials and civic leaders make decisions on social, economic, and environmental problems. Planners present programs and report to interested agencies, businesses, and citizens. Computers are used to gather and analyze information, record and project costs, and forecast future trends.

Education
▸ An advanced degree in urban or regional planning is desirable. A bachelor's degree in planning, architecture, or civic engineering and related work experience may be acceptable.
▸ Courses in housing, urban design, economic development, architecture, engineering, law, earth science, finance, and management are helpful.

Skills Needed
▸ Effective communication skills in both public presentations and written reports. Accuracy in managing and conveying financial plans.
▸ The ability to think in terms of spatial relationships and visualize the effects of plans and designs is essential, as is the ability to judge a plan's effect on the future of a community.
▸ Flexibility to effectively reconcile differing viewpoints.

Career Outlook
▸ The need for urban planners is expected to grow at the average rate in coming years. A growing number of openings in private industry are expected.

Career Activities
1. An official in your town has proposed building a new civic center. What are five questions you think should be answered before the plan is approved?
2. Explain how each of the types of college courses mentioned above would be helpful to an urban planner.

$\mathcal{R}$eview & Activities

Chapter Summary

➤ Most communities have laws and regulations that govern land use and the building quality and safety issues.

➤ Neighborhoods can be carefully planned to be attractive and convenient places to live.

➤ Master planned communities are similar to self-contained towns, providing nearby amenities to residents.

➤ Cooperative housing communities appeal to people who like shared living.

➤ Today's homes must use space wisely to meet needs and wants in a comfortable, convenient way.

➤ Three principal space zones within a home are private, service, and social.

➤ A floor plan is used in evaluating the use of space in a particular home.

➤ Four primary floor plan options are the one-level, two-level, split-level, and split-entry home.

➤ Home buyers are dictating new developments in housing design, which include features that make living as simple and comfortable as possible for everyone in the home.

Checking Your Understanding

1. What is the benefit of planning new housing developments?

2. What are zoning laws? Give an example of what zoning laws may specify.

3. What is the difference between building codes and aesthetic codes?

4. How do planned neighborhoods differ from master planned communities?

5. Give an example of a lifestyle-related change in housing over the last century.

6. Describe characteristics of private, service, and social zones.

7. What is the difference between open and closed plans?

8. Name two basic characteristics to look for when evaluating a floor plan.

9. Compare the advantages of a one-level floor plan to the advantages of a two-level home.

10. What advantages make the split-level home popular?

11. Give an example of a design feature that an architect might incorporate in a home plan to appeal to today's market.

Thinking Critically

1. Predict the consequences of zoning laws that allow commercial buildings in the same neighborhood as residential buildings.

2. What effect would an open-plan design have on the traffic pattern of a home? A closed-plan design?

3. If you could live in a home with one of the floor plan options described in this chapter, which would you choose? What is it about your family's lifestyle that leads you to this choice?

4. Identify as many factors as possible that will effect the way homes are planned and built in the future. Explain your reasoning for ranking three as the most influential.

Applications

1. **Debate the Issue.** Gather information and prepare arguments on whether or not aesthetic codes have a positive effect on communities.

2. **Planned Communities.** Research a community or neighborhood that was preplanned. Write a paper identifying the developer's main goal, how business and/or industry were included, and the types of housing included. Focus on a local example or do your research on the Internet.

3. **Floor Plan Evaluation.** Select a floor plan from a magazine, newspaper, or website that fits one of the floor plan options described in this chapter. Study the floor plan and make a list of its good features. Write an advertisement for this home with the floor plan of your choice. Be specific about why the home is livable and why it's a good choice.

4. **Floor Plan Brochure.** Assume you're a home builder who has constructed a development that features one-story, two-story, split-level, and split-entry homes. Prepare the brochure to promote your development by creating the drawings and writing the descriptions of the homes in this development. In your descriptions, suggest particular layouts for specific clients, depending on their ages, needs, and wants.

5. **Plan for the Future.** Imagine that it is 10 years in the future. Design an innovative home that incorporates popular technologies. Sketch the interior layout and a view of the exterior. Write a description of the home's features and the community in which it will be built.

BUILDING YOUR PORTFOLIO

An employee of a large corporation is relocating and has written to your company, Executive Relocation, Inc., for housing advice and information. She and her husband have two teenage children, as well as an aging parent who resides with them. They would like help in finding a home with an interior design that will be both comfortable and accessible for everyone in the house. You have been asked to write a report evaluating three floor-plan options—the one-level, two-level, and split-level designs—keeping in mind the needs of all members of the family. Use newspapers and magazines to collect possible layouts and home designs that you might submit to the family. Use any other library and Internet resources that seem helpful. In your report, be sure to indicate the advantages and disadvantages of each design. Include your recommendation of a design.

Making Housing Decisions

Choosing a Place to Live

CHAPTER OBJECTIVES

► Explain the steps in the decision-making process.

► Analyze the impact of housing needs, wants, and priorities when choosing a place to live.

► Identify human and material resources that influence housing decisions.

► Contrast different types of community environments.

► Analyze the factors that should be considered when selecting a neighborhood.

► Evaluate the importance of public services in choosing a place to live.

► Summarize and compare multifamily and single-family housing options.

TERMS TO LEARN

- duplex

- efficiency apartment

- fourplex

- garden apartment

- high-rise apartment

- human resources

- low-rise apartment

- material resources

- town house

- triplex

- utilities

*I*magine that your family has decided to move. How would you begin to find a home? How could your family find a place that would suit every member's needs and as many of their wants as possible? This chapter will help you learn how to make the best choices regarding housing. Whether you will be moving soon or in the future, you'll be prepared to handle the situation.

*M*aking Housing Decisions

*C*hoosing a place to live is one of the most important decisions a family or individual can make. One reason is that the costs involved in housing greatly impact the family's financial picture. Beyond that, the choice of location affects the daily lives of every family member, possibly for years to come. Such a decision deserves serious consideration.

THE DECISION-MAKING PROCESS

You've made many decisions in your life. Some have turned out well; perhaps others you later came to regret. Major decisions—and even many smaller ones—are more likely to give satisfying results if you follow this process.

STEP 1: STATE THE SITUATION. Ask yourself: "Why do I need to make this decision? Who else needs to be involved in the decision? Who will be affected by it?"

STEP 2: IDENTIFY YOUR RESOURCES. Think about how resources such as time, energy, and your budget might be helpful in this situation.

STEP 3: LIST THE OPTIONS. Identify all of the alternatives you can think of. The more you can come up with, the more likely that one of them will be a satisfying solution.

STEP 4: WEIGH THE OPTIONS. Consider how each alternative will affect the final outcome. Ask: "What might be the positive and negative results?" Think about what is most important to you, but also how the decision will affect others.

STEP 5: CHOOSE THE BEST OPTION. There may not be a "perfect" solution, but look for one that meets as many of your goals as possible.

STEP 6: CARRY OUT YOUR DECISION. Your decision won't do any good unless you put it into action.

STEP 7: EVALUATE THE DECISION. Ask yourself: "How well did this decision turn out for me and for others? What might I do differently next time?" If you made a poor choice, accept responsibility for it and learn from your mistakes.

Influences on Housing Decisions

Many factors enter into the housing decision. The specific needs of a household or an individual may determine the location or size of housing. Wants and priorities affect housing choices as well, especially in terms of appearance and special features. Also, people take into consideration their resources when they choose a place to live.

NEEDS

Probably the most important factor in making a housing decision is need. A roof over your head is the most important, but there are other needs too. As explained in Chapter 1, housing fulfills a variety of basic human needs.

While all people have the same basic needs, their specific needs differ. For instance, a family of seven people needs more bedrooms than a single person. What other examples of differing needs can you think of?

People choose housing that satisfies their basic needs at the time. When people's life situations change over the years, their housing often changes too. Housing that may have suited a couple when they were first starting out may no longer be suitable when they have children. An older couple might decide to sell a large house and move to a smaller home in a retirement community.

WANTS AND PRIORITIES

Whenever possible, people make choices that also fulfill their wants. Wanting something is not the same as needing it. People may *want* their shelter to provide a swimming pool or a recreation room, but they usually don't *need* it.

Since it's rare to find a home that fulfills all their wants, people must often make choices based on their personal priorities. To one person, a home's appearance might be more important than its comfort. Another person might make the opposite choice. Considerations such as privacy, economy, and convenience might rank differently in importance for you than for someone else. Priorities affect what people want in housing.

Why should evaluating your needs be the first step in choosing a place to live?

RESOURCES

A resource is something that can be used to accomplish a goal. People generally use resources to meet their needs and wants. Both human and material resources are used in making decisions about housing.

Human resources are personal qualities that people possess, including creativity, imagination, knowledge, skills, talent, time, energy, and experience. Knowledge and skills can be especially useful when making housing decisions. For example, a person with knowledge and skills in carpentry might use these resources in updating or remodeling a home.

Human resources are often overlooked. For example, you might think you don't have any skill or talent when it comes to gardening or decorating, when you just haven't had the opportunity to try. By trying your hand at different projects, you may discover talents and skills that you didn't know you had.

Human resources can also be increased. Many community colleges and trade schools offer noncredit classes and workshops in woodworking and in home maintenance and repair. Employees at home improvement centers, garden supply stores, and paint and wallpaper stores can offer advice about many types of projects. Some stores offer free classes, demonstrations, and project

People who have time, energy, and "do-it-yourself" skills may choose to buy a home that needs some work and fix it up.

plans. You can also find expert advice and detailed instructions for projects on the Internet. A willingness to increase knowledge and skills can be a valuable resource when making decisions about housing.

Material resources are tangible assets, such as money, property, supplies, and tools—assets that people may or may not possess themselves. Perhaps the most essential material resource is money, which plays an important role in the choices people make about housing. Whether an individual or family decides to rent or buy, the choices will be limited by the amount of money available. The challenge comes in using money wisely to best meet housing needs.

Material resources other than money can come from communities and other sources. For example, to help maintain an attractive environment, some communities offer free or low-cost trees and shrubs to homeowners.

Before making a decision on where to live and what type of home to live in, individuals and families need to carefully evaluate all of their resources. Sometimes tradeoffs can be made. For example, you might use time and skills to do a project yourself in order to save money. By having a strong understanding of all available resources, the best housing decisions can be made.

Developers Gauge the Market

The housing industry, like any business, walks a fine line between following consumer demand and directing it. On the one hand, architects, developers, and builders may try to create demand by introducing a new housing feature that offers greater convenience or enjoyment. Their hope is that once people start seeing this feature in magazine articles, on television, on websites, and in friends' homes, they will be willing to pay extra for it. This might be termed the "if you build it, they will come" theory.

On the other hand, those in the housing industry must also follow consumers' lead. They watch trends to get an idea of what people will be looking for in a home. For example, one developer noted a survey showing that current home buyers were more concerned about energy costs than those who had bought homes the year before. The developer did additional research and found this was likely to be a long-term trend. Therefore, new housing would need to be as energy-efficient as possible.

The trends tracked may be diverse, with little apparent connection to housing. To what extent are home buyers influenced by stock market trends? Do consumers place more importance on how useful a product is or how easy it is to use? Asking questions like these—and listening to the answers—can pay off in better home sales.

THINKING IT THROUGH

1. Suppose that several automotive groups report that more car buyers are choosing smaller, more fuel-efficient models. How might a wise home developer use that information to plan new homes?
2. Think of the features in your home or another that you're familiar with. What needs do you think the design was meant to meet? Does it succeed? Why or why not?

Choosing a Location

One of the choices people make about housing is its location. A person may need to choose a region of the country, a particular town or city, and a neighborhood. These decisions are based on personal preferences as well as practical concerns.

The location of housing has a major impact on its cost. Generally speaking, certain trends can be seen across the United States:

- Housing tends to be more expensive on the East and West Coasts than in the interior of the country.
- Housing within and near major cities tends to be more expensive than in smaller cities and towns.
- Within major cities, housing costs are generally higher in downtown areas and sections under development.

Climate is one factor to consider when choosing a region in which to live. However, housing costs are higher in areas with the most desirable climates.

TYPES OF LOCATIONS

In general, the locations in which people live can be described as urban, suburban, or rural. Although there are general characteristics for each type of area, it is important to remember that there are variations within each of the three categories. Chicago, Illinois, and Fargo, North Dakota, are both urban areas, but the lifestyle in each is quite different. Both cities offer entertainment and cultural opportunities, but Chicago is busier, noisier, and has more people per square mile.

The convenience of living close to work, shopping, and cultural opportunities appeals to most people who live in cities. Other people choose the slower-paced life available in rural areas. Rural, or country, living offers wide open spaces, less indus-

try (and therefore less industrial pollution), and fewer people. A small town out in the country and a farm far from other populated areas can both be considered rural living. For families who enjoy the outdoors and more privacy, rural living is an attractive choice.

For some people, living in a suburb—a residential area adjacent to a city—provides the best of both city and country living. Suburban living generally offers more open space than city living, while offering some of the same work, transportation, and entertainment opportunities.

How Did They Choose?

Choosing where to live is a decision based on many factors. Work situations, lifestyles, and stages in life are some of the factors that contribute to the choice of location. The following renters and homeowners describe why they chose the location for their homes.

- Single-family homes in suburbs often cost more than those in cities.
- Housing costs in rural areas tend to be the lowest of all.

While these general trends are true, variations can occur in any specific location. A city may have an older neighborhood with single-family homes that cost more than homes downtown. One suburb may have houses that cost less than those in a nearby resort area in the country.

◀ **Gary Talbron:** "My daily schedule in the city is full and hectic. When I was living in the suburbs, I found myself spending too much time traveling to and from work. I decided to move to an apartment downtown that is within walking distance of my office. Although my rent is a little more, I've made up the difference by not having to commute. I've also found that I'm enjoying the city more—the sporting events, concerts, restaurants, and the interesting people I've met."

Luis and Carmen Dominguez: ▶
"About five years ago, Carmen and I were feeling cramped living in the city. The houses in our neighborhood were very close together and allowed for little privacy. Because of our work situations, we knew that a rural location was not for us. Instead, we chose to move to one of the suburbs near the city. We haven't regretted the move for a minute. Although we had to pay more for our home, the real estate taxes are less. There are plenty of recreational opportunities, good schools, and life is a little more peaceful here."

◀ **Carol and Bill Frakes:** "Once my husband I and were both retired, we decided to move to the country. We wanted a place that would allow us to pursue our hobbies. We rented a property with just enough land for my garden and a barn for Bill's pottery studio. The peace and quiet appeals to us, but life can be challenging at times—like digging out after a heavy snowfall in the winter. We sometimes miss the city, but we know it was the right decision for us. We enjoy the fresh fruits and vegetables I raise, and Bill is doing what he loves best. We've made new friends and often get together with them for breakfast at the local coffee shop."

NEIGHBORHOOD

Once the general location has been selected, those who choose city, suburban, and small town living will need to choose a neighborhood. The housing units in a neighborhood are of similar design and price range. Some neighborhoods are made up only of homes, while others include housing, supermarkets, and small shops. For example, Baj Patel resides in a large town house complex about a ten-minute ride from shopping, while Leah Wernick lives with her family above the specialty food store they operate in their neighborhood.

Knowing as much as possible about your future neighborhood is just as important as selecting the right dwelling. When choosing a neighborhood, consider its convenience and condition, the neighbors you would have, and any drawbacks.

Convenience

Most people do not want to spend a lot of time traveling to and from their daily activities. Finding a home close to their place of employment and basic services, such as food stores, is very important to them.

Parents with school-age children might want to live close to schools and recreational facilities. Some families choose a home that is convenient to child care services.

Many residents of cities don't own cars and rely heavily on public transportation. Living near bus or train stops is essential for these people. Suburban housing that is located near major highways might be significant for people who drive into a city to work.

Condition of the Neighborhood

The condition of a neighborhood affects the value of the housing in it. Before moving to a new neighborhood, take a walk around the area. Are the roads and sidewalks in good repair? Is there adequate street lighting and parking? These factors can tell you much about the condition of a neighborhood and assist you in making a better decision about where to live.

Also try to determine the pattern of improvement and growth in the area. If residents are painting, landscaping their yards, or renovating their homes, that's a good sign. Is there much new building going on? Such questions can help you determine whether the quality of the neighborhood is likely to improve, worsen, or stay the same. Many city planning offices can assist you in finding the answers to these questions.

All of these factors are of special concern to people who are buying a home. The value of a home increases or decreases with the value of other homes in the area and with the amount of community involvement shown by residents of the neighborhood.

Neighbors

When neighbors share interests and can rely on each other in an emergency, the entire community benefits. It may be a good idea to learn about the people living in a neighborhood before making a final decision about moving there. Are the neighbors friendly? Do people seem to know and help each other? Families with children should find out whether there are other children in the neighborhood. The ability to form friendships helps people feel more at home in their surroundings.

Drawbacks

No location is perfect. All neighborhoods have problems, but it's best to know about them before moving in. Check the amount of noise and air pollution in the area. Is one street less noisy than another? What plans are there to deal with any vacant buildings that could lead to vandalism or other problems? You might also ask the local police about any safety concerns and whether a community watch program exists. Drive around, ask questions, and be aware of the activity in a community before making a decision.

Friendly neighbors make the transition of moving to a new neighborhood or community much easier.

Assessing Community Services

Imagine what you would do if the trash were not collected from your neighborhood. If your home were to catch fire, would you be able to save it yourself? Like most people, you depend on the community to provide you with certain services. Services vary from community to community. Check out the availability and quality of these services before choosing a place to live.

Prospective residents should investigate the services that are available in the neighborhood they are interested in. They should also find out which of these services are paid for by property taxes, which services residents pay for separately, and how much they cost. These items can, in some cases, add a significant amount to housing expenses.

UTILITIES AND PUBLIC SERVICES

People often take utilities and services for granted. **Utilities** are the electric power, gas, water, and telephone services people use. Public services generally include trash collection, street repair, and sewer systems. Other services, such as snow removal, are also provided in some areas.

PUBLIC SAFETY

A community should have well-trained and well-staffed fire and police departments. Sometimes these services are shared by two or more smaller communities. Rural areas often depend on a volunteer fire department and a county sheriff for protection. The number of staff and distance from your home are factors that can affect response to emergencies. Another consideration is the location of the nearest hospital and ambulance service.

Why do utilities and public services vary according to community or neighborhood?

Why are convenient recreational facilities an important quality of neighborhood or community for many families?

RECREATION

An ideal neighborhood includes space and facilities for recreational activities. These might include soccer and baseball playing fields, basketball courts, parks, and open areas. When deciding on a community, it might be of value to find out whether it has a public park or playground. You might check to see if there is a community swimming pool nearby, a well-stocked public library, museums, movie theaters, or concert halls.

Some of these facilities are provided by residents' tax dollars; others will be paid for by individuals as they are used. A good neighborhood has a mix of both kinds of recreational opportunities.

TAX POLICIES

Tax policies indirectly influence the quality of life in a community. Some communities have much higher taxes than others. These taxes generally pay for better public services and for maintaining neighborhood schools and recreational facilities.

The tax rate, and its impact on the household budget, may directly influence the decision to buy a home in a particular community. Tax rates can also influence a decision to rent in a community, since higher taxes may be reflected in the rent cost.

EDUCATION

For families with children, the quality of the schools in a neighborhood or community holds significant weight when choosing housing. When moving to a new community, it is a good idea to visit local schools, meet the principals, and talk to people in the neighborhood about their experiences with the school system.

There are several things to look for when evaluating a particular school. Are classes overcrowded? What is the ratio of students to teachers? What is the graduation rate at the high school? What does the school spend per student on instruction? Is there an active parent group associated with the school? What plans for improving the school are in place? Is there a community college or university nearby for continuing education? The answers to these questions and more can indicate the quality of education in a community.

Transportation to school is also a concern. If schools are not within walking distance, find out whether adequate busing is provided.

Housing Alternatives

Another factor in the housing decision process is actually choosing the type of housing to live in. There are a variety of housing options available, ranging from single-family homes to multifamily housing. To some people, maintaining one's privacy is the most important consideration when choosing a form of housing. Freedom from maintenance is another reason why people choose one kind of housing over another.

MULTIFAMILY UNITS

Multifamily dwellings are designed to be used by more than one household. Each household within the dwelling has a private living unit. The units may be attached side by side or one above the other, or both.

Multifamily units make the most economical use of land. They frequently offer lower housing costs than single-family housing and come in a variety of styles. This kind of housing is popular with many people.

Apartments

The apartment building is the most common form of multifamily unit. Apartments vary greatly. They range from a separate living unit within a house to several large rooms in a high-rise complex.

A **high-rise apartment** is one of many separate living units in a multistory building generally equipped with elevators. This form of housing is most often found in cities. High-rise apartment buildings may or may not provide extras such as off-street or covered parking, recreational facilities, resident managers, and other services.

A **low-rise apartment**, or an apartment in a building with few floors and no elevators, offers the benefits of apartment living in a more personal setting. A low-rise apartment building may or may not offer laundry facilities, covered parking, or recreational facilities.

A **garden apartment** is a unit in a low-rise building that includes landscaped grounds. These apartment buildings are often clustered around a patio with a fountain or a swimming pool, or an open lawn area sometimes called a *commons*. Garden apartment buildings, more open than traditional low-rise buildings,

Apartment buildings efficiently house many people on a small amount of land.

often have balconies and outside stairs leading to individual units.

An **efficiency apartment** is a unit with one main room, a small kitchen area, and a bathroom. The main room functions as a living, dining, and sleeping area. An efficiency apartment is also known as a *studio apartment*. This is usually the least expensive apartment option in a given location.

Some apartment complexes are built especially for senior citizens or other people with special needs. These complexes may offer assisted living services, such as medical facilities, housekeeping, a central dining room, transportation, and special safety features.

What are the advantages and disadvantages of living in a town house?

While some apartments can be very costly, for many people apartments are the most affordable form of housing. Another advantage is that apartment dwellers usually don't have to take care of outdoor maintenance. On the other hand, apartments offer less privacy than other dwellings.

Town Houses

A **town house** consists of several houses attached together at the side walls. Town houses generally have identical floor plans and are two or more stories high. Each unit has its own separate entrance from the street, and some have a private backyard or patio. Town houses offer more privacy than most apartment units. In addition, town houses require less maintenance than single-family homes since they have only two or three exterior sides and tend to have smaller yards.

Older town houses located in cities are sometimes called *row houses*. Row houses usually have no recreational facilities of their own, and parking may be limited. In suburban areas, some town house complexes provide a swimming pool, tennis courts, or other facilities. These extras tend to increase the cost of renting or buying a unit in the complex.

Duplexes

A **duplex** is one building that contains two separate living units. The units may be attached side by side, with one or two stories per unit, or there may be one unit on the first floor and one on the second floor. Each unit has its own outside entrance.

While a duplex is less private than a single-family home, it may offer some of the same advantages, such as yard space and a quiet residential location. A duplex does not offer the recreational facilities that larger multifamily complexes sometimes do, but is also less impersonal.

Other Multifamily Units

The popularity of multifamily housing has led to the availability of other forms. One option is a **triplex**—three housing units that are attached at the side walls. Another is a **fourplex**—four housing units that are attached at the side walls. These living units generally have two levels and a garage. Unlike town houses, triplexes and fourplexes are not arranged in a straight row. Instead, the structures may be designed in unique shapes. Each entrance often faces a different direction, giving the residents a measure of privacy and the illusion of living in a freestanding unit. The future will probably bring still more designs for multifamily housing.

SINGLE-FAMILY HOUSING

A single-family house is a detached, or separated, dwelling designed to be used by one household. Single-family homes may be large or small, new or old. For example, a manufactured, or "mobile," home (discussed in Chapter 3) is a single-family dwelling; so is a two-story Colonial-style house or a 1930s bungalow.

One of the most attractive advantages of a single-family home is privacy. The walls, ceiling, and floor are not attached to any other living unit, and a plot of land separates each home from the next. However, the land surrounding the home adds to its cost. Owners are responsible for their own outdoor maintenance. Renters may be responsible for maintenance or may have an agreement with the landlord to have maintenance provided.

In areas where many people must be housed in a limited amount of space, single-family homes are probably not the best choice. Multifamily housing uses land more efficiently. However, as explained in Chapter 7, cluster homes and zero-lot-line homes are designed to use land more efficiently than traditional single-family housing developments.

The Choice Is Yours

Choosing a place to live is one of the most important decisions people make. It should be made carefully and with as much information as is available. Needs, wants, priorities, and personal resources should all be honestly identified. The options, in terms of both location and type of housing, should be examined carefully. It's wise to invest some time, energy, and thought before choosing a place to call home.

Another decision that must be made by people looking for housing is whether to rent or buy. Renting lets people choose a place to live without making a long-term commitment or investing a large sum of money. Owning provides financial advantages, as well as a feeling of security and of putting down roots. The decision to rent or own is explored further in Chapter 9.

What do you think the residents of this home took into consideration when choosing to move to this location?

Sharon Thomas

Real Estate Agent

House hunting can be one of the most exciting experiences in your life. It can also be one of the most confusing—especially the first time you do it.

At the agency where I work, I'm known to have a knack for dealing with first-time buyers. But it takes more than sales ability to guide them into purchasing the home that best meets their needs.

"I need to be a good listener—drawing buyers into conversation about their needs, concerns, preferences, and finances."

I have to keep informed about the changing housing market in my area. Research skills are also important. Buyers ask a lot of questions—about everything from the average college entrance scores of the high school to the availability of recycling pickup. I use math skills to offer a buyer quick projections of down payment and mortgage payments.

Most important, though, is an understanding of people and how to deal with them. My success depends on my ability to quickly establish a good rapport with prospective buyers and gain their confidence. This is especially true of first-time buyers, who sometimes judge me almost as much as they judge the houses I show them. They tend to go on their instincts about my professional ability and personal integrity. If they mistrust me on either count, they might reject the homes I show them.

This is a two-way street though. I have to be able to distinguish a serious buyer from someone who makes a hobby of looking. Months may go by between the time the client starts looking and actually closes on a property. The deal may fall through at any point. If that happens, I receive nothing for the hours I've invested, because I work on *commission*, a percentage of the sale price of the home as my fee.

I need to be a good listener—drawing buyers into conversation about their needs, concerns, preferences, and finances. Knowing that one client wants a large dining room or that another objects to electric heating, for instance, can save time for both the clients and me. I try to get feedback about every house we look at. Is the location convenient? Is the yard too large? Is the fireplace a strong selling point with the client or just a nice extra? I keep these things in mind when I look for other homes to show.

This dialogue also helps buyers share their feelings about becoming homeowners. First-time buyers can become anxious as they consider the substantial investment and the other demands of owning a home. I inform them about special financing that's sometimes available to first-time

"I use math skills to offer a buyer quick projections of down payment and mortgage payments."

homebuyers. If they feel they can't afford the homes they see, we go over their finances and expenses again to find a comfortable price range.

In some cases I even advise waiting to buy a home. It's better to lose the commission than to wind up with unhappy customers. This makes good business sense in the long run. Fewer of my sales collapse at the last minute, and my clients are more likely to recommend me to their friends. It's rewarding when former clients decide to sell their houses and they seek me out again.

Career Profile

Real estate agents help people go through the process of buying or selling a home. Other common activities of a real estate agent include arranging home inspections, appraisals, settlements, and advertising.

Education
▸ A high school diploma is required.
▸ Must be able to pass a written exam to become licensed by the state.
▸ Most states require a specified amount of formal training in real estate.

Skills Needed
▸ Knowledge of the housing market, marketplace, and financing and mortgage options.
▸ Understanding of people.
▸ Ability to negotiate successfully.

Career Outlook
▸ While jobs are fairly easy to obtain, the competition in the field can be intense. Real estate agents work principally on commission, sometimes making it difficult to generate a steady income. The turnover rate in real estate is very high. More information can be obtained from the National Association of Realtors, Realtor Information Center.

Career Activities

1. You are choosing homes to show clients who want to buy a three-bedroom home near an elementary school. They would like an eat-in kitchen and a fenced yard. Choose a hypothetical price range for the clients. Then use local real estate ads to select at least three properties you would show them.
2. Assume the same family wants to make an offer on a more expensive home. Their housing costs would consume almost 40 percent of their income. How would you advise them?

Review & Activities

Chapter Summary

➤ The decision-making process is a useful tool when making housing choices.

➤ Before making a housing decision, identify your needs, wants, and priorities.

➤ Consider both the human and material resources available when choosing a home.

➤ Evaluate various locations to determine whether an urban, suburban, or rural environment is preferred.

➤ Consider the advantages and drawbacks of a neighborhood before deciding whether to live there.

➤ The quality of community services can vary widely and should be evaluated carefully.

➤ Many types of housing, both multifamily and single-family, are available.

Checking Your Understanding

1. What specific steps can help you make better decisions?

2. Give examples showing how a need, a want, and a priority might affect a person's choice of housing.

3. Identify two human and two material resources that might enter into housing decisions.

4. How can location affect housing costs?

5. How are urban and rural lifestyles different?

6. How do neighborhoods differ, and how might this affect a family's choice of housing?

7. Why are public services important to the choice of where to live?

8. How can tax policies affect a community?

9. Name four types of multifamily housing.

10. How is a town house similar to a fourplex? How is it different?

11. What is an advantage and a disadvantage of a single-family home?

Thinking Critically

1. Make a list of the human resources you and those in your household possess. How could these resources affect your housing decisions?

2. What would you most like to change about your neighborhood? Do you think the changes would require a small group of people or widespread community involvement? Explain.

3. Suppose your community, because of budget cuts, has to give up two services. Name two services you would be willing to lose. Which services would you insist on keeping? Explain your answers.

4. Imagine that you are working on plans for an assisted living facility for seniors in your community. What type of housing would you build? What types of extras would you include? Where would you build? How many units would the facility include? Give reasons for your choices.

Applications

1. **Housing Through the Life Cycle.** Housing needs, wants, and priorities often change as a person's or family's life situation changes. Projecting into the future, identify your probable needs, wants, and priorities at these stages:

   · Starting college at a university in another state.

   · Age 30, married with two children, ages 6 and 3.

   · Age 55, married, still working but with no children at home.

   · Age 75, retired, wanting to cut down on home maintenance tasks.

2. **Using Resources.** Imagine that your family has decided to build a deck. You want to build it yourselves to save money, but no one in your family has any experience in carpentry. List as many ways as possible that you could find out how to build the deck. Explain what this demonstrates about resources.

3. **Neighborhood Checklist.** Compile a personal checklist of features to investigate before selecting a neighborhood in which to live. Identify what features are most important to you and which you might be willing to give up.

4. **Global Housing.** Using print or Internet resources, research types of multifamily dwellings in a country other than your own. Prepare a short written report describing the housing and how it is similar or different.

BUILDING YOUR PORTFOLIO

You have been asked by the Housing Commission to conduct a study of the housing in your area. Use community resources to answer the following questions:

➤ What seems to be the general trend of growth in the area? Which neighborhoods are growing? Which are beginning to show signs of decline?

➤ What neighborhoods seem to offer the best living conditions for a growing family? For a retired couple? For a dual-income couple? For a single person?

Real estate firms, the chamber of commerce, historical societies, the library, local newspapers, and the Internet are possible sources of information. Write a report summarizing your findings. Also include any recommendations you have for improving housing in your area. You may wish to submit your findings and recommendations to the local housing commission.

Renting versus Buying

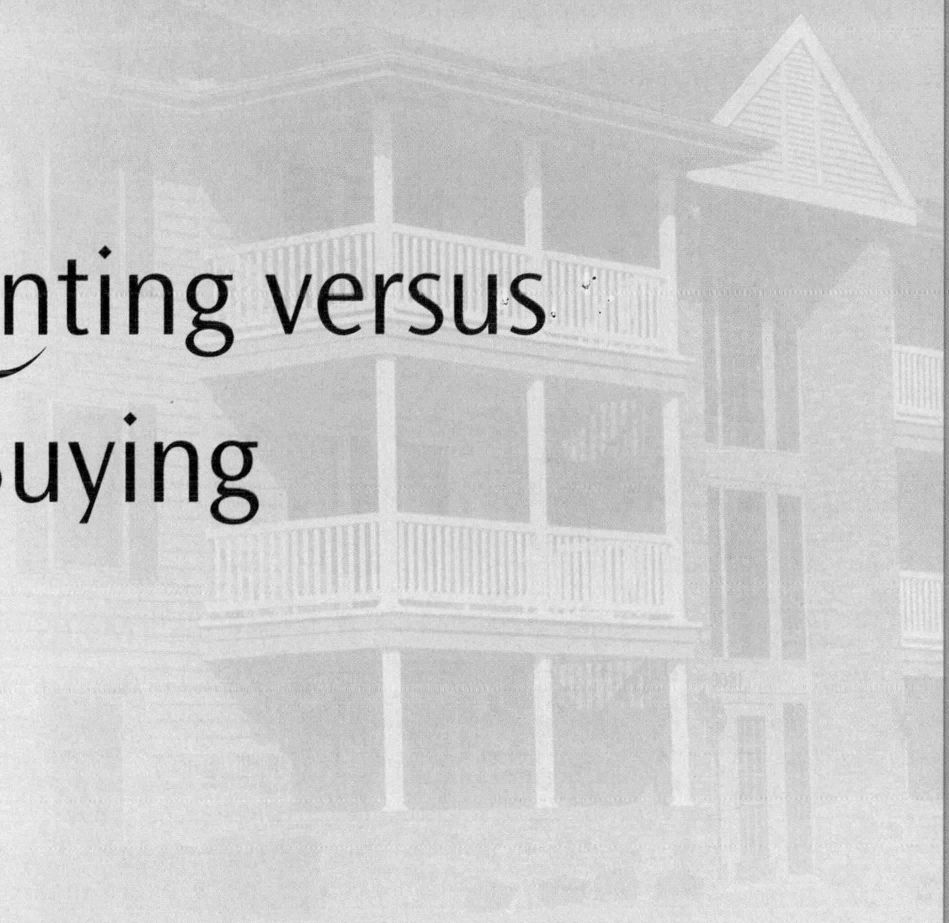

CHAPTER OBJECTIVES

▶ Compare and contrast the advantages and disadvantages of renting or buying a home.

▶ Analyze costs involved in renting and buying.

▶ Assess types of home ownership.

▶ Describe how to determine a realistic housing budget.

TERMS TO LEARN

- closing costs
- condominium ownership
- cooperative ownership
- down payment
- earnest money
- interest
- landlord
- mortgage
- principal
- renter's insurance
- security deposit
- tenant

Some people dream of owning their own home and being able to customize it as they choose. Others prefer to rent a place and have the flexibility of changing residences on short notice without the concerns of selling. Renting and owning a home each have advantages and disadvantages. Understanding these will help you analyze the pros and cons of each in various situations.

Renting: Pros and Cons

Renting means paying money to live in a dwelling that is owned by someone else. **Landlords**, or owners, offer renters—called **tenants**—many types of housing, from small efficiency apartments to single-family houses. Rental housing is available either furnished or unfurnished and in all price ranges.

Whether they're just starting out or have been saving for a home for years, all people make housing decisions at some time in their lives.

ADVANTAGES OF RENTING

A young college graduate with a new full-time job needs a small, inexpensive place to live. A couple with two children want to live in a single-family house, but they know they will be making a job-related move within a year. A retired couple want to try living in a warmer climate for a few months before deciding whether to move there permanently. For these people, and for many others, the best choice may be to rent a home. Rental housing offers several advantages.

PREDICTABLE HOUSING COSTS. Renters typically know what their monthly housing cost will be. They don't have to worry about unexpected repair bills. Money that otherwise might be spent for maintenance and improvements can be saved.

LIMITED MAINTENANCE. For some, a major reason for renting is the limited maintenance responsibilities involved. Yard work, snow removal, painting, and household repairs are generally the responsibility of the landlord. Those who rent single-family dwellings, however, may have to provide their own lawn care and some basic home maintenance.

MOBILITY. Some people don't want to commit themselves to the long-term responsibilities of home ownership. They may have to move often because of their careers, or they may be unsure of the type of housing that will be most comfortable for them. Others may not be sure their income will remain steady for a long period. Renting gives them flexibility.

DISADVANTAGES OF RENTING

While renting a home has many advantages, there are also some possible disadvantages. Renters have limited control and freedom. They also may feel a lack of stability or permanence. In addition, people are at a financial disadvantage when they do not own the home in which they live.

LIMITED CONTROL AND FREEDOM. The major disadvantages of renting relate to control over living space. Renters may have little or no voice in how the building is managed or maintained. They often do not have the freedom to make changes in decor, such as painting and papering walls, without getting the landlord's permission. Some landlords prohibit pets or restrict the number and type of pets that tenants can keep. Landlords may have adults-only policies. Some restrict the hours when a tenant may have guests.

LACK OF PERMANENCE. In general, rental housing does not encourage a sense of community. Tenants may move in and out so often that there's no feeling of permanence or belonging. Unlike homeowners, renters often view their neighbors as strangers and may not get to know them as well.

FINANCIAL DISADVANTAGES. Money spent on rent is not applied toward ownership. After paying rent for years, renters have no investment in property to show for their payments and no tax savings. At the end of the rental agreement period, a landlord

Talking with a landlord about rental restrictions, such as those regarding apartment decor or pets, can help you make a housing decision.

will often raise the rent. The renter must pay the increase or face the disruption and expense of moving. In many cases, monthly rent can cost more than a monthly loan payment for a similar size home.

Buying: Pros and Cons

Owning a home has been a traditional dream for many people because it offers a unique sense of satisfaction. The most common type of housing that is purchased is the freestanding, single-family house set on its own lot. However, units in multifamily dwellings may be purchased. For example, one form of ownership, called **condominium ownership**, involves individual ownership of a unit in a multifamily dwelling, such as an apartment or town house. (You can read more about condominium ownership on page 195.)

The purchase of a home is a major decision, regardless of the type of housing. Like renting, buying has advantages and disadvantages that need to be carefully weighed.

ADVANTAGES OF HOME OWNERSHIP

When choosing home ownership, there are several significant advantages. Some of these advantages include:

FEELING OF BELONGING. Home ownership provides a feeling of stability and a sense of "putting down roots." Many homeowners develop a sense of community awareness and responsibility. Homeowners often want to participate in local government. By doing so, they feel they can help protect the value of real estate in their area and help determine how tax money will be spent.

INDEPENDENCE. While some homeowners must comply with regulations about the exterior designs of their homes, most are free to adapt their homes to meet their needs. They can redecorate to suit their tastes. They can remodel as the household grows or as their needs change. Not only do homeowners benefit from a more livable and attractive home, but improvements can add to a home's value.

INVESTMENT VALUE. Buying a home is an investment. The cost of the home and the money put into maintaining it are not lost, as they are with renting. Rather, the homeowner is exchanging one form of wealth (cash) for another (real estate). Over the last several decades, the value of real estate has generally risen. If a home is kept in good condition, and if the economy is sound, its value will probably rise. Chances are, the owner will be able to sell the home for more than he or she paid for it.

An investment option for some people is to buy a multifamily dwelling—such as a duplex or four-plex—and live in one unit, renting out the rest as a source of income. Owners in this situation become landlords. They must choose tenants carefully, since they will be living close together.

GOOD CREDIT RECORD. Making regular monthly home loan payments to a bank or other institution helps homeowners build good credit records. Prompt payments establish a reputation for reliability that can help people qualify for loans in the future.

TAX ADVANTAGES. Homeowners enjoy income tax savings. With home loans, **interest**—the money that the lending company charges the buyer for a loan—is tax-deductible. This means it can be deducted from the income amount used to figure taxes. Property tax payments are also deductible.

A well-maintained home in a desirable location has the best chance of providing a return on the owner's investment.

Condominium and Cooperative Ownership

What combines the advantages of owning and renting? For many people, the options of condominium or cooperative ownership meet that description.

In the condominium form of ownership, you buy an individual unit in a multifamily dwelling. It might be an apartment, a town house, or a unit in a duplex, triplex, or fourplex. Like any homeowner, you're responsible for home loan payments, property taxes, and interior maintenance. You may sell your home when and to whom you like.

Buying a condominium makes you a member of the owners' association. It also means you are part-owner of common areas, such as hallways, the building exterior, and landscaping. You share in the rights and responsibilities of using and keeping up these areas. Maintenance tasks for common areas are usually turned over to a professional management firm hired by the association. Association members vote on issues concerning the property, such as whether to add lighting to parking areas. The value of your property determines your number of votes. Maintenance and service expenses are paid by monthly fees or dues.

Cooperative ownership is somewhat different. Instead of owning a unit directly, you purchase shares of stock in a nonprofit corporation, which, in turn, owns the property. The price of your unit determines how many shares you receive.

Some members of the cooperative sit on the board of directors, which arranges for maintenance and services.

The board may hire a management firm or delegate the tasks to committees within the cooperative. Additionally, the board may accept or reject the sale of shares—in other words, the sale of a unit. As a shareholder, you receive one vote in making such decisions. You pay a monthly fee to cover taxes and maintenance costs.

Condominium and cooperative ownership share some of the disadvantages, as well as advantages, of both buying and renting. As a corporation, a cooperative has the added risk of financial failure. If shareholders cannot or will not pay the expenses, the cooperative may be forced to declare bankruptcy.

YOU THE CONSUMER . . .

You have been renting an efficiency apartment in the city. The landlord has just informed you that the building will be converting to a cooperative. You must decide whether to stay and purchase shares in the cooperative or find other housing. What information would you want to gather before making a decision? What factors would have the greatest influence on your decision? Why?

DISADVANTAGES OF BUYING A HOME

While owning a home has benefits, there are possible disadvantages to think about, too. These include:

UNEXPECTED EXPENSES. With home ownership comes the responsibility for maintaining the home. Although improvements such as adding a deck or remodeling a kitchen can be planned and saved for, many maintenance expenses arise without warning and need immediate attention. For example, a water heater may need replacing, or a roof may develop a leak. These problems can be expensive. If damage is due to an accident, insurance may pay a por-

Homeowners who are not able to do some home maintenance chores often hire others to do the chores for them.

investing in a house, potential home-owners should realistically assess the amount of time and energy they are willing to spend on maintenance. Condominium owners are not responsible for doing outside main-tenance themselves; instead, they pay a fee for these services.

LIMITED MOBILITY. Buying a home should be considered a long-term investment. It can be costly to sell a home shortly after buying it, because the costs of selling and buy-ing a home are high. A person who knows that he or she may need to move within a year should consider renting rather than buying.

tion of the cost of repair. Often, however, problems arise simply as a result of wear and aging of the home.

TIME SPENT ON MAINTENANCE. The owner of a single-family home is responsible for day-to-day and week-to-week upkeep. Such tasks as yard work, painting, and snow removal must be done periodically to protect the appearance and value of the home. These tasks take time and must be repeated often. Before

$\mathcal{A}$ Closer Look at Costs

Finances are a major factor to con-sider when deciding whether to rent or buy. Both buyers and renters need to consider two types of costs: the initial costs that must be paid once, and the continual costs that must be paid every month or year.

RENTER'S INITIAL COSTS

When looking for a place to live, first-time renters usually pay close attention to the monthly costs that will be involved. Many, however, don't realize that they need to set aside some cash for the initial expenses of moving into rental housing. Awareness of these initial costs can help renters handle them as planned expenses rather than an unpleasant surprise. Typical initial costs include:

APPLICATION FEE. A prospective renter may have to pay a fee when filling out an application to live in a unit. The fee helps ensure that the renter is seriously interested in taking the unit.

CREDIT CHECK FEE. A landlord will probably obtain a credit check on a prospective renter. A credit check tells the landlord whether the renter pays bills on time and whether or not the person has large outstanding amounts charged on credit cards. This kind of confidential information is researched by a credit agency. The landlord may charge the renter the agency's fee.

SECURITY DEPOSIT. Before moving into a rental unit, a renter is usually required to pay a **security deposit**. This fee covers the cost of any future

Planning ahead for such expenses as renting a moving truck can reduce financial stress.

damage the renter might cause to the unit. The deposit may be equal to one or two month's rent. Renters who own pets often must pay an additional security deposit called a *pet deposit*. When the renter moves out, the security deposit is returned if the unit is left in good condition. However, if the renter has damaged the property, the landlord keeps part or all of the deposit to pay for repairing the damage. The pet deposit may or may not be refunded depending on the landlord's policy or the extent of the damage caused by the pet.

ADVANCE ON RENT. Some landlords of rental units require payment in addition to a security deposit. A renter may have to pay one month's rent (or more) in advance before moving in. A landlord considers this advance as a type of "insurance" if a renter moves out unexpectedly, leaving a unit vacant.

MOVING AND OTHER COSTS. When planning for initial expenses, renters should not forget the costs of actually moving into their new home. Professional movers charge a fee to move furniture and other household goods. For an extra fee, they will also pack items in boxes. Renters can save money by renting or borrowing a truck and doing the packing and carrying themselves. In addition to actual moving expenses, there may be a one-time fee for installing or turning on any services that are the tenant's responsibility, such as telephone service, electricity, or cable television.

Careful budgeting for rent, insurance, and utilities can help you meet the continual costs of renting a home.

RENTER'S CONTINUAL COSTS

After moving in, a renter has certain housing costs to pay each month. These include the rent payment, insurance, and perhaps utilities and parking.

MONTHLY RENT. The monthly cost of rental housing is, of course, a major consideration. Rental costs depend on many factors such as the size of the unit, the age of the building, the neighborhood, and the services that are included. A renter may have to give up one feature, such as more space, to gain another, such as paid utilities. Renters who do not already own furniture might consider paying slightly more to rent a furnished apartment.

INSURANCE. Since the landlord's insurance on the building does not cover the tenant's belongings, tenants should purchase **renter's insurance**—a policy that covers their personal property against loss by theft, fire, or other hazards. Personal liability insurance offers protection if someone files a claim against the renter for injuries sustained in the rental unit.

UTILITIES. Sometimes the costs for services such as water, sewer, natural gas, electricity, and trash collection are paid by the landlord and are included in the rent. Other times, the tenant pays for some or all of these utilities, as well as for telephone service. If paying for the utilities is the tenant's responsibility, money needs to be set aside for these costs each month.

PARKING. Some rental units charge an additional fee for garage space. This is particularly true in a city apartment building that has an underground parking garage, where space is at a premium.

BUYER'S INITIAL COSTS

The initial costs of buying a home are usually much higher than those involved in renting. Most people plan for many years before buying a home because of the amount of money involved.

Few people can save up enough money to pay the purchase price of a home in cash. Most people must borrow part of the money to pay for a home. A number of costs associated with financing the purchase of a home arise at the time the purchase is made.

EARNEST MONEY. **Earnest money** is a deposit that a potential buyer pays to show that he or she is serious about buying a home. The money is held in a trust until the deal is final. When the deal goes through, the earnest money is applied toward the payment of the total price. If buyers cannot secure a loan, the money is usually refunded. Buyers may lose the earnest money if they back out of the agreement.

APPLICATION AND CREDIT CHECK FEES. Before loaning a substantial amount of money to buy a home, banks and other financial institutions check the buyer's credit to see whether that person is a good risk. The bank looks to see if the buyer has any large outstanding debts and has the income to pay the monthly bills. The buyer usually has to pay the fee that covers the cost of this credit check.

INSPECTION FEES. When a buyer is seriously interested in a particular home, it is wise to have it inspected. Many buyers hire a professional home inspection company. These firms send a certified inspector to the home to check the structure, the roof, and the plumbing, electrical, and heating systems. The inspector also checks for pests, such as termites. Some firms will estimate the cost of any needed repairs.

DOWN PAYMENT. People are rarely allowed to borrow the entire price of the home they buy. They are usually required to make a **down payment**, or a partial payment of cash, at the

What are the advantages of having a home inspection prior to buying a home?

time of purchase. The down payment may be from 5 to 25 percent or more of the purchase price, depending on what the financial institution requires. The more money a buyer puts down, the less expensive monthly payments will be.

CLOSING COSTS. In addition, buyers are required to pay certain **closing costs**—fees due at the time the purchase is finalized. These fees usually total several thousand dollars. You will read more about closing costs in Chapter 11.

MOVING AND OTHER COSTS. Like renters, homeowners should plan for the expenses of moving and connecting utilities. In addition, they may want to, or need to, spend money on appliances, lawn and garden tools, and other useful items. If they have purchased a newly constructed home, landscaping may be a major expense. Doing landscaping work in stages over several years can reduce initial costs.

BUYER'S CONTINUAL COSTS

Once buyers move in, their monthly costs begin. These include a monthly mortgage payment, property taxes, insurance, utilities, and maintenance of the property.

Owning a home involves other expenses besides the initial cost of the home. What items should homeowners be prepared to purchase?

MONTHLY MORTGAGE PAYMENT. Unlike a loan to buy a car or television, a **mortgage**, or home loan, is long term. Most require making monthly payments for 15 or 30 years, although some are offered for other periods of time.

A monthly mortgage payment includes two components. Part of the payment directly repays a portion of the **principal**—the original amount of the loan. The rest is *interest*, the fee that the lending institution charges the buyer to borrow the money.

At first, most of each mortgage payment goes toward paying the interest on a loan, with a small amount going toward paying the principal. Near the end of the loan term, more money goes toward the principal. This can vary with different types of home loans. Chapter 11 gives more information about types of home loans.

TAXES. Homeowners are required to pay property, or real estate, taxes.

Often this cost is added to the monthly mortgage payment. The taxes are based on the value of the home and are used to pay for such community services as schools, libraries, street repairs, and parks.

INSURANCE. Homeowners should carry property and liability insurance. Property insurance covers the cost of repairing or replacing objects damaged by fire, theft, or other hazards. Liability insurance covers any claims filed against the homeowner by persons who are injured on the property. Most lenders require the buyer to protect the home by purchasing insurance. Sometimes, one-twelfth of the estimated yearly insurance premium is added to the monthly mortgage payment, and the lending company makes payments to the insurance provider.

UTILITIES. Homeowners pay for their own utilities, including water, sewer, telephone, electricity, natural gas or heating oil, trash collection, and cable television fees. The cost of some utilities may be included in property taxes, but most are separate expenses.

MAINTENANCE. As mentioned earlier, homeowners are responsible, directly or indirectly, for the cost of upkeep on their property. A home inspector can point out any possible trouble spots for the buyers. This way, they will be aware of the possibility of any major repairs that may be coming up.

What Can You Spend on Housing?

Before looking for a place to rent or buy, you should decide how much you can afford to spend on housing. One rule of thumb is to spend no more than about 28 percent of gross monthly income on a mortgage payment or rent payment. (*Gross income* is the full amount you earn before taxes are taken out.) However, this varies according to your situation. Some people may want to stretch their budget to spend more on housing, while others prefer to spend less.

Careful planning can help you obtain affordable housing that meets your needs. Take a close look at your financial picture and determine how much you can spend. Also consider what other resources might be available to help you.

ANALYZING YOUR FINANCES

As you read in Chapter 8, a careful account of material resources is a significant factor to consider when making housing decisions. Keep records of your current finances. Be sure to analyze the following:

INCOME. Income is the money received for work done or from investments made. For purposes of housing, it is important to determine monthly and yearly income. Is it steady, or does it vary from month to month? Remember, monthly mortgage or rent payments must be paid whether or not you received income that month.

EXPENSES. It's a good idea to keep track of your monthly expenses for a few months. This will help you estimate upcoming expenses.

Expenses are of two main kinds— fixed and flexible. *Fixed expenses* must be paid regularly, and the amount is fairly constant. Rent is a fixed expense. Many people look upon regular deposits to a savings account as a fixed expense. Certain other types of expenses are *flexible*; that is, they vary in amount and do not occur regularly. Clothing is a flexible expense. Remember to

include payments on existing debts, such as an installment loan for a car, as expenses.

SAVINGS. Both homeowners and renters need to consider the significance of savings as part of their financial plans. Life is full of unexpected—and often expensive—surprises. Without savings, it can be difficult to cope with unplanned needs. Homeowners need money for a down payment and closing costs. They might need money suddenly for expensive home repairs. For a

How might carefully examining your financial picture help you to determine the amount of money available for housing?

renter or homeowner, it may be a need unrelated to housing such as an emergency medical expense. Both homeowners and renters should ask themselves: "How much savings do I have now?" and "What can I save each month?".

STRENGTHENING YOUR FINANCES

After looking at your finances, you may decide to make some changes. Here are some ideas:

- Make a budget—a financial plan.
- Set aside savings first instead of saving what's leftover.
- Reduce flexible expenses.
- Reduce current debt.
- Limit impulse buying. Stick to your plan.
- Continue keeping records so you know how your money is used.

Fixed and flexible expenses change as work and lifestyles change and as households expand and contract. Good money management adjusts spending according to these changes. Knowing exactly where your money is spent can give you

better control in using available financial resources to deal with expenses, including housing.

USING OTHER RESOURCES

Human resources can be used to lower the costs of buying and maintaining housing. People who are willing to invest time, energy, and talent in their homes can save money and at the same time increase the livability of their homes. Someone who builds or assists in building his or her new home lowers the final cost of the home by saving on construction costs. Others save by completing their own home repairs and maintenance. Consumer-friendly products—such as self-adhesive floor tiles, water-based paint, and precut and prefinished wall panels—have encouraged this trend.

People can also use their skills to make things for their homes that might be expensive to buy. For example, a person who sews can design and make window treatments. Someone with plumbing skills can update a bathroom. Doing

Homeowners can save quite a bit of money by doing some maintenance and decorating tasks themselves.

such tasks yourself takes time and energy, but it can also add greatly to the livability, convenience, and value of a home. The money saved can be invested or spent for other needs and wants. Making good use of your human resources can also give a great deal of personal satisfaction and enjoyment.

$\mathcal{D}$eciding to Rent or Buy

Making the decision whether to rent or buy a home is a major one. It is also a personal one that will vary from individual to individual, depending on the situation. There are many factors to evaluate, compare, and analyze when considering housing. Keeping careful records and learning to manage your

finances will make your financial picture clearer. Recognize that the decision to rent or buy a home takes knowledge and planning—tools you will use to make an informed, sound housing decision. Chapters 10 and 11 will discuss specific options for affordable housing in your future.

Judy Flores

Mortgage Loan Officer

The greatest single investment that most people ever make is the purchase of their home. It's very unusual when a homebuyer has enough money to pay cash at the time of the sale. Most buyers need a loan—a mortgage loan—to make their purchase. My job as a mortgage loan officer is to determine whether my bank should provide that loan to them.

"Part of my decision concerns the prospective buyers themselves—whether they are financially able to meet the expenses of the home they want to buy."

Part of my decision concerns the prospective buyers themselves—whether they are financially able to meet the expenses of the home they want to buy. The bank grants mortgages based on my recommendations about which applicants seem to be good financial risks. My ability to make sound judgments is crucial.

I start by gathering information on the financial status of the applicant: his or her annual income, as well as any other assets they have—savings, stock holdings, other property. I verify all this information by running a credit check, contacting the person's employer, and obtaining financial statements.

Next, I list the projected monthly mortgage payments, real estate taxes, and other expenses such as homeowner's insurance. I enter this information into standard mortgage qualification formulas to determine whether the amount the applicant wants to borrow is realistic.

Just as applicants are investigated thoroughly, so is the property they want to buy. Part of my job is making sure the house or condo is worth the asking price and that the seller has clear *title,* or legal claim of ownership. I make sure that the applicant hires experts to inspect the home. They must confirm in writing that it is

structurally sound and free of insect infestation. Copies of all these reports are then submitted for my review. Each application involves a lot of phone calls, paperwork, and attention to detail. I have to handle many applications at one time. A mortgage officer who's disorganized will have a very short career.

If the facts and figures produce a borderline result—showing that the applicant may have trouble paying off the mortgage—I have to make a judgment call. My interviewing skill helps me to put the person enough at ease to gain some insights about character, values, and other issues that may become significant later. I try to find out whether the applicant takes commitments seriously. If two or more people are applying together, I try to evaluate their rapport and their ability to work as a team.

If paying the mortgage will present a real difficulty, I have to reject the

application. Approving it would be a disservice to the lender, and probably to the applicant as well. I have to go with the facts and figures, not with emotions. Luckily, I get to say "yes" to applicants who seem to have what

it takes. Working with the first-time buyers is especially gratifying. I might never these people again, but I feel good about the role I've had in changing their lives for the better.

"Just as applicants are investigated thoroughly, so is the property they want to buy."

Career Profile

Mortgage loan officers assist individuals in applying for loans to purchase real estate or to refinance an existing mortgage. Mortgage loan officers seek to develop good working relationships with commercial and residential real estate agencies, in the hope that when an individual or firm buys a property, the real estate agent may recommend contacting them for financing.

Education
▸ Requires a bachelor's degree in finance, economics, or a related field; training or experience in banking, lending, or sales is advantageous.

Skills Needed
▸ Should be capable of developing effective working relationships with others, confident in personal abilities, and highly motivated. Sales experience is very helpful.
▸ Knowledge of computers and bank applications.

Career Outlook
▸ Employment of loan officers is subject to the upturns and downturns of the economy. When interest rates decline dramatically, there is a surge in real estate buying and refinancing that requires additional loan officers. When the real estate market slows, loan officers can be subject to layoffs.
▸ Since even in economic downturns loans remain the major source of revenue for banks, the fundamental role of loan officers will contribute to job stability.
▸ As in the past, college graduates and those with banking, lending, or sales experience should have the best job prospects.

Career Activities
1. An applicant's credit report indicates that he pays his bills, but consistently pays them late. Write a paragraph explaining how this might affect your approval of the mortgage application.
2. Another applicant currently has ample income to pay the mortgage payments, but she has only worked at her job for six months. Her previous three jobs have all lasted about a year or less. How might this job history influence your decision?

*R*eview & Activities

Chapter Summary

➤ Renting and buying a home both have advantages and disadvantages.

➤ Landlords and tenants are the two parties involved in renting a home.

➤ Cooperative and condominium ownership are examples of purchasing multifamily housing.

➤ Finances are a major factor to consider when renting or buying a home.

➤ Renters and buyers have differing initial and continual costs.

➤ Renters and buyers should carefully determine what they can afford to spend on housing.

➤ Keeping financial records can help in determining how much can be spent on housing.

➤ Human resources can be used to lower housing costs.

➤ Deciding to rent or buy is a personal decision that varies from individual to individual.

Checking Your Understanding

1. Explain why fixed costs and limited maintenance are advantages of renting.

2. What are the financial disadvantages of renting?

3. How can owning a home be a good financial investment?

4. Explain why having responsibility for maintenance might be a disadvantage to homeowners.

5. What might be one drawback to cooperative ownership?

6. Name three initial costs of renting.

7. What is a mortgage, and how is it different from a regular bank loan?

8. What general guideline is given for housing costs?

9. Explain the differences between fixed expenses and flexible expenses.

10. Identify at least three ways a family might strengthen their finances.

11. Identify three human resources that can help reduce housing costs.

Thinking Critically

1. Why is buying a home a major life decision?

2. What types of home repair and maintenance tasks do you currently have the skills to do? Which tasks would you like to learn how to do? Which would you prefer to hire someone to do and why? How might your answers influence your decision whether to rent or buy a home?

3. Compare the main advantages of each of the following: renting a unit in a duplex; buying the entire duplex and renting half of it to a tenant; buying one unit through condominium ownership. Which would you prefer to do? Do you think your opinion will change in two years? In six years? Explain.

Review & Activities

Applications

1. **Develop Case Studies.** Write a fictional case study about two different families or individuals, one that chooses to rent and one that chooses to buy a home. Include a description of characteristics that played a role in the decision, such as life stage, number of family members, and plans for the future. Explain why each decided on either buying or renting.

2. **Analyze Rental Costs.** Research the costs of renting an apartment in your area, using the classified advertisements in a newspaper. Prepare a list of apartments by size (efficiency, one bedroom, two bedroom, etc.), location, and cost. Explain what extra features are offered by the more expensive apartments in each size.

3. **Comparing Housing Decisions.** Interview several older people about housing decisions they made when first starting out on their own. What housing alternatives were available to them? What factors entered into their decisions? How do housing decisions made in years past compare and contrast to decisions people must make today? What factors may account for the differences?

4. **Calculating Taxes.** Property taxes are based on the tax rate and a home's *assessed value*—or the amount of money the tax agency says the home is worth. Suppose a house is assessed at $72,000. If the annual property tax rate is 86 cents for each $100 of assessed value, what would be the taxes on the house? Assume that the next year the house is reassessed at $80,000 and the tax rate is 91 cents for each $100. What would be the new taxes on this house? Why is it important for homeowners to know how their taxes are calculated?

BUILDING YOUR PORTFOLIO

Assume that you have decided to start your own housing locator service. Your clientele will be interested in either renting or buying. What characteristics will make your business different from other locator services? How will you meet the housing needs of your clientele? What fees will you charge for your service? As you create your plan, you may want to contact several housing locator services in your area or on the Internet to find out about the services that they offer. Put your written plan in your portfolio for future reference.

Renting a Home

CHAPTER OBJECTIVES

► Identify factors to consider when assessing rental housing requirements.

► List sources of information about available rental housing.

► Contrast different types of rental housing programs.

► Give guidelines for evaluating rental housing units.

► Analyze the features and conditions of rental agreements.

► Explain the roles of tenant and roommate.

TERMS TO LEARN

• assign

• breach of contract

• evict

• lease

• sublet

• subsidized housing

When you're ready to rent a place of your own, you'll need to make many decisions before you move in. After that, the way you handle your responsibilities as a tenant will affect how you get along with your landlord and the others in the building. If you decide to share your place with a roommate, you'll need to ensure the arrangement goes smoothly. Planning and thought can help you make wise decisions about renting.

Selecting Rental Housing

Selecting rental housing is worth the time it takes to make an informed choice. Most landlords require tenants to sign a rental agreement for at least one year. Also, the cost of moving can be high. Following a plan of action will help you make the best possible selection.

The first step is to think about what your requirements are and decide what to look for. Then you need to find out what's available. After this, you will inspect and compare rental units you are interested in. Finally, when you are close to a decision, you will need to review the rental agreement carefully.

ASSESS YOUR HOUSING REQUIREMENTS

Before beginning to search for rental housing, think about your housing requirements. As you do, remember to consider your needs, wants, and personal priorities. Here are some questions you need to think about:

- What can I afford to spend? Some financial experts say to allow about 28 percent of your monthly gross income for rent, depending on the cost of housing in your area. The information in Chapter 9 can help you analyze your finances.
- What location am I interested in? As you read in Chapter 8, location influences the cost of housing as well as its convenience.
- What type of housing unit would suit me—a house, an apartment, a town house? You may want to review the advantages and disadvantages of various types of housing in Chapter 9.
- How much space do I need? How many bedrooms?

Depending on the type of unit you are interested in, you may need to think about other questions. For example, suppose you have decided to look for an apartment. Do you prefer a low-rise or high-rise building? Would you rather live on an upper floor or at ground level? Each has advantages and drawbacks. Although you may not always have a choice, thinking about such alternatives in advance can make later decisions easier. Consider the following factors:

- Apartments located near stairways, elevators, or entrances may be noisy. Heavy drapes or carpets may muffle some noise.
- Apartments that face a busy street or high traffic area tend to be noisier than those facing quiet areas.
- Apartments in the upper portion of the building may be warmer

What types of security measures would be important to you if you were renting an apartment? A townhouse?

and have poorer air circulation than those on lower floors.
- Ground-floor apartments may be more convenient than those on upper floors.
- Upper apartments may be more secure because they are harder to get to from the street.
- Apartments close to elevators and stairs may have greater risk of theft or burglary.

WHAT IS AVAILABLE?

How do you find out what rental housing is available? You can get started by using various sources of information.

Drive or walk through areas in which you would like to live. Are there any "For Rent" signs posted? A landlord might advertise vacancies on a bulletin board in a local convenience store or other gathering spot.

Newspapers print advertisements for rental housing under the headings. "Apartments for Rent" or "Houses for Rent." In some larger cities, apartments are listed according to the area of the city where they are located. Rental ads usually use abbreviations to save the advertiser space and, therefore, money. Figure 10-1 shows some common abbreviations found in real estate ads.

You can also check for online listings of available rental housing.

These may be posted by newspapers and real estate services. You can search for ads with certain criteria, such as location, number of bedrooms, and price range. Some online listings also have a service that will notify you via e-mail of new ads posted to the site. Because space isn't at such a premium as it is in newspaper advertisements, online ads tend to use fewer abbreviations.

Friends who live in the area you're interested in may know of housing vacancies. Tell them you are looking for a place to live, and describe the kind of apartment or house you want.

Real estate agencies and apartment-finding services often have lists of apartments that are vacant or soon will be. These services provide great help in narrowing down your search in a short time. Some agencies charge renters a fee for their services; others charge the landlord. In some large cities the fee can be as high as one month's rent.

If you are moving a long distance, finding housing may require more research. Some communities have a relocation service that will help you find housing that will meet your needs. You can also find out what is available by subscribing to the local newspaper, contacting the Chamber of Commerce or a real estate service, or using online resources. Some online relocation services offer virtual tours of cities and towns, rental ads, job listings, moving tips and timelines, and other resources. You may also find contact information for potential landlords and view photos of rental units and floor plans.

FIGURE 10-1

Reading Rental Advertisements

Abbreviation	What It Means
appl incl	appliances included
appt only	by appointment only
apt	apartment
avail Nov 1	available November 1
BB heat	baseboard heat
bldg	building
BR	bedroom
c/a	central air conditioning
conven all trans	convenient to all transportation
cpts & drps	carpets and drapes
D/W	dishwasher
EIK	eat-in-kitchen
furn	furnished
gar	garage
grt clst spc	great closet space
grt vw	great view
hrdwd flrs	hardwood floors
immed occ	immediate occupancy
incl h/hw	includes heat and hot water
kit	kitchen
ldry	laundry
LR w/fpl	living room with fireplace
MBR	master bedroom
no lse	no lease
nr bus	near bus
nr bus dist	near business district
pvt entr	private entry
refs req'd	references required
sep DR	separate dining room
utils pd	utilities paid
w/	with
W/D	washer and dryer
WWC	wall-to-wall carpeting
xtra lg	extra large
$400/mo	rent is $400 a month
+ util	utilities paid by tenant

6th & Butler Incredible corner apt. with wide-open views of river and city! 2BR, 2 baths, sep DR, big kit, hrdwd flrs, gar, utils pd.

Riverside Rented by owner, 1 BR, 1 bath, furn, immed occ. Nr. bus. W/D in basement $500/mo + util.

Silverdale Immed occ! 2BR, 1 bath, grt vw, no lse. LR w/fpl, EIK, pvt entr. Call soon to find your great new home!

Capitol Park 3 BR ranch, xtra lg MBR, hrdwd flrs, c/a, attached gar, refs req'd Incl h/hw. Great location. Appt only.

E. 13th & Main Studio apt. Grt vw! Cpts & drps, grt clst spc, BB heat. No pets! New WWC. Nr bus dist. Avail Nov 1.

22nd & Birch Cozy efficiency w/grt vw. D/W, ldry in bldg, c/a. Conven all trans. No lse, $400/mo, utils pd.

7th & Park Spacious new 2 BR, 1 1/2 bath. This garden apt has hrdwd flrs, W/D, LR w/fpl, and cpts & drps. BB heat and c/a. Appl incl. Immed occ, call now! No lse.

Planning a Move

Whether you're moving a few necessities into a college dormitory or a houseful of furniture across the country, preparation is essential to success. A countdown to moving day is useful for organizing the many details you face. Here are some tasks to include in your countdown.

Eight to Four Weeks Ahead

- Decide what to take. This is partly determined by the size of your new place and how you define your needs. Some people use this time to take stock of their possessions and sell or give away things they don't need or use.
- Choose a means of transport. Depending on your needs and resources, you may borrow a friend's truck, rent a moving van, or call professional movers.
- Fill out a change-of-address card at the post office. The post office will forward first-class mail to your new address for up to one year (magazines for 60 days).
- Get a head start on fitting in if you're moving to a new community. Contact the chamber of commerce and tourist bureau. At various websites you might find local history, annual events, area maps, business directories, and an online edition of the local newspaper.

Three Weeks to One Week Ahead

- Cancel utilities, newspapers, and other services as needed. You can use any deposits you get back to order services at your new address, which should be done at the same time.
- Arrange to have accounts closed at one financial institution and opened at a new one, if needed.
- Have your vehicle serviced if you will be driving it a long distance or using it to carry some of the load.
- Pack a survival kit for your first day or two in your new home. Include often overlooked necessities such as eating utensils, a can opener, toilet paper, and soap. Remember, household goods that travel separately may not arrive when expected.

YOU THE CONSUMER . . .

You've been charged with packing your belongings for your family's cross-state move. Your family would like to get by with renting a medium-size van. You've been asked to include only the things you really need, plus a few other valued items. What do you choose to take? How will you gather packing materials, such as boxes and padding? What will you do with your remaining possessions?

Affordable Options

As you look for rental housing, keep in mind that there are three basic categories of rental units. Which ones are available to you depends on your income and the portion of it you can pay for rent.

PRIVATELY OWNED HOUSING. Most rental property is privately owned by individuals and companies. Rental properties are generally owned as investments and are used as sources of income. Tenants pay the full amount of the rent, which is determined by whatever the market will bear.

PUBLIC HOUSING. Public housing complexes with low-cost units are typically found in large cities. This type of housing is designed for low-income families, senior citizens, and those with disabilities. The government builds public housing and rents it to those who cannot afford to pay the cost of private housing. The amount of rent paid is usually set as a percentage of the renter's monthly income. To qualify for public housing, a person cannot earn more than a certain amount, which can vary with each public housing building.

SUBSIDIZED HOUSING. In the case of **subsidized housing**, the government provides assistance payments to private housing owners. These payments help make it possible for families with very low incomes to live in safe, sanitary housing. Government money makes up the difference between what the tenants can afford to pay and what the rent would normally be. Families who live in subsidized housing must meet certain income guidelines. In many areas, the demand for subsidized housing is greater than the supply.

INSPECT AND COMPARE UNITS

Once you have a list of available units that interest you, the next step is to inquire about taking a look at them. Never rent an apartment or house you have not seen, and be sure you see the specific space that is available. Some landlords keep a well-maintained display unit to show prospective renters. Because it's not lived in, the display unit doesn't show signs of normal wear and tear as other units will. Discovering that your unit has cracked walls, peeling paint, or a badly stained carpet after you have rented it is an unpleasant surprise.

You may want to talk with some of the tenants who would be your neighbors. Ask them whether they feel the building is properly maintained and if they enjoy living there.

A good way to keep track of the various units you visit is to compile an inspection checklist. Make notes on the list for every apartment you inspect. Then compare the lists to see which units best meet your needs. In addition to cost and condition of the unit, here are some features to note on your list:

LIVING SPACE. Evaluate the overall layout of each unit you look at. Will your furniture fit? Is there enough storage space? Ask whether a copy of the floor plan is available. The floor plan shows the general layout of the unit and may include dimensions of each room. Comparing floor plans can help you determine whether there is enough living space to meet your needs. If a floor plan is not available, you may want to sketch your own or take pictures of each room.

How could making a checklist for all your needs, wants, and concerns help you in searching for an apartment?

FACILITIES. Does the complex provide facilities such as covered parking, laundry areas, a swimming pool, or a common storage area? Is there an extra fee for any of these facilities?

SAFETY AND SECURITY. If there is a main entrance to the building, is it kept locked at all times? Is there an intercom system for admitting visitors? Are entrances well lighted? Do apartment doors have deadbolt locks and are locks changed when tenants move out? Are there smoke detectors, a carbon monoxide detector, sprinkler systems, and clearly marked fire exits?

MAINTENANCE. Whom do the tenants contact if maintenance is needed? Does the landlord or building manager live on the premises? Are there provisions in the lease that state when the landlord or maintenance workers may enter the unit? Is there a policy on scheduling routine maintenance services?

INDIVIDUAL NEEDS. If you own a waterbed or have a pet, be sure to ask prospective landlords if either is permitted. You may also want to consider how accessible the building is for people with disabilities.

It may be difficult to find an apartment that meets all your requirements. Be realistic and reasonable when making your final decision. Prioritize your needs and wants to identify ones that are most important. Don't be afraid to ask to see a unit for a second time. You should feel satisfied that the unit you select meets as many of your requirements as possible.

Many newer apartment buildings are accessible to people with disabilities.

REVIEW RENTAL AGREEMENTS

Once you've found the place you want to rent, you may feel that there's nothing left to do but say, "I'll take it! When can I move in?" Actually, however, another important step remains. You and the landlord must come to an agreement about the terms of the rental. It's essential that you carefully review all the terms to be sure you understand them. Rental agreements vary widely but take three basic forms: verbal agreements, written agreements, and leases.

Verbal Agreement

A verbal agreement is reached through discussion between the landlord and the prospective tenant. The discussion should cover such things as rent payments, the date payments should be made, and maintenance and repair service. Remember, however, that a verbal agreement will not hold up in a court of law. Verbal agreements are not common. Most people realize that it's wiser to put a rental agreement in writing.

Written Agreement

A basic written agreement outlines certain provisions, such as rental cost. It allows a tenant to rent for an indefinite period of time on a month-to-month basis. This arrangement is a good alternative for renters who move frequently. Some written agreements state that a landlord may tell tenants to move out at any time. This would be a disadvantage for renters who want a feeling of security and stability. Landlords may also dislike the month-to-month agreement because it does not guarantee long-term occupancy of the unit.

Lease

A **lease** is the legal document a tenant signs when agreeing to rent housing for a specific period of time. It is the most binding type of rental agreement. A lease states the rights and duties of the landlord and the tenant. Many landlords require a one-year lease.

The lease should include the following details:

- Address and number of the unit.
- Date tenant will move in.
- List of contents if unit is furnished.
- Cost of unit per month, date monthly payment is due, and where to send the payment.

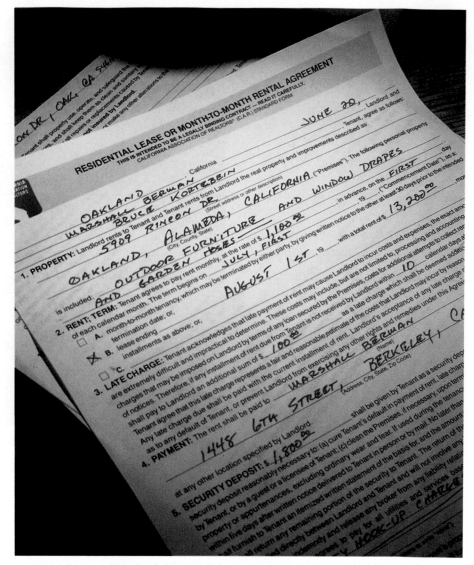

Make sure you understand the rules, rights, and restrictions specified in a lease before you sign it.

- Penalty for late payment.
- Amount of security deposit and conditions for refund.
- Amount of additional fees for such services as trash collection and indoor parking.
- Whether the landlord or the tenant pays for specific utilities, such as electricity.
- Length of time the lease is valid.
- Procedures for renewing the lease.

- Tenant's and landlord's rights to end the lease.
- Statement of responsibility for repairs and maintenance.
- Restrictions, if any. For example, some landlords do not allow pets. There may be regulations about window treatments, putting nails in walls, and painting.
- Landlord's action for tenant's failure to pay the rent.

You should read a lease carefully, even the small print. If you don't understand its terms, ask someone who is familiar with rental agreements to explain it to you. A legal aid service or renters' association in your community or state may be able to provide assistance. You should be able to take the lease with you to check it over. Beware of any landlord who tells you that you must sign the lease on the spot. If there are provisions in the lease you don't like, discuss them with the landlord before signing. Also, never sign a lease until all blanks have been filled in and all your concerns have been answered in writing.

Make sure that any damages you find in the apartment are recorded in the lease by the landlord before you move in. Otherwise, you may be held responsible for this damage when you move out. If you want additional guarantees, such as installation of appliances, have the landlord add them to the lease before you sign it.

The lease should state the options you would have if you had to move out before the lease expired. Some leases require the tenant to pay the rent for the duration of the lease, which can be expensive. A second option is to **assign** the lease, or transfer the lease to someone else. In this case, the original tenant is no longer responsible. A third option is for the tenant to **sublet**, or rent the unit to someone else. This differs from assigning a lease, since the original renter's name remains on the lease. The original renter is still responsible if the rent is not paid or if damage occurs.

The landlord should sign the lease at the same time you do. You should get a copy of the signed lease so that you have proof of the terms and conditions agreed to.

Tenant Rights and Responsibilities

By signing a lease or written agreement, a tenant agrees to assume certain responsibilities. He or she also has certain rights.

Tenants have the right to a safe, habitable rental unit. This means the landlord is responsible for such things as providing plumbing and heating systems that work, installing smoke detectors, and making necessary repairs. Tenants also have the right to privacy. The landlord cannot enter a unit unless proper notice is given or in the event of an emergency. In addition, a landlord cannot discriminate against a tenant because of race or color, national origin, religion, gender, family status, or disability.

Responsibilities of a tenant include abiding by the rules and regulations set forth in the lease. He or she promises to pay the rent on time and to take proper care of the rental space.

If a tenant fails to fulfill his or her responsibilities, a breach of contract exists. **Breach of contract** is a legal phrase for failure to meet all terms of a contract or agreement. Tenants who find that they cannot keep promises agreed to in a lease should talk to the landlord and try to work out the situation. If tenants breach the contract, landlords can **evict** them—legally require them to move out before the lease has expired—and bring a lawsuit against them. Landlords must provide tenants with written legal notice of the eviction. The notice must include the reason for the eviction and the amount of time tenants have to remove themselves and their belongings from the property.

It is the tenant's responsibility to report any repairs that need to be made to a rental unit. It is the landlord's responsibility to make sure the repairs are made in a timely manner.

RELATIONSHIP WITH THE LANDLORD

A tenant may or may not deal directly with the landlord of a rental unit. A landlord may hire a housing manager to handle daily business. Landlords and housing managers are in charge of managing repairs and maintaining building safety. Tenants must know whom to call in case of a problem, as well as who will be collecting the rent.

If repairs are needed on a rental unit, one of a tenant's rights is to receive a written statement discussing the repair, what will be done, and when it will be done. The statement should be signed and dated by the landlord or manager. A specific date should be noted by which all

repairs are to be made. If the repairs are not done, the landlord may be guilty of breach of contract.

Misunderstandings sometimes occur between landlords and tenants. In many cases, tenants bring these problems on themselves by not understanding the rights of landlords. For example, a lease may state that rent is due on the first of the month and that a late charge will be applied if the rent has not been paid by the tenth. Some tenants think this means they have a "grace period" and don't have to pay until the tenth. This is incorrect and can put the tenant at risk for eviction.

The security deposit is another common area of misunderstanding. Some tenants think they should automatically get the security deposit back. Actually, the landlord can pay all or part of the security deposit back within 45 days or keep it to repair any damage. Some people think it's all right not to pay the last month's rent if they have paid a security deposit. These are two separate aspects of a lease. Withholding rent is illegal at any point in the rental period.

When tenants move out they should always return the keys directly to the landlord or housing manager. Keys should never be left in the rental unit. In return, tenants should ask for a receipt for the returned keys.

RELATIONSHIPS WITH NEIGHBORS

Sharing a building with others requires tenants to respect everyone's rights. Tact and courtesy help create good relationships with other tenants in a rental complex. Tenants should clearly understand building policies about such concerns as assigned parking spaces, misplaced mail, loud music, and visitors.

Tenants often develop lasting friendships by meeting others in the building. In some complexes, tenants meet to discuss common concerns. They may also meet for social gatherings. When tenants respect one another, a rental complex can become like a small community, with tenants helping one another out.

When renting a single-family home, it is equally important to get to know and maintain good relationships with neighbors. Even though you don't own your home, you are a part of the neighborhood. You might join the neighborhood association or community neighborhood watch.

Sharing Housing

Several factors can influence a person's decision to share housing with others. Finances are a common reason, especially for those who live in large cities in which housing tends to be more expensive. A group of people in the same situation, such as a group of students sharing housing while at school, is another reason. Some of the advantages of sharing housing include:

- Lower housing costs for people who can't afford an apartment alone or who want to spend less on housing.
- A nicer or larger home than each person could afford to pay for individually.
- Companionship for those people who prefer the company of others to living alone.

Some shared-housing arrangements are more temporary than others. For example, if a friend or relative is having financial difficulties or needs a place to stay on short notice, people often offer a temporary place to live.

New kinds of shared housing partnerships are turning up all the time. One matches up senior citizens with people with disabilities. This enables both to have affordable housing and encourages sharing and companionship. These types of programs are available through government agencies and private organizations.

CHOOSING A ROOMMATE

"How do I go about choosing a roommate?" might be a question you are asking yourself. In some cases, roommates have known each

When choosing a roommate, be sure to express all of your concerns up front to avoid any potential problems in the future.

other through school, work, or just growing up in the same neighborhood. If you don't know someone who wants to share housing, you can still find a roommate with needs similar to yours. Sometimes the best roommates are people who meet only for the purpose of sharing a home. Here are some tips you might find helpful in choosing a roommate:

- Read the newspaper classified advertisements section titled "Roommate Wanted" or "Roommate Needed." College newspapers and workplace bulletin boards often have such ads as well.

- Talk with people you know about your need to find a roommate. Others often know of someone else in the same situation.

- Select a few people that seem to be potential roommates and set up a time to meet them and talk with them. (For safety reasons, don't meet a stranger alone.)

- Discuss your needs, wants, and living habits openly during the roommate interview. Talk about your schedules. How do you each spend your leisure time? Are you neat and tidy or is clutter okay? What other points need to be discussed?

When you are ready to make your decision about a roommate, look over your notes. Which person or persons seem to be the most compatible? If you're thinking of choosing someone you don't know well, ask for references from previous landlords and roommates. It's also a good idea to verify the person's place of employment.

Whatever is decided, be sure that all people involved are in mutual agreement about the living situation. Establishing some "ground rules" for household routines and shared expenses is essential for successful roommate relationships. Open communication and planning make getting along with roommates easier.

GETTING ALONG WITH A ROOMMATE

Roommate relationships can work out well when mutual respect is part of the relationship. People who treat their roommate as they want to be treated get along better. Roommates need to respect each other's schedules, privacy, personal items, and other needs.

As in any relationship, there will be ups and downs, but most problems can be solved with clear communication—talking things through and listening to one another. The following situation shows what can happen when roommates fail to respect each other and ignore basic lifestyle differences before sharing housing.

Why is it a good idea for roommates to agree in advance on household routines and responsibilities?

Marie and Lisa, both employees at a local restaurant, decided to share a one-bedroom apartment. Neither could afford the rent alone, so sharing made sense. Marie worked the night shift, and Lisa worked the day shift—the arrangement seemed as if it would work out well. However, they hadn't considered that their different schedules might cause problems.

Marie was quiet, liked to read, and kept to herself. She also slept during the day. Lisa, who worked during the day, liked to have her friends visit in the evening. Problems arose when Lisa and her friends were so loud that they disturbed the neighbors. Marie received most of the complaints as she arrived home from work in the morning. When Lisa's friends got hungry and raided the refrigerator, they ate most of Marie's weekly food supply. The problems continued for several weeks while Marie ignored the situation. Finally, Marie couldn't tolerate the living situation anymore and asked Lisa to move out.

What issues seem to be at the core of the problems between Marie and Lisa? If you are thinking that Lisa did not respect Marie's rights, and Marie failed to communicate with Lisa about the problems, you are correct. Consideration for others and effective communication are essential ingredients for any living arrangement.

Dividing Expenses

Roommates should discuss expenses and agree on a procedure for dividing them. For the rent payment and regular monthly utility bills, the easiest method is to divide the expenses equally among the people living in the unit. One exception might be the telephone bill, with each roommate paying for his or her own calls.

Some roommates contribute to a common fund from which groceries and other household supplies are purchased. Others purchase the needed items and split the bills as they come in. Would you prefer one of these or another method?

Allocating Household Responsibilities

When establishing household responsibilities, make a list of duties that need to be done and divide the jobs fairly between the roommates. There are several ways that this can be accomplished. Roommates might each have certain jobs they do consistently, such as one roommate shopping for food and cooking, and another cleaning and taking out the trash. Another possibility is to take turns performing tasks. Roommates should come to a mutual agreement about household responsibilities based on what might work best for them.

Feeling at Home

People need to do their homework before they can decide on renting housing. A variety of factors should be considered before finally selecting a place to live, including the type of housing, the services desired, and what monthly cost the budget allows. Knowing your rights and responsibilities as a tenant will help you enjoy your rental property. Respecting others' rights is a way to form and keep good relationships with the landlord and your neighbors. If you decide to share housing, clear and open communication is important to your relationship with your roommate. Think of the research and information-gathering involved in selecting rental housing as a challenge. The final reward is finding the right place to live—a space that becomes home.

Jeanne O'Neill

Resident Manager

Home ownership is usually high on the list of the goals for American families. Renting an apartment seems to be viewed as a second-best option. Why pay rent, people argue, and have nothing to show for it?

Yet there's another side to this issue of where to live. I may be in the minority, but after owning a home and then living in an apartment, I have to say that I prefer apartment living. When my two teenagers and I moved into an apartment, I quickly came to appreciate the conveniences it offered—no major repairs to make, no yardwork to do. Thanks to a conscientious building manager, our experience was a good one.

We'd lived here for about three years when the owner asked me to become the resident manager. I was swayed by the advantages. It would allow me to have time to volunteer at school, live rent-free, and earn a small salary to supplement my part-time job. My job in customer service had given me plenty of experience in dealing with people. I felt confident that I could do the job well.

Now, six years later, the owner of the building has moved to Florida. He may not be here, but I am his representative and I do live here. I experience the same environment and conditions as the other tenants.

Rapport is the real key to managing an apartment building. We have 18 units, and I try to maintain a good relationship with the residents of each one. It takes a lot of skill to monitor the building without disrupting the privacy of the residents or getting too caught up in their demands. We have one chronic complainer, for instance, who even expected me to change his lightbulbs!

"It takes a lot of skill to monitor the building without disrupting the privacy of the residents or getting too caught up in their demands."

I finally had to explain to him, very tactfully, where my responsibilities began and ended.

A description of this job would be hard to write. Basically, I look after the building as if it were my own. I can make minor repairs, but I hire professionals when a job is beyond my skills. I can fix a dripping faucet, but I don't tackle electrical problems. Since I'm also the bookkeeper and bill payer, I do my best to keep the owner's expenses down by hiring people who charge reasonable rates and by getting related work done at the same time.

I also monitor building safety—watching for fire hazards and taking steps to prevent burglaries, for instance. I've taken first-aid training in case of emergencies. There again, I know my limitations. I give each tenant a list of police, fire, and other emergency numbers. I try to keep an eye out for our older residents. If I see that their newspaper hasn't been

"I can make minor repairs, but I hire a professional when a job is beyond my skills."

picked up, I knock or call and ask how they're doing. It's an extra that people really appreciate and that I feel good about doing.

Apparently, the occupants of the building are pleased with the way it's operated. Our turnover rate in units is low, in spite of the inevitable rent increases. Now, my daughter and son-in-law rent a two-bedroom unit here. I'm happy because I can spend more time with my young grandson while doing a job that I enjoy and do well. The owner is pleased because he can enjoy his retirement. It's a win-win situation.

Career Profile

Resident managers collect rent payments and handle other finances of the property, ensuring that taxes, insurance premiums, payroll, and maintenance bills are paid on time. Managers also purchase supplies and equipment for the property, and arrange for repairs that cannot be handled by regular property maintenance staff. They monitor the performance of contractors, and investigate and resolve complaints from residents and tenants. Property managers must understand and comply with provisions of such legislation as the Americans with Disabilities Act and the Federal Fair Housing Amendment Act, as well as local fair housing laws. They must ensure that their renting and advertising practices aren't discriminatory and that the property itself complies with state and federal regulations.

Education
▶ A high school diploma with some experience in real estate is desirable.
▶ College graduates with degrees in business administration, accounting, finance, public administration, or related fields are preferred.

Skills Needed
▶ Good communication, computer, and financial skills, as well as an ability to deal tactfully with people.
▶ Knowledge of a building's mechanical systems is helpful.
▶ Skills in minor plumbing and carpentry repairs are desirable.

Career Outlook
▶ Employment of property managers is projected to increase as fast as the average for all occupations through the year 2008. Many job openings are expected to occur as property managers transfer to other occupations or leave the labor force.

Career Activities
1. Make a list of tasks that would need to be done when a tenant moves out of an apartment.
2. Your phone rings at 1:30 a.m. The tenant in 202 tells you water is dripping into her kitchen from the apartment above. You believe the resident of 302 is out of town. What would you do?

CHAPTER 10

Review & Activities

Chapter Summary

➤ Before looking for a rental unit, determine your needs and wants.

➤ There are many good sources of information about available rental housing.

➤ Three basic rental housing options include privately owned housing, public housing, and subsidized housing.

➤ Evaluating a rental unit involves checking its living space, services and facilities, and any special restrictions that apply to the unit.

➤ Leases are legal, binding documents that a prospective tenant should read and question carefully before signing.

➤ Tenants have certain rights, but also responsibilities to the landlord and to other tenants.

➤ Choosing a roommate carefully, setting ground rules, and communicating openly can help you successfully share housing.

Checking Your Understanding

1. Identify four factors to consider before searching for rental housing.

2. Name three ways to find out about available rental housing.

3. Describe the difference between public housing and subsidized housing.

4. Translate six common abbreviations found in newspaper rental advertisements.

5. What is a lease? How does it differ from a written or verbal agreement?

6. Identify two restrictions that may be found in leases.

7. What three options may be open to a tenant who decides to move out before the lease expires?

8. Identify two rights of tenants.

9. Explain at least three responsibilities renters have to the landlord and to other tenants.

10. What issues should roommates discuss before they move in together?

Thinking Critically

1. What mistakes do you think a person could make when looking for rental housing? What advice would you give to help a person avoid each mistake?

2. Whose rights do you think need more protection, the landlord or the tenant? Explain your answer.

3. Is subletting an apartment a good idea? What are the possible advantages? What are possible disadvantages?

4. If you had the opportunity, would you make a trade with a landlord, such as making basic repairs in exchange for the use of appliances? Why or why not? What services would you be willing to provide in exchange for conveniences?

5. Your roommate is out of a job and is having trouble contributing money to the monthly bills. Your landlord has been calling about the lateness of the rent. What would you do? Explain your answer.

Applications

1. Available Housing Research. Choose a community in a state where you would like to live. Using print or Internet resources, find out facts about the area, such as the population, climate, cost of living, average yearly income, etc. Find out what type of rental housing is available in the area and its cost. Based on your findings, do you still think you would like to live in that area? Explain your answer.

2. Rental Inspection Checklist. Assume that you are looking for an apartment. Develop a checklist that you might use to compare the characteristics of the various rental units you might look at. Share your checklist with the class.

3. Lease Clauses. Write two clauses, or additions, you would add to a standard rental lease. Explain whether you think the landlord would accept the clauses. Why or why not?

4. Roommate Interview. Make a list of questions you would like to ask a potential roommate. Interview a partner, with each asking questions from your lists. From your responses, do you think you would be compatible roommates? Why or why not?

5. Letter of Complaint. Imagine that you have a new neighbor in the apartment directly below you. He stays up late at night with the television or stereo very loud. He has noisy visitors at all hours of the night. You have seen him repeatedly leave his trash in the hallway. Write a letter to your landlord explaining your complaint.

BUILDING YOUR PORTFOLIO

You are in charge of planning a rental housing complex for your community. Write a proposal that indicates the following information:

➤ The area of the community in which you would build.

➤ The type of buildings (low-rise, high-rise, or town houses).

➤ The number of units.

➤ The sizes of the units (numbers and types of rooms).

➤ The rental price range.

➤ The age group of tenants you expect to attract (18-34, 35-64, or 65 and over).

➤ Special features, if any (such as laundry room, pool, or health club).

➤ Why you think the housing complex will be fully rented and financially successful, as well as an important addition to the community.

Buying a Home

CHAPTER OBJECTIVES

- ► Explain factors in determining an affordable price range for a home.

- ► Compare and contrast various ways to finance the purchase of a home.

- ► Evaluate the advantages and disadvantages of new and older homes.

- ► Identify four conditions that affect the resale value of a home.

- ► Summarize the steps in the home-buying process.

- ► Describe the protection provided by homeowner's insurance.

TERMS TO LEARN

- •adjustable rate mortgage

- •amortization

- •appraisal

- •closing

- •conventional mortgage

- •equity

- •escrow

- •graduated payment mortgage

- •homeowner's insurance

- •points

- •survey

Buying a home is a serious financial decision. For many people, a home is the most expensive item they will ever buy. As your housing needs change throughout your life, you will most likely buy and sell more than one home. Real estate agents, loan officers, home inspectors, and lawyers help guide many consumers through the home-buying process and help them become proud homeowners.

Financial Planning: The First Step

Before they began shopping for a home, Seth and Mandy Walsh sat at their kitchen table one evening and discussed their finances. They asked themselves such questions as: How much savings have we accumulated for the purchase of a home? What monthly payment will fit in our budget? How much debt do we currently have? The answers to these questions helped them estimate how much they could afford to pay for a home. By determining the price range they should focus on, buyers can make their search for a home more efficient.

Buying a home is a critical decision. Whether it's the first time you've purchased a home or the fifth time, it should involve much thought and investigation.

INCOME AND BUDGET

A prospective buyer's income is one of the factors that lenders look at carefully to determine how much money they are willing to lend. As you learned in Chapter 9, one commonly used formula states that the monthly mortgage (home loan) payment should be no more than about 28 percent of the household's monthly *gross income* (total earnings before taxes and other deductions are taken out of paychecks). For example, if a prospective buyer makes $2,000 a month, the monthly mortgage payment should not exceed $560. Knowing this, it is possible to calculate how much money the buyer may borrow, based on the length of the loan and the current interest rates.

While the 28 percent guideline is used by many lenders, prospective buyers should also consider their own situation. How much are they willing to spend on housing compared to other items in their budget? How much savings do they want to set aside each month for other financial goals? Questions like these can help families and individuals decide what price range they will be comfortable with.

SAVINGS

Another consideration is how much cash the buyer has for initial expenses. The largest of these is the *down payment*—the portion of the purchase price that must be paid in cash. The down payment and the mortgage work together. A standard down payment is 20 percent. As you can see from Figure 11-1, a larger down payment means a smaller mortgage.

Buyers also need enough cash on hand for the *closing costs* (fees due at the time of purchase). In addition, buyers must keep in mind the cash they may need for other expenses that arise when purchasing a home. Prospective buyers who qualify for a loan on the basis of their income, but do not have enough cash for the down payment or closing costs, must either postpone buying a home or set their sights on a home in a lower price range.

DEBT AND CREDIT HISTORY

Prospective buyers should also take a look at how much debt they currently have. If their credit card balances or other debts, such as car loans, are high, they might not be able to get as large a mortgage as they want. As a general guideline, lenders want to make sure that total monthly debt, including mortgage payments, is no more than about 36 percent of gross monthly income.

Lenders also look at prospective buyers' *credit history,* or their record of paying loans and bills. They want to know whether the buyer makes payments reliably and on time. This information is available to them from credit reporting agencies. Would-be buyers who have a history of skipped or late payments will find it difficult or impossible to get a mortgage loan until they improve their record.

FIGURE 11-1

Down Payment on a Home

Cost of Home	Down Payment	Amount of Loan
$72,000	10% = $7,200	$64,800
$72,000	20% = $14,400	$57,600

$\mathcal{U}$nderstanding Financing

To a first-time homebuyer, obtaining a mortgage loan is often one of the most unfamiliar and challenging aspects of the purchase. The process will be easier if buyers understand the basics of how mortgages work and the terminology involved.

MORTGAGE BASICS

A mortgage contract outlines the terms of a loan between the lender and the borrower. The lender agrees to lend a certain amount of money at a specified interest rate. The borrower agrees to repay the loan according to the terms of the contract, usually by making monthly payments. If the borrower fails to repay, the lender can take possession of the home.

As explained in Chapter 9, only part of each mortgage payment goes toward repaying the *principal*, or the

original loan amount. The rest is *interest*, the fee charged for borrowing the money. Early in the loan, most of each payment is made up of interest. With each payment, a larger portion goes toward principal and a smaller amount toward interest, as shown in Figure 11-2.

Each time a mortgage payment is made, the principal balance—the amount owed to the lender—is reduced. Finally, with the last payment, the principal of the loan has been completely repaid and has a balance of zero. This gradual elimination of the principal is called **amortization**.

As the loan principal is gradually paid off, the homeowner builds equity. **Equity** is the difference between the market value of a property—the price it might sell for—and the principal owed on the mortgage. You might think of it as the home's "cash value" at any given point. For example, suppose a home has a market value of $150,000. If the remaining principal on the mortgage is $100,000, the owner has $50,000 of equity.

In some cases, the monthly mortgage payment includes not only principal and interest, but also a portion of the yearly amount for property taxes and insurance. These are deposited in an *escrow account*. **Escrow** refers to money held in trust by a third party until a specified time. When the taxes and insurance payments are due, the lender withdraws money from the escrow account and makes the payments on behalf of the homeowner.

FIGURE 11-2

Principal and Interest

Sample mortgage: $75,900 for 30 years at 10% interest

Payment Number	Principal	Interest
1	$33.58	$632.50
48	49.60	616.48
180	148.33	517.75
240	244.04	422.04
300	401.52	264.56
360	654.06	5.45

TYPES OF MORTGAGES

There are several types of mortgages that buyers can choose from:

CONVENTIONAL MORTGAGE. This is the most common type of mortgage offered. With a **conventional mortgage**, the borrower pays a fixed interest rate for the length of the loan, usually 15 to 30 years. This interest rate, determined at the time the loan is made, remains the same for the length of the loan. A conventional mortgage is a particularly good choice when interest rates are relatively low.

Consumer Sense

Special Financing Arrangements

Although traditional types of financing work well for many people, alternatives do exist. Private lenders and government agencies offer special financing arrangements. These options are helpful to many prospective homeowners, including some who might not otherwise be able to buy a home.

- **FHA LOAN.** This is a loan insured by the Federal Housing Administration. The FHA guarantees the lender that the debt will be repaid. This encourages lenders to give mortgages to people who might not otherwise qualify. Borrowers can often obtain these loans with a smaller than usual down payment. FHA loans must be obtained from approved lenders, and both the buyer and the home must meet certain qualifications.
- **VA LOAN.** Buyers who serve or have served in the armed forces may qualify for a loan guaranteed by the Department of Veterans Affairs. VA loans offer several advantages. The most important one is that in most cases, no down payment is required.
- **RURAL HOUSING SERVICE.** The U.S. Department of Agriculture's Rural Housing Service offers help to low- or moderate-income families who buy homes in smaller communities. Assistance may come as a direct loan or as insurance for private-sector loans.
- **FIRST-TIME BUYER PROGRAMS.** A variety of government and private programs are designed to help people purchase their first home. Depending on the program, these loans may feature low down payments, easier qualifying, or both.

- **CONTRACT FOR DEED.** A *contract for deed* is an agreement between the buyer and seller that doesn't involve an institutional lender. The buyer pays for the property in installments that include the principal and interest, like a mortgage. The seller then turns over the deed, or legal title. Both parties save money; however, the contract must be carefully written, and read, so that its terms are definite and understood. Buyers should check that the seller has clear title to the property, and thus the right to sell it.
- **EQUITY-SHARING LOAN.** With an *equity-sharing loan*, the buyer partners with an outside party who uses the home as an investment. The investor pays part of the down payment and mortgage payments. When the home is sold, the investor shares proportionally in the equity (the cash remaining after the mortgage is paid off).

YOU THE CONSUMER . . .

You are in the market to buy a home. You have heard of first-time buyer programs and think you might qualify. What additional information would you want or need about such programs? How might you find the information? Identify as many ways as you can.

ADJUSTABLE RATE MORTGAGE. A loan in which the interest rate changes after a certain length of time, usually every one to five years, is called an **adjustable rate mortgage**. Changes in the rate depend on current rates in effect at the time; rates are not determined in advance. How much the rate changes depends on the terms of the mortgage. There is usually a limit on how high the rate can go. Often there is also a limit, or *cap*, on how much the rate can increase in any given year. As with conventional loans, adjustable rate loans are generally paid off over 15 to 30 years.

An advantage of an adjustable rate loan is that the interest rate usually starts out lower than the conventional mortgage rate. An adjustable rate mortgage might be a sound economic choice for people who are not planning to stay in a home for a long period of time. It might also be a good choice for people who are not earning enough to afford a conventional loan at the present time. When interest rates are high, buyers might choose an adjustable rate loan with the expectation that interest rates will come down in the future.

The disadvantage of an adjustable rate mortgage is that the rate changes are unpredictable. Buyers do not know in advance whether their monthly payments will increase or by how much.

GRADUATED PAYMENT MORTGAGE. An option that appeals to many first-time buyers is a **graduated payment mortgage**. With this type of loan, the payments start out low and increase in the later years of the loan, when people are likely to have more income. The advantage over adjustable rate loans is that buyers know in advance how much they will owe each month for the length of the loan.

SHOPPING FOR A MORTGAGE

Mortgage loans are available from many sources, including banks, savings and loans, credit unions, finance companies, and lenders that specialize in mortgages. Prospective buyers are wise to begin shopping for a loan even before they begin their home search. They can compare interest rates and other loan features by phone, on the Internet, or by visiting lenders in person.

Buyers should compare not only the interest rate of mortgage loans, but the number of points. **Points** refer to a one-time fee charged by lending companies to increase their yield on a mortgage. Each point generally equals 1 percent of the mortgage amount. For example, if a lender charges three points on a $50,000 loan, this adds $1,500 to the cost. Although points are usually paid in advance, sometimes they are added to the mortgage and paid out over the length of the loan. In some cases, no points are charged. The decision to charge points is up to the lender.

Meeting with a mortgage loan officer can be a wise first step in the home-buying process. The loan officer can determine a realistic price range for you based on an analysis of your finances.

PREQUALIFYING FOR A LOAN

Many lenders are willing to *prequalify* a buyer for a loan. This means that after obtaining information from the buyer, the lender provides a written estimate of how large a mortgage is likely to be approved. The buyer is not obligated to apply for a loan, and the lender does not promise to approve one. Still, prequalifying has several advantages for buyers. It lets them know how much they can expect to borrow and a maximum price range they can afford. Once the buyer finds a home to purchase, having a letter of prequalification can make it easier to negotiate with the seller. It can also save time in the final loan application process.

Deciding What to Look For

After determining an affordable price range and investigating loans, interested buyers should review the kinds of housing available. There are many housing sizes, styles, floor plans, and methods of construction to choose from.

Buyers must think about what size home would best suit their needs. First-time buyers often start with a smaller home so that their mortgage payments won't be too high. Buyers can't always purchase their "dream home." They can, however, set their sights on a comfortable home in a neighborhood they like with the possibility of moving up to another home later.

Even within a limited price range, there are many types of homes to choose from. By considering their needs and wants, buyers can determine the options that best suit them. Seth and Mandy, whom you read about earlier, discussed the features they wanted in a home. They decided they would rather have a small home in good condition than a larger one that needed a lot of work. They did, however, want two bedrooms so they could use one as an office. They also wanted a home with more privacy than the apartment building in which they currently lived. Seth and Mandy looked at conventional single-family houses, manufactured homes, and town house condominiums. By agreeing to consider more than one type of home, Seth and Mandy increased their chances of finding an affordable home that would fulfill their needs and wants.

NEW HOME OR OLD?

One of the choices home buyers face is whether they would prefer an existing home or a new one. To make this decision, it helps to understand the different ways in which new homes enter the housing market. Buyers should also be aware that both old and new homes have advantages and disadvantages.

New Home Options

People who are interested in becoming owners of a new home can do so using one of four basic approaches. These options vary in cost and in the amount of design freedom they offer the buyer.

DEVELOPMENT HOMES. New homes are often part of a housing development. A housing development is created when a developer, builder, or real estate company buys a large area of land and subdivides it into individual lots on which to build homes. Typically, prospective buyers are recruited before their homes are actually built. They are offered a limited number of similar home designs to choose from, which helps keep building costs down. Buyers make their choice by viewing model homes and reading information supplied by the developer. Once they select a lot, choose a home design, and sign a contract, their home is constructed.

HOMES BUILT ON SPEC. Some builders construct new homes on "spec," which is short for speculation. Construction begins before a specific buyer is found. The builder hopes that the finished home will appeal to buyers and be sold. An advantage for prospective buyers is that they can view the home before agreeing to purchase it. A disadvantage is that buyers have no say in the design and construction of the home.

STOCK HOME PLANS. Many books, magazines, and websites offer stock home plans—predesigned, preapproved plans that are ready for a builder to use. Buyers can select a design that will meet their needs and fit their budget. In most cases, they must also purchase a lot and hire a builder. Some buyers, however, choose to do some of the work themselves to save money.

CUSTOM-BUILT HOMES. People who desire a one-of-a-kind home may choose to have one designed for them by an architect. This option is the costliest but offers buyers the most freedom. They can specify the number of rooms, how they should be arranged, the exterior style, the materials to be used, and hundreds of other details.

Visiting a model home lets homebuyers get an accurate picture of what the home is like. However, people often have to rely on construction plans to envision what their new home will be like.

Buyers who decide to build a new home should find out how reliable the builder is. The local Better Business Bureau keeps records of complaints that have been filed against a building company. Also, the buyer can ask the builder for names and addresses of people who are living in homes built by the company. Buyers should contact these people and ask them if they are satisfied with the builder and the quality of work in their homes. While the home is under construction, buyers should visit the site often to check on construction progress.

Advantages of a New Home

The advantages of new homes are fairly obvious. They are clean and in good condition. They have modern kitchens and usually more than one bathroom. For some new homes, the purchase price may include major appliances, such as a dishwasher and built-in oven. Depending on the situation, the buyer may have freedom to choose exterior and interior materials and designs.

A new home is usually easier to finance than an older one. Sometimes buyers can arrange financing through the developer or builder. Some lenders may accept a smaller down payment for a new home than would be required for an older home.

Since the home is new and in good condition, maintenance costs should be minimal for the first several years. New homes usually cost less to heat because they have been built to follow the latest guidelines on saving energy established by the federal government. They generally have more insulation and more efficient heating systems than older homes.

A new home may also be protected by the Homeowner's Warranty Plan established by the National Association of Builders. This plan provides 10-year protection against defects in the quality of work or major construction flaws. Should such a problem occur, the builder must make the repairs at no cost to the owner.

Finally, a new home is often constructed in a neighborhood in which other new homes of equal quality are built. A new home's value will be similar to that of surrounding homes. Older homes in established neighborhoods vary widely in quality and value.

Disadvantages of a New Home

One disadvantage of buying a new home is that there are often unexpected costs. In some new housing, fixtures such as towel racks, shower doors, and storm windows are not provided. Other costs, such as staining and varnishing woodwork, may not be included in the price of the home. In many cases, the land on which the home is built is not landscaped with shrubs and trees. Fortunately, most builders seed or sod a lawn to make the home look more appealing and to prevent damage to the soil.

Advantages of an Older Home

Many people prefer preowned homes. The age of these homes ranges from several years to a century or more. Many older homes were built at a time when labor and material costs were lower than they are today. Because of this, buyers may get more space for their money and a home that is built of higher-quality materials. Some older homes provide up to 30 percent more living space than a new home of the same selling price.

Older homes often have greater individual character than new ones. Today, most new homes are built in large quantities by developers. Because of this, many of these development houses look alike. Many older homes, on the other hand, vary more. They may also utilize quality construction and materials, such as plaster walls and hardwood floors, that would be costly to duplicate today.

Older homes are usually in well-established neighborhoods. Permanent streets, curbs, and sidewalks have been installed. Landscaping throughout the neighborhood is generally well developed. The buyer can enjoy the beauty of mature trees and lawns.

Fixtures such as towel racks, shower doors, mirrors, and storage shelves aren't always provided in new homes. Is this an advantage to the buyer or a disadvantage?

Disadvantages of an Older Home

A major disadvantage of older homes is the possible costs of repairs. Wiring, plumbing, and interior and exterior surfaces all deteriorate with use and age. Repair or replacement can be expensive. Do-it-yourselfers who have the knowledge, interest, and time to do the necessary repairs can reduce these costs. It's a good idea to check with the seller to find out about any repairs that have recently been made.

An older home may also have structural problems. The basement or roof might leak, or the home may be infested with termites. There may be wall or foundation cracks that need extensive repair work. Many older homes have little or no insulation and inefficient heating and cooling systems. These can result in high utility bills. Depending on when the home was built and whether it has been updated, it may not meet today's high standards for energy efficiency.

Some older homes may actually present a health hazard. For exam-

ple, until the mid-1970s, lead-based paints were used in homes. Lead was used in plumbing systems until the late 1980s. Flaking or chipped lead-based paint and water from lead pipes can cause lead poisoning. Stripping walls and woodwork of lead-based paint and replacing lead water pipes is expensive. If the stripping is not done carefully, home-owners and their children will breathe in poisonous lead dust.

Lenders may require a larger down payment on an older home. However, a buyer may be able to negotiate with the seller to lower the price or change the terms of the deal. The price of a new home is often set by the builder and is usually firm.

Moving into an older home means inheriting whatever decorating features are there. These may or may not agree with the tastes of the buyer. In addition, such items as floor coverings, wallpaper, and paint may be worn out and in need of replacement. These are cosmetic changes, but they do add to costs.

Older homes often include unique features that are part of the architectural structure of the home. What details can you identify in this photo?

*U*nderstanding Resale Value

A home is a large investment. Because of this, buyers will want to choose a home that will increase in value and be easy to resell. Several factors can enhance or detract from a home's *resale value*—the value of the home when sold. The condition and size of the home is one such factor, as well as any special features it may

have, such as a pool, outside deck, or oversized family room. Other important factors in resale value include location, design, taxes and assessments, and improvements.

LOCATION. Many factors determine the value of a location. These include desirability as a residential area; its closeness to public transportation and shopping; the appearance, age, and condition of homes in the area; the quality of the school system; and the distance from industrial and commercial areas. Two homes of similar age and style will be priced differently if one is in a desirable residential location and the other in a deteriorating area.

The site and lot size can also affect the value. Attractive landscaping, a large lot with many trees, or a decorative fence will enhance a home's appearance and make it more valuable. This is part of what real estate agents call *curb appeal*, or the visual appeal of a home when viewed from the street.

DESIGN. Generally, it takes no more material to build an attractive dwelling than a poorly designed one of the same size. However, a good design may make a home more desirable and increase its value because people are willing to pay more for an attractive home. Some styles, too, are more acceptable than others in a particular setting. For example, in a neighborhood of stately old Victorian homes, a split-level home may be more difficult to sell, which can force the price down.

Lending agencies tend to be conservative in their judgement of architectural style. Since the value of a home is determined partly by the price a buyer will pay, the lender is apt to look with greatest favor on a design that has wide appeal.

TAXES AND ASSESSMENTS. Owners pay a yearly property tax to the city, town, or county. This tax is based on *assessed property valuation*, the value of the property as determined by the local government for tax purposes. This is not necessarily the same as market value, which is the amount the property might bring when sold. The market value can be higher or lower than the assessed value. Although the property tax does not add to the initial price of the home, it may affect the price an owner gets when the home is put up for sale. If property taxes are very high, the owner may have difficulty finding a buyer. An owner may have to accept a lower selling price in order to make the sale.

Assessments, too, add to the cost of owning a home and may affect the price. An assessment is a charge made to the homeowner by the local government. This might pay for the owner's share of the cost of an improvement such as widening a street or installing new sewers. Such assessments are more likely in older neighborhoods. Neighborhood association fees are charged to people living in some town houses and single-family homes in particular developments.

What features of the exterior of this home add to its curb appeal?

IMPROVEMENTS. For many reasons, the possibility of remodeling a home may enter into the decision to purchase it. Perhaps a prospective buyer has finally found the "perfect" home—except that the kitchen hasn't been updated since the 1950s. Another buyer may choose a home that can easily be adapted to meet future needs by converting the attic to extra bedrooms. Still another buyer may be looking for a run-down home that can be fixed up and sold at a profit.

Prospective buyers should be aware that remodeling projects affect the resale value in different ways. For example, owners who put in a new kitchen will probably get back about 80 to 95 percent of the cost of the improvement when they sell the home. The percentage depends on many factors: the style of the home, the cost of the home, and the location, among others. Return can be lower if unusual cabinets, colors, or layouts are used. Types of improvement projects that generally have a high rate of return

Weigh the benefits of making costly improvements to a home. What is a possible drawback to making improvements that exceed neighborhood housing values?

are major kitchen and bathroom remodeling, a family room addition, and new vinyl or aluminum siding.

Owners should be careful to keep improvements in line with neighborhood housing values. A remodeling project that will cause the price of the home to exceed the average in the area might not be a wise investment.

The Home-Buying Process

Buying a home is a long and complicated process. If you know the basic steps, however, the procedure becomes much easier. In addition, real estate agents and lenders are ready to help home buyers.

THE ROLE OF REAL ESTATE AGENTS

Some homeowners sell their homes directly to buyers. They advertise in newspapers or put up a "For Sale by Owner" sign in the front of their home. The buyer and seller negotiate the details of the purchase between themselves or with the assistance of their lawyers.

Most homeowners, however, prefer to sell their homes though a real estate agent. A good real estate agent screens prospective buyers and shows the home only to people who are truly interested in buying a home and can afford a home of that price.

When listing a home with a real estate agency, the owner agrees to pay the agent a *commission*, or fee, when the home is sold. The fee is usually from 5 to 7 percent of the selling price of the home. To cover this cost, the owner usually raises the asking price for the home. The buyer, then, actually pays the cost of the agent's fee.

Good real estate agents can also help buyers. Many people begin their search for a home by contacting a reputable real estate agent to find out what's available. An agent helps buyers determine which homes fit their needs and budgets. Effective real estate agents are familiar with local conditions. They can answer questions about neighborhoods, schools, churches, and shopping centers. They should also honestly discuss the advantages and drawbacks of various areas.

An agent can also help negotiate the price with the seller or the seller's agent. However, prospective buyers are often surprised to learn that the real estate agent they are working with may be obligated to protect the seller's interests. This is usually the case unless there is a written agreement that the agent will represent the buyer as a *buyer's agent*. If you're not sure who the agent represents, ask. In either case, the real estate agent who helps a buyer find a home usually shares the commission for selling the home with the seller's agent.

FINDING HOMES FOR SALE

Prospective buyers can learn about homes for sale in several ways. They can drive through neighborhoods they like and look for "For Sale" signs on front lawns. They can read newspaper ads and go to open houses on weekends to walk through homes that are for sale. However, the most efficient way to locate suitable homes for sale is to work with a real estate agent.

Real estate agents keep files with photographs and descriptions of the homes that are listed with them. By looking at these listings, buyers can see what homes are available. At many real estate offices today, buyers can view videotapes of homes or scan computer files. Most communities also have *multiple listing services,* an all-inclusive list of homes for sale in the area. This allows buyers to see homes listed by all real estate agencies that are part of the multiple listing pool.

Many real estate services are also available on the Internet. Online listings of properties for sale may include photos, descriptions, lists of amenities, maps, and agent contact information. Some services also offer "virtual tours" of homes for sale. These allow prospective buyers to see many different views of the home, almost as if they were walking through it. Using these types of services from the agent's office or their own homes can help buyers quickly narrow down their search.

How can a computer and an online service help prospective buyers narrow down their search for a home?

Affordable Alternatives

In addition to traditional ways of finding a home to purchase, other options are available to prospective buyers. These include auctions and urban homesteading.

AUCTIONS. When a homeowner cannot pay the mortgage on a home because of financial difficulties, the lender and the owner may put the home up for auction. In another typical situation, an elderly person who is moving to a retirement home may decide to auction off the home along with many home furnishings. In either case, the home then becomes the property of the highest bidder. Buyers can often acquire homes through auctions at relatively low prices.

URBAN HOMESTEADING. Urban homesteading is one solution to urban decay. In this program, people buy old or abandoned homes at very low prices. They agree to make repairs and live in the home for a specified period of time. The new owners often save money by doing their own carpentry, plumbing, and painting.

These homes can be a good investment. The owners can usually sell the homes for much more than the sum of the original buying price and repair costs. The city benefits by gaining a revitalized neighborhood.

EVALUATING HOMES

Buyers should look at as many homes as possible to get a good sense of the options available within their price range. They will probably look at many that don't measure up to their hopes. It takes time to fit people with the homes that are best suited to them.

When looking at homes, buyers should pay attention to the layout and the number and types of rooms in comparison to what is needed. These factors greatly affect a home's livability. Buyers should also be alert to possible trouble spots. Figure 11-3 shows some of the things to look for.

MAKING AN OFFER

When a buyer finds the right home, he or she can have a lawyer or the real estate agent draw up an *offer-to-purchase contract*. In this contract, the buyer bids for the home by offering a price to the seller. The offer-to-purchase contract includes a legal description of the property to be purchased. It also states the date on which the buyer proposes to assume ownership of the home and other details of the sale.

Along with the offer-to-purchase contract, the buyer submits a check for the *earnest money*. This is the deposit the buyer makes to show he or she is serious about buying the home.

The buyer may ask that the offer-to-purchase contract be worded with certain *contingencies*, or conditions that must be met in order for the sale to become final. For example, most contracts state that the offer is *contingent upon financing*. This means that the buyer agrees to buy the home only if he or she can qualify for an appropriate loan. Another common contingency is a satisfactory report from a certified home inspector. If the specified conditions are not met, the contract between buyer and seller is declared void. The earnest money is returned, and the seller puts the home on the market once again.

Keep in mind that the advertised price of the home is an *asking price*. Owners usually set an asking price that is somewhat higher than the price they actually expect to receive from the sale. Asking prices allow for bargaining.

The amount of bargaining and the final price depend on local economic conditions. Buyers often hear about a *buyer's market* or a *seller's market*. In a *buyer's market*, there are more homes for sale than there are buyers. This condition favors the buyer and pushes prices lower. The buyer can usually purchase the home for below the asking price. In a *seller's market*, there are more people who want to buy homes than there are homes for sale. This condition favors the seller. The buyer may have to meet or exceed the seller's asking price.

Current mortgage interest rates are also a factor in a buyer's or seller's market. If rates are high, people are not as likely to buy homes as when rates are low.

AGREEING TO PURCHASE

If the buyer and seller agree on a price, the offer is accepted. The seller signs the offer, which becomes a binding sales contract. The earnest money is deposited in an escrow account until all the conditions of the sale are finalized.

Once the seller has accepted the earnest money, he or she may not sell the home to someone else even if that person offers more money. If the buyer decides not to buy the home, the seller is allowed to keep the earnest money but is not required to. When the purchase is finalized, the earnest money becomes part of the down payment.

OBTAINING FINANCING

Now that there is a sales contract, the buyer is ready to apply for a mortgage loan. The buyer fills out an application form and provides the lender with information from the sales contract. The buyer must also make a final decision on the type of loan and the amount (depending on the size of the down payment). The lender provides the buyer with information about the loan terms and begins the process of finalizing the loan.

The lender may give the buyer a choice of when to "lock in" an interest rate. A buyer who thinks interest rates may go up in the near future would probably choose to accept the rate that is offered on the day of application. If the buyer thinks interest rates are on their way down, he or she may be able to wait a few days or weeks before locking in an interest rate.

HAVING THE HOME INSPECTED

Although buyers should examine a home carefully before making an offer to purchase it, professional inspections are also part of the home-buying process. Several types of inspections and tests can be involved. Some of them may be required by the lender or by state law; others are optional.

TERMITE INSPECTION. This is the most commonly required inspection. Most purchase contracts state that the seller pays for this inspection and for repairing any termite damage that is found.

Why do you think the deposit put down on a home is called "earnest money"?

FIGURE 11-3

A **VISUAL GUIDE TO...**

Finding the Trouble Spots

When buying a home, especially an older home, there are number of trouble spots you should check for. Many problems can be taken care of with little work or expense; other problems can be costly. If you are seriously considering a home that shows signs of trouble, consult a home inspector or other expert to determine the extent of the problem, possible remedies, and the estimated cost of repair.

ROOF

Ask the age of the roof. Signs of age and possible leaking include curling asphalt shingles, dry and deteriorating wood shakes, and cracked and broken tiles. Water spots on interior ceilings may be a sign of roof problems. Check with a roofing company about the life expectancy of a roof. Roof replacement can be expensive.

OUTSIDE WALLS

Look for blistered or peeling paint, which indicates that paint may have to be removed and new paint applied. On exterior brick walls, look for signs of mineral deposits and cracked or disintegrating mortar joints. These signs may indicate that the mortar needs to be replaced. Repairs can be expensive.

FOUNDATION AND GRADE LEVEL

Look for standing water or ground that slopes toward the foundation. These indicate improper drainage that can lead to uneven settling, foundation cracks, and basement leaks. Check the vertical distance between the ground and wood framing or siding. If there is little or no foundation showing, the wood is susceptible to damage from rot or insects.

INSIDE WALLS

Cracks in walls or ceilings may indicate structural defects or settling of the structure. Both conditions may be minor or serious. Stains on walls and ceilings may result from plumbing leaks, condensation, or missing gutters and flashing. Some repairs can be expensive.

FLOORS

Check for spots that squeak or bounce when you walk on them, or places in the floor that dip or sag. These factors may, but do not always, indicate defects such as sagging floor joists, insect damage, inadequate framing, or concealed fire damage. Repairs for this type of damage can be expensive.

INSULATION

Check under the attic floor and between rafters for insulation; try to learn its R-value. Remove a switch plate cover to check for insulation in exterior walls. Inadequate insulation means higher heating and cooling costs.

WIRING

Identify the age of the wiring. Adequate service includes a 3-wire, 220-volt, 100-ampere capacity. Signs of inadequate wiring include double or triple plugs in a receptacle; old knob-and-tube wiring visible in the attic or basement; use of extension cords; the need to disconnect one appliance in order to use another; the dimming of lights when a major appliance starts up.

Finding the Trouble Spots (Continued)

WATER HEATER

Check the capacity on the label to be sure the size is adequate for your family. Look for leaks and water on the floor around the unit. Most leaks are not repairable, requiring replacement of the water heater.

PLUMBING

Determine the material used for water supply pipes and their approximate age. Lead pipes are found in some older homes and may cause serious health hazards. Galvanized iron or steel pipes can eventually rust from inside, causing clogs and leaks. Flush each toilet to be sure the tank and bowl fill properly. Turn on the faucets to be sure the water pressure is adequate. Low pressure may indicate corroded pipes or problems with the water pump.

SEWAGE DISPOSAL

Ask whether there is a municipal sewage system or an underground septic system (see Chapter 13). If there is a septic system, ask where the underground tank and drain field are located. Also determine the tank size and the last time it was cleaned out.

BASEMENT

Look for signs of moisture (such as mineral deposits) on columns, walls, or floors; cracks in walls or floor; signs of insect infestation, such as cockroaches; and poor drainage around floor drains. Some repairs can be expensive.

FURNACE

Ask about the age of the furnace. Check for rust and cracks. An older furnace may not produce enough heat or may quit working during a period of intense cold. If you have doubts about the furnace, request a thorough inspection from a reputable service.

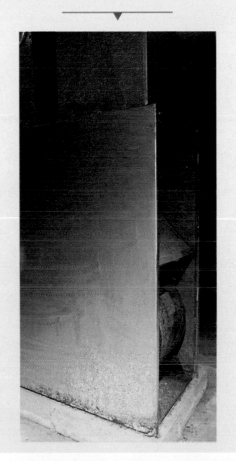

RADON TESTING. Radon is a naturally occurring gas that can pose a health hazard. If present in soil, it can seep into buildings though cracks in slabs or basement floors and walls. Tests can determine whether radon is collecting in the home at dangerous levels. If so, steps should be taken to reduce the levels. Usually this involves sealing cracks and installing a system of vent pipes and fans.

ASBESTOS INSPECTION. Asbestos was formerly used as a building material, most commonly for insulation, but is now known to be hazardous. An inspector should look for the presence of any asbestos—particularly damaged asbestos. If it's found, the seller must decide whether to hire an expert to repair the asbestos or to perform the costly process of removing it. (You will learn more about radon and asbestos in Chapter 26.)

LEAD TESTING. In older homes, the inspector should check for lead water pipes and lead-based paint.

GENERAL HOME INSPECTION. A certified inspector can check the home for structural soundness and ensure that plumbing, electrical, and heating systems are in good working order.

Inspections are well worth their cost to the buyer. It's far better to learn of any problems before the purchase than after. If problems are found, what happens next depends on how the sales contract is worded and the seriousness of the problems.

The seller may agree to take care of needed repairs, the buyer and seller may agree on a lower price, or the buyer may be able to legally back out of the purchase.

OBTAINING HOMEOWNER'S INSURANCE

One of the last steps in the home-buying process is obtaining insurance coverage for the home. **Homeowner's insurance** is a package of insurance protection for the home and its contents. A basic homeowner's insurance policy combines two types of insurance coverage: property insurance and liability insurance.

PROPERTY INSURANCE. This coverage protects the structure and its contents from damage or loss caused by a variety of hazards. These usually include fire, lightning, smoke, windstorms, hail, vandalism, and theft, among others. Depending on where you live, supplemental insurance against floods, earthquakes, and certain other hazards may be purchased in addition to the basic policy.

How much property insurance is needed? The lender will require an amount of coverage equal to the mortgage principal. Many experts recommend purchasing an amount between 80 and 100 percent of what it would cost to replace the structure if it were destroyed.

One way to test for radon is by using a canister. It is opened in the house and is left undisturbed for a specific period of time. The canister is then mailed to a testing lab.

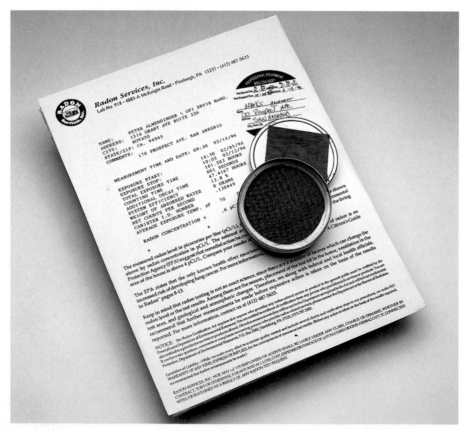

Besides insuring the structure itself, it's important to insure the personal property that it contains—furniture, electronic gear, clothing, and so on. An insurance agent can help the homeowner obtain an appropriate amount of personal property coverage. In addition, to help ensure that personal belongings will be replaced in the event of a disaster, it's a good idea to make a household inventory. The inventory should include a record of items owned, when they were purchased, and what they cost. Pictures or videotape of possessions are good proof of ownership, as well as cancelled checks and credit card receipts. The inventory should be stored in a safe place away from the home, such as in a safe deposit box.

PERSONAL LIABILITY COVERAGE. This type of coverage protects the homeowner in case of an accident. For example, if someone slips and falls on the property, homeowner's insurance would cover any medical expenses. If a tree on the property falls and causes damage to a neighbor's property, the insurance company will likely pay for the damages.

CLOSING THE DEAL

The last step in the home-buying process is the **closing**. This is a meeting at which legal papers are signed and money changes hands, finalizing the deal. The closing is typically attended by the seller, buyer, lender, and any real estate agents involved in the purchase. Sometimes buyers and sellers choose to have their lawyers attend as well.

The buyer must bring funds to pay the down payment and closing costs, generally in the form of a cashier's check. For this reason, the buyer is given a written list of the closing costs ahead of time. Closing costs that must be paid by the seller are also noted and are deducted from the amount the buyer must pay. Here are the typical costs a home buyer can expect to pay for at the time of the closing:

- Origination fee—a fee paid to the lender to process the mortgage application. Sometimes this fee includes the survey, appraisal, and title search.
- Cost of the **survey**—a check to determine the exact boundaries of the property.
- Cost of the **appraisal**—an estimate of the value of the property. This can determine the amount of the loan a lender will agree to.
- Cost of the title search—an investigation to make sure that the seller actually owns, or holds title to, the property and that no one else has any claims against the property.
- Fee for the credit report detailing the buyer's credit history.
- Points—the one-time service charge or fee sometimes charged by lending companies.

- Cost of any required home inspections (unless paid by the seller).
- Attorney's fee—money paid to a lawyer to represent the buyer during the home-buying process.

Once the buyer has signed the mortgage contract, the loan officer issues a check for the purchase price of the home and gives it to the seller. The seller signs the deed to the home, which transfers the title to the buyer. The lending institution generally holds the title to the home until the buyer pays off the mortgage in full.

Once they have taken possession of their new property, most home buyers experience a feeling of pride. They want to protect the large investment they have made by maintaining and improving the property. The potential home buyer has become a proud homeowner.

Even though they enter into a long-term financial commitment, most homeowners are excited about moving to a new home.

Shawna Holt

Model Home Designer

For me, completing the interior design work on model homes is a dream job. In college, I liked learning about architectural styles from the past, but modern interiors are really my favorite.

My employer is a developer who is currently working on his fourth development. This one is called Birchwood. The homes are lovely with lots of natural woodwork and open space. The model homes in Birchwood will help prospective buyers decide which home they want to build.

For each construction project I'm involved with, I might design the interiors for five or six different homes. I also help select colors for brick, siding, shutters, doors, and even the roof. It's vital that these homes have excellent curb appeal. Coordinating the colors is one important key to that success.

"I also help select colors for brick, siding, shutters, doors, and even the roof. It's vital that these homes have excellent curb appeal."

Inside the homes, my work usually involves developing the furniture plan and selecting wallcoverings, window treatments, floorcoverings, lighting, and accessories. I order these items and coordinate the installations. Generally, I have very little time to do all of this work and must complete the project within a reasonable budget.

The work is challenging, but it's exciting. I have developed a group of suppliers I can count on. I know which companies will deliver items, such as furniture, in a timely manner and at a reasonable cost. I'm not able to wait to have walls painted or window treatments installed. My installers are reliable and able to complete a job with little notice.

"I have to be very sensitive to trends and to which designs appeal to a broad audience."

I have to be very sensitive to trends and to which designs appeal to a broad audience. The designs I select must have current colors, fabrics, patterns, and styles. I can't overdo it though! The designs I select have to appeal to a variety of people with diverse taste. The developer I work for builds model homes in different states. That means I have to select designs that appeal to people in a specific region. For example, styles in Arizona are quite different than styles in Oregon. I have to know the style differences and where to purchase the furnishings.

To remain current in the field of interior design I attend national conferences and workshops. I also read several trade publications and monitor new building trends and technologies. Our computer system has been very important in managing our business transactions, records, and maintaining a product resource database.

Career Profile

A *model home designer* plans the space and selects the furniture, wallcoverings, floorcoverings, lighting, and accessories for model homes. They are responsible for ordering and coordinating the installation of the furnishings. The model home designer also coordinates the materials chosen for the homes' exteriors.

Education
▸ A bachelor's degree and Interior Design certification are preferred.
▸ Courses in interior design, principles of design, art, ergonomics, drawing, computer-aided drafting, architectural drawing, lighting, and business practices are helpful.

Skills Needed
▸ Creativity, a sense of design, and an eye for color are required.
▸ A sketching ability and computer-aided drafting skills are necessary.
▸ Visual and spatial aptitude are also important.
▸ Knowledge of the principles and practices of interior design is critical.
▸ Good interpersonal skills are required for working with architects, contractors, suppliers, installers, and other professionals.

Career Outlook
▸ The employment for interior designers is expected to grow faster than average for all occupations through the year 2008. However, the demand for interior designers who focus on model homes is relatively low. More information can be obtained from the American Society for Interior Designers.

Career Activities

1. Study a floor plan of a residence in your community. If this floor plan were a model home, what style would you select for furniture, wallcoverings, floorcoverings, lighting, and accessories?
2. Identify your design selections for a model home in a different region of the country and explain why you think these selections would be appropriate.

CHAPTER 11

Chapter Summary

➤ Financial planning helps buyers determine how much they can afford to pay for a home.

➤ Home buyers may finance their home by obtaining one of several types of mortgages.

➤ Potential buyers should decide what size, type, and age of home would best meet their needs.

➤ New-home options include development homes, homes built on spec, homes built from stock plans, and custom-built homes.

➤ Potential buyers should consider the advantages and disadvantages of new and older homes.

➤ The resale value of a home is an important consideration.

➤ During the home-buying process, buyers are assisted by real estate agents, lenders, lawyers, and home inspectors.

➤ Homeowner's insurance provides financial protection.

Checking Your Understanding

1. Explain how income and savings both help determine what price range homebuyers can afford.

2. What are the distinctions between a conventional mortgage, an adjustable rate mortgage, and a graduated payment mortgage?

3. How can a loan officer help buyers before they begin their home search?

4. Describe two advantages and two disadvantages of buying a new home.

5. What are two advantages and two disadvantages of buying an older home?

6. What are four factors that affect the resale value of a home?

7. Summarize the steps in the home-buying process.

8. Compare a buyer's market to a seller's market.

9. Identify four types of problems that a home should be inspected for.

Thinking Critically

1. Why might someone consider paying less than 28 percent of monthly gross income for housing? Under what circumstances might it be necessary to pay more than 28 percent?

2. When buying a home, would you rather make a down payment that is as large as possible or as small as possible? Explain your answer.

3. What might be the consequences if a homeowner chooses to insure only 40 percent of the home's replacement value?

4. What might cause a home purchase agreement to fall through before or during the closing? How can these situations be avoided?

Applications

1. **Home Buyer's Dictionary.** Use the information from this chapter (and other sources as needed) to make a list of at least ten terms related to home-buying and mortgages. Prepare a "Home Buyer's Dictionary" that clearly explains the terms.

2. **Comparing Mortgage Rates.** Use print or Internet resources to research current interest rates. Make one or more charts to show the following comparisons: conventional versus adjustable rate mortgages; 30-year versus 15-year mortgages; locally available rates versus average rates nationwide. Explain how you would use this information if you were buying a home.

3. **Calculating Mortgage Costs.** Suppose you are buying a $126,000 home. You are making a 20 percent down payment. What is the mortgage amount? If the lender is charging 1.5 points, how much do the points add to the cost of the mortgage?

4. **Comparing New and Older Homes.** Use real estate listings to find six homes for sale in the same community—three that are at least 30 years old and three that are newly built. Based on the asking price and the stated size, calculate the cost per square foot (or square meter). Are the results what you expected? Why or why not? How do you explain the differences or similarities in cost per square foot (or square meter)?

5. **Analyzing Resale Value.** Using detailed real estate listings, choose three different homes in the same price range (within $10,000). For each home, explain factors that you think might increase or decrease the resale value. Which home do you think has the best potential resale value? Why?

BUILDING YOUR PORTFOLIO

You have been hired by a local real estate agency to create a pamphlet called "A Beginner's Guide to the Home-Buying Process." First-time buyers will receive the pamphlet to be informed about basic home-buying procedures and to make them feel comfortable about the process. The real estate agency also hopes to promote its services.

Outline and briefly describe each of the steps in the home-buying process. Be sure to emphasize how the real estate agency is equipped to help new buyers. Design a cover and include any illustrations or pictures clipped from magazines that will help get the information across to new home buyers. Put the finished pamphlet in your portfolio for future reference.

Understanding Construction

$\mathcal{T}$he Basics of Construction

CHAPTER OBJECTIVES

- ► Analyze how a site influences the dwelling that sits on it.

- ► Describe the information shown on a building plan or blueprint.

- ► Describe major components of a home's basic structure.

- ► Evaluate materials used to finish the exterior of a home.

- ► Analyze factors to consider when selecting insulation, windows, and other components.

TERMS TO LEARN

- • cross ventilation
- • flashing
- • flue
- • footing
- • orientation
- • R value
- • topography
- • vapor barrier
- • veneer
- • windbreak

Imagine that you are preparing to build your dream home. You want everything to be perfect. How do you prevent that dream home from turning into a nightmare? Careful planning and learning as much as possible about home construction are the keys to avoiding costly mistakes. You can play an active part in building your dream house by starting with a solid foundation of knowledge.

Understanding Construction

A basic understanding of construction principles is useful even if you will never build a home. Knowing the basics of how homes are constructed can help you evaluate existing housing or tackle home maintenance tasks.

As you explore this chapter, you will discover the way a home is built, from planning the site and structure to laying the foundation, building the frame, and installing the insulation, roof, windows, and doors. You will see that many different materials, people, and technologies work together to build a home that will last a long time.

A home that ideally suits its owners requires selecting the best place to build, carefully choosing a design, and quality construction.

Planning the Housing Site

In building a new home, one of the first points to be considered is the housing site—the specific parcel of land on which the home will sit. Every housing site, or lot, has certain characteristics, such as size, shape, contour, and soil type. The natural conditions of the site can influence how the home is situated on the lot, as well as the style of architecture used. For example, a small lot won't have space for a large one-story home, but a two-story house would work well.

Local zoning laws also affect how the site is used. For example, they may specify the setback distances (how far the building must be from the property lines). Chapter 7 explains zoning laws in more detail.

Prospective home buyers and renters should think about how the characteristics of the site could influence the quality of life in the home. The site, and whether it has been used effectively, can either enhance a home or detract from it.

ANALYZING CHARACTERISTICS OF THE SITE

The topography of the land is one aspect of the site. **Topography** refers to the contour, or slope, of the land and its other physical features. A site might be flat and low-lying, or it might be sloped. Topography influences the housing style a person can choose when building a home. Sloping land might lend itself to a multilevel home, whereas such land might not be suitable for a long, rambling ranch style.

The characteristics of the ground on which the housing will rest affect planning, construction, and maintenance. Land that is flat, well drained, and free of rocks is generally the easiest and least expensive to build on. Not all sites are like that, however. Poorly drained soils may cause swampy yards, wet basements, sewage problems, and poor plant growth. In a cold climate, water trapped in poorly drained soils will freeze and expand, sometimes causing sidewalks, driveways, and foun-

Building a house on a hillside requires special plans to protect the land from erosion and keep the house on solid footing for years. What styles of houses are suited to hillsides and sloping land?

dations to crack and bulge. People shopping for land should visit the site while it is raining to check for drainage problems. Any special design or construction modifications required to counteract poor drainage will increase building costs.

PLANNING THE ORIENTATION

The **orientation** of a home is its position on the lot and the direction the home faces. Ideally, a home should be oriented so that residents can enjoy sunshine, gentle breezes, and the natural beauty of the housing site. The principles of good orientation apply to all types of housing. For instance, awareness of orientation can help a person choose one apartment unit over another.

What Influences DESIGN?

Adapting to the Lay of the Land

Adapting to a region is one housing trend that never goes out of style. Structural and design elements that respect an area's climate, soil, geography, and resources have influenced both historic and modern buildings.

- *Climate.* In coastal Louisiana, homes are often built up off the ground to avoid problems caused by high humidity and low terrain. A steeply pitched roof sheds the heavy rains the region is known for, while a deep porch protects the house beneath.

- *Resources.* The "big woods" of the north live on in some modern homes. Logs are fashionable accents for mantels, porches, and furnishings. Some luxury homes wear the facade of the pioneers' humble log cabin, although greatly refined.

- *Natural Disasters.* In earthquake-prone San Francisco, it's what inside that counts. Earthquake protection measures include bolting homes to their foundations, strengthening garage doors, reinforcing chimneys with steel, and installing plywood in crawl spaces. All help protect against the shearing forces of earthquakes.

Technological advances sometimes change the need for a design feature. High ceilings, which encourage air circulation, were once favored for cooling homes in warm climates. Today, air conditioning is common. When high ceilings are used today, it is for their design effect rather than any cooling benefit.

THINKING IT THROUGH

1. What environmental features affect the design of homes or any of their systems in your area?
2. Historically, how were home designs in your area adapted to the land?

Properly situating a house on the building site allows natural heating and cooling from shade, sunlight, and gentle breezes. *How could the porch protect the interior of this house in the summer?*

In regions with cold winters, exposure to the sun is especially important. The south and west sides of a dwelling receive the most sunlight. For this reason, rooms that are the center of family activity—usually the kitchen and the family room, living room, or great room—are best located on the south or west side. Such design features as large windows can combine with the orientation to make the interiors of rooms bright and sunny.

Homes also need some protection from the hot summer sun. An overhanging roof, or the use of awnings to provide shade, may help screen

A family room that faces south or west is a pleasant place to spend a winter day as the sun warms the room.

Using Sunlight Effectively

For natural warmth and light, homes need exposure to sunlight. Sunlight and fresh air help prevent dampness, mildew, and rot. A home oriented to receive maximum sunlight will need less artificial lighting. Also, the general placement and angle of a home can make a great difference in home energy use and conservation.

the direct rays of the sun. The roof overhang should project far enough to shield windows from the summer sun, yet allow the rays to penetrate windows in the winter, when the sun is low in the sky. Limiting sun exposure is especially important in hot climates.

Planning Effective Air Flow

As climates vary, so do the methods used to create air flow in housing. In warm climates, a dwelling should be oriented so that it takes advantage of pleasant breezes. Ideally, natural **cross ventilation**, or the air flow created when air travels in one side of the home and out another, should be a significant factor when building any home. Windows are the major means for providing cross ventilation. Cross ventilation is a natural way to keep a home cool during warm weather.

In areas with cold winters, the home should be protected from strong, cold winds. As few windows as possible should face north. A garage could be placed on the north side of the home to shelter the home from winds.

In both hot and cold climates, the natural elevation of the housing site may influence the effect of winds. A

A line of trees or shrubs is an excellent way to shelter a house from cold winds. If planting trees or shrubs along the north side of a home is not possible, what other feature could provide protection?

home on a hilltop is more likely to be exposed to strong winds than one nestled in a valley. This can be an advantage in a warm climate and a disadvantage during winter months in a cold climate.

Something that protects a housing site from strong winds is called a **windbreak**. Rows of trees and shrubs are often planted around isolated homes to act as windbreaks. Walls and fences may also be used for this purpose. In cold climates, some people even build a home in the side of a hill to shield it from the winter wind.

Choosing the Best View

Whenever possible, homes should be oriented to take advantage of desirable views. Large windows can help. A porch or patio will also add to the residents' enjoyment of attractive surroundings.

Sites with an unattractive view may be creatively changed to hide the undesirable features. For example, if a home is next to a commercial parking lot, building a fence or planting trees can camouflage an unattractive view.

Architectural Drawings

Once the building site is chosen, the owners select a floor plan that best suits their needs and the site's topography. (Guidelines for evaluating a floor plan are discussed in

Chapter 7.) Architectural and construction drawings—sometimes referred to as *prints* or *blueprints*—are drawn up or selected. They are thoroughly checked to be sure they meet

FIGURE 12-1

Common Architectural Symbols

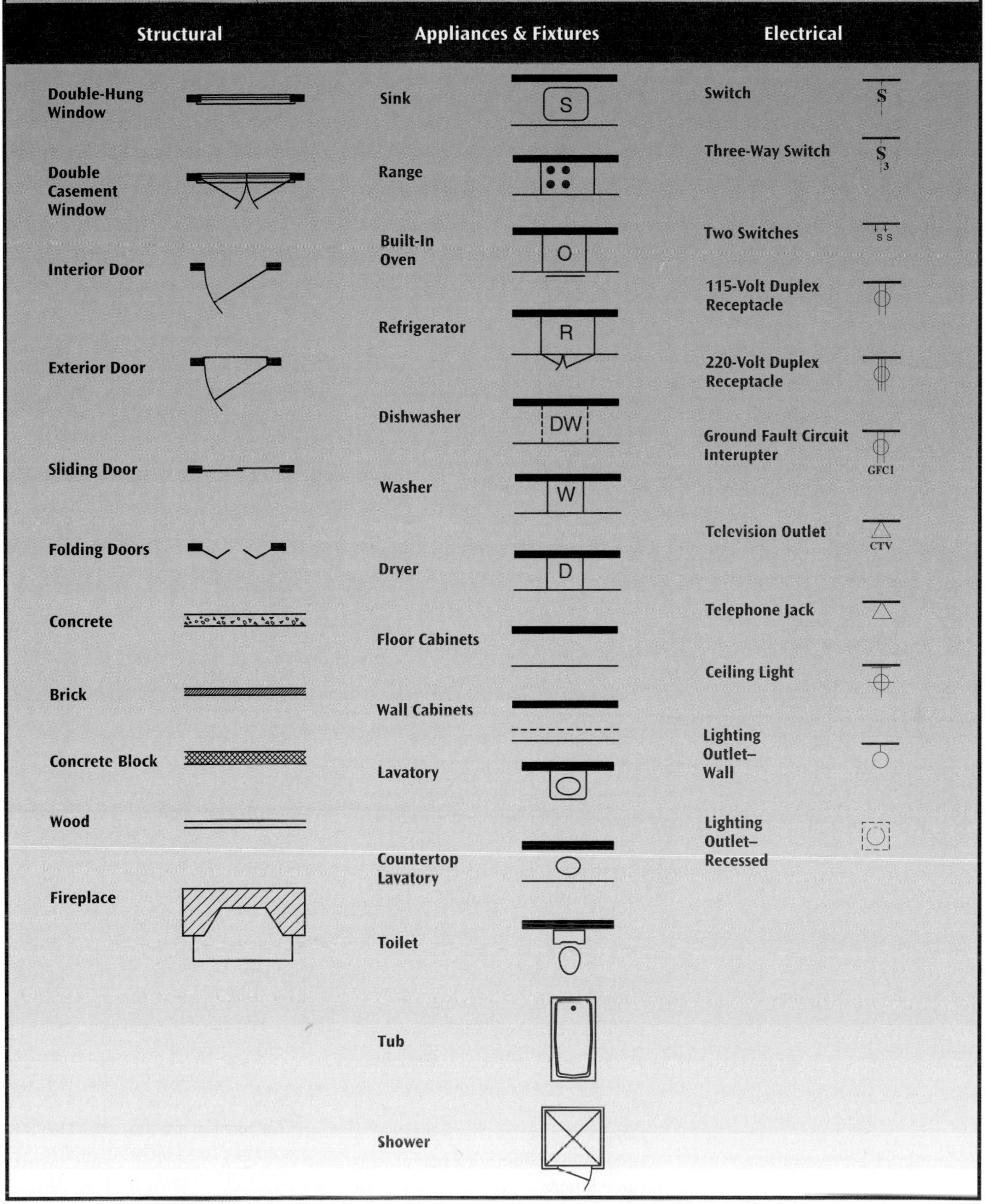

Structural
Double-Hung Window
Double Casement Window
Interior Door
Exterior Door
Sliding Door
Folding Doors
Concrete
Brick
Concrete Block
Wood
Fireplace
Appliances & Fixtures
Sink
S
Range
Built-In Oven
O
Refrigerator
R
Dishwasher
DW
Washer
W
Dryer
D
Floor Cabinets
Wall Cabinets
Lavatory
Countertop Lavatory
Toilet
Tub
Shower
Electrical
Switch
S
Three-Way Switch
S 3
Two Switches
S S
115-Volt Duplex Receptacle
220-Volt Duplex Receptacle
Ground Fault Circuit Interupter
GFCI
Television Outlet
CTV
Telephone Jack
Ceiling Light
Lighting Outlet–Wall
Lighting Outlet–Recessed

all building codes and regulations. Building codes specify construction techniques and materials to ensure that the home is safe and well built.

Architectural drawings are technical drawings that provide information about the appearance and construction of a building. There are several kinds of architectural drawings. The most common are floor plans and elevations. Other drawings give information about the foundation, framing, and other aspects of construction.

FLOOR PLANS. These show the layout of rooms as if viewed from above. Floor plans include a lot of information because builders use them as a guide for constructing the home. A basic floor plan includes information about the size and location of walls, doors, windows, stairs, closets, fireplaces, cabinets, and major appliances. From the basic floor plan, specialized floor plans are developed. For example, there may be separate floor plans for the electrical, plumbing, and heating and air conditioning systems. If all of the information were placed on one floor plan, the drawing would be too crowded and hard to read.

ELEVATIONS. Elevation drawings show vertical surfaces as if viewed by someone standing on the ground or on the floor. Exterior elevations show the front, back, or sides of the structure. Interior elevations show interior walls.

Many architects use computer-aided design (CAD) programs to help them generate drawings. With a CAD program, architects can make drawings on a computer, change the plans as needed, and print multiple sets of the finished plans in a fraction of the time it would take to draw them by hand. Several sets of prints are usually required for the construction of a home. One set of prints is filed with the local government. The builder also needs prints at the job site.

Since there's only a limited amount of space on a print, it's impossible to show all the information needed. Symbols are used as a type of building shorthand. Common architectural symbols are shown in Figure 12-1 on page 257.

The Basic Structure

Once plans are drawn up or selected, the process of turning the architect's ideas into a reality can begin. The builder transforms a set of plans on paper into a solid structure that will provide shelter, and more, for years to come. The process begins with the home's underlying structure: the foundation and frame.

This chapter explains how a home is built using *conventional construction*. In other words, materials will be measured, cut, and assembled piece by piece on the job site. Chapter 3 describes the options of a systems-built home or a manufactured home.

THE FOUNDATION

The foundation is the underlying base and support of a home. It consists of the footing and the foundation walls. The **footing** is a continuous concrete base that supports the foundation walls below ground level. Foundation walls extend from the footing to the floor and support the load of the structure above.

The type and size of footings should be suitable for the climate of a particular area. Footings may be located from 1 to 6 feet (0.3 to 1.8 m) beneath ground level. They should be placed on solid, undisturbed soil below the *frost line*—the depth to which frost penetrates soil in that climate. If footings are placed above the frost line, the soil under them could freeze and expand, possibly causing the foundation to crack. Homes built in areas prone to natural disasters, such as earthquakes, must follow stricter building codes. This may include placing foundations on flexible and reinforced moorings that absorb the wave of the earthquake.

There are three types of foundation construction. Homes may be built with a basement, a crawl space, or a slab foundation.

Home with a Basement

After the exterior dimensions of a home with a basement have been staked out, the earth is excavated down to the proper level, often about 7 feet (2.1 m). Once the excavation is dug, the footing is poured for the perimeter of the building. The footing is generally 12 inches (30 cm) thick and 24 inches (60 cm) wide. Other footings are also poured to serve as a base for interior columns that help support the floors.

Most foundation walls are made from poured concrete or concrete block. They are built upon the footings and form the walls of the basement. The foundation walls are generally 10 to 12 inches (25 to 30 cm) thick and about 8 feet (2.4 m) in height. They extend above the ground level 4 to 12 inches (10 to 30 cm) to protect the frame structure of

the home from soil moisture and insects. The concrete floor of the basement is poured at a later time after parts of the plumbing and possibly heating systems are installed.

Foam plastic inserts can be placed inside the concrete blocks as the basement walls are being constructed. The inserts provide additional insulation to improve the energy efficiency of the home. Pre-insulated concrete blocks are also available.

Waterproofing the foundation is the next step to seal the foundation against damage by moisture. Waterproofing material is applied on the outer face of the foundation wall starting just below the final ground level down to, as well as on top of, the footing. In addition, to reduce the danger of water damage, many builders customarily place drain pipes around the footings and,

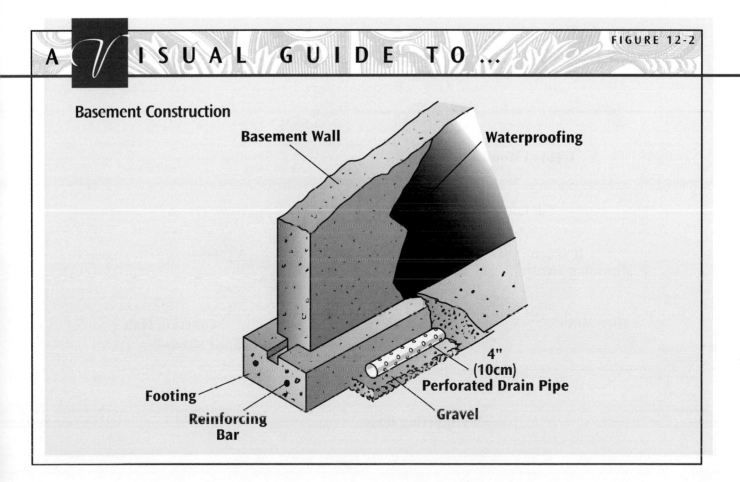

FIGURE 12-2

A VISUAL GUIDE TO...

Basement Construction

Basement Wall

Waterproofing

4" (10cm) Perforated Drain Pipe

Gravel

Footing

Reinforcing Bar

in some areas, under the concrete floor. The pipe collects any water and directs it to nearby drains. Figure 12-2 shows these waterproofing features.

In parts of the country where termites are common, a termite guard should also be installed. A *termite guard* is a metal shield fastened on the top of the foundation walls before framing begins. This shield prevents termites from getting into the wood structure of a building.

Home with a Crawl Space

A home with a *crawl space* has about 18 to 24 inches (45 to 60 cm) of space between the ground and the bottom floor of the home. That means the foundation walls are much shorter for a home with a crawl space than for one with a basement. The crawl space leaves just enough room to crawl under the structure to reach electrical wiring and parts of the plumbing and heating systems.

The floor of a crawl space may be soil or gravel. It is covered with a plastic material that runs up onto the foundation walls to prevent

moisture from rotting the wood floor above it.

Home with a Slab

A home with a slab foundation has no basement or crawl space. The concrete footing and short foundation walls under the home hold up a slab—a poured layer of concrete about 4 inches (10 cm) thick. In warm climates where frost is not a problem, a thickened edge slab—which combines the footing and concrete slab into one unit—may be used. Figure 12-3 shows a slab foundation.

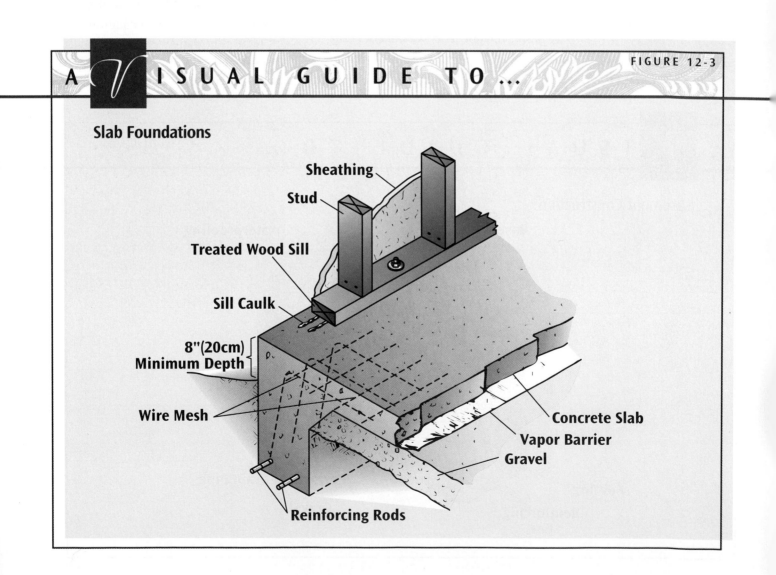

A VISUAL GUIDE TO...

FIGURE 12-3

Slab Foundations

Sheathing

Stud

Treated Wood Sill

Sill Caulk

8"(20cm) Minimum Depth

Wire Mesh

Reinforcing Rods

Concrete Slab

Vapor Barrier

Gravel

Parts of the plumbing and heating systems are often put in place before the slab is poured. A system of welded wire rods—called *rebarring*—is also put in place before the concrete slab is poured. These rods reinforce the concrete and prevent cracking.

THE FRAME

The frame is the skeleton of the housing structure. It supports the wall and roof materials and distributes their weight to the foundation. If the frame is not constructed properly, the structure may sag or even collapse.

Most home framing is done with wood or new wood technology products. However, builders are increasingly using alternative building materials, such as steel. Nearly every wood-framing component has its steel counterpart. Steel framing is priced about the same as wood, and the quality control is much tighter. Steel can withstand termites, fire, and severe weather and will not shrink or settle over time. Steel framing also can be designed to withstand earthquakes and hurricanes. Steel framing can be used for framing floors, walls, and roofs. Chapter 3 describes other materials that are used for framing homes, such as engineered wood products and plastic.

THE FLOOR FRAME. The first piece of the floor frame attached to the foundation wall is the sill plate. The floor frame is built on top of the sill plate. When a second or third floor is added, those floors are built on top of wall frames. The floor frame consists of girders, joists, and subflooring. Standard floors are built to hold a uniform load of 100 pounds per square foot. In areas where homes may need to withstand natural disaster, floors are designed to hold 185 pounds per square foot to help minimize damage. See Figure 12-4 for more information on floor frames.

THE WALL FRAME. The wall frame is built on top of the floor frame. The wall frame supports the ceiling, upper floors, and roof and serves as a nailing base for wall finishes. It includes the vertical studs and horizontal plates, as well as headers above doors and windows. Figure 12-5 shows and explains these components of the wall frame.

Standard construction practices use 2 x 4 wood studs placed every 16 inches (40 cm). If steel framing members or the deeper 2 x 6 wood studs are used, the spacing can be increased to 24 inches (60 cm). With the high cost of lumber, this practice reduces building costs.

Some interior walls support the floors and roof above, in addition to separating rooms. These interior walls are known as *load-bearing walls*. Homeowners will want to keep this in mind if they are planning to remodel, especially when changing the size or shape of a room. A load-bearing interior wall should never be removed unless a beam is put up to take its place. Otherwise the upper floor or roof will lack sufficient support. On the other hand, a *nonbearing wall* does not support any weight from the structure and it may be removed.

THE CEILING AND ROOF FRAMES. The roof frame consists of a series of rafters that support the weight of the roof. Carpenters nail the bottom outer end of the rafters to the top of the outside walls. If steel framing is used, joints are fastened with screws rather than nails.

The slope of the rafters establishes the roof pitch, the angle of the roof. In general, the steeper the slope of a roof, the less likely it is to leak. On most roofs the rafters extend past the edge of the exterior wall to provide an overhang, which prevents water from running down the walls and also shades the home. See Figure 12-6 for more information on ceiling and roof framing.

FIGURE 12-4

A VISUAL GUIDE TO...

Floor Framing

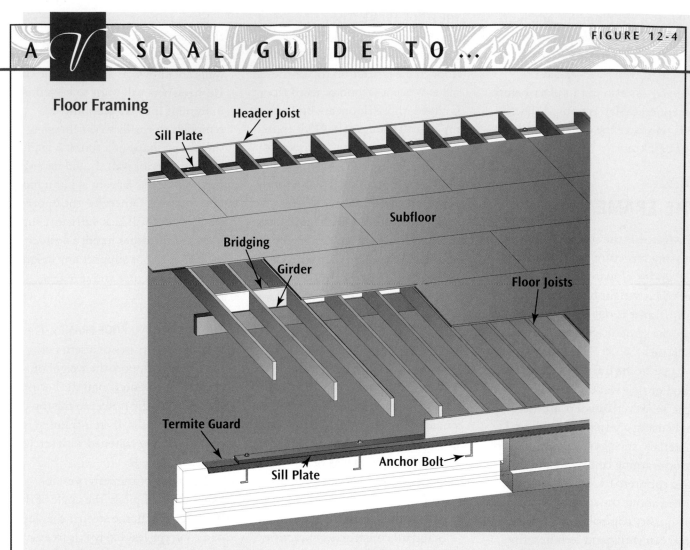

Header Joist

Sill Plate

Subfloor

Bridging

Girder

Floor Joists

Termite Guard

Sill Plate

Anchor Bolt

TERMITE GUARD

A sill sealer (strip of insulation) and sometimes a *termite guard* are placed on top of the foundation wall.

SILL PLATE

The first piece of lumber, called a *sill plate*, is bolted to the foundation wall with galvanized steel *anchor bolts*. (Anchor bolts are set about 6 ft. (1.8 m) apart into the concrete of the foundation walls before the concrete hardens.)

FLOOR JOISTS

Floor joists are attached to the sill plate and support the flooring.

BAND JOISTS

The ends of the floor joists are nailed to the *band joists* (also called *rim joists*).

GIRDERS

Girders—major support beams—help support the floor joists. A girder is made of wood or steel and placed at right angles to the floor joists.

BRIDGING

Bridging consists of wood or metal braces, either horizontal or criss-crossed, nailed tightly to the joists. Bridging distributes the load from one point over several joists, making them all work together. (If floors squeak, it often means that bridging is not nailed tightly or is missing entirely.)

SUBFLOOR

The floor frame is covered by the *subfloor*—rough flooring made of plywood sheets or other panel stock or tongue-and-groove boards. Subflooring is nailed directly to the floor joists to hold them in line.

FIGURE 12-5

A VISUAL GUIDE TO...

Wall Framing

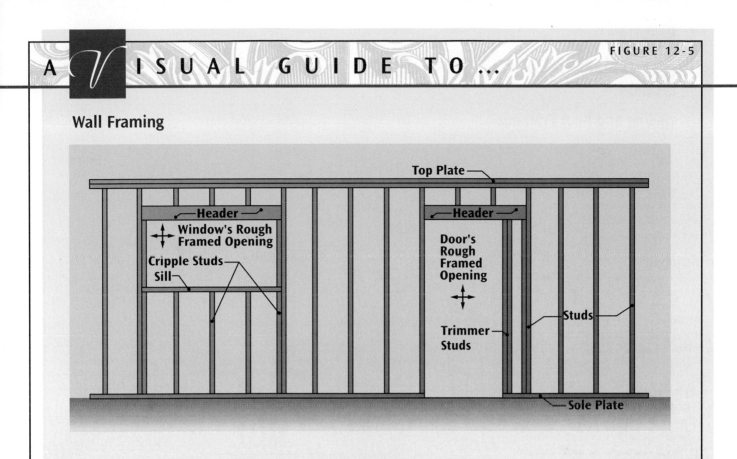

STUD

A *stud* is a vertical wall framing member. Wood studs are generally spaced every 16 inches (40 cm). If larger wood members or steel framing is used, walls may be framed at 16 or 24 inches (40 or 60 cm).

PLATES

Studs are attached at the top and bottom to horizontal members called *plates*. A double top plate consists of two lapped pieces of lumber spiked together.

HEADER

The *header*, or lintel, supports the load above a door or window opening.

Finishing the Exterior

Once the basic structure and frame have been built, work on the exterior of the home begins. The care that is taken in finishing the exterior, and the materials that are used, will greatly affect the home's appearance and the safety and comfort of the occupants.

THE WALLS

The rough finish and final finish of exterior walls are important for the home to be fire-resistant, waterproof, and energy-efficient. Various materials are used.

FIGURE 12-6

A VISUAL GUIDE TO...

Ceiling and Roof Framing

CEILING JOISTS
Ceiling joists support the ceiling and often act as floor joists for second floors and attic floors. They also support the bottom ends of the rafters.

RAFTERS
Rafters support the roof. They extend from the exterior walls to the ridge.

RIDGE
The *ridge* is the horizontal beam at which the two slopes of the roof meet. It is the highest point of the roof frame.

ROOF TRUSS
A *roof truss* combines a joist, rafters, and supports in one preassembled unit. Trusses are assembled at a factory and delivered to the job site, where they are attached directly to the top plate.

OVERHANG
Rafters or roof trusses often extend past the edge of the exterior wall to provide an *overhang*.

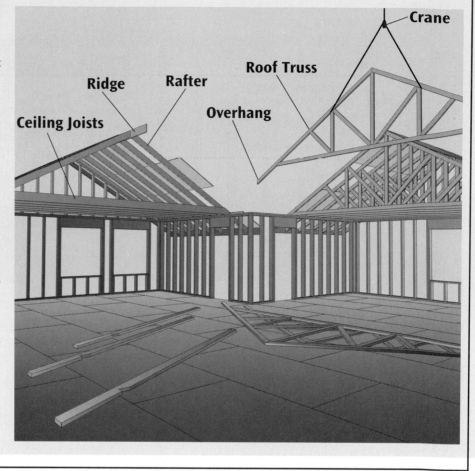

The Rough Finish

Rough boarding, also called *sheathing*, is applied to the outside of the roof and wall framing. It usually is in the form of 4 ft. x 8 ft. (1.2 m x 2.4 m) panels. Sheathing is generally moisture-resistant and helps brace the frame against the wind by joining the floor framing and studs.

Sheathing can consist of plywood, foam, or *oriented strand board (OSB)*. OSB is a product made from strands of wood fibers that are bonded together with water-resistant or waterproof adhesives.

After the sheathing is up, builders usually wrap the home with a heavy waterproof material. This creates a protective envelope that keeps out water and moisture. Wrapping the home also helps reduce heat loss by keeping insulation dry and closing the small cracks and holes in the rough boarding to keep out wind.

Once a house is framed, the sheathing is applied to the outside face of the walls and roof. A waterproof barrier provides further protection. How does the waterproof barrier also reduce heat loss from the home?

The Final Finish

Since exterior wall coverings have a tremendous impact on the appearance and overall maintenance of a home, homeowners should select them with care. The most common materials are wood, aluminum, and vinyl. Masonry siding materials are also used. The choice depends on the area's climate and the preference and budget of the homeowners.

WOOD AND OSB SIDING. Wood is a commonly used siding material. It's strong, a good insulator, easy to assemble, and suitable for a wide variety of exterior styles. Wood siding is milled from cedar, redwood, pine, or cypress. One side is smooth and the other rough. Wood siding may be made into clapboards, vertical boarding, or horizontal boarding. *Clapboards* (KLA-buhrds) are narrow overlapping boards that are thicker on one edge than the other. They are more weatherproof than vertical and horizontal boarding, which are applied without overlapping.

OSB siding is a popular alternative to the high cost of wood. It is available in a variety of styles. Plywood siding is another economical type of wood siding that comes in a variety of textures.

MANUFACTURED SIDING. Siding is also made from materials other than wood.

- Siding made of aluminum or steel is durable and resists weather and

"Curb appeal" is what builders and real estate agents call a home with an attractive exterior appearance. One way to achieve that all important first impression is with quality siding. What products could a homeowner choose for siding a house other than wood?

corrosion. Because of metal's reflective qualities, this type of siding helps lower heating and cooling costs. Aluminum does dent, and it may conduct electricity. Steel, on the other hand, is dent-resistant. It is one of the most durable of all prefinished siding materials.

- Vinyl siding is also fairly durable and requires no maintenance. It is less likely to dent and doesn't conduct electricity. However, it is brittle and more likely to crack or break under extreme weather conditions. Although vinyl and aluminum can suit many geographic locations, you may not want to use them if you live in areas where hailstorms are common.

- Fiberglass siding looks like wood shingles and comes in a variety of natural wood colors. It does not need to be finished or painted.

MASONRY SIDING. Masonry products include brick, clay, tile, stone, concrete block, and stucco. In some situations, masonry products are used to construct the entire exterior wall. In other situations, a **veneer**—an overlay material that provides an ornamental finish—is used to create the look of a masonry wall. Masonry veneer walls are used in many areas of the country. Masonry construction is often more expensive than wood construction. However, it is usually less expensive to maintain and lasts longer.

Paints and Finishes

Siding made of wood products must be protected against the elements. Wood and plywood siding can be either painted or stained and sealed, while OSB siding must be painted.

Primer should be applied to exterior wood before painting. A coat of primer serves as a sealer and prevents paint waste that occurs from untreated wood absorbing the paint.

For paint, the choice is between water-based and oil-based. Good water-based paints expand with changing temperatures without cracking the paint film. They are easy to spread, dry quickly, and have good color retention.

Oil-based paints are harder to spread and take longer than water-based paints to dry. They can, however, hide imperfections better than many water-based paints and offer good stain resistance. Many oil-based paints are harmful to the environment because they are a major source of *volatile organic compounds* (VOCs). VOCs combine with sunlight to form ground-level ozone, an ingredient in smog. Paint manufacturers are developing hypoallergenic paints, sealers, and finishes that are durable, much safer, and VOC-free.

THE ROOF

Since the roof protects the home's interior from the weather, roofing materials must be strong and weatherproof. Light-colored roofs are popular in hot climates because they help keep the home cool. By reflecting sunlight, lighter roof colors can reduce cooling loads 20 to 50 percent. Common roofing materials include asphalt, fiberglass, vinyl, wood, clay tile, slate, concrete tile, and metal.

Wood siding needs to be painted for a finished look. Why is it important to use a primer before painting?

SHINGLES. Shingles are thin pieces of material laid in overlapping rows that cover roofs. Asphalt shingles are the most widely used roofing material because of their fire-resistant qualities, attractive appearance, and low cost. In general, the heavier the shingle, the longer its life will be. Asphalt is also the easiest type of shingle to install and the most economical to repair. Fiberglass and vinyl shingles are similar to asphalt shingles and come in a variety of textures and colors.

Wood shingles and *shakes*, a thicker shingle, are attractive but may cost from 50 to 100 percent more than asphalt. They are treated with fire-retardant and decay-resistant chemicals. Wood shingles and shakes are most often used in parts of the country where cedar, redwood, and cypress trees grow.

SLATE AND TILE. In places with hot sun and little snowfall, roofs are often covered with clay tile, slate, or concrete tile. Slate and tile are usually chosen for their design qualities. If properly installed, they are fireproof and make the strongest roofing materials. However, they tend to crack in a cold climate. An alternative to slate is cement fiber, which costs less and is not as heavy.

Roofing materials vary, depending on the climate. For example, a steel roof is very durable and weather resistant. *What types of roofing materials are on the homes in your neighborhood?*

STEEL. Steel roofs are very durable and provide excellent protection against severe weather, even hailstorms. A steel roof can last longer than 50 years, and the metal can be recycled. Steel roofing materials can be made to look like traditional materials and come in a variety of colors. The initial cost of a steel roof is higher than shingles, but considering that the steel roof lasts over twice as long, the long-term cost is less.

OTHER METALS. Metal roofing made of lead, zinc, copper, or aluminum tends to be popular in warm, dry climates. Metal roofing is fireproof, but can be noisy in heavy rain, hail, or sleet.

Installing the Roof and Chimney

Most roofing materials are applied in a standard way. First the roof frame is covered with sheathing, then with roofing felt. This process keeps out moisture. Then, starting at the outer edge of the roof, a starter strip of shingles (or other roofing material) is applied. The roof should be shingled in straight lines, and the distance between the shingles should always be equal. Wind-resistant roofing materials and methods are often used on homes in areas prone to hurricanes or tornadoes.

Flat roofs are not shingled. Instead, several layers of building paper may be applied with a special compound and then covered with gravel or marble chips. Flat roofs are economical to build. They are most practical in areas where there's little or no snowfall. The weight of snow can damage a flat roof.

As a construction crew finishes applying the roofing materials, flashing is installed around the chimney. **Flashing** consists of strips of sheet metal. It is placed around the chimney and other roof openings and in the roof valleys. Flashing insulates the roof from the chimney and prevents moisture from leaking through the roof openings.

A chimney has two parts: a **flue**, which is a vertical shaft through which smoke and hot gases are carried to open air, and the walls, generally of brick, which surround the flue. The flue is usually lined with stainless steel or terra-cotta clay. The smooth surface of this lining allows the hot gases to rise quickly. The top of the chimney is called the *cap*. A stainless steel screen should be built into the cap of the chimney to prevent updrafts from carrying sparks out onto the roof and to keep out leaves, birds, and small animals.

Metal flashing, such as that used around chimneys, protects the home from water seepage.

INSULATION

Proper insulation is one of the keys to a comfortable, energy-efficient home. The purpose of insulation is to reduce the passage of heat through the walls and roof. If the insulation is installed properly, the home will feel warmer in winter and cooler in summer.

The effectiveness of insulation depends on its **R value**. The R value of insulation is a measure of its capacity to resist winter heat loss and summer heat gain. The higher the R value, the better the insulation.

Builders and home buyers have learned that is it easy and cost effective to increase insulation beyond the minimum levels required by building codes. Recommended levels for outside walls range from R-11 in warmer climates with minimal heating requirements to R-28 for cold climates. Depending on the climate, other desirable R-value ratings range from R-22 to R-49 for attics and ceilings, R-11 to R-25 for floors, and R-11 to R-19 for basements and crawl spaces.

The R value of an insulation product is generally given per inch. To determine the total R value a product will provide, multiply the thickness of the insulation by its R value per inch. For example, if an insulation product has an R value of 5, you can use 2 inches (5 cm) of it to get an insulation value of R-10.

Vapor Barriers

Vapor barriers are materials that help reduce drafts and prevent moisture from getting into a home. Barrier materials include asphalt-laminated paper, aluminum foil, and foil-backed gypsum board. Rolls of plastic film are also used as vapor barriers to envelop entire walls and attic areas. The vapor barrier can be part of the insulation.

Vapor barriers should be properly installed to prevent moisture damage in walls and ceilings. A vapor barrier should face the warm side of the wall. This means placing the barrier toward the *inside* of the wall in cold climates and toward the *outside* of the wall in warm climates (assuming the home is air conditioned).

Forms of Insulation

There are several common kinds of insulation. The basic types include flexible, loose-fill, foam, rigid, and reflective.

FLEXIBLE INSULATION. This type of insulation comes in two forms: blanket and batt. Both types consist of a fibrous, porous material that is usually made of fiberglass. *Blanket insulation* is covered with paper on one side and a vapor barrier material on the other side. Blanket insulation comes on a long roll. Tabs on the sides of blanket insulation allow it to be fastened easily to the studs.

Properly installed insulation at the recommended R-value will provide years of comfort in this new home. It will also help hold down heating and cooling bills.

Batt insulation (blanket insulation cut into shorter lengths) is often uncovered and is also made of a fibrous material, such as fiberglass. It may or may not have a vapor barrier on one side. Some forms of batt insulation are made to stay in place without the usual fastening method.

LOOSE-FILL INSULATION. Loose-fill insulation can be poured, blown in, or packed by hand. The most effective use is in floors. Materials used are fiberglass, vermiculite, perlite, and cellulose. Because loose fill is made up of short fibers, it tends to settle. This can cause cold spots to occur. When part of a wall is warm and part is cold, condensation may cause paint to blister and wood to rot. Care must be taken to distribute loose-fill insulation evenly and to replace the insulation when it begins to break down with age.

FOAM INSULATION. Foam insulation is pumped through a tube to the location where it is to be applied. Foams generally expand after application to fill all cracks and crevices. A newer type of foam insulation is *CFC-free foam*. It has no *chlorofluorocarbons* (CFCs), which deplete the earth's ozone layer. One advantage of foam is that it always fits perfectly, conforming to the shape of the space. Spray foam insulation is typically easier to install, safer for the environment, and more energy efficient than traditional batt insulation. Foam works particularly well in steel-framed buildings. Care must be taken when using foam in existing structures since the foam can crack existing walls as it expands.

RIGID INSULATION. These rigid foam panels can serve as rough wall boarding as well as insulation. An aluminum foil facing is sometimes attached to the panels as a vapor barrier.

REFLECTIVE INSULATION. Reflective materials include aluminum foil, tin-coated sheet metal, and coated paper. Because these thin materials are very effective in keeping heat from entering a home, they are more likely to be used in warmer climates. These materials may be used between studs and in attics. The reflective surface should face an air space at least ¾ inch (2 cm) deep to maintain reflective and insulating properties.

WINDOWS

There are many types of windows from which to choose. Since they are both functional and decorative, windows should be chosen with care. Windows come in many different styles. See Figure 12-7 to learn the terms for various parts of a window.

Frame Materials

Over the years, wood has been commonly used for window frames and sashes. Both the inside and outside of plain wood frames must be painted or stained every few years. All-wood frames are generally more expensive than other types of frames.

Aluminum and vinyl window frames are lightweight and come in a variety of factory finishes and designs. Their light weight makes them easy to install and remove. However, metal frames conduct heat and cold. Wood frames are better insulators than metal frames.

Many people prefer window frames that are a combination of wood and another material. Aluminum-clad and vinyl-clad wood frames don't need to be painted and are good insulators. Whatever type of frame material is chosen, the windows need to be installed correctly so there is no air leakage that causes drafts.

Types of Glass

A single thickness of glass is a poor insulator. By sealing two or three panes together as a unit, much better insulation is provided. The sealed air space between panes provides the insulation and reduces heat loss. This space can be filled with argon gas to further improve the insulating qualities of the window. With double- or triple-pane windows, moisture is less likely to condense on the side of the window that is indoors, as often happens with single-pane glass.

Low-emissivity (or low-e) glass is often featured in newer thermal windows. It has a clear coating that helps keep heat inside in winter and outside in summer. Low-e glass blocks out ultraviolet rays and helps reduce fading of upholstery fabrics and drapes. However, because it keeps out the sun's warmth, low-e glass may not be desirable in the south windows of homes designed for passive solar heating.

On older windows, insulation can be improved with storm windows. These are second windows installed outside the regular window. The air space created between the two windows provides insulation.

Certain other kinds of glass are used for special purposes. Tempered plate glass is made to be extra strong. Because of its strength, it is used for sliding glass doors. Patterned glass, sometimes called *obscure* glass, has a textured surface. It allows light to pass through, but no one can see through it. It may be used for privacy purposes in bathroom windows or for windows in exterior doors. Laminated, shatterproof glass is recommended for homes in hurricane and tornado areas.

DOORS

Many styles of doors are available. They may be made of wood, metal, fiberglass, or some combination of these materials. Flush doors have a smooth surface. Panel doors have sunken or raised sections. Molding may be added to a flush door to give the appearance of panels. Some styles include windows.

Most doors come prehung in a wood or metal frame that consists of a head jamb and side jambs. Exterior entrances also have a threshold at the bottom.

FIGURE 12-7

A VISUAL GUIDE TO...

Windows: Parts and Styles

SASH

The *sash* is the framework that surrounds the window glass. If the window can be opened and closed, the sash is the part that slides or swings open.

LIGHTS

The *lights* are the areas of glass. If each sash has one continuous glass area, it is described as *single light*. A *divided light* window has several smaller areas of glass within each sash. In a true divided light window, *muntins* are the strips that hold individual small pieces of glass within the sash. In modern windows, muntins are more likely to consist of a decorative grid that fits over a single light. The grid gives the look of divided lights but may be removable for easy window cleaning.

FRAME

The frame surrounds and holds the sashes. The *head jamb* is the top of the frame. The sides are called *side jambs*. The bottom is called the *sill*.

TRIM

Decorative trim can be added around the window after installation. The trim around the top and sides of the window is called *casing*. Some windows have casing along the bottom as well. Others have a ledge at the bottom, called a *stool*, with an *apron* below the stool.

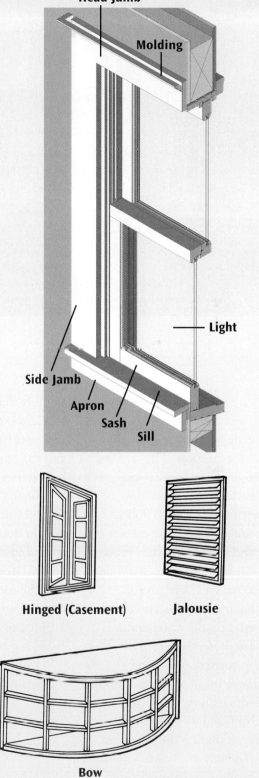

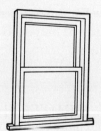

Double-hung

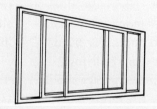

Gliding Sash

Hinged (Casement)

Jalousie

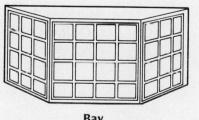

Bay

Bow

The design of the main entrance to a home affects both its appeal and weather protection.

Doors are either solid or hollow. Hollow doors are lighter in weight than solid doors and are generally used only for interiors. They are less expensive, but they are also less sound-resistant.

For exterior use, a solid door is recommended. It provides greater security and is more weather-resistant. An insulated door, such as one with a steel outer "skin" and a polyurethane foam core, conserves energy better than a wood door.

For extra protection from the weather, a storm door may be installed in front of an exterior door. Storm doors include glass for protection from cold weather and a screen for ventilation during warm weather. The frames are made of metal, fiberglass, or wood. Storm doors are not recommended for areas of the home that are exposed to more than a few hours of direct sunlight each day. Heat trapped in the space between the storm door and the exterior door can damage the exterior door.

Building codes require some areas to have fire-rated doors. For example, the door between the living space and an attached garage should be fire-rated. The fire rating indicates how long it would take the door to burn. Common ratings are 20, 60, and 90 minutes.

Exterior doors are hinged so that they swing inward. Whenever possible, they should swing against a blank wall. The same is true for interior doors. For safety, interior doors should never be hinged to swing into a hallway.

WATER PROTECTION

Additional details for the exterior of a home are important in keeping rainwater or melting snow from damaging the structure. These include the finish grade, gutters, and downspouts.

FINISH GRADE. To raise the level of the ground around the home or to eliminate holes that often result from excavation, sand and gravel are usually used as fill. The *finish grade*, or finish level of earth next to the foundation, should be contoured to slope away from the home to prevent rainwater from seeping into the basement or crawl space. The finish grade should also be kept below the top of the foundation. This will keep ground moisture from coming into contact with any of the wood construction, which could eventually cause the wood to rot.

GUTTERS AND DOWNSPOUTS. Rainwater falling from a sloping roof will erode the soil and damage plants and shrubs close to a home. A *gutter*—a horizontal open trough, generally at the eaves or edges of the roof—catches rainwater that drains off the roof.

Wire or mesh guards keep downspouts clean and free of leaves and sticks while allowing rainwater to filter through. Why is it important to clean out trapped leaves from gutters?

The gutter is attached to a vertical pipe called a *downspout*, or a *rain leader*. It carries the water down to the ground. At the bottom, the downspout is connected to a ground drain or to a downspout extension to carry rainwater away from the foundation of the home. Gutters need to be kept clean and clear of leaves, sticks, and other materials that can block the water from draining off.

Andy Algava

Roofer

Home roofing problems can lead to thousands of dollars' worth of damage if not discovered early and properly repaired. It's the homeowner's job to check regularly for problems. It's my job to track down the cause of those problems and correct them.

"Water that seeps through a roof may run horizontally before collecting indoors, so a good roofer must understand water collection and drainage patterns."

I started learning the roofing trade when I was in high school as a helper in my uncle's roofing repair business. I liked working outdoors, and learned enough by watching to think that I'd make a good roofer myself. After graduating from high school, I entered an apprenticeship program where I received both classroom instruction and hands-on training. Now I work for my uncle as a professional roofer, qualified both on new construction and repair of old.

Most of our business is from homeowners with leaking roofs. Our first step is to locate the source of the leak, which can be the hardest part of the job. Water spots inside the house are good clues but don't always lead straight to the answer. Water that seeps through a roof may run horizontally before collecting indoors, so a good roofer must understand water collection and drainage patterns. Poor drainage can lead to leakage, especially with flat or low-pitched roofs; water may also seep though loose or broken shingles.

Whatever the problem, the repair technique we choose depends partly on the type of roof and the way it's covered. The solution may be simple: sealing roof seams with tar, or replacing or covering worn shingles with new ones. Sometimes the decision is

Besides knowledge and technical skill, roofers need the physical strength to handle the work. This job requires a lot of climbing and carrying heavy equipment. We often work in unpleasant weather conditions, too, although we don't take unnecessary risks. Still, the roofing trade has one of the highest accident rates of any trade or profession. As a result, we teach and stress safety practices in all phases of the job.

more complex. For instance, many roofs are covered with several layers of material. I need to decide how many of these layers must be replaced in order to correct the problem. When roof shingles are curled or buckled, I need to examine them to determine whether just those few shingles need to be replaced or whether the roof must be replaced entirely.

To make decisions like these responsibly, roofers must learn about the different kinds of roofs and the variety of materials used to cover, protect, and repair them. I take this part of the job very seriously, since my decision can mean the difference between a homeowner spending several hundred dollars and several thousand. More importantly, it can mean the difference between spending money on a solution or throwing it away on a costly mistake.

"Besides knowledge and technical skill, roofers need the physical strength to handle the work."

Career Profile

A *roofer* installs roofs for new homes and buildings and makes repairs or reroofs for existing ones. Some roofers may also waterproof foundation walls and floors. Roofs are made of tar or asphalt and gravel; metal; rubber or thermoplastic; or shingles, which are made of asphalt, slate, fiberglass, wood, tile, or other material. Roofing work is very strenuous and involves heavy lifting, climbing, bending, and kneeling. A roofer also has to be able to work outdoors in all types of weather.

Education
▸ A high school diploma is recommended.
▸ Can develop skills through on-the-job training but may take several years to gain experience working with all types of roofing applications.
▸ If at least 18 years old, a 3-year apprenticeship program is offered consisting of 2,000 hours of on-the-job training annually. In addition, 144 hours annually of classroom instruction in math, safety, and tools are given.

Skills Needed
▸ Good problem-solving skills and attention to detail.
▸ Must be in good physical condition to be able to perform heavy lifting, climbing, bending, and kneeling. Also need good balance.

Career Outlook
▸ Employment opportunities are expected to experience average growth.
▸ Roofing employment opportunities are generally easier to find during the spring and summer, when most roofing work is completed.

Career Activities

1. The home repair industry as a whole is often cited as one in which unethical workers take advantage of clients. Why do you think this happens? How does that perception hurt the industry?
2. Based on the educational requirements above, what is the average number of hours per year an apprentice spends learning the trade?

Chapter Summary

- The characteristics of the housing site affect the housing built on it.
- Knowing how a home is constructed can save you time and money and help you avoid potential problems.
- Architectural drawings provide information about the appearance and construction of a building.
- The foundation and frame form the basic structure of a home.
- Exterior construction includes covering the frame and applying a final finish to the outside walls and the roof.
- Common kinds of insulation are flexible blankets and batts, loose fill, foam, rigid, and reflective.
- There are several types of windows and doors, each with its own characteristics.
- Exterior details of a home can help protect it from the weather.

Checking Your Understanding

1. Give three reasons why a home should be oriented to use sunlight effectively.

2. What information does a floor plan show about a structure?

3. What function does a footing have in construction?

4. Identify two characteristics for each of the following: the floor framing, the wall framing, and the roof framing.

5. Identify the pros and cons of manufactured siding.

6. Compare the different types of roofing materials. What benefits does each have?

7. What does the R value of insulation mean? Why is it important?

8. What is the purpose of a vapor barrier?

9. Identify at least three improvements in window frame materials and glass.

10. Discuss how the finish grade, gutters, and downspouts are important for the exterior of a home.

Thinking Critically

1. Suppose you are a home buyer, and you have narrowed your search to three homes—one with a slab, one with a crawl space, and one with a basement. What would be your first, second, and third choices? Why?

2. Imagine that you are building a home in a southern coastal area. What climate-related conditions would you need to consider in choosing siding, roofing, and windows?

3. Justify the use of insulation in a home to a person who wants to save money by not installing it.

Review & Activities CHAPTER 12

Applications

1. **Identifying Symbols.** Find an example of a floor plan by using resources such as books, magazines, encyclopedia articles, or websites about architecture or construction. Identify the meaning of the symbols used on the floor plan. Then write a brief paragraph in which you describe the building shown in the plan.

2. **Builder Questionnaire.** Prepare a list of questions you would ask a builder about a house you want built. Be sure to include questions about the construction method, exterior materials, and energy-efficient elements that will be included.

3. **Construction Checklist.** Imagine that you are having a new house built. You want to keep track of the many steps in the process of home construction. Develop a checklist for each phase that you would use to evaluate whether the work was done properly.

4. **Build to Suit the Area.** Make a chart with the following column headings: Climate, Foundation, Roofing, Siding. Choose three different climates and write them in the first column of the chart. Fill in the other columns with options suitable for each climate.

5. **Energy-Efficiency Expert.** For each of the following thicknesses and R values of insulation, find the total R value that the product will provide. Then determine where in a home that amount of insulation is suitable.
   a. 1½ inch (3.8 cm) thick with R-7 per inch = R-?
   b. 1½ inch (3.8 cm) thick with R-11 per inch = R-?
   c. 2¼ inch (5.7 cm) thick with R-16 per inch = R-?

BUILDING YOUR PORTFOLIO

Assume that you are an architect for a home design firm. Create a consumer information brochure that explains your preferences for choosing particular exterior design options for buildings in your area. Use the following topics as a guide:

➤ Roofing and siding
➤ Window types
➤ Exterior doors
➤ Energy-efficient elements
➤ Disaster-proof materials or methods, if desired

Interior Construction

CHAPTER OBJECTIVES

► Explain the roles of contractors and subcontractors.

► Describe safety features of electrical systems.

► Summarize characteristics of the plumbing, heating, cooling, and ventilation systems.

► Evaluate options for interior features such as stairways, walls, ceilings, and floors.

TERMS TO LEARN

- cesspool
- circuit breaker
- conduction
- contractor
- convection
- fuse
- ground fault circuit interrupter (GFCI)
- ground wire
- panel box
- radiation
- recovery rate
- septic tank
- subcontractor
- thermostat

The construction of your new house is going great. The contractor says that the builders are ready to start work on the inside. This is your chance to find out all about the inner workings of a home. Even if you are not going to be the owner of a newly constructed house, you'll benefit from knowing what goes on behind the walls and under the floor of a home.

The Inner Workings

In Chapter 12, you learned about the framing of a home, the finishing of the exterior, and the installation of insulation, windows, and doors. Now you will see the hidden inner systems: electrical, plumbing, heating, cooling, and ventilation. You'll also find out about finishing the interior of a home.

CONTRACTORS AND SUBCONTRACTORS

Many people work together to construct a home, including contractors and subcontractors. A **contractor** is a person who oversees a construction project. This person may own the construction company or may be an employee hired by an owner, developer, or management firm. Contractors are also called general contractors or construction managers. Contractors oversee construction supervisors and workers, coordinate building schedules, and supervise all design and construction processes for the duration of the project.

The contractor is the person who ensures the success of a construction project by coordinating the work of subcontractors and workers. Name three skills that you think a contractor must possess.

One of the contractor's main jobs is to supervise the hiring of subcontractors. **Subcontractors** are workers hired by contractors or homeowners to perform a specific function in the construction of a home. Bricklayers, electricians, drywall installers, carpenters, heating and cooling specialists, plumbers, painters, floor-covering installers, and other subcontractors work together to complete a home. Before choosing subcontractors, owners or contractors need to check on reliability and past performance on other jobs.

Most building jobs have a completion deadline. Therefore, the contractor must be very careful in scheduling subcontractors so that all the work can be completed according to plan and on time. A problem can arise when, for example, a painter has been scheduled to do wall treatments and the finish work on the drywall is not yet done. Unfortunately, some problems can't be anticipated, such as delays in deliveries of materials. These problems can sometimes cause building projects to fall behind schedule. It's the job of the contractor to see if time can be made up on some other part of the project.

By planning carefully, the contractor is able to coordinate the installation of the internal systems that make up a home. These systems include electric wiring, plumbing, heating, cooling, and ventilation.

Electric Wiring

Houses built today have electrical systems that can handle the increased power needed by computers, entertainment centers, and more appliances. Electricians wire a house in accordance with strict codes that ensure safe supply of the necessary power.

One of the first systems to be installed in a home is the electrical system. Codes set by state and local governments generally require that home wiring installations meet high safety standards because electricity is potentially dangerous.

Electric power is sent to communities through a network of overhead wires or underground cables. Underground service is considered more desirable since there is less chance of storm damage that may interrupt power.

The main electrical supply line runs from the public lines to each home, entering through an electric meter that measures the amount of current used. A power company worker reads the meter to determine the amount of electricity used during a certain period. The power company then bills the resident according to usage.

CIRCUITS

A **panel box**, also called a service entrance or fuse box, is a device that controls the distribution of the electricity to the home wiring system. This system is made up of circuits. A circuit carries electricity to a specific area of the home. Heavy-duty appliances, such as refrigerators, ranges, and clothes dryers, usually require separate circuits. Lights and small appliances within the same area may share one circuit.

The number of circuits depends on the lighting system, the number of electric *receptacles*—or outlets—needed, and the number and types of appliances to be used. The popularity of home computers and entertainment centers has resulted in an increased need for circuits and receptacles in homes. A good electrical plan provides an ample number of circuits so the owner can add new electrical devices and appliances in the future without costly rewiring.

For safety, a main switch at the panel box can be used to disconnect all the home's power from the main

Consumer Sense

Checking the Panel Box When the Lights Go Out

Fuses or circuit breakers in the panel box control each circuit in the home. When a circuit is overloaded, the circuit breaker switches off ("trips") or the fuse melts ("blows"). If this happens, first correct the source of the overload, then follow the steps below.

- **TO RESET A BREAKER:** Flip the switch to the ON position. With some manufacturers' models, you must first flip the switch completely to the OFF position and then to the ON position.
- **TO CHANGE A FUSE:** For safety, stand on a dry surface and use only one hand. Turn off the main power supply. Grasp the blown fuse and turn it counterclockwise until it is out of the panel box. Replace with a new fuse of the correct capacity (measured in amperes or "amps").

YOU THE CONSUMER . . .

One of the fuses in your panel box has blown five times in the last two months. What options do you have for identifying and solving the problem? Which would be the best choice? Why?

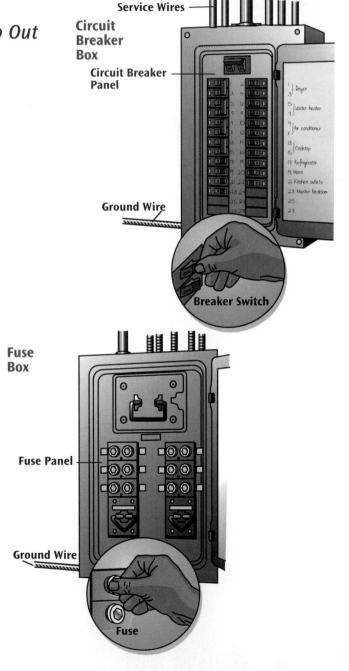

Service Wires

Circuit Breaker Box

Circuit Breaker Panel

Ground Wire

Breaker Switch

Fuse Box

Fuse Panel

Ground Wire

Fuse

supply line. Fuses or circuit breakers in the panel box control power to each circuit in the home. **Fuses** and **circuit breakers** are safety devices that stop the flow of electric current in an overloaded circuit. Newer homes have circuit breakers, but older homes may still have fuses.

Here's how fuses and circuit breakers work. Each circuit is designed to carry a specific amount of electricity. If too many appliances are used on one circuit, the demand for electricity is too great and the circuit becomes overloaded. This could cause the wires to overheat and start a fire. Fuses and circuit breakers prevent that from happening. When a circuit is overloaded, the fuse melts or the circuit breaker switches off, cutting off the power. See the feature on page 282 for information on how to reset a breaker and change a fuse.

A *surge protection device* (SPD) can be used to protect equipment, such as computers, from damage due to power surges. It filters out sudden increases in power created by a local power company or a storm. Several types are available. For best protection, use a central unit that protects the whole home at once. It is installed with its own circuit breaker as close as possible to the panel box. SPDs can be installed in new or older homes.

RECEPTACLES

Current building codes require that wall receptacles, or outlets, include a ground wire connection. A **ground wire** is an electrical conductor that is connected to the earth. The ground wire provides protection in case there is an abnormal flow of electric current. Electricity naturally seeks the ground, so a grounding system provides a safe path for the electricity. If this safe path were not provided, any problems in the circuit could produce a shock that could seriously injure or kill a person. An electrician can tell you whether the receptacles in your home are grounded.

Some appliances have plugs with two flat prongs and one round one. The round one serves as a ground connection. These plugs are designed to be used in modern receptacles that have three slots. People who live in older homes that do not have three-slot receptacles can use a grounding adapter plug to convert a two-slot receptacle for three-prong use. A grounding adapter plug should be used only if the electrical service is grounded. To ground the adapter plug, loosen the screw on the receptacle's cover plate. Slip the adapter's grounding wire under the screw, then tighten the screw again.

Present building codes require that all electrical receptacles near plumbing or water have **ground fault circuit interrupters** (GFCIs). GFCIs are receptacles that guard people against electrical shock. For example, if a current makes contact with water and a person comes into contact with the current, normally

the result would be serious shock to the person. However, a GFCI senses the drop in current through the receptacle, and the circuit interrupter stops the current flow before injury can occur. People who live in older homes without GFCI receptacles can have them installed.

Additional safety devices for electrical receptacles may be needed in homes. Families with small children should place safety covers over the receptacles. These prevent a child from putting a paper clip or other metal object into an outlet and receiving a shock. For outdoor use near a yard or patio, weatherproof receptacles help keep out moisture.

Building codes require that all electrical outlets in bathrooms have a ground fault circuit interrupter. How does a ground fault circuit interrupter work?

lumbing

The term "plumbing" refers to the system of pipes used to carry water into the home and water and waste materials out of the home. The plumbing system must be built according to regulations established by state and local boards of health. This set of rules, called the *plumbing code*, is designed to ensure that the community has pure drinking water and adequate sanitary waste disposal.

In most cities, water is supplied by a publicly maintained system with water from wells, lakes, or rivers. The water goes through a purification process that destroys disease-producing microorganisms and makes it safe to drink. Generally stored in a reservoir, the water either flows to consumers by gravity or is pumped through service pipes.

PIPES

Plumbers install pipes that supply water to a home (*supply pipes*) and carry off wastes and odors (*waste and vent pipes*). Supply pipes have shutoff valves that make it possible to turn off water in part of the system when repairs are needed. Pipes may be made of copper, brass, iron, steel, or plastic.

Plastic has become very common for plumbing pipes. It resists rust and corrosion and is economical to install. Plumbers can bend plastic pipes between wall studs, floor joists, and other obstructions for faster, easier installation than is required for metal piping. However, these benefits should be weighed against possible drawbacks. In the event of a fire, plastic pipe can release toxic chemicals. In addition, plastic waste pipes tend to be noisier in use than metal ones.

FIXTURES

Various plumbing fixtures are available for use in bathrooms, kitchens, and utility rooms. Most modern fixtures are made of cast iron with a porcelain enamel coating, china, stainless steel, or prefabricated plastic. Each type has its advantages and disadvantages.

PORCELAIN ENAMEL. Porcelain enamel on cast iron is often used for bathtubs, toilets, and sinks. These fixtures come in colors to fit any decorating scheme. Porcelain-coated sinks are easy to clean, but they can chip and may become permanently stained by some substances. Scouring powder and drainpipe cleaner shouldn't be used on porcelain.

Water supply pipes carry hot and cold water to fixtures in bathrooms, kitchens, and utility rooms. What are the advantages of copper pipes versus plastic pipes?

CHINA. China fixtures are made of clay fired at a high temperature. They are resistant to ordinary acids and cleansers and are used for toilet bowls, toilet tanks, and sinks. China fixtures are available in many colors and styles. They are heavy and durable but can crack or break.

STAINLESS STEEL. Stainless steel is commonly used for sinks. It is durable and rust resistant. A satin finish is usually used to hide water spots. Compared to other types, stainless steel sinks are easier to install because they are lighter in weight.

PREFABRICATED PLASTIC. Bathtub and shower units made of prefabricated plastic are popular in new home construction and home improvements. The entire unit is molded in one piece. These units install easily and don't require costly on-the-job trim and finishing. Countertops with molded sinks are good choices for bathrooms and kitchens. They offer easy care and come in many patterns and colors.

Prefabricated plastic countertops with molded sinks are popular choices for many homes. The units install easily and are easy to maintain.

WATER HEATERS

Homes need a reliable supply of hot water for bathing, washing dishes and clothes, and other uses. There are two basic types of water heaters: storage and on-demand.

A *storage water heater* is the most common type. It consists of a tank to hold the water and a burner or unit underneath the tank to provide heat. Water can be heated by electricity or gas. The size of the water heater needed depends on the appliances and the number of people in a household. Generally, a 50-gallon (190-L) water heater is recommended for most households.

In addition to a storage water heater's capacity, it's important to consider the recovery rate. The **recovery rate** indicates the average amount of water that will be heated in the tank in one hour. The higher the recovery rate, the more hot water will be available during peak demand periods. Since a water heater is a long-term investment, homeowners should try to anticipate their needs in the years ahead.

Most of the new storage water heaters come with an energy-efficiency rating on the outside. Some models are sold with insulation built into the shell. Insulation is important because storage water heaters keep water constantly heated even when no one is using water. High-efficiency water heaters can use 10 to 50 percent less energy than conventional models. The efficiency of older models of water heaters can be improved by wrapping a layer of insulation around the water heater to prevent heat loss.

If there is not enough hot water in the home when it's needed, the storage water heater may be too small or its recovery rate may be too low. Perhaps sediment has formed on the inside, decreasing the storage tank's capacity. The tank should be drained periodically to remove sediment.

On-demand, or tankless, water heaters are another option. On-demand water heaters don't use a storage tank. They hook up directly to a supply line and heat water only when needed. This can result in great energy savings. The drawback is that on-demand heaters have a lower flow rate.

Other energy-efficient models include:

- A heat pump water heater that extracts heat from the outdoor air or ground.
- Models that capture "waste" heat from air conditioners and deliver it to hot water storage units.
- Solar water heaters, which often can provide nearly half of a household's hot water demands.

Energy-efficient options should be considered when a water heater must be replaced. Many times the least expensive water heater to purchase is the most expensive to operate—for the environment as well as the household.

SEWAGE DISPOSAL

Wastewater and sewage flow from fixtures to a system of underground piping. This piping is connected to a public sanitary sewer, a septic tank and disposal field, or a cesspool.

In many public sewer systems, sewage is carried through cast-iron piping for a distance of at least 5 feet (1.5 m) from the building. Then it may be carried through another type

of piping. Sewer pipes and water supply pipes should be kept as far apart as possible in order to prevent any leaks in the sewers from contaminating the water supply.

For buildings not connected to a public sewer system, the sewage may be disposed of through a **septic tank**. This tank is a large concrete box, generally buried underground. In it, solids settle and eventually decompose due to bacterial action. The liquids overflow into a system of pipes or drain tiles laid underground in an area called the *disposal field* or *drain field*. The liquids gradually seep out of the pipes or tiles and into the soil. After several years of use, the septic tank must be cleaned and the residue removed.

Houses not on a public sewer have a septic system. Strict standards must be met for homes using this system in order to avoid polluting nearby groundwater or rivers and lakes.

A cesspool is another way to dispose of sewage. A **cesspool** is a system that collects sewage and lets it gradually seep into the surrounding earth. In many urban areas, local health regulations don't allow cesspool use because of the dangers of contaminating nearby soil and water.

In some cases, septic tanks and cesspools may develop problems. Overloading can occur if gutters and swimming pools are connected to the system. High-foaming detergents and other cleaning products may interfere with the necessary bacterial action in septic tanks and cesspools. Mechanical waste disposers fill cesspools very quickly, resulting in the need for more frequent cleaning.

Heating the Home

People living in cold-weather climates require efficient heating systems designed to keep them comfortable. Most people feel most comfortable at temperatures of 70–75°F (21–24°C). However, *humidity*—the amount of moisture in the air—affects the temperature at which people feel comfortable. When the right amount of humidity is in the air, people may feel just as comfortable at 65–70°F (18–21°C).

To see how home heating systems work, it helps to understand the three types of heat movement: conduction, convection, and radiation.

Conduction is the transfer of heat from a body of higher temperature to one of lower temperature by direct contact. For example, when you step on a cold floor with your bare feet, you feel the heat leave your feet through conduction.

Convection is the transfer of heat by means of air flow. For example, warm air naturally rises to the highest point in a room or home. The most common way to provide heat

Radiators for a steam heat system heat the room through a combination of radiation and natural convection.

in a home is through convection. Air that has been warmed by a furnace is circulated through each room.

Radiation is the transmission of heat by means of rays traveling in straight lines from a source. The classic example of radiation is the sun. Its heat does not come through physical contact, nor is it blown. People receive warmth directly from the sun's rays.

TYPES OF HEATING SYSTEMS

Do you know what type of heating system is used in your home? Common systems include warm air, steam, hot water, and radiant heat. Figure 13-1 explains how each type of system works.

Heating systems may be fueled by gas, oil, or electricity. Gas and oil are usually used with furnaces and boilers. Furnaces and boilers are rated for energy efficiency. The rating is the ratio of heat produced to the energy consumed on an annual basis. Electric heat is usually the most expensive and inefficient way of heating a home. In Chapter 14, you'll learn about alternative heating methods that are energy efficient.

Most heating systems are controlled by a thermostat. A **thermostat** is a temperature-activated switch that turns the heating system on and off to keep the temperature of a home at a set level. Usually, thermostats are electrically operated. Programmable thermostats can save

Heating Systems

FORCED WARM AIR SYSTEM

Air is warmed by a furnace, then propelled by a blower through ducts to registers in each room. The air circulates, heating the room by convection. Cooler air returns through another system of ducts. For best efficiency, the hot-air ducts need to run through the center of the building and be insulated. A filter usually cleans the air before it is reheated and recirculated.

- Provides the fastest method of raising room temperature.
- The same ducts can be used for a central air-conditioning system.
- Leaky, uninsulated ducts allow heated or cooled air to be lost in attics, crawl spaces, and unfinished basements.
- Heated air may dry out skin and furnishings unless a humidifier is added.
- Circulating air tends to stir up dust, which can aggravate allergies.
- Ducts take up valuable space.

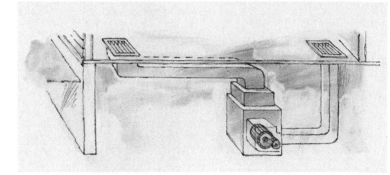

WARM AIR GRAVITY SYSTEM

Similar to a forced warm air system except that there is no blower. Warm air from the furnace rises upward through the ducts and into the rooms by natural convection. When the air cools, it becomes heavier and drops to the floor of the room, then into return ducts by gravity.

- Quieter than a forced warm air system.
- Can't be installed in a home that does not have a basement.
- Ducts take up valuable space. Leaky ducts cause loss of heat in unused spaces.
- Air cannot be filtered or humidified by the furnace.

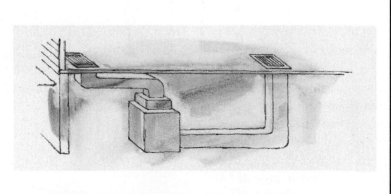

Heating Systems (Continued)

STEAM SYSTEM

Water is heated in a boiler, which generates steam. The steam is forced by its own pressure through pipes to heating fixtures—either radiators or convectors. *Radiators* (shown here) heat the room by a combination of radiation and natural convection. *Convectors* are upright or baseboard fixtures that heat the room by convection.

- Raises room temperature quickly.
- Clean—doesn't stir up dust.
- Difficult to maintain an even temperature in the home.
- Heating pipes may freeze during severe weather.
- Doesn't provide for cooling and ventilation.
- May be noisy.

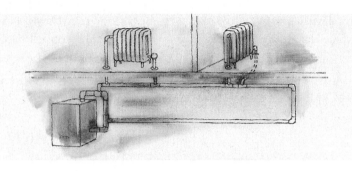

HOT WATER SYSTEM

Water is heated in a boiler, then circulates through pipes to radiators or convectors. In a forced hot water system, the water is circulated by a pump. In a hot water gravity system, the boiler must be located in the basement; warm water rises by natural convection, and cool water drops by gravity.

- Quiet and clean. Efficient and economical.
- May take longer for rooms to reach the desired temperature.
- Heating pipes may freeze during severe weather.
- Doesn't provide for cooling and ventilation.

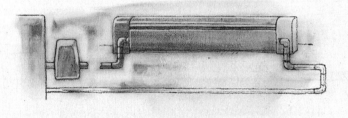

RADIANT HEAT SYSTEM

Heating elements—either hot-water piping or electric wiring—are hidden in the floor, ceiling, or baseboards. Heat radiates from the elements.

- No registers, radiators, or convectors to affect furniture placement.
- Quiet and clean.
- Hidden heating elements can be difficult and expensive to repair.
- Electric radiant systems lose efficiency over time.

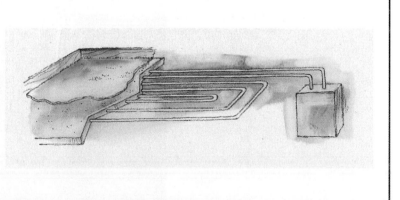

energy and money by reducing the amount of time a heating system operates. When a home is not occupied, or when everyone is asleep, less heat is needed. A programmable thermostat can be set to raise and lower the temperature at certain times each day. Some programmable thermostats allow different times and temperatures to be set for each day of the week.

CHOOSING A HEATING SYSTEM

Based on its location, building materials, and method of construction, each home has specific heating needs. Designers of quality systems can help in the selection of a system and will guarantee performance. For example, they may guarantee that the system will provide a temperature of at least 70°F (21°C) at the lowest recorded temperature in your area.

For most people, choosing a heating system is a financial consideration. However, the purchase price is really less important than the operating costs. Those costs are determined by the level of heat required, the climate, the type and cost of the fuel used, the home's insulation, and the efficiency of the system.

Another important consideration is indoor pollution. To reduce the buildup of harmful fumes within a home, homeowners need to select heating equipment that uses sealed combustion technology, which means an air supply directly vented into and out of the appliance. Many people are also concerned about the heating system's impact on world pollution and conservation. Expert advice is crucial to the selection and installation of a heating system.

FIREPLACES AND STOVES

Would you want to have a fireplace or a wood- or coal-burning stove in your home? Fireplaces and stoves have many advantages. Some homes use these as a supplemental—or even main—source of heat.

Heating a home with wood requires extra work. Wood must be cut or purchased and stacked. The fire must be fed for continual heat. Wood prices are generally lower than gas and oil or electricity, but burning wood does contribute to air pollution. Environmental regulations in some areas control the use of wood furnaces and stoves.

Traditional built-in fireplaces are made of masonry, which is stonework or brickwork. Many modern fireplaces are made of metal, or metal encased in stone to give a more traditional appearance. These fireplaces are often less costly to install, and the metal case provides a safer, more durable unit.

Gas fireplaces give a cozy look with more convenience than burning wood. They are also better at providing continuous high heat than wood-burning fireplaces.

Wood-burning stoves require less attention than fireplaces and hold their heat longer. Although the stoves are efficient, some states concerned with the environment strictly regulate wood burning.

Fireplaces contain a *firebox*, the recessed area in which the fire is built. The floor, or *hearth*, extends out in front as a precaution against flying sparks. The *mantel* is the facing around the fireplace, including any shelf above it.

When the fire is burning, smoke goes up into the smoke chamber to the chimney flue (the inside shaft) and then to open air. Every fireplace must have its own flue. Otherwise, smoke from one fireplace may be carried to another by drafts. At the top of a fireplace, as it meets the chimney, there should be an adjustable damper. When the fireplace is not in use, close the damper to prevent heated or cooled air from escaping up the chimney.

Although popular, fireplaces have disadvantages. They are expensive to build, can cause drafts, and require attention and maintenance. In addition, they waste heat (up to 90 percent) and create a potential fire hazard. To help prevent heat loss through the chimney, glass doors are available to cover the fireplace opening when not in use. Glass doors with vents along the top can be kept closed while a fire is burning, yet they allow heat to enter the room through the vents.

Gas-fired and electric fireplaces don't use wood, yet produce fires that look like wood-burning ones. Gas fireplaces are increasing in popularity for several reasons. They are cost-effective and provide continuous high heat. Gas fireplaces can be vented directly outside; they require no chimney or indoor air.

Wood- or coal-burning stoves are also popular. These may be made of steel, cast iron, or soapstone. In many cases, stoves are used as supplements to a home's central heating system.

A stove may be placed inside an existing fireplace, using the fireplace flue for venting. Freestanding stoves can be placed within a room to radiate heat in all directions.

Some special safety precautions should be observed when installing a freestanding stove. There must be adequate clearance between the stove and the floors, walls, and ceiling. The stove also must be placed on a fireproof base, such as metal, brick, or concrete.

Stoves have the advantages of fireplaces without some of their disadvantages. They don't cause drafts, require less attention, and hold heat for several hours. They also use less fuel.

Cooling and Ventilation

Just as heating systems are a priority for people living in areas with cold weather, cooling systems are important to people who live in areas with warm seasons or year-round warm temperatures. Equally important is ventilation in the home.

COOLING

In warm climates or in areas where spring and summer weather bring high temperatures, people often install cooling systems in their homes. Air conditioners remove excess moisture while they cool and circulate air.

There are two main types of air conditioners: room air conditioners and central air-conditioning systems. A room air conditioner is enclosed in a cabinet that fits into a window or wall. These units cool the air and blow it into a room. Room air conditioners come with different cooling capacities, measured in BTUs (British thermal units). It is important to choose a unit with the right capacity for the room. A general rule is that 12,000 BTUs are needed for every 500 square feet (46 square meters) of floor space.

A central air-conditioning system has a large unit located outside the home that, with the help of the furnace blower and ducts, supplies cool air to each room. Central air conditioning can be built into a new home or installed in some older homes by adding it to a compatible heating system. The home may need additional insulation to help the air-conditioning system operate efficiently and economically. Central air conditioning is controlled by a thermostat, just as heating systems are. For the best energy efficiency, the size of the air conditioner needs to be matched carefully to the size and cooling needs of the home.

Newer air conditioners use a refrigerant that does not deplete the ozone. Federal appliance standards require that all new air conditioners be rated for energy efficiency. The Seasonal Energy Efficiency Ratio (SEER) helps consumers choose air conditioners with less energy consumption and pollution.

VENTILATION

Ventilation refers to supplying a home with fresh air and keeping air circulating throughout a home. This can help to reduce odors, stale air, and indoor pollution levels.

In the past, ventilation in homes was provided accidentally through air leaks. However, in order to reduce energy loss, advances in building techniques have made homes more airtight. This can result in air within homes becoming stale and trapping pollutants and moisture.

One solution is to install an active, or mechanical, ventilation system. A basic whole-house system consists of a fresh air inlet to bring in outside air, ducts to distribute the air, exhaust fans to remove the stale air, and a timer to control the system cycle. The benefits include improved indoor air quality, fewer drafts, improved health, and lower utility bills. In some areas, active ventilation systems are required by the building code. An example of an active ventilation system is shown in Figure 13-2.

Ventilation can also help cool a home. Many homes have a *whole-house fan* installed in the ceiling to pull air from the living space into the attic. Unlike an active ventilation system, a whole-house fan does not run continuously. A manual switch is used to turn on the fan when the outdoor temperature is lower than the indoor temperature. The fan pulls hot indoor air up into the attic, allowing cooler outdoor air to enter through open windows. Whole-house fans are most effective in climates with warm days, cool nights, and low humidity.

Roof vents are another important component of ventilation. Attics must have roof vents so that warm, moist air can escape. Roof vents may be installed in the soffit area, along the roof ridge, or in gable ends. Crawl spaces, too, must have vents to provide air flow.

Some rooms in a home require special ventilation for health, as well as for comfort. These rooms include the kitchen and bathrooms.

In kitchens, indoor pollution and humidity levels can be high. Cooking smoke can leave walls and cabinets sticky and hard to clean.

More importantly, it can irritate your eyes, nose, throat, and lungs. Gas appliances can produce toxic fumes as well. Exhaust ventilation solutions include range hoods and ceiling or wall fans that vent heat, smoke, moisture, and odors outside. Some range hoods act as filters to remove smoke, fumes, and other materials from the air.

The big problem in bathrooms is water condensation, which can allow mold and mildew to grow. It can also rot drywall, moldings, and window frames, as well as rust fixtures and damage insulation. When an

exhaust fan ducted to the outdoors is used, moisture is removed ten times faster than without such a system. Some fans are automatically activated when humidity builds up in the bathroom.

For safety, the room in which the furnace and the water heater are kept must be well ventilated. If necessary, this can be accomplished through ducts and fans that bring fresh air in or draw room air out.

FIGURE 13-2

A VISUAL GUIDE TO...

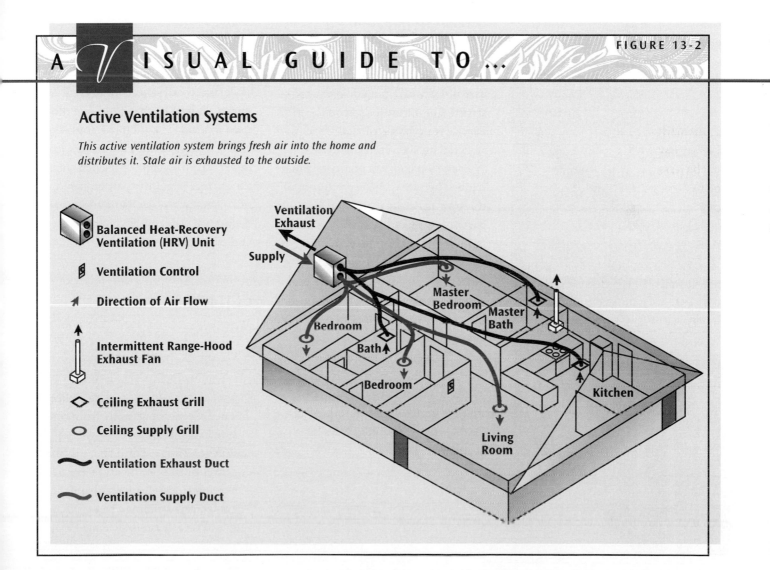

Active Ventilation Systems

This active ventilation system brings fresh air into the home and distributes it. Stale air is exhausted to the outside.

Balanced Heat-Recovery Ventilation (HRV) Unit

Ventilation Control

Direction of Air Flow

Intermittent Range-Hood Exhaust Fan

Ceiling Exhaust Grill

Ceiling Supply Grill

Ventilation Exhaust Duct

Ventilation Supply Duct

Ventilation Exhaust

Supply

Master Bedroom

Master Bath

Bedroom

Bath

Bedroom

Living Room

Kitchen

Finishing the Interior

After all the mechanical systems are in place, work can begin on more visible interior components: the finish construction. Now the interior can take shape with the addition of stairways and finished walls, ceilings, and floors. After this is done, the more decorative elements, such as floor coverings, can be installed.

STAIRWAYS

A home may have one or more main stairways connecting different levels of living space. It may also have a service stairway leading to the basement. Most main stairways are assembled with premade parts constructed of hardwoods, stone, or tile. Service stairways are usually constructed on site, from softwoods.

Each step consists of a riser and a tread. The *riser* is the vertical part of the step; the *tread* is the horizontal part you walk on. Generally, a riser is built at a height of 7½ inches (19 cm) and a tread at a depth of 10–11 inches (25–28 cm).

For a short stairway, it is safer to have either one or three steps. Research shows that people fall more frequently where there are only two steps. The size of the risers or the treads should be uniform on a stairway so that people don't stumble. Handrails should always be installed.

WALLS

Many types of wall materials are available for housing today. Figure 13-3 summarizes the characteristics, advantages, and disadvantages of the common wall finish materials.

One of the best materials for interior wall and ceiling finishes is plaster on lath. *Plaster* is a hard, white finish made of lime or gypsum, sand, and water. *Lath* is the base to which the plaster adheres. Today, lath is made of metal mesh or sheets of drywall that are nailed to the studs. By using special tools, plaster walls can be textured.

Because the installation of plaster on lath is costly, sheets of drywall—nailed directly to the studs—are often used instead. The joints between the sheets of drywall are concealed with tape and a thin coat of plaster, then the surface is painted, wallpapered, or covered with tile. Paint and other decorative wall coverings are discussed in Chapter 19.

CEILINGS

Most ceilings are flat and set at right angles to walls, but innovative designs are sometimes used instead.

- *Shed ceilings* expand vertical space. They ascend diagonally from one side in a single slope.
- *Gabled ceilings* expand space in the center of the ceiling and have two sloping sides. (Both shed and gabled ceilings are sometimes referred to as *vaulted ceilings*.)

Stairs need to be easy to walk up or down for people of all ages. Would a home based on universal design features have stairs?

Homeowners need to consider wall finishes carefully. Some, such as masonry or textured plaster, would be difficult to change later.

FIGURE 13-3

Interior Wall Finishes

Material	Characteristics	Advantages and Disadvantages
BRICK	Warm, earth look; forms interesting patterns.	Resists fire; durable; low upkeep; poor insulator for its thickness.
CONCRETE	Massive appearance; may look institutional; can be colored and textured.	Durable; low upkeep; fireproof; can be painted; poor insulator unless separate insulation added.
PLASTER	Smooth; no joints; can be given texture.	Durable; can be finished in many ways; may crack.
PLASTIC (PANELS, TILE, SHEETS)	A variety of textures and colors.	Durable; easy to clean; easy to install; moisture-resistant.
TILE (GLAZED, CLAY)	A variety of sizes, shapes, and colors.	Easy to clean; durable; reflects noise; resists water and stains; requires strong base such as cement or plaster.
WALLBOARD	Smooth finish; joints must be taped.	Durable; moderate cost; can be finished many ways; fire resistant.

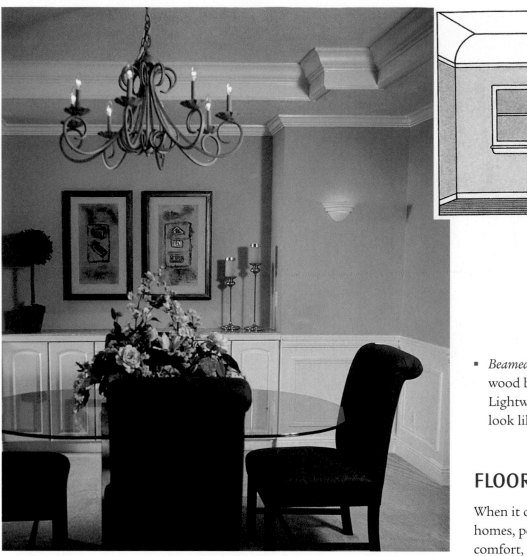

A tray ceiling is flat with edges that angle down to the walls. A coved ceiling (see drawing) has a curve where the walls and ceiling join.

- *Beamed ceilings* feature decorative wood beams over a plaster ceiling. Lightweight materials finished to look like wood are also used.

FLOORS

When it comes to flooring for their homes, people are concerned with comfort, convenience, durability, and appearance. They have many styles and materials to choose from, each with its own characteristics. Materials for floors can be divided into two types: finish flooring and floor coverings.

Finish Flooring

Finish floor materials are considered a permanent part of the floor. These materials include wood, engineered wood, ceramic tile, concrete, slate, stone, and brick.

WOOD. Wood is the most popular finish flooring. It is attractive and comfortable to walk on. Oak is the most commonly used hardwood.

- *Coved ceilings* have walls and a ceiling that flow into each other by means of a curved surface.
- *Dropped ceilings* are lower than the rest of the ceiling area. This type of ceiling accents or defines an area of a room, such as a dining area.
- *Tray ceilings* feature edges that angle out and down to walls.

Ceilings may be constructed from materials such as plaster or drywall. The following are some other options:

- *Stamped metal ceilings*, which were popular in the 19th century, are being manufactured again.
- *Acoustical tile ceilings* are ceilings with a porous material that can absorb sound. They are useful in high-noise areas, such as recreation rooms.

Wood flooring is usually made in strips that fit together with *tongue-and-groove* joints. The tongue-edge projection of one board fits into a groove cut along the edge of another board. Strip flooring is fastened to the subflooring with nails. It comes in prefinished (factory-stained and sealed) and unfinished styles.

Hardwood planks, which are wider than strips, are also used. They are usually attached to the subfloor with screws. The screws are covered with wood plugs, giving the floor an Early American look.

Wood floors may also be laid with small pieces of wood arranged in different designs, such as herringbone and checkerboard. This type is called *parquet* (par-KAY). Parquet is available in prefinished squares that can be easily installed.

Whatever type of wood floor is chosen, the finish is also important. A low-gloss finish hides scratches better than a glossy finish. Polyurethane finishes provide excellent protection for wood.

Engineered wood floors consist of several layers of wood glued at right angles to each other (similar to plywood). The top layer is a hardwood veneer. Unlike solid wood, engineered wood floors can be used in areas that may be damp. They are stapled to subflooring or glued directly to a concrete floor slab. Some tongue-and-groove boards can also be glued to each other and then installed over a foam pad. This type of installation is called a floating floor because it is not nailed or glued to a subfloor or concrete slab.

CERAMIC TILE. Ceramic tile is often used in bathrooms, kitchens, and entryways because it is durable, moisture-resistant, and easy to clean. It can also be used in other rooms, such as dining areas and sunrooms. Tiles come in many sizes and shapes. The spaces between the tiles are filled with a cementlike substance called *grout*. Tiles should be installed on a solid, even surface in order to prevent cracking.

CONCRETE. Flooring made of concrete is easy to clean and extremely durable. However, the hardness of concrete can make it hard to stand or walk on for long periods of time. Previously, concrete was used only in garages and utility areas. New technologies for coloring concrete and creating textures have made concrete an attractive finish floor option for other rooms as well.

Parquet wood floors can be arranged in different types of geometric patterns. Why is this style of flooring often used in a small area such as an entryway?

Concrete flooring isn't just for garages anymore, as you can see with this flowing design. What are some advantages of concrete flooring? What are some disadvantages?

SLATE, STONE, AND BRICK. Slate, stone, and brick may be used on both indoor and outdoor floors. These materials are often used for patios, porches, and entrance halls. However, like concrete, they are not comfortable to stand on for lengthy periods.

When choosing a floor material, consider how a room will be used and how much traffic there might be. For instance, brick wouldn't be the best choice for a bedroom because it is cold and hard. There may be architectural limitations as well. For instance, a stone or brick floor is very heavy. A room where these are used requires special framing to carry the additional weight.

Floor Coverings

Unlike finish flooring, floor coverings are not considered permanent. When a floor covering becomes worn, it is removed and replaced. Floor coverings may be installed directly over the subfloor or over a finish flooring material, such as a hardwood floor.

Carpeting is a popular floor covering. It creates a warm feeling in a room, absorbs sound, and is comfortable to walk on. For areas that require a nonabsorbent floor surface, such as kitchens and bathrooms, vinyl or laminate floor covering is often used. These are durable, are easy to clean, and come in a wide range of colors, patterns, and textures. These and other types of floor coverings are discussed in greater detail in Chapter 19.

Finish Trim

Toward the end of the home construction process, carpenters generally install the finish trim. They put up *moldings*—the decorative strips of wood around a room. For example, crown molding might be installed around the top edges of walls along ceilings, baseboards along floors, and trim around windows and doors.

From the Inside Out

Understanding the interior construction of your home and its systems can make living there easier and more enjoyable. Many repair problems can seem overwhelming unless you know something about a home's hidden mechanical systems. This knowledge can help you understand what is involved in maintaining, repairing, or replacing home systems. In addition, understanding a home's systems and construction enables renters or potential buyers to recognize possible trouble spots and to deal with them—whether that means patching a crack in a plaster wall or calling an expert to repair a heating system. It all adds up to being informed and knowing that you can deal with any home maintenance or repair situation that arises.

Even if you never have a new home built, understanding housing construction can help you maintain and repair your home. How can understanding housing construction help potential homebuyers?

Anson Ly

Electrician's Apprentice

Some parts of our environment are such a part of our lives that we take them for granted and forget how crucial they are. Electricity is a prime example. So much of what we do depends upon readily available electricity. Count the number of outlets in the rooms of your house and the number of wires that lead to each.

We even have extension cords and multi-plug boxes to increase our opportunities to use electricity.

News reports in recent years of "rolling blackouts" show what can happen without electricity: elevators stop between floors, traffic lights at busy intersections don't function, and refrigeration for food in stores and restaurants is lost.

My father advised me years ago to learn the electrician's trade. "There will always be a need for skilled electricians to install equipment and repair it," he said. I followed that advice by entering an apprenticeship program after high school. An apprentice works under a skilled professional to learn a trade and become qualified in it. That's the path I took, and I have never regretted it.

My apprentice program was four years of on-the-job training in using, caring for, and safely handling the tools and materials of the electrician's trade. In addition, I was required to take a minimum of 144 hours of classroom instruction each year. The subjects ranged from drafting, wiring layout, and blueprint reading to applied mathematics and electrical theory. Safety, of course, was stressed; safety codes were studied and followed at all times.

"There will always be a need for skilled electricians to install equipment and repair it."

My work as an electrician can be physically demanding; much of it takes place in partially completed structures, where we are exposed to the elements. We sometimes have to work while standing on ladders or kneeling in confined spaces, yet it's very rewarding work.

When I finished the apprenticeship I was able to assemble and install the electrical systems for light, heat, power, air conditioning, and refrigeration. I chose to work for an electrical contractor as part of a team of electricians. I hope someday to start my own business, specializing in working with a builder of new homes.

Because electricians work with small, color-coded wires, they must have good eyesight with normal color vision and above-average finger dexterity. Mechanical aptitude is also helpful. Interpersonal skills—dealing with people—are also very important. One of the things I enjoy most about my job is the variety of people I meet; the changing location of job sites keeps my work interesting. I need good listening skills, too. When my job supervisor gives me directions, I have to be sure I pay attention and understand what to do; a lot depends on my attention to detail.

"One of the things I enjoy most about my job is the variety of people I meet."

Career Profile

An *electrician's apprentice* works with a licensed electrician to learn all areas of the trade, including installing and assembling the electrical systems for light, power, heat, refrigeration, and air conditioning. The electrician's apprentice can learn the trade informally by working as a helper for an experienced electrician, or by completing an apprenticeship program. The apprenticeship program is a four-year program that provides on-the-job training, in addition to 144 hours of related classes annually. If the electrician's apprentice completes the apprenticeship program, then a test can be taken to be certified as a skilled electrician.

Education
▸ A high school diploma or equivalent is required.
▸ Courses in mathematics, electricity, electronics, mechanical drawing, science, and construction are helpful.

Skills Needed
▸ Good health, agility, and dexterity.
▸ Good color vision.

Career Outlook
▸ Employment opportunities are good since fewer people have become skilled in this area in recent years.

Career Activities
1. List all of the uses for electricity in your school and your home.
2. Research the impact of electrical shortages using library or Internet sources. How do these events affect an electrician's work?

Chapter Summary

- ➤ Understanding the interior construction of a home can help you make sound decisions when building, remodeling, buying, or renting.
- ➤ Safe, efficient home electrical systems are regulated by state and local codes.
- ➤ Plumbing systems bring water into the home and carry out water and waste materials.
- ➤ Homes can be heated using warm air, steam, hot water, or radiant heating systems, as well as fireplaces and wood-burning stoves.
- ➤ Cooling systems include room air conditioning units and central air conditioning.
- ➤ Ventilation systems circulate fresh air, control odors and moisture, reduce pollution, and may provide cooling.
- ➤ Finishing the interior involves stairways, walls, ceilings, and floors.
- ➤ Choosing wall, ceiling, and floor finishes is based on personal taste, ease of installation, sound absorption, and ease of maintenance.

Checking Your Understanding

1. How do the roles of contractors and subcontractors differ in building a new home?
2. What do a fuse and a circuit breaker have in common?
3. Describe how a ground fault circuit interrupter works.
4. What materials are commonly used for plumbing pipes and fixtures?
5. Describe the difference between convection and radiation. Name a heating system using each.
6. How can a programmable thermostat reduce utility bills?
7. With what type of heating system would a central air-conditioning system be most compatible? Why?
8. Explain why ventilation systems are more essential now than they were years ago.
9. What safety factors should be considered when planning a stairway?
10. Name at least three types of finish flooring. Describe a benefit of each type.

Thinking Critically

1. Imagine that you are the general contractor for your own home. The plumber you've hired won't be ready to start for three weeks, yet the hot water heater is due to be installed in one week. What are the possible consequences of this situation? What would you do? Why?
2. Many new homeowners are willing to pay more for better heating, plumbing, and electrical systems, while economizing on furnishings. Explain the logic behind these choices.
3. A new homeowner has asked you for advice on finish flooring for a family room. What type would you recommend and why? What factors might influence your decision?

Applications

1. **Homes of the Past.** Interview an older relative, friend, or neighbor about some aspect of interior construction from the past. It may be an experience he or she had with heating, plumbing, electricity, or other home systems. If you cannot interview a person, use encyclopedia articles, books, or the Internet to learn about construction methods in the early 1900s and to find information on earlier systems and their disadvantages.

2. **Create a Visual Guide.** Clip photos from magazines or print pictures from the Internet of interior wall finishes and finish flooring. Prepare a visual resource that new homeowners could use by describing the advantages and disadvantages of each finish you find. Check local newspaper ads or stores to determine the costs of the finish flooring and add that information to your visual resource.

3. **Determine the Better Buy.** Imagine that you are replacing a damaged living room ceiling with drywall panels. The ceiling measures 14 ft. x 18 ft. (4.3 m x 5.5 m). Drywall panels come in two sizes: a 4-ft. x 8-ft. (1.2-m x 2.4-m) panel that costs $4.89 per panel, and a 4-ft. x 12-ft. (1.2-m x 3.6-m) panel that costs $7.19 per panel. How many panels of each size would you need to complete the ceiling? Which size panel is the better buy? (Note: Count any partial panels needed as one whole panel.)

4. **Future Fixtures.** Draw a design for "The Fixture of the Future." It can be for a utility room, kitchen, or bathroom. Use your imagination and think of all the features you would want. In addition, write a paragraph describing the fixture and its benefits.

BUILDING YOUR PORTFOLIO

You just got a job with a contractor to design a web page for prospective customers that explains the types of home heating systems. The contractor has suggested that the web page might include cartoons and illustrations to create interest. Design the layout of your web page using a computer or by hand. Create the illustrated information in which you clearly describe the types of systems available. You may use print or Internet resources, such as home repair manuals and encyclopedias, to help you find pictures of unfamiliar systems.

CHAPTER 14

Housing, Landscaping, and the Environment

CHAPTER OBJECTIVES

► Evaluate the importance of resource management.

► Identify traditional and alternative energy sources.

► Explain the features of energy-efficient heating and cooling systems.

► Describe ways in which home designers, builders, and consumers can conserve energy, water, and other resources.

► Give examples of ways in which outdoor living areas can expand a home's living space.

► Explain how landscaping can enhance a home.

TERMS TO LEARN

- active solar heating systems
- energy audit
- fossil fuels
- geothermal energy
- landscaping
- passive solar heating systems
- resource management
- retrofitting
- U value
- Xeriscaping

Do you turn off the lights when you leave a room? Do you turn down the heat at night in the winter? If so, you are already starting to do your part in protecting our natural environment. The environment provides people with just about everything they need to live, including food, water, fuel, and building materials. There are many steps in building and maintaining a home that can be taken to preserve our natural resources. Here is your opportunity to learn how you can play a more active role in protecting our environment.

Housing and Resources Management

For years, people assumed that sources of food, heat, and housing materials would always be there when needed. As supplies decreased and prices rose, however, people became more conscious of conserving the environment—that is, using it wisely.

Throughout the country, scientists, engineers, and architects have created model homes designed to make the best use of the environment at minimal cost. These homes are virtually self-sufficient, using very little energy from outside sources. Almost everything, including waste products, is recycled. Solar water heaters, solar ovens, devices that convert sewage to fertilizer, greenhouses, and gardens all help provide food and fuel with a minimum of pollution.

Even though not all people can work this closely with nature, they can still use natural resources wisely. Whether people build their own homes, buy them, or rent them, they are making decisions that affect the environment.

Preserving the natural environment is essential for our future well-being. For many home owners the goal is to create a home and landscape that are environmentally and socially responsible. Protecting the environment is a matter of resource management. **Resource management** is the wise use of natural resources—that is, the building materials, energy sources, and everything else that nature supplies. When it comes to your home, resource management covers a wide range of issues: everything from

This style of home, called a geodesic dome, has less surface area than a "box-type" house and is therefore easier to heat and cool. Why is it important that all households be concerned with resource management?

insulation to energy-efficient argon-filled windows to energy-saving appliances to less-polluting paint. As you learned in Chapter 3, green building is a way to design, build, and operate homes to use our resources efficiently. Conserving land, water, and energy and managing consumption extend beyond building a home. In our daily lives, we need to strive for sustainability. *Sustainability* means meeting the needs of people today without forfeiting the well-being of future generations.

Managing resources means making tough decisions. Do you choose the product that's least expensive or easiest on the environment? Is it worth spending more on extra insulation and a heat pump to reduce your heating bills? Do you spend the time and effort it takes to seal the home against cold drafts each winter, or do you just turn up the heat?

How to use your resources so they'll do the most good is often a judgment call. This chapter discusses environmental issues and describes solutions for sustainable living. From there, it's up to you to make choices that are right for you.

Using Energy Efficiently

People use huge amounts of energy to heat, cool, and light their homes and to operate appliances. Every time you turn on the television, blow-dry your hair, or run the dishwasher, you are using energy. Two steps you can take immediately to reduce your household's energy needs are to lower the thermostat in cold weather to 68°F (20°C) or below and raise the thermostat to 78°F (26°C) or above when using central air conditioning.

Some homes, buildings, and products are designed to be more energy efficient, and those with outstanding energy efficiency earn the honor of being labeled ENERGY STAR. For more information about ENERGY STAR homes and products, see page 314. Chapter 24 gives specific information about energy-efficient kitchen and laundry appliances.

Turning down the heat in the winter is an excellent way to conserve energy. You can compensate for the lower temperature by wearing warm clothing.

ENERGY SOURCES

One of the first steps in understanding how to use energy efficiently is to know where it comes from. Traditional sources of energy have been oil, coal, and natural gas. They are called **fossil fuels** because they were formed in the earth from the remains of prehistoric animals or plants. These fuels are nonrenewable, which means they can be used up. As the supply diminishes and demand continues, fuels become more expensive. Burning fossil fuels also adds pollution to the environment, increasing health hazards and contributes to climate change.

Hydroelectric and nuclear power plants do not depend on fossil fuels, but they do have other limitations. To help meet future energy needs, researchers are developing alternate sources of energy, such as solar, wind, and natural steam power.

Traditional Fuels

Natural gas is a clean-burning fuel (unlike coal, which gives off fumes and solid particles). Natural gas is the fuel used by most households in the United States. It is used in furnaces as well as water heaters, ranges, and clothes dryers. Natural gas does not require storage space in the home because it is brought in through underground pipelines. Therefore, natural gas can be used only in areas that have gas pipelines.

Two other types of gas—butane and propane—are also used for heating and cooking. These forms of liquid petroleum (LP gas) are sold in pressurized tanks. The gas is liquid in the tank but burns as a vapor.

Fuel oil is also used by millions of people to heat their homes and water. Fuel oil is stored in tanks, either in the home or in the yard, often underground. Oil does not

burn as cleanly as natural gas, which adds to air pollution. Because of this factor, some people do not want to use it.

Although the United States has large coal reserves, only a very small percentage of households use coal for heating their homes and their water. However, large utility companies burn coal to generate electricity, which reaches homes through electrical wires. Almost every home in America has electricity to power lighting and appliances. Electricity is also used for heating and cooling, although heating with electricity is relatively expensive.

Burning coal pollutes the air. These pollutants can contribute to health problems such as asthma and lung disease. They are also a major cause of urban smog and acid rain, which harms trees and pollutes lakes hundreds of miles from the place where the coal is burned. Burning coal also releases carbon dioxide into the atmosphere, contributing to global climate change. Coal can be treated to make it burn more cleanly, but the process is expensive.

Until about 1850, wood was the major source of fuel. Although wood alone could not supply enough fuel to serve modern needs, it can be a second source of home heating. The advantage of using wood for fuel is that it is a renewable resource; users can plant new trees. Unfortunately, heat from wood fires escapes up the chimney along with the smoke.

Alternative Energy Sources

In addition to gas, oil, coal, and wood, other energy sources are being used to supply energy needs. These sources include hydroelectric, nuclear, solar, geothermal, and wind power. Forms of energy that are renewable and do not pollute are often referred to as *green energy*.

HYDROELECTRIC POWER.

Hydroelectric plants use the moving water of rivers to drive electrical generators. Hydroelectric plants supply 9 percent of the power generated in the United States and account for about half of all renewable energy used. Hydroelectric power is clean and renewable. Water is not destroyed in the production of electricity. Building dams and reservoirs, however, can significantly impact surrounding areas and affect wildlife. The amount of hydroelectric power is not likely to increase significantly because there are few remaining sites in the United States that are appropriate for new hydroelectric plants.

NUCLEAR POWER.

In a nuclear power plant, reactors fueled by uranium produce heat. The heat is used to make steam, which drives turbines. The turbines in turn power the generators that produce electricity. Thirty years ago, some experts thought that nuclear power plants would someday produce most of the world's electricity. Today we are aware that there are many difficulties and dangers in operating nuclear plants. Radiation leaks have occurred in nuclear plants in several countries. Accidents at nuclear plants can pollute the local land with radioactive material. Because the contaminated material is also vented into the atmosphere, the pollution can spread around the globe. Nuclear waste is hard to dispose of because it remains hazardous for centuries. Finally, nuclear plants are very expensive to build.

SOLAR POWER.

The sun is the most powerful energy source available to us. The energy the sun delivers in only 40 minutes could operate all the factories, machines, and vehicles and heat all the buildings on the earth for an entire year. Technological advances have resolved many of the problems previously experienced with solar energy, but we are still learning how to maximize the use of this energy.

Burning coal and fuel oil leads to pollution in many communities. What other forms of energy are cleaner?

Hydroelectric plants can produce huge amounts of energy. Even though this is a renewable source of energy, why is it unlikely that more sites will be created?

Because it is clean and plentiful, solar power is an appealing alternative energy source. As you will read later, the sun's energy can be used to heat homes. Some power plants use the sun to generate electricity. With advances in technology, ways to use solar energy will increase.

GEOTHERMAL ENERGY. Heat from the earth's interior is **geothermal energy**. Beneath the surface of the earth, the ground remains at a relatively constant temperature throughout the year. Home systems that use geothermal energy take advantage of this by transferring heat stored in the earth or in ground water into a building during the winter, and transferring it out of the building and back into the ground during the summer. The ground, in other words, acts as a heat source in winter and as a natural air conditioner in the summer.

WIND POWER. More and more utility companies are building "wind farms" to supply a clean, renewable source of energy. For example Colorado now offers most residents the option of using wind power. Parts of California are well known for the windmills that line the highways. Wind farms in Iowa and Minnesota provide enough electricity to supply almost 200,000 Midwesterners. The Midwestern wind farms alone save about 300,000 tons of coal and 500,000 tons of carbon dioxide emissions.

ENERGY-EFFICIENT HEATING AND COOLING SYSTEMS

Although alternative energy sources are becoming more widely used, Americans still rely primarily on traditional fuels. As a result, we all need to use these fuels wisely. On the average, heating accounts for about one-third of home energy use and can double in colder areas. Choosing wisely in the areas of home heating and cooling is very important. Heating and cooling systems are broadly referred to as *HVAC* (heating, ventilating, and air conditioning). Each of the heating systems you learned about in Chapter 13 is available in energy-efficient models. Remember to look for the ENERGY STAR label on furnaces, boilers, air conditioners, and other HVAC sys-

These modern windmills—called wind turbines—are reliable sources of energy. Are there wind turbines in your region of the country?

tems. ENERGY STAR-labeled equipment uses 10 to 20 percent less energy than standard-efficiency models.

In addition to the traditional heating systems, engineers have developed more advanced heating and cooling systems to conserve fossil fuels and reduce pollution.

Heat Pumps

A study by the United States Environmental Protection Agency (EPA) named geothermal heat pumps (GHPs) as more efficient heating and cooling systems over other types of equipment including high-efficiency gas furnaces and air conditioners. While the purchase price of a geothermal heat pump is higher than a gas furnace, money is saved in operating and maintenance costs. Geothermal heat pump installations in both new and existing homes can reduce energy consumption 25 percent to 75 percent compared to older or conventional replacement systems. For further savings, GHPs can be equipped with a "desuperheater" that provides hot water. Geothermal heat pumps are environmentally clean, too. All heat pumps require electricity to run the compressor. However, they use less electricity than conventional systems. ENERGY STAR-labeled heat pumps are more energy efficient than other heat pumps.

A geothermal system consists of a series of pipes buried in the ground. Liquid circulates through the pipes and absorbs the heat from the ground. A geothermal heat pump removes the heat from the fluid in the pipes and transfers it to the house. In the summer, excess heat is transferred back into the ground. Conventional ductwork is generally used to distribute heated or cooled air from the geothermal heat pump throughout the building. About half a million geothermal heat pumps are being used today for heating and cooling throughout the United States in residential, commercial, and government buildings.

Solar Heating

Another option is to use solar energy to heat homes. This process can be either active or passive. **Active solar heating systems** require mechanical devices that collect and store the sun's heat and then distribute it throughout the house when it is needed. Active solar heating systems are usually designed to provide 40 to 80 percent of the home's heating needs. This type of heating system is expensive, for two reasons. First, the components are often costly and must be custom fitted to the house, so installation costs are high. Second, the house needs a backup heating system for periods of cloudy weather and severe cold. Small systems, such as wall air panels and window box collectors, are a simpler and less expensive option for those who only want to heat one or two rooms.

Solar energy is an environmentally friendly way to provide energy for a home. In addition to solar panels, new developments in technology have created solar roofs. If planning to use solar energy as the main heat source in a home, what do homeowners and contractors need to consider?

Passive solar heating systems make direct use of the sun's heat without mechanical systems. They use features such as windows and masonry walls to collect and store heat. Figure 14-1 further explains solar heating systems.

Heat Recovery Ventilators

A *heat recovery ventilator* is an energy-efficient device that uses heat energy that would otherwise be wasted. Heat recovery ventilators remove stale air from the house in winter, but first they extract the heat from the air and keep it indoors. Similar technology transfers heat outside to cool a home. Heat recovery ventilators are popular with consumers in Canada and are gaining popularity in the United States.

CONSERVING ENERGY THROUGH DESIGN AND CONSTRUCTION

No matter what type of heating and cooling systems they use, homes can be designed and constructed to save energy. For example, an ENERGY STAR home uses 30 percent less energy for heating, cooling, and water heating than a home based on the Model Energy Code. Builders and residents are becoming aware that wasting energy is neither economical nor efficient. The ongoing energy use of a building is probably its greatest environmental impact, so designing buildings for low energy use is a priority. Also, while it costs money to make a home energy-efficient, those who live in it will save on energy costs for years to come. In addition, these homeowners will enjoy greater comfort, better indoor air quality, and lower maintenance costs.

FIGURE 14-1

A **V**ISUAL GUIDE TO...

Solar Heating Systems

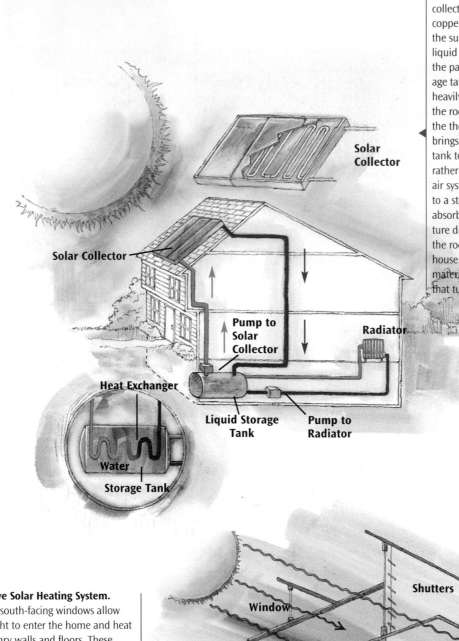

Solar Collector

Solar Collector

Pump to Solar Collector

Radiator

Heat Exchanger

Liquid Storage Tank

Pump to Radiator

Water

Storage Tank

Active Solar Heating System. Large solar collectors are located on the roof. The solar collectors contain absorber panels, usually copper with a black coating that absorbs the sun's heat. If a liquid system is used, liquid passes through pipes coiled behind the panels and transfers the heat to a storage tank of water. The storage tank is heavily insulated to reduce heat loss. When the room temperature in the home drops, the thermostat activates a pump that brings the heated water from the storage tank to radiators. Some systems use air rather than liquid for heat transfer. In an air system, the sun's heat is moved via fans to a storage bin filled with rocks. The rocks absorb the heat. When the room temperature drops, fans distribute the heat from the rock bin though ductwork in the house. Another type of system uses roofing materials with built-in photovoltaic cells that turn sunlight into electricity.

Passive Solar Heating System. Large south-facing windows allow sunlight to enter the home and heat masonry walls and floors. These materials collect and store warmth for times when the sun is not shining. An overhang above the windows shades them from too much heat in the summer. However, in winter the sun is lower in the sky, so its heat penetrates the windows when it's needed most.

Shutters

Window

Masonry Wall

Wise planning can help make a home energy efficient. What features of this home help conserve energy during cold winter months?

As you've learned, improved insulation, advanced windows, tightly sealed and insulated ducts, high-efficiency heating and cooling, and reduced air infiltration from drafts are important ways to conserve energy. There are also basic design features that can contribute to energy conservation.

Energy Efficiency in Architectural Design

Architects and builders know that, by following certain principles, they can reduce a home's heating and cooling costs. Consider these factors when choosing a new or existing home:

- The smaller the roof, the less the heat loss. Compact, two-story houses are best in cold climates because there's less roof in proportion to the total floor area.
- The color of the roof also affects the amount of heat a home loses or retains. Light colors reflect heat and dark colors absorb it. Therefore, light-colored roofs are better in warmer climates because they lower air-conditioning needs. Dark roofs are better in colder climates because they reduce heating needs.
- Sunrooms, skylights, and large windows provide passive solar energy if they face south. Dark walls absorb light and store heat. In regions with cold weather, family rooms and living rooms should be placed where they get afternoon sun.
- If large windows are used in cold climates, they should face south. Storm windows or insulated glass should also be used.
- Window shades and awnings can help keep out sun and heat. Overhangs and porches can keep out sunlight during summer months. Light-colored walls also reflect heat.

This home is ideally suited for its warm climate. What features do you notice that make it efficient to keep cool during warm summer months?

- The smaller the wall area, the more easily a structure can be heated or cooled. Square buildings are energy efficient. Rambling L-shaped and T-shaped homes are the most difficult to heat or cool efficiently.
- Rooms such as the kitchen, family room, and living room, where most activities take place, should be in the same part of the home. That way, other areas of the home can be closed off to conserve on heating and cooling.

Consumer Sense

Money Isn't All You're Saving

ENERGY STAR *Homes*

The energy Americans use to watch television, heat and cool the house, light a room, and take a shower, plus other household activities creates about one-fifth of all pollution generated in the country. Homes with products that use less energy generally use fewer natural resources and pollute less. With this connection in mind, the United States Environmental Protection Agency (EPA) and the Department of Energy (DOE) have put their stamp of approval on homes, buildings, and products that use less energy without sacrificing design, quality, or performance.

The voluntary ENERGY STAR Program includes appliances, heating and cooling equipment, TVs, VCRs, computers, buildings, new homes, exit signs, water coolers, and more. Products, homes, and buildings with outstanding efficiency ratings can earn the ENERGY STAR label. Even some kinds of light bulbs qualify. ENERGY STAR labeled homes are inspected and tested by an independent third party. Homes that meet program standards receive a label that is affixed to the home's electrical box.

These are some of the features that contribute to a home's ENERGY STAR status:

- Added and improved insulation, and technologically advanced windows promote a constant temperature throughout the home. Rooms stay warmer in cold weather and cooler in hot weather.
- Heating and cooling system components, including furnace, water heater, and central air ducts, are designed to work with minimum waste. ENERGY STAR components carry longer warranties. Some ENERGY STAR builders guarantee that utility costs will not exceed a certain amount.

- Refrigerators lower energy use through increased insulation, tighter door seals, and more efficient motors.
- In dishwashers, booster heaters raise the temperature of water as it enters the washer, while the home water heater stays at a lower setting. Other features let you match cycles to cleaning needs and to dry with air instead of heat.

While energy efficiency may increase the purchase price of ENERGY STAR homes, lower maintenance and utility bills add up to savings over time. Appliances built for efficiency tend to last longer with fewer repairs. They even run more quietly. The investment may also pay off in a higher resale value when owners become sellers.

YOU THE CONSUMER . . .

Your search for a new home has come down to two choices. One has been designated an ENERGY STAR home; the other has not. The asking price for the ENERGY STAR home is about 15 percent higher than the other. How do you decide if the ENERGY STAR home is worth the added cost? What other factors related to maintenance and utilities do you consider in making this decision?

- Ceiling height can influence room temperature because warm air rises. In warm weather, high ceilings collect rising room heat that can be pulled outside by exhaust fans. In cold weather, however, high ceilings make a room more expensive to heat. Ceiling fans can be used to move heat back down into the living space.
- A *vestibule*, or entryway with an outer and inner door, reduces heating and cooling costs. When people enter through the outer door, they close it behind them *before* opening the inner door to the home. This helps prevent outside air from entering the home.
- Closets and storage areas placed on the coldest side of the house (the north side) act as insulation for the living areas. This can save on heating costs.
- An attic fan or whole-house fan will help cool the house.

The design of earth-sheltered homes is very energy efficient. Would you enjoy living in this type of home? Why or why not?

Earth-Sheltered Homes

The earth-sheltered home features an energy-efficient design. It is usually built into the side of a hill so that only the south wall is exposed. The south wall has large windows to let sunlight in, allowing passive solar heating. The tops of the other walls may be exposed enough to let light in through smaller windows. The roof area of the home is covered with a layer of earth to insulate it. Since the ground temperature stays around 50-55°F (10-15°C) all year, this natural insulation greatly reduces heating and cooling costs.

Construction of an earth-sheltered home may cost more, since it must withstand great earth pressures and moisture. However, in the long run, the energy savings may make up for the initial costs.

Despite its energy efficiency, the earth-sheltered home does not yet enjoy widespread acceptance. One reason is that it doesn't fit into traditional residential neighborhoods.

Insulation, Caulking, and Weatherstripping

High-quality insulation, caulking, and weatherstripping can save energy. By reducing heat loss, they decrease fuel consumption and lower heating and cooling bills.

Insulation, discussed in Chapter 12, is laid, sprayed, or blown into areas in walls and ceilings, wrapped around pipes, or otherwise used to keep a home warmer in cold weather and cooler in warm weather. One area that is often overlooked when insulating is the ductwork that distributes heated and cooled air through the home. The ductwork is usually located in attics, basements, and other spaces not heated or cooled. The conditioned air traveling through the ducts can leak out into these spaces. Leaky, uninsulated ducts waste energy. Foil tape, fiberglass tape, or advanced duct tape need to be applied to seal the joints, and ducts need to be insulated.

Getting a home ready for the winter takes time but the effort shows up in lower utility bills.

Weatherstripping is a strip of material installed around the edges of windows and doors to exclude outside moisture and air. Some types of weatherstripping for windows are adhesive-backed foam rubber or vinyl. Interlocking metal sections of weatherstripping are often nailed around doors. *Caulking* is a pastelike substance, often made of silicone, that can be applied inside or outside a home wherever air or moisture can enter. On the outside of a home, this might be around windowsills or any location where the siding meets window or door frames.

Energy-Efficient Windows

Research shows that windows account for about one-quarter of a house's heating load and half of the cooling load. Energy efficiency needs to be one of the main concerns when selecting windows. One way to tell a window's energy performance is the U value. The **U value** is the measure of a window's capacity to resist winter heat loss. The U value, like the R value that measures insulation, helps you make informed decisions. The lower the U value, the better the window. For example, a window with a U value of 0.15 means high thermal performance. In warm climates, windows need to prevent heat gain. This measurement is called solar heat gain coefficient, SHGC. Lower SHGC numbers mean better performance. Here are several ways windows can be made energy efficient.

- Windows with a layer of air between the panes of glass help prevent heat or cooling loss.
- Double- or triple-paned windows that have argon gas sandwiched between the panes can cut down substantially on heat loss in cold weather or heat gain in warm weather.
- "Cool windows" save on air-conditioning costs. They use a tinted, coated glass (such as low-e glass) to let light in but filter out the heat.
- Windows with another type of coating on the glass absorb solar heat in cold weather and reflect it in warm weather.
- Tubular skylights through the roof use the sun for lighting interiors but avoid the drawbacks of leaks and energy loss that can be associated with regular skylights.

Experts predict that windows will soon be as well insulated as walls. Consumers should choose the types that best fit their climates.

Retrofitting Homes

The process of making a home that is already built more energy efficient is called **retrofitting**. Many steps can be taken to conserve energy, from using weatherstripping on windows and exterior doors, to sealing leaky ducts, to building a solar room to collect heat. Insulation can be added to attics, outer walls, and heating ducts. Windows can be replaced with new energy-efficient designs, or storm windows may be added.

For a small fee, most utility companies will evaluate the energy efficiency of a home. This **energy audit** is an inspection of the home to determine where heat loss may be occurring. The energy advisor will suggest ways to seal leaks and reduce energy use.

While new homes are usually well insulated, many older homes lack adequate insulation. They can be retrofitted by adding insulation to exterior walls and attics.

Energy Conservation Practices in Commercial Buildings

Using energy efficiently is very critical to owners of commercial buildings. Energy conservation is not only important for wisely using our natural resources, but for an owner of a large company savings on energy bills can impact company profits.

Architects and designers work with owners of commercial buildings to design facilities that conserve energy and still maintain a comfortable environment. Here are some examples of how this can work:

- **Building envelope.** Energy conservation for the building's envelope (exterior) focuses on insulation technologies, windows, and solar shading devices. Insulation technologies have been improving by addressing the problems associated with air infiltration in construction and eliminating toxic foaming agents. Windows have been improved by using energy conserving coatings, films, and inert gases to fill window cavities rather than air. The Hooker Chemical building in Niagara Falls, New York, is an excellent example of a structure designed to conserve energy by using movable solar shading devices. These units are horizontal louvers that minimize solar heat gain in the building while allowing daylight to enter.

- **HVAC systems and maintenance.** Heating, ventilating, and air conditioning systems are a major focus for energy conservation practices. Buildings consume a great deal of energy through heat loss and cooling. In fact, chillers are the single largest energy consumers in commercial buildings. These machines create

peaks in energy usage during summer afternoons. The industry has improved the efficiency of chillers by reducing the amount of energy required to operate the equipment.

- **Lighting.** Lighting consumes about 40 percent of the total electricity budget in commercial buildings. Energy conservation with lighting involves reducing the amount of energy required to operate light fixtures and the energy required for cooling equipment. Energy required to cool a space is especially critical in a retail store because the light fixtures that enhance merchandise generate a great deal of heat. To understand the amount of heat generated by a light bulb think about the last time you touched a hot light bulb. Evolving technologies to reduce the energy consumption of lighting includes

improvements in compact fluorescents, halogen technology, LED technology, and fiber optics.

You, the *Designer*

Imagine you are part of a design team responsible for planning energy conservation for a new grade school located in Miami, Florida. Decide what energy conservation characteristics you would recommend for the building. How would these recommendations vary if the grade school was located in Minnesota? Give rationales for your choices.

Using Water Wisely

Water is essential to daily life. People use it for drinking, cooking, bathing, washing clothes, scrubbing floors and windows, and flushing the toilet. In fact, households in the United States use 40 billion gallons (151.4 billion L) of water every day. Considering that two-thirds of the earth is covered by water, you might think that conserving water is not necessary. Think again. Less than 1 percent of the world's water is suitable for people to drink. About 97 percent is in the oceans and therefore has a high salt content. Another 2 percent is in the form of glaciers and polar ice. With the growth of world population, it is important to conserve water. In many areas, periodic droughts result in water shortages. Pollution is another threat to the water supply. To conserve and protect water, governments, businesses, and individuals must work together.

GOVERNMENT CONSERVATION EFFORTS

Government agencies manage and protect the water supply. They regularly test all major sources of water. They also monitor potential sources of contamination, such as housing developments with septic systems or industries with chemical storage tanks.

Activity. People in Pennsylvania withdraw 1.3 billion gallons (4.9 billion L) of groundwater every day for domestic, agricultural, and industrial uses. Assign several students to find out how much water your state or city uses each day, broken down by purpose, if possible.

Through zoning and building codes, septic system permits, and other measures, local governments can control the amount of water used. One county in California prohibits lawns from taking up more than 20 percent of the landscaped area in some housing developments. This helps cut down on the amount of water used for lawns. Many other communities have issued watering schedules, such as permitting residents to use water for lawns only on odd or even days, according to their street addresses.

Many cities and towns have water-treatment plants that help recycle water. In some plants, wastewater is treated and purified, then discharged into the ground where it seeps back into natural places. In this way, water is sent back to its original sources and later converted again into drinking water.

WATER-SAVING FIXTURES AND APPLIANCES

Many manufacturers are redesigning fixtures and appliances with water conservation in mind. For example, a new "smart" dishwasher constantly monitors wash load conditions.

One way to conserve water is through water-wise landscaping. What are other ways for households to conserve water?

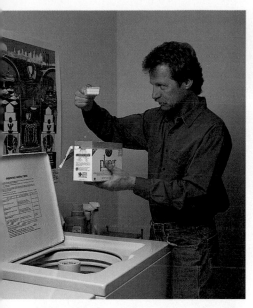

Remember to only do the laundry when you have a full load. How else can you conserve energy when doing the laundry?

Grinding mechanisms remove food particles; so there's no need for pre-rinsing, which saves both water and time. The dishwasher runs just long enough to get the dishes clean, then shuts off automatically. This saves both water and energy.

A horizontal-axis washing machine uses the same tumbling

action as a dryer and uses over 40 percent less water than a standard washer. Its electronic controls monitor tumbling and spin speeds and keep clothes from balling up. These machines have an added convenience: because there's no agitator in the way, it's easy to wash bulky items like bedspreads and parkas. One model saves 19 gallons (72 L) of water per load, or about 8,000 gallons (30,283 L) a year.

Water-saving fixtures for the bathroom and kitchen are available. Modern toilets are designed to use only 1.6 gallons (6 L) of water per flush. An electronic faucet that reduces water usage by 85 percent runs only while hands or objects are beneath it.

Water-efficient showerheads use less than 2.5 gallons (9.5 L) of water per minute. That saves the typical household 12,000 gallons (45,425 L) of water a year. It also means that less energy is needed to heat water and clean and process wastewater, reducing the carbon dioxide emitted into the atmosphere by water treatment plants.

CONSERVING WATER DAILY

You and the members of your household can take measures to conserve water in your home. You can also encourage government action. Here are just a few things you can do to help preserve water supplies.

- Run washing machines only with full loads. Use the water-saving feature if your machine has one.
- Wash dishes by hand with minimal water use or use the energy-saver cycle on a dishwasher.
- Take shorter showers. If taking a bath, fill the tub with only a few inches of water.
- Contact a pollution-control agency or county extension agent for advice on how to dispose of hazardous household waste. Don't dump toxic substances, such as oil-based paints, paint thinners or solvents, cleaning fluids, or motor oil, on the ground or into storm sewers.
- Fix leaky faucets and toilets that run continuously. Even a small leak can waste gallons of water.

Using Building Materials Wisely

People have always used materials from the environment to construct their homes. Many of these materials, such as stone and metals, are nonrenewable. With the construction of 1 to 2 million new homes in the United States each year, some supplies of natural building materials are running out.

As discussed in Chapter 3, much can be done to conserve building material. When natural resources are processed into building material, by-products such as wood chips and sawdust can be used to make particleboard for flooring, shelves, and ready-to-assemble furniture.

Recycling protects our environment. Materials that are recycled don't add to the problem of overflowing landfills and making new products out of recycled materials takes less energy.

For more efficient use of materials, builders can use plentiful materials in place of those that are scarce. Materials that are easier to process can be substituted for those more difficult to manufacture.

RECYCLED BUILDING MATERIALS

There are several ways waste materials can be recycled into building materials for sturdy and attractive homes.

- Old newspapers can be made into material for subflooring and wall paneling.
- Steel from old automobiles can be used for framing and roofs.
- Aluminum beverage cans can be processed into material for house frames.
- Glass bottles can be crushed and used to make brick, driveway pavement, and floor tile.
- Plastic soft-drink bottles can be made into polyester carpeting.
- Discarded car tires can be melted and mixed with crushed glass for driveway surfaces.

- Ashes can be used in making concrete.
- Clay soil contaminated with petroleum products (possibly from the ground around a gas station) can be used to make paving bricks.
- Old wooden doors can be remilled to make stair rails and hardwood floors.
- Newspapers can be made into blown cellulose insulation. The shredded newsprint is first treated with cornstarch (an adhesive) and boric acid (a fire retardant).

- Door and window moldings can be constructed of recycled materials. One such material is made from wheat straw, newspaper, wood, and plastic. It is stronger and less expensive than wood, and it doesn't warp, split, or need painting.
- A lumberlike material for outdoor decks is made from plastic bags, industrial sawdust, and other wood waste. It needs no preservatives and won't crack, splinter, or rot.

Outdoor Living

As people have developed more awareness of protecting the environment, they have also developed a greater appreciation of enjoying the environment. More and more people are finding that when good weather arrives they want to spend time outdoors. Outdoor living spaces have become extensions of a home's interior. By making good use of outdoor living spaces, people can even cut down on how much space they need inside their house.

DESIGNING THE OUTDOOR LIVING SPACE

The first step is to consider the best place for an outdoor living space.

Most people prefer outdoor living areas to be accessible easily from the home. Does the house design facilitate adding a large front porch or a porch that wraps around the side? What about a multilevel deck on a sloping building site? Some homes are ideal for a patio that extends off the main living area. Screened porches are popular in some areas of the country, and interior courtyards are found in many Southern and Southwestern homes.

Just as when originally planning the house, designers create their plans for outdoor living areas based on the terrain of the site and how much space is available. They must consider where the house is on the lot, what people will see from the street, what household members will see from inside the house, where the active-use areas are, and the location of existing trees and shrubs. They spend time studying the sun and shade, wind and breeze, and sights and sounds.

Three- or four-season rooms are increasingly popular. These rooms are meant to be permanent. The walls feature lots of energy-efficient windows that can be opened for fresh air or closed to shut out the weather. Such rooms have doors leading to the main part of the home that can be left open or closed off.

Homeowners need to think about how the outdoor space will be used. In some cases, the homeowners want an area for casual entertaining. A brick fireplace or barbecue grill may be the main feature of the area. Some homeowners even go to the extent of adding an outdoor kitchen, which makes the most sense in parts of the country that remain warm most of the year. A family with small children might set aside an area for a swing set, sandbox, or playhouse. Sometimes people just desire a place to sit back and enjoy the fresh air.

Adding a three-season porch can bring the outdoors in. During warm months, windows can be opened to bring in the fresh breezes. During very cold weather, the doors to the rest of the house can be sealed to conserve on energy costs.

More and more people are adding outdoor living areas to their homes and using them for casual entertainment.

Imagine the pleasure of sleeping outdoors on a breezy summer night. A screened-in porch can be an ideal fair weather bedroom. A couch or futon that easily turns into a bed provides comfortable seating during the day and a cozy bed at night.

Remember energy conservation for outdoor areas, too. Trees provide needed shade in the summer and good windbreaks in the winter. Shading the area also can be done by extending the roofline on the house or with awnings and umbrellas.

CREATING THE OUTDOOR LIVING SPACE

Once the outdoor living space is thoroughly planned, construction can begin. This can range from a simple concrete pad for a patio to an elaborate structure that would follow the same construction process as a house.

Flooring for a patio or interior courtyard could be concrete, brick, tile, or paving stones. Wood decks offer the homeowner a readily available and relatively simple way to create functional, pleasing outdoor features. Wood for outdoor space must withstand all kinds of weather as well as insect attacks. It must be strong and resist wear, splintering, and warping. Naturally decay-resistant woods are redwood, cypress, and western red cedar, but they are expensive. Treated lumber is more economical and is satisfactory for most projects. Pressure-treated wood is the best choice. Recycled plastic is an environmentally wise and economical choice as well. It is made to resemble wood and does not warp or rot.

Walls with screens may be added to define the space, or a fence may edge the space. For safety reasons, raised areas need railings. Wood or plastic lumber can be used here as well. Plantings and rocks can also be used to frame a space naturally.

Of course, seating will need to be provided. In some instances, seating is built into the deck design. Freestanding outdoor furniture is available in a wide variety of styles and price ranges. Look for materials that can withstand the use they will be given. For example, furniture that will be outdoors on a patio needs to be more durable than pieces inside a covered porch.

When nighttime use of outdoor living spaces is desired, lighting can be added. Solar-powered lights work well in many cases. Electricity can be added to some spaces easily, or lights from the house may be directed to the outdoor living area. One final important aesthetic consideration for outdoor living areas, as well as the house, is the landscaping.

More homes are being designed with porches, decks, and patios to allow people to enjoy the outdoors. Older homes can be retrofitted with these features as well.

$\mathscr{L}$andscaping—The Finishing Touch

A home's site can be greatly enhanced through landscaping. **Landscaping** refers to the ways people use plants and objects to enhance or change the natural environment around the exterior of their homes. Landscaping should be planned carefully. It needs to take into account the basic characteristics of the housing site.

THE PURPOSE OF LANDSCAPING

Well-planned landscaping enhances the exterior appearance of the home and the outdoor living spaces. Depending on the choices that are made, landscaping can serve a variety of purposes. For example, it can enhance the privacy, safety, and beauty of a property. It can provide shade, block unpleasant sights and sounds, affect wind patterns, reduce maintenance, and provide areas for specific uses. Figure 14-2 illustrates some landscaping ideas.

Landscaping plans are usually determined by the amount of space available and the needs and wants of members of the household. Most houses have plantings close to the building, which can make the house look more appealing. Landscaping around an outdoor living area increases its appeal. People who enjoy gardening might clear a sunny area with good soil for growing flowers and vegetables.

FIGURE 14-2

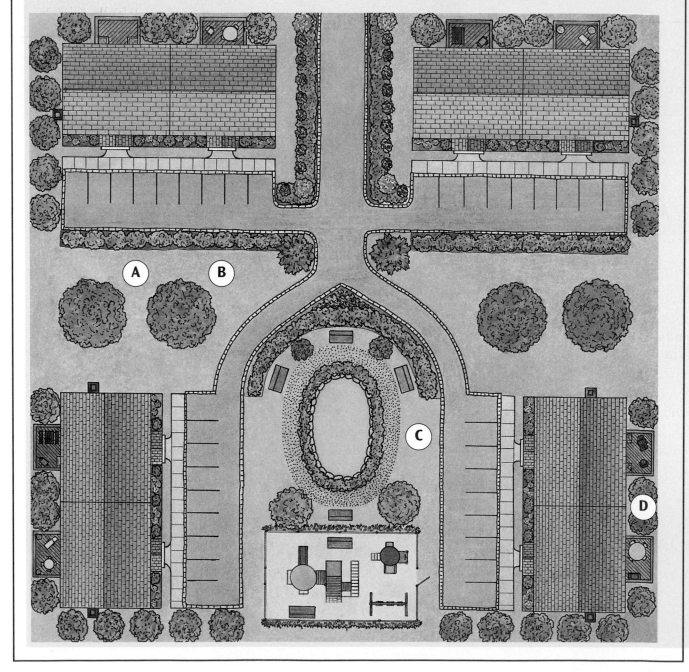

Landscape Planning

In this apartment complex, landscaping has been carefully planned to achieve several purposes.

A Grassy lawns with large shade trees provide safe areas for children to play.

B A row of shrubs separates each lawn area from the adjoining lot.

C Benches, flowering plants, and a reflecting pool create a central place for residents to relax and socialize.

D Small trees and shrubs shield each building from the noise and view of nearby streets.

DESIGNING THE LANDSCAPE

Whether a landscape is designed by a professional or by homeowners, good planning is the key to a successful outcome. Here are some of the steps involved in planning a landscape design.

- Determine how much time will be spent taking care of landscaping. Areas that are orderly and elaborate require more time to keep looking attractive. Natural plantings require less time.
- Assess the site over a period of time. Observe and keep track of details, such as which areas get sun and shade at different times of year.

- Consider the needs, wants, and lifestyle of the residents.
- Sketch a plan that shows the general location of landscape features, such as existing and planned trees, hedges, patios, flower beds, and play areas.
- Choose specific varieties of plants. To do so, first identify the characteristics desired (for example, a low-growing, red flowering annual). Check gardening books and catalogs to find plants that match those characteristics and are suitable for the climate. Local plant nurseries and county extension offices can also help you learn which types will grow best in your area.

USING NATURAL ELEMENTS

Natural elements—whether found on the site or added—are a major part of most landscaping plans. They include materials such as soil and rock as well as various types of plants.

Soil and type of terrain are basic features a landscaper must begin with. Landscapers can either work with the existing terrain, or they can alter the terrain to make it more attractive. Soil containing the right nutrients and the correct balance of sand, silt, and clay encourages plant growth. Landscapers who work with soil that lacks these qualities must fertilize the ground or look for other ways to enhance the land.

Trees and shrubs can serve to accent the landscape design and provide natural shade. Depending on the type, trees may also provide flowers, fruit, fall color, or winter greenery. When planted in rows, trees and shrubs can serve as a natural privacy fence or outline the boundaries of specific areas within the property.

Flowers add color and beauty to a landscaped area. They can be planted in beds along hillsides, around borders of lawns, or in pots and planters on patios and courtyards. Flowers vary in the amount of care they need. Some flowers, called *perennials*, never need replanting and continue to bloom year after year. Others, called *annuals*, must be planted each season. The climate of an environment affects whether you should add flowers to a site and your decision about the kind of flowers to plant. Some homeowners like to plant meadow seeds for wildflowers to replace grassy lawns.

Attractive landscaping adds a great deal to the visual appeal of a house and can make the environment more pleasant for everyone.

Many homeowners enjoy planting flowers and tending to their yards. What type of plants could be added to a yard to feed wildlife?

Groundcovers include grasses and various types of low-growing plants. Grass is the most common groundcover. Some grasses are suited to particular climates. In dry areas, having grass lawns is not ecologically sound since watering is required. Certain grasses grow well in shade, while others need full sun. Grass needs more maintenance than do other groundcovers. Vines, woody plants, and other groundcovers are perennials. Depending on the variety, groundcovers may bloom with tiny flowers, lose their leaves, or sprout cones. Groundcovers other than grass are often used in shady areas or where mowing is difficult. Choose plantings that are natural to an area because they will require less watering.

You might not think of rock as a landscaping element, but it has many uses. Flat paving stones can be used to form walkways or a decorative driveway. Small colorful rocks can keep weeds out of planting beds. Large rocks can serve as accents in a landscape design. Rock gardens are attractive and easy to maintain. In dry climates, combinations of rock and native plants are a popular—and often necessary—alternative to grassy lawns.

Don't overlook the possibilities of edible landscaping. Popular plantings include fruit and nut trees, strawberries as groundcover, and blueberry bushes. Consider planting for wildlife, too, such as birds, squirrels, and other small animals. Contact the extension office in your county or a local plant nursery for tips on which edible landscaping varieties grow best in your area.

USING MANUFACTURED ELEMENTS

Few landscape designs rely exclusively on natural elements. Manufactured elements such as fences and walkways often play a role in design.

Fences are used for decoration as well as privacy. Several types of fences are available, but two of the most popular are the *picket fence* and the *rail fence*. A picket fence is made of small vertical stakes held together by horizontal bars at the bottom and near the top. A rail fence is made of horizontal boards or bars supported by vertical posts.

Walkways and footpaths help define the space by adding a framework, and they make moving around a landscaped yard easy. Railroad ties, paving stones, and bricks are popular choices.

Outdoor lighting can have two purposes. It's a practical way to add beauty to a yard or common area. Certain types of lights can also provide safety and security at night. Low-voltage, solar, or spotlights can illuminate flowers and plants. Lights on stairs and along walkways help prevent falls. Spotlights—some motion-activated—can add to the security of entrances, garages, and outdoor areas.

LANDSCAPING TO SAVE WATER

Landscaping to conserve water is called **Xeriscaping** (ZIHR-uh-skay-ping). The key is choosing plants that are native to a geographic area or to another region with a similar climate. These plants need extra watering the first year, but once lished, they thrive on nothing more than natural rainfall. Here are some other water conservation tips.

- **Water early.** If you must water lawn and garden, do so in the early morning or in the evening to reduce evaporation.
- **Choose locations of plants carefully.** Plants that are sheltered from strong winds and glaring sun need less water.
- **Keep only a small lawn area.** Lawn grass soaks up water like a sponge. It needs more water and more pesticides than most other plants, and it requires more maintenance. For an open look, try wildflowers or prairie grasses instead. Groundcovers, such as vinca and pachysandra, look invitingly green and are easy to care for. Include decks and patios as part of the landscaping to reduce mowing and watering.
- **Keep grass long.** If you do have a patch of lawn, don't mow it too short. Taller (3-in. [7.6-cm]) grass blades shade the ground and

Lighting can make a house look more attractive by illuminating landscaping and structural features. Outdoor lighting can make a home safer as well.

reduce evaporation of soil moisture. They also develop deeper root systems that use water more efficiently.
- **Don't overfertilize.** Too much fertilizer makes plants need watering more often.

- **Avoid using sprinklers.** About half the water from a sprinkler evaporates before it ever touches the ground. A soaker hose or drip irrigation system works more effectively.

*Y*ou and the Environment

Housing and the environment can work together. Architects and builders can create successful, energy-efficient housing with methods and materials that do not harm the earth. People can make their homes energy efficient by using alternative energy sources, by installing better insulation and sealing ducts, and by purchasing more efficient technology. They can also conserve energy and water in many ways in their daily lives. Thought, planning, and access to environmentally-friendly materials and methods can enable people to respect the environment while retaining the quality of life they want.

Grant Shepherd

Landscape Architect

Landscape architects help others enjoy life. That's how I look at my job—or I guess I should say—the jobs that make up my career. Landscape architects work with a variety of other professionals including architects, engineers, construction contractors, urban planners, business administrators, and environmental scientists. We use our hands and our heads to analyze outdoor space, and then we create and present a design project for approval.

My career started as a volunteer in high school helping the staff of a nursing home with its grounds. We removed litter and and planted trees, shrubs, and flowers. The local horticultural society sponsored the project and helped us understand the principles of sunlight and shade, soil types and drainage. We contacted the Audubon Society about placing bird feeders and attracting colorful birds. Our group helped put in safe walkways so the residents could enjoy time outdoors. It was great to see people take a renewed interest in their surroundings.

That experience, and the yardwork I did to earn money for college, helped me realize that people don't just care about what's inside their homes. What's outside matters too! I chose a university with a strong landscape architecture program that included lots of emphasis on CAD design. Not surprisingly, the school had a lovely campus. One course, required for all landscape majors, requires designing a landscaping improvement for some part of the campus.

"Landscape architects help others enjoy life."

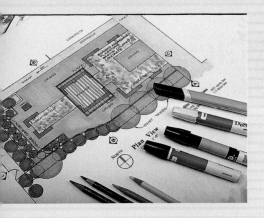

Business leaders have us designing a golf course. I've also worked with companies building single-family homes in a new subdivision, as well as those constructing a downtown high-rise with indoor gardens. I am particularly excited about a new project. A local hospital has just hired us to create grounds and green spaces to refresh and calm those undergoing trying circumstances. The result of this work is always satisfying.

As I've worked in the landscape architecture field, I've realized just how important "people skills" are in my work. My internship with a state agency gave me experience working with other professionals as we redesigned a state park campground. We visited the site time and again to analyze the "lay of the land." We took soil and plant samples and met with contractors. CAD drawings helped us visualize and convey plans for new roadways and level camping areas, as well as hiking trails and scenic views. The ultimate goal was to provide visitors with opportunities to enjoy nature, while not destroying its delicate balance.

Many landscape architects are self-employed, but I work for an engineering firm that offers landscape services. The design projects people hire us for are many and varied. Some of my colleagues are busy creating a proposed shopping center.

"People don't just care about what's inside their homes. What's outside matters, too!"

Career Profile

Landscape architects design projects and conduct impact studies to ensure building and recreational space is used safely and well. Projects can be as basic as creating "green space" within an industrial complex, or as exotic as the landscaping of a resort or wildlife refuge area.

Education
▸ A bachelor's degree, plus an internship, in landscape architecture is required. Master's degrees are desirable for areas of specialization. Licensing via the L.A.R.E./Landscape Architects Registration Examination is required in 46 states. Contact the Council of Landscape Architectural Registration Board for more information.
▸ Courses include surveying, CAD, site design and construction, ecology and environmental science, urban and regional planning.

Skills Needed
▸ Communication and writing skills are essential, since landscape artists develop design presentations, proposals, and impact studies.
▸ A knowledge of computer applications, including word processing, desktop publishing, and spreadsheets aid the work of the landscape architect. The ability to draft and design using CAD software is essential.
▸ Strong analytical skills, in addition to artistic talent, are needed as the landscape artist works both in the office and on-site.

Career Outlook
▸ Employment is expected to increase as fast as the average growth in construction. The growing demand for recreational areas will determine the trend. Due to low start-up costs, landscape architects often are self-employed.

Career Activities

1. Take a walking tour of a local business or retail district to study landscape design. Discuss in class what you liked about the designs you saw and what you would change.
2. Create your own garden design. You can also create a design that can be developed in planting containers.

Chapter Summary

- Housing can be designed or adapted to protect the environment.
- Most traditional fuels, such as oil, coal, and natural gas, are nonrenewable.
- Conservation and use of alternative energy sources can relieve energy shortages and reduce pollution.
- Advanced heating and cooling systems, such as heat pumps, are energy-efficient choices for homes.
- Architectural design that considers such factors as shapes of homes, colors of roofs, ceiling height, and placement and efficiency of windows can help people save energy.
- Water waste is decreased and pollution levels lowered by carefully planned construction and landscaping, water-saving habits, and efficient equipment.
- Use of natural building materials can be reduced by using recycled materials.
- Outdoor living areas are extensions of a home's interior that are often used for living space, relaxation, and casual entertainment.
- Landscaping can improve the outside environment of a home.

Checking Your Understanding

1. What is resource management, and how does it benefit the environment and people?
2. Identify the three types of traditional fossil fuels and state a disadvantage of each.
3. List three alternative energy sources.
4. Describe how a geothermal heat pump works and how it conserves energy.
5. What is the difference between active and passive solar heating?
6. Identify four ways that architectural design can help conserve energy.
7. Name three ways to retrofit a house for better energy efficiency.
8. Describe three recycled building materials that can be used in home construction.
9. What is the purpose of landscaping?
10. Give an example of how landscaping can provide privacy for a housing site.
11. Define Xeriscaping and give four examples.

Thinking Critically

1. Why should people care about conserving water if there is no shortage in their area?
2. What do you predict will happen in the future if people do not actively conserve natural resources?
3. Should conservation be voluntary, or should it be enforced by law? Give reasons for your answer.
4. Imagine that you want to donate money to a research group that will either come up with new recycled materials for building or invent energy-efficient heating systems. You must tell the group which alternative you think is more important and why.

Applications

1. **Writing Conservation Slogans.** Design three bumper stickers to promote water or energy conservation. Make the sayings as memorable as possible. For example: "Save water: Sing shorter shower songs."

2. **Analyzing Energy-Efficient Homes and Products.** Choose an energy-efficient product that has been used in, or would be suitable, for housing in your area. Identify the advantages and disadvantages of the technology used.

3. **Evaluating Building Materials.** Look around your classroom at the walls, ceiling, floor, windows, and door. Write down what material or materials you think each is constructed of. Then suggest what type of recycled building material or energy-efficient product could be substituted for it, or how you could make the existing room more energy efficient.

4. **Landscape Drawing.** Cut out a picture of the exterior of a home from a magazine or sketch one on a piece of paper. Cut out pictures of outdoor living spaces and landscaping elements to create a landscaping plan. Write a brief summary explaining why you chose these specific landscaping elements.

5. **Publish on the Web.** Assume that a local contractor has asked you to contribute an article for a website about innovative outdoor living spaces people could build in your area. Write a brief fact sheet highlighting your choice, its advantages and disadvantages, and how it could be developed.

BUILDING YOUR PORTFOLIO

You have decided to enter an article contest sponsored by *21st Century Homes* magazine. The theme for the contest is "Homes of the Future." In 900 to 1,500 words, entrants are to describe creatively a home that efficiently uses land, water, and building materials. Before you begin writing, investigate some interesting projections about housing of the future on the Internet or in the school's media center. You might also interview a housing professional in regard to his or her predictions about future housing trends. Begin with realistic predictions about housing trends and use your imagination to fill in the details.

Using Design

$\mathcal{T}$he Elements of Design

CHAPTER OBJECTIVES

► Describe the elements of good design and why they are useful.

► Explain the feelings that space can convey, and suggest how to change the apparent size of a space.

► Demonstrate ways to use line to create specific effects.

► Analyze the effects created by forms and shapes in particular designs.

► Illustrate how texture can be used to create desired effects.

TERMS TO LEARN

- color

- form

- harmonious design

- line

- space

- texture

*H*ave you ever walked into a room for the first time and been struck by how pleasing it looks or how welcoming it feels? Chances are the look and feel of this room—the design—didn't just "happen." The person who designed the room used the elements and principles of design to create the desired effect. Some people seem to be able to do this by instinct, but anyone can learn to use design elements and principles.

*B*lueprint for Success

*F*rom a very young age, humans are sensitive to order. People like things that are balanced and orderly. Pre-schoolers' drawings, for example, often show a sense of order.

The guidelines used by artists, designers, and architects to create pleasing, orderly designs are called the elements and principles of design. Rather than restrict the designer, the design elements and principles provide a general roadmap to follow that helps ensure success. The elements of design include:

- Space
- Line
- Form
- Texture
- Color

As you learn to recognize these elements, you will increase your design sensitivity. You'll see how the components of a piece of furniture, a room, or entire home combine to give an overall design impression.

With greater awareness of design elements, you can begin to look for and plan design in little things as well as large: from the arrangement of objects on a dresser to the placement of furniture in your room. When paired with the principles of design—which you'll read about in Chapter 17—an understanding of design elements can help you create a pleasing, comfortable environment that reflects your personal tastes.

The elements and principles of design were used in planning this functional living space, a favorite spot for family and friends to gather.

Space

Dictionaries list nearly a dozen meanings for the term "space." As an element of design, **space** is the three-dimensional expanse that a designer is working with, as well as the area around or between objects within that expanse. The two parts of this definition state the two aspects of space that a designer must consider—the size of the overall design space and the arrangement of objects within that space.

LARGE AND SMALL SPACES

City planners work with huge spaces in which they place buildings, homes, parks, streets, and other large components. For most people, however, design space is more confined. They may have an entire house or apartment to work with, or just a room, or even only part of a room.

Different-sized spaces convey a range of feelings. Large, open spaces give many people a feeling of freedom and sometimes of luxury. Too much empty space, on the other hand, can make people feel lonely and uncomfortable. If you've ever been alone in a room meant to hold hundreds of people, you may have felt that way. A room with a high ceiling or too few furnishings sometimes has the same effect. The empty parts of the room look much larger than the smaller areas containing furniture. The emptiness of those areas appears exaggerated.

Have you ever felt confined in a room with a low ceiling or in a crowded space? That feeling isn't unusual. On the other hand, well-designed small spaces can make people feel snug and secure. The feeling of these spaces is generally one of privacy or intimacy. People often seek this kind of space when they want to talk with others or relax alone.

ARRANGING SPACE

Whatever the size of the space, people have two general design choices—fill the space or leave much of it empty. How much space is filled and how the furnishings are arranged should be determined by the effect you want to achieve. It's possible to arrange small spaces to make them appear larger, and arrange large spaces to make them appear smaller.

To make a smaller space appear larger, keep as much space open as possible by limiting the number of furnishings. Select relatively small furniture of a plain design. Avoid using lots of patterns. You might install mirrors to visually enlarge the room. Another strategy is to choose furniture that has a dual purpose. A shelf unit with cabinets, for example, might hold books, photos, a television, and a CD player. The same unit might also have a door that pulls down to become a small desktop when needed.

When space is too large for its purpose, it can be divided with permanent or temporary room dividers or screens. You can also divide space by arranging furniture in small clusters, almost as if each group were within walls. There are also design tricks to make the space appear smaller. You might, for example, use area rugs to visually divide a large room.

As you arrange space, consider the feelings that the space conveys. Keep in mind that the effect space has on people also depends on how line and form—two other design elements—are used within that space.

Even in a large loft, it's possible to arrange furniture to make a conversation area warm and inviting.

*L*ine

Line is often called the most basic design element. **Line** delineates space, outlines form, and conveys a sense of movement or direction. Lines delineate space when they intersect to create two-dimensional planes. Examples of this are the lines that mark the edges of a wall, floor, or ceiling.

Lines can be used to convey a sense of strength, serenity, gracefulness, or action. One place to see how line conveys a sense of movement is in the distinct lines that make up some fabric and wallpaper patterns. Stripes are an obvious example. The outlines of objects and the lines formed by groups of objects also convey movement and direction. An example is a row of windows.

All lines are either straight or curved, and are placed in a direction—vertical, horizontal, or diagonal. Lines can be combined to make zigzags or other variations. Combining lines and placing them in a design in certain ways can create specific effects and feelings.

CREATING EFFECTS WITH LINE

A variety of lines is desirable in a room design. However, confusion results when lines and shapes aren't used harmoniously. The use of line can also have an effect on how space is perceived. For example, lines can be used either to separate or unify space. The effect happens because when people see a line, their eyes tend to follow along the line from one end to the other.

Another effect that line can create is increased height. If you've been inside a home with tall windows, you may have noticed they seem to add height and strength to the room. The illusion of greater height is, again, created by the eye. As you look at a tall window or long draperies, your eye is drawn in a vertical direction—up and down—emphasizing the vertical space. That visual effect also works when a short person wears clothes with vertical stripes.

Width can be emphasized too. Low sofas and bookshelves draw your gaze around the room and create the illusion of greater width. The same effect can be achieved with smaller objects. By aligning the tops of picture frames in a wall grouping, you create the effect of a continuous line.

The Mission-style furniture complements this bedroom. How would you describe the lines?

CONVEYING FEELINGS WITH LINE

Lines may suggest various feelings because they remind people of human characteristics. A horizontal line may suggest rest because people and animals sleep in that position. A vertical line may suggest action because humans are upright when they walk. Runners lean forward and their bodies form diagonal lines. Diagonal or zigzag lines convey excitement and movement.

By placing lines in certain combinations and directions, you can create restful feelings or exciting ones. A bedroom with mainly diagonal or zigzag lines might not convey the calm feeling desired for sleep. Horizontal lines and a few decorative patterns would seem relaxing and more soothing. In a workout room or a game room, crisscrossing lines would contribute to an exciting decor. Curved lines have a graceful effect. In nature, curved lines are the most common. Circles, curves, and ovals are likely to be perceived as more natural and free than straight ones.

Too many lines in a room can carry the intended effect to an extreme. Many sharp angles and competing lines can cause continu-

The graceful curved lines of the desk and window treatment soften the sharp angles of the window and wall molding. How would it look instead with straight draperies hanging at the sides?

ous eye movement in the viewer. This creates a feeling of tiredness and confusion. If a busy design is confined to a small area, however, a point of interest is created. For instance, placing a small rug with a zigzag pattern on a bare wood floor in front of a solid-color sofa achieves interest without dominance.

The characteristics of line in fabric and wall coverings are easy to

identify. Not so obvious are the lines indicated by entire objects. For example, a tall bookcase, as a whole, creates a vertical line against the wall. Sometimes, too, line can evoke an emotional response simply because of its own beauty. The graceful curve of an archway, a stairway, a vase, or a mirror catches the eye.

Form

Another design element that can easily be seen is form. **Form** describes the shape and structure of solid objects. Form may be two-dimensional or three-dimensional. Walls and rugs are examples of two-

dimensional forms. They have length and width but little or no depth. Three-dimensional forms, such as chairs and other furniture, have depth in addition to length and width.

CREATING EFFECTS WITH FORM

Form, like line, can be used to achieve certain effects. Large, heavy objects, such as a piano or sofa, usually give a feeling of stability. Their massive appearance adds a solid feeling to a room.

Another way to create stability in design is to place several small objects together. Two chairs and a table placed close together, for example, have a visual effect similar to a large sofa. Long, low tables achieve the same effect because of their shape.

Placement of form can also create the appearance of instability. When the bottom of an object is too small in proportion to the top, the object looks as if it might topple over. When you say that something is "top-heavy," you are recognizing this quality in the object. A triangle balanced on one of its three points is a classic example of a top-heavy form. A chair that tips over easily may have legs that aren't far enough apart. Like the triangle, it has a base that is too small.

Weight is an interesting factor in considering form. A designer is more concerned with an object's *apparent*

weight than its actual weight. Sometimes the same form can appear lighter or heavier based on its color or texture. For instance, the form of a beige sofa against a beige wall may not appear especially heavy. The same sofa with a denim slipcover against that light-colored wall would have more apparent weight.

The forms of the upholstered furniture give this living room a solid feeling. How do you think delicate furniture would look in its place?

Harmonious Design

A designer strives to combine forms in a way that creates a **harmonious design**—a design in which every item fits well with the others. Homes in some new developments or older city neighborhoods often have similar designs with only minor variations. They may be related in form, size, and color. The similarities are often the result of the homes having been built around the same time, perhaps by one builder.

In furniture, too, it's important that forms harmonize with one another. Suppose that you have a long sofa with a simple curving line and are looking for a table to go with it. Which would create a harmonious arrangement—a large table that echoes the curve of the sofa or a small antique telephone stand?

The small stand in the example is quite different in form from the sofa. Often when forms that are very different from one another are placed together, the effect isn't satisfying. As you work with the design elements, try to increase your awareness of form. Ask yourself the following questions: Is this form right for its intended function? Does it add to the stability of the room or detract from it? Does it blend well with other forms in the room? As you learn to answer such questions with ease, you'll know that you are developing an eye for analyzing good design form.

Row houses in San Francisco are a classic example of harmonious design in architecture. The concept of harmony is also important in interior design.

Texture

An object's **texture** is the appearance or feel of its surface. When you run your fingers over the surface of something, your sense of touch reveals the *tactile texture*—the feeling of roughness or smoothness—of that surface. You can often predict what a surface will feel like from its appearance. Modern printing techniques, however, can fool the eye.

What appears to be a rough-textured wall covering may be smooth paper printed to make it look rough. These surfaces have a smooth tactile texture, but a rough *visual texture*.

Responses to texture are personal and subjective. Do you prefer rough, nubby textures or smooth ones? Do you feel comfortable in rooms with strongly contrasting textures? Your response to the texture of an object can influence your reaction to the whole form or space. For example, have you ever admired the form of a sofa or chair from a distance, but found at close range that you disliked its texture?

SPECIAL EFFECTS WITH TEXTURE

Texture can influence the way people feel in a room. Plush, deep-pile carpet and furniture covered with soft fabric provide a sense of comfort. Nubby, rough materials convey a feeling of ruggedness and stability. Smooth velvets and heavy brocades suggest luxury. Glass, metal, and stone give a feeling of coolness.

To suggest a formal mood in a living room, you might choose a Persian rug and an oil painting for the wall. For a casual look, you

Consumer Sense

Adding Texture to Surfaces

Adding the impression of texture can transform plain surfaces—whether they're walls, doors, furniture, or accessories—into something eye-catching and unique. Decorative painting and *faux finishes* can give flat surfaces more of a three-dimensional, textured look. *(Faux,* pronounced "foe," is the French word for false.) With the right painting technique, surfaces can be made to resemble stucco, antique metal, brick, or stone.

Most of the techniques use water-based latex paints and glazes over a semigloss latex base coat. Using these paints allows for easy cleanup with soap and water. Other common household items, such as masking tape, plastic wrap, combs, and feathers, are sometimes used.

These techniques require a bit of practice. One way to try your hand is to start with a small project—such as a tray or box—before moving on to something bigger. This gives you a chance to perfect your technique.

Here are some of the most popular methods:

- **SPONGING.** First, a base coat of paint is applied to the entire surface. Then a natural sea sponge, dipped in paint, is used to create the texture. The sponging can be applied in several layers with different colors, or it can be a single application.
- **RAGGING.** A ragged (RAGD) finish begins with a base coat over the surface. Then a wad of fabric (such as muslin or corduroy) or even plastic wrap is used to dab another color of paint on the surface.

- **FAUX GRANITE.** The first step in creating a granite look is to apply a base coat. Next, sea sponges dipped in paint are used to create the spotted look of granite. The number of applications depends on the granite you are trying to duplicate. Some looks call for five or six colors.
- **FAUX MARBLE.** Creating the look of marble is one of the more difficult decorative techniques. After the base coat is applied to the surface, a natural sea sponge is used to add another color. Thin, round artist's brushes, or sometimes feathers, are used to create the veining of marble. After applying vein lines to the surface, a soft brush is used to soften the lines.

YOU THE CONSUMER . . .

Suppose you would like to add some texture to the white walls in your entryway. Compared to wallpapering the area, what might be the advantages of using one of these decorative techniques? What disadvantages might there be? How could you learn to use these techniques?

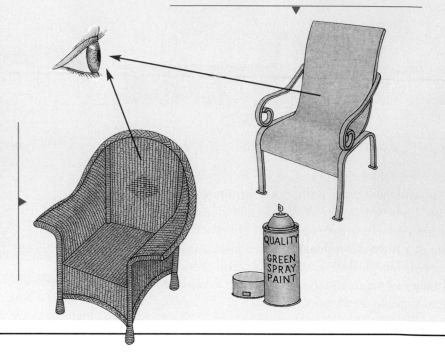

How Texture Affects Apparent Color

The perceived color of a surface is the result of some light waves being reflected from the surface while other waves are absorbed by it. The texture of a surface affects the way it reflects light, and thus its color.

The surface of this metal chair—painted with green paint—is *smooth*.

A smooth surface *reflects* much of the light that strikes it.

The smooth surface reflects light in straight, orderly lines to the eye.

The surface of the metal chair appears light green to the observer.

The surface of this wicker chair—painted with green paint—is *rough*.

A rough surface *absorbs* much of the light that strikes it. The light that is reflected is sent in various directions, creating shadows on the surface.

Although painted the same color as the smooth metal chair, the wicker chair appears darker to the observer.

QUALITY GREEN SPRAY PAINT

---

might hang a swag of dried flowers on the wall and choose a jute rug for the floor.

Texture can also affect the apparent size of an object. For instance, a chair covered in a rough, loosely woven fabric may seem larger than the same piece covered in a smooth, satin-like fabric.

Another interesting aspect of texture is the way it affects color. In general, smooth textures appear lighter in color than rough textures. Figure 15-1 illustrates this phenomenon and its relationship to vision.

TEXTURE AND VARIETY

Texture is useful for adding variety and interest to a room. For example, you might break up a smooth wall by hanging an antique quilt or an arrangement of baskets or decorative plates on it.

Careful planning is important, however. Watch out for undesirable effects, such as designs that use too many different textures. Limiting the number of textures to a few will help you avoid this problem. Through experience, you will develop confidence in using this element of design.

Color

All elements of design are important, but most designers agree that **color** is the most significant. People are able to express their individuality with color. It's possible to set a mood or create an illusion with color. You can even make a warm room seem several degrees cooler—and a cool room can actually feel warmer.

The design elements you have read about so far can be used to create certain effects. When you combine them with color, however, the possibilities become much more exciting. You will see why when you read more about this important design element in Chapter 16.

Color is a design element that most people enjoy working with. Can you pick out other elements of design in this cheerful room?

Using Design Elements

Paying attention to all the elements of design really makes a difference in design. Ashley was inspired to redecorate when she came home from a weekend visit at her friends' new condominium. She spent the next Saturday afternoon at the mall and came home to duplicate some of her friends' ideas. Her purchases included a fringed throw for the sofa, a patterned rug, an ornate mirror, and some paint for an old rocking chair that had been in the garage.

After painting the large rocker and hanging the mirror, Ashley surveyed the results. She had to admit that the change wasn't what she'd anticipated. The colors and textures didn't look the same in her apartment. The rocking chair made its corner seem crowded. The mirror took up too much space on the narrow wall.

Now that you have learned about the elements of design, can you figure out what Ashley did wrong? If you said that Ashley needed to take into account the form and characteristics of her existing furnishings, you're right. The size and layout of her apartment, as well as the lines, colors, textures, and lighting there, affected her design success. Considering the elements of design is important—whether you're designing a room from top to bottom, or just adding some special touches.

John Harding

Space Planner

The next time you are in a large office complex, look closely at the furnishings and how they are arranged. The design of such spaces is usually the work of an interior space planner, a specialized field within interior design. Space planners generally develop plans for commercial offices or other large institutions—selecting the furniture, equipment, and lighting and determining how it will be arranged. In addition to applying the principles of good space design, a space planner must understand the types of environments that encourage productivity.

I became interested in space planning when I was an intern at an architectural firm in Dallas. Our company was hired to redesign an office complex for a major corporation. What we found was poor, almost chaotic, use of the space. The reception area was too far from the main entrance. People who needed privacy for conversations were sitting very close to other employees. Many employees had to stack files and paper on the floor. Lighting was inadequate in many areas.

It was obvious that these employees needed a better environment to work effectively. It took us six months to transform the office complex. Once the job was completed, some of the employees sent notes to thank us for creating an environment that made it exciting to come to work. I really liked the idea of using my skills to make a positive difference in the attitudes of people, so I decided to find a full-time job as a space planner.

The firm I currently work with specializes in office space planning. Large corporations all over the world hire us to develop space plans and specifications. Specifications usually include choosing furniture, equip-

> *"We found poor, almost chaotic, use of the space."*

new products, technology, and concepts. I read trade magazines and attend space-planning conferences. Conferences give me an opportunity to attend workshops and presentations, and to talk to the manufacturer's representatives about their new products. Every year there are new furniture designs, fabrics, and office systems. I use the Internet to get product information and find design solutions. Actual plans are developed using computer-aided drafting and design (CAD) software. In the future I'm sure that the Internet and other technology will continue to transform the way that space planners work and offices function.

ment, materials, and lighting. Our firm places a great deal of emphasis on effective lighting.

International companies are especially exciting to work for. To develop a space plan for these companies requires an understanding of that country's culture. Cultures differ, for example, about how they view privacy and social interaction. One culture might require heavy doors for private office spaces to assure privacy, whereas a closed office door might offend in another culture. Every situation is unique. It is exciting to learn about the differences and plan accordingly. We always conduct a thorough assessment of the employees' needs before we start a project. By interviewing employees, we identify how they do their job and what they need to be successful.

My profession is always changing. We have to constantly keep up with

"By interviewing employees, we identify how they do their job and what they need to be successful."

Career Profile

Space planners design the space and specify the furniture, equipment, and lighting for public buildings, and commercial or institutional establishments, such as offices, restaurants, hotels, and retail stores. Space planners often work for architectural or interior design firms.

Education
▸ Space planners normally need a bachelor's degree.
▸ Courses in interior design, principles of design, art, ergonomics, drawing, computer-aided drafting, architectural drawing, and lighting are helpful.

Skills Needed
▸ This profession requires both the ability to sketch and draw freehand, and computer-aided drafting and design proficiency.
▸ The ability to handle detail work accurately is required.
▸ Visual and spatial aptitudes are important.
▸ Knowledge of the principles and practices of interior design is critical.
▸ Good interpersonal skills are required for working with clients, interior designers, architects, and other professionals.

Career Outlook
▸ Space planners are in high demand. As the need for professionally designed offices, restaurants, and other institutions continues, job openings are expected to increase. More information can be obtained from the American Society for Interior Designers.

Career Activities

1. Study how space is arranged in your school library. Sketch a design for a new plan for the library and give your rationale.
2. Devise ten questions you might ask an accountant to determine how his or her office should be planned.

Chapter Summary

➤ When used with the principles of design, the five basic elements of design can help ensure the success of a design project.

➤ Space is the three-dimensional expanse that a designer is working with, as well as the area around or between objects within that expanse.

➤ The feelings conveyed by large spaces are different from those conveyed by small spaces.

➤ The size of space can be changed physically or visually.

➤ Line delineates space, outlines form, and conveys a sense of direction.

➤ Various line arrangements create specific feelings.

➤ Form, like line, can be used to achieve stability and other effects.

➤ A good design uses forms that harmonize with one another.

➤ Texture influences how people feel in a room.

Checking Your Understanding

1. Identify and describe the elements of design.

2. What feelings might be conveyed by a very large space?

3. Describe one way to make a large space appear smaller.

4. Explain one way to create the appearance of extra height in a room.

5. Give an example of a way to use line to emphasize the width of a room.

6. What feelings do these lines suggest: horizontal, vertical, zigzag?

7. Explain the difference between actual weight and apparent weight. Give an example.

8. What term describes a design in which every item fits well with the others?

9. Describe textures used in formal and in informal design.

10. How can the texture of an object affect the appearance of its color?

Thinking Critically

1. Give examples of a room or other space that you felt was too large, one that seemed too small, and a space that felt comfortable. Analyze the reasons why each space created that impression. What design changes might make the first two spaces seem more comfortable?

2. What types of lines dominate the exterior of your school building? Which are used most in your classroom? What design effects are created by these lines?

3. Describe two versions of the same room (such as a living room or bedroom). For the first version, describe furnishings that you would include to create a feeling of stability. For the other version, describe similar items of furniture that would have a lighter form.

4. If you wanted to purchase a sofa, why would it be necessary to bring the sample of fabric home before placing the order?

Applications

1. **Internet Assessment.** Working with a partner, visit interior designers' or real estate agents' websites to find actual room designs. Find examples of design elements and discuss their use in the various settings.

2. **Elements of an Era.** Locate photos of two living rooms, dining rooms, bedrooms, or kitchens that depict styles from two different eras—for instance, modern and Victorian. Write a brief essay focusing on the way line is used in the two settings. Are there other differences in the way design elements were used?

3. **Space Exploration.** Find photos that illustrate at least three of the following: a large space which is mainly empty; a large space that has been divided in some manner; a large space that's filled; a small space which is rather empty; and a small space that has been filled. Mount the photos on a poster board. Label them and indicate what you perceive the mood or feeling of each room to be.

4. **Harmonious Housing.** Select a street or neighborhood in your community as an example of homes with harmonious design. Sketch or photograph a scene showing several of the homes together. Write a paragraph explaining the features that make the structures harmonious.

5. **Texture Board.** Collect samples of fabric and carpeting that represent different textures. Cut them so they are all the same size. Classify the samples as either formal or informal. Mount them on a sheet of poster board and label the types of fabrics.

BUILDING YOUR PORTFOLIO

Your client is an insurance agent who is leasing space in a new office building. She has hired you to design a waiting area for her clients. The agent tells you that most of the time the room would be used by no more than three or four people. She wants them to feel comfortable, but also wants to convey that they can trust her with their business. The waiting area is 8 ft. x 12 ft. (2.5 m x 3.6 m). Write an essay describing the ideas you would present to her. Address all of the elements of design in your comments: space, line, form, texture, and color.

Color and the Design Process

CHAPTER OBJECTIVES

- ► Analyze how color can be used to create moods and illusions.

- ► Explain how primary colors are used to produce other colors on the color wheel.

- ► Describe the effects of intensity and value on various hues.

- ► Identify the characteristics of different types of color schemes.

- ► Describe factors to consider when planning a color scheme.

TERMS TO LEARN

- accented neutral
- analogous
- color scheme
- complement
- complementary
- hue
- intensity
- monochromatic
- pigments
- shade
- split-complementary
- tint
- triadic
- value

The duplex your cousin just rented has a great location, but needs to be repainted. The walls are dirty, and the dark, low ceilings give the rooms a closed-in feeling. Your cousin finds a note from the landlord offering to buy the necessary paint. "No wild colors" is the postscript at the bottom. Your cousin turns to you and asks hopefully, "Do you want to help choose a color scheme?"

The Magic of Color

The words *color* and *magic* seem to go hand in hand. Perhaps this is because color affects how people feel. It can evoke memories or emotions or trigger certain thoughts in your mind. It can even play tricks on your eyes. Some psychologists study people's color perception and other attitudes, feelings, and responses to colors. Designers often rely on the psychological effects of color to help them achieve their goals. Individuals can do the same as they plan new color combinations for their homes.

SETTING A MOOD

Color influences how people feel. Because colors create certain moods, they should be chosen carefully. Red, for example, can make people feel bold, excited, or even nervous. Orange, which is less aggressive, may make them feel friendly, hopeful, and full of energy. Blue is generally subdued and is often used to create a calm feeling. However, large amounts of dark blue can be a poor choice because it can be depressing. Many greens have a calming influence.

Did you know that yellow can be effective in rooms used for studying? It suggests cheerfulness and happiness. If you want to enhance the appearance of natural light in a room, yellow is a good choice. Gold has a similar effect, but is considered more formal.

Neutral colors such as whites and grays evoke certain feelings as well. An all-white room has a simple, clean look, but can lead to feelings of isolation. For some people, too much gray can result in a lack of energy.

Builders often use the same neutral tint throughout a new home, but it's unlikely that you would choose to have every room in your home the same color. One reason is because of the specific moods that colors can create. Another is because living with color is enjoyable for most people.

How would you describe the feeling of this room—warm or cool? Which of these two living rooms do you prefer? Why?

WARM AND COOL COLORS

It's possible to feel warmer or cooler because of a color. In general, colors associated with the sun—red, orange, and yellow—are called warm colors. Red-orange conveys the most warmth of any color. Blues and greens—colors that capture the essence of the ocean—are called cool colors.

However, depending on the base, or undertones, of the color, it's quite possible to have a relatively warm green or cool yellow. Blues appear warmer when red is added to them; the opposite is true when green is added. Making a wise color selection in a design scheme can change the feeling of warmth or coolness in a room even if the temperature stays the same.

The colors you choose will depend partly on the purpose of the rooms. Cool colors are popular in bedrooms, bathrooms, and home offices because of their relaxing effect. Warm colors are especially suitable in areas of activity.

ILLUSIONS WITH COLOR

Color can fool the eye. At the same distance, warm-colored objects appear closer than cool-colored ones. You can visually enlarge a small room, for example, by painting the walls a cool color.

Dark and light colors also create illusions. A high ceiling that is painted a dark color will seem lower, and a light color will cause a low ceiling to appear higher. Bold, bright colors make objects stand out. On a tan sofa, your eye would be drawn to turquoise pillows; white pillows would be less likely to be noticed. A dark walnut bookcase seems to fill more wall space against an ivory wall than a bleached oak bookcase against a deep blue wall.

Remember that repainting can be time-consuming. You are more likely to get the effect you want the first time with some advance planning. You want to be happy with the results for a long time.

Components of Color

The endless array of colors makes the process of choosing colors for a room design quite challenging. Learning about colors and how they combine with one another will give you greater confidence in color selection.

THE SCIENCE OF COLOR

Color is a property of light. Light is made up of energy rays of different wavelengths. Each wavelength is a separate color. When sunlight passes through a prism, the rays are bent. Because each wavelength bends a different amount, the light is separated into its component colors: red, orange, yellow, green, blue, indigo (a deep blue), and violet. The display is called *visible spectrum*. The red rays, which are the longest, bend the least. They appear on one side of the spectrum. The shortest rays are violet. They are on the opposite side of the spectrum because they bend the most. A spectrum also appears when the sun's rays pass through water vapor to form a rainbow. Have you ever noticed that the colors always appear in the same pattern?

All objects contain **pigments**, substances that absorb some light rays and reflect others. The colors that you see are the reflected light rays. For instance, when light strikes a red chair, all the rays in the light are absorbed except the red rays. The red rays bounce off the surface and we see the chair as red. Most objects reflect some of the rays in the light that hits them. If no light is reflected, the object is black. If all light is reflected, it is white.

THE COLOR WHEEL

You have probably seen the color wheel before. It's a helpful tool for visualizing how different colors are related to one another. The placement of each color on the wheel is significant. Use Figure 16-1 to analyze the relationship of the colors on the color wheel.

Have you ever seen a rainbow with colors in a different order than the one shown here?

FIGURE 16-1

A VISUAL GUIDE TO...

The Color Wheel

The color wheel is a circular arrangement of colors. The sequence of colors on the wheel is fixed. This color wheel has been expanded to display shades and tints.

PRIMARY COLORS: yellow, red, and blue. These colors are basic—they cannot be created by mixing other colors.

SECONDARY COLORS: orange, violet, and green. These colors are made by mixing equal parts of two primary colors. Secondary colors appear on the color wheel halfway between the primary colors that make them.

TERTIARY COLORS: yellow-orange, red-orange, red-violet, blue-violet, blue-green, and yellow-green. Tertiary (TUR-shee-air-ee) colors are also known as "intermediate" colors. They are created by combining a primary color with a neighboring secondary color.

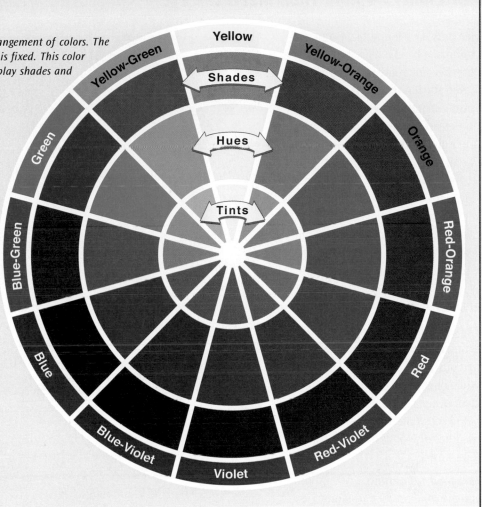

THE LANGUAGE OF COLOR

Several special terms refer to the different qualities of color. Learning these terms will help you better understand and analyze color. By using the language of color, you can communicate your color ideas much more precisely.

The specific name of a color is its **hue**. Hue is the feature of color that makes one color different from others. Each color on the color wheel is a hue.

Black, white, and gray don't appear on the color wheel because they have no hue. Technically, they are not colors at all, but often they're called *neutral colors*. Because they're neutral, they tend to blend well with other colors.

Color Choices—More Than Meets the Eye

Researchers have found that certain colors can make people relax, feel more hungry, become more or less aggressive, and even show more creativity. These physical, mental, and emotional responses occur even though you aren't aware of them. That makes color a powerful tool in the interior design of public and commercial spaces.

How does it work? That's not yet completely understood. Still, designers who are aware of specific colors' effects can take advantage of them. They can suggest color schemes that create an effect appropriate for the space. Here are some examples:

- **The dentist's office.** Imagine yourself sitting in the reception area, waiting nervously for your name to be called. While magazines can distract you, the color of the room and furnishings can help keep you calm. Blue is often used because of its ability to minimize anxiety.

- **Fast-food restaurants.** The next time you are in a fast-food restaurant, check out the color scheme. Chances are you will find lots of red and orange. Why? Red increases your appetite. Orange can add excitement and help you make quick decisions.

You will eat and leave more quickly so someone else can take your place.

- **Schools.** One study tested the effects of color by repainting half the interior of a New York City school. The halls were painted a muted pink, while the classrooms became blue, green, cream, and beige. The results were astonishing. In the repainted half of the school, students' attention span, cooperation, and grades improved. The student body hadn't changed, but the new colors helped to bring about a greatly improved atmosphere.

- **Offices.** In an office where lawyers meet clients, dark wood can convey a sense of security and permanence. If cubicles house graphic artists, light blue can enhance creativity—or purple can spark imagination. Neutrals like beige and gray, when used without sufficient accent colors, can be depressing and unfriendly. That's not conducive to productivity. Cream and light yellow are more cheerful and improve concentration.

You, the Designer

Imagine you are part of a design team responsible for the color schemes in a remodeled hospital. Decide what colors you would recommend for patients' rooms. What colors would you use in waiting areas for patients' families? Give reasons for your choices.

Intensity

The brightness or dullness of a color is called its **intensity**. Purity and strength are other terms for intensity. You can lessen a color's intensity by mixing it with its **complement**, the color that is opposite it on the color wheel.

Intense or pure colors are bright and stimulating. Objects with high color intensity seem larger and closer than objects with low intensity. Colors of low intensity are more muted. Muted colors generally create a calmer effect than highly intense or pure colors. In the 1970s, orange was such a popular color that many people had bright orange carpeting installed. It wasn't long before some realized that a large area of such an intense color wasn't easy to live with.

Value

The lightness or darkness of a color is its **value**. The basic hues in the color wheel are considered middle or normal values.

Adding white to a hue raises its value, or lightens it. The result is a **tint**, a hue that is lighter than its normal value. For example, pink is a tint of red. Peach is a tint of orange.

Adding black to a hue lowers its value, or darkens it. The result is a **shade**, a color that is darker than its normal value. For example, navy is a popular shade of blue. Rust is a shade of orange.

Tints and shades are considered to have the same hue as the original color, but they have a different value. Figure 16-2 summarizes some of the ways colors can be mixed to produce new colors.

Color chips from paint manufacturers are typically arranged from tints to shades.

FIGURE 16-2

Creating Colors

Types of Colors	Examples	How They're Mixed
Secondary Color	orange green violet	red + yellow yellow + blue blue + red
Tertiary	red-orange yellow-green blue-violet	red + orange yellow + green blue + violet
Tints	pink peach lavender	red + white orange + white violet + white
Shade	navy maroon forest green	blue + black red + black green + black

Color Schemes

With so many individual colors to choose from, how can you be sure the combination you have chosen will be pleasing—not just to you, but to others? Although color preferences are personal, designers have established certain tried and true ways of developing color schemes. A **color scheme** is a combination of colors selected for a room design in order to create a mood or set a tone. You can create pleasing color schemes based on the color wheel, as described in Figure 16-3.

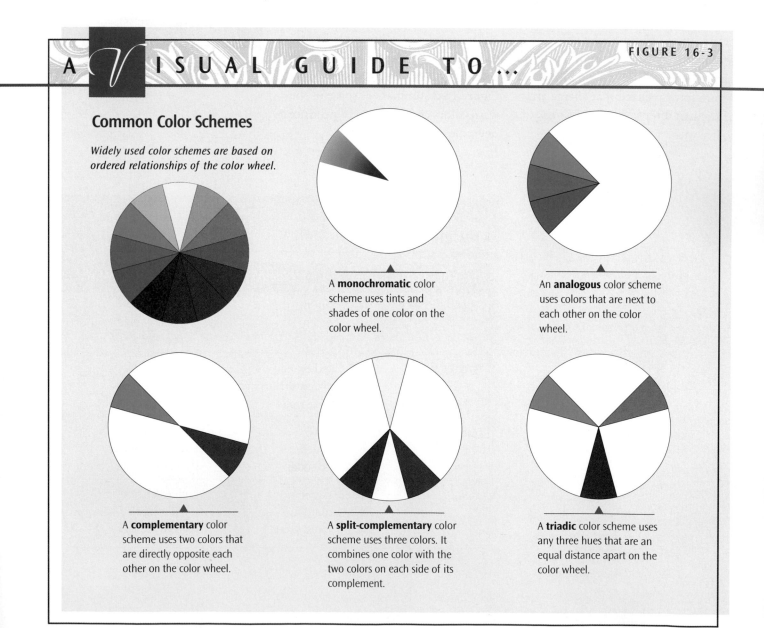

FIGURE 16-3

A VISUAL GUIDE TO...

Common Color Schemes

Widely used color schemes are based on ordered relationships of the color wheel.

A **monochromatic** color scheme uses tints and shades of one color on the color wheel.

An **analogous** color scheme uses colors that are next to each other on the color wheel.

A **complementary** color scheme uses two colors that are directly opposite each other on the color wheel.

A **split-complementary** color scheme uses three colors. It combines one color with the two colors on each side of its complement.

A **triadic** color scheme uses any three hues that are an equal distance apart on the color wheel.

White, black, and gray can be used to create a *neutral color scheme.* Color schemes based on beige and brown are also typically regarded as neutral. It's common for people to fear making mistakes with color and feel "safer" working with neutral color schemes. Many people find that these color schemes are also easier to live with than color schemes based on vibrant colors. Professional designers often encourage clients to use more color.

To provide contrast, a small amount of bright color is sometimes used in a neutral color scheme. The result is called an **accented neutral**, or "neutral-plus," color scheme. In a beige family room, for instance, red lamps, pillows, and picture frames might be added for contrast. The occupant of a rather sterile-looking apartment might paint one wall of the white living room a shade of apricot for emphasis.

Bright colors, such as red, yellow, and blue, are often seen in children's rooms. This softer look was achieved by using less intense hues. What is this color scheme called?

What is the name of this bedroom's color scheme? If the red accents were removed, what would it be called?

PLANNING COLOR SCHEMES

One type of color scheme is not better than the others. In many instances, a color scheme that is satisfying in one setting may be disappointing in another. One individual or family may like a color scheme that another person would not. To be successful, a color scheme should suit the place, the people, and purpose for which it's intended.

Factors to Consider

Take plenty of time choosing colors for a color scheme. Consider the following factors before making the investment of money and time.

MOOD. Decide on the mood you hope to create. Do you want the effect to be active or restful? Formal or casual? Sophisticated or relaxed? What colors would you choose for a sophisticated look?

PEOPLE. If others will share the space in a home or office, ask for their input about colors. You may not be able to please everybody, but avoid using a color in a common area if someone really doesn't like it.

STYLE. The style of the room and your furniture may influence your choice of color. For example, a room with Spanish-style features and stucco walls is often painted a shade of white. You might favor muted Williamsburg tints, such as a dusty green, in a colonial-style home.

TIME. The amount of time you'll spend in a room is also a consideration. Many people reserve dramatic color schemes for areas where they spend little time, such as an entryway or stairway. Another option is to use the intense color on one wall only. Such an accent wall is relatively simple to change.

EXISTING COLORS. Most people have to accept some room components they can't change without substantial expense: carpeting, ceramic tile, countertops, draperies, and furniture. If so, they can plan a color scheme that incorporates the colors of those elements.

The colors in this dining room appear across from each other on the color wheel. Is this color scheme complementary or monochromatic?

ADJACENT ROOMS. When there's an archway or an open passage between two rooms, you can see parts of both rooms at the same time. That doesn't mean colors have to be the same, yet you'll want to consider how they harmonize. To create a unified look, many designers believe that one color, called a *signature color*, should run throughout a home, even if only in small amounts.

LIGHTING. Lighting, both natural and artificial, has a significant effect on color. When a room has a great deal of bright natural light, for example, white walls may seem too stark and glaring. Muted or cool colors might be a better choice. On the other hand, a room without much natural light will seem brighter if a warm color is used.

Different kinds of light change the way colors appear. Did you ever buy a shirt that you thought was a certain color, only to find that it looked completely different when you brought it home? The difference in lighting was probably responsible. Natural light shows objects in their true colors. Different kinds of artificial light, on the other hand, can make colors appear more blue or yellow than they really are.

For all of these reasons, it's important to choose colors under lighting conditions similar to those in the room you are designing. Bring paint, wallpaper, flooring, and fabric samples home. Look at them at various times of the day and evening. They can look different, depending on the light at the time. (You will learn more about lighting in Chapter 22.)

SELECTING COLORS

After considering the factors that affect your color choices, you can begin to finalize a color scheme. It may begin with a *color concept*, such as a teen saying she wants her bedroom to be yellow and blue. In any event, start with the dominant color. This may be a favorite color, the color of a rug or a piece of furniture,

or a color that sets the mood you hope to create. It should be a color you (or the client) enjoy and can live with. Remember, a general rule of thumb is to avoid too much or too little color. Consider that intense colors in large quantities may overpower the room. Limiting their use to accents may be a better option. Substituting a tint or shade of the color is another alternative.

To select the additional colors, you might use the color wheel. For example, suppose that you decide to use various shades of blue and blue-green in an analogous color scheme. A light tint of blue for the walls might be combined with brighter blue-green accents. For color scheme ideas, look through magazines to find rooms with colors that appeal to you. You may also find color

schemes that you like in a painting, fabric, wallpaper, or even in your favorite dishes.

As you make choices, ask yourself if the colors you're considering have *color harmony*. The colors should relate in a way that is pleasing and satisfying when you look at them together. If you don't like something about the color scheme or you're indifferent toward it, keep looking for other options.

Creating a Color Sample Board

When planning a color scheme, it's helpful to make a preliminary sample board, or collage, of the colors and materials that may be used. The sample board provides an idea of how the different colors, patterns, and textures will look together. To make a sample board:

- Use pins or thumb tacks to mount samples on a foam-core board so you're able to move swatches around and change your plan.
- Gather as many actual samples as you can of the materials you plan to use: paint, wallpaper, fabrics, flooring, even wood finishes. If you can't obtain actual samples, approximate the colors using colored pencils, paint, or pictures from magazines.

Existing colors must be taken into account when selecting a color scheme. If the buyers of this home wanted a lighter color scheme in their dining room, what existing features would they have to consider?

If you like a color at the store, why should you take it home before making a final choice?

- Vary the size of the samples so that they are in the same proportion to one another as the real objects. For instance, the carpet sample might be three times the size of the fabric swatch you're considering for a window treatment.
- Arrange the samples to reflect the relationship of objects in the room. Place the swatch of the sofa fabric next to the paint sample for the adjacent wall, for example.
- Evaluate the color scheme. Look at your sample board at various times of the day and evening. If you're dissatisfied, make changes until you find a pleasing combination.
- Use the color wheel to analyze your final scheme. Did you settle on any of the combinations discussed in this chapter?

If you're using paint, you should realize that paint samples may not accurately represent how the paint will look on the walls. Before you make a final decision, paint a large section of a wall and allow it to dry. Make sure the color meets your expectations before painting the entire room. Also keep in mind that the larger an area you cover with a color, the darker it will appear.

Color Scheme Success

Imagine that you're back at your cousin's new home, where the chapter began. During the past three weeks, you helped your cousin choose a new color scheme. Now you're here to see the results. The place has been transformed. Since the dark ceilings were primed and painted an off-white, the closed-in feeling is gone.

The kitchen's only window looks out on the shaded backyard. Now that the blue walls and cabinets have been painted a tint called soft rose, the kitchen has lost its dreariness.

The bedroom faces the sunny side of the house and is filled with light most of the day. For the walls, your cousin selected a soft, cool green that harmonizes with the room's pale blue carpeting. With her favorite shade of blue as an accent color, and the addition of some plants, the room has an airy feeling of coolness and serenity. Your cousin used the same periwinkle blue for the chairs and accessories in the kitchen. In the bathroom, she placed a periwinkle rug on the floor and blue glass bottles on a shelf.

The front door is now painted a deep shade, similar to a terra cotta flowerpot. You had suggested a neutral color called "oyster" for the living room. As a test, your cousin painted the wall by the front door. But when you look at it, you agree with your cousin that the oyster tint doesn't work. As your cousin puts it, "This looks too cold. I want something warmer and more cheerful." What will you suggest?

When you know how to work with colors, creating pleasing effects can be fun rather than intimidating. If you take the time to learn the characteristics of individual colors and how to work with them effectively, then you can combine this knowledge with that of the other elements of design to create an interesting interior that will be a pleasure to live in.

Blue and white has been a popular kitchen color scheme for decades. How do you think this room would "feel" if the cabinets and walls were also blue?

Julia Sanchez

Color Specialist

You know that color is everywhere, but did you know it's also an important industry? The study of color includes its scientific, technical, artistic, psychological, and historic aspects. What could be more interesting than to work in a field that is so diverse and ever changing?

"To begin color selection, I start by researching the theme the designer has identified."

My interest in color started when I was taking art classes in high school. I loved mixing colors together to create new ones. I was also fascinated by how people have different reactions to a color. Some people didn't like orange, but most people seemed to like blue. I wondered how manufacturers could decide on product colors with wide appeal.

Today, I'm a trained color specialist. I work for a company that designs home and office products, including fabrics, wallcoverings, paint, and floorcoverings, that are sold around the world. My job is to assist in the selection of colors for the products.

To begin color selection, I research the theme the designer has identified for the new products. For example, if the theme is related to Egyptian interiors, I research the colors and historical significance associated with that period. It's very important to be historically accurate. I go through the same research process if the designer's theme is to reflect a specific era, such as the 1950s.

Communicating a specific color is complicated because everyone has a different impression of a color name. If I recommend that a fabric be sky blue, there could still be confusion. Our fabric manufacturer might select a different shade of sky blue than

colors is especially important to designers and manufacturers in the interiors industry. Many products are very expensive to manufacture. Therefore, these corporations want to make sure their products are manufactured in the "popular" colors. In the 1970s avocado green and harvest gold were popular appliance colors. Today, white and black are in highest demand, but that may change. I anticipate a great deal of international influence on color and trends in the future.

what I had in mind. The wrong shade could mean a significant loss of sales for our company. One means for communicating color is with the Munsell color chart, which is used worldwide. The chart includes samples of each color with a specific number. When I want to specify moss green, I look at the Munsell chart, write down the specific number, and then provide this number to the manufacturer. The fabric manufacturer consults the Munsell chart and fabricates the right color. It works great!

Besides communicating about color, I need to be very aware of color trends. I am a member of the Color Marketing Group and the Color Association of the United States. These organizations forecast which colors will be popular in the coming seasons. Identifying future trends in

"Communicating a specific color is complicated because everyone has a different impression of a color name."

Career Profile

A *color specialist* works with designers and manufacturers to select colors for fabrics, wallcoverings, floorcoverings, accessories, lighting, and furniture. This specialized individual can work in a variety of industries such as furniture, textiles, paint, appliance, and environmental design.

Education
▸ A Bachelor of Arts or higher degree is preferred.
▸ Courses in art, art history, color theory, principles of design, interior design, and physics are helpful.

Skills Needed
▸ Creativity, a sense of design, and an eye for color are required.
▸ Sketching ability is useful.
▸ Ability to keep abreast in the field of interior design is essential.
▸ Color specialists need good interpersonal skills for working with interior designers, manufacturers, managers, and other professionals.

Career Outlook
▸ Demand for color specialists should remain strong, since manufacturers and consumers are interested in new colors. More information can be obtained from the National Association of Schools of Art and Design.

Career Activities
1. Study several photographs of interiors. Identify the color schemes that are used in the various rooms.
2. Select different colors for these interiors and explain why you think these colors would be successful.

Chapter Summary

- Specific colors can influence your mood and create illusions.
- Color is a property of light. An object's color results from the way pigments reflect light that strikes the object.
- The color wheel is used to identify relationships between colors.
- A color can be described in terms of its hue, intensity, and value.
- Various types of color schemes can be created by using the color wheel.
- To design an effective color scheme, first consider the uses and characteristics of the room.
- Creating a color sample board can help you coordinate colors in a room.

Checking Your Understanding

1. Choose any three of the following colors and identify the moods each can create: red, orange, blue, yellow, green.

2. How can warm and cool colors be used to create illusions?

3. What happens to sunlight when it passes through a prism?

4. Explain how the primary colors are used to create secondary and tertiary colors. Give specific examples of each.

5. What is intensity? Give two examples showing the effects of intensity.

6. What is the difference between a tint and a shade?

7. Compare a monochromatic color scheme to an analogous color scheme.

8. How can you use the color wheel to create a split-complementary color scheme?

9. What is a signature color in a home? Why might you use one?

10. Describe at least three factors that should be considered when choosing a color scheme.

Thinking Critically

1. Would it be acceptable for an interior designer to choose colors without consulting the client? Why or why not? Give examples to support your answer.

2. Assume you are working with clients who want a rather intense red used as the dominant color for one of the rooms in their new home. What would you suggest to satisfy their request? Why?

3. Imagine that you are designing a color scheme for a couple's retirement home. The wife loves most shades of blue, but her husband doesn't care for blue. He prefers greens. What would you do?

4. What is a trendy color or color scheme today? Do you think it's likely to be popular for only a short period of time? Why?

Review & Activities CHAPTER 16

Applications

1. **Effective Color Schemes.** Look through magazines or newspapers to find pictures of three rooms that use color effectively. Analyze and describe the type of color scheme in each room. Why do you think each was chosen for that particular room? What makes each color scheme effective and appealing?

2. **Light and Color.** With a partner, observe a variety of objects under natural light and artificial light. Note the changes in color appearance under each type of light. Do you and your partner agree on the changes in appearance? If not, what might cause you to disagree?

3. **Color Inspiration.** Choose a fabric swatch, wallpaper sample, picture from a calendar, or photo of a piece of artwork that is very appealing to you. Plan a color scheme around your choice. Create a sample board of your color scheme, placing the item you originally chose at the center. Explain the type of color scheme you created and how you arrived at your choices.

4. **Expressing Personality with Color.** Imagine that you are about to visit the home of a family you have never met. You have been told that your hosts are cheerful, friendly people with an easygoing lifestyle. Write a descriptive paragraph to convey how you would expect their home to look and why, focusing especially on color.

BUILDING YOUR PORTFOLIO

You've been hired to plan a color scheme for a spacious, sunny great room in a contemporary-style home. This combined kitchen and family room is the central activity zone for your clients and their six-year-old twin boys. They want new furniture and floor coverings and are willing to have the walls and kitchen cabinets painted. Existing colors include a red brick fireplace, dark green kitchen countertops that resemble marble, and a white range and refrigerator. Create a sample board that shows your proposed color scheme. In writing, explain why you selected these colors. Place your completed sample board and explanation in your portfolio.

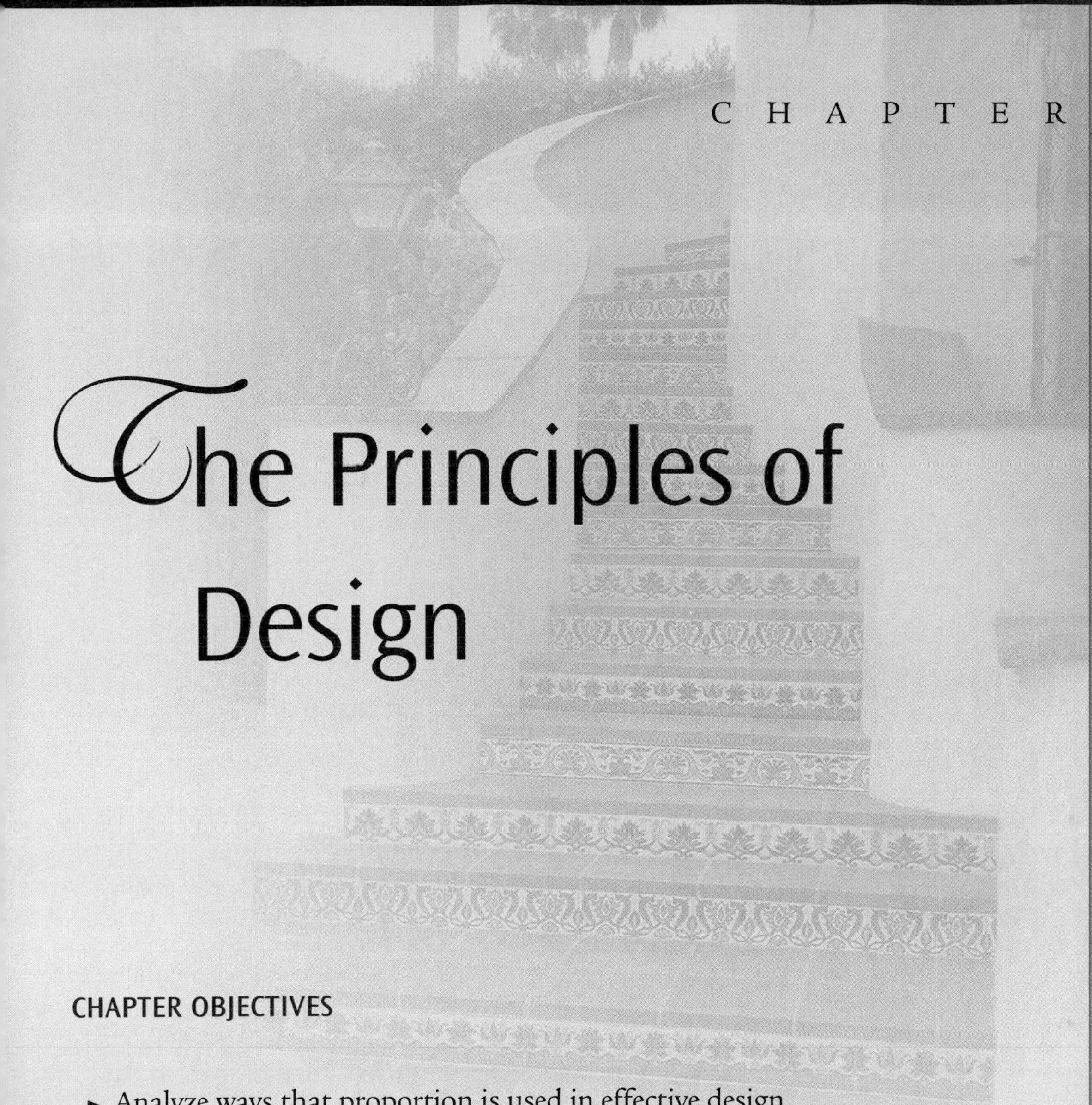

The Principles of Design

CHAPTER OBJECTIVES

► Analyze ways that proportion is used in effective design.

► Analyze scale and the ways it is used in design.

► Implement the types of balance.

► Explain ways to achieve various types of rhythm.

► Describe how to create emphasis.

► Assess the importance of balancing unity with variety.

TERMS TO LEARN

- asymmetrical balance
- eclectic
- emphasis
- golden rectangle
- golden section
- gradation
- opposition
- proportion
- radiation
- repetition
- rhythm
- scale
- symmetrical balance
- transition
- unity

Learning about the various elements of design is only part of a designer's education. Knowing how to work with the design elements involves recognizing the *principles* of design—proportion, scale, balance, rhythm, emphasis, unity, and variety. With a little practice, you'll be able to assess how these principles are used in good design.

Proportion

Ignoring the first design principle—proportion—may be the most common reason that a room setting just doesn't look right. **Proportion** refers to the size relationships that can be found within an object or design.

In math class you've learned that proportions are often expressed as ratios. If a table is twice as long as it is wide, the proportion of length to width may be expressed by the ratio 2 to 1, sometimes written 2/1 or 2:1.

It can take practice to learn to "see" proportion. Consider the example of a rectangular area rug with an intricate pattern. What proportions can you identify? You might think of these:

- The length compared to the width.
- The size of the border area compared to the middle of the design.
- The size of the middle of the design compared to the rug as a whole.

- The rug's area compared to the entire floor area.
- The amount of each different color in the design.

Each of these size relationships can be expressed as a ratio, and each is an aspect of the rug's proportions. Whether or not the rug appeals to you depends in part on the proportions that were chosen by its designer.

From experience, designers know that certain proportions create a more pleasing effect than others. For example, most people generally prefer rectangles to squares. Think about how often you see rectangular rugs, windows, picture frames, and chests of drawers compared to square ones. On the other hand, a rectangle that is too long and narrow can create a sense of discomfort—it may not "look right." In that case, its proportions are not pleasing.

Another general rule is that unequal divisions of space are often more appealing to the eye than equal divisions. For instance, suppose you decide to enhance a room design by draping a patterned throw over the back of a large upholstered chair. You could fold and place the throw so that it covers the top half of the chair's back. However, it might be more visually interesting to drape it so that unequal areas of throw and chair fabric are showing.

THE GOLDEN SECTION

Thousands of years ago, some of the ancient Greeks studied proportion in art and mathematics. One idea that fascinated them was a certain way of dividing a line into two segments. If you divide the line at just the right point—somewhere between one-third and one-half the distance from one end—something unique happens. The ratio of the larger segment to the smaller segment will equal the ratio of the whole line to the larger segment. This special way of dividing a line has come to be called the **golden section**.

Paying attention to design elements and principles is important in every room of a home.

In the golden section, the ratio of ab to bc is the same as ac to ab.

Many designers feel that dividing a line or form according to the golden section is more visually pleasing than dividing it exactly in half or in any other way. For example, you might use this principle when deciding where to place tiebacks on a drapery—not halfway between the top and bottom of the window, but approximately at the point of the golden section.

THE GOLDEN RECTANGLE

Imagine dividing two identical lines according to the golden section, then using the four resulting segments to create a rectangle. The ratio of the long side to the short side will reflect the golden section. This special rectangle is called the **golden rectangle**. It is thought by many to be the most visually satisfying rectangle—not too skinny, not too square.

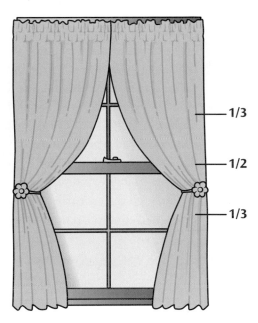

The golden mean is the division of a line anyplace between one-half and one-third of its total length. These curtains are tied back at the golden mean for this window.

The sides of this golden rectangle represent a ratio of 1 to 1.618. Due to careful study of the ratio by Greek sculptor Phidias, the ratio was also given the name "phi."

From Math to Mozart—"Golden Rules" of Proportion

The *golden section* and the *golden rectangle* (explained on the previous page) began as mathematical concepts. Any golden rectangle, no matter how large or small, is based on the same ratio. When you divide the length of the long side by the length of the short side, the result is approximately 1.618. This special number is called the *golden mean*. Some other names for it are "golden ratio" and "divine proportion." It appears in many different areas of mathematics.

Through the centuries, the golden mean and its related concepts have had a major influence on the creative arts. Here are some examples:

- *Music.* Certain compositions by Mozart and Beethoven appear to be divided into parts according to the golden section. Whether this was done purposely is unknown. Another composer, Bartok, deliberately used the golden section to structure some of his pieces. The golden section even figures in the design and construction of violins.

- *Visual Arts.* The proportions of Greek sculptures often seem to be based on the golden section. In some of his drawings, Leonardo da Vinci sketched in golden rectangles to guide the proportions of human faces and figures. People have found golden rectangles in analyzing many other works of art.

- *Architecture.* The Parthenon in Athens, Greece, is the most commonly cited example of the golden rectangle in architecture. Some experts maintain that the Great Pyramids in Egypt are based on the golden section. In the 20th century, architect Le Corbusier used golden rectangles in some of his structures in various ways, such as for the shape of windows.

In recent years, new ideas about these "golden rules" have arisen. Some people question whether an exact golden rectangle really appears in as many works of art and architecture as has been claimed. Others point out that almost any shape of rectangle can be found in a painting or a building if you're looking for it. Whether the golden rectangle is more pleasing than others is also open to debate.

In spite of these differing opinions, it's certainly true that the golden section, golden rectangle, and golden mean are among the many ideas that have influenced design over the years. By using them to guide proportions, you can create designs with classic appeal.

THINKING IT THROUGH

1. Look around your home or classroom for examples of rectangular shapes, such as a desk top, window, picture frame, or rug. Measure each rectangle, then divide the length by the width. Which shapes come close to being a golden rectangle?

2. Use print and Internet resources to read more about claims that have been made linking the golden mean, section, or rectangle with a particular work of architecture or art. What is the supposed link? What evidence is presented? Do you find it convincing? Why or why not?

An easy way to approximate a golden rectangle is by using this pattern of numbers: 2, 3, 5, 8, 13, and so on. (To remember the sequence, notice that each number is the sum of the two preceding numbers.) A rectangle with dimensions based on two consecutive numbers in this sequence—such as 3 : 5 or 8 : 13—will be close to the shape of a golden rectangle.

The golden section and the golden rectangle have influenced design for centuries. The feature on page 372 explains more about how these ideas originated and the impact they have had.

RECOGNIZING GOOD PROPORTION

Visually pleasing proportion is usually referred to as "good" proportion. The best way to learn how to recognize good proportion is to study the shapes and sizes of actual objects, rooms, and homes. Look at the relationship among features. As you do, keep in mind the guidelines just discussed.

Proportion is vital in architectural design. Well-proportioned structures are pleasing to the eye. Try to identify exteriors in which the walls, windows, and roof create a visually appealing whole.

Some proportional relationships are easier to pick out than others. The relationship between wall areas and windows is fairly obvious. Ideally, when several windows are the same size, the space between them should not be the same width as the windows. For instance, an architect would be unlikely to space three 30-inch-wide windows 30 inches (76 cm) apart from each other. Making the space between the windows narrower or wider than the actual width of the windows would appear more interesting. To achieve a visually pleasing proportion, regardless of the period or the style of the home, the openings and the solid proportions shouldn't be equal.

Considering proportion is also important when you buy furniture and accessories. Take notice of whether the base of a lamp is in pleasing proportion to the shade, for

Examine the windows of this apartment building. Did the architect take proportion into account when it was designed?

example, or how the thickness of a table's legs relates to their length.

When you see proportions that seem pleasing to you, try to figure out why they're appealing. With practice, you'll be able to recognize good proportion.

Scale

Imagine that you're sitting at a writing desk in a swivel desk chair. The chair is so large that your feet dangle, your knees bump the edge of the desk, and you have to hunch forward to write. When you get up to leave, you try to push the chair into the knee space of the desk, but it won't fit. What's wrong? Obviously, the chair is too large for the desk—and for you. You could also say that the chair is out of scale. **Scale** refers to how the size of an object or a space relates to human beings and to other objects or spaces in a design.

Scale is not the same as proportion. A particular lamp may be well proportioned in itself, with a pleasing ratio of shade to base. However, to be in scale with a room design, it must also be the proper size in relation to the other furnishings. A large lamp might be the right scale for a heavy-looking library table, but out of scale if placed on a compact nightstand. Similarly, a miniature accent lamp on a triple dresser would also be the wrong scale.

In a small den, an oversized coffee table in front of a loveseat would be out of scale. The table would overwhelm the room and make it seem crowded. There might be too little space for other furnishings. In contrast, a spacious room sparsely furnished with small furniture would be equally out of scale. This is a common problem when people move from a small house or apartment to a much larger home with higher ceilings.

Jamie learned the hard way that furniture pieces should be in scale with one another. She bought a beautiful china cabinet because it was half price and the finish was similar to her dining table. When it was delivered, however, the new cabinet looked much more massive than it had in the large furniture showroom. In comparison, her dining table and chairs seemed to have shrunk. Unfortunately, Jamie bought the cabinet at an "all sales are final" clearance. She had to live with the displeasing effect caused by the difference in scale.

THE HUMAN SCALE

Because homes and furniture are built for humans, it is important to use the human figure in evaluating their scale. Rooms and furnishings should be designed for the individuals who will use them. Lack of appropriate scale can cause both physical and visual discomfort. For example, pictures and mirrors should be at eye level. If they are hung too high on the walls they will not only detract from the design, but be difficult for people to see and enjoy.

Sometimes special scale is necessary, as in a child's bedroom or playroom. Here, adult furniture would be out of scale. Chairs and a table designed on a child's scale would be more appropriate. Low chests and shelves are suitable to store belongings within a child's reach.

Human scale should be taken into account when selecting furnishings for home and non-residential environments that children use frequently.

Scale—A Principle of Design That Can Inspire

Researchers have found that the scale of an object can have a profound effect on people. For example, many people are intrigued by the tiny scale of furniture and accessories in a miniature house. In contrast, people can feel overwhelmed by the size of dinosaurs in a museum. Scale has this impact when there are extreme differences in size between an object and the human body.

For centuries, designers and architects have understood how scale affects people. They have used strong vertical lines and tall spaces to increase the contrast in size between people and structures. When people walk into these spaces, they tend to have an immediate emotional response. Here are some examples of large-scale structures and the feelings they are intended to inspire.

- **Chartres Cathedral.** This cathedral was built in the countryside of France in the late 12th and early 13th centuries. Its soaring vertical spaces were designed to fill people with a sense of both personal humility and the glory of the divine. The size and height of the cathedral are emphasized by its isolated setting in an open, flat field.

- **Taj Mahal.** After his wife's death in 1629, Shah Jahan, the emperor of India, ordered a magnificent tomb to be built for her. The enormous scale of the Taj Mahal and the use of precious marble expressed the emperor's intense feelings for his wife.

- **Palace at Versailles.** This royal residence was built in the mid-17th century for King Louis XIV of France. The king wanted to demonstrate his superiority over the people of France and other countries. He intended for the vastness and luxury of the palace to impress and demoralize people.

- **U.S. Capitol Building.** The immense Capitol dome, completed in 1866, has come to symbolize the American government. Walking in the Rotunda—the vast interior hall beneath the dome—leaves visitors with a lasting impression of the power of democracy.

You, the *Designer*

Imagine you are part of a design team responsible for designing a courthouse. Decide what you would recommend for the shape and size of the structure. What design would you recommend for the entrance of the structure? Give reasons for your choices.

Balance

People feel most content with a sense of order and balance. You probably know this from experience. Balance is the design principle that provides a feeling of equality. Balance in design occurs when the amount, size, or weight of objects on both sides of a center point is equal, or when unequal objects or groups of objects appear to be equal. The two main techniques for achieving balance are symmetrical balance and asymmetrical balance.

SYMMETRICAL BALANCE

Symmetrical balance, also known as *formal balance*, is the most obvious balanced relationship. In **symmetrical balance**, the arrangement of forms on one side of an imaginary central line is the mirror image of the forms on the opposite side. Symmetrical arrangements seem to convey dignity and quiet. They suggest a feeling of rest and calm because both sides of the arrangement are of equal interest. Many impressive buildings throughout history have been designed with symmetrical balance.

Inside a home, consider a furniture arrangement in front of a fireplace. To create symmetrical balance, you might arrange two upholstered chairs facing each other in front of the fireplace, which would act as the center point. Suppose that you also placed a rug between the chairs and hung a painting above the mantel. If you drew an imaginary line though the center of the painting, fireplace, and rug, both halves would appear the same. This mirror image of one side looking just like the other illustrates symmetrical or formal balance.

Applying the basics of symmetrical design is a good place for beginners to start when trying to achieve balance. If this type of balance is overused, however, a monotonous appearance can result.

ASYMMETRICAL BALANCE

A design with **asymmetrical balance** is one in which elements on either side of an imaginary central line are unmatched, but appear to be in balance. To use the fireplace example again, the two upholstered chairs could be placed on one side of the fireplace, balanced with a loveseat on the other side. Another name for asymmetrical balance is *informal balance*. East Asian design often makes use of asymmetrical balance.

Which type of balance was implemented in this bedroom—symmetrical or asymmetrical?

Different sizes, forms, textures, and colors can be combined to achieve asymmetrical balance. For example, a round object can balance a square object of similar size. Two or more smaller objects can balance one large one.

When using asymmetrical balance, be sure to consider objects' *apparent weight* rather than their actual weight. For instance, a small, dark object could balance a larger, light-colored item, in spite of their size difference. That's because the dark object has more apparent weight. As you learned earlier in this unit, warm, intense colors and rough textures suggest heaviness, whereas pale, cool tints and soft, smooth textures suggest lightness.

The objects on either side of the lamp balance the top of this small chest.

Rhythm

You can find rhythm in the back of a chair, in the pattern of a quilt, or in the folds of draperies. **Rhythm** is the principle that suggests connected movement between different parts of a design. It might be created with colors, lines, forms, or textures. Sometimes rhythm is referred to as *continuity*. It can add interest to an area, but to avoid monotony, it should not be overused. Rhythm can be achieved in various ways, including repetition, radiation, gradation, opposition, and transition.

REPETITION. Rhythm is most often achieved by **repetition**, which is the act of repeating. The repeating pattern might be as simple as *A A A A,* in which the letter A might represent a window, a spindle in a stairway railing, or a pattern in a wallpaper border. The repetition might be an *alternating* pattern, such as *A B A B A B* (think of a checkerboard); or *A B C A B C,* with three different elements repeating.

Repeating rhythm helps to lead the eye from one point to another. A specific color repeated at various points in a room setting creates a sense of rhythm, as does a repeated design in flooring. Woodwork that runs around the top or base of a wall also introduces a rhythm that leads the eye from place to place.

The repeating lines in the wallboard, and even the starfish, develop a sense of rhythm in this colorful studio.

RADIATION. Rhythm in design can also be achieved by radiation. **Radiation** occurs when lines radiate, or move outward, from a central point. Chairs arranged around a round table are an example of radiation. To achieve rhythm through radiation in design, you might group small pictures around a large one. Tieback curtains, which lead the eye to the top and center of the window, are also an example of rhythm through radiation.

GRADATION. When objects increase or decrease in size, the eye tends to follow the line created. **Gradation** is a gradual increasing or decreasing of color, size, or pattern. For example, different sizes of candles, arranged from tall to short, lead the eye from one candle to the next.

A gradual change of form is usually more pleasing than an abrupt one. When forms gradually change from low to high, as in a pyramid arrangement, your gaze glides up the slope. On the other hand, if you see one small form perched on top of a much larger one, your gaze is "jumpy," darting back and forth.

Repetition and radiation are both apparent in this tile design.

OPPOSITION. When lines come together to form right angles, the result is termed **opposition**. Examples of opposition include the square corners of a doorway, draperies that hang straight down, and a sofa with the arms at right angles to the back.

TRANSITION. When lines change direction by flowing in a curve, or when curved lines lead the eye from one object to another, the result is called **transition**. Arched doorways, draperies with flowing swags, and a sofa with a back that curves into the arms are examples of transition.

Nesting tables are a classic example of gradation. Can you think of another example?

Emphasis

The terms *center of interest* and *focal point* can be used to describe the principle of design called **emphasis**. Dramatic structural features—such as a colorful stained glass window, a stone fireplace, or a winding staircase—are likely to be focal points because they draw attention. However, the rooms in your home don't need such features to have a center of interest. You might create emphasis with a large cabinet or an eye-catching framed poster. The focal point doesn't have to be valuable or expensive. It might be a brightly painted headboard or a large ceramic pitcher filled with silk tulips.

Instead of one large object, a center of interest can be created with a collection of smaller ones. For a grandparent, it could be a framed collection of grandchildren's colorful drawings. Collections don't have to be large to be emphasized. For instance, Michelle has dozens of teapots in her collection. By displaying only five or six at a time, her teapots have more of an impact than a large, cluttered display.

The decision to emphasize a particular area or feature is a personal one. When choosing an item or feature to emphasize, keep in mind that it should be dominant, but not overpower the rest of the room design.

Emphasis may also be used in reverse. If you don't want to call attention to a feature in a room, allow it to blend in with the background. For example, you might choose to paint woodwork the same color as the walls so it doesn't stand out.

In most settings a large floral arrangement is a simple way to create a focal point.

$\mathcal{U}$nity and Variety

A quart of paint transformed these four mismatched chairs into a harmonious grouping.

Unity occurs when all the parts of a design are related by one idea. When there is unity among design elements, the result is design harmony. A harmonious design has consistency of style.

You can create unity by choosing items with similar characteristics. For example, you might select furniture and accessories that all have curved lines. The similarity of line will help the room look "tied together." Don't confuse unity with sameness, however. It's not necessary, or even desirable, for all the furnishings in a room to match.

Without some variety, rooms can be predictable and monotonous.

Variety is possible when different styles and materials are combined. The **eclectic** style of decorating involves mixing furnishings of different styles and possibly from different periods. This works as long as the styles and materials are compatible. For instance, modern furniture might be mixed with more classic styles as long as all the pieces have similar proportions and a similar finish. Familiarity with the elements and principles of design helps ensure success when creating an eclectic decor.

Variety adds interest to a design, but confusion can result if variety is carried too far. One common mistake is to use a different decorating style in each room of a small home. Having Victorian decor in the living room, for example, and a chrome and glass table in the adjacent dining area creates a feeling of conflict. This lack of unity may make compact living quarters seem even smaller.

UNITY AND ARCHITECTURE

Too much variety can also undermine architectural design. Some builders use many styles and materials in one structure. A design that lacks unity can be unattractive.

To be effective, unity and variety must be combined to create an overall harmonious effect. For example, owners of contemporary homes may achieve unity and variety by integrating the house design with the landscape around it. To blend with the surroundings, natural building materials are often used. Emphasis on horizontal lines also creates a feeling of unity with the landscape. Expanses of windows, combined with large wall areas, create a pleasing mix of unity of line and variety of texture.

Most types of homes can be unified by carrying exterior design features inside. Traditional furnishings might be used in a Cape Cod house. The furniture in a modern home could have the same clean, simple lines and shapes as the outside.

Applying Design Principles

The principles of good design apply in any setting. When David and his brother, Marcos, decided to share a house, they each already had a variety of furnishings. There was a comfortable sofa that had belonged to their parents, plus several chairs and end tables they brought from their respective apartments. By paying attention to their form, color, and style, the brothers were able to select which pieces to have in the living room and which to move to the bedrooms. They painted four mismatched chairs the same color to use at their table in the eat-in kitchen.

Between the two brothers, they owned a total of seven wall clocks of unusual styles. Grouping them on the wall above a low bookshelf made an interesting focal point for the living room. With some imagination, along with knowledge of the elements and principles of design, Marcos and David created a stylish, eclectic living area.

Design principles can be combined to create a striking, yet very livable decor. What design principles are evident in this room?

Visual Merchandiser

Kate Lin

As a child, I loved to window shop during the holiday season. All of the big stores in town were so beautifully decorated. Some had lights all around the display windows. Department stores even wrapped up the appliances with bows and ribbons. They seemed more like toys than dishwashers or washing machines. What I liked best, though, was to walk by the big toy store. The owner would place battery-operated toys together in the display case. Watching these toys run was like watching a parade.

Today, as a visual merchandiser, I'm responsible for putting together the very scenes that I used to admire. I try to create for other people that same sense of delight and excitement. I start working on the design months before a holiday or event.

Visual merchandisers design, install, and construct displays in store windows and inside the stores to attract attention. We construct backdrops, install background settings, gather props, arrange mannequins and merchandise, and place descriptive signs.

A store's success is affected by its visual merchandisers because they can often encourage people to come into the store. My goal is to get shoppers to notice products they might not have considered buying otherwise.

I got started in the field with a summer job at a smaller department store. It helped that I had worked in set design for my high school's plays. In high school, I took courses in art, woodworking, and mechanical draw-

"A store's success is affected by its visual merchandisers."

ing. Many visual merchandisers go on to community or junior colleges. Fashion merchandising schools, fine arts institutes, and interior design schools are also good places to get valuable training.

Some visual merchandisers specialize in one area. I started out arranging furniture displays at a department store. After several years I accepted a job as a display director in a home furnishings store. I'm responsible for supervising and coordinating all activities connected with display. I consult with the store manager and decide which items should be displayed. My long-term goal is to be a sales promotion director or head of store planning for a major department store.

"I start working on the design months before a holiday or event."

To succeed in my job, you need to be well organized and good at working with others. Probably the most important skill to have, though, is a good eye for design. When they're used properly, design elements can turn a dull display into an eye-catching one.

Career Profile

Visual display merchandisers design, construct, and install displays in store windows and showcases in order to direct customers' attention to the merchandise being sold. They construct backdrops, choose and install background settings, gather props, arrange mannequins and merchandise, and place descriptive signs. Holidays and big sales events provide the busiest times of year for a visual display merchandiser.

Education
- A high school diploma is required.
- College courses that would be beneficial include merchandising, business administration, marketing, psychology, art, woodworking, and mechanical drawing.
- Some stores will provide on-the-job training.

Skills Needed
- Good communication skills and the ability to work well with others.
- Creativity with a good eye for color and detail, and a sense of balance and proportion.

Career Outlook
- Job opportunities depend on retail sales, which depend on the economy.

Career Activities
1. Choose a product and design a display area for that product.
2. Choose a holiday and decide what decorative home accessories you would display in a shop window. Give a rationale for your choices.

Chapter Summary

➤ Applying the principles of design to the elements of design helps achieve satisfying results.

➤ The terms *proportion* and *scale* both refer to size relationships. Proportion refers mainly to relationships within an object. Scale refers mainly to relationships of one object to another.

➤ A design can use symmetrical or asymmetrical balance to create a sense of equality.

➤ Various types of rhythm suggest connected movement in a design.

➤ An item that draws attention provides a point of emphasis.

➤ Successful design utilizes both unity and variety.

Checking Your Understanding

1. Identify and define the principles of design.

2. What is meant by the "golden section"? Why is it significant?

3. Why might a small, antique chair not look "right" with an oversized desk?

4. What is the human scale?

5. What challenge does a child's room present when applying the principles of design?

6. Explain the difference between symmetrical balance and asymmetrical balance. Which is considered more formal?

7. Explain and give an example of achieving rhythm through three of the following: repetition, radiation, gradation, transition, and opposition.

8. What are two architectural features commonly chosen for emphasis?

9. Why is unity alone not enough to create a good design?

10. Give an example of how interior and exterior designs can be unified.

Thinking Critically

1. How might you deal with scale in a home where some family members are larger than average and others smaller than average?

2. You have seen an ad showing a coordinated grouping of furniture at a great price. It consists of a sofa, two matching chairs, two end tables, and a coffee table. You are concerned that using all the pieces would make your small family room look crowded. What pieces would you be able to do without? Why? What might be the advantages and disadvantages of buying a furniture grouping?

3. Why is an eclectic style often the choice of young people in their first homes?

Applications

1. **Object Proportion.** Choose a basic piece of furniture or an accessory such as a lamp, an end table, or a chair to illustrate proportion. Draw various examples of the item to illustrate both good and poor proportion. Ask your classmates to identify which of the objects aren't in good proportion.

2. **Assessing Architecture.** Using a guide of area homes that are for sale or a real estate agency's website, examine photos of homes. Choose three examples that exhibit good use of proportion and three that do not. Identify the features that relate to proportion.

3. **Balance.** Think of at least three items you might display on a fireplace mantel. Sketch at least two possible arrangements using different types of balance. Explain how your arrangements achieve balance. Which do you think is most successful? Why?

4. **Rhythm.** In magazines or feature sections of a newspaper, find at least five pictures of rooms that show types of rhythm patterns. Label each picture according to the type of rhythm displayed: repetition, radiation, gradation, transition, or opposition. Make a classroom display using everyone's examples of each type.

5. **Emphasis.** Choose one room of your home and determine its focal point. Explain why it is a center of interest.

6. **Display Case Design.** You have been asked to design a display case for your school. It will be placed outside the room where the school board meets. Decide on the "message" you want the display case to send. What objects will you include? What will you make the focal point and why?

7. **Design Principles Evaluation.** Make a checklist to use when evaluating a room for use of elements and principles of design.

BUILDING YOUR PORTFOLIO

You are helping a couple whose five-year-old grandson is coming to live with them. Their spacious guest bedroom currently has a neutral color scheme with cream-colored carpeting, but they want it redesigned as a permanent bedroom for their grandson. Prepare a list of questions you might ask the clients. What questions would you like to ask the child? Decide on possible responses. From your mock interview, write a description of the room you would propose. Include as many elements and principles of design as possible, focusing on scale, emphasis, color, texture, form, and space. Cut photos from magazines and catalogs and sketch your ideas to illustrate your presentation to the family.

Planning Interior Environments

Developing a Design Plan

CHAPTER OBJECTIVES

► Identify the first five steps in developing a design plan.

► Analyze the importance of learning about clients' characteristics.

► Describe factors to examine when taking an inventory of an existing environment.

► Complete a scale drawing of a room and its furnishings.

► Explain how to develop a preliminary budget.

► Evaluate the importance of having a design resource file.

TERMS TO LEARN

- clearance space

- contingency fee

- inventory

- multipurpose rooms

- prioritize

- scale drawing

- template

Imagine a dream come true. Your family has won the grand prize in a contest—a brand new house. The builder will finish it to your specifications, within a certain budget, of course. How would you go about making this unfinished house into a home, personalized just for your family? Would you know where to start?

Good Design Requires Planning

Some interior designers recommend removing everything from a room to get a fresh perspective of the room's potential.

Designing the interior of a new house is like starting with a blank canvas. You could shop at a wide variety of stores to select materials and furnishings. You then put all the pieces together to finish the dream house.

A shopping spree can be fun, but without careful planning you could run into problems. Since there is a certain amount of money to spend, you must budget carefully to make sure you can purchase all the things you need. The furnishings, window treatments, and floor and wall coverings chosen must be attractive, meet your family's needs, and be able to withstand the wear and tear that's ahead.

Everyone is more likely to be pleased with the end result if a design plan is followed. A good design plan is the starting point of designing the interior of a home.

THE ELEMENTS AND PRINCIPLES AS DESIGN TOOLS

In the last unit you learned about color, form, line, space, and texture. You studied proportion, scale, emphasis, unity, variety, and the various types of balance and rhythm. The knowledge you've gained about using the design elements and principles will be indispensable tools in creating an effective design plan. Now it's a matter of figuring out how to approach a project.

STEPS IN A DESIGN PLAN

Fortunately there is a process that may be used for almost any design project—an efficiency apartment, a recreation room in a basement, or an entire home. Following the process helps both professional designers and novices to develop pleasing, livable rooms.

This chapter introduces the ten steps of a design plan. The first five steps are explained in detail in this chapter. Next you will learn more about backgrounds, furniture, lighting, and accessories—the materials used to develop a design. With the knowledge from those chapters you'll be able to move on to Steps 6 through 10. They will be explained in Chapter 23. Figure 18-1 below shows all ten steps.

FIGURE 18-1

Steps in the Design Process

STEP 1. Identify the project.

STEP 2. Assess client characteristics.

STEP 3. Analyze the environment.

STEP 4. Develop a preliminary budget.

STEP 5. Compile a design resource file.

STEP 6. Plan use of space.

STEP 7. Choose a style and color scheme.

STEP 8. Select backgrounds, furniture, lighting, and accessories.

STEP 9. Present the design.

STEP 10. Modify and implement the design.

Working through the design process involves creativity, along with concrete activities such as measuring, calculating, and budgeting.

$\mathcal{B}$eginning the Design Process

Starting a design project is exciting. It may be tempting to jump ahead and select colors and furnishings rather than take time for the first few steps of the process. Your design, however, will be more successful if you lay a solid foundation for the project.

The first five steps in the design process draw on a variety of skills. Good communication skills are needed to gain the information you need to begin a project. Next you will draw on your analytical skills to evaluate the area to be designed. Have your calculator ready as you estimate costs. Then, use your creativity to find ideas that might work well.

Step 1: Identify the Project

Imagine that you have been an interior designer for two years. During that time, you have used the design process on dozens of projects. More than once, working through all of the steps has kept you from making mistakes or impractical suggestions.

Your initial task is to help clients clearly identify the design goal. Just what is it that they're hoping to achieve? Perhaps they are trying to simplify their lives and want an uncluttered living area, or maybe they want to change a bedroom into a home office.

Today you are meeting with a new client, Mrs. Woo, a second-grade teacher and mother of two teens. The family lives in an older home with an L-shaped formal living and dining room. Mrs. Woo wants to convert the space into a more casual family room the family can enjoy and where Austin and Tina, her children, can spend time with their friends.

To develop a realistic plan, you'll need to determine the approximate amount that Mrs. Woo is considering spending. Is it $1,000, or $5,000, or more? Obviously, the scope of projects can vary greatly. One may involve redesigning an entire house, including structural changes. Another might be updating a color scheme and finding new accessories to give a fresh look to a single room. How long the client plans to live in the home may affect the scope of the project.

The desired time frame should also be assessed. Unless changes are minimal, implementing a plan will take some time. Often people have an event driving a design project—having a kitchen completed by Thanksgiving or redecorating because of an upcoming wedding. In the Woo household, the teens would like the changes made as soon as possible, but Mrs. Woo's realistic goal is for completion by the end of the summer.

Even if you are decorating for yourself or your family, it's important to define the goal. For example,

if your younger sister has asked you to help make her bedroom look more grownup, you will still need to evaluate the project and its proposed budget and time frame. What changes would she like to see? Are your parents willing to pay for curtains and a comforter or is the plan to do more to the room? Does your sister want the room ready for her slumber party next weekend or is she willing to wait longer to achieve the new look? The timeline needs to be realistic for the amount of work to be done.

Design projects may range in complexity from one corner of a room to an entire home.

Working with an Interior Designer

There's a common myth that only the wealthy hire interior designers. When the possible savings to clients is taken into account, however, the services of an interior designer are more affordable than many consumers think. Interior designers are able to purchase products at a special discount. Plus, they are able to prevent costly mistakes.

A designer will explain the design process and the services that he or she will provide. Generally, a designer can design and draw the floor plans of the project; specify and order furniture, materials, equipment, and lighting; and oversee the construction and installations. For a successful design solution there are some things that the client should do, too. Consider these points when choosing and working with an interior designer:

- **HIRING PROCESS.** Most designers report that new business comes not from advertising, but rather from other satisfied clients. Consumers are advised to interview two or three interior designers before making a choice. They should look at the designer's portfolio of past work. Does the designer listen well and communicate clearly? If clients seem to have little idea of what they want, a good designer can help them decide. Is the designer certified by the American Society of Interior Designers (ASID)?
- **EXPENSES.** While interviewing interior designers, it's vital to inquire about fees. Most charge by the hour. Hourly rates typically range from $50 to $300. Other designers charge a flat fee or by the square foot. Some are paid a straight commission.
- **BUDGET.** It is important to have a budget in mind prior to talking with a designer. If consumers are uncertain about the possible cost of a project, they should identify a maximum amount that they're willing to spend. The interior designer should be able to help them get the most return on their investment.
- **SAVING TIME.** When working with an interior designer, there are several things that can be done in advance to expedite the process. Clients should think about how they plan to use the space. They can consider which items they want to try to reuse in a new project. Also, clients should clarify their personal likes and dislikes so they can convey them to the designer.
- **COMMON FEARS.** Some consumers fear that an interior designer will impose his or her own taste on the project. On the contrary, the designer's job is to determine how to achieve the client's preferences. Another myth is that a designer will encourage clients to start from scratch, buying everything new for their project.

YOU THE CONSUMER . . .

You and a friend are discussing the value of interior designers. Your friend insists that most people can save a lot of money—and do a good job of decorating—without the services of an interior designer. Do you agree or disagree? What are advantages of working with a professional interior designer?

Step 2: Assess Client Characteristics

Success in a design project begins with matching possibilities for the room design with the habits, likes, needs, and wants of the people who will use it. Designers usually use one or more **inventories**—surveys that identify characteristics that will affect the design plan. You could provide a written questionnaire for clients to complete, but it's often better to interview them in person. For many projects, you will need to consider both the family's ideas and those of the individual person or people who will use the room most. Take careful notes for future reference.

Multipurpose rooms are increasingly common. They can help to expand the available space in a home.

A FAMILY INVENTORY

In a family home, it's important to create a design plan that pleases everyone. Sometimes, of course, compromises will need to be made. However, it's usually possible to develop a design that the family will find both attractive and functional. You will need to learn about their lifestyle and their expectations for the room or area.

Lifestyle

Begin by discussing the family's lifestyle. Tailor your questions according to the area to be designed. For a kitchen, you might ask what their morning and evening routines are like. Where are various meals usually eaten? How is the kitchen involved in a typical weekend?

Lifestyle and interior design are related in several ways. Your clients' answers to your questions will help to formulate your design plan. If the project is for your own home, discuss these considerations with your family to be sure everyone is in agreement.

ACTIVITIES. Some rooms are used for one main purpose. Others are **multipurpose rooms**, or used for many things. As the designer, your role is to identify and accommodate all main functions that take place there. One room might serve as a guest bedroom/sewing room/home office all in one! Start by asking the family members what the room needs to be designed for.

ENTERTAINING PREFERENCES. Will the room be used for entertaining? If so, are the occasions usually formal or informal? What would be the usual number of guests? The maximum number? Is there entertainment-related equipment that should be in the room—a television, VCR, music system, piano, game table, pool table, microwave oven, storage for games and music? How would food be served? Knowing where food and beverages will be consumed affects which floor coverings and upholstery fabrics to consider.

HOBBIES. Do family members have hobbies? Do those require any special storage needs? Is there a collection that might be displayed as part of the design?

STUDY AND WORK. Where do family members prefer to read? Study? Pay bills and do household paperwork? Are they online? Mrs. Woo needs space to grade papers and work on lesson plans. Austin and Tina have desks in their bedrooms where they do most of their homework. For group projects, however, they want space to invite classmates to work with them.

Preferred Atmosphere

What are the family's overall style preferences? Is it formal or informal? Rustic or traditional? Sleek and stylish or soft and cozy? Do they like antiques or prefer a modern look? Keep in mind that each room is part of the home as a whole. Although every room may have a look of its own, all should have a similar feeling.

Ask family members about their color preferences as well. It's unlikely that all will share the same favorite color, but you can bypass any color that someone truly dislikes.

Future Considerations

Once a room is completed, it's apt to stay that way for some time. That's why the family should consider changes that might occur in the future. Is it possible that they'll be getting a pet or adding to the family? For instance, Mrs. Woo anticipates that her father will spend winters with them after he retires. Tina will leave for college in two years.

NONRESIDENTIAL INVENTORIES

What if your design project is not in a home? Interior designers often plan other types of interior environments as well. These may range from a corporate meeting room to a restaurant interior. It's important to query the client about the purpose of the room, the characteristics of people who will use it, and their needs. For example, how might the decor you plan for an orthodontist's office, where most of the patients are preteens and teens, be different from what would be suitable for a heart specialist's waiting area?

Universal design should also be considered. For instance, the payment counter should accommodate a person in a wheelchair who is writing a check.

Step 3: Analyze the Environment

Perhaps you're redesigning just one or two rooms in a home. Why might it be important to walk through and assess the rest of the house? The reason is because some features in the other parts of the home may very well influence your design plan.

THE ENVIRONMENT INVENTORY

Start your inventory by jotting down the exterior style of the house or apartment building. Certain styles of homes lend themselves to specific decorating styles. You shouldn't feel limited to that one style, however. Continue with the inventory by assessing these existing factors:

NUMBER AND PLACEMENT OF ROOMS. Note the number and type of rooms in the home. If additional space is needed, could part of an attic or basement be converted?

ACTIVITY ZONES. You studied about three types of zones in Chapter 7. Identify the current private, social, and service zones of the home. Do

The right furnishings can help make up for inadequate storage in a home. *What might be stored in the furniture in this living room?*

they need to be improved? Can this be achieved within the scope of the current project?

STORAGE AREAS. Ask whether there is adequate storage. Are there belongings, such as books or sporting goods equipment, that need more space? Count the closets, paying attention to their size and what they're currently used for. Look at other built-in cabinets, as well.

FURNITURE AND ACCESSORIES. Assess the current furnishings. Are there pieces in good condition that the client wishes to use in the redesign?

Would they work in a new design? Would refinishing or reupholstering make them more desirable? What current accessories does the client want to keep in the redecorated area? Which could be moved to a different location?

CONDITION OF BACKGROUNDS. Try to gauge not only the condition, but also the appeal, of the current flooring, walls, and window treatments. What looks worn or dated? Would it be attractive again if it were cleaned or refinished? Are there features that the client particularly likes?

ENERGY CONSIDERATIONS. Keep energy efficiency in mind when assessing an environment. Are existing windows and doors tight? Would replacing a tile floor with carpeting minimize drafts in a room? Is better air circulation needed?

ELECTRICAL AND LIGHTING. Is the home's electrical service adequate for existing lighting and equipment and for any that might be added? If in doubt, consult an electrician. Often electrical service must be upgraded to accommodate new kitchen appliances, lighting, and entertainment equipment. Pay attention to the lighting in the various rooms. Will it be sufficient for the new design? Would it be worthwhile to increase natural light by adding or enlarging a window? You will learn about various types of lighting in Chapter 22.

SAFETY. Every home must meet basic safety requirements, but sometimes more specific needs must be addressed. Will young children live in the home or visit frequently? How about an older adult or someone with a disability? If so, think about features such as childproofing, grab bars, and door handles. Look for things that could be a danger to anyone—a stairway without a railing, spindles placed too far apart on a deck railing, slippery floors, and glass doors without special safety glass.

TRAFFIC FLOW. You'll recall learning about traffic patterns in Chapter 7. Does furniture placement make the current traffic pattern awkward? Perhaps furniture is too large for the space and there's inadequate **clearance space**, the additional space furniture takes up when it's in use. At a dining table, for instance, people typically take up about 20 in. (51 cm) of floor space, but need another 12 in. to 16 in. (30 cm to 41 cm) to pull back their chairs. Figure 18-2 lists some standard clearance spaces.

FIGURE 18-2

Standard Clearance Spaces

Living Room/Dining Room	
Minor traffic pathway	1.5 ft.–4 ft. (0.46 m–1.2 m)
Major traffic pathway	4 ft.–6 ft. (1.2 m–1.8 m)
Space between coffee table and chair or sofa	1 ft.–1.5 ft. (0.3 m–0.46 m)
Leg room in front of chair	1.5 ft.–2.5 ft. (0.46 m–0.76 m)
Space around table and occupied chairs for serving	2 ft. (0.6 m)
Conversational Grouping	
Sofa, two end tables, two chairs, and coffee table	6.5 ft. x 14 ft. (2 m x 4.3 m)
Kitchen	
Space in front of cabinets	2 ft.–6 ft. (0.6 m–1.8 m)
Space between appliances	4 ft.–7 ft. (1.2 m–2.1 m)
Bedroom	
Space around bed (any size) or between twin beds	1.5 ft.–3 ft. (0.46 m–0.9 m)
Space between dresser and bed; space to pull out dresser drawers	3 ft. (0.9 m)
Bathroom	
Space in front of toilet	1.5 ft.–2 ft. (0.46 m–0.6 m)
Space between bathtub and opposite wall	2.5 ft. (0.76 m)

DEVELOP PRIORITIES

Few people are able to change everything when they move or redecorate. Budget or other restrictions usually limit what can be done. A designer can help clients **prioritize**, or rate their wants and needs in order of preference. The key is to change the things that will make the most difference.

MEASURE SPACE AND FURNITURE

Prepare to try out furniture arrangements by measuring the room. (Note that since most material amounts are given in customary measures, metric equivalents are not given here.) Use a metal measuring tape. First draw a rough sketch; then transfer measurements to graph paper. Use a pencil to make a **scale drawing** with each square representing a given number of inches or centimeters. (A common scale is ¼ inch = 1 foot.) Then measure permanent features, such as doorways, windows, built-in cabinets, and fireplaces. Transfer them to the drawing, accurately portraying their location.

Using the chart of architectural symbols on page 257, indicate any other special features. Also mark the location of heating and cooling registers.

A conversation area is most comfortable when people are seated from 4 to 10 feet apart.

To make a scale drawing, it's necessary to measure the room and the furnishings that will be arranged there.

Then measure furniture that will be kept in the new design plan. Record the length and depth of each piece at its longest and deepest point. Draw the pieces on graph paper using the same scale as the drawing of the room. Cut out and label each silhouette. Another option is to use ready-made **templates**, cutout patterns of furniture and appliances that may be traced. Make sure they represent the size of the furniture you're considering.

Some designers transfer the room and furniture measurements directly to a computer software program for home design. They complete much of the design plan on the computer. Chapter 23 discusses this option in more detail.

Make sure you have a copy of the scale drawing with you when you shop. It will eliminate guesswork about whether a piece will fit.

Scale Drawings

Graph paper is convenient to use for scale drawings. Measure the room, decide what scale to use, and draw the floor plan.

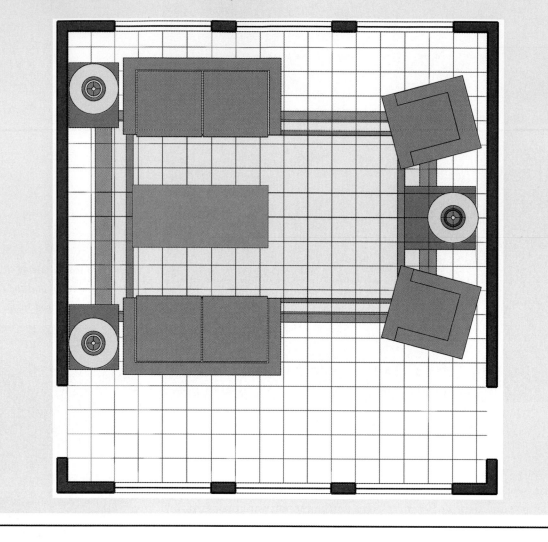

CONSIDER FURNITURE NEEDS

For many people, arranging the furnishings in a room is a favorite aspect of the design process. At this stage of the process, your plan for furniture placement doesn't have to be definite. Before moving on to the next step, however, it's helpful to know the number and types of pieces you want to incorporate in the floor plan.

Is there room for two loveseats, as shown above in Figure 18-3? Or would a sofa and two or three chairs work better for your seating arrangement? It's desirable to have a tabletop or another surface near each seat so a glass or book may be set down. You'll learn more about arranging space in Step 6, which is covered in Chapter 23.

Step 4: Develop a Preliminary Budget

The budget for an interior design project may include wall coverings, floor coverings, window treatments, upholstery fabric, furniture, lighting, and accessories. The cost may also include wages for an upholsterer, as well as labor for installing wall coverings, floor coverings, and window treatments. If you plan to do some work yourself, remember to factor in the cost of tools you will need to buy or equipment that you will have to rent.

Architectural and interior design fees might also be included in the budget. Additional money might be needed to pay electricians, plumbers, and carpenters. To plan for unexpected expenses, it's a good idea to add a **contingency fee**, which is *an additional percentage of the total cost of the project*. A 20 percent contingency fee is often used for a project.

Once you have developed a preliminary list of all items that will be changed, you can begin to estimate the cost of the project. To determine realistic costs you may visit local retail stores, review catalogs, or conduct a search on the Internet. Estimates for upholstery fabrics and coverings for walls, floors, and windows will require you to perform calculations. An example of a budget for an interior design project appears below. To the total, you would add the estimated fees for your design work, as page 394 explains.

FIGURE 18-4

Preliminary Budget for an Interior Design Project

ITEM	Color/Style	Quantity	Estimated Cost	Amount Budgeted	Remarks
SOFA	Leather	1	$1,500	$1,500	Allow 12 weeks
CHAIRS	Wing	2	$800 ea.	$1600	
PAINT	Satin finish	3 gal.	$25 ea.	$75	Paint sale in June
CARPET	Berber	40 sq. yd.	$33 per sq. yd.	$1320	Includes cushion and installation
WINDOW TREATMENT	Sheers	25 yd.	$18–$20 per yd.	$500	Client will sew and paint
LAMPS	Brushed steel	2	$150 ea.	$300	Check prices on the Internet
VASES	Modern	2	$100 ea.	$200	
CONTINGENCY FEE			20% of total	$1,100	
TOTAL				$6,595	

CALCULATE MATERIALS

As part of the budget process, you will need to determine how much or how many you need of particular items. If you need four dining room chairs, figuring the total cost is easy.

For wall, floor, and window coverings, however, careful measuring and calculation are required. This section explains the process for various background materials.

Paint

Determine the amount of paint required for a room by measuring the room and calculating the square footage that will be painted. For example, in estimating the paint needed for a room 12 ft. x 30 ft., follow these steps:

1. Measure the length of each wall, add the lengths together and total.

   12 ft. + 12 ft. + 30 ft. + 30 ft. = 84 lineal ft.

2. Multiply the length of feet around the room (your answer in #1) by the height of the ceiling to determine the total number of square feet.

   84 ft. × 8 ft. (ceiling) = 672 total sq. ft.

3. A gallon of paint will cover approximately 350 sq. ft. to 400 sq. ft. To allow ample paint, divide the total number of square feet (your answer in #2) by 350 to find the number of gallons of paint.

   672 ÷ 350 = 2 gal. of paint

Wallpaper

To determine how much wall covering to order, follow Steps 1 and 2 as explained for paint. Your answer again would be 672 ft. Then to figure the required number of rolls:

1. Divide the total number of sq. ft. by 36. (A single roll of wallpaper covers approximately 36 sq. ft.)

   672 ÷ 36 = 18.67 or 19 single rolls

2. For every two openings (doors and windows), subtract one roll of wallpaper. If the paper has a repeating pattern *do not* deduct for the openings. Example:

   19 – 2 (2 doors and 2 windows) = 17 single rolls of wallpaper

Most wallpaper is actually sold in double rolls. How many would you order—eight or nine?

Resilient Flooring or Carpeting

To determine the amount of vinyl, plastic laminate, tile, or carpet required, measure the size of the room. For example, in estimating the amount of floor covering for a room 12 ft. x 30 ft. you would:

1. Measure the length of each wall and multiply the length by the width.

   12 ft. × 30 ft. = 360 total sq. ft.

2. Most carpet is sold by the square yard. To calculate that number, divide the total square feet by 9.

   360 ÷ 9 = 40 sq. yd.

Rugs

Area rugs are priced according to size and quality. To estimate the price of an area rug, consult a catalog or check at a store. Standard sizes in feet include: 2 x 4, 2 x 8, 4 x 6, 6 x 9, and 9 x 12.

Window Treatments

To determine fabric yardage required for a window treatment, measure the area to be covered by the window treatment.

1. Measure the width and length of the area to be covered by the window treatment.

45 in. (width) × 84 in. (length)

2. To give fullness to the window treatment, multiply the width by 2 or 2½. If you are using a sheer fabric, multiply by 2½ or 3.

45 in. × 2 = 90 in.

3. Determine the number of widths of fabric required by dividing the width including fullness (your answer in #2) by the width of the fabric. (Home decorating fabrics are often 54 in. wide.)

90 in. ÷ 54 in. = 1.67 or 2 widths of fabric

4. To determine the length of each width of fabric you must add 12 in. to the length of the window treatment. This extra foot is needed for the hem and heading on the window treatment.

84 in. + 12 in. = 96 in. fabric required for each width

5. Determine the total length of fabric required for the window treatment by multiplying the number of widths (your answer in #3) by the length of fabric required for each width (your answer in #4).

2 × 96 in. = 192 in. of fabric required

6. Fabric is sold in yards. Thus you must convert the number of inches required into yards. Divide the length of fabric required for the window treatment (your answer in #5) by 36 in.

192 in. ÷ 36 in. = 5⅓ yd. of fabric required

Upholstery Fabric

To determine the amount of fabric required for upholstery, refer to Figure 18-5. It gives the sizes of common upholstered furniture and the approximate yardage. More specific charts are available for other pieces or special upholstery treatments. For sofas with button tufting, add two yards of fabric.

FIGURE 18-5

Approximate Yardages for Upholstery

Furniture Piece	Number of Yards
Sofa, 6 ft. (1.8 m)	12 yd. (11 m)
Sofa, 7 ft. (2.1 m)	14 yd. (13 m)
Sofa, 9 ft. (2.7 m)	18 yd. (16.5 m)
Wing Chair	7 yd. (6.4 m)
Club Chair	8 yd. (7.3 m)
Dining chair with upholstered seat and back	2 yd. (1.8 m)
Square ottoman	3 yd. (2.7 m)

Step 5: Compile a Design Resource File

To convey their likes and design ideas, clients often have photos and articles they have saved. Designers also maintain their own extensive resource files.

As part of the file, it's helpful to take "before" photos of the area to be designed. You'll enjoy comparing them to the finished project and they'll be useful for completing the next steps of the design process. If the project isn't in your own home, you might videotape the room to have as a reference while you're working.

FIND SOURCES OF IDEAS

Finding outstanding designs to include in a resource file of designs isn't difficult. There are a number of sources.

- Decorating and women's magazines show photos of well designed rooms.
- Furniture and accessory catalogs are an excellent source of ideas.
- A growing number of informative websites are devoted to interior design.
- Sunday newspapers frequently run features on home design.
- How-to books and interior design reference books are available at bookstores and the library.

Organize your file by separating the clippings and photos into categories such as bedrooms, family rooms, dining rooms, kitchens, etc. You may also include product brochures and samples of wallpaper, paint, and fabric in the appropriate file. These may be picked up at stores and home improvement centers.

If the project is in your own home, have your family look through the clippings, separating them into designs they do and don't like.

A design resource file can provide inspiration when you're considering redecorating.

The Next Steps

Following the first five steps in developing a design plan provides you with a solid foundation for your project. Once you study about backgrounds, furniture, lighting, and accessories, and how to select them, you'll be ready to finalize your design with Steps 6-10 in Chapter 23. In that chapter you will learn how to plan space; select a style, a color scheme, and other design components. Then you'll explore various methods of presenting a design, and, finally, implementing the plan.

Whether design work involves a new home like this one or a much older home, following the ten steps in the design process is beneficial.

Elizabeth Jackson

Interior Designer

In many large cities, rents are sky-rocketing. Young working people find that the housing they can afford is much more compact than the homes where they grew up. To make the most of the space they have, many of these people turn to an interior designer. This is the type of challenge I enjoy very much.

I begin by analyzing the rooms to identify any design problems. I consider the clients' needs, wants, and budget. Using my knowledge of space, color, proportion, and other elements, I devise a plan that helps the space work for the people living there. Accomplishing this requires artistic talent, color sense, imagination, good business judgment, and the ability to work with many details.

"The basic goal of interior design for a smaller room is to lighten it up—literally and figuratively. I show people how to trick the eye into believing the room is larger."

The basic goal of interior design for a smaller room is to lighten it up—literally and figuratively. I show people how to trick the eye into believing the room is larger. For example, smaller pieces of furniture not only take up less space, but also make a room seem less cramped. Because white and pale shades reflect the light and seem to enlarge the area, they are best for walls and ceilings. For clients who like bright or deep colors, I suggest using them as accents.

Anything that calls attention to the spaciousness overhead also helps an area look larger. Ceiling moldings can be painted to help define the upper half of the room. A patterned border, vertically striped wallpaper, and tall pieces of furniture such as bookcases all direct the eye upward. Suspending plants from the ceiling not only draws the eye upward but also uses that space well.

Ample lighting makes every inch of a small room more noticeable. I usually avoid draperies on windows. Instead we use sheer curtains, and add blinds or shades for privacy. Mirrors are great for fooling the eye into seeing more space than is actually there. Glass tabletops and shelving let you see through them to the area beyond.

Eliminating clutter is the best way—and the least expensive way—to "free up" a room. Clutter makes a room look crowded. This can be a real challenge in a tiny apartment. I encourage clients to display large collectibles in higher locations. Pottery vases or trophies work well on top of bookcases or cabinets. Baskets or decorative plates can be a real asset when mounted at the top of a wall. To avoid countertop clutter, I suggest storing small appliances under the counter. The no-clutter rule also applies to walls—one large painting

or object sometimes works better than clusters of small ones.

I believe that attractiveness and usefulness go hand in hand. If the space is well designed, even the smallest home can feel comfortable, bright, and interesting. Some people find they actually prefer the convenience of a small place. One client told me, "One small room that suits you perfectly is better than three spacious ones that don't."

"Eliminating clutter is the best way—and the least expensive way—to 'free up' a room."

Career Profile

Interior designers work on the interiors of homes or other buildings to create designs that will be efficient and can meet the needs of the clients. The interior designer has to consider the size and shape of the rooms, the colors that will be used, the materials needed, the efficiency of the design, and what works with the clients' budget and meets their taste. Another important aspect of the interior designer's job is to make sure that all designs follow building code and legal regulations. The interior designer often uses CAD (computer-aided design) tools to allow the client to visualize what the final design will look like. Interior designers may have a specialty such as kitchens, living rooms, or office space.

Education
▸ Must pass the National Council for Interior Design qualification exam to become licensed; 21 states and the District of Columbia require the license.
▸ A bachelor's degree and two years of experience within the field are required for licensing.
▸ Certification by American Society of Interior Designers (ASID) preferred.

Skills Needed
▸ Must be creative, imaginative, and able to follow changing trends.
▸ Experience in architecture is helpful.
▸ Must have excellent writing, speaking, and nonverbal communication.
▸ Needs to be a self-starter to be able to meet deadlines.

Career Outlook
▸ Although the outlook for employment in this field is good, there is also a lot of competition for jobs. Education and talent are needed to succeed.

Career Activities
1. What suggestions would you have for clients who were finding it difficult to get rid of clutter in their small home?
2. Your client is interested in a collection of heavy furniture that is rather massive. How would you discuss scale and proportion with the client? Write a paragraph detailing your comments.

Chapter Summary

- There are ten recommended steps to follow in developing a design plan.
- The design process involves taking several types of inventories.
- Follow the design plan process for both personal projects and those for clients.
- Lifestyle plays a key role in creating a design to suit a family or individual.
- Features and furnishings of the current room should be examined, and measurements taken.
- Calculating the required amount of design materials is necessary to prepare a preliminary budget.
- A design resource file is a helpful source of ideas and inspiration.

Checking Your Understanding

1. What are the first five steps in developing a design plan?
2. How is timing involved in the initial stage of a design plan?
3. What types of questions are asked in a personal inventory?
4. Give an example of a multipurpose room.
5. Name at least five factors that should be analyzed when an environment is inventoried.
6. What are three places in a furniture arrangement that require clearance space?
7. What features should be shown in a scale drawing?
8. Explain how to measure for carpeting or vinyl floor covering.
9. What is a contingency fee? What is the average amount recommended?
10. What are three types of items that might be included in a design resource file?

Thinking Critically

1. Explain the risks of tackling a design project without a plan.
2. In trying to follow a time frame when working with painters, carpenters, plumbers, etc., what advantage might an interior designer have over a homeowner?
3. When interviewing clients about their lifestyle and home, why is it important to ask questions tactfully?
4. Some designers recommend that clients live in a home for a while before redesigning it. Why might they make that suggestion?

Applications

1. **Developing an Inventory.** Prepare a list of questions to pose to clients who are planning to update their kitchen and the adjacent family room. Keep in mind that your goal is to discover their needs and wants.

2. **Drawing to Scale.** Measure your bedroom or another room in your home. Measure the furniture in the room. Draw the room and furnishings to scale on graph paper. Use architectural symbols to indicate doors and windows.

3. **Calculating Wall and Floor Coverings.** You would like to give a new look to a dining room that measures 14 ft. x 16 ft. The ceiling is 8 ft. high. The room has one window and two doorways. How many gallons of paint would be needed for the room? How many rolls of wallpaper with a repeating pattern?

4. **Comparing Costs.** The paint you want to buy for the dining room cited above costs $22 per gallon. Quarts of the same type of paint are $10.99. The pre-pasted wallpaper you're considering costs $13 per single roll. It has a repeating pattern. How much would you spend on paint for the room? How much would the wallpaper cost?

5. **Reality Pricing.** List on a sheet of paper: leather sofa, brass table lamp, coffee table, ceiling fan, 8-ft. x 10-ft. rug, computer desk, and dining table with four chairs. Next to each item, write an estimate of how much you think it might cost. Using catalogs, the Internet, or newspaper ads, determine an actual average cost of such an item. Were your estimates high or low? Discuss your findings with classmates.

BUILDING YOUR PORTFOLIO

You are helping your uncle with a design plan for the living room of his townhouse. He would like new coverings for the floor, walls, and windows. He is also interested in purchasing a new sofa. Within two years he expects to be transferred to another city. Make at least one suggestion for every component that he wants to change. Explain the rationale for your ideas. What would be the most expensive item in the budget? For what would you try to spend the least amount of money?

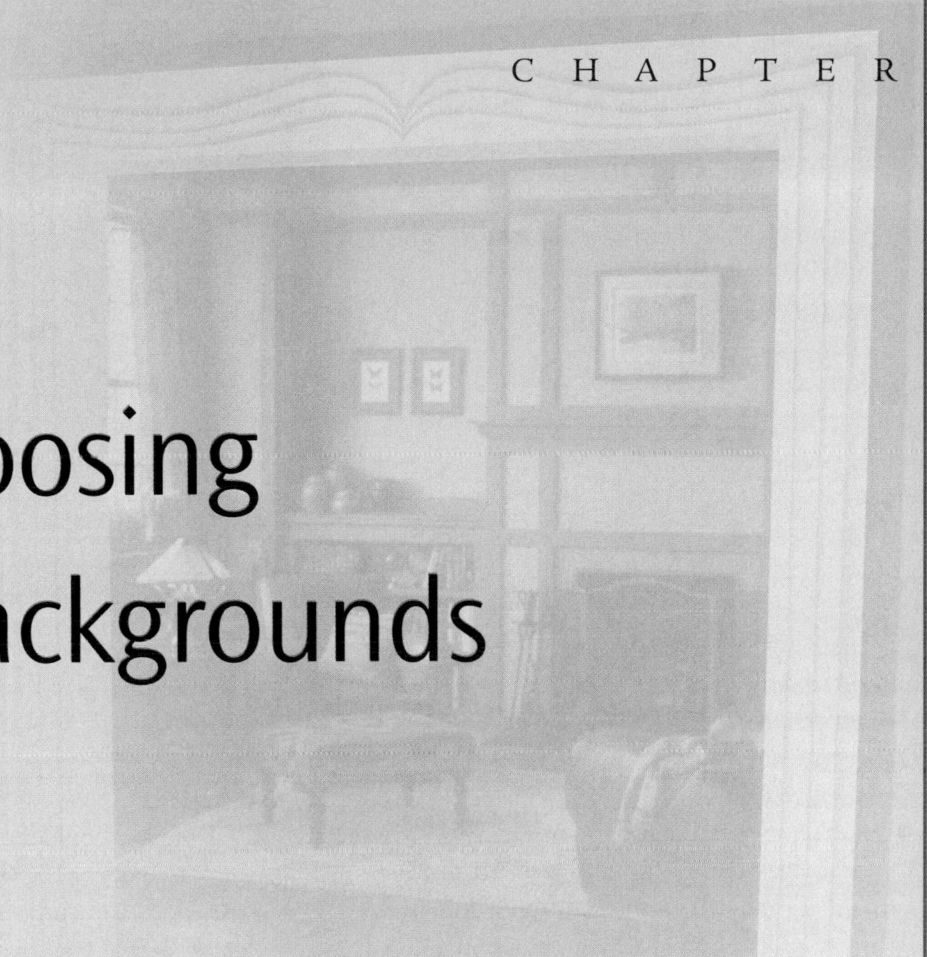

Choosing Backgrounds

CHAPTER OBJECTIVES

▶ Explain what backgrounds are and why they are important.

▶ Assess the fiber content of various home textiles and backgrounds.

▶ Evaluate various types of floor coverings for specific uses.

▶ Compare the characteristics and uses of various wall coverings.

▶ Suggest options for ceilings.

▶ Describe characteristics of various window treatments.

TERMS TO LEARN

- alkyd paint
- blinds
- chair rail
- latex paint
- moldings
- pile
- plain weave
- primer
- resilient flooring
- satin weave
- stenciling
- swag
- twill weave
- valance

Why do many people consult interior designers? Often, it's for expert help choosing coverings for their walls, floors, and windows. Along with the ceiling, these are the backgrounds of a room. Together, these surfaces affect more than the room's appearance. They also contribute to the feel, the sound, and sometimes the energy efficiency of the room.

The Role Backgrounds Play

Backgrounds are easy to overlook or take for granted. If they are missing or out of proportion, however, they become quite noticeable. It is best to make some decisions about background areas before going on to other parts of your design.

Backgrounds help set the mood of a room. The materials, patterns, colors, and textures you choose for the background elements all contribute to the mood, which may be formal or informal. It may be calm and quiet or vibrant and exciting.

Sound is also affected by backgrounds. Soft, textured materials tend to absorb sound, while smooth, hard surfaces don't. What would the noise levels be like in a room with thick carpeting, compared to one with a wood floor?

In some rooms the background may actually be the focal point of the room. This is true when there is some special quality, such as a dramatic beamed ceiling or a floor-to-ceiling window. In other rooms the background goes almost unnoticed, serving only to provide a setting for the furnishings.

ENERGY-EFFICIENT BACKGROUNDS

Some backgrounds can help save money on heating and cooling bills. When Jesse and Kiara Dixon remodeled their home, they learned they were fortunate that some existing characteristics of the home could be adapted to conserve energy. One such feature was a very large window on the south side of the house. It let plenty of light in the family room, much of it shining on the brick fireplace wall.

Architectural features may be an asset or they may present special challenges when designing the background of a room.

Other backgrounds are also capable of boosting energy efficiency. For instance, plush carpeting and some ceiling tile have an insulating effect. Foil wallpaper may reflect heat. A built-in cabinet or bookcase can help insulate an outside wall.

COLOR CONSIDERATIONS

You have already studied characteristics of particular colors in Chapter 16, but there are some special factors relating to background color.

Windows that open to an attractive view form their own background. What other benefits might be gained from these windows?

The Dixons invested in rough quarry tile for the floor. They eliminated the sheer curtain panels that filtered the sunlight, opting for heavy insulated draperies instead. Every morning they opened the draperies fully. The tile floor and brick wall absorbed the sun's heat during the day, then released it at night. Every evening the Dixons drew the draperies to hold in the stored heat. In hot weather, they installed a canvas awning over the window and closed the draperies as needed.

Public and Private Choices—Backgrounds for Hotels

Some of today's hotels have several thousand rooms. Try to imagine the number of hotel guests, employees, and rolling luggage that might pass through the lobby on any given day. Then it's understandable why interior designers must carefully evaluate the suitability of different types of floors, wall treatments, and upholstery for both the hotel's public and private areas. Public areas include the lobby, restaurant, banquet facilities, meeting rooms, halls, and swimming pool/recreational areas. Guest rooms and adjoining bathrooms are considered private areas.

Hotel owners generally have a decorating theme or a particular image they want to convey. The theme may be determined by the hotel's location. For instance, for a hotel located in Hawaii, a tropical theme is likely. If a hotel caters to business travelers, it might strive for a look of calm efficiency—perhaps soothing colors and a streamlined look.

Durability and ease of maintenance are two other key characteristics designers look for in choosing background materials. Many manufacturers have commercial lines of their products for high-use situations. Here are some examples of factors designers keep in mind when choosing materials:

- **Hotel lobby and reception.** Guests get their first impressions from the lobby and reception area. Thus it's very important that this area is both attractive and well maintained. Materials should be of a high quality, be able to withstand very high traffic, and reflect the theme of the hotel.

- **Dining room.** Various dining areas in a hotel may have distinct images. Catering to people who are in a hurry,

a coffee shop might be bright and open. A formal dining room might be given a darker, more relaxed atmosphere. In both cases, the colors chosen should be appealing to the appetite. Background materials must be able to withstand food and beverage spills. Walls need to be protected against damage from the backs of chairs. It's also desirable for materials to provide some soundproofing. A dining area with only hard surfaces can be noisy, making conversation difficult.

- **Guest bedrooms.** Designers have greater flexibility in selecting backgrounds for guest rooms and suites. Durability is a factor, but less so than in the public areas of the hotel. No matter how large or small the hotel is, there are three requirements that should be met. Materials should have

soundproofing qualities. Window treatments should be able to darken the room during the day. The room should be able to be easily cleaned and maintained.

You, the *Designer*

Imagine you are part of a design team responsible for selecting background materials for a new hotel in a major city. Decide what types of floorcoverings, fabrics, and wallcoverings you would recommend for the lobby. What would you suggest for the guest bedrooms and bathrooms? Give rationales for your choices.

- Because the light in a room is uneven, color will seldom look the same in every spot.
- The way light strikes the wall can affect how dark or light a color appears. Colors may even appear different from one season to the next.
- Doorways, windows, and fireplaces all affect the color in a room. How does color change when it reflects through a doorway? Won't an uncovered window be black at night?
- Furniture reduces the amount of background color. An entertainment center, for instance, covers much of a wall. A sofa obscures part of the floor.
- Remember that reds, oranges, and yellows make a room seem warmer. Greens, blues, and violets generally create a cooler feeling.
- For passive solar heat, the color of the mass that stores the heat (tile, brick, or concrete) should be dark. The surfaces that reflect the heat (walls, ceilings, and furnishings) onto the thermal mass should be light.

Textiles in the Home

Imagine a home with smooth ceramic tile floors, polished wood chairs, gleaming glass tables, and shutters at every window. It sounds interesting, but isn't something missing? Without textiles—fabrics—most people wouldn't consider a house a home. To select backgrounds and home furnishings effectively, it's important to understand textiles and the fibers that are used to make them.

The hard surfaces of the blinds, table, chairs, and tile floor are made more appealing with the softening effect of the textiles.

TYPES OF TEXTILES

Consider the abundance of textiles in your home. You probably have carpeting or a rug, upholstered furniture, pillows, and curtains—and that may be just in the living room. There are many more items, of course, in the kitchen, bathroom, and bedrooms. Chair cushions, placemats, towels, linens, and bedspreads are all home textiles.

FIGURE 19-1

Principal Fibers for Carpet and Home Textiles

Common Synthetic Fibers

MATERIAL AND COMMON USES	*Advantages*	*Disadvantages*
ACRYLIC *Blankets, rugs, some carpet*	Appearance and feel of wool Low static level Resists mildew and moisture	Subject to pilling
NYLON *Very popular for carpeting; rugs*	Very durable Easily maintained Resists matting Mold-, mildew-, and moth-proof	Generates static unless treated Subject to pilling and fading Attracts dirt
OLEFIN, POLYPROPYLENE *Carpeting (especially indoor/outdoor and Berber); decorative rugs; may be combined with acrylic or nylon*	Strong, easily maintained Nonabsorbent Resists stains and static Extremely colorfast Inexpensive	Crushes easily Limited colors and designs unless combined with other fibers Sensitive to heat
POLYESTER *Curtains; scarves for window treatments; pleated shades; draperies; fiberfill; bedding; upholstery; carpeting (including newer PET polyester)*	Soft, durable Resists soil Resists stains (PET polyester) Easily dyed Often blended with cotton	Generates static electricity Subject to stains and pilling Not absorbent In carpeting, lower grades don't wear well
RAYON *Draperies; bedding; slipcovers; upholstery; tablecloths*	Absorbent; easily dyed Drapes well Can be washed with care Resists insects Sometimes combined with acetate	Wrinkles easily if untreated Shrinks in hot water Highly flammable Susceptible to fading
NYLON/POLYESTER BLEND *Carpeting (especially Berber)*	Durable Easy to maintain Combines advantages of both fibers	Limited colors

Slipcovers are a very popular way of updating furniture. Some consumers choose to make their own. What type of fabric would you select for such a project?

FIGURE 19-1 (Continued)

Principal Fibers for Carpet and Home Textiles

Natural Fibers

MATERIAL AND COMMON USES	Advantages	Disadvantages
COTTON *Chintz and other upholstery fabric; curtains and draperies; throw rugs; towels; bedding*	Strong and durable Absorbent Washable or dry cleanable Easily dyed Often blended with polyester	Wrinkles Shrinks unless treated Soils easily Very flammable if untreated Not mildew-resistant
FLAX (LINEN) *Draperies; upholstery; tablecloths; kitchen towels*	Strongest natural fiber Withstands frequent laundering Lint-free and absorbent Ages well	Wrinkles easily Highly flammable Relatively expensive Not mildew-resistant
SILK *Draperies; upholstery; lampshades; wall coverings*	Strong and smooth Very absorbent Dyes well Drapes and retains shape well Stain- and wrinkle-resistant Washable or dry cleanable	Expensive Weakened by bleach and light Spotted by water unless treated Not insect-resistant Yellows
WOOL *Plush and Berber carpeting; fine rugs; blankets; upholstery; draperies*	Soft and durable Resilient Long lasting Soil- and fire-resistant Easily dyed Resists fading and abrasion	Relatively expensive Not resistant to moths Can shrink May cause an allergic reaction Hard to clean once deeply soiled

Fibers

Fabrics start out as tiny fibers. The fibers are twisted together into yarns, then the yarns are woven into fabric. Figure 19-1 describes some of the most common fibers used today. It explains characteristics that make them useful or unsuitable for specific items. For example, cotton rugs are fine in the kitchen, but carpeting made of cotton would be a poor choice.

Fibers are classified as natural or synthetic. Cotton, wool, flax (linen), and silk are *natural fibers* because they come from plants and animals.

Nylon, polyester, polypropylene, acrylic, and rayon are several common *synthetic fibers*. They are man-made with chemicals and other materials. Natural and synthetic fibers are often combined to blend the best qualities of both.

Weaves and Finishes

Most home decorating fabrics are woven, although leather is an example of a nonwoven material. In weaving, two or more sets of threads are interlaced at right angles. The *warp* is the set of threads that run lengthwise. The *weft* is the set of threads that runs crosswise. Figure 19-2 illustrates three basic weaves: plain, twill, and satin.

The *Jacquard weave* is used to produce brocades and damasks, rich-looking fabrics that are found as draperies, upholstery, and bedspreads. These fabrics are woven on special looms and usually feature large, elaborate designs.

FIGURE 19-2

A VISUAL GUIDE TO...

Basic Weaves

If you examine a piece of fabric under a magnifying glass, you will likely discover one of these weaves:

Warp

Weft

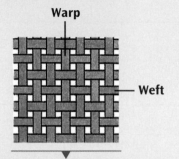

Plain weave is a simple pattern as strong in one direction as it is in the other. This pattern should wear evenly. The plain weave is used for percale and muslin sheets and pillow cases. Many curtains also have a plain weave. How would you describe the way the warp interacts with the weft to create a plain weave?

Warp

Weft

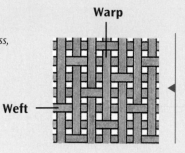

Satin weave is a pattern distinguished by long "floats," which are formed when each warp thread passes over a certain number of weft threads at one time before passing under one. The floats give satin fabric its characteristic sheen. Satin fabric, silk, and rayon are woven in a satin weave.

Warp

Weft

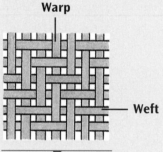

Twill weave is a pattern with diagonal lines or wales. A wale is formed when a weft thread passes over two or more warp threads before passing under a warp thread again. The twill weave produces a firm, strong fabric. Denim and gabardine are examples of fabrics that use this weave.

Carpeting, upholstery fabrics, and table linens are commonly treated to resist stains. Some fabrics have had a finish applied to make them flame resistant. Other fabric treatments help reduce wrinkling, shrinkage, fading, and static.

TEXTILE LAWS

The federal government protects consumers with regulations for textiles. The Flammable Fabrics Act established standards for apparel fabrics, as well as home items such as rugs, carpeting, and mattresses.

Two others focus on letting consumers know what they're buying. The Textile Fiber Products Identification Act specifies what must appear on labels: fiber content and percentage, the product's manufacturer, country of origin, and care information. Another labeling act is strictly for wool products.

Floor Coverings

Floor coverings are usually the most expensive component of a design project. One way to justify the cost is to regard them as the foundation of the room. Another is to realize that quality floor coverings pay off in years of good service. Durability is important because most floors are subjected to dirt and spills, the weight of furniture, and heavy traffic.

As you read in Chapter 13, finish floor materials, such as wood, brick, and ceramic tile, are laid over the structural flooring and are part of the floor. They are often installed when the home is built and provide a durable, long-lasting surface. Finish floorings are not always desired for every room, however. Floor coverings are popular choices.

The type of flooring chosen depends largely on the purpose of the room, the amount of traffic flowing through it, how much maintenance the floor requires, and whether it coordinates with the decorating scheme of the room. The lifestyles of the occupants must also be taken into account. Resilient flooring, carpeting, and rugs are all possible choices.

RESILIENT FLOOR COVERINGS

Resilient flooring is flooring with a semi-hard surface that returns to its original shape after stress. For instance, if a frying pan were dropped on a resilient floor, the floor would resist denting. Resilient floor coverings are warmer and quieter to walk on than hard floor materials such as wood and ceramic tile, but they aren't quite as durable. The resilient floor coverings that are used most often are vinyl and plastic laminate flooring.

It can be difficult to tell the difference between wood and plastic laminate flooring. What other backgrounds are apparent in this bedroom?

- Vinyl resists many stains, including grease and bleach. It is durable and easy to clean and comes in a vast assortment of patterns and colors. Most varieties have a no-wax finish with built-in luster. Vinyl flooring is sold in tile and sheet form. The tiles are 12 in. x 12 in. (30 cm x 30 cm). The sheets, or rolls, are sold in 6-ft. and 12-ft. widths (1.8-m and 3.7-m).
- Plastic laminate flooring is made of fiberboard that is covered with a photo reproduction of wood grain or other material. A top layer of plastic provides protection. Laminate floors are installed as floating floors over a foam pad. They are durable and comfortable to stand on. They also resist dents and scratches.
- Asphalt, rubber, and cork are other types of resilient flooring. They are used in homes less often today.

CARPETING

Carpeting is a preference of many people, in at least part of their home. Besides insulating the floor against drafts, carpeting cuts down on noise and provides a feeling of comfort. Slips and falls are less likely to occur on well-anchored carpeting than on bare floors.

New manufacturing techniques and advancements in fiber chemistry have resulted in carpeting that is more durable, attractive, and easier to maintain than ever before. People no longer have to avoid light-colored carpeting for fear of soiling. Some carpet fibers feature permanent protection against tough stains.

Carpet selection involves much more than choosing a color. You also have options in pattern, texture, and durability. There's striped carpeting, floral prints, plaids, and even some that glow in the dark! With the wide array of carpeting on the market, choosing a knowledgeable carpet dealer is essential. He or she can help you examine *performance ratings* of various carpets, provided by many manufacturers.

Size and Installation

Wall-to-wall carpeting provides an unbroken area of color and texture and can make an area seem spacious. The same color is often used in several rooms to help unify the design. *Broadloom* carpet is carpeting manufactured in rolls up to 15-ft. (4.6-m) wide, but 12-ft. (3.7-m) rolls are standard. Seams are taped or sewed together, and the entire carpet is fastened to the floor with tackless strips or by gluing.

Carpet tiles come in various sizes. They are easy to install and are convenient because an individual piece of soiled or worn tile can be replaced.

Quality

The density of a carpet's **pile**, or nap, helps determine its quality. The pile is the visible surface of the carpeting. The amount of pile in car-

peting is called the average pile yarn weight. It should be sufficient to prevent crushing. Contrary to popular belief, the *depth* of the pile doesn't necessarily make a carpet more durable, although it might make it feel more luxurious. Carpet density can be checked by bending back a piece of carpet and noticing the amount of space between the yarns and how the yarns are attached. This is called the *grin test*.

Fiber content and construction also help determine carpet quality. While some high-quality carpeting is made of wool, more than 95 percent of carpeting today is created with manufactured fibers. Nylon is by far the most popular, followed by polypropylene carpeting. Many Berbers are made from polypropylene, also known as olefin.

A relatively new type of polyester called *PET* is being used more often because of its resistance to stains and fading. Recycled plastic containers are used in the production of PET. Acrylic carpeting was common at one time, but is rarely seen today because of its tendency to become fuzzy. Refer back to Figure 19-1 on pages 416-417 to review the characteristics of various fibers that are used in carpeting.

Texture and Construction

In years past, almost all carpeting was woven on looms. Today, however, about 90 percent is constructed

Tufted carpet. Yarn is threaded into a backing with needles, secured with adhesive, and then cut or left looped.

FIGURE 19-3

A VISUAL GUIDE TO ...

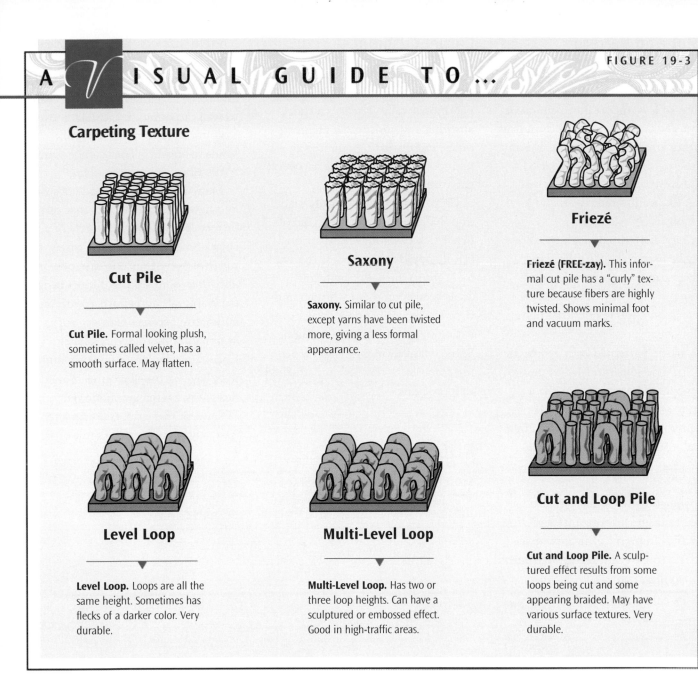

Carpeting Texture

Cut Pile

Cut Pile. Formal looking plush, sometimes called velvet, has a smooth surface. May flatten.

Saxony

Saxony. Similar to cut pile, except yarns have been twisted more, giving a less formal appearance.

Friezé

Friezé (FREE-zay). This informal cut pile has a "curly" texture because fibers are highly twisted. Shows minimal foot and vacuum marks.

Level Loop

Level Loop. Loops are all the same height. Sometimes has flecks of a darker color. Very durable.

Multi-Level Loop

Multi-Level Loop. Has two or three loop heights. Can have a sculptured or embossed effect. Good in high-traffic areas.

Cut and Loop Pile

Cut and Loop Pile. A sculptured effect results from some loops being cut and some appearing braided. May have various surface textures. Very durable.

by *tufting*. With this method, the yarn is inserted with threaded needles into a backing material. The tufts are then glued to the backing. Carpets can also be knitted into an uncut loop pile. Another construction process, needlepunch, is used to produce a lower-cost product often used as indoor-outdoor carpeting. It has a flat surface rather than a pile.

It's possible to choose a neutral color and still achieve great visual interest with carpeting. New machines produce textures ranging from squares to diamond shapes.

Carpet yarns made of a variety of fibers can be looped, twisted, or cut to create many different textures and

to influence the quality of the carpet. For example, plush carpeting has upright loops cut to form an even surface, providing a luxurious effect. Figure 19-3 shows how other carpet textures are created.

Color and Pattern

The decorating scheme of a room is often determined by the carpet color, so it is important to choose it carefully. Examine a carpet sample at various times of the day and evening in the room where it will be used. That way you can tell what it will look like in different types and levels of light.

Chapter 16 discussed how color may be used to create different effects and feelings. You can use these principles when choosing a carpet color. Remember that light colors make areas seem larger.

Carpets patterned with geometric or floral designs can suggest design elements to be repeated in the wall and window treatments. A rule of thumb is to use a small pattern in a small room and reserve large patterns for larger rooms. Patterned carpets are practical, since they don't show dirt easily. Tweed can also be used to disguise footprints and dirt. Practical in high-traffic areas, tweed carpets consist of multicolored yarns looped together.

Carpet Cushion

A quality under padding, or *carpet cushion*, can extend the life of a carpet dramatically. It acts as a shock absorber and adds to the comfort, quiet, and insulating qualities of carpeting. It also prevents the carpet or rug from sliding.

Carpet cushion is typically made of polyurethane foam, fiber, or rubber. Thick cushion feels luxurious, but it should always be less than ½ in. (1.3 cm) thick. For high traffic areas, a cushion that is thinner and firmer is recommended. Berber carpet requires a thin, dense cushion. Some relatively inexpensive carpeting comes with the cushion attached to its backing.

RUGS

Most rugs are a type of carpeting. The difference is that they aren't fastened to the floor. Rugs are made in one piece and have finished edges. They are usually rectangular or oval and come in many sizes. Unlike wall-to-wall carpeting, rugs can be moved from room to room or from one home to another. They can be turned to distribute wear more evenly.

Many large rugs are made of wool and have colorful designs that can be incorporated into the style of a room. Smaller accent rugs, often made of polypropylene, add personality to a room setting. Motifs range from animals and sports to seasons and natural scenes. Carpets, rugs, and mats constructed of plant fibers, such as sisal, coir, rush, and jute, have become favorites of many designers. Softer, synthetic versions of some of these fibers are an alternate way to capture the same look.

Wall Coverings

Walls are the largest background space in a room. There are a variety of factors to consider when choosing wall coverings. These include the condition of the walls, the cost involved, the function of the room, the look desired, and lifestyle. The most common wall coverings are paint, wallpaper, and paneling.

Paint is generally the least expensive wall covering. When walls have a lot of cracks, however, it can be less time-consuming to wallpaper or panel. Fabric, mirrors, cork, and even carpeting are sometimes used as wall coverings. These wall coverings bring additional textures and patterns into a room.

Wall painting has been elevated to an art. There are many styles of faux finishes, such as the sponge painting shown here. Different colors can be combined to create effects ranging from subtle to dramatic.

Neutral colors are often used on walls, regardless of the type of wall covering chosen, because they are less overpowering than more vivid colors. However, tints, shades, and intense colors can also fit in a carefully planned design.

Washable surfaces are recommended for bathrooms, kitchens, children's rooms, and hallways, because walls in those areas tend to become soiled sooner than bedrooms or living rooms.

PAINT

Properly preparing walls to paint often takes more time than actually applying the paint. Walls should first be washed. Then tiny cracks and nail holes should be filled with spackling compound and a putty knife. Sometimes a special primer needs to be applied before repainting. Usually white in color, **primers** are sealants that makes surfaces nonporous and keep out humidity. Some are formulated to cover stains.

A gallon of paint covers 350 to 400 sq. ft. (28 to 37 sq. m). Many premixed colors of paint are available. However, paint can be specially mixed to match almost any color. Consumers can buy paint that dries in 30 minutes, doesn't drip, has little or no odor, and resists rust and mildew. There are two main types of paint.

- **Solvent-based paint.** This type of paint may be oil or a synthetic resin called **alkyd** (AL-ked). Alkyd dries more quickly than pure oil paint and doesn't contain lead. It produces a durable and washable surface and is often chosen for walls and ceilings in bathrooms and kitchens, where splatters and grease are likely to build up. A solvent, such as mineral spirits, is used to clean paintbrushes.
- **Latex paint.** Latex is a water-based, quick-drying paint. It is easy to apply. However, latex does not adhere well to some surfaces, such as bare wood and surfaces previously painted with alkyd paint. In such cases, the surface should be sanded and/or a primer should be applied first. Cleanup with warm water is fairly simple. Latex paint is considered more environmentally safe than solvent-based paint.

Paints are available in various finishes: gloss, semi-gloss, satin or eggshell, flat (dull), and textured. Glossy paints are easiest to clean, but flat paints typically look more formal. Textured paint adds interest, but may be difficult to clean and to remove.

Decorative Painting

An array of special effects can be created by using a sponge or fabric to apply color over a contrasting base coat. Usually more affordable than wallpapering, the techniques can add a richness and transform a plain background. One technique involves spattering paint; others involve removing wet glaze from a surface by dragging or combing with a tool. See page 343 for details about several faux finish techniques

In **stenciling**, patterns are created by using a special brush to apply paint through cutout areas in a template. An up-and-down motion of the brush is used with very little paint to create shading and to prevent the paint from seeping under the stencil. Stenciled designs are often applied along the top border of a wall or around windows and doors.

Several painting techniques and wall coverings were used in this kitchen and eating area. How many can you find?

WALLPAPER

Decorative paper has been used to cover walls since the 16th century in Europe—and since colonial times in America. Today's wallpaper is available in an almost limitless assortment of patterns and colors. It's possible to achieve many design effects not possible with paint. Wallpaper can even change the apparent dimensions of a room, making it seem smaller or larger.

Vinyl and vinyl-coated papers are the best-selling wallpapers today. They are especially suitable for kitchens, bathrooms, and children's rooms. Most are water- and stain-resistant, making them easier to clean.

Specialty papers are also available. Foil paper can make small rooms appear larger. Heavy embossed paper, which has raised surface areas as part of the design, is used to create a formal effect. Fabrics and natural fibers backed with paper can provide interesting textures.

The wallpapering process involves several steps. Walls need to be *sized* before hanging wallpaper. Sizing is a very thin coating that makes the wall tacky, allowing the paper to stick better. Prepasted wallpaper is soaked briefly in water before hanging. Other papers require that paste be spread on the back. The strips of wallpaper are cut, hung, and trimmed.

Some wallpaper is strippable, which means that it can be removed from the wall easily. Other types, especially older papers, must be removed by steaming and scraping.

Before purchasing wallpaper, bring home a sample and hold it against the wall. Sometimes it's possible to have the retailer order a large sample piece. Before hanging, check that all rolls have the same batch number. Wallpaper that is printed at one time is given a number. Even though all the rolls of a given pattern have the same design, the colors may vary slightly from batch to batch.

Most wallpaper has a pattern repeat that must be matched from strip to strip. This must be taken into account when calculating how much to order.

Wallpaper Borders

Wallpaper borders are popular and relatively inexpensive. They can be pasted over coordinating wallpaper or a painted surface. Typically, borders are placed at the top of a wall, at a midway point, or above a countertop. Borders are easy to install, but it's helpful to have another person hold one end of the long strip.

Most borders are sold in rolls containing 15 ft. (4.6 m).

Some self-stick borders may be peeled easily from the wall without leaving any residue. They are ideal for individuals who rent their homes.

PANELING

Paneling can provide a feeling of warmth. It can also camouflage imperfect walls. Available in many price ranges, paneling requires little maintenance. Most paneling is sold in sheets that measure 4 ft. x 8 ft. (1.2 m x 2.4 m).

- **Solid wood paneling.** Solid wood paneling is attractive but costly. It comes in many varieties, from white pine to dark walnut.
- **Manufactured paneling.** Manufactured paneling is a more economical option. It is created by bonding a thin layer of fine wood to a less expensive wood backing. This paneling, like solid wood paneling, requires a protective finish to seal it against stains and water.
- **Laminated plastic paneling.** This paneling is constructed much like the plastic laminate that is popular for countertops. It consists of layers of paper and resins baked at high temperatures and under extreme pressure. The top layer can be printed in any color or pattern, including wood grain.

MOLDING

Moldings are strips of shaped wood used for trim or ornamentation in a room. Their main purpose is to finish off a window, door, or wall. Providing an elegant finished look, *crown molding* is a wide trim used on walls next to the ceiling. Some moldings are more functional than decorative. For example, baseboard moldings hide the break between the wall and the floor, keep dirt from accumulating in the crack, and prevent damage to the wall at floor level.

A **chair rail** is molding that runs horizontally across the wall about 3 ft. (0.9 m) from the floor. Chair rails prevent the backs of chairs from damaging walls, but are installed mainly for their decorative appeal. Paint might be applied below the chair rail, and wallpaper above.

Try to picture this room without the wallpaper. How do you think it would look if the walls were painted white or another solid color?

Ceilings

Ceilings in elegant homes built long ago were sometimes painted with murals and designs or inlaid with tiles In homes constructed since the beginning of the 20th century, however, less attention has been paid to the decorating potential of ceilings. Beams and other special treatments are sometimes used in modern homes, but they add to the cost of construction.

The average height of a ceiling is 8 ft. (2.4 m), although higher ceilings are common in older homes and in some rooms of many new ones. Higher ceilings lend a feeling of dignity, and sometimes freedom, to a room. Ceilings that are lower create a warm and informal room. If they are too low, however, a cramped feeling can result. Lower ceilings lower the cost of construction and also heating and cooling.

Several tricks can be used to make ceilings seem higher or lower than they really are. Ceilings seem higher when wallpaper or paint is extended a short distance onto the ceiling. Wallpapers with vertical lines also create a feeling of added height. Ceilings appear lower when a border is applied at the top of the wall and when the ceiling color is extended a short distance down the wall. Painting a dark color or covering with patterned wallpaper also lowers the apparent ceiling height.

Acoustic ceiling tile has several benefits. The tiles can serve as insulation, absorb sound, and hide stained or cracked ceilings Larger ceiling panels, 2 ft. x 2 ft. (0.6 m x 0.6 m) and 2 ft. x 4 ft. (0.6 m x 1.2 m), are commonly suspended from metal channels that form a grid in the ceiling. This system is often used to lower a high ceiling and to hide plumbing and wiring. Twelve-inch (30 cm) square tiles are typically stapled to strips of wood that have been nailed to the ceiling. They may be glued directly to an existing ceiling if it is level.

Ceilings with wood beams are a feature in some homes. How could you achieve the look of solid wood in the beams without incurring the cost?

Window Coverings

Window coverings, also called window treatments, often play a starring role in a room's design. A dramatic window treatment can have a tremendous impact on the style of a room. The style of the window itself and the view from the window both influence the choice of treatment. Window treatments can also help control the home environment by regulating the amount of light, cutting down on noise, and providing insulation and privacy.

TYPES OF WINDOW TREATMENTS

Consumers have many, many options for window treatments: dozens of types of curtains, draperies, shades, blinds, shutters, and valances. Often more than one type is used at the same window. Combining them with special window hardware multiplies the number of possible looks. Figure 19-4 on pages 428-429 illustrates a sampling of popular window coverings.

Curtains

Constructed of unlined fabric or lace, curtains offer a variety of colors, patterns, and textures. They may be sheer to medium weight.

Sheer curtains may either stay closed or be drawn open on a rod. Sheers are often used behind draperies. They look best when they are very full.

Mainly used on doors, *sash curtains* are hung close to the glass and are

The molding on the wall and the decorative rod contribute to this room's formal look. Can you identify the window treatments that have been combined at this window?

gathered on rods at both the top and the bottom of the window. *Café curtains* are often used in kitchens and bathrooms. *Tiebacks* are another popular type of curtain. Tiebacks edged with ruffles are called Priscilla curtains.

Draperies

Traditional draperies have *pinch pleats* and are hung from a track called a *traverse rod*, which allows them to be opened and closed by pulling on a cord attached to the rod (called drawn draperies). Draperies may also be tied back at the sides of the windows. Stationary drapery panels hang at the sides of the window but can't be pulled across to cover it, making them most suitable when there isn't a need for privacy.

Tab-top curtains are often hung from decorative rods. For which rooms or room styles would this style of curtain be a good choice?

FIGURE 19-4

A **V**ISUAL GUIDE TO...

Window Treatments

Draperies with sheers. Often found in formal rooms, extending to the floor. Drapery fabric is usually heavier than curtain fabric. This sheer curtain fabric lets light in during the day.

Café Curtains with valance. Panels cover part of the window, usually the bottom portion. They are either shirred (gathered) on a rod (shown) or attached with rings, clips, or fabric loops (tabs).

Tieback Curtains with fringed valance. Two curtain panels may meet at the center or cross over each other and then be held back with cord, fabric, or hardware.

Draped Scarves. Graceful "scarves" are made of sheer or semi-sheer fabric. Decorative hardware is part of the look.

Swag and Jabots. Swags drape across the top of a window. Jabots (jab-OZE) or cascades hang gracefully down the sides. May be used over other window coverings.

Valance. This very popular top treatment may have pinch pleats (shown), gathers, or hang from a rod or mounting board. Typically, valances cover no more than the top third of the window.

Window Treatments (Continued)

Roman Shade. Accordion pleats are formed when Roman shades are raised; otherwise they are flat. They are made of various weights of fabric, or woven with bamboo, metal, or wood.

Roller Shade and Cornice. Roller shades may be plain or decorative and are often trimmed with fringe. A cornice is similar to a valance, but is sturdier.

Balloon Shade. This shade balloons at the bottom when raised. An *Austrian shade* has rows of scallops from top to bottom.

Shutters with valance. Shutters may cover an entire window or just the bottom half. They may be used with or without curtains.

Blinds with curtains and valance. Horizontal blind slats may be from ½ to 2 in. (1.3 to 5 cm) wide. May be wood (shown), metal, plastic, or fabric-coated. Wood provides best insulation.

Vertical Blinds. Often used at patio doors and large windows, the vanes or slats are wider than horizontal blinds. They may be rotated 180 degrees to control light.

Draperies have decorating advantages, such as focusing attention on a window or changing the apparent proportions of a wall area. They can be used to hide uneven walls or unsightly pipes. Draperies can even suggest a window where there is none, or a wider window instead of a narrow one. Many are washable like most curtains, but some must be dry cleaned. Vacuuming helps keep them clean. Drawn draperies are energy efficient, especially when lined with a special insulating fabric. They also absorb sound.

Top Treatments

Top treatments are decorative and also serve to hide window hardware. The **valance**—a short length of fabric placed across the top of a window—may be used alone, as well as with most other window treatments. It is often a gathered or pleated fabric that matches or blends with the rest of the window covering. There are many styles of valances. A *blouson* (BLUE-zahn) or balloon valance may be stuffed with tissue paper for a puffy look. A *cornice* has the same purpose as a valance, but has more structure. It is often constructed of wood, which may be painted, stained, or padded and covered with fabric.

A **swag** is a piece of fabric that is draped gracefully across the top of a window. It is attached to both sides of the window frame at the top.

Window Hardware

Some curtain and drapery hardware is intended to be functional and not seen. For instance, combination rods have up to three rods in one, one curtain rod or traverse rod for each part of the window treatment. For example, a double rod can accommodate curtains and a valance. Decorative hardware, on the other hand, is meant to be seen and enhance the window treatment. Most decorative wood or metal rods have a diameter of 1, 1½, or 2 in. (2.5, 3.8, or 5 cm). The ends of the decorative rods are called *finials* and endcaps.

Various types of hardware that hold fabric back to the sides of the window are called sideholders. They are used to tie back curtains or to hold back scarves. Brackets, sconces, and swagholders may be installed at the top of a window to hold rods or fabric.

Shutters

Originally designed to keep out heat and cold, shutters give a simple, uncluttered look to a window. They work well with traditional decors. *Shutters* are vertical sections of wood or manufactured material hinged together, much like a folding door. The sections of traditional shutters have crosswise slats called *louvers*, which vary in width. Some use a fabric insert rather than louvers. Interior shutters are usually painted or stained.

Shades

Shades range from very plain to very ornate. Most may be used alone or with another window covering. Inexpensive *roller shades* come in a variety of colors. Usually mounted at the top of a window, they are made of cloth or vinyl and sometimes are trimmed with fringe. They can also be laminated with fabric or wallpaper. Roller shades may be made of room-darkening, light-filtering, or heat-reflective materials. Vinyl shades are washable.

A *Roman shade* is a shade that lies flat against the window when down and can be drawn up by a cord into a series of horizontal accordion folds. A *balloon shade* is similar to a Roman shade, but a puffed effect is created when the shade is raised.

Pleated shades are usually made of a solid piece of fabric and are raised or lowered with cords. They have horizontal accordion folds that are evident even when the shade is down. *Cellular shades* are similar, but have a double layer of fabric with air space between, making them better insulators.

Blinds

Blinds are made of a series of evenly spaced slats that may be opened or closed by cords. The entire blind may also be raised and lowered, or pulled across a window, by cords. One reason for their popularity is their ability to provide privacy or to let in almost full light. Blinds are more tedious to clean than other window coverings.

Horizontal blinds, traditionally called Venetian blinds, have horizontal slats. The narrowest slats are used in mini-blinds and micro-blinds. *Vertical blinds* are blinds with vertical vanes that are usually 3½ in. (9 cm) wide. Most draw to one side of the window.

COMPARING COST AND OTHER FACTORS

Personal tastes, budget, and the necessary upkeep are all factors in choosing window coverings. Design details—the type of window and its placement, the scale and proportion of window coverings, and the color scheme of the room—also influence the choice. For some types of windows in certain settings, you may even decide not to have a window covering.

Money-wise, you'll find that custom and made-to-measure window treatments are the most expensive. Ready-made valances, curtains, and draperies are less costly because they're mass-produced. Many people choose to hire a seamstress or to make their own window coverings. Pattern companies have made the job easier than you might think. Some designs require little or no sewing. In most cases, valances and curtains can be sewn for a fraction of the cost of custom-made window treatments.

The same window can look very different when the window covering is changed. Which of these two looks do you prefer? What circumstances might lead you to choose the one on the left?

Annie Shay

Textile Specialist

Textiles are both beautiful and technical. Being able to work harmoniously with these two extremes is what my profession is all about. I work in New York City as a textile specialist. The designs at my company range from historical reproductions to bold contemporary designs.

I became interested in this profession while I was working as an interior designer for a firm in Philadelphia. I created almost all of the new fabric designs for our clients. Unfortunately, textile design was only one small division of the firm, and I wanted to work with fabrics all of the time.

The company I work for now sells its fabrics and wallcoverings to interior designers and architects. Designers can view our samples at design centers in the U.S., Canada, and England. Designers can also buy our fabrics and wallcoverings to use as samples in their design studios. As a textile specialist for our firm, I work with our clients, fabric designers, and textile manufacturers.

My interior design background helped to prepare me for my profession. I've also taken advanced chemistry and textile courses. Chemistry classes have helped me with the technical aspects of understanding the properties of textiles. I have focused on fabric and upholstery flammability standards. Our firm sells a lot of fabric to designers specifying materials for commercial buildings. These fabrics must meet flammability standards by preventing ignition, flame spread, and smoke development. They have to be durable to withstand extensive use and abuse.

> *"Textiles are both beautiful and technical. Being able to work harmoniously with these two extremes is what my profession is all about."*

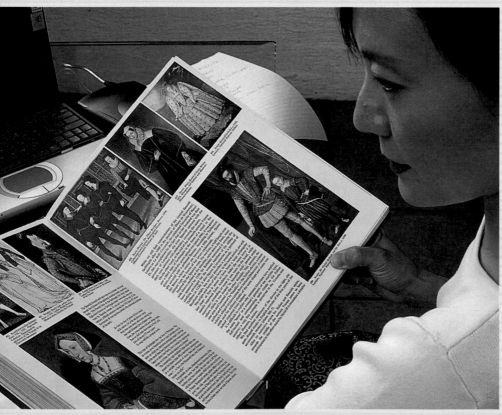

library will reserve them for six months. That helps ensure that another textile manufacturer won't attempt to duplicate our designs.

Textile designs available on the Internet also help to inspire our new collections. Unfortunately, computers don't really provide good color rendition. I'm sure this will improve in the future and I'll be using the Internet more than ever.

My job is to blend these technical components with the beauty of a design. Each year our firm creates two new fabric collections. Each collection might have 20 new designs in a variety of colors. I work with the designers in developing these new collections. We are inspired from a variety of sources. Inspiration could come from a historic event or sometimes we refer to a textile museum.

We have an excellent textile museum in New York that is available to professionals in the textile industry. The museum has an enormous collection of fabrics from around the world. Some are extremely old. To see the fabrics, I make an appointment with the curator of a specific collection. I can check out the fabrics that have inspired me and share them with our designers. If we develop new designs from these fabrics the

"Inspiration could come from a historic event or sometimes we refer to a textile museum."

Career Profile

Textile specialists use their knowledge of textiles to develop specifications for interior fabrics, including upholstery and window treatments. Their work involves studying flammability standards, energy conservation, and maintenance. A textile specialist will work with textile designers, researchers, and manufacturers to develop new products.

Education
▸ A Bachelor of Science degree is required. Advanced degrees are becoming more desired as employment opportunities increase.
▸ Courses in chemistry, physics, textiles, computer-aided drafting, principles of design, fire protection, and safety are helpful.

Skills Needed
▸ A technical aptitude and the ability to understand chemistry are required.
▸ Knowledge of research practices and theory is necessary.
▸ Knowledge of the principles and practices of interior design is critical.
▸ Good interpersonal skills are required for working with fabric designers, researchers, interior designers, and other professionals.

Career Outlook
▸ Demand for textile specialists should remain strong, since consumers are interested in new fabrics. More information can be obtained from the American Society for Interior Designers and American Society for Testing Materials.

Career Activities

1. Select several upholstery and window treatment fabrics. Examine the following characteristics of the fabrics: weave, fiber content, and soil-resistant treatment.
2. Identify ideal fabrics for upholstery and window treatments and explain why you think these fabrics would be suitable for each purpose.

Chapter Summary

➤ The backgrounds of a room are an essential part of its design.

➤ Some background materials reduce energy consumption in the home.

➤ A variety of synthetic and natural fibers are used in home textiles.

➤ Resilient floor coverings are sturdy, need little maintenance, and return to their original shape after being stepped on.

➤ Choosing carpeting or rugs requires considering a variety of factors.

➤ Paint, wallpaper, and paneling are the most common wall coverings.

➤ Decorative ceilings and moldings can be used to change the apparent dimensions and the overall effectiveness of a room design.

➤ Choosing from among the many types of window coverings impacts the look of a room.

Checking Your Understanding

1. What are three ways in which backgrounds can have a significant effect on a room?

2. How can you find out the fiber content of most textile items?

3. What are two types of resilient flooring?

4. What is carpet pile? Is carpet with deep pile more durable than carpet with a shorter pile?

5. Why is the "grin" test done? How can it help you evaluate carpet quality?

6. What type of paint might you choose to be long lasting in a bathroom? Which level of gloss? What type of wallpaper?

7. Why is it important that all rolls of a wallpaper pattern you are using have the same batch number?

8. Why might you want a ceiling to appear lower? Give an example of a way to achieve that look.

9 What are two ways window treatments affect the interior environment of a room?

10. How does a Roman shade differ from a roller shade as it is raised?

Thinking Critically

1. A friend's uncle is selling an unused roll of carpet at what seems to be a reasonable price. It looks nice, but you're not sure what kind of carpet it is. He thinks it's made of olefin. Would you buy it for your family room? What if it was for a spare bedroom? Explain your decisions.

2. Make a list of at least six rooms in a home. Recommend either resilient flooring or carpeting for each room. Explain your choices.

3. Which wall, floor, and window coverings do you think that you might try to install or apply yourself? Which would you hire a professional to install? Explain your decisions.

4. In what situations might you decide to leave a window uncovered? Explain your answer.

Applications

1. **Textile Hunt.** Look around your home and classroom for examples of various textiles. Look for evidence of their fiber content and make a chart of your findings. Try to find objects made from at least three different fibers. List the item and what it's made of, such as: "area rug—polypropylene; bathroom curtains—cotton/polyester blend."

2. **Working with Wallpaper.** Look through a wallpaper book that contains pictures of rooms decorated with some of the wallpaper patterns. Compare the actual wallpaper with the pictures. Does it look like you had visualized it? Would it be more pleasing if portions of the room were painted or paneled? Share your observations with the class.

3. **Letting Light Shine.** Choose three styles of windows from those shown on page 271. For each style, sketch one window treatment that would provide privacy and one that would highlight the view. Be sure to consider any window hardware or movement for each style.

4. **Recycling Research.** Use print or Internet resources to research recycled and energy efficient materials that are used in interior design backgrounds. Possible topics include carpeting and carpet cushion. Write several paragraphs about your findings.

5. **Bargain Backgrounds.** Imagine that you want to design an attractive living room with a very limited budget. The room has two windows and two doorways and is 12 ft. x 18 ft. (3.6 m x 5.5 m). Using the information presented in the chapter, try to choose inexpensive coverings for the floor, walls, windows, and ceiling. Perform the calculations introduced in Chapter 18 to estimate the cost of the materials. Present your ideas to the class, using examples from catalogs if possible. Explain your choices.

BUILDING YOUR PORTFOLIO

Your client has converted a 12-ft. x 15-ft. (3.7-m x 4.6-m) sunporch into a guest bedroom. This will mainly be used every winter by her mother who lives with her for several months. Her mother occasionally relies on a cane when she walks. She enjoys quilting and watching the birds in the backyard. Blues and peaches are her favorite colors.

Although the contractor tied the room into the home's existing heating and cooling system, it is slightly cooler than the rest of the house. The new bedroom's large window faces the north.

Submit a proposal identifying the materials and colors you would suggest for the floor, walls, ceiling, and window treatments. Sketch the window treatment you select. Write an explanation of your choices.

Recognizing Furniture Styles

CHAPTER 20

CHAPTER OBJECTIVES

▶ Identify factors that influence changes in furniture design.

▶ Describe general points that can be helpful in understanding furniture style periods.

▶ Compare formal and informal furniture styles.

▶ Identify and describe major styles of American furniture from 1600 to the present.

▶ Describe the types of furniture choices available to today's buyer.

TERMS TO LEARN

- adaptations
- antique
- cabriole leg
- chair table
- gateleg table
- highboy
- japanning
- modular furniture
- reeding
- reproduction
- trestle table
- trundle bed
- turning
- veneer
- Windsor chair
- wing chair

Chairs, tables, beds, and other basic furniture pieces have remained for centuries, but their styles have changed significantly over time. Many things have influenced style changes. One example is changing expectations. At first people were concerned primarily about the function of furniture. In time, the way it looked became equally important.

Changing Styles

Some furniture styles are identified by the historic era in which they were first made. Such "period pieces" are often named for the king or queen who was in power when the furniture was built. Other styles of furniture are named for the person who originated the design, or for the general design movement of the time. Some historical designs have become classics. Surviving examples are now found in museums or are owned by collectors. Other designs have been passing fads.

In this chapter you will learn how to recognize major furniture styles. Some will appeal to you more than others. Try to base your judgements on how well each piece meets its function and how well each style encompasses the elements and principles of design you learned about in Unit 5. Investigate whether appearance or function was the top priority when each furniture style was created.

WHY DESIGNS CHANGE

In addition to changing expectations, many other developments affect furniture design. Available materials, methods of manufacturing, and changes in lifestyles and tastes are a few examples.

MATERIALS AND MANUFACTURING.

New manufacturing techniques and materials influence furniture design. Modern synthetic materials have different properties than traditional wood, thereby creating potential for new designs. Traditional wood chairs, for example, are carved. Some plastic chairs, however, are molded from liquid plastic. As a new material is developed, furniture makers experiment with different processes using that material. As processes are refined, new design possibilities may open up.

It's only since the 1990s that home office furniture designed to accommodate computers has been available. In this case, new designs were developed to meet a new need.

LIFESTYLE CHANGES. Furniture designs have often reflected the time during which the pieces were made and the lifestyles of the people who used the furniture. For instance, during the 18th century in France and England, much of the furniture was formal and elegant, reflecting the lifestyle of the royal courts. On the other hand, the furniture built by the early colonists in the New World was much plainer and more informal. What factors do you think influenced the designs of the colonists?

CHANGES IN TASTE. The styles people prefer today are different from the styles people liked during other periods of time. Tastes change from era to era. These changes are influenced by several factors, including lifestyle, fashion, and needs. Just think how a computer desk of the 21st century differs from a desk from an earlier century.

Understanding Furniture Styles

Categorizing furniture styles by specific periods is convenient, but it can be difficult to place an unknown piece. You will have greater success in identifying furniture styles if you are familiar with the following points.

OVERLAPPING STYLE PERIODS. There is no definite beginning or end to any period. Typically, styles develop gradually. Often a certain country or region sets the fashion for others. In the 19th century, styles became pop-

ular in America later than they did in Europe. Can you identify which countries or regions influence furniture styles today?

Furniture that incorporates designs from two periods is referred to as *transitional*. When you study different periods, you will detect trends that indicate the general direction of change as one period blends into another.

The dates given in this chapter refer to the period when the styles were most popular in America.

Modern furnishings tend to be less formal than many styles of the past. Why do you think that's true?

designs, a new cycle of designs begins.

Furniture pieces from different periods are apt to look good together if the pieces are taken from the same stage within each period. For example, simple early New England pine furniture may blend well with equally simple Modern-style or contemporary pieces.

FORMAL AND INFORMAL. Formal furniture styles originated mainly in Europe in the 18th century. Some formal styles were ornate. Others had classical lines. All formal styles were elegant, since they were created for the wealthy.

Furniture for the common people of the same era was usually made with simple hand tools. These pieces were often plainer, smaller versions of formal styles.

Formal pieces of various periods can be grouped together successfully if they have similar lines. Simple informal furniture of various periods, sometimes called country-style furniture, also has a common bond.

You'll get a better feeling for the period a style belongs to if you think of furniture in terms of the people who used it and the homes it occupied, not just the dates associated with it.

GOING THROUGH STAGES. Most periods begin with simple, basic designs. As time goes by, designers tend to add more decorative features and designs may become very elaborate. When people grow tired of these

$\mathcal{D}$esigns that Last

Good design is not limited to a single period. Although only a small percentage of all furniture sold today is truly new, experimental, or contemporary in design, many people prefer a contemporary look. As

time goes by, some of the contemporary styles will be successful. Those styles will be copied and in time become "traditional." Remember, at one time colonial style was contemporary.

Well designed furniture tends to survive over the years, partly because collectors recognize and value its excellence. Everyday, consumers help perpetuate good designs. There is a large demand for **reproductions**, or accurate copies of originals. Many people also buy antiques—furniture made in an earlier period. By law in the United States, a piece of furniture must be 100 years old to be classified as an **antique**. However, the term is often used informally to mean "old." Generally, if an antique has been refinished or changed significantly, it is less valuable.

Colonial Period, 1600-1780

This chapter focuses on American furniture. You will see that most styles of American furniture, especially in the 17th and 18th centuries, were influenced by English styles. For this reason, this chapter concentrates on the English impact. Other influences came from France, Italy, Germany, and the Netherlands. Furniture reflecting all these styles can be purchased today.

The colonists adapted foreign styles to make furniture that was practical for everyday use. They used tools and materials that were available to them. Thus, furniture made in America during colonial times was often simpler than European furniture of the same style and period.

What details make this piece of furniture characteristic of the Jacobean era?

SEVENTEENTH CENTURY

English and other European styles were introduced in the colonies in several ways. Some were brought by trained furniture makers who emigrated from Europe. Others were copied from European designs. The distance and difficult communication between settlements in America and the differences in available materials caused regional differences in how particular styles evolved.

The first two successful English colonies in the New World were Jamestown (1607) and Plymouth (1620). The furniture style of the time is often referred to as *Jacobean* (jak-uh-BEE-uhn) style, after James I, England's reigning king. (*Jacob* is the Latin word for James.) Jacobean was the dominant style during the time of the Pilgrims.

Jacobean furniture was heavy and rectangular, with geometric or floral carvings. Rounded forms, such as legs and spindles, were made by a method called **turning**—adding shape by using a *lathe*. A lathe spins wood against a cutting tool, held by the furniture maker, which cuts away various parts of the wood to different depths. Modern versions of the lathe are used today.

Stools and benches were more common than chairs during this period. The few chairs that were used had straight backs and hard plank seats. Cushions were not introduced until the last half of the 17th century.

First, the colonists chose oak for their furniture, as they had in England. Then they turned to more plentiful hardwoods, such as maple, beech, ash, and hickory. Regardless of the wood used, the furniture was often painted black, red, or yellow.

Homes of this period were sparsely furnished and had little storage room. Since there were no closets, chests were especially important. Colonists used them mainly for storage, but also as seats, tables, and even beds. Chests were generally rectangular with hinged lids. The side panels could be either ornately carved or very plain.

Cupboards were also important for storage, but they were considered a luxury. Cupboards often contained shelves at the bottom for linens and clothing and an enclosed upper section for silver and glassware.

Tables were less common than chests. Some of the tables that were used were designed to conserve space. For example, the draw-top table had leaves that could be pushed beneath the tabletop when the table wasn't in use. The **chair table** was also popular. It was a chair that had a large back that protected the occupant from drafts, which could be tipped forward to form a table. Very large trestle tables were also used. A **trestle table** was a table with a long rectangular top and a wide vertical support at each end. To offset its size, the top could be removed, and thus the table was easier to move.

Because most houses were small, bed space was limited. Four-poster beds, wooden cradles and trundle beds were used. A **trundle bed** has a low bed that can be stored under a higher bed during the day.

WILLIAM AND MARY STYLE, 1700-1725

The next important furniture style—William and Mary—was named for the royal couple who began their rule of England in 1689. William, who was Dutch, brought Dutch traditions and craftspeople to England.

This William and Mary highboy, with its delicate and intricate design, provided storage space for clothing. It has **bun feet.**

The delicate furniture style that evolved was also influenced by the French court style of Louis XIV and by an earlier Italian design.

The chairs of the William and Mary period reflect a strong Asian influence. The curved back replaced the straight back of the Jacobean chair. Seats were often woven from *rushes*—the stems of marsh plants. These were more comfortable than the wooden plank seats of the previous periods. American furniture makers quickly adapted the William and Mary style.

In the American colonies, William and Mary furniture was marked by a lightness not found in Jacobean furniture. It featured fine carvings and trims, which reflected the growing prosperity of the colonists. Fine **veneer**—a thin layer of more expensive wood—was glued to less expensive wood furniture for a better appearance. Velvets and silks were

The gateleg table was introduced in the 17th century. The pull-out legs gave good support to the expandable tabletop.

used to upholster chairs made of deeply carved walnut, birch, and maple, creating an elegant look.

After the chair, the table was the most common type of furniture. The **gateleg table**—a table with legs on each side that swing out to support drop leaves that are pulled up from the sides—was popular during this period.

As their wardrobes grew, colonists needed more storage space. For the first time, the chest of drawers became an important piece of furniture. The **highboy**, a chest of drawers mounted on legs, was developed in this period. The delicate William and Mary highboy is an example of a style being refined over time. For example, this furniture often had brass handles instead of wooden knobs. The highboy soon replaced the cupboard as the fanciest piece of furniture in the home.

QUEEN ANNE STYLE, 1720-1755

In the early 18th century, the colonists adopted a furniture style known for its graceful, curved lines. This style had become popular with the middle class in England during the reign of Queen Anne. The Queen Anne style was influenced by the furniture of the Netherlands and Asia. Queen Anne furniture was slender and flowing, featuring curved rather

What Influences DESIGN?

Asian Influences on Design

The Far East has made significant contributions to European and American design heritage. Merchant and whaling ships brought cargoes of beautiful silk, ivory, and porcelain to major ports in England and the American colonies. Ship captains and officers brought back lacquerware and pieces of furniture. These imports from China and Japan helped inspire European-American housing designs and furnishings.

The finish known as *japanning* was popular beginning with the William and Mary period. It simulated a process of lacquering traditional in the Far East. In America, much of the japanning was done in Boston.

Some of Thomas Chippendale's later designs showed other strong Asian features. One such feature was Oriental fretwork, mainly on the tops and sides of case goods. *Fretwork* is fancy, open-cut patterns. Straight legs also reflected the Asian influence.

Asian designs also influenced design in other ways. In colonial America, versions of Chinese patterns were used on wallpaper and furniture. Chinese-style latticework also appeared in architectural designs and on staircases and fences.

More than 100 years after Chippendale's time, architect Frank Lloyd Wright was fascinated when he visited the Japanese pavilion at the World's Columbian Exhibition in Chicago. Wright began collecting colorful Japanese prints and later traveled to Japan. Principles of Japanese design can be seen in almost all of Wright's work. This influence includes an emphasis on simplicity, horizontal lines, asymmetrical balance, and the use of natural materials.

THINKING IT THROUGH

1. Look at the dining room chairs on pages 452-453. Do any appear to have an Asian influence? Why?
2. How does the Far East seem to be influencing design in the 21st century?

than straight lines. The **cabriole** (KAB-ree-ohl) **leg**, *a leg that curves out at the middle and then tapers inward just above an ornamental foot*, is a characteristic of the Queen Anne style.

Sometimes the wooden surfaces of this furniture were varnished with "japan," a glossy black lacquer. The process of applying glossy black lacquer to furniture is known as **japanning**. Furniture makers of the period felt that the technique gave the furniture an oriental look.

The Queen Anne style brought a number of innovations in sofa and chair design. For the first time, upholstered furniture became widely available. Queen Anne style furniture was more comfortable than that of any previous time. One popular style was the fully upholstered **wing chair**, an armchair with a high back and high sides (or "wings," designed to give protection from drafts. The wing chair remains popular today.

A simpler piece of furniture from this period, the Windsor chair, has

also retained its popularity. The **Windsor chair** is a chair with stick legs and a spindle back inserted into a saddle-shaped plank seat. It was originally made in Windsor, England, but was soon produced throughout colonial America.

CHIPPENDALE STYLE, 1755-1780

Around the middle of the 1700s, two developments changed the course of furniture design: the increasing popularity of mahogany wood and Thomas Chippendale's book of furniture designs.

Chippendale was a popular cabinetmaker and furniture designer in England. Chippendale's company produced furniture in a variety of designs, including his own. In 1754 he published a book of furniture designs—the first such book ever published. Although the book didn't introduce new styles, people found

This Queen Anne table is simple but elegant. The cabriole legs echo the curves of the top.

The decorative details appear on the inside of this Chippendale desk, as well as the outside. Contrast the ball-and-claw feet of this period to the feet of the Queen Anne table.

Windsor chairs were often made from different woods and painted so all the parts would match.

Chippendale's interpretations of existing styles very exciting. The book's influence on furniture making was widespread. Wealthy Americans wanted to furnish their homes with Chippendale designs.

Several distinctive details marked Chippendale's work. S-shaped chair and table legs ending in *claw-and-ball* feet were a common feature of his early work. His later oriental-inspired designs had straight legs. The *camelback sofa* was also his design. This well-known piece is distinctive for its curved back and sides. Decoration on Chippendale's furniture often included shells, leaves, and flowers carved into the wood.

Compared to the delicate designs of the Queen Anne style, Chippendale furniture appears heavier and more solid. Part of the illusion of weight comes from the use of mahogany. The properties of this wood, widely available for the first time, allowed craftspeople to produce elaborate designs more easily.

*P*ostcolonial Period, 1780-1840

The colonists' declaration of independence in 1776 ushered in many changes in political thinking and lifestyle. After the Revolutionary War, there were changes in furniture styles. Designs in both Europe and America were influenced by the delicate, balanced lines of classical styles of ancient Greece and Rome. This overall style is often referred to as *Neoclassicism*. Two basic styles predominated during this time in America: the *Federal* and the *Empire* (ahm-PEER).

FEDERAL STYLE, 1780-1820

The term *Federal* is often used to denote the furniture of the earlier of the two classical styles. As you read in Chapter 6, this was also the term used to describe the architecture of the time. The Federal style was most popular in New York, Washington, and Philadelphia, each of which served as the federal capital of the new country at different times after the Revolutionary War.

The Federal-style sofa shown here was influenced by the designs of ancient Greece and Rome. This style became popular after the Revolutionary War.

The architecture of the Federal period was straight-lined and uncluttered. Federal furniture was similar in style. Designs were small and rectangular, and the furniture was light, delicate, and symmetrical.

The first furniture to have features of the Federal style was actually designed in England in the 1760s by the Scottish architect Robert Adam. Adam designed furniture to harmonize with the delicate, airy rooms of his Georgian-style buildings. Adam's buildings emphasized function but were also decorative. He used plaster walls, ceilings decorated with classical designs, and raised moldings.

Two rival English designers—George Hepplewhite and Thomas Sheraton—simplified Adam's designs. This reduced manufacturing costs and made the furniture more accessible to the middle class. In no time, Adam's designs were famous.

Hepplewhite and Sheraton displayed both similarities and differences in their individual designs. One way to compare the two is to analyze their chairs. A typical Hepplewhite chair has tapered legs and a decorative back in the shape of a shield, an oval, or a heart. Sheraton's chairs had rectangular or square backs. The legs were slender and tapered, sometimes decorated with reeding. **Reeding** is decorative carving consisting of vertical lines that resemble thin reeds—stems of tall grass. Sheraton also favored painted surfaces and inlaid decoration.

Both Hepplewhite and Sheraton published important design books in the late 1780s and the early 1790s. These books had a tremendous influence on American furniture makers. By the beginning of the 19th century, the classical Federal style was the leading fashion.

EMPIRE STYLE, 1820-1840

The Empire style takes its name from the rule of the French emperor Napoleon I. The original Empire style was created by Napoleon's official court architects and interior designers. The style spread rapidly throughout Europe. In America, the Empire style flourished for about 20 years, during the last half of the Neoclassical period.

The Empire style is a continuation of the Neoclassical style, but with a much stronger emphasis on historical accuracy. Whereas the Federal style was mostly uncluttered and symmetrical, the Empire style was elaborate and much more dramatic. Designers began to copy ancient furniture directly. They also incorporated Egyptian decoration, because of Napoleon's campaigns in Egypt.

What features of the Empire style can you find in this table?

In America, the most famous of the Empire designers was Duncan Phyfe, a Scotsman who had emigrated to New York. Phyfe used such classical designs as leaves, swans, eagles, and dolphins, as well as urn-shaped pedestals and dog's-paw and lion's-paw feet. His shop was well known for pedestal tables with curved legs and brass feet. Phyfe was also known for his chairs with a back shaped like a lyre—a musical instrument resembling a small harp.

Reeded legs are characteristic of Thomas Sheraton's Federal furniture.

As America's population grew, so did the demand for furniture. Phyfe is credited with incorporating the factory method into his workshop. Furniture makers began to standardize their designs and to keep some finished furniture on hand. Rather than ordering custom-made furniture, customers bought what was immediately available. With the industrial revolution, making furniture moved from being a craft to being an industry. In some cases, mass production caused the quality of furniture to decline.

SHAKER FURNITURE

A plain and simple style of furniture existed along with Federal and Empire furniture. It was created by the Shakers, a religious group that had settled in New England. The Shakers emphasized utility, not ornamentation. Although the furniture was very plain, it had graceful lines and proportions. Shaker designs didn't achieve much popularity in the 1800s, but today the furniture is popular.

Why do you think Shaker furniture is admired more today than when it was made?

Victorian Period, 1840-1900

Many different and often contradictory styles developed during the Victorian period, which coincided with the reign of England's Queen Victoria from 1837-1901.

Following a trend similar to that of Victorian architects, furniture makers of the day revived styles of earlier periods. Among the major revival styles of the period were Gothic, Elizabethan, Rococo (or "French Antique"), Louis XVI, and Italian Renaissance. Near the end of the period, some heavy, ornate pieces showed a Turkish influence. Actually, these so-called revival styles were not historically accurate. Inspired by earlier styles, Victorian furniture makers relied on their imaginations to create elaborate and fanciful designs. Many of these styles were little more than fads, however.

Victorian furniture is characterized by highly carved dark woods and curved lines.

Advances in technology encouraged more elaborate details and fancy upholstery fabrics. Victorian sofas and easy chairs can be recognized by their curving lines, inlaid floral patterns, and rich upholstery.

Victorian tables, desks, and cabinets were also ornate and heavy-looking. There was a great demand for rosewood, a tropical wood with a dark, reddish brown grain. It was usually finished to a high luster. When it became possible to manufacture large pieces of veneer, furniture makers often applied a veneer of rosewood to a pine backing. Later in the period, many tables and cabinets were made of black walnut. Marble, iron, and brass were also used in Victorian furniture.

One of the most famous names of the Victorian period was a German cabinetmaker named John Henry Belter. In New York, Belter invented a technique for bending strips of wood around a wooden frame by using steam and pressure. The wood surface was then elaborately carved,

This is one of William Morris' wallpaper designs using stylized forms from nature.

giving an almost lace-like appearance. Belter's furniture was mass-produced, and his designs were popular and influential.

DESIGN REFORM

Toward the end of the Victorian period, some designers and furniture makers reacted against the excessive use of ornamentation. They called for a more natural use of materials and a return to handcrafted furniture.

The most famous reformer was William Morris, an English artist

and designer. Morris paid close attention to the basic line, structure, and proportion of furniture. Much of his furniture was handcrafted and unaffordable for the average person. Nevertheless, his ideas of design reform had an important influence on other furniture makers and designers. Morris summarized the aim of design reform in a famous statement: "Have nothing in your house that you do not know to be useful or believe to be beautiful." Do you agree with this advice?

Modern Period, 1901-Present

In stressing the importance of function, Morris looked ahead to the Modern period. During the first two decades of the 20th century, furniture designers did not make a radical break from Victorian styles. However, many designers did become interested in simpler forms. Many of these forms were abstract; that is, they didn't resemble recognizable forms. Modern furniture used very little decoration. Furniture contained fewer parts and was built out of newly invented materials. Designers were also fascinated by the growing possibilities offered by modern machines.

How does this International-style dining room furniture differ from traditional pieces of the same type? What characteristics of this style appeal to you?

Modern Scandinavian designers returned to the use of wood, this time with a natural, hand-rubbed finish. Many American furniture makers have also followed this trend. The combination of innovative designs and mostly manufactured materials gives most International-style furniture a distinctive machine-made look.

CONTEMPORARY DESIGNS

Although the period in which we are now living can still be termed Modern, there is a general trend toward softening the harshness of early Modern designs. It is difficult to identify the leading contemporary style. We are too close to it to judge it yet. No doubt historians will someday find a name for today's style, but it won't be *contemporary*. They will use that word to describe their own style.

Nevertheless, most designs today do have certain characteristics. The following points apply to many pieces of contemporary furniture:

- Contemporary designs aren't confined to one nation or continent. Designs may originate in the United States, Italy, Germany, or other countries. This furniture rarely embodies traditional designs or national characteristics, so it's usually difficult for the average person to tell where a certain design originated.
- Contemporary furnishings usually utilize architectural materials such as marble, wood, glass, stone, and plastics. These contribute interesting textural contrasts. Furniture is arranged so that the

Mies van der Rohe's Barcelona chair was a very modern concept for 1929.

INTERNATIONAL STYLE

Architect Walter Gropius founded the Bauhaus (BOW-hows) school of design in 1919 in Weimar, Germany. Gropius wanted to unify architecture, interior design, and furniture design. Followers believed that furniture should not include details that didn't contribute to its function.

The plain, functional style that was developed by Gropius spread to other countries, including the United States. Known as the International style, it is completely nontraditional.

Early designers in the International style abandoned the use of wood and other natural materials. Instead, they used chrome-plated steel tubing and manufactured materials. More recent furniture in the International style often makes use of molded plastic and glass.

shape stands out clearly against a simple background. Bold design, as well as color, may be used.

- Furniture shapes are designed for the human form. Before plastic came into use in furniture manufacturing, people had to adapt to the shape of the particular seat, whether it was a crude 17th century wooden bench or an overstuffed Victorian sofa. In each case, the material used for the seat limited its form. A plastic seat, however, can theoretically be shaped to fit any person who might use it. In practice, because of mass production methods, such individualized shapes haven't been made. Modern plastics, however, has provided designers a new freedom of expression.

- Freedom of design, along with an emphasis on convenience, has made modular furniture popular. **Modular furniture** consists of standardized pieces (modules) that can fit together in a variety of ways, like building blocks. Modular furniture can be arranged and rearranged to suit the changing needs of the people using them. Some pieces have been designed to serve more than one purpose. Sofas may convert into individual seats or beds. Storage units may be stacked to form room dividers. You'll learn more about modular furniture in the next chapter.

- Furniture may now be influenced by the work of engineers and chemists. Finishes that are durable and almost indestructible are now available. Designers are experimenting with other new materials. They use clear, see-through plastic, for example, to make furniture that seems to take up little space in a room.

Although contemporary furniture is usually created of new materials such as plastic, glass, and metal, the use of such traditional materials as wood and fabric is not ruled out. These materials give a feeling of warmth that is lacking in furniture made solely of metal or plastic.

Most people strive to protect their furniture from wear, but others think that aged wood with wormholes, nicks, and cuts is aesthetically superior to new wood. Because the amount of antique wood is limited, techniques have been developed to make wood look as if it's from an earlier era. *Distressing* wood is one process in which new wood is made to look old. The color and the texture of the wood are changed by first scraping the surface of the wood and then rubbing it with a piece of smooth metal. This process is used when older furniture needs repair or a new part, or when a furniture designer wants to create the look of age.

REPRODUCTIONS AND OTHER TRADITIONAL PIECES

Today, about one-fourth of all consumers select contemporary designs in furniture. The rest choose designs that are based on other periods or come from other countries.

Designs from the past may be used in three ways. One is to furnish a home with antiques. This is difficult because scarcity and demand have made good antiques very expensive. Another method is to select reproductions—exact copies of originals. All reputable manufacturers identify reproductions so they cannot be confused with antique originals. A third method is to use **adaptations**, that is, furniture in the style of old designs. For example, furniture in the Victorian style may have many features characteristic of the Victorian era without being an exact copy of any one piece.

Mixing furniture of different styles—such as pieces of folk art, antiques, reproductions, adaptations, and handmade furniture—creates a uniquely American look. Natural wood, earthy colors, plants, and pottery are also typical of this look. Wicker furniture, twig furniture, refinished furniture, and American Victorian pieces can be combined in informal ways to provide comfort and beauty. Americans now consider flea markets, resale shops, house sales, and rummage sales as sources of this new furniture.

AWARENESS OF STYLES

Today, more furniture styles are available than ever before. For example, you can purchase a William and Mary gateleg table, a Windsor chair, a Chippendale cabinet, a Shaker chest, and a Modern-style dining set—possibly all from the same furniture store.

Being able to recognize different furniture styles will allow you to analyze your personal tastes. Awareness of various styles will help you choose styles to create pleasing rooms for yourself and others. You will also be better able to judge new furniture styles as they become available.

Traditional styles are still quite popular. This dining set is based on Queen Anne furniture.

FIGURE 20-1

A VISUAL GUIDE TO...

Dining Chairs Through Time

What differences and similarities do you see in the various styles? What influences can you make from this timeline about changing lifestyles and tastes?

1770
CHIPPENDALE STYLE
(THOMAS CHIPPENDALE)
- Decorative, open back
- Fabric seat
- Carved leg with claw-and-ball foot

1650
JACOBEAN STYLE
- Straight, rectangular back
- Wooden plank seat
- Straight legs

1785
FEDERAL STYLE
(GEORGE HEPPLEWHITE)
- Decorative back in shape of shield
- Fabric seat
- Tapered legs

1710
WILLIAM AND MARY STYLE
- Curved back
- Leather back and seat fastened with brass-head nails
- Elaborately turned front legs

1825
EMPIRE CHAIR
(DUNCAN PHYFE)
- Decorative lyre-shaped back
- Fabric seat
- Curved, decorated legs

1730
QUEEN ANNE STYLE
- Decorative, rounded back
- Fabric seat
- Cabriole leg with ornamental foot

FIGURE 20-1
(CONTINUED)

A VISUAL GUIDE TO...

Dining Chairs Through Time (Continued)

1889
VICTORIAN STYLE
- Rounded, tufted upholstered back
- Rounded, upholstered seat
- Curved, carved legs

1946
MODERN STYLE (CHARLES EAMES)
- Molded to fit human form
- Plywood seat and back
- Molded, wooden legs

1909
**MODERN STYLE
(FRANK LLOYD WRIGHT)**
- Straight slat back
- Rectangular seat
- Straight, rectangular legs

1957
**MODERN STYLE
(EERO SAARINEN)**
- Molded plastic back
- Aluminum pedestal
- Cushioned seat

1928
**MODERN BAUHAUS STYLE
(MARCEL BREUER)**
- Woven cane back
- Rectangular cane-and-steel-tube seat
- Steel tube legs

1984
**POST-MODERN STYLE
(ROBERT VENTURI)**
- Bent plywood construction
- Wide, tilted seat
- Painted pattern

Jaime Orduno

Furniture Restorer

For several years I owned an antique shop in my hometown. Finding the old pieces of furniture to sell in the store was a big part of my work, but repairing and refinishing them was the best part. I would take a chair or table that had been neglected for years in someone's attic and give it a new life. The hands-on work was so enjoyable that I sold the store and now specialize as a furniture restorer.

"Once the right method of restoration is determined, I write up a contract detailing the work to be done and the cost, including the profit I want to make."

I'm good at what I do, but I'm not skilled at everything. Although I was trained in both metalwork and wood-working, I refer tasks like restoring cracked tiles to other craftsmen. That still leaves me a big range of work: from patching an old picture frame to replating a silver tray. I never get bored, for I rarely do the same thing two times in a row!

Furniture restoration is truly an art and a craft; yet it's a business, too. I have to listen carefully to what each client wants done. Some people have trouble describing what they want, so it helps if I can envision the finished product and convey that idea to the customer. Once the right method of restoration is determined, I write up a contract detailing the work to be done and the cost, including the profit I want to make. I charge a deposit, usually 20 percent of my estimate of the final cost.

An example will best show what I do. Recently, a woman brought in a chest of drawers that had been hers as a child, and her mother's before her. Inside the drawers I detected traces of eight different layers of paint. The top and sides of the chest were made of maple, but the drawers were pine—not an unusual combination of woods 100 years ago. Wooden flowers were carved across each

When the customer came to pick up the chest, her reaction was as rewarding as the work had been. She said this heirloom combined her childhood memories with her adult taste. Moments like that may be the most satisfying part of this job—to think that I'm preserving not only furniture, but also heritage and history.

drawer front. The customer wanted me to strip the chest and repaint it to match her bedroom. I explained that antiques are worth more unstripped, but she said, "I don't want to sell it. I want to use it and enjoy it."

First I stripped off all the old layers of paint. Next, I used a palm sander on the bare wood, though I had to sand the carved flowers and the vertical molding by hand. After preparing the surface for paint, I painted everything except the top of the chest with two coats of cream-colored gloss paint. After it dried, I painted the carved flowers and vertical molding in pastel colors—allowing each color to dry before I painted the next. To create the look of marble on the top of the chest, I had to use a number of intricate techniques along with several types of specialty paints and glazes.

"I'm preserving not only furniture, but heritage and history."

Career Profile

A *furniture restorer* takes furniture that is old, broken, or damaged in some way and makes it look like new. This process includes sanding, stripping, cleaning, polishing, and repairing. Then the furniture restorer uses stains, finishes, or paint to achieve the look that the client wants. A furniture restorer has to work with many different chemicals and sometimes power tools, so it is important to follow safety procedures to avoid the risk of injury.

Education
▸ No formal degree is required.
▸ Training is completed on the job.
▸ Courses in furniture woodworking are helpful.

Skills Needed
▸ A thorough knowledge of woods and other materials.
▸ A good eye for detail.
▸ Patience and persistence.
▸ Some physical strength required in order to move pieces of furniture.

Career Outlook
▸ Employment opportunities are good. The rising cost of furniture will encourage more people to have furniture restored.
▸ People appreciate quality furniture and quality work.

Career Activities

1. You have purchased some old and antique furniture to repair and resell. How can you find the approximate age of the pieces? When might you decide to refinish a piece?
2. You are starting a furniture restoration business of your own. Brainstorm some visual aids you might use to help your customers. Take your two best ideas and describe what they are and how they would be used.

Chapter Highlights

- ➤ Furniture styles change over time for many reasons.
- ➤ Design periods overlap and go through stages.
- ➤ Furniture from most periods includes both formal and informal styles.
- ➤ Most traditional American furniture styles were influenced by designs that had been popular in England and other European countries.
- ➤ Today buyers can purchase contemporary furniture, or they can choose furniture with designs from earlier periods—antiques, reproductions, or adaptations.
- ➤ Knowing how to recognize furniture styles can help you analyze your personal tastes and choose appropriate styles for yourself and others.

Checking Your Understanding

1. What five factors influence changes in furniture design?

2. What is meant by "transitional" furniture?

3. Explain the stages that most furniture style periods go through.

4. Contrast formal with informal furniture styles.

5. How does the William and Mary style differ from the Jacobean style? Give an example of each.

6. How did the lines of Queen Anne furniture differ from those of previous furniture periods?

7. Identify three characteristics of Chippendale furniture.

8. List the major characteristics of furniture in the Federal style and the Empire style. Name a designer for each style.

9. Identify three characteristics of contemporary design.

10. How do antiques, reproductions, and adaptations differ?

Thinking Critically

1. Discuss the following statement. "The history of furniture styles can be viewed as an ongoing argument." Describe the ways that each style period "argues" or contrasts with the period directly preceding it. Why do you think that this has happened?

2. Which style of furniture do you think best emphasizes function? Explain your choice.

3. Why do you think American colonists began to make more of their own furniture and to import less from England?

4. What factors do you think motivate today's furniture buyers most? Why?

5. Do you prefer contemporary furniture or designs from the past? Give examples of your favorite furniture pieces, and explain their appeal to you. You might also identify styles that you find unappealing or inappropriate to your needs.

Applications

1. **Colorful Terms.** Use print or Internet resources to learn how at least five of the following terms relate to furniture: bat wing, fretwork, bonnet top, ears, finial, Marlborough, slat, piecrust top, and apron.

2. **Famous Books.** Research one of the furniture style books by Chippendale, Hepplewhite, or Sheraton. Report in what ways the book affected the evolution of furniture designs.

3. **Biography.** Use print or Internet resources to learn more about one of the furniture designers featured in this chapter. Write a brief report about the individual and his contributions to design.

4. **Future Furniture Styles.** Draw a picture of a living room or bedroom in the year 2050. Including styles from our time and earlier, as well as styles that might develop in the future, that you think will endure. Write a brief description of your drawing in which you explain the choices you made.

5. **Back to Bauhaus.** Research the Bauhaus movement and the influence it had on furniture in America. Identify at least three well-known furniture designers who were affiliated with the school.

BUILDING YOUR PORTFOLIO

Choose one furniture style on which you will become an "expert." Using print or Internet resources, research information on the style. Study examples of the various stages of that style. Find information that will help you do the following:

➤ Discuss the historic, economic, and social highlights of the time period when the style originated.

➤ Discuss previous styles that influenced the style.

➤ Collect illustrations of the style and describe it.

Share your information by giving an oral report with visual aids.

Selecting Furniture

CHAPTER OBJECTIVES

► Evaluate materials commonly used to make furniture.

► Identify quality features to look for when evaluating furniture construction.

► Explain the options available when shopping for furniture.

► Summarize guidelines for caring for furniture.

TERMS TO LEARN

- bamboo
- case goods
- joint
- multipurpose furniture
- particleboard
- plywood
- warping
- wicker furniture
- wrought iron

*I*magine life before furniture. You might have a rock to lean your back against, but sleep directly on the hard ground. Today there's furniture for every purpose—sitting, eating, sleeping, studying, and storage. The challenge is choosing the most attractive, useful, and durable pieces for the available space—all within a budget.

*F*urniture Materials

The first step in evaluating any piece of furniture is to check the type and quality of the materials used. Of the variety of materials used in the construction of furniture, the most common are wood, metal, glass, and plastic. Each of these materials can be used alone or in combination with others.

WOOD

Wood is the most common material, especially for case goods. **Case goods** are furniture pieces that are not upholstered. Chests, desks, and tables are examples of case goods. Wood is both beautiful and durable. It can withstand a great deal of weight and is fairly easy to repair. Both hardwoods and softwoods are used in furniture construction.

Hardwoods include cherry, maple, pecan, oak, walnut, mahogany, birch, and ash. Their strength, beautiful natural grain, and resistance to denting make them desirable for furniture construction. They are preferred for fine furniture.

Examples of softwoods are pine, fir, redwood, and cedar. Softwoods, generally speaking, dent more easily, have a coarser grain, and cost less than hardwoods. They are commonly used for interior parts of case goods. Pine is often used for constructing country-style furniture because the cracks and dents that may occur in pine give this furniture its characteristic rustic look. Redwood is coarse and splintery but is weather-resistant. For this reason, many outdoor furnishings are made of redwood.

Common hardwoods and softwoods are described in Figure 21-1 on pages 462-463. Furniture makers select these woods for furniture construction based on the cost and the different properties of the wood. Possible furniture construction uses for various woods include veneer, solid wood, and particleboard.

VENEER. Most wood furniture produced today is made with *veneer*—an ornamental overlay placed over a base material. The veneer may be a thin layer of fine wood; several thin sheets of lesser quality wood that are dyed, glued, and pressed together; or plastic laminate. The base material is often plywood. **Plywood** consists of three, five, or seven layers of less expensive wood glued together. Some plywoods can be purchased with a fine veneer finish on one side.

Because of the high-quality glues used, veneered wood is strong. It also resists shrinking and warping. (**Warping** means losing its straightness.) Veneers show off the unique characteristics of the wood used. Because it requires a smaller amount of expensive wood, veneered furniture is usually more economical than solid-wood furniture of the same type. A major disadvantage of veneered wood, however, is that it's difficult to repair if damaged. Sanding and refinishing are impractical because of the danger that the veneer might peel off.

Veneer can be used to create a beautiful piece of furniture.

SOLID WOOD. When furniture is made of solid wood, whole pieces of the same wood are used to make the exposed surfaces—for example, tops, sides, and door and drawer fronts. The interior construction of the furniture, however, may use a wood of lesser quality.

Unlike veneered wood, solid wood can be turned and carved. When it's damaged, solid wood can be sanded and refinished. One disadvantage is that changes in humidity may cause the wood to crack, swell, and warp. Its relatively high cost is another disadvantage.

PARTICLEBOARD. Parts of inexpensive furniture and higher priced furniture are often made of **particleboard**—a combination of wood shavings, veneer scraps, chips, and sometimes sawdust that is mixed with glue and pressed together under heat. Particleboard, though less expensive and more durable than solid wood and veneer, is less desirable. Because of its appearance, it is widely used on parts of furniture that are concealed, such as the insides of doors and drawers and the backs of bookcases. Furniture makers use particleboard for the shelves of bookcases because it doesn't warp as easily as solid wood. Particleboard can be used as a base for wood or plastic laminate veneer.

Wicker furniture is lightweight, easy to carry, and can be used in almost any room.

OTHER WOOD PRODUCTS. Some styles of furniture use whole slender growths of wood. **Wicker furniture** is furniture that is woven of thin, flexible twigs, branches, and stems, often from willow trees. Wicker has been popular since the 1800s. Once the furniture has been woven, it is usually varnished or painted. The best quality wicker has smooth surfaces; neat, well-wrapped joints; and legs that stand evenly for stability. **Bamboo** is a fast-growing, woody, tropical plant. Its sturdy stems can be used in furniture making. Bamboo is particularly popular for casual furniture.

METAL

Metals are also used in furniture construction. Some common furniture metals are iron, steel, aluminum, brass, and copper. All are strong and durable.

Iron is the most frequently used metal for furniture. **Wrought iron** is a tough, durable form of iron that can be hammered and bent into different shapes. It is suitable for decorative accessories, table and chair frames, and lawn furniture.

Steel can also be used for decorating purposes and, because of its

Wrought iron furniture is sturdy yet decorative and fits with many different decorating styles. What types of wrought iron furniture have you seen?

FIGURE 21-1

Characteristics of Various Hardwoods and Softwoods

Hardwoods: Woods from deciduous trees (lose leaves annually).

TYPE	Cherry	Maple	Pecan	Oak	Walnut	
CHARACTERISTICS	Close-grained; durable; resembles unfinished mahogany; darkens with age.	Very strong; grain is usually straight and fine; Bird's-eye maple and curly maple have unusual grains.	Strong and tough; open-grained; machines well; glues moderately well.	Strong; durable; widely available; open-grained; glues well. White oak and red oak used for furniture.	Medium hard; beautiful grain; strong; ideal for carving.	
USES IN THE HOME	Fine furniture and cabinets.	Early American and contemporary furniture; fine flooring.	Furniture.	Fine furniture, unfinished furniture, cabinets, and architectural details.	Fine furniture, cabinets.	

strength, for exposed furniture legs and arms. When combined with chromium, steel becomes *stainless steel*. Stainless steel doesn't rust and maintains a shiny appearance. Brushed steel is currently popular.

Aluminum is one of the most adaptable metals. It is inexpensive, easy to care for, and lightweight. Because it doesn't rust, it is ideal for outdoor furniture. Aluminum can be formed into many shapes, making it especially suitable for such items as lamp bases. One drawback is that aluminum dents.

Copper is both durable and rust-resistant. Copper can be shaped by hammering or heating, then casting the metal in a mold. You may find it in lamps and hardware, such as doorknobs and drawer pulls. Brass is made by mixing zinc with copper. Both brass and copper take a high polish but will tarnish if not protected by lacquer. Since they reflect nearby colors, brass and copper

blend well with most interiors. They are chosen for their beauty, color, and texture and are commonly used in decorative accessories such as lamps and fireplace screens.

Because the construction details of metal furniture can be seen, you can easily spot poor quality and design flaws. A drawback of metal furniture is that it's more difficult to repair than wood.

Softwoods: *Woods from coniferous (conebearing) trees.*

Mahogany	Birch	Pine	Cedar	Redwood
True mahogany considered ideal for furniture and cabinets. Fine grain; uniform texture; strong; polishes well. Philippine mahogany (lauan) is coarser and inexpensive.	Fine texture; close grain; sands poorly; can be stained to resemble mahogany; walnut; or maple.	Lightweight; even-textured; soft; dents easily.	Durable; close-grained; easy to finish; pleasant scent.	Lightweight; moderately hard; resists decay; strong.
Fine furniture, cabinets. Philippine mahogany used for inexpensive furniture and trim.	Tabletops; furniture parts requiring strength; cabinets.	Early American, country, unpainted, and inexpensive furniture.	Chests and closets.	Outdoor furniture, fences.

GLASS

Glass is a popular material in the production of furniture. Glass used for furniture should be *tempered* (treated for safety and durability). It should be free of bubbles, scratches, and other defects. Glass is used for tabletops and for the doors of china cabinets and display cabinets. When using glass in furniture, designers usually combine it with a wood or metal frame to secure the glass.

The openness of this glass-topped table would make it ideal for use in a small space. Would this table be a good choice for an outdoor space?

PLASTIC

The versatility of plastics has permitted many innovations in furniture design. Manufacturers and designers have experimented with it to form new shapes and surfaces. Plastic can be molded, for example, to form tables and chairs.

Plastic furniture is available in a variety of colors and can be made to look like other materials, such as wood or marble. It may also be transparent. Transparent objects give the illusion of space and help avoid an overcrowded look in a small room.

Thin sheets of plastic laminate can be glued to wood panels as veneer to form the tops or sides of tables, desks, chests, and other pieces of furniture. Because plastic resists spots, scratches, and other abuse, this process is especially popular for furnishings that are heavily used. The laminate can be any color or design, including woodgrain.

A definite advantage of plastic is its cost. Mass production makes plastic furniture available at a low cost. On the other hand, some plastic furniture may grow dull and lose its color. In addition, if the finish is marred, it's difficult to repair.

The size and bulk of an entertainment unit can overpower a room. How does the use of a mirrored door on this piece affect its apparent size?

Basic Furniture Construction

Imagine that you're looking for a small dresser. You find two that you like at the same store. They look similar—both are oak and their hardware is about the same. One costs $100 more than the other, however. You wonder what makes it more special than the other. The likely answer is the way it was constructed.

Once you understand the materials used to make furniture, it may be even more important to know how pieces are constructed. As you've learned, wood is the most common furniture material. It forms the structure of most case goods, as well as the frame for upholstered pieces. Knowing how to judge quality wood construction can help you make the best choices for the money you have available—your own or a client's.

When you compare the two dressers, for example, from different price ranges, you can observe quality differences. Figure 21-2 shows general signs of quality construction.

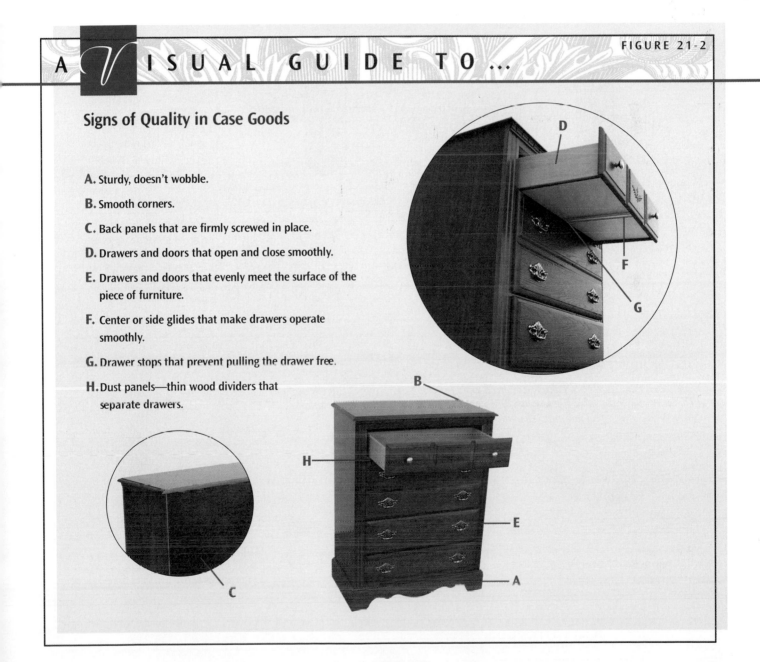

FIGURE 21-2

A VISUAL GUIDE TO...

Signs of Quality in Case Goods

A. Sturdy, doesn't wobble.

B. Smooth corners.

C. Back panels that are firmly screwed in place.

D. Drawers and doors that open and close smoothly.

E. Drawers and doors that evenly meet the surface of the piece of furniture.

F. Center or side glides that make drawers operate smoothly.

G. Drawer stops that prevent pulling the drawer free.

H. Dust panels—thin wood dividers that separate drawers.

FIGURE 21-3

A VISUAL GUIDE TO ...

Common Wood Furniture Joints

The most commonly used joints for furniture construction range in complexity from the butt to the dovetail. A rule of thumb is that the more complex the joint, the sturdier the construction.

TONGUE AND GROOVE
The projection, or tongue, on one piece is inserted in a groove cut into the other. Used in flooring materials and paneling, as well as furniture, such as tabletops.

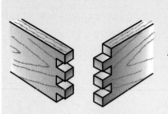

FINGER OR BOX
Square notches are cut into the ends of each piece of wood and then fitted together. Because the notches are square, they can sometimes be pulled apart. Used on lower quality furniture.

DADO
A groove is cut across one piece of wood so that the other piece fits snugly into it; generally used for holding shelves or drawer bottoms in fixed positions.

RABBET
A groove is cut in one piece of wood to receive the other. Not a sturdy joint; should not be used on pieces that must withstand continual movement, such as a drawer.

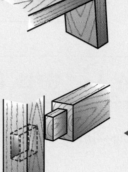

MORTISE AND TENON
A projection on one piece of wood fits into a hollowed-out space on the other. When glued, this forms a strong joint that holds well under strain. Has many uses, such as attaching a bar between two chair legs.

MITERED
Two edges are cut at 45-degree angles and joined to form a square corner. The joint is glued and sometimes reinforced.

DOVETAIL
A series of flaring projections on one piece fit into a series of grooves in the other; can take strong pulls or strains. A good joint for drawers.

JOINT REINFORCEMENT

Rabbet and mitered joints are often reinforced to add strength to their weak structures. More stable joints are sometimes reinforced, especially in fine furniture. The illustrations below show some of the devices and methods available to strengthen wood furniture joints.

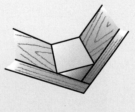

SPLINE
A thin strip of wood is inserted into grooves where two pieces come together.

DOWELS
Small wooden dowels are glued into holes of the pieces being joined.

GLUE BLOCK
A small block of wood is attached with glue and/or screws where two sides come together.

JOINTS

A **joint** is the place where one piece of wood is connected to another. Some joints are concealed. Others are exposed and are part of the furniture design. Joint structure can be simple—placing one board against another—or it can be intricate and complicated. The structure of a joint and how it is held together determine its strength. Figure 21-3 shows some common wood joints, how they are used in furniture, and methods for strengthening joints.

Various methods are used to hold joints together. Wood joints are usually glued to add strength. Nails and screws may also be used. For reinforcement, glue blocks, splines, dowels, biscuits, and corner blocks can be added to joints.

When evaluating wood furniture, check to see that appropriate joints have been used and that they are tight and strong. The drawers in a desk, for instance, must support the weight of the contents, as well as withstand frequent opening and closing. Check whether joints have been glued and nailed. Staples don't provide enough support. Also, check to see if joints are reinforced.

Some molded metal and plastic furniture may not have joints. Other pieces have joints that are bolted, welded, or riveted. Joints should be smooth and sturdy enough to hold up under normal use.

Various finishes can be used to change the appearance of a piece of furniture.

FINISHES

Once constructed, the outer surfaces of wood furniture are prepared for receiving a finish. Finishes are applied to protect the wood from moisture, heat, warping, and abrasions that may occur during use. Finishes may also be used to enhance or change the color of the wood or to decorate it.

The minimum preparation for finishing requires sanding the wood smooth. In some cases, bleach is applied to wood for decorative purposes. Bleach removes some of the natural color of the wood and can give it a worn or weathered look. Other finishing substances include:

- Stain, which adds color without covering the natural grain.
- Clear varnish, which emphasizes the grain pattern and protects the wood.
- Clear lacquer and polyurethane, which provide a protective finish.
- Hand-rubbed oil, which penetrates the wood and brings out the natural grain. Oil used on fine wood furniture gives it a soft shine, or *patina*.
- Paint, which is generally used to cover the grain of less expensive woods.

Some pieces are finished to resemble a more expensive wood. For example, if you see a label on a piece of furniture that reads "oak finish," this means that another material or

Better quality furniture has a clear, smooth finish that enhances the wood grain and brings out of the color of the wood.

Upholstered furniture provides more comfortable seating than hard surfaces. Would this chair be more appropriate in a casual or elegant living room? Why?

UPHOLSTERED FURNITURE CONSTRUCTION

Upholstered furniture—chairs and sofas with padding, springs, and cushions—provides a soft surface on which to sit and relax. Upholstered furniture was rare until the end of the 18th century. It became common after 1850, when more thought was given to a comfortable lifestyle. Since then, many changes have occurred in upholstering.

The basic elements of all upholstery construction are the frame, springs, padding, cushions and upholstery fabric. Check these features carefully. They indicate the quality of a piece of upholstered furniture. Figure 21-4 summarizes what to look for.

Frames and Springs

The frame is the skeleton structure of a chair or sofa. It is a vital, but unseen, part of the furniture. The frame of an upholstered piece should be constructed of a strong hardwood, such as birch or maple. The wood should have been dried in a kiln to prevent warping. Look for joints heavily reinforced with dowels, corner blocks, and glue. Screws may also be used. (Nails or staples don't provide enough support.)

Springs are another important consideration. *Coil springs* are used to make high-quality furniture. Each spring is hand-tied and anchored to

wood—usually an inexpensive wood—has been finished to resemble oak.

It is also important to check the finish of metal furniture. Brass and copper pieces may be lacquered. Those that aren't will require occasional polishing. Sometimes an entire piece may be made of the surface metal. A key term to look for on the label of metal furniture is "plated." At other times an underlayer of inexpensive metal is plated with a more attractive metal, such as brass, chrome, or copper. Eventually, plated metals can wear thin and expose the underlayer. If the label doesn't mention the type of finish used on the furniture, ask the salesperson. Find out the best way to care for the finish.

webbing or to steel bands at the back of the piece. Less expensive furniture uses the *convoluted spring*, which consists of zigzag strips of steel. Before purchasing, sit on the chair or sofa to test the "give" in the springs. They shouldn't strike the frame when bounced on lightly.

Padding and Cushions

Padding materials are used to cushion the frame, making upholstered furniture more comfortable. Similar materials are used to form or stuff cushions. Several types of fillings and padding are used today.

- Polyester and polyurethane foam are good materials for padding the frame. They hold their shape well and resist moths and mildew.
- Solid polyester or polyurethane foam cushions are very durable and provide good support.
- Cotton and shredded foam compress over time.
- Down is the most expensive filling for cushions and gives a very soft feel.

Also look for features that can add extra durability. Loose back cushions and seat cushions give twice the wearing surface because they can be turned. Extra arm covers protect the arms of furniture, which tend to wear and show soil first.

Loose cushions may be stuffed with a block of polyurethane foam or a polyurethane core wrapped in polyester fibers, cotton, or down. The polyester-covered polyurethane core has a soft feel and a plump appearance. Down, which is very expensive, is used only in the highest quality furniture. If the loose cushions are zippered, open one end and examine the filling.

FIGURE 21-4

A VISUAL GUIDE TO...

Signs of Quality in Upholstered Furniture

Look for these signs of quality construction when evaluating furniture:

A. Durable, stain-resistant fabric.

B. Protective covers for arms.

C. Snugly filling cushions.

D. Threads secure and trimmed.

E. Fabric patterns match.

F. Solid foam or down cushions.

G. Hand-tied coil springs anchored to steel bands.

H. Reinforced joints.

I. Hardwood frame.

J. Padded edges.

K. Durable padding material.

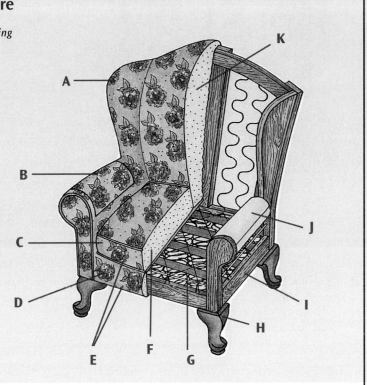

Regardless of the padding used, you should not be able to feel the framework or springs through the upholstery. The fact that so much of the furniture construction is concealed by the outer covering makes selecting upholstered furniture difficult. Read labels carefully and question the salesperson about the pieces you're considering.

Loose back cushions and seat cushions give twice the wearing surface because they can be turned. What else can be done to extend cushion durability?

Upholstery Fabrics and Materials

Upholstery fabrics are specially made for covering furniture. The major features that determine the suitability of an upholstery material for a particular use are its appearance, feel, durability, color, pattern, and cost. Additional considerations may be the fabric's ability to resist fading and soil and to be cleaned, along with its flammability. Uphol-

Leather furniture is durable and, with proper care, will be attractive and comfortable for years. Better quality leather furniture is evenly colored and is free of blemishes.

Figure 21-4 summarizes the characteristics you should look for in quality upholstered furniture.

BED CONSTRUCTION

You spend about one-third of your life sleeping. A good bed supports your body as your muscles relax. If your body is not properly supported during sleep, your muscles may ache in the morning. A soft bed provides little support. For this reason, a firm bed is usually recommended, especially for people with back problems.

Generally speaking, an adult with a traditional bed should purchase a new mattress and springs every ten years. Evaluate bed frames as you would any other case goods. Selecting a mattress and springs requires some additional knowledge.

stery fabrics are either woven or nonwoven, with tightly woven fabrics the most durable choice for upholstered furniture. See the feature "Choosing Fabrics for Furniture" for additional buying guidelines.

Leather and vinyl are also used for upholstering. Although leather costs more, it gives a special look and feel. Well-made leather pieces are also durable, though stains, cuts, and scrapes can be a problem. Vinyl is durable, easy to clean, and much less expensive than leather. Some people don't care for it, however, because it can be cold in the winter and sticky in the summer. Vinyl is also very difficult to repair.

Judging Upholstery

When you evaluate upholstered furniture, check the outer fabric for a general indication of quality. If the fabric has a pattern, check to see that the pattern matches where pieces come together in visible areas. Are the seams straight? Are the hems and pleats even? Is the fabric made of strong fibers in a durable weave that will wear well? Refer back to the chart on pages 416-417 for characteristics of various fibers that are used in upholstery and other home textiles.

When judging the fabric, read the label for information on fiber content. Has it been treated with water or stain repellent? If there's a warranty on the fabric, learn what it covers and how long it lasts.

Mattresses and Springs

Choosing a mattress can be difficult because you can't see inside it. You must rely on labels and salespeople for much of your information. Stores often have cut-away models that show the interior construction of particular brands and models.

The most common mattress is the innerspring mattress. Its firmness and comfort are determined by a series of coil springs that vary in size, number, placement, wire thickness, and padding. A quality mattress

Choosing Fabrics for Furniture

When buying new upholstered furniture or recovering an existing piece, it's often possible to choose a specific fabric to be used. Upholstery fabrics are usually labeled by grades—for example, Grade A, Grade B, and Grade C. Grade A is usually the most expensive fabric and Grade C the least. A higher grade doesn't necessarily indicate that a fabric is better quality. Expense depends on the cost of the fiber used, the construction method, and the difficulty of dyeing or printing the piece. Consider these points when making a decision:

- **COLOR AND PATTERN.** Upholstered pieces tend to be large (sofas, chairs, etc.), and they have a major impact on a room. The color and pattern of the fabric should fit into your overall design.
- **FIBER CONTENT.** In Chapter 19, you learned the characteristics of common fibers used in decorating fabrics and other home textiles. If a fabric is made from a blend of fibers, it will have some of the characteristics of both. Check the label for the fiber content.

- **TIGHTNESS OF WEAVE.** Hold a sample of the fabric up to the light. Fabrics that allow less light to show through are woven more tightly and tend to give longer wear.
- **STAIN RESISTANCE.** Some fibers, such as nylon, attract stains more than others. In addition, some fabrics have an applied stain-resistant finish. This is often worth the extra cost.

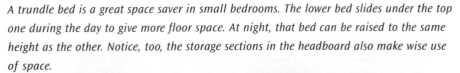

YOU THE CONSUMER . . .

You are choosing an upholstered easy chair for a family room. There are small children in the family. The sofa has a large floral pattern and the curtains are a subtle stripe. What pattern of fabric might be a good choice for the chair? What other specific fabric characteristics would be important?

A trundle bed is a great space saver in small bedrooms. The lower bed slides under the top one during the day to give more floor space. At night, that bed can be raised to the same height as the other. Notice, too, the storage sections in the headboard also make wise use of space.

should have at least 300 firmly anchored coils, good padding around each coil, and a tightly woven cover with a reinforced border to prevent sagging. The fabric must be fire-resistant.

Foam mattresses are also available and are popular choices for people with allergies. A foam mattress is about 6 in. (15 cm) thick. It's made of foam or plastic, with thousands of holes or cores cut in it. The more holes there are, the softer the mattress will be. Foam mattresses are light, distribute weight evenly, and rarely lose their shape.

The mattress of a bed rests on top of springs. The mattress should not be placed directly on the floor because air must circulate around it to keep it dry and free of mildew.

The size and number of springs determine their quality. *Box springs*—a series of coils attached to a base and then padded and covered—provide the most support, but they are also the most expensive. Less expensive coil springs are the same as box springs but are not padded and covered. Flat springs are attached to a frame and may have metal bands supporting them. Inexpensive flat springs provide the least support and often sag. Usually springs and mattresses are purchased as a set. Don't spend money on recovered and reprocessed mattress sets, however.

Water Beds

Some people find a water bed more comfortable and supportive than a standard mattress. When the heavy-duty plastic water bag is filled, it produces a mattress that conforms to the body's curves and gives good support. Water bed mattresses need to be heated.

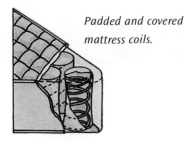

Padded and covered mattress coils.

A major disadvantage of water beds is their tremendous weight. A standard-size water bed weighs about 1,600 lbs. (726 kg). A strong foundation, as well as a special frame, is required to support it. Be sure that your home can support a water bed before you buy one. If you rent, check for any restrictions on water beds.

Futons

Another popular alternative to the traditional bed of mattress and springs is a futon. At night, a futon is a bed. During the day, it can be folded to serve as a sofa. For this reason, people can economize by buying a futon.

A futon has a wood or metal frame and one or more layers of mattresses. The highest quality futons come with a rope webbing, a 3-in. (7.6-cm) cotton mattress, and a 3-in. (7.6-cm) wool mattress. The webbing—firmly woven fabric strips that are interlaced—prevent the mattresses from falling between the slats of the frame.

Futons look like a couch or chair during the day and transform into a bed at night. Modern futons have firm mattresses and quality frames to provide a comfortable night's sleep.

Shopping for Furniture

Furniture is a major investment. It's easy to fall in love with the look or style of a piece. However, there are other considerations. Ask yourself if the piece is functional—will it serve intended needs well? Design, construction, and ease-of-use all relate to function. Is the size of the piece right for the space you have?

Accumulating furniture is usually a gradual process. Start with an overall plan and set priorities for what's most important to buy first. For instance, is a new sofa a priority? Perhaps you'd be satisfied to put a slipcover over an older loveseat and spend your money on a comfortable chair for reading. Buying less expensive furniture allows you to furnish a home more quickly, but items may need to be replaced sooner. If you buy more costly pieces, you will have to get by with less, but what you have should last longer. Which strategy is best for you?

Looking for versatile pieces is one way to compromise. You may be able to buy fewer items if they are **multipurpose furniture**—pieces that serve more than one need. A sofa bed or futon can turn a living room into a bedroom. A table can be used for dining and for paperwork.

Improvising with non-furniture materials is another way to stretch your furniture dollar. You've probably seen shelves made from bricks and boards. A simple desk can be made by placing a flat door across a pair of filing cabinets. Outdoor furniture is yet another option. You can use it indoors now and outdoors later. Canvas director's chairs, for instance, look good in informal arrangements. In what other ways can you improvise?

WHAT ARE YOUR OPTIONS?

There are numerous ways to buy furniture for your home while sticking to a budget. Depending on your preference, you can buy new or used items. You can also buy unfinished or unassembled furniture.

NEW FURNITURE. Try to shop for new furniture at reputable stores that carry brand names. Then you can be more assured of the quality of the furniture. In addition, most manufacturers offer guarantees against flaws. Watch local media for sales. At certain times of the year, most furniture stores reduce prices.

USED FURNITURE. Used furniture, especially case goods, can be a very good buy. The key is to check for signs of quality. Auctions, thrift shops, flea markets, garage and estate sales, and newspaper advertisements are excellent sources of

The graceful lines of today's outdoor furniture make it suitable for use in casual indoor living spaces. Later, as a family budget grows and more furniture can be added, the outdoor furniture can be moved outdoors.

People and Furniture on the Move

Today's generation is the most mobile in history. In the past, people often remained in the town where they were born for their entire lives. In contemporary society, that social pattern has changed. You may share an apartment with friends in college, then move halfway across the country to take a full-time job. As your career and life advances, you're likely to live in a series of homes in a variety of locations.

The furniture industry keeps track of such trends. They know that many of today's consumers want furniture that's easy to move and reuse in a different home. The same buyers are also looking for style at an affordable price.

For many, modular furniture is a good choice. Modular furniture comes in sections that can be stacked or arranged in a variety of ways. Perhaps you've seen wall or storage units that are made up of interchangeable sections. Sofas, too, are available in modules that can be used together or apart. Modular furniture can be taken apart, moved, and rearranged in a new setting.

Are there any disadvantages? There are several points to keep in mind:

- With some modular furniture, you are responsible for assembly and that's not always easy. Some furniture goes together easily. Other types need more work. If your skills or the components you're given aren't the best, you could end up with the Leaning Tower of Storage!

- The quality of modular furniture varies greatly. The materials and hardware used in some brands are less durable than in more expensive furniture pieces. Check what you are getting. Does the manufacturer use hardwood or less expensive particleboard? What type of finish is used? Will pieces withstand the amount of use you'll give them?

- When buying quality modular furniture, consider whether the design of the pieces is something you'll like five or ten years from now.

THINKING IT THROUGH

1. Talk to someone who has purchased, assembled, and used modular furniture. Find out about the ease of assembly, durability, and overall satisfaction with the product. Compare your findings with those of your classmates.
2. Use print and Internet sources to compare the costs of similar modular pieces. Write a list of questions you would like answered before making a purchase.

used furniture. Some stores specialize in used furniture. If you like the design of a piece, but not its finish or color, consider refinishing or painting it. Many products are available that give striking results. Reupholstering or adding slipcovers can update chairs and sofas.

UNFINISHED FURNITURE. Unfinished furniture has not been stained, varnished, or painted. Because it must be finished by the consumer, this furniture is usually less expensive. It comes in a wide variety of styles. Less expensive pieces are typically made of pine. Often, the joints are glued or nailed. Better quality items are made of hardwood and have dovetailed joints and reinforced corners.

UNASSEMBLED FURNITURE. Some stores offer ready-to-assemble furniture. Because the manufacturer can mass-produce the pieces and doesn't

have to assemble them, they cost less than other furniture. Some of this furniture can be taken apart for storage or moving. Many pieces, however, require permanent gluing as part of the assembly process. Before buying, be sure to look at an assembled model of the piece you want.

Unfinished, unassembled furniture can be a good way to decorate a new home if the owner has the ability and time to assemble and finish the furniture.

Caring for Furniture

Both upholstered pieces and case goods require careful treatment and regular maintenance to keep them looking good and make them last. Most manufacturers include instructions for the proper care of each piece of furniture.

UPHOLSTERED FURNITURE

All fabrics tend to fade if exposed to the sun for a long time. Position upholstered furniture away from sunny windows. If that isn't possible, close the window coverings. Other light sources can also cause fading.

Dirt and soil can damage fabric. Regular vacuuming of upholstery can prolong its life. Periodic dry cleaning by a specialist is recommended, or use a dry-cleaning foam.

No matter how careful you are, accidents occur sometimes. Remove spots immediately so the stain doesn't set.

CASE GOODS

Dust and soil are abrasive and can scratch a fine wood finish. Regular dusting will help. Waxes and polishes should be applied occasionally to provide a protective finish. Don't wax more than once every few months, however, to prevent wax build-up. Use only polishes recommended for furniture.

Occasionally, cuts and scratches occur on case goods. Some home remedies are helpful for blemishes on wood. Minor scratches can be treated with wax sticks. Choose a wax stick that matches the color of the furniture. Rub the wax into the scratch, then smooth the wax with a soft cloth. Finally, apply a polish.

If watermarks appear after a wet glass has been left on an unwaxed surface, use fine steel wool to gently rub in wax or polish. Another method is to place a thick blotter over the ring and press it with a warm iron until the ring disappears. The best solution, however, is prevention. Use coasters or trivets.

Furniture, like other costly items, should be considered an investment. You don't want to waste your money on furnishings that won't last. Therefore, gather all the information you can before making a purchase. Whatever your style preference, budget, or lifestyle, you have many options. Once you've made your purchase, take care of it. By maintaining your furniture, you protect your financial investment as well.

Zack Danz

Furniture Showroom Salesperson

Looking back, I'd say my interest in furniture began with my grandmother. When I visited her as a child, she told me fascinating stories about an old table that had been in the family for over a hundred years and about a chest that her grandfather hand-carved. Now my folks have those same pieces of furniture in their home, blended with new ones like the ones that I sell today as a furniture showroom salesperson.

"In my work, I'm amazed by the huge number of furniture options people have today, many more than in my grandmother's time."

In my work, I'm amazed by the huge number of furniture options people have today, many more than in my grandmother's time. Old furniture is getting harder to find, so many people now turn to reproduction pieces. Other people prefer more modern designs. I like helping customers find what they need to create a comfortable home environment in the style that suits them.

While I was in high school, my interest in furniture led me to take a couple classes in housing and interior design. What I learned comes in handy in the store when we create room arrangements for customers to walk through. We like to show furniture in ways that give people ideas they might use in their own home.

My first job in this business was part-time in a large retail store's furniture department. Now I work full-time for a home furnishings store. To stay knowledgeable, I take courses and workshops in furniture construction, preservation, and interior design. I have to know about furniture construction and safety, as well as appropriate care. You never know when you're going to have to talk about the hardness or softness of woods, or the security of a table's joints. People come in with budget limits in mind, so I also have to

understand how different financing arrangements can work for them. Sometimes I work with customers who are interested in the certain historical designs, such as Victorian or Queen Anne. The Internet is a useful information source.

I've been learning to use new software that helps customers see what an upholstered piece looks like in the fabrics available. We put the sofa or chair on the screen, the customer chooses a favorite fabric, and with the click of a few keys, there it is. This really helps our customers make a decision they won't regret.

I think you could say that one of the best skills I've developed is an ability to read the customer well. One customer may have a visual plan for an entire room, yet another has only a vague idea. Some customers bring in sketches and floor plans for me to evaluate. I listen carefully and answer questions in order to figure

"With a tactful approach, I'm able to show respect for each individual's design choices."

out what they need from me. With a tactful approach, I'm able to show respect for each individual's design choices.

Working in furniture sales has shown me that the company's success—and mine—depend on the kind of representative I am. If I'm professional and come across as caring and helpful, the customer is happy and so is my supervisor. Moving up to a better position last year and receiving nice commissions on my sales makes me feel pretty good too.

Career Profile

A *furniture showroom salesperson* assists customers in buying furniture. This individual must explain furniture construction and design features, showing various models and colors. Positions are available in a variety of environments, ranging from the large retail store to the smaller, competitive shop geared toward home design.

Education
▸ At least a high school diploma or the equivalency is required. Advanced degrees are important for advancing to a sales management position.
▸ Courses in business, housing, interior design, furniture construction, and related computer design applications are helpful. Retail sales experience is a plus.

Skills Needed
▸ People skills with an eye to customer service and good written, verbal, and nonverbal communication skills are necessary to the successful furniture showroom salesperson.
▸ The ability to complete appropriate financial transactions and retail sales paperwork correctly is required as accuracy is often monitored.
▸ Knowledge of the product, as well as the ability to assist the customer with computer-aided design choices, is increasingly important.

Career Outlook
▸ Employment opportunities are expected to be good and to rise as fast as the average as retail sales are expected to increase with population growth. Part-time employment is also often available.

Career Activities
1. Using Internet or print resources, find and price furniture for a family room. Offer at least two alternatives for the room.
2. Imagine that you are working with a customer who is dissatisfied with a product's quality. In pairs, play out the situation. Have the class analyze the use of verbal and nonverbal communication.

Chapter Summary

- The four most commonly used materials for furniture construction are wood, metal, glass, and plastic.
- Knowing how to evaluate joints, finishes, and upholstery materials helps consumers determine the quality of a piece of furniture before purchasing it.
- The basic elements of all upholstered furniture construction are the frame, springs, padding, cushions, and upholstery fabric.
- Before buying a traditional bed, shoppers should evaluate the mattress, springs, and frame.
- Consumers have a number of options for finding quality furniture.
- Furniture requires proper care and repair to retain its value and usefulness.

Checking Your Understanding

1. What furniture material is most commonly used for case goods?

2. Name one advantage and one disadvantage for each of the following: veneer, solid wood, particleboard.

3. What are the advantages and disadvantages of metal furniture and plastic furniture?

4. Which type of joint is stronger—a rabbet or dovetail?

5. How can you evaluate the springs of a piece of upholstered furniture?

6. What are three things to look for when buying a mattress?

7. What is a futon? Why is it considered a multipurpose piece?

8. In addition to buying new, ready-to-use furniture, what other furniture purchase options are available?

9. What is the difference between unfinished and unassembled furniture?

10. Identify two tasks that should be part of regular care for upholstered furniture and two for case goods.

Thinking Critically

1. If you were planning to buy a piece of upholstered furniture, what three signs of quality would be most important to you? Why?

2. What techniques might a manufacturer use to try to conceal poor-quality construction? What can consumers do to guard against such problems?

3. Which characteristic would be most important in the choice of upholstery fabric for an outdoor bench, a family room sofa, and a recliner? Why?

4. Identify ways furniture needs might differ at each stage of the life cycle.

5. If you were furnishing an apartment, what furniture might you buy new? Used? Unfinished? Unassembled? Give reasons for your answers.

Applications

1. **Choosing Outdoor Furniture.** Your aunt has asked you to help shop for furniture for her screened porch. The porch has a roof, but wind and rain come through the screens during storms. What materials would you suggest for the furniture? What materials would you avoid? List as many ideas as possible. Then write a detailed description of the pieces you would choose.

2. **Analyzing Case Goods.** Using an example of case goods that is available to you, sketch the piece and identify the locations and types of joints. Write an analysis of why these joints are suitable or unsuitable for each situation.

3. **Evaluating Furniture Sources.** Brainstorm all the types of places you could buy furniture. Make a chart summarizing the advantages and disadvantages of each source.

4. **Tracing Trends.** When radios, television sets, and phonographs were first manufactured, they were enclosed in decorative wood cabinets and were considered furniture. Write a paper discussing the evolution of these early models to the entertainment centers of today.

5. **Downsizing.** Your neighbor is moving to a retirement living center. He will have his own room, but meals will be shared with other residents in a dining room. He can take along four or five of the following pieces to furnish his new room: an antique cherry desk, mahogany china cabinet, twin bed with maple headboard, queen-size bed, upholstered recliner, cedar chest, maple nightstand, wicker loveseat, and oak dresser. What would you advise him to take? Why? Write a list of ideas for your neighbor about how he might make the room seem spacious and more like home.

BUILDING YOUR PORTFOLIO

Casual Living, a new furniture manufacturer, has hired you to design an advertisement for its recliner lounge chair. The advertisement will run in several home magazines. Keep the following information in mind as you prepare the art and the words for the advertisement. The chair—for everyday use—is both attractive, comfortable, and durable. The company's market research shows that working men and women over age 30 are the primary market for the chair. Begin by reviewing other advertisements for furniture. Then design your ad, making sure to include the following elements:

➤ A sketch of the recliner lounge chair with a member of the target market using it.

➤ A description of the materials and construction methods used. Include types of joints.

➤ A brief summary of what benefits the chair offers the buyer.

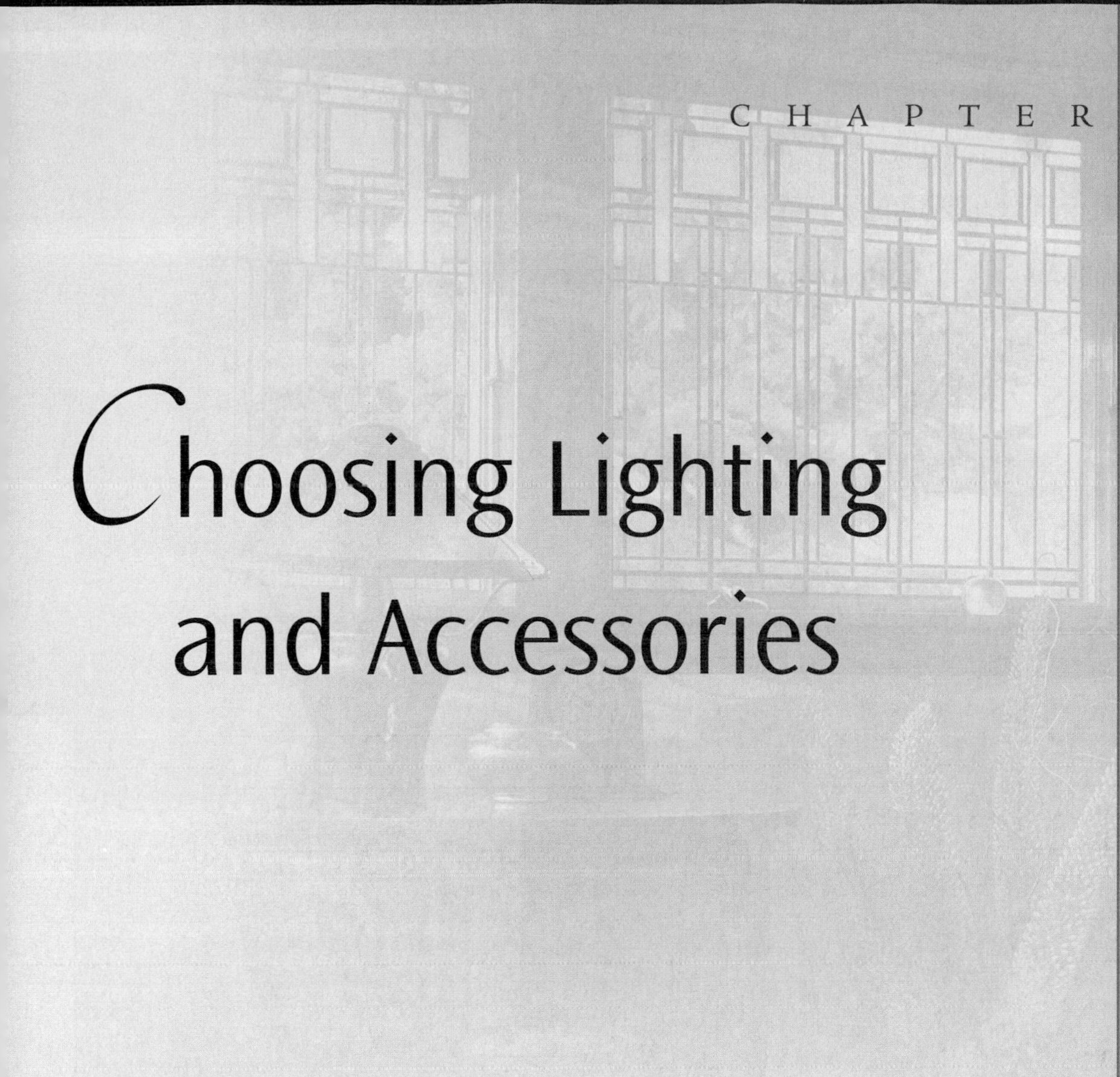

Choosing Lighting and Accessories

CHAPTER OBJECTIVES

► Explain the function of different kinds of lighting.

► Describe different types of light sources and fixtures.

► Summarize guidelines for choosing appropriate lighting.

► Suggest ways to use accessories to personalize a home design.

► Describe how to display accessories attractively.

TERMS TO LEARN

- cornice lighting
- cove lighting
- downlights
- fiber optic light
- fluorescent light
- halogen bulb
- incandescent light
- light emitting diode (LED)
- luminous ceiling panels
- soffit lighting
- strip lights
- valance lighting
- wall washers

Shed some light on your home and brighten up your world. Have you ever noticed how lighting can affect your mood? Imagine the impact of a light bringing to life a brilliantly colored painting. Recall how a sunny room in December makes you forget about the winter wind. Lighting can turn an ordinary room into a work of art. Add to that your own special accessories on tabletops and walls and you've got a home that reveals the uniqueness of you.

$\mathcal{L}$ ighten Up

Not only can you set a mood with light, you can create subtle drama with light. But if a room is too dark or too overlit, it will appear unattractive, no matter how beautifully decorated it is. Properly used, lighting can emphasize the best features of a room and your furnishings.

Lighting also affects the way a room can be used. For example, if the only light in a room is a dim bulb in an overhead fixture, chances are you won't be reading in that room at night. Inadequate lighting can create eyestrain, affect your comfort level, and result in accidents. Proper lighting contributes much to everyone's comfort and safety.

In the daytime, lighting can come from sunlight. The sun's intensity depends on the time of day, the season, and the weather. This natural light is also affected by the number, size, and location of windows; the kind of window treatments; and the orientation of the room to sunlight.

It's important to consider both natural light and artificial light when planning a room. As you read in Chapter 16, sunlight consists of a mixture of colors. The color of sunlight varies with the time of day and orientation of the room. Afternoon light from the south and west has a "warm" cast, toward the red end of the spectrum. Light from the north is "cool," which makes colors seem bluish. Light from the east has an effect somewhere in between.

Of course, at night, on cloudy days, or in rooms without windows, you must depend on artificial light. Some lighting fixtures provide *direct lighting*—light that shines on specific areas. *Indirect lighting* is reflected off ceilings and walls. It's also more diffused, or softer, than direct light.

Attractive and comfortable rooms combine lighting from different sources, such as this room's use of natural light from windows, a wall lamp, and overhead ceiling fixtures.

WHAT'S IN A BULB?

The light you get from any fixture depends on the bulb used. Bulbs are categorized by their type and their wattage. The higher the wattage of a bulb or tube, the greater the intensity of light. Be aware that some fixtures can be used safely only at a certain level of wattage—check the labels on the fixture. Different bulbs produce different effects. Three-way bulbs allow a user to select from three levels of light when used with a three-way fixture. A dimmer switch allows the user to lower the light level and vary the mood of the room. The sources of artificial light are incandescent, fluorescent, halogen, fiber optics, and light emitting diode.

THE PURPOSES OF LIGHTING

Lighting professionals identify three main types of lighting in a home—general, task, and accent. Rooms need at least two of these types. Understanding the nature and purpose of each type of lighting, as well as the light fixture options available, will help you make effective lighting choices.

GENERAL LIGHTING. Also known as background or ambient lighting, general lighting provides just enough light so that you can see everything in a room. It also helps soften the shadows and harsh contrasts that can be caused by other lighting. General lighting is most effective when both direct and indirect sources of light are combined.

TASK LIGHTING. Tasks such as reading require more intense light than general lighting provides. Task lighting focuses light on the area where it is most needed—for instance, a desk lamp illuminating a desk top. To provide the best task light, shades should be shaped so that more light is directed downward than upward.

ACCENT LIGHTING. A light aimed directly on a specific object to create a dramatic effect is called accent lighting. Accent lighting can be used, for example, to highlight a special painting. For the most dramatic effects, accent lighting should be three times brighter than general lighting. You can achieve that with increased bulb wattage or a light-focusing fixture.

Table lamps often provide task lighting for reading or can be used to provide a comfortable glow on an entryway table top.

INCANDESCENT LIGHT. Light produced by electricity passing through a tungsten filament in a glass bulb is called **incandescent light**. Light from an incandescent bulb tends to be warm and flattering. Bulbs are available in a variety of shapes and either clear or frosted. A frosted coating reduces glare and produces a softer light. Small, clear bulbs—sometimes used in chandeliers and wall lights—produce a sparkling effect. Colored bulbs bathe everything with the color of the coating. Reflector bulbs have a silver or aluminum reflective coating inside that directs the light forward giving better beam control. Reflector bulbs put approximately double the light on a subject as a regular bulb of the same wattage. Incandescent bulbs are available in 15 to 300 watts.

FLUORESCENT LIGHT. A visible light produced when chemicals inside a sealed glass tube transform ultraviolet rays is called **fluorescent light**. Fluorescent bulbs produce various color casts but some give off the true color created by natural sunlight. Fluorescent bulbs are usually long, straight tubes; but they may also be circular, U-shaped, or shaped like regular incandescent bulbs. Fluorescent tubes produce more light than the same wattage incandescent bulbs. Also look for the new, compact fluorescent bulbs (CFLs). They screw into regular incandescent lightbulb sockets. They cost more than incandescent bulbs but will last up to ten times as long. CFLs can create electronic interference and shouldn't be used with dimmers or electronic timers.

HALOGEN BULBS. A special type of incandescent light is produced by a **halogen bulb**—a bulb containing pressurized halogen gas, which makes it more efficient than a regular incandescent bulb. Halogen bulbs are usually smaller than regular bulbs, but they produce a whiter, more intense light. Although halogen bulbs are more expensive, they also last longer. Halogen bulbs have disadvantages. They become very hot when in use and can cause serious burns. A typical halogen bulb burns at 1000°F (450°C).

FIBER OPTICS. Fiber optic cable, consisting of hair-fine strands of glass, was developed for clear, high-speed communication. However, it's also being used for lighting. Currently, **fiber optic light** is used primarily in museums and for displays because it emits no heat and no ultraviolet rays. Light flows through the glass strands and is focused at the other end.

LIGHT EMITTING DIODES (LEDS). LEDs are considered by many to be the next major evolution in lighting. In each **light emitting diode** is a silicon "chip" about the size of a grain of salt and made of crystals. A small electrical current passing through the chip generates the light. An LED bulb can last 100,000 hours or more. That's ten times longer than compact fluorescent bulbs and 133 times longer than incandescent bulbs. Residential use of LED technology is just getting started.

TYPES OF LIGHTING FIXTURES

The lighting fixtures in a home may be structural or nonstructural. Structural lighting fixtures are built into the home during construction or remodeling. Nonstructural lighting fixtures can be replaced or moved from one location to another fairly easily.

Structural Lighting

Structural, or built-in, lighting fixtures and their wiring are usually hidden from view. They are also permanent. Figure 22-1 shows examples of structural lighting that can be used in homes.

Nonstructural Lighting

Nonstructural lighting consists of fixtures that can be moved or replaced. Nonstructural lighting includes various ceiling and wall fixtures, as well as portable lamps. Most nonstructural fixtures use incandescent, halogen, or compact fluorescent bulbs. Only buy light fixtures that have the Underwriters Laboratories (UL) seal, showing that the fixture meets safety guidelines.

Look for the Underwriter's Laboratory seal on light fixtures.

FIGURE 22-1

A VISUAL GUIDE TO...

Structural Lighting

Valance lighting consists of a light source (usually a fluorescent tube) mounted over a window and hidden by the window valance. The valance is a bracket that is open at the top and bottom, allowing light to be directed both upward and downward. Bracket lighting is similar to valance lighting but is used on a wall rather than over a window.

Luminous ceiling panels consist of fluorescent tubes placed above plastic panels. They may cover all or part of a ceiling and provide good general lighting in kitchens, workrooms, and baths.

Cove lighting is similar to cornice lighting but directs light upward toward the ceiling. Cove lighting can give a room the appearance of added height.

Soffit lighting is a light source enclosed in a box-like structure that directs light downward. Usually, a plastic panel at the bottom of the soffit diffuses the light. Soffit lighting is often used over kitchen and bathroom sinks.

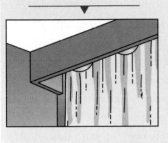

Strip lights are rows of incandescent bulbs or fluorescent tubes around the top or sides of a mirror. They are usually used in bathrooms or dressing areas.

Downlights direct a beam of light from the ceiling downward. They may be used for accent lighting or general lighting. *Recessed downlights* are set flush in the ceiling.

Wall washers are small recessed ceiling lights that spread light over a wall from ceiling to floor. For best effects, the fixtures should be placed the same distance apart and 2 ft. to 4 ft. (61 cm to 122 cm) from the wall (the higher the ceiling, the greater the distance). Wall washers light the wall evenly and de-emphasize texture.

Cornice lighting is a concealed light source (usually a fluorescent tube) that is mounted near the junction of wall and ceiling and directs light downward. Cornice lighting is often used to highlight wall hangings or wall groupings.

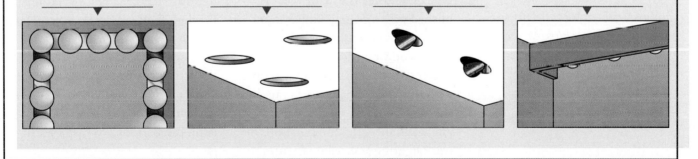

When choosing nonstructural lighting, consider the following:

- Ceiling and wall fixtures are commonly used for general lighting. The fixtures come in a variety of styles ranging from an elegant chandelier to a modern hanging pendant to a wall sconce.
- Track lighting consists of a series of light fixtures called *cans* attached to a strip mounted on the ceiling. Usually these fixtures are spotlights that can be swiveled, rotated, and angled toward specific areas. They can be moved to different locations along the track. The light cans should be aimed at a 30-degree angle to prevent light from shining in anyone's eyes and to avoid disturbing reflections and glare.
- Portable canister spotlights can be placed on the floor to produce accent uplighting on specific objects. Some people use special bulbs in floor canisters to provide growing light for large, stationary plants.
- Lamps are very versatile forms of portable lighting—both direct and indirect—as well as task lighting. A well-equipped lighting store will carry table lamps, floor lamps, clip-on lights, mini-reflector spotlights, and desk lamps. An endless variety of styles of lamps and shades are available.

DECORATING WITH LIGHT

How much light is enough light? That depends on the purpose of the room. A kitchen or workshop needs brighter light than a family room. Generally five portable lamps can nicely light a 12-ft. x 20-ft. (3.7-m x 6-m) room.

Designing with light, though, is much more than just having enough light. Good lighting is usually made up of a number of effects that create a balance between areas of illumination and subtle pools of shadow. One of the biggest lighting mistakes is to overlight a room. On the other hand, too much contrast between bright and dark areas of the room tires the eyes. The decorating in a room will need to be considered when designing the lighting. Light is reflected by smooth surfaces and light colors and it is absorbed by textured fabrics and dark colors. Combinations of structural and nonstructural lighting that produce downlighting, uplighting, wall-washing, and accent lighting will help create the look you want.

Downlighting, the most common type of lighting, is usually accomplished with a ceiling fixture or one of the types of structural lighting. If there is only one downlight in the center of the room, you can end up with a gloomy appearance because the floor is well-lit but the ceiling and walls are dark. Combinations of track lighting and ceiling fixtures can help solve this problem. *Uplighting*, or reflecting light off the ceiling, can be achieved with many of the structural lighting fixtures, wall sconces, or tall floor lamps. Uplights enhance a sense of height making a room appear spacious.

Wall-washing can make a room seem wider. To create dramatic shadows with wall-washers, mount the lights closer to the wall, only 6 in. to 12 in. (15 cm to 30 cm) away, and space the lights evenly. Direct the lights downward to create pools of light.

When decorating with light, accent lighting shouldn't be confused with task lighting. Accent lighting highlights chosen features of a room, such as a painting or a stone fireplace. Accent lighting works best when the fixture and bulb remain hidden, so recessed ceiling fixtures or hidden upright can lights are ideal.

"Painting with light" is a talent you can master once you learn the basics. Each room of the house has its own lighting needs. There are even software lighting design programs that will help you plan how to light a room for the effect you want.

Entryways, Hallways, and Stairways

The entryway is the first introduction your guests will have to your home, so you want to make the lighting engaging and welcoming. A pendant light is a good choice. Hang it high enough to be out of everyone's way. You'll find dozens of attractive fixtures at a lighting store. If the entryway is large enough to accommodate a small table, a table lamp can be added to cast a warm glow.

Cove or bracket lighting achieves nice effects in hallways and helps provide a feeling of spaciousness. Accent lighting could illuminate artwork or family photos on the walls, and a recessed downlight could provide accent lighting for artwork hung at the end of a long hallway.

Lighting in Retail Stores—A Means to Sell Merchandise

Retailers have learned that lighting plays a very important role in merchandising. Psychologists have examined how lighting affects perceptions, feelings, and responses. Similar to what has been learned about color, responses to lighting may be physical, emotional, and mental. Retailers use this information to attract people to their store and induce them to buy. That makes lighting a critical component to successful businesses.

How does it work? Lighting creates an image of the store, highlights merchandise, allows the merchandise to be evaluated, and motivates consumers to buy. The key to success is the appropriate quality and quantity of light. A logical pattern of brightness directs shoppers to special displays and aisles. It is very important to select lighting that also enhances the colors of merchandise.

Understanding the appropriate quality and quantity of light helps designers suggest lighting plans that help to sell merchandise and promote the image of the retail store. Here are some examples of how this can work:

- **Cosmetic Retail Store.** A cosmetic retail store was interested in using lighting to sell more cosmetics. To accomplish this goal they designed a store that was located on the second floor of a building. To go to the store you had to use an elevator. The elevator waiting area had a lot of mirrors and lighting that made complexions look gray. After you bought and wore some of the store's cosmetics you were required to use an elevator that was placed in another area with many mirrors and this lighting was designed to enhance complexions.

- **Specialty Stores.** Specialty stores sell jewelry, flowers, artwork, or high-end clothing. These retailers are generally interested in having an accurate color rendition that allows a consumer to see the true colors of the merchandise. For example, retailers select lighting that enhances the glitter and color of jewelry. Museum stores select lighting that reveals the beauty of art and reproductions.

- **Discount Retail Store.** Generally a discount retail store will use economical lighting that is not attractive. This helps to reduce the operating and fixture expenses for the business. One discount retail store in California purchased a building with existing light fixtures. Since the fluorescent lights were hidden in the ceiling they were very concerned that the lighting would give the impression to their customers that it was not a discount store. Thus, at a great expense they removed all of the existing lighting and replaced it with exposed fluorescent lights that were suspended from the ceiling. The lighting wasn't attractive, but it gave the impression to the consumers that the company was keeping their expenses to a minimum in order to maintain the lowest prices possible.

You, the
Designer

Imagine you are part of a design team responsible for selecting lighting for a floral shop. Decide what lighting you would recommend at the entrance. What lighting would you recommend for the floral displays? Give rationales for your choices.

In many rooms of the house, safety is a major factor in selecting lighting. That's why lighting needs to be accessible when a person first enters any room. Lighting for safety is very important in the entryway, hallways, and stairway of a home. To prevent accidents, stairs should be lit at the top and bottom, with switches provided in both places. For safety in hallways, lighting fixtures need to be placed every 8 ft. to 10 ft. (2.4 m to 3 m). It's also an important safety precaution to keep light from causing a glare or shining directly into anyone's eyes. Recessed downlights are a good solution.

Living Room and Family Room

Consider all of the uses these rooms get and you'll understand the variety of lighting you'll need. A combination of structural and nonstructural lighting achieves the best effects. General lighting will work wonders when entertaining or watching TV.

Dimmer controls allow you to pick the light level you want. Wall washers or valance lighting lend a dramatic flair to the room, or track lighting could be used as accent lighting to show off your favorite artwork. Upright can lights placed on the floor would spotlight plants and cast dramatic shadows on the wall.

Task lighting is needed for reading or working on projects. The ideal reading light in a living room or family room is a floor lamp placed to the right or left of your shoulder and slightly behind so it casts a beam on the seat of your favorite reading chair. Use a high-wattage bulb or choose a three-way bulb so that you can adjust the light level to the need. The bottom of the shade should be at eye level to reduce glare. Select a lamp style that works well with the room and add a dark shade to reduce overall light or a sheer lamp shade for maximum output.

Dining Room

Dining room lights need to be attractive as well as functional. A chandelier or pendant light is used most often. Adding a dimmer allows the intensity of the light to be adjusted for activities ranging from homework to a formal dinner. Track lighting can provide lighting accents on the table. Cornice lighting can illuminate wall decorations. Wall sconces could set off a buffet or built-in cabinet. Choose fixtures that work well together and complement the furniture. The most common lighting mistake in the dining room is to select a too small light fixture that looks out of scale. The rule of thumb for the appropriate size is to pick a chandelier that is no less than 6 in. to 12 in. (15 cm to 30 cm) smaller than the width of the table. The fixture should hang no more than 30 in. (76 cm) above the tabletop.

Kitchen

A large ceiling fixture or luminous ceiling panels will supply plenty of general downlighting. Choose a fixture that takes fluorescent tubes for energy efficiency. With only an overhead light, though, you may find that you're working in your own shadow at the sink or range. Soffit lighting or track lights can direct the light where needed. Small fluorescent lights under the cabinets put an extra task light on the countertops. Mount the lights close to the front of the cabinets to avoid glare on the work surface.

Many rooms can benefit from a combination ceiling fan and light. What is the advantage of the fixture allowing independent operation of the light and fan?

The recessed downlights provide general lighting in this dining area while the chandelier directly illuminates the table. Why would you choose to add a dimmer switch to the chandelier?

LIGHTING CONTROLS

You may find as you arrange the lights in a room that the way to achieve the perfect balance is by dimming some lights and turning up others. In order to recall those level settings easily, you need lighting controls. A sophisticated dimming system allows you to create and save multiple preset lighting scenes, sort of like a speed dial setting on a telephone. You could program the living room lights to dim to just the right level for watching a DVD on the home entertainment system or brighten the room for a family card game. In addition to automated systems, there are dimmers that allow you to manually adjust the level of light you want in a room.

Bedroom

An overhead light from a recessed fixture, ceiling fixture, or a light that is part of a ceiling fan will take care of general room needs. In addition, a bedside light is a must for people who like to read in bed. The trouble is that sometimes the light shines in the eyes, not on the page. One remedy is a table lamp with a shade diameter of at least 14 in. (36 cm). The bottom of the lamp shade should be at eye level when the person is reading.

Bathroom

Safety is a main concern for lighting in the bathroom. A ceiling fixture or recessed downlights can provide overall room light. Add lights around the bathroom mirror to provide task lighting. Use strip lights on either side or across the top of the mirror, rather than a downlight to avoid shadows.

Programmable lighting controls allow homeowners to preset lighting scenes for just the right balance of light in a room.

SAVING ENERGY WITH LIGHTING

In a typical energy bill, lighting accounts for 10 to 15 percent. Much of that is unnecessary consumption due to lights left on in unused rooms or using inefficient incandescent bulbs. Turning off the lights when you leave a room seems like an easy habit anyone could develop, but technology can help handle forgetfulness. Occupancy sensors on lights can detect activity within a room and switch off the lights if no activity is detected. Occupancy sensors operate either by ultrasonic, which detects sound, or infrared, which detects heat and motion. Motion sensors are ideal for homes with children or others who may have trouble reaching a light. Motion sensors on outdoor lights are an energy-efficient way to have lights for security and safety without having to keep a light burning.

Incandescent lights are the most power hungry. If using incandescent lights, choose reflector bulbs for energy savings. A 50-watt reflector bulb can put as much light on an object as a 100-watt regular bulb. A better choice, however, is a compact fluorescent lamp using about 75 percent less energy while producing the same amount of illumination. They also last about ten times longer than an incandescent bulb. High-efficiency fixtures that use fluorescent light tubes are another alternative. They are often found in kitchens, laundry rooms, basements, and garages.

As the cost of LED bulbs drops, LEDs may be the most economical type of lighting to choose. An LED bulb currently on the market has ten white light LEDs mounted in a standard light bulb base. It uses less than 1.5 watts of electricity.

Accessories

After you've finished selecting the furniture and lighting for a room, the next step is choosing accessories. These personal touches make it your home. They also tell your guests something about you. Accessories are the items that give a room personality.

There are endless possibilities for accessories. Maybe you have a collection of sports memorabilia you want to display. Perhaps you like plants and floral arrangements. It doesn't matter whether the objects are sophisticated or simple, elegant or rustic. What matters is that they mean a lot to you. What is important, though, is learning how to display your treasures in a way that shows them off and that complements the room. Although accessories are considered decorative, they can also be functional. A room divider, for example, separates living space, while its design makes a personal statement. Whether functional or purely decorative, no room is complete without these final touches.

How would you describe this room if all the accessories were taken away?

The accessories around the fireplace help highlight it as the focal point of the room.

When planning wall decorations, keep these basic principles in mind.

- Hang items approximately at eye level for most people. When hanging shelves and baskets, place them high enough to avoid being bumped by anyone.
- Consider the proportion between the wall decoration, the wall, and nearby furniture. A single, small item will look lost on a large bare wall, but it might be just right over a small end table. The rule of thumb is that the art should not be wider than the piece of furniture under it and should be no smaller than half the piece's length.

Personal taste dictates whether a few or many accessories are preferred.

WALL DECORATIONS

Paintings, posters, tapestries, prints, and even sculptures can be found adorning the walls of many homes. Pictures and other items hung on the walls give a room a warm, personal look. Wall mirrors make a space look larger while adding elegance. Wall clocks serve both design and functional purposes. A shelf display of brightly colored bottles sets a casual tone. A row of thick volumes of poetry might set a more formal mood. Even the surface of the wall itself can be decorated, using wallpaper borders or stenciling. Stenciling is a subtle and traditional type of wall decoration. Patterns are created on the wall by painting through cutout areas in templates.

- If the wall has a highly patterned background, use simple wall decorations, such as a mirror in a plain frame. If you want to hang a busy picture against patterned wallpaper, select a wide mat—a white or colored border between the picture and the frame.
- For art, pick a frame that complements both the room and the piece of art.
- Position a mirror where it will create an illusion of space and depth and where it will reflect something pleasing. For example, rather than hang a mirror over a fireplace, hang a wall decoration you like there. Hang the mirror on the opposite wall and everyone in the room can enjoy the glow of the fireplace.
- Use lighting to enhance the color and texture of wall decorations. The light shouldn't distort the colors or create glare on the item. Avoid fluorescent lights because they emit UV rays that can damage art. To avoid overheating artwork, use low-wattage lighting of no more than 25 watts.
- Choose hanging hardware appropriate for the weight of each piece.

Get the Hang of Wall Groupings

If you don't have a large item to hang on a large wall, create a grouping, such as several related prints or a collection of related objects. You can even group different subjects by using color to create a unified look. If you're working with pictures or photographs, frame them similarly and put the same color mat around them.

When creating a grouping, use an uneven number of items for a more pleasing arrangement. Arrange the items into a geometric shape, such as a rectangle, oval, or triangle. Position the pieces so there is one strong vertical or horizontal line in the grouping. If you want to add height to a room, use vertical arrangements. Use horizontal arrangements to add width to the room. Position large pieces low and group smaller pieces by size and shape. The midpoint of the grouping should be at eye level. Balance light and dark colors throughout the grouping. Remember the elements and principles of design you learned in Unit 5.

The space between the items is important, too. If the space is too narrow, the items lose their individuality. If the space is too wide, the group does not appear cohesive.

Before you start pounding nails in the wall, figure out the most pleasing way to arrange the items. Software drawing programs are a very convenient way to experiment until you achieve the look you want. There are also two simple methods you can use without a computer.

Method 1

1. Collect the items you want to group, trace their outlines on paper, and cut them out.
2. Tape the paper silhouettes on the wall, trying out different arrangements to see which is most appealing.
3. Insert the nails or hangers through the paper, remove the paper, and hang the wall decorations.

Method 2

1. Piece together newspaper to create the size of the wall space.
2. Lay the paper on the floor and arrange the wall decorations until you achieve a grouping that is balanced in size, shape, and weight.
3. Trace their outlines on the paper and tape the paper to the wall. Insert the nails or hangers through the paper, remove the paper, and hang the items.

Care of Wall Decorations

Hang paintings and other decorations away from sources of dirt or damage. Sunlight can damage photographs and artwork over time. Special UV-coated glass can help protect images, but even behind UV glass art and photographs will fade after years of sun exposure. Always hang treasured pieces or family heirlooms out of direct sunlight.

Mats on artwork can become dingy over time. You can learn how to cut mat board yourself or take the art to a framing shop to have the work done. Ask for acid-free mat board that doesn't leave a line on the artwork or discolor.

Explain why each of these different types of groupings works well.

Fabric wall hangings, quilts, and other woven or cloth decorations may discolor if exposed to direct sunlight. They may also require periodic cleaning to maintain their attractive appearance.

ADDITIONAL ACCESSORIES

Many other types of accessories can be used to enhance a room's design. You don't have to search for expensive items to display. It's more important to choose items that reflect your identity and interests. Here are just a few ideas of accessories you might display:

- Family photographs, souvenirs, and other personal mementos.
- Simple, everyday objects such as candlesticks, bowls, baskets, and vases.
- Natural items, such as interesting rocks or branches.
- A small, dramatic piece of sculpture.
- A stack of your favorite books next to a sofa or on the fireplace mantel along with some candles and plants.

Accessories can personalize the private zones of a house, too. What types of lighting do you find in this room?

Try mixing different kinds of items and styles to achieve a popular eclectic look. For example, pair unlikely style partners such as antique with modern or rough with shiny. Accessories are also more interesting when placed in groupings. As with wall decorations, arrange the objects in uneven numbers for visual interest. Try organizing them by pattern, color, or theme. Careful thought will result in an interesting effect rather than an appearance of clutter. Think of tables or shelves in the home as an empty canvas just waiting to be filled with interesting colors, shapes, and textures. If you're unsure what goes together, color is a good guide. Then vary the heights. Place low objects toward the front and the taller ones in the back.

Plants—living or artificial—can enliven a room inexpensively and are one of the easiest ways to incorporate color into a room. If you plan to use living plants, their location will also be determined by the amount of light they must receive. An arrangement of fresh, silk, or dried flowers can add color and beauty to any spot in a room.

A decorative screen can serve as a backdrop to embellish a room's décor or to divide an area. Screens come in a variety of designs.

Unusual lamps can serve as accessories in a room setting.

Spruce up a sofa with pillows to add softness to a room. Choose an accent color that picks up other accessories around the room to tie it all together. Rich fabrics that would be too overwhelming on large furniture can be introduced on decorative pillows. Use a variety of fabrics or choose pillows in your favorite color and vary the texture of the fabrics.

Don't overlook ways to save energy through accessories. For example, filling a bookcase on an outer wall with books provides extra insulation. A bright throw can add color and warmth.

CHOOSING ACCESSORIES FOR NONRESIDENTIAL SPACES

Even businesses want to add a personal touch to the work environment. Textured wall hangings, paintings, art posters, sculptures, and fountains can be found everywhere from the front office of a factory to the reception area of a doctor's office. Designers who select the accessories for nonresidential spaces strive to set a tone for visitors and employees. Does the company want to convey strength, cutting-edge technology, or stability? Maybe their message is "Your comfort is our business." For example, guests arriving at a luxury hotel may be greeted by ornate oil paintings in the lobby. A software development company might choose abstract wall hangings and modern sculptures to convey that they are on the cutting edge of technology.

Some museums offer art leasing programs for businesses. Art can be exchanged on a revolving schedule to make new pieces available for viewing on a regular basis. Some private galleries offer the same arrangement. Next time you visit a local business, take the opportunity to see what their accessories say about them.

Sometimes a piece of furniture sets a theme for accessories. In this case, the painted armoire gives the illusion of additional accessories. What would be the benefits and drawbacks of such a piece?

Rod Walker

Lighting Specialist

In my work as a lighting specialist I visit the homes of potential clients to evaluate their lighting needs. The houses may be well built and the furniture of good quality; yet there is often not one place in the living room or the family room where there is sufficient light for specific tasks, like reading or working on a computer.

"Part of my job is to advise clients on the amount and type of lighting needed for the various activities within their residence."

An important part of my job is to discuss my clients' lifestyles and then advise them on the amount and type of lighting needed for the various activities within their residence. As with furniture, lighting should contribute both to the overall effect of a room and to the comfort of its occupants. Just as an interior designer does, I contribute to the livability of both new and existing housing—but through the single factor of home lighting.

My clients could easily go to a general merchandise store and pick out lights that fit in with their decorating scheme. However, when they come to my lamp and lighting fixture shop, they can get answers to their questions about correct lighting. I recommend minimum light levels for various tasks, using lists of recommended levels published by the U.S. Department of Agriculture, the Illuminating Engineering Society, and the manufacturers of lighting equipment. For instance, a lamp with bulbs totaling 150 to 200 watts should supply ample light for studying. However, I know that if a room has dark walls, dark furniture, and little light from other sources, 200 watts may not be enough.

I use a light meter to measure how many footcandles of light are given off in different areas of a room; I can then determine whether the client has enough of the correct type of lighting for her or his activities. In some cases, other items or techniques can create the correct lighting atmosphere. Something as simple as painting a room a lighter color can add light, as can keeping light fixtures clean. It's all part of the work of a lighting specialist.

To determine just how much light each room has, I measure the amount of light in each area in which an activity is planned. The amount of light is measured in units called *footcandles*. Each footcandle represents the quantity of light that would be produced by a candle as it shines on a surface one foot away. Reading and playing cards require 30 footcandles of light under normal circumstances. Ironing or shaving demands more light, about 50 footcandles. Writing a letter or working in the kitchen requires 70 or more footcandles of light.

"Something as simple as painting a room a lighter color can add light, as can keeping light fixtures clean."

Career Profile

Lighting specialists assist customers with their home or office lighting needs. They help the customer choose the lighting that will be most effective and comfortable in a particular area. If activities ranging from reading to watching television are performed in one room, a light that can be increased and decreased is beneficial. A lighting specialist is familiar with the types of light needed for various activities, whether in the developing of a new home or adding an accent light to an already lighted room.

Education
▶ A high school diploma is required.
▶ Courses in electrical or electronic engineering provided by colleges or technical schools are helpful, and they are required for management positions.

Skills Needed
▶ A knowledge of the properties of light and how light is best suited to different activities.
▶ Sales ability is beneficial.

Career Outlook
▶ Employment opportunities should remain steady for the future.

Career Activities

1. Imagine that you have been hired to light a home library that has dark paneling, high ceilings, and a dark ceramic tile floor. Using library or Internet resources, find pictures of lighting you would use. Write a brief description of why you made those choices.
2. With a partner, study the effects of lighting. Devise a simple experiment, such as determining how much light is reflected off a light surface versus a dark surface. Conduct your experiment and share the results with the class.

CHAPTER 22

Chapter Summary

➤ Various daily activities require different types of lighting.

➤ Specific light sources and fixtures meet different needs.

➤ Safety and purpose of lighting are two of the factors to consider when choosing lighting.

➤ "Painting" a room with light is using a balance of light fixtures and light treatments.

➤ Accessories enhance the appearance of a room.

➤ Wall decorations and accessories can be organized by size, color, or theme for an attractive effect.

Checking Your Understanding

1. Describe the difference between direct and indirect lighting.

2. Give an example of general, task, and accent lighting. Explain the function of each.

3. Which type of light bulb lasts the longest? How much longer than the others does it last?

4. Which structural lighting fixtures direct light toward the ceiling? Which direct light toward the floor?

5. Name three types of lighting you could use in a dining room.

6. What are the two types of occupancy sensors? How does each work?

7. Name four factors to keep in mind when hanging a picture or other wall accessory.

8. Name five items other than wall decorations that could be used as accessories to enhance a room.

Thinking Critically

1. Plan lighting for a living room that is used by two people. One person is bothered by bright light. The other complains about not being able to see when the lights are dim. How can this problem be resolved?

2. Describe what type of lighting fixtures you would choose for your bedroom. Which type of artificial light would you pick? Why?

3. How would you use accessories and lighting to transform a living room containing only a sofa and three wood tables of varying sizes? Discuss the kinds of accessories you would use, how many, and where you would put them.

4. What types of wall decorations would you choose to hang in a room with bright floral wallpaper? What would you avoid hanging in that room?

Review & Activities   CHAPTER 22

Applications

1. **Evaluating Lighting.** Evaluate the lighting in your home. Do the general lighting and task lighting meet everyone's needs? How could you add accent lighting? Discuss your evaluation with your family. Suggest ways the lighting could be improved.

2. **Painting with Light.** On a piece of graph paper or using a computer, make a floor plan of a living room that is 15 ft. x 17 ft. (4.6 m x 5.1 m). Leave a doorway at one end. At the other end of the living room include sliding doors that open onto a patio. Arrange a sofa, chairs, and tables in your plan. Then determine how you will light the room using downlighting, uplighting, wall washing, and accent lighting. Draw the light arrangements on the plan and include a written description of why you chose the lighting. For example, wall sconces could be added to illuminate a painting.

3. **Arrange a Wall Grouping.** In a catalog, find pictures of three wall accessories you like. Cut out or copy the pictures and mount them on a sheet of paper or scan the photographs into a computer. Make a series of sketches showing three different ways to group the wall accessories.

4. **Decorate a Business.** Imagine that you own a hotel in a large city. Search on the Internet or through catalogs to find pictures of accessories and wall decorations you would put in your lobby to create a particular mood or image. Present your choices and give your rationale.

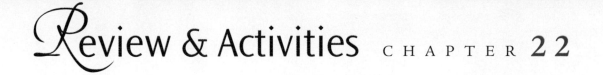

BUILDING YOUR PORTFOLIO

You have been hired to decorate the walls of a couple's new home. You must design a wall arrangement for the blank wall above the fireplace and for the one over the sofa. The clients have several interesting hand-crafted items they collected while on vacation in Mexico. They would also like to display photographs of their families, as well as some of the wife's framed needlework. Draw the arrangements you would use. Include information explaining each item.

Completing and Presenting the Design

CHAPTER OBJECTIVES

► Describe the final five steps in the design process.

► Identify factors to consider when planning how to use a space.

► Evaluate the advantages of computer-aided design.

► Suggest a style and a color scheme for an interior design project.

► Suggest backgrounds, furniture, lighting, and accessories for an interior design project.

► Compare various types of visual representations used by interior designers.

► Demonstrate how to implement a design plan.

TERMS TO LEARN

• elevation

• overlay

• pictorial drawing

• rendering

• sample board

In the preceding chapters, you learned how to analyze the various aspects that make up a design—from backgrounds to accessories. You're now ready to proceed with your design plan. In Chapter 18 you studied the first five steps in a design plan. This chapter helps you complete the design by following Steps 6-10. You will plan how to use the available space. Next, you'll select a style and color scheme. Then you'll be ready to choose backgrounds and fill the space with furnishings. In the last two steps you will present and implement your design.

Step 6: Plan Use of Space

Think about your favorite room. How would it look without any furnishings? Quite different! Every room is a blank box waiting to be designed. Satisfaction with the finished room depends largely on how well you use that space in your design.

A functional room arrangement is one in which the space meets the needs of its occupants. No matter how attractive a room is, if it is difficult to use or move around in, those who use it will be uncomfortable.

Whether the space you're planning is spacious and elegant or casual and cozy, it should be designed according to the needs of the people who will use it.

ARRANGING SPACE

When beginning the actual design of a room, review the purposes the room serves. What items of furniture go together? If you want a comfortable spot for reading, for example, you'll probably want a lamp and small table within easy reach of a comfortable chair. This could be described as a *functional grouping* because the pieces work together to meet one purpose or activity.

Next, consider the features of the room itself as shown on your floor plan. Furniture needs to be arranged in a way that doesn't block doors, windows, heating and cooling vents, or electrical outlets.

On your floor plan, sketch in the way people would walk through the room. Traffic patterns must be logical and convenient. People should be able to walk easily from place to place without disrupting others. As you try out various furniture arrangements, consider their impact on the traffic patterns. What would be the advantage of choosing furnishings that could also be successfully arranged in other ways?

Also remember to allow for clearance space, the space left around furniture so that it can be used. Refer back to the chart of standard clearance spaces on page 398. The height of furniture should also be considered. When furniture is drawn to scale on a floor plan it may appear that you have a great deal of clearance space. However, a drawing on a floor plan represents only two dimensions of an object—length and width. The third dimension—height—can reduce the apparent openness of a space. Try to visualize the bulk and height of the furnishings you choose as they will look in the finished room.

A thoughtfully arranged room is functional and pleasing to look at.

This is the time to incorporate your knowledge of design elements and principles. As you plan your furniture arrangement, there are several factors to keep in mind.

- Don't overcrowd a room. Leave some open space for a feeling of airiness.
- Attempt to balance the room. For example, using the same size and quantity of furnishings on opposite walls can help create a feeling of balance.
- Create a focal point by highlighting an interesting feature. For instance, grouping chairs around a fireplace draws attention to that part of the room.
- Consider the views from one part of the home to another, as well as to the outdoors. You can use furniture groupings to direct attention away from unwanted views or toward pleasant ones.

An area rug helps define this conversation grouping. Do you think sufficient clearance space has been allowed?

- The orientation of a room might determine its arrangement. For instance, if a room had many windows with a northern exposure, it might feel cozier with the seating arranged in another part of the room.
- Use your imagination. Sometimes an unusual arrangement—placing a piece of furniture at an angle, for instance—will solve a problem or create an interesting effect.

Room by Room

Because each area of a home has a specific purpose, it has special requirements when it comes to arranging furniture. In planning any room, always consider first how it will be used.

LIVING ROOMS AND FAMILY ROOMS. In many homes, the family room serves the same function as a living room. Either room can be a place to relax and entertain. However, in a home that has both, a living room is often more formal and a family room is designed primarily for comfort.

- Sofas, chairs, and loveseats are possible seating options. Sectional sofas offer flexibility because the sections can be grouped in different ways. Arrange the seating so that people can talk without having to raise their voices. L- or U-shaped arrangements are popular. Be sure to determine a focal point such as a fireplace or a large window with an outdoor view.

- Provide a convenient surface for reading materials or refreshments near the seating. You might use an end table, a coffee table, or a sofa table—even a chest, teacart or bench. Choose pieces that are in proportion to the sofas and chairs nearby.

- The living or family room might include electronic entertainment equipment. Although these items need not be the focal point of the room, they should be placed for easy access. Entertainment centers are useful for holding such equipment. They may be open or closed from view with doors.

DINING AREAS. The table usually takes up so much space that you may be limited in the ways you can arrange the other furniture in the room—a hutch, china cabinet, or serving cart, for instance. In a small dining room, consider using a drop leaf or gateleg table, which can be collapsed to a smaller size when not in use.

Be sure to allow space for chairs and movement around the table. Provide a clear pathway between the dining table and the kitchen.

Dining rooms are a luxury that many homes don't have. When space is limited, round and oval tables require less space than a table like this one.

BEDROOMS. Because of its size, the bed is usually the focal point of a bedroom. The head of the bed is often placed against the longest wall. Twin beds may be placed side by side or at right angles to one another. Bed placement usually depends on the other furnishings that must fit in the room. The size and shape of the room, as well as the location of the doorway, windows, and closets are also factors that play a role. Sometimes it's necessary to put a bed against a window, making warm window coverings a wise investment. Try to leave space on both sides of the bed for bed making. If that's not possible, use casters so the bed may be easily rolled away from the wall.

- Most people want a small night-stand next to their bed. If possible, place chests and dressers near the closet, leaving space to open doors and drawers. Also leave some open floor space for dressing.

- Perhaps you'd like to incorporate a sitting area or work area in a spacious bedroom. A movable screen can be a practical way to separate areas. In small bedrooms, consider double-duty furniture. For example, a dressing table may also serve as a desk.

- A child's bedroom is often a multipurpose room. Children read, play, study, pursue hobbies, and store toys in their rooms. Modular storage units and multipurpose furniture are ideal there. Consider flexibility and furnishings that will grow and adapt to the child's needs.

Interior designers now spend relatively little time at the drawing board. What would account for this?

HOBBY AREAS. A guest bedroom may double as a studio, a sewing room, computer room, exercise room, or workshop for crafts and hobbies. Analyze the activities planned for the room and the needs of those who will use it. Careful arrangement of furniture and equipment can make the room serve more than its original purpose. Placing a sofa bed in the room, for instance, is a space saver.

DRAWING PLANS

In years past, design work always involved drawing by hand. To make neat, accurate drawings, designers use drawing pencils, T-squares, triangles, and compasses. They add labels and dimensions using precise hand-lettering techniques.

Planning on graph paper is still a good option, particularly for fairly limited projects. However, designers today typically use computers and software to create design plans. Even do-it-yourself designers can produce plans using reasonably priced home-design software on their personal computers.

Floor plans are probably the most common type of design drawing. Architects use them to design the layout of rooms and areas in a home. While a floor plan gives you the view from above, an **elevation** is a diagram that provides a side view. Interior elevations show one wall as seen from the center of the room. With an elevation, you can see the relative heights of furniture, walls, windows, doorways, and other architectural features.

FIGURE 23-1

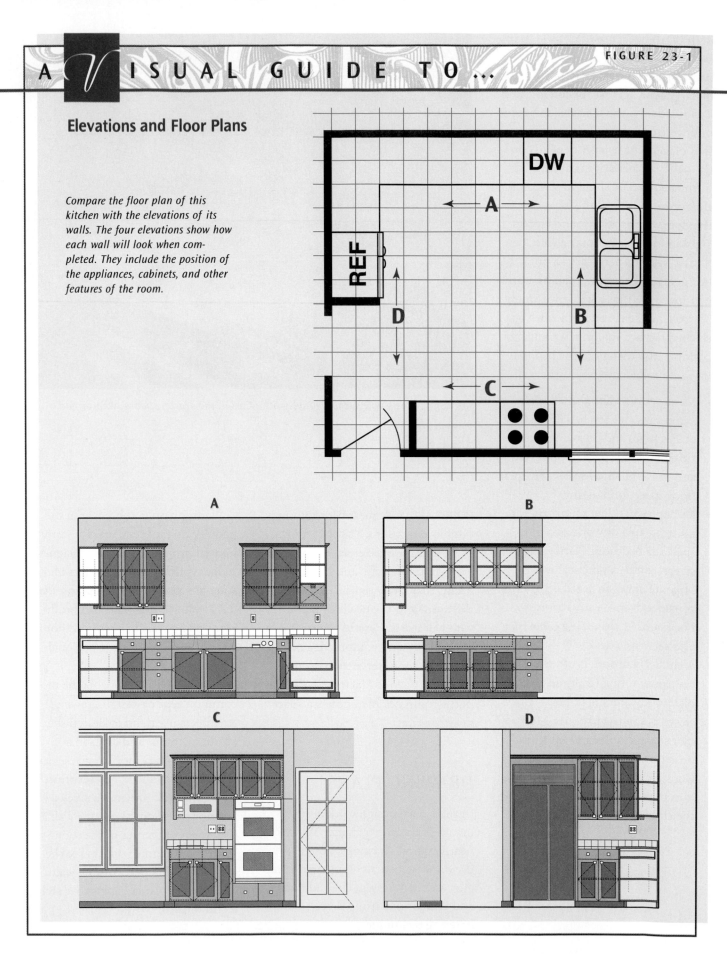

A VISUAL GUIDE TO ...

Elevations and Floor Plans

Compare the floor plan of this kitchen with the elevations of its walls. The four elevations show how each wall will look when completed. They include the position of the appliances, cabinets, and other features of the room.

DW

REF

A

B

C

D

One common use for interior elevations is to show the arrangement of cabinets on a kitchen or bathroom wall. Figure 23-1 on page 506 shows such a sample kitchen.

Computer-Aided Design (CAD)

Designers and drafters commonly make construction drawings, interior designs, and other drawings using a computer. With CAD programs, designers can prepare drawings and make changes to them

One of the many benefits of CAD is that it helps take the guesswork out of custom ordering furniture.

Consumer Sense

What to Look for In Interior Design Software

Are you in the market for a CAD-based interior design program for your computer? Try not to be swayed by the first colorful package you spot on a store shelf. It may turn out to be exactly the software you're looking for, but read the box very carefully before you purchase it. Software is usually not returnable once it's been opened. Prices can vary considerably from one source to another, but there's more to compare than price. Consider these points:

- **YOUR EXPECTATIONS.** Do you want to produce professional plans or is it for your own use? Some software is a learning tool and is easy to use, but isn't capable of producing original room designs. Some professional programs are very powerful, but more difficult to learn. Will you want to scan in a floor plan, choose from the program's floor plans, or draw in your own on the screen? Do you want a program that includes actual furnishings from selected manufacturers? The more you know about what you hope to achieve with the software, the happier you will be with your purchase.

- **YOUR EXPERIENCE.** Have you used a design program before? If not, talk to someone who has had experience with the product you're considering—a friend, teacher, or salesperson. You might also find a rating of the product in a software magazine. Check the package to see if a tutorial is included. A user manual and toll-free number for technical support are other valuable features.

- **YOUR COMPUTER.** Does your computer system have the minimum requirements necessary to run the program? (Requirements should be listed on the package.) For best viewing results, you should have a 17-in. (43-cm) monitor or larger. You will also need a scanner and scanning software if you intend to scan plans.

YOU THE CONSUMER . . .

Visit a store or an Internet site to learn about at least two brands of interior design software. Create a checklist comparing the features of each product. Which software would you purchase? Why?

CAD is useful for planning nonresidential environments, as well as residential interiors.

faster than can be done by hand. As a result, designers have more time to spend developing creative designs. In some instances, for relatively routine designs, the cost to the client is less. Individual designers and small design firms realize that, by using design software, they are in a position to accept larger and more complex design projects.

Computers create straight lines, precise angles, and perfect circles of the exact dimensions required. Once a designer enters basic information about a room, CAD programs can produce accurate floor plans that can be changed in an instant. In a keystroke, designers can duplicate standard appliances and pieces of furniture, conventional plumbing and electrical fixtures, and identical windows, doors, and closets.

Design programs create views that seem to be almost three-dimensional, as realistic as a photograph. This can help the designer and clients judge how pieces will actually look in a room. Color schemes can be changed with the click of the mouse button.

Many furniture and fabric manufacturers have put their catalog collections, including descriptions and prices, on CD-ROM. Designers can view these materials without leaving their studios.

Step 7: Choose a Style and Color Scheme

After completing your floor plan, the next step is to make final decisions about style and color scheme. These two aspects will dramatically impact the appearance of the space. Therefore, it's very important to consider your selections carefully. In a residence, the style and color scheme selected will reflect the personal preferences of the family members. In nonresidential settings, designers consider the accepted preferences of the general population.

STYLE

Of all the interlocking pieces in the design puzzle that must fit together, the style probably has the greatest impact on the room's overall effect. The *style* is the overall characteristics of a design. As you learned in Chapter 20, a style might be the characteristics of a specific period of time, region, or a designer. A style might also be a feeling, such as formal, informal, stark, or cozy. A style gives focus to a room. Although it may not always be obvious, style influences how people feel about the room. Remember that Chapter 20 focused on historic American furniture. There are other popular styles based on furniture from other countries.

It's best to choose a style early and keep it in mind as you work through the entire design process. Style may be based on special possessions that clients want incorporated in the design plan. If, for example, a client wanted to use her grandparents' Mission-style oak furniture from the 1920s, you would probably suggest the Arts and Crafts style for a unified look or mixing Mission-style and modern furnishings.

The home itself might already have a distinctive style. Generally, architectural details help influence the style for an interior. You should not feel limited to that one style, but don't stray too far from the look, either. For instance, a country look would probably appear out of place in a very contemporary home in the city, but a Scandinavian style would work well. French country would be too formal for a lakeside cottage, whereas a more relaxed, rustic look would suit the cabin and its setting.

In selecting a style, you'll be aided by the clippings in the design resource file that you developed in Chapter 18. Once you select a style that pleases you or the clients, strive to make all the elements and principles of design support the selection. The colors, patterns, textures, furniture, and accessories you choose will be linked by that one common denominator—the style.

You have already studied several furniture styles in depth. Here are some characteristics of room design that go with the respective styles that were introduced in Chapter 20.

COLONIAL. This style from America's early days is very simplistic. Generally rooms are small, have low ceilings and a large fireplace as the focal point. Walls are often painted white and the ceilings have exposed beams. Floors of wide wooden planks are covered with braided rugs. Fabrics are simple with designs of checks and small prints. Quilts are often used as an accessory.

QUEEN ANNE. This style is relatively formal. Often the rooms are large with high ceilings and classical architectural details. Walls are covered with wood paneling or wallpaper. Simple window treatments use luxurious fabrics. Known for elegance, the Queen Anne style incorporates mahogany and walnut woods, along with silk fabrics and silver accessories.

VICTORIAN. A flamboyant and elaborate style, Victorian interiors generally have carved wooden panels. Stenciled architectural designs often form a border near the ceiling. Elaborate side and top window treatments accompany lace curtains next to the windows. Fringe, tassels, and dark, rich colors are used on furniture and accessories.

This open interior is well suited for entertaining. How would you classify its style?

MODERN. Modern interiors are simple and unify technology with art. The focus is on the horizontal line and monochromatic colors. Black, cream, and white are frequently used on walls and fabrics. Wood floors are often bleached to reinforce the use of white. Window treatments are minimal—many windows have no covering at all. Steel, black leather, and stone are popular materials for furniture and accessories.

COLOR SCHEMES

In Chapter 16 you learned about factors to consider in choosing colors. At this point, you now have more to think about than which colors go well together. You must decide what colors support the style you chose and how to distribute them throughout each room.

Do you want the room to feel warm or cool, calm or vibrant, spacious or cozy? You may use the color wheel as a guide to help in selecting a color palette for the design.

Consider the color of wood tones of furniture, floors, and woodwork and how it relates to other choices. Guard against choosing a shade or hue just because of its current popularity. You might end up with the latest fashion trend, but be unhappy if it's not the right color for you or your clients.

Remember to consider a compatible color scheme for the entire home. Each room should have a color scheme that complements colors used in the other rooms. This is especially important for areas next to each other.

Step 8: Select Backgrounds, Furniture, Lighting, and Accessories

Now you are ready to select the elements that comprise the interior. Once your choices have been made, you will be ready to revise the preliminary budget you prepared earlier in Step 4 of Chapter 18.

BACKGROUNDS

As you recall from Chapter 19, floors, walls, ceilings, and windows make up the background of a room. Deciding which materials, colors, patterns, and textures to use is the part of the design process that many people enjoy most.

Part of the goal should be making sure the choices harmonize with the overall style of the room. If you were designing a bedroom with a Victorian theme, you might choose plush carpeting, floral patterned wallpaper, and velvet draperies with swags and tassels. Different choices would be made, of course, if you were designing a country-style bedroom.

Budget is usually a guiding factor in making final choices for backgrounds. Try to focus on the changes that will have the greatest impact. For instance, you might postpone plans to add a crown

The warmth and softness that carpeting lends to a room setting is one reason for its ongoing popularity. The price per yard varies greatly from one carpet to another.

molding where the ceiling and wall meet to allow the installation of durable laminate flooring that would visually enlarge the room. You might opt for an inexpensive window covering to allow for new wallpaper. You could add the crown molding and window treatment later.

FIGURE 23-2

A Completed Budget for an Interior Design Project

ROOM	Item	Mfr.	Number/ Name	Color	Quantity	Estimated Cost	Actual Cost	Remarks
LIVING ROOM	Sofa	XXX	23452	Blue	1	$1,400	$1,600	12 weeks to manufacture
LIVING ROOM	Chairs	XXX	14530	Floral	2	2 @ $800 = $1,600	$1,700	
LIVING ROOM	Paint	XXX	345	Blue Mist	3 gal.	$90	$99	Client will paint
LIVING ROOM	Carpet	XXX	47878584	Oatmeal	40 sq. yds.	$1,250	$1,550	Call installers
LIVING ROOM	Sheers	XXX	34767	Ivory	25 yds.	$500	$525	Paul will sew and install. Reuse rod.
LIVING ROOM	Lighting	XXX	46763767	Brass	2	2 @ $200 = $400	$360	Check Internet prices
LIVING ROOM	Vases	XXX	3565	Black	2	2 @ $100 = $200	$260	
AMY'S ROOM	Bed	XXX	4783	Oak	1	$800	$650	Double size
AMY'S ROOM	Rug	XXX	Coir	Bleached	8 ft. x 11 ft.	$340	$360	
AMY'S ROOM	Curtains	XXX	567243	Ginger	10 yds.	$180	$280	Paul will sew
AMY'S ROOM	Fan	XXX	67238	White	1	$125	$115	
SUBTOTAL						$7,085	$7,499	
CONTINGENCY FEE—20%						$1,417		
DESIGN SERVICES @ $70/HR.						$2,800	$2,800	Actual hrs. to be charged
TOTAL						$11,302	$10,299	

FURNITURE, LIGHTING, AND ACCESSORIES

Once you've chosen the backgrounds, you are ready to select furniture, lighting, and accessories and arrange them to the best advantage. This is one of the most challenging parts of the design process, but it can also be very rewarding as the design truly takes shape.

Using the information you collected in Steps 2 and 3 of the design process, you have a basic idea of the types of furnishings to include. Furniture choices for any room must be guided by the function of that room.

Whether you're evaluating a room's existing furniture or shopping for new pieces, think about what styles might best contribute to the design theme. Use what you learned in Chapter 21 to evaluate the quality of furniture materials and construction. At the same time, focus on how the furniture will fit into the space available. Use the floor plan and furniture templates you made in Chapter 18 or design software to try out various room arrangements.

Finally, think about lighting and accessories. If you have followed all the steps in the design process, and if you have made good use of design elements and principles along the way, the result should be a design plan you can be proud to present to a client or implement yourself.

BUDGET REVISIONS

Now that you have selected your backgrounds, furniture, lighting, and accessories, you may replace estimated costs with the actual prices of items you have selected. Figure 23-2 illustrates a revised budget for a sample interior design project. Note that specific information about manufacturers and model or style numbers are included in the revised budget.

Step 9: Present the Design

Design is a visual process. Can you imagine trying to design a room using only words? Fortunately, designers can use more than words to express their ideas. Whether they are created with a computer or with more traditional tools, certain basic types of visual aids are useful in the design process. You're already familiar with floor plans and elevations. Pictorial drawings, models, and samples and collages are other visual aids. Some or all of these are often used when a designer presents a design plan to a client.

TYPES OF DRAWINGS

Various drawings are used sometimes to help clients visualize a design concept. They include perspectives and renderings, fairly complex drawings that demand a great deal of skill and practice. Because of the expense, these drawings are seldom created for residential interiors. Some design and architectural firms hire an artist to create them for nonresidential and contract interiors.

Artists and designers use pen and ink, colored pencils, markers, watercolors, or airbrushes and paint to add texture and color to their drawings. Visual representations, such as drawings and models, can be prepared by hand or on a computer.

FIGURE 23-3

A **V** I S U A L   G U I D E   T O ...

Pictorial Drawings

*Which of these draw-
ings is a one-point per-
spective drawing?
Which is the two-point
perspective drawing?
What kind of informa-
tion do you get from
perspective drawings
that you don't get from
floor plans?*

Samples and collages are still best prepared by hand.

Perspectives

When you look at floor plans and elevations, you see only one surface at a time—either a top or a side view. These types of drawings do a good job of conveying information about the exact size and shape of objects, but they don't show how objects look in real life.

To provide a realistic view of how a finished room will look, designers may use pictorial drawings. A **pictorial drawing** is a drawing that shows the viewer several surfaces of objects in the room simultaneously. This is more like a picture than a diagram. Figure 23-3 illustrates pictorial drawings.

Pictorial drawings typically use *one-point perspective* or *two-point perspective*. A one-point perspective drawing of a room shows what is seen when the viewer looks directly at the opposite wall. The central feature of the perspective drawing is the wall you are facing; but it also shows parts or all of the two adjacent walls, the ceiling, and the floor. A two-point perspective drawing features two walls. It illustrates what you see when looking at the corner where the two walls meet. Again, ceilings and floors are included in the drawing.

Renderings

As part of the presentation, interior designers may include a floor plan, wall elevations, or pictorial drawings of the room, as well as sketches of furniture or other details. Presentation drawings are similar to the drawings used during the design process. However, they are often more detailed or have special enhancements added.

A designer's preliminary drawings may simply be rough pencil sketches that preserve ideas for later reference. To prepare drawings for the final presentation, the designer may make a rendering. A **rendering** is a drawing in which the designer adds realistic details, such as textures, shadows, shadings, and color. The designer may use pen and ink, watercolor, or CAD software to make the rendering.

Similar techniques may be used to enhance floor plans and elevations, giving them greater depth and realism. Some presentation floor plans include not only furniture, but also figures of people or arrows showing the traffic flow through the rooms. Presentation elevations are useful for showing design details and the finish of materials for kitchen or bathroom cabinets. Looking at Figure 23-4 on the next page, you can compare the floor plan before and after color rendering.

Sometimes, to avoid making changes on the basic drawing, enhancements and special details are added with an overlay. An **overlay** is a sheet of transparent, or see-through, material that is placed over a basic drawing. The overlay can be raised and lowered to show the drawing with and without extras. Overlays can be used to show alternative color schemes, furniture arrangements, and other design ideas.

TYPES OF VISUAL REPRESENTATIONS

Besides drawings, designers use a variety of visual representations to help a client visualize the design concept. Designers will prepare presentation boards, samples, collages, illustrations created with computer-aided design software, and models. These representations help to illustrate the style, color scheme, space plan, and the backgrounds, furniture, lighting, and accessories selections. Visual representations help to ensure that clients are fully aware of what the interior will look like and what they will be purchasing. It is important to make adjustments at this step because it can be very costly to change purchases once items have been ordered.

Presentation Boards

Most clients want to see and feel actual samples of fabrics and other materials before making decisions. For this reason, designers may prepare a **sample board**—a piece of illustration board with mounted samples of proposed wall coverings, floor coverings, upholstery, and window-treatment fabrics. A separate sample board is prepared for each room being designed.

FIGURE 23-4

A VISUAL GUIDE TO ...

Renderings

A basic floor plan (top) can be made into a rendering (below) to help the client visualize the finished room.

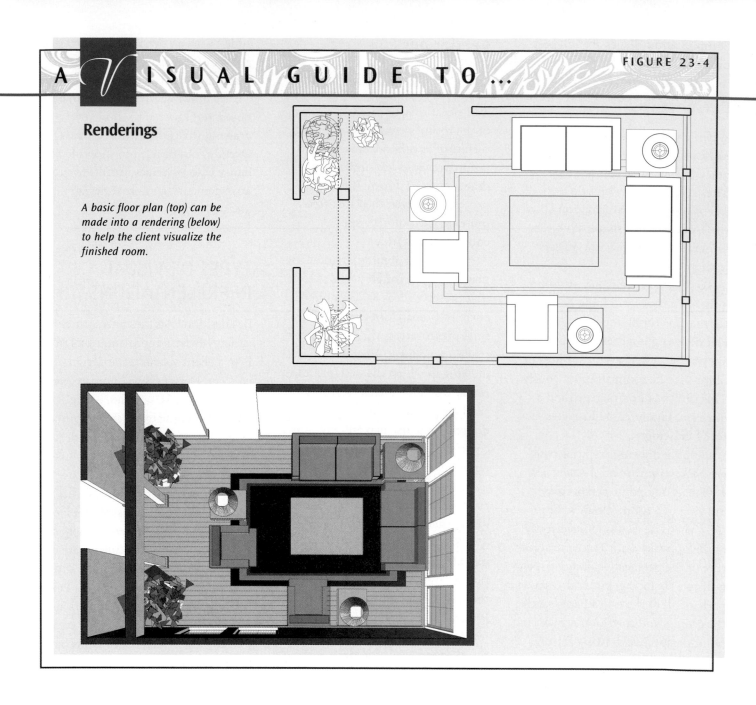

The layout of the sample board should reflect the elements and principles used in designing the room. The size of the samples is usually in proportion to the size of the real objects they represent. For example, the fabric swatch for a sofa should be larger than the sample for a pillow. In addition to the samples, a floor plan and pictures of furniture and accessories may be glued to the board. Label each clearly. Information about furniture manufacturers, dimensions, fiber content, and other details may accompany the sample board.

In Chapter 16, you read about making a color scheme collage from samples of fabrics, floor coverings, paint, wallpaper, and wood grains. Samples allow you to see the exact colors and patterns of materials. You can also feel their textures and observe the effects of shiny or dull finishes. Even the most sophisticated CAD programs have not yet eliminated the need for actual samples.

Computer Presentations

Drawings created with CAD software can be printed out on paper for a traditional presentation. One of the advantages of using the computer is the ability to present the plan right on the computer screen.

Some interior design software packages and manufacturers on the Internet allow clients to choose from furnishings and fabric samples shown in realistic detail on the computer screen. After the clients make their selections, they can view an entire room on the screen as if they were looking at a photo of the finished project.

For even greater realism, a series of images can be prepared, each showing the design from a slightly different angle. The images are stored by the computer and "played back" in sequences, like frames in a movie. This technique creates the illusion of walking through a room.

Models

Even a pictorial drawing provides only one view of a room. Sometimes what is needed is a three-dimensional model. A model is the best way to get an overall sense of a design because it lets you observe all the elements in the room from any angle.

In the past, the only way to create a model was to physically build one. A simple model of a room or a house can be made by gluing photocopies of the floor plan and the wall elevations to a stiff backing, then cutting them out and fastening them together. Detailed models, complete with furniture and backgrounds, are a more time-consuming and expensive option.

Instead of constructing physical models, many designers now use computer models. A computer model is not really three-dimensional, since it exists on a flat computer screen. It does, however, give the illusion of three dimensions. The image can be rotated and viewed from a variety of angles. Unlike physical models, computer models can easily be changed so the designer

What does a sample board offer that a computer presentation can't?

can experiment with design alternatives. Different versions of the model can be stored in computer memory for later comparison. Computer models have become the tool of choice for evaluating how a design will look and function in real life.

A PROFESSIONAL PRESENTATION

Once professional designers complete a design plan, they are ready to present the proposal to the client. This demonstration, or presentation, of the plan is the way interior designers communicate their ideas. Only then can the client visualize how the room or home will look when the design plan has been implemented. If the client wants to change the plan, it can be revised before actual work begins. The presentation, then, can save time and money and help ensure the client's satisfaction.

An oral presentation of a design generally has three parts: introduction, discussion of the design, and summary. The introduction identifies the main features of the design and emphasizes how the design satisfies the client's motives and needs.

The discussion section presents the designer's detailed analysis of the design solutions. A designer will generally focus on the current problems associated with the space and identify how the proposal will help solve the issues. The summary section reviews the client's motives and the key features of the proposed design. After the presentation, there is a question and answer discussion between the designer and the client.

Step 10: Modify and Implement the Design

Often, a client requests certain changes after the design plan presentation. The designer incorporates these and gets the client's approval. This often requires budget changes, as well.

The final step in the design process is to implement the design. This step involves developing a projected timeline, ordering purchases, and scheduling installations. The timeline for the project is generally tied to a budget. For example, if you are renovating your entire home you will probably have to do so in phases over several years. If you are working on one room you might be able to afford to complete the project in one phase. Examine your budget and determine a timeline that is affordable. Figure 23-5 provides an example of a timeline for implementing a design project.

Placing the orders for your purchases should be included in your timeline. There are many factors that can determine how long it might take to receive an item for your project. For example, if you find lamps at a local store, you can purchase them immediately. In contrast, a custom sofa could take

FIGURE 23-5

Timeline of an Interior Design Project

PURCHASES	Order Date	Received	Installation Start Date	Completion Date
LEATHER SOFA	May 1	Aug. 4		
WING CHAIRS	July 1	Sept. 6		
PAINT			Aug. 20	Aug. 24
CARPET	July 1	Aug. 21	Sept. 3	Sept. 4
VALANCES	July 10	July 28	Sept. 8	Sept. 8
LIGHTING	July 1	Aug. 1		
VASES	July 1	July 15		

twelve weeks to arrive from the manufacturer. Sometimes fabrics or wall coverings are behind in production, which results in a delay. As you develop your timeline, contact suppliers for estimated delivery dates.

INSTALLATIONS

To coordinate your project you will also want to consider when installations should occur. Generally, the first workers on the job are electricians, plumbers, and carpenters. Painters and wall covering installers do their work next. Flooring is then installed, followed by window treatments. The room is then filled with furniture, lighting, and accessories.

Communication

The implementation phase is the time when communication between clients and their interior designer is critical. At the start of a project, an interior designer should give the client a projected timeline for completion. Along with the timeline, a written contract should also be submitted that outlines costs, items purchased, fees, and designer/client responsibilities. As the project proceeds, the designer should maintain frequent communication with clients to let them know when items have arrived, any delays, and installation dates.

Sometimes a manufacturer discontinues a product that's part of the design plan. In that event, a designer should immediately notify the client and suggest appropriate substitutes.

Good communication skills help clients build trust in their interior designer. Throughout the ten steps of the design process, frequent communication ensures the clients' complete satisfaction with the finished design.

Jason Kim

CAD Specialist for Interior Design

I've been interested in computers as long as I can remember. My current job as a computer-aided design (CAD) specialist is to develop drawings on the computer. About two years ago I started working for an architectural/engineering firm in Miami. The firm designs buildings and interiors for corporations and residences all over the world. Our architects develop the designs of the buildings. They take into account the function, safety, and economical needs of our clients. The engineers develop the mechanical aspects of the buildings including heating, ventilating, and air conditioning.

As the architects and engineers develop the designs, they give me their ideas and sketches. I take the sketches and draw the plans using the CAD software. These drawings are saved on the computer, which makes it very easy to revise and duplicate drawings. Our firm has designed hotels, retail stores, and several office complexes. We have also designed homes for people here in the U.S., and in Canada, Greece, and Japan.

Working as a CAD specialist requires a variety of skills. Obviously you have to really enjoy working at a computer. I am in front of the monitor at least 30 to 40 hours a week. Some of my time is spent talking with the architects and engineers. We have to work as a team. That makes it especially important to appreciate the value of compromising and building consensus.

Our last project involved a new hotel in Puerto Rico. The architects and interior designers worked with

"As the architects and engineers develop the designs, they give me their ideas and sketches."

Since technology is always changing, I have to keep up with the changes in drafting software packages. I try to go to special classes at least twice a year to learn about a new system or to get training for an update for a software system I am currently using. I use the Internet to learn about changes in the field and new products.

our clients to identify the objectives, requirements, and budget of the project. I was responsible for drawing the floor plans, elevations, sections, electrical plans, mechanical system plans, specifications, and perspectives. To be able to draw these plans, I have developed a basic understanding of construction techniques, interior systems, building codes, zoning laws, fire regulations, and accessibility standards. During the design process of the hotel, I had to redo the drawings over and over. If I had to do this manually it would have required a tremendous amount of time and expense.

It's very important that I monitor the details of a project. I think our firm is able to develop better designs by using the CAD software and our clients are able to easily visualize our concepts.

"Working as a CAD specialist requires a variety of skills. Obviously you have to really enjoy working at a computer."

Career Profile

CAD specialists for interior design prepare technical drawings and plans on the computer for architects, interior designers, and engineers. Drawings include floor plans, elevations, sections, electrical plans, mechanical system plans, specifications, and perspectives. The drawings are for commercial and residential buildings.

Education
▶ Most employers prefer to hire individuals with drafting training received at a technical institute, community college, or a 4-year college/university.
▶ Courses in drafting, computer-aided drafting, interior design, mathematics, science, and engineering technology are helpful.

Skills Needed
▶ A mechanical aptitude and the ability to draw freehand and detailed work accurately are required.
▶ Visual and spatial aptitude is also important.
▶ Knowledge of the principles and practices of interior design is critical.
▶ Good interpersonal skills are required for working with architects, interior designers, engineers, and other professionals.

Career Outlook
▶ CAD specialists for interior design are in high demand during this decade. As technology continues to advance job openings are expected to increase. More information can be obtained from the American Design Drafting Association and the Accrediting Commission of Career Schools and Colleges of Technology.

Career Activities
1. Locate a copy of a residential floor plan. Draw the floor plan using a computer-aided drafting system.
2. Select furniture for the floor plan and explain some of the best solutions for the space.

CHAPTER 23

Chapter Summary

➤ A good furniture arrangement is comfortable, functional, and attractive.

➤ Today, many designers use computer-aided design programs rather than hand drawings.

➤ The elements and principles of design are used to create a style. The color scheme, backgrounds, furnishings, lighting, and accessories in the design plan all contribute to the style.

➤ Designers use a variety of drawings and other visual aids to visualize and present a design plan.

➤ When giving a presentation, a designer can show the client enhanced drawings and sample boards, or present the entire design plan on a computer screen.

➤ Implementing a design plan includes preparing a projected timeline, ordering purchases, and scheduling installations.

Checking Your Understanding

1. What are the final five steps in the design process? List them in the order they should be done.

2. Identify four factors to consider when designing an efficient, functional furniture arrangement.

3. How does an elevation differ from a floor plan? When would a designer use an elevation?

4. What advantages does computer-aided design have over drawings done by hand?

5. Identify four characteristics of an interior done in the Modern style.

6. Name three types of visual aids a designer might use to create a design.

7. Explain the difference between the two kinds of pictorial drawings.

8. Explain the purpose of renderings and overlays.

9. List three elements that could be included when constructing a sample board.

10. Describe how to develop a timeline for an interior design project.

Thinking Critically

1. Imagine that you are redesigning a bedroom for a client. She is so fond of a particular grouping of furniture that she wants to order a dressing table, three dressers, and a nightstand to go with the queen-sized bed. How might you show the client that was too much furniture?

2. Are handmade models ever better visual aids than those on a computer screen? Why? Do you think the traditional drawing methods will continue to be used in the future? Why or why not?

3. In preparing a timeline for a design project, why do you think you should build in extra time to the schedule?

Applications

1. **Budget Basics.** Imagine that you're working with a family who wants to convert a spare room into a home office/den. They would like a hardwood floor, wood paneling, new lighting, custom Roman shades, and an oak computer desk. Their budget won't accommodate so many improvements, however. How would you help them settle on a plan? What alternatives might you suggest?

2. **Software Survey.** Obtain catalogs that describe software for home computers, or visit a store that sells software. Observe the software that's available for planning home interiors. Read the catalog or package descriptions. Then determine the capabilities and cost of each program. Make a chart summarizing your findings. Share it with your class.

3. **Gaining Style Practice.** Identify a style for the lobby of a law firm. Based upon this style select the color scheme, backgrounds, furniture, lighting, and accessories that could be used in the lobby. Present your work to your classmates.

4. **Internet Survey.** Go to a search engine on the Internet to identify manufacturers and retailers of interior products. Visit the sites to learn about products and information that are available. Then identify the types of products that manufacturers or retail sites offer, price ranges, and delivery policies. Make a chart summarizing your findings. Share it with the class.

5. **Drawing Practice.** Make a simple pictorial drawing of one room in your home or school. You may prepare your drawings by hand or use computer software if it's available. Display your work in the classroom.

BUILDING YOUR PORTFOLIO

The owners of a large Victorian home have hired you to redesign an area that was once the servants' quarters adjacent to the kitchen. Currently the space is used for storage, but the couple wants it converted into a private bedroom and bathroom for their nephew who will be attending college in their city. Begin the project by making a list of the 10 steps in the design process. (Refer back to Chapter 18, if necessary.) For each step, write a paragraph or more detailing what you would do to complete that segment of the design process. Include a list of questions you would ask the clients. For Step 10, prepare a sample timeline of the project.

Designs For Living

Kitchens, Laundry Areas, and Baths

TERMS TO LEARN

- island
- master bath
- peninsula
- vanity
- work center
- work triangle

CHAPTER OBJECTIVES

► Explain basic principles for designing efficient kitchens, laundry areas, and bathrooms.

► Compare options for cabinets, countertops, and fixtures.

► Describe considerations in planning electrical, lighting, and ventilation systems for these areas.

► Point out ways to incorporate universal design features in kitchens, laundry areas, and bathrooms.

► Give guidelines for shopping for appliances.

Of all the rooms in a home, the kitchen, laundry area, and bathrooms are often the most interesting and challenging to design. Increasingly, they are called upon to be both high-tech and high-comfort, to serve multiple purposes, and to express individuality and flair. This chapter will help you design and equip new or remodeled kitchens, laundry areas, and baths that are efficient, safe, comfortable, and appealing.

$\mathcal{P}$lanning Kitchens

Kitchen designs should reflect the needs, wants, and lifestyle of the household they serve. Before planning a kitchen, consider the following questions.

- Which meals will usually be prepared in the kitchen? Will they be elaborate or simple meals?
- For how many people will food usually be prepared?
- Who will prepare the meals? Will there be more than one cook at a time?
- Will young children or aging adults be active in the kitchen?
- Should the kitchen accommodate physical limitations, such as vision or hearing impairments, special mobility problems, or wheelchair accessibility?
- How many appliances and gadgets are to be stored in the kitchen?
- Will the kitchen be used for eating as well as food preparation?
- What other activities will be carried out in this space—such as doing laundry, watching TV, accessing the Internet, doing homework or projects?
- How much entertaining involving food preparation does the household do?
- Will the kitchen need to change and adapt as the occupants age and their lifestyles change?

Analyzing the answers to these questions can help you discover features the kitchen should have. For example, if two or more people participate in meal preparation, the kitchen must be arranged so that the cooks don't get in one another's way. If there are children or family members with special needs, ways to meet their needs should be part of the design.

DESIGNING AN EFFICIENT LAYOUT

What makes one kitchen easier to work in than another? The answer is not size, but efficiency. An efficient arrangement allows meal preparation and cleanup to be completed using less time and energy. No matter how small or large a kitchen, planning an efficient layout will make it more convenient and pleasant to use. A first step is to plan the work centers.

Work Centers

Preparing a meal usually involves several different tasks, such as getting food from the storage area, measuring and mixing, cooking, and cleaning up. For the most efficient meal preparation, each task should be performed in a **work center**, an area of a kitchen especially equipped for a particular chore.

Most work centers are built around a major appliance or fixture and include both counter and storage space. A well-planned kitchen includes three basic work centers: food storage, cooking, and cleanup. Some kitchens also have mixing and planning centers, as well as other specialty centers.

FOOD STORAGE CENTER. The refrigerator is the focus of fresh food storage. Food that doesn't require refrigeration can be stored elsewhere. Some people find it convenient to store spices, sauces, mixes, and such staples as rice near the range. Canned food can be stored in a cabinet or pantry.

COOKING CENTER. The focus of the cooking center is the range (or, in

Efficiently organized kitchens are divided into work centers.

some kitchens, a separate cooktop and oven). If possible, part of the countertop should be made of stainless steel, ceramic tile, or other heat-resistant material, so that hot pans can be set directly on the countertop.

If a microwave oven is used for meal preparation, it should also be located in this area. If the microwave is used primarily to heat snacks, it can be placed near the refrigerator instead. Other items that belong in the cooking center are small cooking appliances, such as a toaster or electric skillet; pots, pans, and utensils used for cooking; pot holders and hot pads; and serving bowls.

CLEANUP CENTER. The cleanup center includes the sink and the dishwasher, if there is one. A garbage disposal, recycling bins, and perhaps

a trash compactor might also be part of the cleanup center.

Some kitchens are designed with dual cleanup centers. One may be designed for washing dishes, while a secondary sink in another part of the kitchen handles tasks such as washing vegetables. This arrangement is especially convenient when more than one person works in the kitchen at a time.

Many people prefer to store dishes, glassware, and silverware near the cleanup center so that these items can be put away easily after washing. The cleanup center also needs storage space for dishwashing detergents, scouring powder, dishcloths, and towels.

Some kitchens have an additional sink that allows a second cook to wash vegetables and fruits and prepare salads. The lower counter height makes it convenient for a seated user.

MIXING CENTER. The mixing center is where much food preparation takes place. For convenience, it is best located between the refrigerator and the sink or between the sink and the range. Mixing bowls, knives, cutting boards, and utensils used for stirring and measuring should be within easy reach. Small appliances, such as an electric mixer and a blender, might be located on the countertop or in a nearby cabinet. Foods used most often in cooking and baking—such as flour, sugar, and spices—should also be within easy reach.

PLANNING CENTER. If there's enough room, a planning center is a useful feature. Planning centers are a convenient place to plan meals and store cookbooks. Many people also use a planning center for coordinating family messages and schedules, making telephone calls, paying bills, and filing household records. Planning centers range from a small table and chair to office areas that include a computer or Internet appliance.

OTHER CENTERS. A large kitchen might have additional work centers. For example, many kitchens have a serving and eating center. An alternative to storing dishes, glassware, and silverware in the cleanup center is to store them along with linens near the serving center.

People who bake frequently may want a baking center. A baking center might include a marble surface for kneading dough and making pastry and extra-wide storage spaces for appliances and bakeware. A socializing center, or casual seating area, is becoming more popular in today's kitchens. Such an area allows family members and friends to visit with the cook while he or she prepares the meal. Other specialized work centers incorporate areas for laundry, sewing, and maintaining indoor plants.

The Work Triangle

One clue to a kitchen's efficiency is its **work triangle**—the triangle formed by drawing imaginary lines to connect the sink, range or cooktop, and refrigerator. Because most kitchen work occurs in this area, it should be the basis for kitchen design. The triangle should not be so small that the kitchen is cramped or so large that the work centers are inconveniently far apart. Ideally, the total length of the sides of the triangle should be between 12 ft. and 22 ft. (3.7 m and 6.7 m). To accommodate a wheelchair, a work triangle should be 14 ft. to 24 ft. (4.3 m to 7.3 m).

A work triangle functions best when the three sides are nearly equal, with the sink located between the refrigerator and the range. If possible, traffic passing through the kitchen should not cross the work triangle.

Today's lifestyles may require adaptations to the work triangle. For example, more space than the recommended minimum may be needed when more than one person will be cooking at a time. The addition of extra work centers, such as a food prep sink, may affect how the basic work centers are arranged. Even with new ideas emerging, the work triangle concept remains a useful way to evaluate kitchen efficiency.

Common Kitchen Layouts

Kitchen cabinets and appliances usually are arranged in one of four basic shapes: one-wall, corridor, L-shaped, and U-shaped. In addition, any of these basic layouts can be varied by adding an island or a peninsula. An **island** is a freestanding storage and countertop unit. A **peninsula** is a countertop that extends out into the room, with one end attached to a wall or a cabinet. Figure 24-1 on pages 532–533 illustrates these basic layouts and variations.

An island can make a work triangle more functional in a large kitchen. Would an island be a good idea in a small kitchen?

Kitchen Layout Options

Kitchen layouts are influenced by several factors, including available space and budget. Ideally, the layout is based on a work triangle, which is formed by drawing imaginary lines to connect the sink, range, and refrigerator.

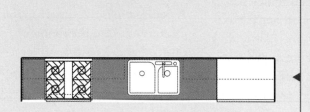

ONE-WALL KITCHEN

The range, sink, refrigerator, and cabinets are arranged along the wall. The one-wall kitchen is sometimes at the end of a living room and may be concealed by a set of folding doors or a screen.

ADVANTAGE:
- Saves space. A practical choice in apartments or other small homes.

DISADVANTAGES:
- Very limited storage and counter space.
- If stretched out to allow more storage and counter space, work centers may be too far apart.

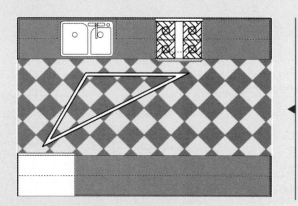

CORRIDOR KITCHEN

Appliances and cabinets are arranged along two walls, with an aisle between them. Both ends of the kitchen may be open, or one end may be a wall.

ADVANTAGE:
- Usually has a compact, efficient work triangle.

DISADVANTAGES:
- The work triangle may be too cramped to allow more than one person to work in the kitchen at a time.
- If both ends are open, people walking through the kitchen can interrupt meal preparation.

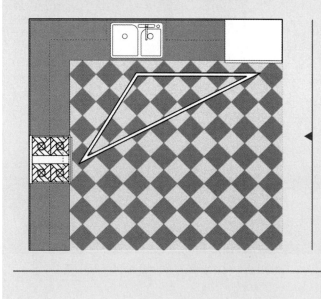

L-SHAPED KITCHEN

Appliances and cabinets are arranged along two adjoining walls. This arrangement permits an open area that may be used for dining.

ADVANTAGES:
- The work triangle is not interrupted by traffic.
- More than one person can work conveniently in the kitchen.
- More continuous counter and cabinet space is possible than with one-wall and corridor layouts.

DISADVANTAGE:
- Corner storage might not be fully accessible.

Kitchen Layout Options (Continued)

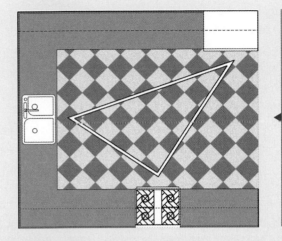

U-SHAPED KITCHEN

Appliances and cabinets are arranged along three adjoining walls. Some U-shaped kitchens also have an island in the middle of the U.

ADVANTAGES:
- Usually has more continuous counter and cabinet space than any of the other layouts.
- A major appliance may be placed along each wall so that the sides of the work triangle are equal.

DISADVANTAGE:
- Corner storage may not be fully accessible.

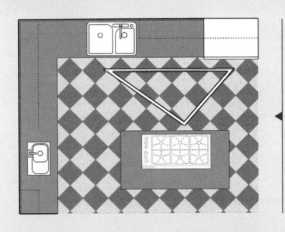

ADDING AN ISLAND

Any of the basic kitchen designs can be altered by adding an island—a freestanding base cabinet. The island may contain a second sink, a cooktop, or a chopping block. It may simply provide extra counter and storage space. It may also be used as an eating area, with stools for seating.

ADVANTAGE:
- Offers many options for making a kitchen more functional.

DISADVANTAGE:
- Can be a traffic obstacle if not well planned.

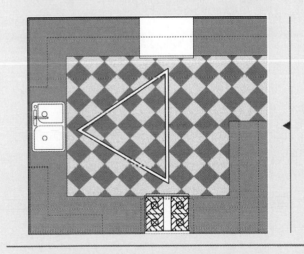

USING A PENINSULA

A peninsula countertop extends out into the room. Usually there's a cabinet below the peninsula countertop. There may also be cabinets suspended from the ceiling directly overhead. Like an island, a peninsula can be used for many purposes.

ADVANTAGES:
- Can serve as an open divider between the kitchen and a dining area or family room.
- Can be used to add a fourth countertop to a U-shaped kitchen, as shown here.

DISADVANTAGE:
- Some people may not like the openness of a peninsula.

Making a Floor Plan

To plan the layout of kitchen cabinets and appliances, draw a floor plan to scale. (See Chapter 18 for directions on making a floor plan.) Use templates to determine the best locations for cabinets and appliances. Be sure to double-check the floor plan before work begins and appliances are ordered. Once the plumbing, equipment, and cabinets have been installed in a kitchen, moving them is usually complicated and expensive. Before you implement your plan, check it against the guidelines listed in Figure 24-2 below.

FIGURE 24-2

Do's and Don'ts When Planning Kitchen Layouts

DO	DON'T
✓ Provide adequate working space for more than one person, if possible.	⊘ Don't place a range under a window. Window curtains could catch fire, drafts might extinguish a pilot light or a flame, and the window would be difficult to clean.
✓ Allow enough clearance for stooping and for opening appliance and cabinet doors and drawers.	⊘ Don't install cooktop burners and a built-in oven next to each other. This creates a fire hazard.
✓ Allow at least 5 ft. (1.5 m) of space between opposing counters in a corridor or U-shaped kitchen, or one with an island.	⊘ Don't install a built-in oven above convenient reach. The oven will be difficult to load and unload, which could result in burns.
✓ Allow space for a chair or a stool so that a person can sit down to perform tasks.	⊘ Don't place the refrigerator next to the range or built-in oven unless they are separated by insulating material. Heat from the range or the oven will cause the refrigerator to overwork.
✓ Arrange the sink, refrigerator, and range in an efficient work triangle.	
✓ Allow at least 18 in. (46 cm) of counter space next to the door of the refrigerator.	⊘ Don't locate a dishwasher where a person could easily fall over the dishwasher door when it's open.
✓ Allow at least 21 in. (53 cm) of counter space on either side of the cooktop.	⊘ Don't crowd appliances into corners with little or no work space around them.
✓ Allow 18 in. to 24 in. (46 cm to 61 cm) of counter space on both sides of the sink.	⊘ Don't put appliances near doorways where they could be damaged by opening and closing doors.
✓ Allow at least 36 in. (91 cm) of counter space in the mixing center.	

CHOOSING CABINETS AND FIXTURES

When planning the layout of a kitchen, you're working mainly with ideas, measurements, and drawings. When you begin shopping for components such as cabinets, countertops, and fixtures, the kitchen in your imagination takes its first steps toward becoming real. Looking over the available choices can be an exciting experience. For lasting satisfaction with kitchen components, be sure to consider their practical aspects as well as their appearance.

Cabinets

Most kitchens include base cabinets and wall cabinets. Base cabinets, which rest on the floor, are usually 24-in. (61-cm) deep. Wall cabinets, placed on the wall above the countertop, are usually 12-in. (30-cm) deep. Standard widths range from 9 in. to 48 in. (23 cm to 122 cm). Cabinets can also be custom made to any size.

When a kitchen is being designed, the color or finish of the cabinets is usually chosen first. This provides a starting place for selecting countertops, floor and wall coverings, and window treatments. Light-toned cabinets give a feeling of spaciousness, whereas dark-toned cabinets create a feeling of warmth and coziness.

Kitchen cabinets can be constructed of hardwood, softwood, plastic laminate, or metal. The most durable cabinets have solid hardwood doors, drawer fronts, and frames. Oak and cherry are popular because of their strength and beauty but are relatively expensive. Particleboard, which costs less, is often used for the sides and shelves. The interiors of all cabinets and drawers should be smooth. They should also have a laminated or lacquered surface for easy cleaning with a damp cloth.

Cabinets are available with many special storage features, such as:

- Cutlery drawers to store knives safely.
- Deep drawers with upright dividers to keep baking pans in order.
- Fold-out pantry units that provide one-item-deep storage.
- Roll-down doors attached to the upper cabinets to hide small appliances from view when they're not being used.
- Corner cabinets with easy-access designs, such as a turntable or hinged pullout racks.

Special storage features in cabinets, such as a pullout pantry spice rack (left), pullout shelves (middle), and dropdown drawer (right) allow kitchen planners to make excellent use of compact spaces.

Countertops

Countertops should be attractive and durable. The ideal countertop material would withstand chopping, grinding, cutting, hot dishes, and stains. Unfortunately, there's no one material with all these features. Figure 24-3 compares several popular countertop materials.

Kitchen Sinks

Sinks and faucets are available in styles, materials, and colors to suit every kitchen design and need. Sinks may be round, square, or oval; be deep or shallow; and have single, double, or triple bowls. Some sinks are designed for special-purpose use, such as cleaning and draining vegetables. Some have a specially fitted cutting board and strainer. Materials used for sinks include stainless steel, porcelain, and acrylic. You may want to review the discussion of fixture materials in Chapter 13.

OTHER KITCHEN DESIGN CONSIDERATIONS

For health and safety, a kitchen needs sufficient electrical circuits and outlets, proper lighting, and good ventilation. Choosing background materials for walls, floors, and window treatments is another aspect of kitchen design.

FIGURE 24-3

Countertop Materials

MATERIAL	Advantages	Disadvantages
PLASTIC LAMINATE	Economical Range of colors Easy to maintain	Scratches easily Scorches easily Difficult to repair
SOLID SURFACE (ACRYLIC OR POLYESTER COMPOUND)	Can be worked into different shapes and integrated sinks Easy to clean Range of colors and stone-like finishes Durable Resists germs and mildew	Can scorch Expensive
WOOD, BUTCHER BLOCK	Good for chopping and slicing	Will spot from spills and water Scorches Germs can breed
CERAMIC TILE	Durable Easy to maintain Resists scratching Resists scorching	Surface can be uneven Objects dropped on it often shatter Grout must be sealed
NATURAL STONE (SUCH AS GRANITE)	Durable Resists stains	Expensive
MARBLE	Good for making pastry or candy	Stains easily Expensive
CONCRETE	Can be worked into different shapes and integrated sinks Range of colors Resists scratching Resists scorching	Stains easily Prone to crumbling and cracking
STAINLESS STEEL	Resists stains Resists scorching Easy to clean Can include an integrated sink	Shows scratches Shows fingerprints Can dent Expensive

ELECTRICAL CIRCUITS AND OUTLETS.
Large kitchen appliances must have electrical circuits separate from the circuits for the rest of the home. Electric ranges, cooktops, ovens, and other heavy-duty appliances each require a separate 240-volt circuit. If extra circuits are included in the circuit panel during installation, additional appliances can be added in the future.

Many small appliances are used in today's kitchens. Ample outlets (receptacles) make using these appliances easier. Spacing between outlets should be approximately 5 ft. to 6 ft. (1.5 m to 1.8 m), never more than 10 ft. (3 m). Local building codes may specify the placement of outlets. To reduce the risk of electrical shock, any outlet near a water source should be equipped with a ground-fault circuit interrupter (GFCI).

LIGHTING. Within a kitchen, various areas have different lighting needs. For example, work centers require bright lights, but an eating area can have softer lighting. Plan the lighting as you draw the floor plan so that the necessary electrical wiring can be installed. You will probably want an overhead light for general lighting, as well as task lighting for the sink, cooktop, and countertop work areas. Refer to Chapter 22 for more information on lighting in the kitchen.

VENTILATION. Steam, odors, and condensation are often a problem in a kitchen. Adequate ventilation can help. Local building codes may establish the type and amount of ventilation required for kitchen equipment.

Ventilation systems are often part of the range. Whenever possible, the range ventilation system should exhaust air to the outdoors through a duct. The most common choice is a *range hood* or *canopy hood* located above the cooktop. Another option, called a *downdraft system*, uses a vent in or near the cooktop itself.

A *recirculating range hood* does not exhaust air to the outdoors, but merely filters it and returns it to the room. This type of range hood is able to remove some smoke, grease, and odors, but has no effect on steam or heat. A recirculating range hood should not be used with a gas cooktop because it doesn't remove combustion gases from the air.

BACKGROUND MATERIALS. The kitchen floor should be easy to maintain, withstand heavy traffic, and complement the rest of the kitchen decor. Options include vinyl, tile, laminate, wood, ceramic tile, and carpet. Select a wall covering that is water- and mildew-resistant, as well as easy to clean. Paint, vinyl-faced wallpaper, plastic laminate sheeting, and ceramic tile are good choices. Also be sure window treatments are easy to clean and, if used near a heat source, nonflammable. See Chapter 19 for more information on floor coverings, wall coverings, and window treatments.

UNIVERSAL DESIGN AND KITCHENS

There are numerous ways to include universal design features in a kitchen so that it's easy for everyone in the family to use—whether they're school-aged children, aging adults, people with vision problems or hearing impairments, or wheelchair users. Figure 24-4 shows some typical adaptations.

Kitchenaid®, a division of Whirlpool

A canopy hood over the cooktop removes steam and heat. Why is it a good idea to choose a hood that also includes a light?

Universal Design Features in Kitchens

Features such as these can help make a kitchen safe and accessible to people of all ages and abilities.

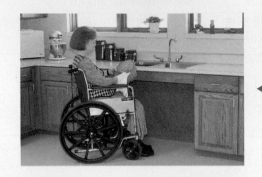

FLOOR PLAN
- Extra-wide doorways and traffic areas.
- Room for a wheelchair user to turn around 180 degrees.
- Enough clear floor space at cabinets, appliances, and work centers for wheelchair users to maneuver.

COUNTERTOPS AND CABINETS
- Counters with rounded edges.
- Color-contrasting borders at the edges of counters.
- Lower and higher counters for people of varying heights.
- A counter on a crank-operated unit that can be raised or lowered to a convenient work height.
- Counter areas without base cabinets, allowing wheelchair accessibility.
- Extra toe space under cabinets for wheelchairs.
- Large, easy-to-grip, D-shaped cabinet pulls.
- Lighting to illuminate cabinet interiors.
- Turntable storage aids.
- Pull-out shelves in base cabinets.
- Pull-down shelves in wall cabinets.
- Safe storage for household chemicals and sharp objects, out of children's reach.

APPLIANCES
- Side-by-side refrigerator/freezer.
- Cooktop, wall oven, and microwave oven lowered to a height convenient for all users.
- Range or cooktop with controls positioned on the side or front.
- Dishwasher installed next to a chair-accessible space.
- Dishwasher raised 9 to 12 inches (23 to 30 cm), or dishwasher drawer substituted, for easy loading and unloading without bending.
- Large, easy-to-read electronic touch-pad control panels.

FIXTURES
- Sink in a motorized unit that can be raised or lowered at the touch of button.
- Single-lever faucets with scald protection.
- Pull-out step under the sink for children to use.

FLOORING
- Nonslip, nonglare flooring.
- Color-contrasting borders on floors near solid obstacles.

Choosing Major Appliances

The cost of appliances often makes the kitchen the most expensive room in the home. When selecting any major appliance, it's important to shop carefully.

APPLIANCE SHOPPING TIPS

The first step when shopping for an appliance is research. Consumer information is available in print or online from many sources, including consumer magazines and product manufacturers. By studying this information, you can find out about available models and their features.

As you do your research, give careful thought to your needs and wants. Which features are most important to you? What is your price range? The answers to these and other questions will help you narrow down the choices when you actually start shopping.

Whether you are reading consumer information or visiting stores, keep the following factors in mind. They are important considerations when buying appliances.

SAFETY. Research the safety features of various models. Look for the Underwriters Laboratories (UL) certification seal on electrical appliances. This seal means that the product has been tested and meets established safety standards. On gas appliances, the seals of the Association of Home Appliance Manufacturers and the American Gas Association also mean that the appliance meets safety and performance standards.

PERFORMANCE. Consumer magazines test products and publish performance ratings. You may decide to pay extra for a model that performs better—for instance, a dishwasher that gets dishes cleaner or tends to need fewer repairs. On the other hand, you may discover a bargain model that performs almost as well as more expensive ones.

ENERGY USE. The more energy an appliance uses, the more it will cost to own. The difference on your monthly utility bill can be significant, especially over the 10- to 20-year life of an appliance. See "Choosing Energy-Efficient Appliances" on page 540 for more information. On the next several pages, you'll read about some of the energy-savings features available for each type of appliance.

Why is it important to consider the energy-efficiency rating of a water heater?

LISTED

The Underwriters Laboratories (UL) certification seal.

Choosing Energy-Efficient Appliances

When buying kitchen and laundry appliances, look for energy-efficient features. You'll save money in the long run and help the environment, too.

- **COMPARE ENERGYGUIDE LABELS.** Manufacturers of refrigerators, freezers, dishwashers, and clothes washers are required by law to include an EnergyGuide label. This label shows the estimated annual energy consumption for that model. It also shows the range, from lowest to highest, of energy consumption for other models. This allows you to compare the efficiency of competing brands and similar models.

- For significantly more energy-efficient appliances, look for those displaying the ENERGY STAR symbol. For more information about the ENERGY STAR program, see Chapter 14, page 314.

Money Isn't All You're Saving

YOU THE CONSUMER . . .

Create a poster or web page design to inform consumers about the advantages of choosing energy-efficient appliances. You may want to include graphs or tables showing how much money a family can save over 15 years and the benefits to the environment. Arrange to display your work in your school, the local library, or neighborhood stores.

SPECIAL FEATURES. Generally, models with more and better features cost more. If no appliance has all the features you want at a price you can afford, you'll need to set priorities.

SIZE. Capacity—how much it can hold—is important for some appliances, such as refrigerators and washing machines. Measure to see whether the appliance will fit through doorways and into the space you plan to put it. Allow clearance for opening the appliance door and for ventilation, if needed.

STYLE. Freestanding and small portable appliances are better choices for a person who moves frequently. Built-in appliances can be expensive to install.

APPEARANCE. Choose appliance colors that will blend well with the walls and cabinets. Neutral colors work well in most color schemes and will allow you to remodel in the future without having to replace the appliances.

PURCHASE PRICE. Compare prices at several retailers to find the best buy. Ask about charges for delivery and installation of the appliance. Check to see if any stores or manufacturers are offering rebates. Some stores offer financing arrangements or special financing rates.

WARRANTY AND REPAIRS. Most appliances come with a *warranty*, which protects you in case the product is defective. Investigate the length and type of warranty offered by the manufacturer or the retailer. What type of service does the store offer? What is the cost of a service call? You can read more about appliance warranties in Chapter 27.

REFRIGERATORS AND FREEZERS

For keeping foods cold, the most common choice is the two-door combination refrigerator-freezer. The freezer compartment may be above, below, or beside the refrigerator compartment.

The recommended size of the refrigerator compartment depends on the number of people in the household. For two people, 16 cu. ft. (0.4 m³) is recommended. Add 1.5 cu. ft. (0.04 m³) for each additional person. Some families may want or need a roomier refrigerator than these guidelines suggest. Generally, the larger the refrigerator, the more energy it uses. The most energy-efficient size is 16 cu. ft. to 20 cu. ft. (0.5 m³ to 0.6 m³).

Modular refrigerators are an alternative to the traditional refrigerator-freezer. Separate drawer-type modules can be placed in convenient locations around the kitchen. The temperature and humidity in each can be adjusted to suit a particular type of food—one module for fresh fruits and vegetables, for example, and another for dairy products and meats.

Separate freezers enable consumers to keep large quantities of frozen foods on hand. These range from large upright or chest-style freezers to smaller models that can be installed under a kitchen counter.

Refrigerators and freezers can be purchased with a variety of special features. Here are some examples:

- An automatic ice maker.
- Ice cube and cold water dispensers on exterior doors.

Some refrigerators include separate compartments for fruits and vegetables that allow the user to set those temperatures separately. Why is this an advantage?

Look for adjustable shelves that allow you to arrange the height according to the items. How are the glass shelves beneficial?

- A self-defrosting freezer. This eliminates the need to remove frost manually that would otherwise build up on the freezer walls and reduce energy efficiency.
- A power-saver switch that can save energy during periods of low humidity.
- Separate compartments with individual temperature controls for fruits and vegetables, cheese, and meats.
- Glass shelves, a feature that prevents dripping to shelves below.
- Deep door compartments that can hold large items such as gallon beverage containers.
- Electronic controls that sound an alert when the door is left open or the unit needs repair.
- Slide-in, microwave-safe containers for storing leftovers.
- A pull-down opening on exterior doors that allows quick access to snacks and beverages. This saves energy by reducing the number of times the main door is opened.
- Movable shelves that crank up or down easily to fit in tall items.
- A built-in touch screen and bar code scanner that keeps track of the household's food inventory and can go online to order items from a local store.

RANGES, COOKTOPS, AND OVENS

Ranges combine surface cooking units and one or more ovens in one appliance. For many years a freestanding range was considered standard equipment, and it's still the most popular choice. Consumers can also choose a drop-in or slide-in range. Both are designed to give a "built-in" look when installed between cabinets.

An alternative to the range is to use two separate, built-in components. A built-in cooktop is installed in a countertop. The area beneath it can be used for storage or left open to accommodate a seated user. A built-in oven is typically installed in a wall, though it may also be installed in a cabinet or island. It may be a single or a double unit. One advantage of separate units is that both the cooktop and the oven can be installed at any convenient height.

Gas or Electric?

Debate continues as to whether gas or electricity is better for cooking.

For surface cooking, many people prefer gas burners because the temperature can be adjusted instantly and precisely. However, electricity is often preferred for oven cooking because it keeps the temperature more even and is a safer heat source for children and older adults. To get the best of both options, you might choose a gas cooktop and an electric wall oven. Energy cost is another consideration. On the average, a gas appliance costs less than half as much to operate as an electric one, provided the gas appliance has electronic ignition instead of a pilot light. Check with a local utility company for a comparison of gas and electric costs in your area.

Types of Surface Cooking Units

The different types of surface cooking units vary in cost, heating characteristics, and type of cookware that can be used. Before making a selection, find out as much as you can about the options currently available. Here are some points to consider.

Cooktops come in many configurations to suit a cook's preference. Some may choose fewer burners combined with a built-in grill while another cook may like the option of more easy-to-clean burners. Microwave ovens meet the needs of today's on-the-go families.

- Gas burners or electric coils are standard on many cooking units.
- Sealed gas burners are easier to clean than standard burners but are less energy efficient.
- Smooth cooktops are made of glass-ceramic. When not in use, they provide extra work space. The heating elements, which are below the surface, may be gas burners, electric coils, induction coils, or halogen lamps.
- Halogen elements and induction elements are more energy efficient than conventional electric coils. Solid disk elements and smooth cooktops using electric coils are less efficient.
- Modular cooktops can be customized with interchangeable units, such as grills, griddles, rotisseries, steamers, and woks.

Types of Ovens

Several types of ovens are available, each with its own cooking characteristics. Many kitchens have more than one oven. If a range or wall oven has two separate oven compartments, they may be of different types.

CONVENTIONAL. A conventional oven uses gas or electricity to heat the air in the oven compartment. Some gas ranges also have a separate broiler compartment. With electric ovens and most self-cleaning gas ovens, broiling is done in the oven compartment.

CONVECTION. A convection oven is similar to a conventional electric oven but uses fans to circulate heated air over the food. As a result, heat is more evenly distributed and food cooks more quickly.

MICROWAVE. In a microwave oven, tiny waves of energy cause food molecules to vibrate against each other. The resulting friction creates heat within the food. The cooking power of a microwave oven is measured in watts. The higher the wattage, the faster the food will cook. Microwave ovens cook much faster than conventional ones, but they are not as effective at browning foods.

HALOGEN. In this type of oven, powerful halogen lights cook in about one-fourth the time of a conventional oven. Halogen ovens are generally higher priced than conventional ovens.

RAPID COOK. A rapid-cook oven uses a combination of convection or conventional heat and microwave energy to cook food much faster than a conventional oven. Rapid-cook ovens can bake, broil, roast, and toast foods. These ovens are more expensive than conventional or convection ovens.

COMBINATION. Ovens are available that can be used for more than one type of cooking, such as conventional/convection or halogen/microwave.

Other Features

Special features are available on many ranges, cooktops, and ovens. Consumers must weigh the added convenience or energy savings against the extra cost of appliances with these features. Here are some examples:

- Self-cleaning or continuous-cleaning ovens. Because it has better insulation, a self-cleaning oven uses less energy for cooking than one without a cleaning feature. If you use the self-cleaning feature more than once a month, though, you'll end up using more energy than you save.
- Other features for easy cleanup, such as a lift-up cooktop, removable knobs, and a removable oven door.
- Electronic ignition on gas ranges and cooktops. This feature eliminates the need for a continuously burning pilot light, saving energy.
- Electronic touch controls.
- Programmable ovens that can start cooking at a preset time and shut off automatically. Some let you store frequently used settings in memory and activate them at the touch of a button.
- A warming drawer to keep foods warm until served.

DISHWASHERS

Dishwashers are available in both built-in and portable models, with a variety of wash and temperature cycles. Portable dishwashers can be transported easily. They are ideal for renters and people who move frequently. However, they must be wheeled to the sink and connected to the faucet before each use. Built-in dishwashers free the sink for other activities while the dishwasher is in operation. They make less noise than portable models because the surrounding cabinets act as sound barriers.

Some dishwashers sanitize the dishes, eliminating household bacteria. Look for certification by National Sanitation Foundation to select a sanitizing dishwasher.

Many people believe that dishwashers waste heat and water. Actually, they conserve energy. They use less hot water than washing dishes by hand. Newer model dishwashers use as little as 4 gal. (15 L) of water and have a water preheater that adds further to the energy savings. You can store a day's worth of dishes in a dishwasher and wash them at night, when energy rates are often lower. Many models have an energy-saving switch that permits dishes to be dried by air rather than heat.

Drawer-type dishwashers are installed like drawers in a cabinet. These units use energy and water efficiently. A pair of dishwasher drawers can be run independently for small loads or together for large loads. When the drawers are placed just under the counter, a person does not need to bend down to load and unload dishes.

DISPOSAL UNITS

Disposal units provide a quick and convenient way to eliminate waste. They are installed beneath the sink, where they are connected to the drain. They grind up food scraps so the particles can be flushed down the drain.

A continuous-feed disposal is turned on and off by a switch mounted on the wall. Scraps are added as the disposal is operated. Batch-feed disposals grind scraps a batch at a time. They are operated by turning or pushing a drain stopper. This type may cost less to install and is safer to use.

WASHING MACHINES

Washing machines wash, rinse, and spin-dry clothes automatically. Most have controls that adjust the speed of agitation from delicate to heavy-duty, the temperature of the water from hot to cold, and the water level from very low to full. Some washers feature extra-large-capacity tubs. Machines are also available with automatic dispensers that add soap, bleach, and fabric softener.

Dishwasher drawers offer space-saving features and allow users to wash just a few dishes without wasting energy and water. Why does this type of dishwasher work well in a universal-design kitchen?

A stacked clothes washer and dryer allow homeowners to locate these appliances in a small, yet convenient space.

Many washers have energy-saving features. One example is separate controls for wash and rinse temperatures. Another is a suds-saver feature, which saves the wash water from lightly soiled loads for reuse. For even greater energy efficiency, you may want to choose a horizontal-axis washing machine. It's described on page 319 in Chapter 14.

Computer technology enables the most sophisticated and expensive machines to be programmed in advance for different types of loads. To carry out the cycle, the user merely has to press one button.

CLOTHES DRYERS

Gas dryers are less expensive to operate than electric dryers. All dryers have time and temperature controls. Some have an energy-saving feature called "electronic sensor drying." This feature enables the machine to measure, or "feel," the degree of moistness in the clothes and shut itself off when clothes are dry. An electronic ignition on gas dryers eliminates the need for a continuous pilot light.

Most dryers feature an automatic cool-down period. This feature is especially useful for permanent-press clothes. At the end of the cycle, the clothes continue to tumble for a timed interval with the heat off. This makes them more comfortable to handle and reduces wrinkles. Some dryers feature a removable rack that permits tennis shoes, stuffed toys, and wet mittens to be dried without tumbling.

SPACE-SAVING LAUNDRY APPLIANCES

Several options make it possible to fit a laundry center in a small space. For instance, a stacked washer and dryer can be used. This unit has a full-sized, top-loading washer on the bottom with a dryer stacked on top.

Washer-dryer combinations are also available. The user puts in clothes, chooses the settings, and comes back to clean, dry clothes. Small combination units can fit under a counter or in a closet.

Another solution is a portable washer and dryer. Portable washers are filled and drained at the sink. Small, portable dryers plug into any standard electric outlet and require no special wiring or venting.

Planning Laundry Areas

Many homes have laundry areas. They range from a closet just big enough to hold a washer and dryer to a separate room large enough to also be used for sewing and crafts.

CHOOSING A LOCATION

A laundry center can be located in almost any part of the home that provides these basic requirements:

- Hot and cold water supply lines and drains. To reduce the cost of construction or remodeling, choose an area near existing plumbing lines. If possible, provide a floor drain beneath the washer in case it overflows or the hoses leak.

- A 240-volt electrical outlet for an electric dryer, or a gas line for a gas dryer.
- Proper ventilation for the dryer's exhaust system. This can be achieved by locating the laundry near an outside wall.

A laundry area is often located on the main floor near a side, back, or garage entrance. The area can double as a mud room for removing dirty or wet garments and footwear before entering the home.

The kitchen can be a convenient location for a laundry center. The person washing clothes can do other household tasks at the same time. However, soiled clothes shouldn't be handled in the same area where food is prepared. A closet off the kitchen may be a good option. Folding doors can hide the laundry equipment when not in use.

Another possible laundry location is in or near a bathroom or sleeping area. This might be a step saver, since these are areas where most soiled clothes and linens are collected. One drawback to a sleeping-area location is that laundry equipment is noisy. Doing laundry will need to be limited to times when people are not sleeping. Insulation in interior walls can help mask the noise of laundry equipment.

A basement laundry room is yet another option. This keeps soiled clothing and linen, as well as the noise of the washer and dryer, away from living areas. However, a basement location is less convenient. In addition, basements are sometimes damp, which promotes the growth of mold and mildew on items stored for a long time.

At one time, washing machines and dryers were kept out of sight in the basement. Many of today's homes include laundry rooms on the main floor. Why is this an advantage?

PLANNING FOR EFFICIENCY

Activities associated with laundering include storing soiled clothes and linens, washing, drying, sorting, folding, and ironing. All of these tasks can be easier when you have the right equipment and the space is arranged in an orderly manner. When planning a new or redesigned laundry area, include as many of the following features as possible.

- A washable floor covering.
- Proper lighting that does not create shadows over the washer or dryer.
- Storage space for detergent and other laundry supplies.
- Baskets, bins, or carts for sorting and carrying laundry.
- A sink near the washing machine for hand laundering or presoaking stains.

- A clothesline or rod for line drying.
- Horizontal racks for drying items flat.
- A rod or hooks for hanging items as they are removed from the dryer.
- A countertop or other flat surface for folding laundry.
- Space to set up an ironing board near an electrical outlet. When not in use, the board can be hung on the wall or on the back of a door. Another option is an ironing board that folds into its own cabinet built into the wall.

UNIVERSAL DESIGN AND LAUNDRY AREAS

In keeping with the philosophy of universal design, laundry areas can be planned to accommodate a variety of individual needs. Some compact washers are only 32 in. (81 cm) high, with the controls mounted on the front. They are easy to use from a seated position. A dryer door that swings to the side, rather than down, provides easier access for wheelchair users. Placing the dryer on a platform reduces the need to bend or stoop while loading and unloading. People with limited vision appreciate easy-to-read controls with an audible tone that signals when clothes are dry or when the dryer's lint screen needs cleaning. Braille control panel overlays and instruction books are available for some models of washers and dryers. Lowering the work table or counter and leaving open space underneath will accommodate seated users. As in the kitchen, provide single-lever controls for faucets and D-shaped handles on storage cabinet doors.

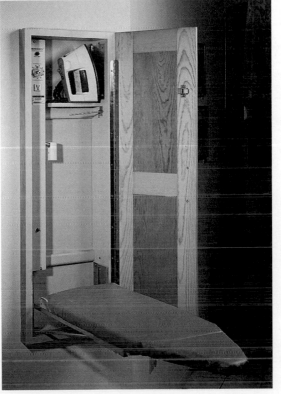

This ironing board can be folded up and tucked away when it is not needed. What other efficient features would you add to a laundry area?

*P*lanning Bathrooms

Although a typical home has only one kitchen and laundry area, most have more than one bathroom. Bathrooms may range from small and basic to large, multipurpose spaces. Adding or remodeling a bath is a common home improvement project. Whether you're planning a remodeling project or a new home, give careful consideration to bathroom design.

Many newer or remodeled homes include a **master bath**, a full bath that is part of the master bedroom area. It often borrows design elements from the adjoining master bedroom. A large master bath can serve as a relaxing retreat or an exercise studio.

Locating a bathroom close to existing drainage pipes reduces construction costs. If that location is unsatisfactory, however, the best long-term solution may be to spend the money for pipe work and locate the bathroom where it will be most convenient.

PLANNING THE SIZE AND LOCATION

Bathrooms are identified as full, three-quarter, or half-baths, depending on the number of basic fixtures included. A *full bath* has a minimum of a sink, a toilet, and a bathtub. The term *three-quarter bath* often refers to a bathroom with a sink, a toilet, and a shower, but no tub. A *half-bath,* or powder room, contains only a sink and a toilet.

If a home has only one bathroom, it should be a full or three-quarter bath located off a main hallway. If there is more than one bathroom, the most common arrangement is to locate at least one full bath in or near the sleeping area and a half-bath near the living area.

Many newer homes have a master bath that is an extension of the master bedroom. The bathroom is often designed specifically to meet the needs and tastes of the homeowner.

The bathroom might also be positioned to provide a sound barrier between quieter and noisier parts of the home. For example, when placed between a family room and a bedroom, it can help prevent noisy activities in the family room from disturbing sleep. Insulating bathroom walls can help provide a sound barrier.

When making a bathroom floor plan, design and measure the layout carefully. Once fixtures have been installed, they're expensive and difficult to move. Allow enough space in the bathroom for safety and comfort. Check local building codes for minimum dimensions and other requirements. Consider whether more than one person at a time might want to use the bathroom to get ready for school or work. If so, you may want to include two sinks and perhaps partitions to separate different areas.

SELECTING FIXTURES AND CABINETS

Much of a bathroom's decor is determined by the fixtures and cabinets chosen. Fixtures come in many colors and may be made of porcelain enamel, china, stainless steel, or prefabricated plastic. Chapter 13 provides more information on these choices. You may also want to review the discussion of water-saving fixtures in Chapter 14.

Bathtubs

Bathtubs may be rectangular, square, round, or oval. They are usually enclosed by walls on three sides. However, there are exceptions. Freestanding tubs with ball-and-claw feet are sometimes chosen for a Victorian look. Tubs may also be sunken into the floor or built into

a platform anywhere in the room. Whirlpool bathtubs include water jets for massaging muscles.

For safety, some bathtubs are equipped with nonskid bottoms and grab bars. Both safety and comfort can be enhanced with a soft bathtub. This type of tub, made from the same tough plastic as automobile bumpers, becomes more cushioned when hot water is added. It has a high-density foam core that helps insulate the heat, improving energy efficiency.

Showers

Installing a shower head above the bathtub creates a *tub shower*. A walk-in *stall shower* is another alternative. A compact stall shower is a good solution for a small bathroom.

This bathtub is built-in and encased with tile, which also protects the bathroom wall. Many people find that plants do well in the humidity of the bathroom and provide a pleasant atmosphere.

One-piece shower units made of molded plastic are an easy way to add a new shower to a bathroom. Another option for shower walls is tile. The disadvantage of tile is that the grout must be kept in good condition or the walls will leak.

The shower head may be fixed in position on the wall, adjustable, or handheld. Some shower units have multiple spray heads. Instead of a shower curtain, sliding panels or a swinging door may be used to keep water inside the shower area. Shower doors are usually made of safety glass or plastic and may be patterned to provide greater privacy.

Toilets

Toilets can be mounted on the wall or on the floor. The water tank may be above the bowl (high-line) or at the same level (low-line). In some models, the tank and bowl form a single unit.

Building codes in some states require new or replacement toilets to be *ultra low flush* (ULF) models. These use no more than 1.6 gal. (6.1 L) per flush, as compared to older toilets that used as much as 5 gal. (19 L) per flush.

Bathroom Sinks

Bathroom sinks—also called washbasins and lavatories—come in several different styles.

- A *wall-hung* sink has open space beneath, which helps make a small bathroom seem roomier.
- A *pedestal sink* is supported by a freestanding base. Many pedestal sinks are artfully shaped, giving them a look of sculpture.
- An *inset sink* is set into a countertop. The cabinet beneath provides storage.

- An *above-counter basin* looks like a decorative wash bowl set on the counter. The plumbing extends down through the counter.

The standard height for bathroom sinks is approximately 32 in. (81 cm) from floor to rim. Placing the sink at this height makes it especially convenient for children and people who use a wheelchair.

This appears to be a decorative wash bowl, but it is actually an above-counter basin with the plumbing hidden in the decorative cabinet.

Cabinets and Countertops

Like kitchens, bathrooms may include wall and base cabinets. A base cabinet in a bathroom is called a **vanity**. It conceals sink pipes as well as provides counter space and storage. (You can read more about bathroom storage in Chapter 25.) Materials used for vanity tops include marble, plastic laminate, solid surface, enameled cast iron, and fiberglass.

OTHER CONSIDERATIONS

To be safe and efficient, bathrooms, like kitchens, require a certain degree of technical planning. When designing a new bathroom or remodeling an old one, think about the following considerations.

ELECTRICAL OUTLETS. Bathrooms may require several electrical outlets to accommodate personal appliances, such as hair dryers, curling irons, electric shavers, radios, and clocks. Any outlet near a water source should be equipped with a ground-fault circuit interrupter (GFCI).

LIGHTING. For safety, bathroom lights should be wall or ceiling mounted and operated with wall switches. A lamp knocked into the bathtub or sink could cause a fatal shock. Chapter 22 provides more information about bathroom lighting.

VENTILATION. Steam from a hot bath or shower causes condensation to form on mirrors and walls. Without proper ventilation, wallpaper will start to peel and mildew will grow.

The best solution is an exhaust fan that vents to the outside.

FLOOR AND WALL COVERINGS. Choose a floor covering that will not be slippery when wet and that can be cleaned easily. Avoid flooring that is damaged by water or shows water spots. Vinyl and tile are popular choices. As in the kitchen, select a mildew-resistant, easy-to-clean wall covering.

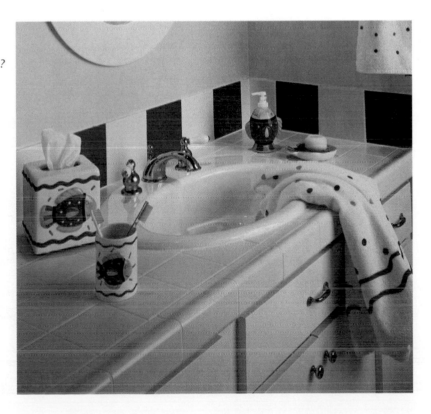

A vanity provides extra storage in a bathroom to avoid clutter on the counter as well as conceal the plumbing. What are other ways to add extra storage in a bathroom?

UNIVERSAL DESIGN AND BATHROOMS

When designing a bathroom, remember the varying abilities of people who may use it now or in the future. To make a bathroom accessible to everyone, consider these universal design features:

- Wide doorway and extra floor space.
- Grab bars placed near toilets and tubs.

- Elevated toilet seat added to a standard toilet.
- Shower with a seat.
- Shower doors that retract and pivot for easy access.
- No-sill, doorless shower stall and rolling shower chair.
- Hand-held shower head.
- Single-lever shower controls.
- Barrier-free sink with the faucet toward the front and a side drain that places the pipes away from the user's knees.

- Tiltable mirror at the sink.
- Faucet with a retractable spray handle to allow shampooing from a chair.
- Low counter for access by seated users or young children.

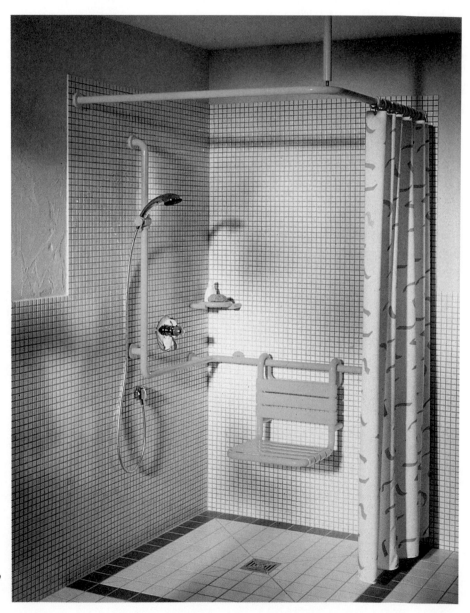

A no-sill, doorless shower allows access to people with impaired mobility.

Low-Cost Updates

You can improve the appearance of a kitchen, laundry area, or bathroom without major remodeling. One or more of the following suggestions may provide just the right decorative touch.

- Hire a professional to repaint appliances or put a new porcelain coating on fixtures. Both are much less expensive than replacement.
- Instead of installing new cabinets, paint or refinish the existing ones, or replace just the cabinet doors and fronts.

- Brighten up the room by replacing hardware such as cabinet knobs and handles, towel bars, and faucets.
- To change the color scheme or add an accent color, use towels, throw rugs, a shower curtain, and window treatments.

- Choose a coordinated set of accessories that harmonizes with the room's style. Add interesting accents such as baskets or candles.

You can get a new look at a reasonable cost by redecorating a kitchen or bathroom. Wallpaper is an excellent option for providing a bright change. What type of wallpaper is best for a kitchen or bathroom?

Kitchen Planner

Yvette Allen

I frequently hear homeowners and renters complain that the kitchen is not "right." It's too small to move about when cooking, the appliances or cabinets are in the wrong places, or there is no place to gather for coffee and conversation. Other rooms may be spacious and well designed; but if the kitchen doesn't meet the tastes and needs of those who use it, the house scores low on the livability scale.

> *"Whenever possible, I follow the principles of universal design: plan a kitchen for people of all physical abilities and ages."*

I'm a kitchen planner; I design kitchens that are attractive and practical for the people who use them—including people with special needs. Whenever possible, I follow the principles of universal design: plan a kitchen for people of all physical abilities and ages. If a person has a weak grasp, I might fit the range controls with enlarged soft covers and attach wide plastic loops to door and drawer handles. For a person with a disability, a usable kitchen can open up a whole world of independence and capability.

A thorough knowledge of kitchen design principles is a given requirement in my job, along with a working knowledge of basic construction, ventilation, and local building codes. In addition, I need to keep up with the latest trends in home appliances and fixtures, ergonomics, and even cooking methods. It helps to have an artistic eye, and I can't imagine succeeding as a kitchen designer without knowing how to use CAD programs for planning!

Each job begins with a meeting with the family to find out their schedules, habits, and preferences. This helps me determine the kitchen's traffic patterns and the work area requirements. Together we come up with a plan to fit their unique lifestyle—for example,

whether children play a part in preparing meals or whether there is a gourmet cook who combines cooking with entertaining quests. Last year I even designed a professional baking center for a woman who wanted to run a business from her kitchen.

I apply the same principles and give my best effort to all clients, regardless of how much money they want to spend. Budget, nevertheless, is a determining factor. Modest budgets require a special kind of creativity. I concentrate on useful, good quality appliances and fixtures and a few well-chosen decorative elements, using designer tricks like revolving shelving devices to store contents of cabinets. In one small home I was able to convert inexpensively a closet into a pantry area to store food and extend the kitchen. As you can imagine, designing a kitchen to fit a restrictive budget keeps my math skills sharp.

"Each job begins with a meeting with the family to find out their schedules, habits, and preferences."

Preparing and sharing meals with family and friends is a wonderful part of life; people should enjoy that to the fullest. I'm proud to say that my work makes a meaningful contribution to that goal.

Career Profile

A *kitchen planner* works with clients to develop an attractive, practical, and efficient kitchen that fits their tastes and needs. This includes being able to design kitchens for people with special needs. The kitchen planner will assist clients in determining the most useful fixtures and appliances and the most efficient way of organizing them. The kitchen planner needs to be informed on current appliance design and new cooking techniques. A kitchen planner also needs to know building regulations and have an understanding of electrical and ventilation systems. Of course the final design must remain within the client's budget. Kitchen planners utilize CAD (computer-aided design) programming to allow the client to visualize the final product before the work begins. Status as a Certified Kitchen Designer (CKD) may be attained after seven years of training.

Education
▸ A minimum of an associate's degree is required.
▸ Some companies require a degree in Interior Design.
▸ After seven years of training, an individual can become a Certified Kitchen Designer (CKD).

Skills Needed
▸ Knowledge of construction and building codes is necessary.
▸ Must be computer literate, with knowledge of CAD.
▸ Creativity and a good eye for color and balance are essential.

Career Outlook
▸ Employment outlook is good but can fluctuate with changes in the economy.
▸ More employment opportunities can arise with the building of new homes and the remodeling of older homes.

Career Activities
1. Interview a family member or neighbor about any likes and dislikes of his or her kitchen. Create a kitchen design based on the available space and your "client's" needs. Prepare a presentation of your design including a brief summary of the interview with your client.
2. Look through print and online resources to find the latest kitchen technology. Create an idea file that you can share with others. Write a brief description of each item explaining why a homeowner may want to choose it.

Chapter Summary

➤ A well-designed kitchen is based on the needs of the family, has work centers for specific tasks, and is arranged efficiently.

➤ Cabinets, countertops, and fixtures should be chosen with their practical aspects in mind.

➤ Electrical outlets, lighting, and ventilation are important considerations.

➤ Universal design features can help make kitchens, laundry areas, and bathrooms easier for everyone to use.

➤ Before selecting appliances, research the available choices.

➤ Laundry rooms and bathrooms should be conveniently located.

➤ The right equipment and arrangement of space can make a laundry room more efficient.

Checking Your Understanding

1. Name two appliances or tools you would find in each of the three basic kitchen work centers.

2. Define *work triangle* and describe its ideal characteristics.

3. Compare the ventilation needs of a kitchen, laundry area, and bathroom.

4. Give an example of a specific lighting or electrical need in a kitchen, a laundry area, and a bathroom.

5. Why is it important to consider energy efficiency when shopping for appliances?

6. What is the difference between a conventional oven and a convection oven?

7. Name four possible locations for the laundry room in a home.

8. Identify three features that make a laundry room more efficient.

9. What features help make it possible for two people to efficiently use a bathroom at the same time?

10. Describe four styles of bathroom sinks and name an advantage of each.

11. Identify three features that make a bathroom more accessible for someone who uses a wheelchair.

Thinking Critically

1. What problems might result if a kitchen does not have an efficient work triangle and well-planned work centers?

2. Kitchen remodeling is one of the most common alterations new owners make to old houses. Why?

3. What features in a laundry area would encourage children to launder their own clothes? What safety features would be needed?

4. How might the concept of kitchen work centers apply to the design of bathrooms?

Review & Activities CHAPTER 24

Applications

1. **Work Triangle Analysis.** Take measurements in an actual kitchen or obtain a scale drawing of a kitchen floor plan. Determine the distances between the sink, the range or cooktop, and the refrigerator. Compare the results to the ideal dimensions of the work triangle. Assess the efficiency of the kitchen's layout. What improvements can you suggest?

2. **Appliance Sales Presentation.** Choose a kitchen or laundry appliance. Make a poster, graphic aid, or web page design illustrating the various styles and features available. Use brochures from appliance dealers, newspaper advertisements, or information from the Internet to help you. Using your finished work, make a sales presentation to your class.

3. **Laundry Room Design.** Create a plan for a laundry room. It should provide for doing basic laundry tasks efficiently and incorporate at least five universal design features. Sketch the floor plan. Provide a description of the size and type of appliances and the features that make the laundry room efficient and accessible.

4. **Bathroom Design.** Design a master bathroom that emphasizes comfort and relaxation. Research products and design options using print or Internet resources. Sketch the floor plan and describe the fixtures, flooring, and accessories you would choose.

BUILDING YOUR PORTFOLIO

Your firm, Innovative Kitchen Planners, has been hired by the Perez family to help them plan how to remodel their kitchen. You have been asked to work with them. There are two school-age children in the family. Ms. Perez does not work outside the home. She does part-time tailoring in her home and makes most of her children's clothes. Mr. Perez is a pastry chef who enjoys testing new recipes at home. Their family room is adjacent to the kitchen, so they would like a kitchen that allows them to engage in their separate tasks and still be near each other. Plan a kitchen that will accommodate all members of the family. Prepare a written summary of your plan. Include sketches, photos, or illustrations to explain your ideas.

558

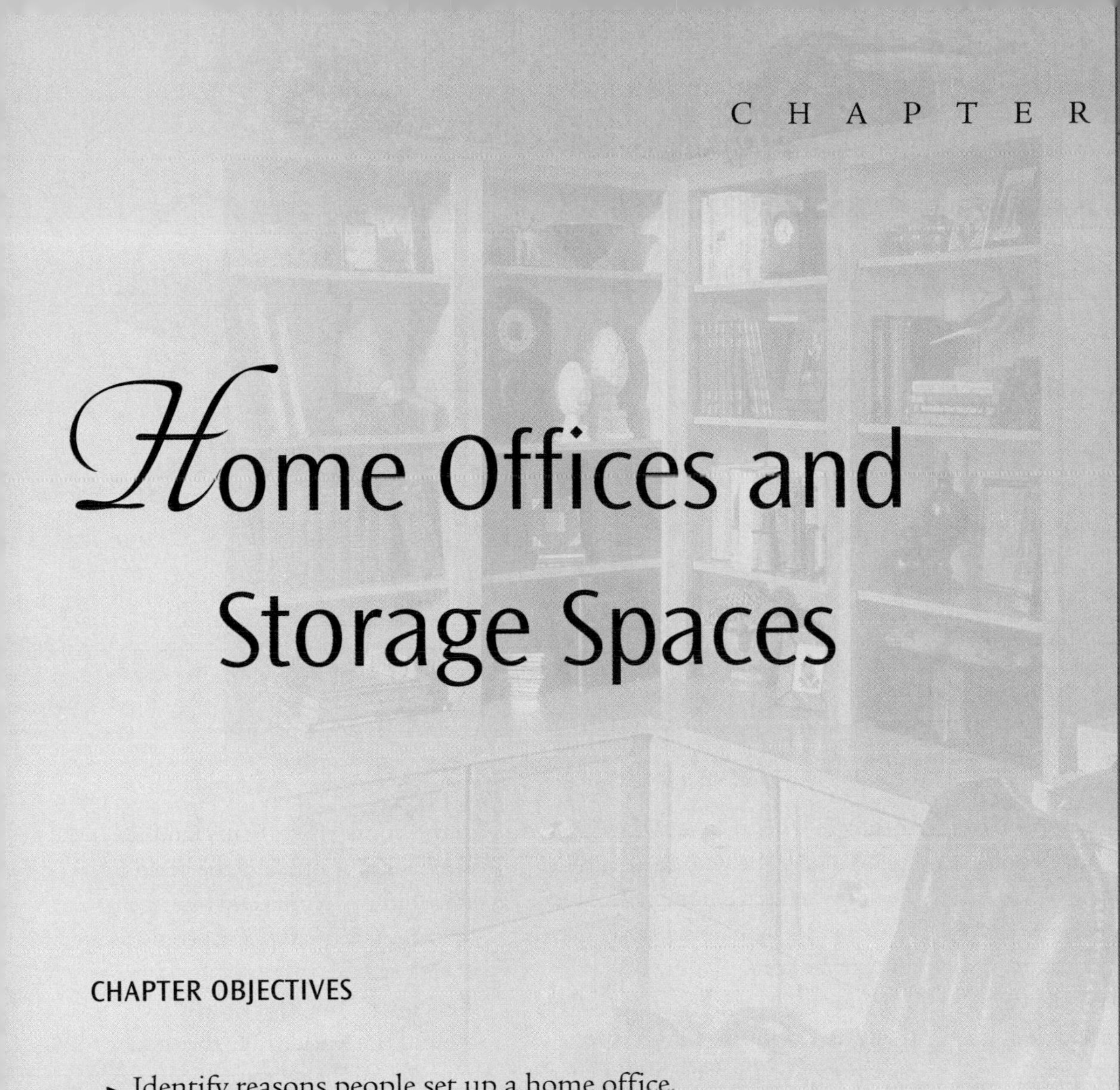

Home Offices and Storage Spaces

CHAPTER OBJECTIVES

▶ Identify reasons people set up a home office.

▶ Describe considerations for choosing a location for a home office.

▶ Explain guidelines for arranging work zones in a home office.

▶ Identify ergonomic features of office furniture

▶ Create an efficient plan for storing possessions in the home.

▶ Describe a process for organizing a closet.

TERMS TO LEARN

- closed storage

- ergonomics

- open storage

- telecommuter

Imagine that you have the opportunity to work from your home. How will you create a comfortable and productive work environment? You have also been wanting to make better use of storage space to help reduce clutter in your home. This chapter will help you make efficient use of the space, fit in your new home office, and make your home more livable.

*H*ome Offices

The dream of working at home has turned into reality for many people. There are millions of home office workers and the numbers continue to grow. Many home workers are telecommuters, also called teleworkers. **Telecommuters** are people authorized by their employers to work from home using computers, modems, fax machines, and teleconferencing equipment to handle their work responsibilities. Telecommuters are accustomed to accessing all the information they need from their company via computer connections. Some companies require telecommuters to come into the office for scheduled meetings or work in the office one day a week. Other home office workers are entrepreneurs who run their own businesses from their homes.

There are many advantages to working at home. Long commutes no longer eat up extra hours of the day. At-home workers often manage their own schedules, and they get to spend more time with their families. The downside of a home office for some people is that they never get away from work.

Home office workers also find they are responsible for all aspects of running an office. They are in charge of creating their own productive work environment. They need to make careful plans to ensure they create the best surroundings for their work.

USES FOR A HOME OFFICE

How do you get started creating a home office? First, consider all its uses. Not every home office is used by an entrepreneur or telecommuter. There are millions of employees who have created a space that serves as an after-hours extension of their business office. Students often do homework in the home office. Some families use the home office as the place to store family records and manage finances and bills. Many people use a work station to access the Internet and e-mail family and friends around the world. Take the time to consider all the potential uses for the space to prepare the best plan.

LOCATION

Where should a home office be located? That depends on what type of work will be done there and what space is available. Almost any room can be converted to an office or rearranged to include one. Home offices range from a corner of the family room to an entire room. If the space is to be used only occasionally, a 2-ft. x 5-ft. (0.6-m x 1.5-m) space provides enough room for a work area and filing space. For example, a section of a bedroom could be used with freestanding panels to separate the work area from the rest of the room. Sometimes an extra wide hallway, storage space under a stairwell, or a closet can be converted to a functional, small office space.

For someone who works full-time at home, though, a larger, professional work space is needed. The perfect space is a separate room that encourages creativity and productivity. With a separate space, the home worker can keep business materials and equipment all in one place to promote maximum efficiency. Setting aside a room strictly for business also helps separate home activities from work activities.

For families who need a home office in order to manage finances or do homework, an efficiently organized space in a corner of a room will be adequate. How has the use of laptop computers changed the look of home offices?

When the home office is the full-time work environment for an entrepreneur or telecommuter, a space designated specifically as a home office is a requirement.

One essential first step for someone planning to work full-time at home is to check the zoning laws that affect the location. Zoning laws may restrict the types of businesses that can be run from a home, particularly if clients will be visiting the home.

Today, more new homes are being designed to include space for a home office. Often, the office space has a separate outdoor entrance.

When an existing home is used, adding a separate office usually means using existing space for a new purpose. If a quiet area is needed, choose a room with a door that's away from the main activity of the home. An extra bedroom is often the first choice. A bedroom usually has closet space for storage and windows to let in natural light. Other options include converting a seldom-used dining room, finished basement, loft, attic, or part of a garage.

Designing a Home Office

Once the space for the home office is chosen, the next step is developing a design plan. The daily activities required to do the work, as well as the worker's habits, needs, and personality, need to be considered. Some workers like to keep things out of sight and have a clean workspace. Others prefer to have items displayed and spread out.

Jamar Adkins, an interior designer, is starting his own company and will work out of his home. He begins the design process, as he would with a client, by listing all the activities he does in an average day.

He uses his computer for developing design plans and doing paperwork. While designing, he spreads out brochures and samples of items he wants to incorporate in his design. In addition, Jamar has a library of reference books and files of samples and product brochures plus business records. He also keeps backup computer disks of all of his work. Jamar meets with clients in their homes and businesses, so he doesn't need a conference table in his office.

As Jamar analyzes his list, he divides it into zones of activity,

much like a kitchen is divided into work centers. Activities that are done most often will be assigned the primary work space. In Jamar's office, this includes the computer zone and the work station zone where he spreads out samples and designs. The library zone consists of the brochures, samples, and photos that Jamar uses frequently. These need to be placed in an active storage area that is easily accessible. His reference books are used less often, so they are placed in a bookcase just outside the primary work area. A file cabinet holds business-related papers. Materials that he uses less often and his backup computer disks are placed on shelves in the closet.

PLAN THE SPACE

One benefit of a home office is the opportunity to create a space that both feels comfortable and works well for the person using it. Most people want their office to be both efficient and have a personal touch.

Just as a living room or family room is decorated to suit a person's lifestyle, a home office can be, too. When developing a design plan for an office space, consider the individual's personality as well as work habits.

Before filling the room with furniture, you need to decide how to arrange the space. As with designing any other room, the place to start is to measure the area carefully and make a graph paper or computer floor plan. Next, measure any existing furniture and equipment that will be used. If additional pieces will be needed, visit office stores and consult catalogs to find out what is available. Then, start to match activities with equipment, workspace, and storage so you can decide what additional items may be needed. Try out different arrangements on your floor plan.

Here are some guidelines for designing home offices:

- Keep the activity zones in mind and plan how to arrange furniture and equipment into different centers of operation.
- Arrange the main work area in an L-shape or U-shape. Start with the desk or work surface and determine placement of the computer work station, bookcase, and filing cabinets. If the computer station is where most of the work is done, start with that. A compact L-shape work zone takes about 5 ft. (1.5 m) on one wall and 6 ft. (1.8 m) along another. Place a swivel chair in the middle so that by turning or rolling slightly, everything is within reach. If the room is carpeted, put a plastic pad under the chair.
- When seated, the computer, telephone, and a file cabinet should be within easy reach.

- Plan for plenty of work surface. A desk should be at least 24 in. (61 cm) deep and a minimum of 36 in. (91 cm) wide.
- Strive to create an ergonomic work space. **Ergonomics** is an applied science concerned with designing and arranging things so that they are safe, comfortable, and efficient for people to use. An easy rule of thumb is that an ergonomic work environment is an adjustable one that facilitates frequent changes of body position and avoids eye-straining glare from light sources.
- Use vertical space. For example, tall, narrow bookcases can hold many things without taking up much floor space. Consider a rolling filing cabinet that can be stored under the desk. A corner bookcase can optimize wasted space.
- Be sure to plan for enough storage space. Figure out how to put in as many cabinets, cubbyholes, and storage units as possible without overcrowding the space. No matter how organized workers are, they always need more storage space than they think. Don't forget about storage space for paper, pens, office supplies, research materials, and other work tools.
- Store similar items together. Put most frequently used items in a handy place, such as on the middle bookshelves. Put less frequently used items in less convenient places or in another room.

SELECT OFFICE FURNITURE

Few people have an unlimited budget for a new home office. Most people just starting out aren't able to do everything they would like at once. As with other rooms, it's helpful to make a master plan, then decide what basics are needed now and which items can be added later. A basic office setup usually includes a desk or writing surface, a computer area, a chair, a filing cabinet, and shelving for books and references.

There are choices for every budget and for every type of space. An unused table might function as a work surface. A desk can be made by placing a flat door on top of two filing cabinets. Many companies lease furniture, as well as computer equipment. Leasing can be a viable solution for outfitting a business without putting out a lot of money all at once.

Office furniture comes in a variety of styles from ultramodern steel to classic oak. No matter what style is preferred, there are a few points to keep in mind. A computer station needs to be ergonomically designed with adjustable sections for a keyboard, mouse, and monitor. Correct placement of the components helps prevent fatigue and other problems.

An ergonomically designed office system allows the user to make adjustments to fit his or her needs for comfort and efficiency. What ergonomic features can you identify in this office?

Another space-saving technique is to select pieces that serve more than one function. For example, a low filing cabinet could also serve as a computer printer stand. Some desks come with an optional shelving unit at the back. What other multiuse options can you think of?

Adjust the top of the monitor so it is slightly lower than eye level. Place the keyboard directly in front of the user and at a height that keeps the wrists relaxed but not bent. Some desks feature legs that allow the user to adjust the height. Choose a desk with enough space to work effectively. Some come with built-in drawers; others are open. Keep overall storage needs in mind when deciding which option is best.

Modular furniture makes it easy to rearrange the office. Many furniture manufacturers offer office systems that create a "mix and match" plan. A person starts out with the basic plan and adds new pieces as the budget allows. Modular furniture is available in both modern and traditional styles.

For people who plan on moving or adding to an office, modular furniture is the answer. They can start out by buying a few pieces and easily add on as their needs and budget grow.

The most important part of a home office is a good chair. It is worth paying a little more to get an ergonomic design. An ergonomically designed chair is one that has a contoured backrest, a seat that is dense enough to hold a person's weight, adjustable arms, and adjustable chair height and seat height. An office chair needs five legs for stability and wheels for ease of movement.

CHOOSE OFFICE TECHNOLOGY

One reason there is such growth in home offices today is the widespread use of computers. Powerful desktop computers are available today at lower prices. The amount of equipment needed depends on the reason for and use of the office. One business owner might need a computer, a printer, a telephone with an answering machine, and a fax machine. Another might need more extensive equipment to compete with larger companies. For example, a consumer writer could use the same word processing and desktop publishing software as the magazine assigning the work does. Freelance designers can use the same illustration and CAD software as a large firm. Telecommuters can stay in touch with their managers via a web-cam for conferences and meetings.

One option to save space and money is choosing one multitask machine instead of several separate ones. For example, there are printers that also serve as a fax machine, a scanner, and a photocopier.

One very important aspect of a home business is safety and security of data. Electrical surge protectors for electronic equipment will protect

Technology enables workers to compete in a global marketplace without leaving home.

against loss from electric current fluctuations. Home workers need to back up all their computer data on a regular basis. They can use backup disks or tapes to protect their files against computer viruses and failure. A fireproof box can be used to protect electronic files, important paperwork, and legal documents.

THE POWER SUPPLY

A home office often needs a lot of electrical power for a computer, printer, scanner, copier, answering machine, fax machine, and lighting.

In addition to a dedicated business telephone line, a well-equipped office has a fax line that may also be a computer modem line. Some people prefer using a cable modem in their computer, which cuts down on an extra phone line for a modem.

Have an electrician check out the space before moving in all the equipment. Additional outlets may need to be added or electrical service into the house may have to be increased. The worst time to have new phone lines or outlets put in is after the room is filled with furniture and equipment.

SELECT LIGHTING

One important final consideration for a home office is lighting. Both glare and low light levels lead to eyestrain. A well-planned home office has indirect lighting and task lighting. Overhead lights to illuminate the entire room can provide indirect lighting. Task lighting on desks and work areas can be adjusted in angle and level of intensity to light up the computer, projects, or papers on the desk. Natural lighting from windows can make a home office cheery and comfortable, but care needs to be taken to be certain it doesn't produce glare. Positioning the computer monitor away from the window or the screen at a 90-degree angle to the window can solve this problem. Window coverings such as blinds can further reduce unwanted light.

The recessed downlighting in the soffit provides general lighting for this office area. What function do the lights under the cabinets perform?

The Storage Challenge

In just about every room of the house, people look for ways to tuck away all the things that create clutter. By devising and using a convenient system to store your belongings, you will be able to find what you need easily and it will stay in good condition.

The challenge is somewhat different in every situation. The number and type of items to be stored varies. The amount of available space and each person's natural "neatness quotient" does, too. However, it's possible for everyone to develop a workable system. It takes setting a goal and planning and maintaining a good storage system.

The Demand for Storage Space

Take a look through real estate ads and you'll find many that draw attention to homes with "lots of closet space." Storage space, it seems, is an asset that seems just as desirable as an extra bathroom and new carpeting.

Early people needed a safe place for storing food, but today's needs extend far beyond the kitchen. What is behind the modern home buyer's demand for storage space? A number of explanations may apply.

- *Less space.* Years ago most houses had an attic for storing everything from out of season clothing to holiday decorations to family treasures. Then, many homes were streamlined and had less storage space. Now, it's in demand again.

- *More things.* Some people believe that society is becoming increasingly *acquisitive;* the desire to acquire things has grown. Advertising has a lot to do with creating a desire for new products. Rapid advances in technology also fuel the acquisition habit by producing "new and improved" models before people have mastered or worn out the old ones. All of these possessions have to be kept somewhere.

- *More money.* In the past, many people felt fortunate to have two pair of shoes. However, decades of strong economic growth, put more money in the pockets of more people. Buying more was encouraged to keep the economy thriving.

- *More years.* Today's longer lifespans give time to accumulate more possessions. Many items are discarded along the way, of course, but sometimes people have trouble letting go of unused possessions.

The original storage need has not been forgotten either. As shelves full of canned soups and microwavable meals will attest, people still need a place for their food.

THINKING IT THROUGH

1. Estimate what percentage of your home is taken up with storage. Compare the square footage of closets and other areas used for storage, including corners of basements or the garage and outdoor sheds.
2. Suggest three ways to convert underutilized or "wasted" space into storage space.

Planning Storage

Simply having a place to put things isn't enough. An effective storage plan draws on your analytical and decision-making skills plus your creativity. You need to identify what needs to be stored (and what doesn't). Often you must find solutions to the need for additional storage space. Then, you need to choose the best equipment and methods to make the plan work.

ASSESS STORAGE NEEDS

Whether you are reorganizing storage for one room or a whole house, the first step is to identify what needs to be stored. Go through the area and simply make a list of all the items. Entries might range from a "vacuum cleaner" to "three dozen books."

As you make your list, identify things you no longer use. Having less to store immediately frees up space. If you find yourself saying, "This might come in handy someday," you probably don't need it. Unless something has special meaning for you, if you haven't used it in two years, you can probably give it away or sell it and not miss it.

Next look at your list of remaining items and group those that are

similar. As a general rule, similar things should be stored together. Is there a specific area or room in which it would be best to store certain groups of items?

If what you have to store will fit conveniently in the storage space you have available, you can skip the next step. However, most people find they need additional storage space to organize their possessions effectively.

FIND ADDITIONAL STORAGE OPTIONS

Every drawer and cabinet is already full or overflowing. Where will you find more space?

First, realize that storage can be open or closed. In **open storage**, stored items are visible. In **closed storage**, doors or drawers conceal items. Both types are important.

Next, look both for unused space that might be used for storage and for ways to maximize the space you already have. Each room's unique features need to be considered.

Finding storage "opportunities" means using your creativity as well as analytical skills. For instance, this window seat provides comfortable seating as well as convenient storage. What other creative storage ideas do you see?

Possibilities in a bathroom might range from adding a shelf around the entire room to fitting in a small chest or adding a vertical shelving unit over the toilet. Colorful baskets could hold often-used toiletries.

In the kitchen, you can attach a small shelf or bin to the underside of an upper cabinet. This can be used to store spices, cookbooks, or other small items. Look for small appliances that can be mounted under cabinets as well. Benches with under-seat storage might replace chairs at the table.

What about extra storage space in the family room, living room, and bedrooms? Cabinets, chests, and desks are designed specifically for storage. Look, too, for pieces that do double duty. A large stool might open to reveal storage space. An old trunk could serve as a coffee table and store games, pillows, or rarely used items.

In the bedroom, you might substitute a small chest of drawers for a bedside table. Some beds have drawers built into the base, but you can devise your own. Purchase storage boxes designed to fit under the bed or put wheels on old dresser drawers and roll them underneath.

Be creative! Virtually every nook and cranny can be cleverly used. Empty suitcases can store out-of-season clothes. High shelves can be added to closets for more space.

CHOOSE STORAGE ORGANIZERS

Although storage may seem tight, the options for storing and organizing have never been so plentiful. Whole stores are dedicated to storage equipment. You can spend thousands of dollars on custom storage for a home or do wonders with a very limited budget.

Go back to your list of items to be stored. First, identify those that are used most often. Then identify the type of storage preferable or possible for each item. Shelves can easily hold everything from towels to canned goods. Drawers are ideal for folded clothing, kitchen utensils, and other small items. A few hooks can hold a bathrobe, belts, or coffee mugs.

Next analyze your existing storage spaces. Are there ways they can be used more efficiently? Can the items in them be stored more conveniently?

You don't have to buy an expensive, sophisticated storage system. However, it's a good idea to look at items in all price ranges of what's available for ideas. For example, roll-out shelves might be most convenient. You could, instead, use inexpensive plastic containers for various stacks of items and pull those out to access what's in them. Maybe you don't have space for small cubbyholes, but you can add a long shoe bag to the inside of a door to hold small items. A tie rack could double as a jewelry holder.

Choose what you do buy with an eye to flexibility. For instance, adjustable shelves allow you to adapt space to the height of the objects being stored. Modular storage pieces can be assembled in different configurations as needs change. With basic carpentry skills, you can also make your own storage pieces.

Group similar items together and then devise a way to store them. With a convenient place for keeping items, they are more likely to be kept neatly than just piled up in the back of a closet.

ARRANGE ITEMS

When your storage systems have been selected and installed, you can begin to implement your plan. The final step in organizing storage is to arrange stored items in a systematic way. When doing this keep these principles in mind.

- Arrange items according to frequency of use. Items used every day or quite often should be stored within easy reach—on low shelves, near the front of shelves, in top drawers, at the front of the closet. Items used less frequently can be kept on top shelves, in bottom drawers, or at the back of a closet. Rarely used items can be stored on high shelves or in an attic, basement, or garage.

- Arrange commonly used items in places and at levels that are accessible to everyone. For instance, in the kitchen, put the plates and bowls on cabinet shelves that are within the reach of the shortest person. Put children's toys and videos where they can access them. Store any dangerous medications, materials, or equipment in locked cabinets.

If you can't find a tool, you can't use it. Organized storage puts everything within reach and allows the users to get to the task at hand rather than waste time looking for a tool.

- Devise ways to remember where things are. Items that are visible are easiest to find. Labels are a great help. When storing things in out-of-the-way places, mark the containers and keep a list of what's where.

- Arrange items for safe storage and easy access. Heavy objects are best stored at waist height because they are difficult to move. Avoid stacking items of different shapes and sizes; they could easily topple.

Organizing Your Closet

In every home, clothes closets are a major storage facility. Although most closets have good storage potential, they seem to invite disorder. Most people do eventually clean their closets. However, the large number of items stored—along with constant, hurried use—causes closets to become messy. If "Clean my clothes closet" is at the top of your to-do list, here are some suggestions.

CLEAN OUT. The first step in reorganizing your clothes closet is to clean it out. Pull out items you no longer need or want. If the thought of doing the entire job all at once overwhelms you, try cleaning in stages. Spend a little time on your closet every day until the job is done.

TAKE INVENTORY. As you remove items from the closet, put everything you no longer need or want

Organize a closet by grouping similar items and select storage systems that fit your needs. How did the person who organized this closet create additional useful space?

into three stacks—those to be given away, those to be sold, and those to be discarded. This step often yields a surprising amount of closet space for the clothes and accessories you want to keep.

GROUP SIMILAR ITEMS. You can group garments according to type, season, or color. Another good way to categorize clothes is by top half of the body (shirts, sweaters, jackets), bottom half (skirts, pants), whole body (suits, dresses, robes), and special-occasion. During this step, decide how each garment and accessory should be stored. You'll want to hang some items and store others flat.

DIVIDE SPACE. Now you know how much and what type of space you need. Whether your closet is a reach-in or a walk-in, you can adapt the space to the items being stored by installing a system of rods, shelves, drawers, hooks, containers, and racks. You can purchase ready-made components, kits, or build your own modular storage units.

Hanging space can be increased substantially by adding a second, lower rod partway across the closet. You may have to raise the original rod. Place the upper rod about 80 in. (203 cm) above the floor. Place the lower rod about 40 in. (102 cm) above the floor. Shirts, jackets, and skirts can be hung from both of the stacked rods. Long coats, slacks, or dresses can hang from the original upper rod.

Seasonal clothing and seldom-used items can be stored in boxes and tucked away on top shelves in the closet or kept under the bed. What items do you have that could be kept in storage containers?

Shelves and drawers are very useful in closets. Overhead shelves can be installed for storing blankets, out-of-season clothes, and suitcases. You could line the floor with narrow shelves for shoes. You might place a chest of drawers in a large closet.

Don't overlook closet doors, floors, and walls. You can purchase specially designed closet hooks and racks to make use of this space. A shoe rack for the floor keeps shoes in order. Hooks can be secured to the back wall of the closet and used to hang clothes and accessories that you wear infrequently.

Many types of containers, including small plastic bins and wire baskets, are available for storing clothes and accessories on closet shelves. Some containers are designed to be stacked on the floor. Others are designed with a side flap that drops when the cover is lifted so the contents are easy to reach. Storage containers can be made using regular cardboard cartons as a base and colorful paper for decoration.

Lisa Harmoning

Professional Organizer

I make my living from the clutter that other people collect in their homes and offices—and not by selling it at garage sales! I'm a professional organizer: In that role, I help people sort, organize, and store their belongings. It makes their life easier and their surroundings neat and attractive.

I started my business almost by accident. When I was home with my newborn son, I forced myself to work on my overstuffed bedroom closet. The results were so rewarding that I decided to overhaul the other six closets in our house. The downstairs closet caught a friend's eye; she offered to pay me to do two of hers. That job led to two more, from her sister and neighbor; word of mouth took over from there.

As you can easily understand, my strongpoint is organization. I have a knack for creating an environment that makes it much easier to keep things in order. While I've taken on all kinds of organization jobs, my specialty is closets. They just seem to invite mess and overcrowding, so reorganization makes a dramatic difference in the way they look and function.

To reorganize a clothes closet, I begin by removing all the contents, asking the owner to set aside all items that are used regularly—at least once every two weeks. Next is the tough part: I ask people to identify items they no longer need. This pile is never as big as it could be. I have to use tact and persuasion to help clients pare down their belongings.

Once the number of items is reduced, I discuss possible ways of organizing and renovating the closet in line with the needs of the owners.

"As you can easily understand, my strong point is organization."

the design, I begin the work. There are many storage products on the market now, with new ones being developed all the time. Through the professional organization I belong to, I'm able to buy these at a much lower cost than retail.

The final step is to install the equipment and put everything back in the closet. I've become a pretty good shelf installer, and I often create more hanging space by using double rods, one above the other.

People are delighted with their new, orderly closets. Not only is the space more efficiently arranged with everything easy to find, but there often is some room to spare. When my customer buys new items, they can be added in an orderly way that makes it likely that the closet will stay well organized.

Clothing needs and choices are really different from person to person. Many people also store things besides clothes in their clothes closet. I always see if some can go elsewhere to free up space.

The next step in the process is to decide how to organize the items to be kept. That requires analyzing the types of items and determining the best use of the space. I make a rough sketch of the reorganized closet, using shelves, hooks, bins, and rods. Then I calculate the number and size of shelves and other organizers that will be needed. For more complex jobs, I utilize a CAD design program to show what the finished project will look like and to determine materials and costs. Once the client approves

> *"There are many storage products on the market right now, with new ones being developed all the time."*

Career Profile

Professional organizers can run their own business or work in an office setting. They assist individuals in many different areas, such as space planning, time management, business organizing, financial record keeping, paper management, or room organizing. Although there are many other areas in which professional organizers can provide assistance, they often specialize in one or two. A professional organizer helps an individual get organized and provides training techniques to help keep them organized.

Education
- A high school diploma is recommended.
- Noncredit courses are available as seminars or over the Internet.

Skills Needed
- Organizational skills are a necessity.
- Math skills are needed and computer skills are helpful.

Career Outlook
- Employment opportunities are expected to grow quickly as more people work and can benefit from assistance in the home or in the office.

Career Activities

1. Do a quick check of your own closet and categorize the clothes according to how often you use them and their size. How long do you think it would take you to organize your closet? Is it work that you would enjoy?
2. Imagine that you have been hired to design storage for a bedroom closet that is 6 ft. (1.8 m) wide. Using both open and closed storage systems, organize the closet space efficiently and logically. Draw your design to scale using graph paper or a computer program.

CHAPTER 25

Review & Activities

Chapter Summary

➤ Home offices are used by entrepreneurs, telecommuters, family members for managing finances, and students in the family for doing homework.

➤ A home office can be set up in an extra bedroom, basement, attic, study, garage, or part of another room depending on the home worker's needs and the space available.

➤ Daily work activities are divided into zones to help plan the arrangement of a home office.

➤ Office furniture comes in many styles, but the main consideration should be choosing ergonomically designed pieces.

➤ Additional needs for a home office are up-to-date office technology, adequate electrical power, and proper lighting.

➤ Shelves, drawers, hanging storage, and containers are commonly used to store items.

➤ You can create additional storage space by using existing space more efficiently or by converting space into useful storage areas.

➤ Analyzing all your storage needs and allocating your storage space to meet these needs are part of planning for storage.

➤ There are four main steps to follow in organizing a closet.

Checking Your Understanding

1. Give two reasons why it would be best for a full-time home office worker to have an office that is a separate room.

2. What two shapes are the best for arranging a main work area. Why?

3. Name three ways space could be used vertically in a home office.

4. What would you look for when selecting a computer station and a chair for a home office?

5. What is the difference between indirect lighting and task lighting?

6. Identify three places in a home where unused space might be converted to storage space.

7. List the steps to follow when implementing a storage organization plan.

8. What is the difference between an open and a closed storage system?

9. What principles should be followed when systematically arranging items for storage?

10. What are the four main steps in organizing a closet?

Thinking Critically

1. If you were starting a business, how would you divide your budget between office furniture and technology? Explain your answer.

2. What would be the advantage for a mother of two young children to place her home office in the family room? What would be the disadvantage? How could the mother help lessen the impact of the disadvantage?

3. How might storage problems differ between a large, two-story home and a small efficiency apartment? Discuss how the storage problems for each type of home can be solved.

4. Suppose you were asked to mediate a heated discussion between two friends who share a small apartment. One friend is messy; the other is neat. The messy friend leaves his clothing and art supplies everywhere. The neat friend keeps his things orderly. Considering what you have learned about storage, what would you suggest that will help these two live in harmony?

Applications

1. **Design a Home Office.** Choose one of the careers covered in this textbook and plan a home office space for the person. Write a brief description of what activities would be performed in the office and what furniture and office technology the person would need. Draw a simple floor plan of how the space would be utilized.

2. **Telecommuting.** Interview a telecommuter about the pros and cons of working at home. If you do not know a telecommuter, research the subject on the Internet. Write a brief report on why you would or wouldn't enjoy working from your home.

3. **Space Planning.** Find a floor plan for either a two- or three-bedroom home. Using a colored marker, outline all of the existing closets and storage spaces. Evaluate how adequate you think the storage is for the home. Then determine how additional storage could be gained in the house. Number the plan as to where you would create additional storage and then write a brief description of what each additional storage area would be, such as built-in shelving under the stairs to the basement. Exchange your plan with a classmate and evaluate the work you are given.

4. **Creative Storage.** Using a software program or freehand drawing, create your idea of the perfect freestanding, modular wall system for a bedroom. Include pictures or symbols, or both, to indicate the items stored in the system.

BUILDING YOUR PORTFOLIO

Imagine that you are part of a design team responsible for selecting furniture for home offices. One of your clients is going to start her own landscape architecture business and work out of her house. She plans to turn an unused bedroom into her office. Using catalogs, sales flyers, or the Internet, locate furniture you would recommend for her office. Draw a floor plan with the furniture in place and be prepared to present your work to your client along with a price list for purchasing the furniture.

Home Safety and Security

CHAPTER OBJECTIVES

► Identify common home health hazards.

► Describe ways to prevent home accidents.

► Describe ways to make a home safe for young children.

► Explain safe and effective use of smoke alarms and fire extinguishers.

► Identify ways to improve home security.

► Suggest strategies for improving home safety for people with specific special needs.

TERMS TO LEARN

- asbestos

- asphyxiation

- carbon monoxide

- combustible

- flammable

- radon

- thermal burn

One of the basic human emotional needs is to feel safe and secure. For most people, the place they feel safest is their home. Homes, however, can present a risk of pollutants, accidents, and security problems. Fortunately, there are steps you can take to increase the likelihood that you, your family, and your possessions will remain safe from harm. The information in this chapter will help you plan and implement strategies to make your home the safe place you want it to be.

Reducing Health Hazards

People have become increasingly aware of the harm pollution causes to the natural environment. Pollution can also be a problem in the home. Some indoor pollutants may make people feel mildly ill. Others may have no noticeable effect at first, though, over time, they can cause serious health problems. By taking a few precautions, families can reduce the health hazards of pollution and enjoy greater peace of mind.

POLLUTANTS IN THE AIR

The majority of indoor pollution problems are airborne—carried by or through the air. There are several indoor air pollutants. Some are natural and some are the result of technology. How much indoor air pollution a home has is influenced by the building materials and equipment used, how the home is used, and where it is located.

Carbon Monoxide

Any furnace, heater, stove, fireplace, or water heater that burns gas, kerosene, or wood produces poisonous gases. One of the most dangerous of these gases is **carbon monoxide**—a colorless, odorless gas that is readily absorbed by red blood cells when breathed in. If the red blood cells absorb carbon monoxide instead of oxygen, the body doesn't get the oxygen it needs. The symptoms of carbon monoxide poisoning can range from headaches, nausea, and heart problems to **asphyxiation**—loss of consciousness or death from lack of oxygen.

All heating devices should be checked regularly to be sure they're working properly. Every home using gas appliances should have a carbon monoxide detector, a device that monitors the air and sounds an alarm if a dangerous level of carbon monoxide is detected.

Radon

Radon is another dangerous gas to guard against. **Radon** is a radioactive gas that occurs naturally in some types of soil and rock. Usually radon escapes into the atmosphere and causes no harm. However, if it seeps into the home—through cracks in the foundation—it can build to harmful levels. Breathing high concentrations of radon increases the risk of lung cancer. Home test kits are available to measure radon levels. If tests show high levels of radon, simple steps such as sealing cracks can be taken to reduce the levels.

Asbestos

Many older homes contain **asbestos**, a flame-retardant mineral substance. Before 1978, asbestos was used in many building materials that were installed in hundreds of thousands of homes and buildings. Unfortunately, the discovery came later that tiny fibers of asbestos, when inhaled, could cause lung cancer. This danger arises when asbestos crumbles or is otherwise damaged. Homeowners should never try to remove or seal off suspected asbestos. That task must be performed by a professional.

Other Air Pollutants

Indoor air quality can be affected by chemical vapors from carpeting, insulation, and other materials. Other substances that pollute indoor air are molds and bacteria, tobacco smoke, and fumes from cleaning products and pesticides.

There are several steps you can take to preserve and improve air quality. First, keep your home clean and well ventilated. Try to keep moisture levels low in the home. This will help prevent the growth of molds and bacteria. Choose cleaning products and other materials that are free of known pollutants. An air purifier that removes dust, mold, bacteria, and odors from the air can also be used.

LEAD

Lead is a toxic metal that can be found in old paint, water, soil, and air. Sometimes it penetrates a home's water supply. If lead enters the body, it can cause behavioral and developmental problems, particularly in young children. In most cases of lead in water, the cause is traced to lead water pipes or lead-based solder (SAH-der) used to join the pipes. Lead solder has been prohibited since 1988, but many homes still have lead pipes. If you think your home has lead pipes, contact your local health department or water company to find out how to have your water tested. Meanwhile, before use, it is wise to let faucets run until the water runs cold to flush out any lead that might have accumulated in the pipes.

Homes built before the 1970s may have lead-based paint. Lead particles from the paint can get into household dust, which may be breathed or swallowed and can cause lead poisoning. Children may eat chips and flakes of peeling paint. To reduce the risk of lead poisoning, repair peeling paint and keep the house clean.

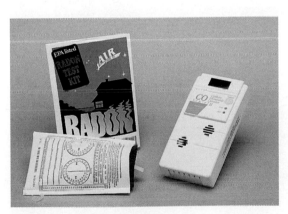

Inexpensive yet potentially lifesaving devices for the home include carbon monoxide detectors and radon testing kits. What is the difference between carbon monoxide and radon poisoning?

Preventing Accidents

Every year more than 20,000 Americans die as a result of home accidents. Thousands more suffer long-lasting injuries. Some home accidents result in lifelong disabilities. The most common types of accidents that occur in the home are falls, electric shock, and burns. Fortunately, most home accidents can be prevented by taking some simple precautions.

- Use sturdy step stools to reach high places.
- Install grab bars on walls in tubs and showers and use nonskid bathtub mats.

Homes with steps and stairways present additional hazards. Make certain that any changes in floor level are obvious and that the area is well lighted. Provide secure handrails. Avoid leaving items on stairs where they can be tripped over.

Outside the home, keep sidewalks swept and clear of trash and clutter. Cracks in the sidewalk should be repaired and uneven sections replaced. If you live where the winters are cold, keep sidewalks and steps free of ice and snow.

FALLS

Falls account for most home injuries. Many falls occur because of defects in flooring, clutter, or lack of adequate lighting. Falls also result when people hurry or use poor judgement, such as standing on an unsteady chair to reach a high shelf.

To reduce the risk of falling, follow these home safety tips:

- Wipe up spills immediately.
- Repair loose tiles and tears in carpeting promptly.
- Anchor rugs firmly to the floor with double-sided adhesive tape or rubber backing.

This step stool is designed to help people reach high places. Using an unsteady chair in place of a step stool is a major cause of falls.

ELECTRIC SHOCK

Severe electric shock is powerful enough to knock a person down, cause unconsciousness, or interrupt breathing and heartbeat. Electric shocks in the home result mainly from the misuse of electrical appliances. Learning the safe way to handle appliances and making safe use an everyday practice will decrease your risk of electric shock. Each appliance comes with specific warnings, but some cautions apply to all. For example, never clean or service appliances while they are plugged in. When disconnecting an appliance, don't pull on the cord, as this tends to loosen or break the wires. Instead, grasp the plug with your thumb and forefinger and pull gently to remove it from the outlet.

Because water is a good conductor of electricity, never touch electrical appliances with wet or damp hands. Don't use electrical appliances near sinks or bathtubs. A hair dryer, for example, could accidentally fall into a bathtub or sink full of water. If someone tried to pick it up, an electric current might pass through the person's body even with the appliance turned off.

Plugging too many appliances into one receptacle (outlet) can overload the circuit and might damage the wiring. An electric circuit is the path electric energy follows from the source of electric power to one or more electrical fixtures or receptacles and back.

Faulty electrical systems can cause or contribute to electrical accidents. All electrical systems should be installed according to the National Electrical Code. Homeowners should arrange to have a professional check their electrical system about every five years and replace defective parts as necessary.

Fuses and circuit breakers are built-in safety devices in an electrical system. Both protect electrical circuits from damage caused by too much current. An excess of current can be caused by a fault in the circuit or by an outside event, such as lightning. Fuses and circuit breakers both work by interrupting the electrical circuit, thus stopping the flow of electric current.

To reduce the risk of electric shock when using small appliances, ground fault circuit interrupters (GFCIs) are required in kitchen, bathroom, and outdoor receptacles in new homes. A GFCI detects changes in current that are too slight to activate a regular circuit breaker or fuse but great enough to produce serious shock. When a GFCI senses that the electrical current flowing to an appliance is beyond its normal load, the GFCI shuts off the flow of electricity to the appliance.

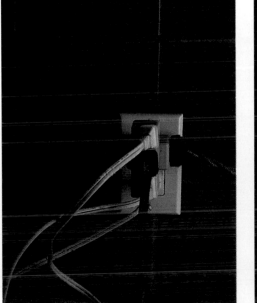

Too many appliances plugged into an outlet can overload a circuit and possibly damage the wiring. Instead, plug in only the appropriate number of appliances and use ground fault circuit interrupters in kitchen and bathroom receptacles.

BURNS

Becky Martello was cooking dinner for the family. As Becky removed a pan from the burner, her loose shirt sleeve swept across the flame and caught fire. Clothing is often very **combustible** or **flammable**, which means it is capable of burning quickly. Fortunately, Becky remembered what to do when clothes catch fire: STOP, DROP, AND ROLL. She escaped with only minor thermal burns.

A **thermal burn** is an injury caused by hot liquids, hot surfaces, or flames. Other types of burns may be caused by chemicals and by electricity. Many thermal burns are caused by carelessness while cooking. Becky for example, should have been wearing close-fitting clothing while working near an open flame. Long hair should be tied back. Keep flammable materials, such as towels, paper, and plastic, away from the range or cooktop. Turn pan handles toward the center of the range to prevent accidental spilling of hot food. Use potholders and oven mitts when handling hot containers of food.

Following safety precautions in the kitchen can help prevent thermal burns. What precautions has this person taken?

The "Mr. Yuk" symbol is used to warn children that they should not eat or drink a substance. It can help protect them from taking in any poison. In what areas of the home would you use "Mr. Yuk"?

CHILDPROOFING THE HOME

Very young children are naturally curious. They also have a lot of energy. Dozens of things attract their attention. They want to get close, to touch, and perhaps to taste each one before crawling, climbing, or running to the next attraction. Because they're unaware of the potential dangers in the home, their need to explore and experiment can lead to accidents. It's up to adults and older children to keep young children safe. Here are some ways to make a home safer for young children.

- Install a gate across stairway openings.
- Install safety catches on all windows.
- Insert safety plugs into all unused outlets.
- Arrange electrical appliance cords so young children cannot get tangled in them or pull down appliances by the cord.
- Keep small items out of reach. Children can easily choke on coins, marbles, and other small objects.
- Avoid using furniture with sharp corners or glass tops. Sharp corners in the home can be padded by attaching strips of foam rubber. Special cushions can also be purchased.
- Fasten bedding so a baby cannot pull it over his or her head.
- Tie up cords from curtains, drapes, and blinds so that children cannot get tangled in or choked by them. Keep the crib away from windows with hanging cords.
- Keep pillows and stuffed animals out of the crib while the baby is sleeping.
- When carrying hot liquids or foods, make sure the baby isn't crawling nearby.
- Always test bath water to make sure it's not too hot. Use nonslip mats or stickers in the bottom of the tub. Never leave a baby alone in a tub, even for a second.

Installing a gate across stairways is one safety precaution needed in homes with small children.

- Store medicines out of reach. Brightly colored pills and liquids may look like candy to a child.
- Keep houseplants out of reach. Some can be poisonous.

- Store poisonous substances such as cleaning products in high, locked cabinets. Put safety latches on the doors of low cabinets to keep children out.

Preventing Fires

Of all possible home accidents, fire is the most feared because of its potential to kill and seriously injure people, destroy possessions, and devastate lives. Thousands of people die each year in residential fires. Property losses are in the billions of dollars.

Becoming familiar with the main causes of home fires can help you take actions to prevent them. Many fires are caused by:

- Careless smoking or children playing with matches or lighters.
- Faulty wiring or electrical equipment.
- Unattended or improperly extinguished wood stove and fireplace fires.

- Flammable liquids or oily rags stored near a heat source.
- A space heater too close to combustible materials, such as drapes or a bedspread.
- Combustible materials too close to hot surfaces of wood-burning stoves.
- Chimneys and flues clogged with soot and dirt.
- Use of flammable substances, such as aerosols, in cooking areas or near heating units.
- Buildup of grease in exhaust fans and vents.
- Ignition of a gas leak.

A fire goes through four stages. In the first stage, the fire smolders. Invisible, toxic (poisonous) gases may be produced even though there's no flame, smoke, or noticeable heat. A fire may smolder for hours. In the second stage, some smoke and more toxic gases are produced. In the third stage, flames erupt and begin to spread. During the fourth stage, there is high, uncontrolled heat. In this stage, toxic gases expand rapidly.

Most fires start in the kitchen. Three-quarters of the people who die in house fires are trapped upstairs by fires that start downstairs. The majority of these people don't die from burns; rather, they are asphyxiated in their sleep by the toxic gases produced by the fire.

No matter how careful people are about fire prevention, fires can happen in any home. To minimize the danger if a fire starts, you can purchase fire-safety devices to handle minor fires.

Some people use space heaters in their homes to provide additional comfort in rooms. What safety precautions need to be taken with a space heater?

SMOKE ALARMS. Fire experts believe that smoke alarms are the most important aid in saving lives and property. Smoke alarms detect poisonous gases in the first stage of a fire and sound a loud buzzer to alert residents to the danger. Small and relatively inexpensive smoke alarms can be wired into a home's electrical system, plugged into a receptacle, or operated by batteries.

Ideally, there should be a smoke alarm in every room except the kitchen and bathroom. (These rooms aren't good locations because smoke alarms can be set off by cooking fumes and steam.) At the very least, there should be one alarm on each level of the home, including one near the kitchen and each sleeping area, and one near the furnace and water heater. They should be installed near the ceiling, and away from windows, doors, or heating vents that might divert smoke from the unit. Once smoke alarms have been installed, they need to be tested regularly to be certain they are working. Replace batteries at least annually.

FIRE EXTINGUISHERS. Several types of fire extinguishers are available for putting out small fires. Water extinguishers deliver water under pressure and are effective on ordinary combustible materials, such as wood, paper, or cloth. Foam extinguishers and dry-powder extinguishers will douse flammable liquids such as fat, oil, and alcohol. A third type of extinguisher contains a gas, such as carbon dioxide, to smother electrical fires. This last type must be used carefully, because the gas can also asphyxiate people.

Because the kitchen range is the most likely place for a fire to begin, an extinguisher for smothering grease fires should be located in the kitchen. Place it where it can be grabbed without having to reach across the range. A grease fire can also be smothered by sprinkling it with baking soda or salt, or by covering the pan with a lid. Special "fire blankets" can also smother most fires that begin at the range. Some homeowners install indoor sprinkler systems that turn on in case of a fire emergency, but these are expensive.

All adults and teens should know how to operate the fire extinguisher. Young children, however, should be taught to run for help if fire breaks out—not to fight it. Fire professionals advise everyone to use extreme caution when deciding to fight even a small fire. If the fire isn't immediately extinguished, their advice is to leave the building, then call the fire department from a safe location.

The contents of many fire extinguishers lose their effectiveness after a period of time. Check your fire extinguishers to see if they have expired. If they have, follow the manufacturer's directions for renewal or recharging.

A HOME FIRE SAFETY PLAN

Schools and other public buildings are required by law to have a fire safety plan for evacuating the building. A fire safety plan is just as important for your home. When the smoke alarm goes off, you and your family must know how to get out of the home quickly and safely.

The first step is to plan possible escape routes. For each room or area of the home, plan at least two ways to get outside. Alternate routes are back doors, windows, balconies, and fire escapes.

If you live in a high-rise or other multifamily building, check the hallways for a diagram of possible escape routes from the building. Remember, never use an elevator during a fire. If the power goes out, you could become trapped in the elevator.

Make sure your escape routes are usable. Check all windows to make sure they open easily. If necessary, purchase escape ladders for upper-story windows. In a high-rise building, be sure that fire escapes are functioning and that fire exits are neither blocked nor locked.

Designate a place for all family members to meet after escaping from the building. People have lost their lives by going back into a burning building to look for someone who was already outside.

Plan a fire drill with your family to practice escaping from your home in a hurry. In case of a fire emergency, you'll be able to think more clearly if you have planned ahead.

Once you have an escape plan, draw a diagram showing all escape routes and the location where you will meet. Post it where everyone in the household can see it. Make sure everyone is familiar with the escape plan. Explain the procedures for escaping from a fire, as listed below.

- Don't stop to gather valuables or call the fire department. Leave immediately.
- Crawl on your hands and knees. Since heat and toxic gases rise, the cleanest air will be close to the floor. If you are in bed, roll to the floor instead of sitting up.
- Shout to alert others as you exit.
- Use the escape routes you planned ahead of time.

- When you come to a closed door, feel it first. If the doorknob is hot, DO NOT open it! Use an alternate route. If the door isn't hot, brace your body against it and open it slowly. If you feel a rush of hot air, close the door and use an alternate route.
- Close all doors behind you.
- Once outside, go to the designated meeting place.
- If you're unable to escape, close the door of the room first, then open a window a few inches and breathe through the opening. Wave your arms, a sheet, or a curtain out the window to attract attention.

To increase safety, ask family members to sleep with bedroom doors closed. A closed door will hold back a fire for a long time and slow down the passage of smoke.

Practice your escape plan by holding fire drills twice a year. Since the hours between 11:00 p.m. and 6:00 a.m. are the most dangerous from the standpoint of fire safety, it's a good idea to hold at least some drills after dark. A fire safety plan and regular drills can greatly increase your family's chances of escaping a fire safely.

Promoting Security

How safe is your neighborhood? Some people believe that they live in a safe neighborhood where crime is unlikely. Unfortunately, break-ins and robberies can and do happen anywhere. According to statistics from the Federal Bureau of Investigation, one out of every six American homes will be burglarized at some time.

Burglar-proofing a home is something everyone should think about. Fortunately, there are security devices you can install and several security measures you can take to help keep your home, family, and possessions safe.

they are to keep trying. Of course, too many security devices can make it inconvenient to go in and out. In the end, you must compromise between what makes you feel secure and what level of inconvenience you're willing to put up with. Minimum protection begins with secure doors and windows.

SECURITY DEVICES

Burglary is committed by people who take advantage of carelessness or neglect. In other words, the more difficult you make it for burglars to break into your home, the less likely

There are many home security devices available, ranging from simple mechanical devices to complex electronic ones. Your local police department is an excellent source of information about their effectiveness.

DOOR LOCKS. Police recommend installing a deadbolt lock on each exterior door. The bolt should extend into the door jamb a minimum of 1 in. (2.5 cm). Unlike common spring locks, deadbolts can't be opened by a credit card or a screwdriver.

For safety reasons, it's best not to have windows beside exterior doors. If the doorknob is too close to a window, a burglar could break the window, then reach inside and unlock the door. Another solution is shatterproof glass in windows that are installed next to doors.

SECURE DOORS. A strong door lock is worthless if the door itself is weak and can easily be kicked in. All entrances to a home should have a door with a solid wood or metal core. The door frame should be solid. It should also be strong enough to prevent a burglar from

Deadbolt locks provide extra security on exterior doors. Locks that can be opened from either side by a key are best.

easily prying it away from the door with a crowbar. Hollow-core doors made of soft, thin wood are suitable for closets and interior rooms, but they are too weak to provide the security needed for an entrance door.

Sliding glass doors present a particular problem because they can easily be forced open. Special locks prevent forced sliding. A thick wooden dowel or a broomstick placed in the door track can also keep the door from being opened. If the garage is attached to the house, make sure the connecting door to the living area is secure.

WINDOW LOCKS. Most types of windows come equipped with locks, but these alone don't ensure security. For example, traditional double-hung windows with thumb-turn locks can be easily pried open. Keyed locks might be added for extra protection, especially for the first-floor windows. However, keyed locks shouldn't be used on windows in sleeping areas, because they might slow down escape from fire.

DOOR VIEWERS AND CHAINS. Some intruders ring the doorbell and try to get invited in. Others force their way inside once you've opened the door. Always identify a visitor before opening the door. If there's no window to look out, install a door viewer. A door viewer is a small hole in the door. The hole is fitted with a metal cylinder and a lens that allows a wide-angle view of the person at the door.

Why is it important not to open the outer door to your home if you don't know who is on the other side?

An inside door chain provides little security for identifying visitors. An intruder could easily force the door against the chain and break it loose.

ALARM SYSTEMS. Even the best of locks may not keep burglars from attempting to enter a home. The next line of defense is alerting residents, neighbors, or the police that a break-in is underway.

A number of electronic alarm systems are on the market. Some are as simple as an electronic barking dog that is triggered by attempts to force a door or window. Some other systems are very complex and include electronic eyes and motion detectors. Sensing that someone is trying to break in or has already entered the home is one part of an electronic alarm system. The other part is the response.

Electronic home security systems can detect when there is an attempted forced entry and sound an alarm in the home or trigger an alarm that summons the police.

Alarm responses also vary widely. In some alarm systems the only response is a loud noise. The hope is that the noise will frighten the intruder away and alert everyone else that there's trouble. Some alarm systems are connected to a central processing station that alerts the police when the alarm is triggered. Often, private companies send an armed response team to investigate triggered alarms. In some alarm systems there is a "FIRE" button that residents can press to alert the fire department in case of a fire emergency.

To select an alarm system that will be right for your needs, consider several factors. First, think about your neighborhood. What is its reputation for burglary or burglary attempts? Consider the layout of your home. Is an alarm system appropriate? What about your budget? What can you afford? Your local police department is a good source of advice for making a decision about alarm systems.

LIGHTS, INTERCOMS, AND MIRRORS. Correctly placed light is another safety device. Place floodlights over exterior doors, including the garage door. Some floodlights have a motion detector that causes them to turn on whenever they sense movement. Parking areas and walkways should also be well lighted and clear of structures and foliage that could conceal someone. In multiunit buildings, every hallway and stairway should have adequate lighting. An intercom system can help keep unwelcome people out of multiunit buildings. The intercom allows residents to identify people who ring the main entrance doorbell. The residents then use a remote door-lock release to let authorized visitors enter.

Elevators should contain mirrors positioned so that a person about to enter the elevator can see if anyone is already inside. Use good judgement before entering an elevator occupied by someone you don't know. Elevators should always have an alarm button in working order inside the elevator. When riding in an elevator, try always to stand within easy reach of the alarm button.

SECURITY MEASURES

In addition to installing security devices, there are several security measures people can take to lower their risk of becoming a victim of burglary. For example, make the exterior of the home visible. Trim trees and shrubs so that they don't cover doors or windows. Planting small thorny bushes underneath windows might discourage burglars from hiding there.

Try to disguise the fact that your home is vacant when you're away. Ask a trusted neighbor to pick up newspapers and mail and to open and close the shades or drapes. Use an automatic timer to turn lights on at dusk and off at the usual bedtime. The timer can also turn on a radio. Keep garage doors closed at all times.

There was a time when most people knew their neighbors and assumed that most of them would look out for one another's property. As lifestyles changed, it became less and less common in some neighborhoods to know one's neighbors. "Mind your own business" became the social guide for more and more people. Home security increasingly became an individual endeavor. Some people who reject this trend have tried to regain the idea of shared responsibility by forming neighborhood crime watch groups. Neighbors attend regular meetings, get to know one another, and agree to watch out for one another's property. Thieves may be less likely to burglarize homes in such a neighborhood.

Lights on the exterior of a home not only make it look attractive, they also add security. What other security measures has this homeowner taken?

Meeting Special Needs

A home that is safe and secure for the "average" person may present problems for a person with a disability or someone with diminished abilities due to age. The following ideas for increasing safety and security are in keeping with the philosophy of universal design—designing homes for people of all ages and physical needs.

IMPAIRED MOBILITY. For those who use a cane or a walker, or who simply have difficulty walking, falls are a constant household danger. A highly polished floor, a loose rug, or a chipped piece of tile can be especially treacherous. Safe floor coverings are essential. Throw rugs shouldn't be used. Here are some other home modifications to prevent falls:

- Trim doorway thresholds so that they are flush with the floor or extend no higher than ¼ in. (6 mm).
- Provide handrails on each side of a staircase and along hallways. Handrails should extend 18 in. (46 cm) beyond the last step.
- Install grab bars and rubber flooring in the bathroom.
- Provide a seat in the tub or shower.
- Provide sturdy chairs, preferably with arms, to make it easier to sit down and stand up.
- Provide a place to sit while preparing meals, in case the person becomes tired.

A motorized stairway chair lift can be installed to help a person with impaired mobility reach other levels of a home.

When designing to accommodate wheelchair users, safety and security are especially important. For example, if a space beneath a kitchen sink is left open so a wheelchair user can roll up to it, the pipes must be insulated to prevent burns. Devices such as sound- or motion-activated lights and wheelchair-height peepholes can help increase security.

People with limited mobility—as well as those with other disabilities, problems of aging, or chronic illnesses—can benefit from a system that allows them to summon help at the press of a button. In case of an emergency, users simply press the button on a device worn around the neck or wrist. The button signals the home telephone to dial a preset number automatically, which might be a hospital or a central dispatch office. The source of the incoming call is automatically identified, and assistance is sent.

IMPAIRED VISION. People who have reduced vision and those who are blind have an increased risk of accidents. For those who have trouble distinguishing objects, it may be necessary to increase the amount of lighting in the home. Increasing the contrast between objects and their backgrounds increases their visibility. For example, placing a light object against a dark background makes it easier to see. The following measures can also make homes safer for the visually impaired.

- Mark the edges of steps with wide strips of contrasting adhesive tape.
- Clearly label and store any poisonous substances. Use very large type or braille, depending on the severity of the impairment.
- Remove furniture that has sharp corners, glass tops, or is easily tipped over.

- Install a telephone with oversize numerals or numerals printed in braille. Preprogram emergency and frequently used phone numbers if possible.

IMPAIRED HEARING. Certain measures can help people who have impaired hearing. An electrician can install wiring that substitutes a flashing light for the ring of the doorbell and telephone. Some smoke alarms have flashing lights as well as a warning sound. Another helpful device is a portable, vibrating timer, which can be used as a kitchen timer. By alerting a person with impaired hearing to check the progress of cooking food, the timer can help to prevent fires.

This telephone is especially equipped to assist a person with a hearing impairment. What other home devices could be installed?

Design Issues for Special Healthcare Facilities

Millions of Americans suffer from some form of dementia, such as Alzheimer's disease. As the illness progresses, an individual who has dementia experiences disorientation, confusion, and memory loss. These characteristics present unique challenges for interior designers who are responsible for planning healthcare facilities, such as nursing homes.

A major concern for designers is creating an environment that is supportive and safe for residents. Designers plan an environment that specifically addresses the patients' needs. Special considerations include the following:

- *Space.* Many people who suffer from dementia spend a great deal of time walking. Medical professionals realize the value of a small unit where the patient can't get overly fatigued or lost in an unfamiliar hallway. As the disease progresses, most patients spend very little time in their own room. Instead, they spend waking hours in a combination living room/dining room/activity area. When weather permits, some residents enjoy going outside. A fenced garden or courtyard should include a path that is designed in a circular pattern.

- *Furniture Arrangement.* To help orientation and to prevent falls, it is important to minimize furniture and clutter. Rooms and objects should not be rearranged. Large clocks and calendars help to orient residents to the day and time. Sense of touch is especially important to patients with dementia. Quilts, wall hangings, and other textured objects are often placed on the walls.

- *Security.* It's essential that the unit have safeguards for keeping patients inside unless they're accompanied by another adult. Windows should not be large enough for a person to climb out. Outside doors should be locked or equipped with alarms that sound when they're opened. To help steady patients who have trouble walking, the hallways should be lined with handrails. For safety, floor coverings should be the same throughout the facility—all carpet or all vinyl. It's common for patients to fall when they step from a carpeted floor to a smooth one.

- *Storage of Belongings.* Residents welcome having familiar items in their rooms, such as family photos or a special afghan. Memory loss causes people with Alzheimer's disease to misplace items. Therefore, patients shouldn't have access to money, jewelry, and other items of great value. Medications, razors, and scissors are not stored in patients' rooms.

You, the

Designer

Imagine you are part of a design team responsible for planning the wing of a nursing home for individuals with dementia. Decide what safety precautions you would recommend for the patients' rooms. What would you suggest for the shared living area? Give rationales for your choices.

Bryon Weber

Lead Abatement Specialist

Asbestos and lead are recognized today as threats to health and even to life. Asbestos is no longer used in insulating materials, but it remains a danger in older buildings where inhaling asbestos fibers can cause lung disease. Similarly, though lead paints are no longer sold for use in homes, older buildings frequently have paint, varnish, and plaster that contain lead compounds.

The danger is not only that paint and plaster chips may be eaten by young children, but that lead may be taken into the body by breathing in dust. My job as a lead abatement specialist is to reduce the dangers from lead by removing it from homes and buildings, especially when they are about to be renovated or demolished.

"The danger is not only that paint and plaster chips may be eaten by young children, but that lead may be taken into the body by breathing in dust."

My training to be a lead abatement specialist included a course on hazard reduction and training in specialized cleaning techniques and procedures for removing and sealing paint. The course met the Environmental Protection Agency (EPA) regulations. I became certified and went to work for a company that specializes in lead and asbestos abatement.

If homeowners suspect a lead paint problem, they call in a risk assessor who inspects the home and offers a plan of action. Options may include: (1) remove and replace doors and molding containing lead paint; (2) encapsulate the painted surfaces by coating them with a special paint that binds the lead and prevents it from leaching out; (3) enclose interior surfaces with drywall and seal them with caulking; or (4) wet-sand surfaces and then plane them down.

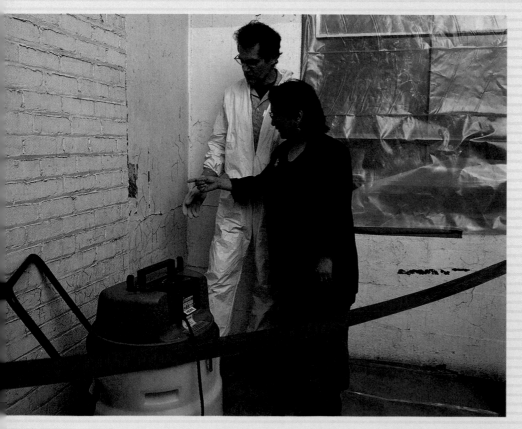

My job is to go to a home in which a lead hazard has already been identified. I wear special protective equipment, including a mask and disposable suit. I seal off each room as I work on it to prevent dust from escaping. In addition to other tools, I use a high-tech vacuum that has a HEPA (high-efficiency particulate arrestor) filter.

When I speak to groups about lead-paint safety, I urge them not to try to remove the paint themselves; the problem can become worse if it's done incorrectly. I suggest ways for them to protect themselves and their families, such as: thoroughly rinsing mops and sponges after cleaning dusty areas, washing children's hands often, removing shoes before entering homes, and making sure children eat nutritious meals. That last suggestion may sound odd, but it's been shown that children who eat low-fat dairy products and foods such as spinach, beans, and lean meat actually absorb less lead into their systems.

I take satisfaction from my work as a lead abatement specialist, for I know I provide a valuable service. I am especially thankful that my efforts have probably spared the lives of young children by keeping lead paint and plaster out of their environment.

"I wear special protective equipment, including a mask and disposable suit."

Career Profile

Lead abatement specialists remove lead from buildings that are going to be demolished or renovated. They also remove lead from residential homes. Prior to the late 1970s, lead was a very common component that could be found in paint, plumbing fixtures, and pipes. It was then discovered that lead entering into a person's bloodstream could cause health risks. Any lead that is now found in buildings needs to be removed. A lead abatement specialist has to wear personal protective equipment before entering into any work site, including a personal air monitor that gauges how much lead the worker is being exposed to. There are several different methods a lead abatement specialist may have to use to remove the lead. Once the lead has been removed, it is placed into a special container for proper hazardous waste disposal.

Education
▸ High school diploma is required.
▸ A license is required and can be obtained by completing a 40-hour training program.
▸ Technical training is often provided on the job.

Skills Needed
▸ Good math skills.
▸ Good physical strength.

Career Outlook
▸ Employment opportunities are expected to be good, since more emphasis is being put on safety.

Career Activities

1. An important part of this career is safely following procedures. Using a science textbook or online resource, research a simple laboratory experiment and make a list of all the safety precautions that need to be followed.
2. Research the adverse side effects of lead poisoning in young children. Create a public service announcement to share with your community or plan a web page to reach a broader audience.

Chapter Summary

➤ Health hazards caused by indoor pollutants can be monitored and possibly prevented.

➤ The most common types of home accidents are falls, electric shock, and burns.

➤ Specific precautions can be taken to lower the risk of accidents to children in the home.

➤ Becoming familiar with the main causes of home fires can help you take actions to prevent them.

➤ The more difficult it is for burglars to break into your home, the less likely they are to make repeated attempts to enter.

➤ A home can be modified to be a safe and secure place for people with special needs.

Checking Your Understanding

1. Identify at least three pollutants that can be found in the home.

2. Why is it important to childproof a home?

3. Identify six ways to help prevent falls.

4. Explain the function of GFCIs.

5. Where do most home fires start? Why?

6. For minimum coverage, where should home smoke alarms and fire extinguishers be installed?

7. What features of a door can promote or decrease home security?

8. What factors should be considered when selecting an alarm system?

9. Describe three ways to modify a home to make it safer for a person whose vision is impaired.

10. Explain three ways to modify a home for someone with impaired hearing.

Thinking Critically

1. A weekend guest complains of headaches after sleeping in a bedroom near the furnace room. What might be the cause? What precautions should the homeowner take?

2. Some people claim that "accidents never happen to them." Explain what's wrong with this type of thinking.

3. Discuss the saying, "You can never be too careful," in relation to home security. Do you agree with it? Describe what you would do to promote security in a home of your own.

4. The Stein family is shopping for a new home. Although their household includes no one with a physical impairment, the Steins still want to evaluate potential homes with regard to people with special needs. Explain why this might be important.

Applications

1. **Effects of Indoor Pollutants.** Use print or Internet resources to find out what "sick building syndrome" is. Prepare to report on the causes, symptoms, and ways in which people are attempting to alleviate the problem.

2. **Investigating Pollutants.** Using print or Internet resources, investigate one of the following: carbon monoxide; radon; asbestos. Find out how it is produced and how it affects the cardiopulmonary system. Share your findings.

3. **Home Safety Campaign.** Design posters or web pages that illustrate important aspects of home accident prevention. Use catchy slogans and appealing illustrations to make the point of your campaign clearly and emphatically.

4. **Home Security Systems.** Research the types of security alarm systems currently available and report on how different systems work. If possible, report on models that might be available in the near future as well.

5. **Neighbors Working Together.** Think about what you could do to start a neighborhood watch group in your area. What would you ask neighbors to do for each other? How would you help neighbors identify suspicious activities? Prepare a letter that would invite neighbors to a first meeting and explain the purpose of the group.

6. **Providing for Special Needs.** Suppose someone in your household must temporarily use a wheelchair. Make a list of changes and strategies that you and your family might carry out to make your home safe and comfortable for this person.

BUILDING YOUR PORTFOLIO

Your community is hiring a home safety inspector, and you want the job. The inspector will visit homes and help homeowners check for safety and security hazards. Write a letter of application for the position that explains your views on home safety and security. Include a brief plan for carrying out your job and a sample checklist for one area of safety or security that you will use as you inspect homes. Put your work in your portfolio for future reference.

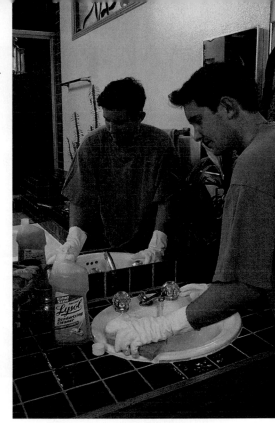

Bathroom fixtures should be cleaned at least once a week.

FIGURE 27-1

Suggested Cleaning Schedule

TIME FRAME	Tasks
DAILY	• Wash dishes • Wipe kitchen counters and cooktop • Clean kitchen sink • Sweep or vacuum kitchen floor • Make beds • Straighten all rooms • Take out garbage
AT LEAST WEEKLY	• Vacuum carpeting • Shake out small rugs • Dustmop, sweep, or vacuum noncarpeted floors • Clean bathroom fixtures • Wash kitchen and bath floors • Clean inside of microwave • Dust furniture; polish if needed • Dust accessories • Change bedsheets • Do laundry • Clean washer and dryer lint filters
MONTHLY OR BI-MONTHLY	• Wash mattress pads and turn mattresses • Wash windows and mirrors • Clean refrigerator (defrost if needed) • Clean oven • Vacuum drapes, upholstered furniture, and lampshades • Clean dust buildup from ceiling fans • Wipe blinds • Straighten and clean kitchen shelves and drawers • Straighten closets
EVERY FOUR TO EIGHT MONTHS	• Clean closets • Wash blankets, bedspreads, bedskirts • Clean drapes and curtains • Clean woodwork, walls, and ceilings • Vacuum refrigerator coils

SCHEDULES

Maintaining the standard of cleanliness you decide on will be much easier if you set up a cleaning schedule. How frequently a cleaning task needs to be done depends on the task and circumstances and on personal preferences. For example, dishes should be done more frequently than laundry. A person with few clothes and towels will need to do laundry more often than someone who has more.

The suggested cleaning schedule on this page offers recommendations for organizing a cleaning schedule. Once you have decided on your schedule, getting the correct tools and supplies and working out efficient cleaning routines for each area will help you stick to the schedule.

TOOLS AND SUPPLIES

The right cleaning tools can make a job go faster and often give more satisfactory results. Having the tools, however, doesn't help unless they are used. A lot of people keep their homes quite clean with little more than a vacuum, broom, cleaning cloths, sponge, bucket, mop, and all purpose cleaning solution. Some people have every cleaning gadget on the market and still find it difficult to keep their homes clean. The following list includes some basic cleaning tools and products as well as a few items you may not have thought of using for cleaning. Which items on the list do you use?

- Vacuum cleaner. An upright cleaner generally cleans carpeting better than a canister cleaner, but a canister cleaner may be easier to handle and have more attachments for cleaning furniture, drapes, and blinds.

- Hand-held vacuum for vacuuming furniture, stairs, and cleaning up spills.
- Broom, soft brush, and dustpan for cleaning wood and resilient floors.
- Soft paintbrushes for dusting hard-to-reach places such as pleated lampshades, corners of cabinets.
- Disposable foam paint applicators for dusting blinds and between slats on louvered doors.
- Putty knife for scraping hardened splashes and drips on kitchen counters.
- Dust mop for noncarpeted floors.
- Stiff bristled brush for scrubbing floors and tile, an old toothbrush for getting to corners.
- Mop and bucket for cleaning floors.
- Brush for cleaning toilet.
- Sponges and dust cloths.

- Cleaning solutions and polishes. Read labels when selecting products to be sure they're appropriate for the material to be cleaned. Ammonia, for example, may remove the finish from no-wax floors.
- Step stool or stepladder for reaching high places.

Storing cleaning supplies in a convenient place for use makes cleaning more efficient. If you have two or more bathrooms, for example, you may find it practical to buy a toilet bowl brush and a set of cleaning products for each bathroom and store them there. Similarly, in a two-story home, it's convenient to keep the cleaning supplies, products, and tools used to clean each floor on that floor. Another solution is to store cleaning supplies and products in a basket that can be easily moved from room to room as you clean.

Many cleaning products are toxic. Most are poisonous if taken internally; some can cause serious damage to the skin and eyes on contact. To prevent accidents, follow these rules:

- Store all cleaning products out of the reach of children.
- Always read and follow label directions when using cleaning products.
- Never mix cleaners together.

CLEANING ATTITUDES AND ROUTINES

Cleaning may not be your favorite activity, but there are ways to make cleaning time seem shorter and less of a task. First, enlist help. Everyone should help keep the home clean. Even children can be assigned cleaning jobs such as dusting, emptying wastebaskets, and straightening.

When dividing up cleaning chores, consider work or school schedules, abilities, and preferences. One method that works for many people is to have everyone choose items from the cleaning schedule that he or she will be responsible for. The items that no one chooses can be written on slips of paper and drawn from a hat. To keep everyone happy, renegotiate the list of cleaning responsibilities every four to six months. That way, no one will feel stuck forever with a job they particularly dislike.

The cleaning process can be less like work if you approach it with a positive attitude. Set a timer and see how fast you can finish a room. Make the atmosphere cheerful. Play music and work to the rhythm. Do chores together and visit as you work. Think of cleaning as an opportunity to improve your health. Use cleaning sessions as part of your exercise program. Pay attention to your body movements and work on your posture. Finally, cleaning, like most vigorous activities, is an excellent way to reduce stress.

A positive attitude toward cleaning can help lighten your cleaning chores. However, the best attitude in the world will not hold up long with an inefficient cleaning routine. Your cleaning routine is the course of action you follow to clean. Although periodically you'll want to take a little more time to do a more thorough job, you can clean major areas of your home in minutes if you have an efficient routine. Figure 27-2 on page 604 explains routines for quick cleaning of kitchens, bedrooms, baths, and living rooms. Whether you use these routines or develop your own, see if you can cut down on the time it takes to clean.

When people think of ways to have a good time, cleaning the bathroom usually isn't at the top of the list. A good attitude does make a difference. Think of some ways to make cleaning more enjoyable.

Quick-Clean Routines

You can complete your cleaning chores efficiently by following these quick-clean routines.

BATH

1. **Clear the floor.** Put rugs, wastebaskets, etc., outside the room.

2. **Wipe sink area.** Use a damp paper towel to pick up hair around sink.

3. **Sweep or vacuum floor.**

4. **Loosen dirt and soap scum.** Pour toilet bowel cleaner in toilet. Spray tub, outside of toilet, shower walls, and shower door or curtain with appropriate all-purpose cleaner. Leave to soak.

5. **Clean vanity.** Move everything that sits on the vanity counter to one side. Spray the cleared side and sink with cleaner. Wipe off with a sponge. Move everything to the other side and repeat. Put items back in place.

6. **Touch-ups.** Work your way around the room. Spray and wipe shelves. Wipe fingerprints from doors and light switches.

7. **Rinse fixtures.** Use a sponge and cool water to wipe down tub, shower, and lastly the toilet. Swish toilet bowl cleaner around bowl and under rim with brush. Flush.

8. **Shine glass and chrome.** Spray mirror and faucet with glass cleaner and wipe with paper towel or cloth. Clean window if needed.

9. **Mop floor.**

10. **Finish up.** Empty wastebasket, shake out rugs. Put everything back in place.

BEDROOM

1. **Make bed.**

2. **Pick up and straighten.** Pick up and put away any clothing and other items that have been left out. Straighten shelves, dresser top, etc. Gather everything that belongs in another room into a box or basket and set it in the hall.

3. **Vacuum or dustmop floor.**

4. **Dust and polish.** Move around the room, using furniture polish and a clean dry rag to dust and polish furniture.

5. **Shine glass.** Go the opposite way around the room, using glass cleaner to clean mirrors, glass accessories, and windows, if necessary.

6. **Finish up.** Return items in the box to their rightful place.

FIGURE 27-2
(CONTINUED)

A V ISUAL GUIDE TO...

Quick-Clean Routines (Continued)

LIVING ROOM

1. Pick up and straighten. Pick up and put away any items that are out of place. Straighten shelves, coffee table, and so forth. Gather everything that belongs in another room into a box or basket and set it in the hall.

2. Vacuum. Use attachments to vacuum furniture, bookshelves, blinds, and windowsills. Start with the highest item and work down. Next, vacuum floor.

3. Dust and polish. Using a feather duster, soft brush, or rag, dust light fixtures and items on tables. Polish wood furniture.

4. Shine glass. Use glass cleaner to clean mirrors, glass furniture and accessories, pictures, and television screen.

5. Finish up. Return items in the box to their rightful place.

KITCHEN

1. Sweep floor.

2. Pretreat spots. Check for dried spills and spots on floor, range, or cooktop, and counters. Spray with cleaner and leave to soak.

3. Soak drip pans. Remove range drip pans and burner rings and put in warm soapy water in the sink. Leave to soak.

4. Wipe appliances. Wipe inside of oven with a damp rag. Scrape off baked-on food. Clean outside of range with a rag and cleaner. Wipe off other appliances.

5. Discard. Open refrigerator and remove food that should be discarded. Wipe shelves and door.

6. Clean counters. Slide everything to one side of counter. Spray on cleaner and wipe clean, then slide everything back in place.

7. Scrub. Use a plastic scrub pad to clean the range parts in the sink. Drain sink and rinse parts. Dry and replace on range. Wash sink.

8. Shine glass and chrome. Use glass cleaner to polish faucet and glass accessories.

9. Exit mopping. Mop the floor. Start at the farthest corner of the kitchen and work your way out the door.

REDUCING CLEANING TIME

How much time are you willing to devote to cleaning your home every week? Think about this question before you go furniture shopping. Select furnishings with maintenance requirements that match the time you have to maintain them. You can also reduce cleaning time in other ways.

CHOOSE EASY-TO-MAINTAIN FURNISHINGS. Although all furnishings need some care, many products now available are designed to be low maintenance. They can be kept clean with a minimum of time and effort. For minimum-care kitchen flooring, choose no-wax vinyl in a pattern and color that doesn't show dirt readily. For furniture, carpeting, and window treatments, look for stain-resistant fabrics and fibers. Labels usually give maintenance requirements.

STOP DIRT AT THE DOOR. An excellent way to cut down on the time spent cleaning your home is to keep dirt from ever entering. Place doormats outside and inside every entrance. Choose sturdy, rough-textured mats that will remove dirt from shoes and boots and hold up in all kinds of weather.

REDUCE CLUTTER. The fewer items you have, the less there is to clean. First, get rid of things you don't need or really want. One way to weed out clutter is to get three medium-sized cartons. Label them "Keep," "Toss," and "Can't Decide Today." Go through an area and sort items by assigning them to the appropriate box.

Once the area has been cleaned, decide on the best place to store or display the things in the "Keep" box and put them there. Take another look at the items in the "Can't Decide Today" box; if you still aren't sure, date the box and store it out of sight. In a few months, check these items again. Sell or give away all usable items in the "Toss" box.

Once your home is de-cluttered, keep it that way. These rules will help.

- Put things away. Don't leave something where it doesn't belong, even temporarily.
- Don't keep a broken object that you might fix someday. Fix it now, or give it to someone who will.
- Before buying anything, decide where it will be stored or displayed. If you can't think of a place, don't buy the item.
- Keep only what you need. If you want a magazine article, for instance, clip it and recycle the rest of the magazine.

CLEAN AS YOU GO. You can keep big cleaning jobs from building up by taking time to clean as you go through the day. For a start, always clean up spills as soon as they happen. A moist spill is much easier to clean than a hardened one. Straighten rooms before you leave them—stack magazines, fluff cushions, remove items that don't belong there. Store dirty dishes in the dishwasher, if you have one. Rinse and stack them by the sink, if you don't. To prevent soap scum buildup, after a bath or shower, quickly wipe off the shower door or curtain and rinse out the tub.

Donate all the useful belongings you have tucked away but never use. You'll appreciate being free of clutter and other people will be able to make good use of the items.

Outdoor Maintenance

Just as it is important to keep the inside of your home clean, it is important to keep the outside maintained as well. This type of maintenance should be part of your maintenance schedule to help keep the outdoor living spaces of your home attractive and comfortable.

There are some special tools needed to perform some outdoor maintenance tasks. These generally include tools that cut through plants and soil, such as lawn mowers, trimmers, and weed cutters. Other items include pruning shears, rakes, hoes, and shovels.

OUTDOOR MAINTENANCE TASKS

Depending on where you live, outdoor maintenance tasks will vary. For example, a person who lives in a warm climate may have to mow the lawn for a longer season than someone who lives in a climate where it snows in the winter. However, a person who lives in a cooler climate may have to shovel snow in the winter.

Other factors that affect the amount of outdoor maintenance tasks are the size of the lawn and the amount of landscaping. Generally, the more landscaping materials and plants there are, the more maintenance required.

Some outdoor maintenance tasks are only done at certain times of the year. In the spring, for example, summer-blooming flowers are planted. Raking fallen leaves and removing dead foliage after a frost are done in the fall.

Preventive Maintenance

"A stitch in time saves nine" is an old proverb that certainly holds true in the case of home maintenance. The meaning of the proverb is that fixing something at the first sign of trouble is a lot easier than fixing it after the damage has gotten worse. The primary purpose of preventive maintenance is to deal with home repair problems as soon as you're aware of them. That way you'll prevent minor problems from becoming major ones. A secondary purpose is to keep up the appearance of the home. Several areas of the home benefit from regular preventive maintenance.

Weather Blocking

Did you know that 50 to 70 percent of the energy used in the home is for heating and cooling? That's a considerable investment of money and other resources. To protect this investment, it's a good idea to make sure that energy is not wasted. *Weather blocking*—taking steps to reduce energy waste—is energy insurance.

Many products on the market assist homeowners in saving energy. Homeowners might find some of these items helpful:

- **INSULATION.** Placing foam rubber pads and gaskets beneath cover plates and around electrical outlets prevent air seepage from these boxes. Your utility company may offer them to customers for the asking.
- **WINDOW SEALS.** Inexpensive kits of plastic film help form an airtight seal around windows. Indoor kits contain film that you press into place using double-sided tape, then heat-shrink to fit with a hair dryer. Outdoor kits include film and molding strips that you cut and fit as needed.
- **PULLEY SEALS.** These small rectangular caps help prevent air from escaping from pulley weight holes in older double-hung windows. Screws and adhesive backing hold the seal in place.

- **WEATHERSTRIPPING.** Leaks around windows and doors waste a remarkable amount of energy. For weatherstripping windows, adhesive-backed foam is an inexpensive, convenient choice. Gaps between doors and frames can be closed with spring metal weatherstripping, a ribbon of durable metal that pushes back against a closed door. Adhesive-backed, vinyl V-strips are less sturdy but easier to install.
- **DOOR SWEEPS.** This hinged device attaches to the door jamb to draw the door across the frame for a tighter fit. It can be cut to fit doors of different sizes, and can close gaps of up to ½ in. (1.25 cm).

YOU THE CONSUMER . . .

Your family is doing an informal energy audit of your home. Your task is to identify places in your room and the kitchen where weather blocking might be useful. What locations do you find? How do you decide if these need weather blocking? What type of weather blocking do you suggest?

JOINTS

Where two housing surfaces come together at a joint, an opportunity exists for moisture, air, and insects to enter. Problems may occur where siding meets the foundation or roof, where plumbing or electric lines enter the home, and around doors and windows. Many of these joints are sealed by caulking. **Caulking** means applying a sealing compound to make a joint watertight and airtight. A variety of caulking compounds are available in hardware and home improvement stores.

One easy home maintenance task is applying caulk around windows. How does caulk help cut down on energy consumption in a home?

Often homeowners feel that cleaning out gutters is an endless task. You can avoid clogged gutters by covering them with mesh guards.

Over time, as caulk dries with age and the joined building materials swell and shrink at different rates, the caulk often cracks or pulls away from one or more surfaces. Damaged caulk is fairly easy to repair. You need a caulking gun and caulking compound. Acrylic latex caulk is a good general-purpose sealant that dries fast and can be painted.

Caulking is necessary inside the home, as well. Seal joints where interior walls meet with windows and exterior doors, along the edges of resilient floors, and to fill gaps between walls and baseboards. You can buy heavy-duty, water-resistant caulk in a tube for sealing the joints around tubs, sinks, and showers. Check interior and exterior caulk at least once a year.

Follow these steps when applying caulk:

- Remove old caulk with a paint scraper, putty knife, or screwdriver. Load a caulking gun with the appropriate kind of caulk. Cut the tip to the size needed.
- Place the tip at one end of the joint you want to caulk.
- Hold the gun at a 45-degree angle. Squeeze the trigger lever as you pull the gun toward you or downward in a smooth motion.

GUTTERS AND DOWNSPOUTS

Uncontrolled water from rain and melting snow can ruin roofs and siding, seep into windows and do interior damage, and erode lawns. To control drainage, gutters should be installed at the bottom of all sloped roofs. Connected to the gutters are downspouts that carry the water to ground level. Downspouts may lead directly to underground drainage systems or simply release the water onto the ground some distance from the house. Concrete or heavy plastic slabs, called "splash guards," are often placed at the outlet of a downspout to direct the water flow away from the foundation. If the gutters or downspouts

Downspouts serve to carry water away from a home's foundation. Splash guards at the bottom of downspouts prevent erosion from running water.

Draining the water heater on a regular basis can help prolong its life.

are broken or clogged, or if splash guards are broken or missing, water may collect in an area where it can seep into the foundation or basement.

Roofs and roof drainage systems should be checked at least twice a year. After autumn leaves have fallen and before spring rains start are the best times. Check for missing shingles, loose sections, and leaking joints.

Roof drainage systems can become clogged, especially if leaves fall nearby. Using a sturdy ladder, inspect and clean out gutters. To prevent further accumulation, you can install mesh guards or wire cages.

WATER HEATERS

Drain water heaters once a year to allow sediment that collects in the bottom of the tank to drain out. Also check the thermostat on the water heater. If your hot water must always be cooled with large amounts of cold water before it can be used, you're wasting energy and money. Turn the thermostat down.

The water in the water heater is under pressure. As a safeguard, most water heaters have a pressure relief valve located at the top. The valve is designed to leak water if the pressure inside builds up

beyond a predetermined level of safety. Excess pressure could result in a dangerous explosion. Every six months, test the pressure relief valve by lifting the test lever. When you lift the lever, it should release hot water through the overflow. When doing any maintenance on a water heater, remember that the water is very hot—usually between 120° and 150°F (49° and 66°C). These temperatures can cause serious burns and scalds.

FURNACES

More than half the heating systems in the United States are forced-air systems. These systems warm air with a burner and circulate it through a network of ducts with a fan or blower. Cool air returns to the furnace through a return duct. Forced-air heating stirs up dust and dirt. A filter in the return duct catches these particles and sends clean air through to the furnace. If the filter becomes clogged, it blocks the flow of air. This makes the furnace work harder. It also wastes energy and may lead to insufficient warming.

If your home uses forced-air heating, check the furnace filter every month. Open the filter compartment door, slide the filter out, and hold it up to the light. If you can see through the filter, it's good for another month. If not, replace it.

AIR CONDITIONERS

Routine maintenance of air conditioning systems is important to help keep them operating efficiently. Air conditioning units should be cleaned and checked at the beginning and the end of each season.

A room (window) air conditioner, like a furnace, contains a filter that traps pollen, dust, and dirt. If the filter becomes dirty or clogged, cooling performance is affected. A dirty filter can be washed with warm soapy water. If the filter has deteriorated, replace it.

A central air conditioning system is a split system, with some of the components installed outdoors and some indoors. Because it sits outdoors, dirt, leaves, grass, and other debris can easily get into the condenser unit and reduce the unit's efficiency.

Clean both room and central air conditioning units to remove leaves, dirt, and other debris. Always follow the manufacturer's instructions when cleaning a room air conditioning unit. Also check the manufacturer's instructions about any other maintenance tasks that are necessary.

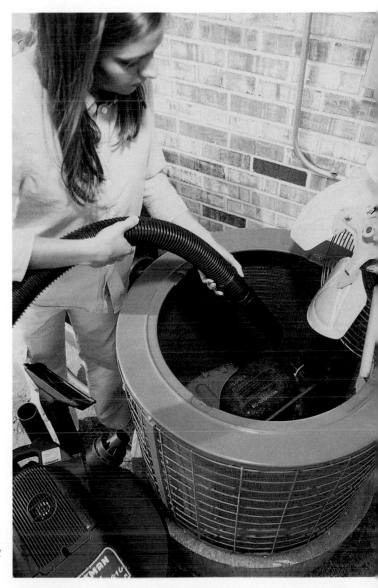

Air conditioners run more efficiently when they are clean. At the beginning of the season, remove leaves and dirt from the condenser unit.

Home Repairs

Normal wear and tear, the elements, pests, and natural decay occasionally result in a need for home repair. There are numerous home repairs that you may be able to handle yourself. You might tighten hinges to fix a sagging door or install a new lock to increase home security. You can learn how to replace broken screen panels or stop a leaking faucet by replacing a washer. Books, magazines, newspaper articles, and Internet sites give step-by-step directions for doing these and other home repairs. Home improvement centers, as well as some hardware and lumber stores, have experts who will give you advice on specific problems.

As you do more and more repairs yourself, your skill and confidence in handling repairs will increase. There are some repairs, however, that should always be left to professionals. Leave such work as rewiring a home or replacing water supply pipes to qualified electricians or plumbers. Gas-leak problems should be handled immediately by your gas supplier. Air conditioner and furnace repair should be done by a qualified technician. Major structural repairs—replacing a roof, for example—are also probably best left to professionals.

Many home repair situations develop gradually. For example, a door might sag a little more each week, until you discover weeks later that it's scraping the carpet when it is opened or closed. Even then, you have time to plan the repair and carry it out. Emergency home repairs are an entirely different matter. When the toilet overflows, for example, it must be attended to immediately. Everyone should learn to handle home repair emergencies. Figure 27-3 shows what to do if a pipe bursts, the lights go out, there's no hot water, a sink stops up, or a toilet overflows. To prepare before an emergency strikes, locate and label the main shutoff valves for water, natural or propane gas, and electricity in your home.

The home repairs you can do yourself will go much more smoothly if you have the right tools and materials for the job. Many clerks who sell materials are able to help you choose the one that's right for your job. Although the tools you need will vary from job to job, Figure 27-4 shows some items for a basic home repair tool kit.

FIGURE 27-3

A VISUAL GUIDE TO...

Emergency Repairs

WATER PIPE BURSTS

1. Place bucket under pipe to catch water. If water is shooting up, place a large towel over the top to direct water down.

2. Turn off water at main shutoff valve. (Located near the point where the main water supply pipe enters house. Could be outdoors or in basement.)

3. Turn on all faucets in the home to drain pipes.

4. Call a plumber to replace damaged pipe.

LIGHTS GO OUT

1. If you were using a small appliance, unplug it.

2. Determine how widespread the problem is. If it's the entire neighborhood, call your electric company to report the power failure. If it's your home, go to Step 3.

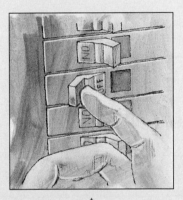 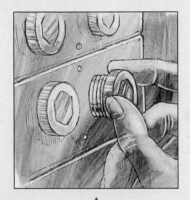

3. If you have a breaker box, check to see whether any breakers have been tripped (usually has a red marker showing). Flip it to "off," then back to "on."

4. If you have a fuse box, check for blown fuses by looking at the thin metal filament inside the glass. If it's blackened or broken, unscrew the fuse and replace it with a new one.

NO HOT WATER

1. If there is water on the floor around the water heater, shut off the water inlet valve and close the gas shutoff valve or cut off electricity to heater. Call a plumber.

2. If there is no water on the floor, and the heater is gas, check to see if the pilot light is lit. If it's electric, check the fuse box or circuit breaker box to make sure it's getting power. (See "Lights Go Out.") Follow the manufacturer's directions to restart the heater. If it doesn't work, wait 15 minutes, then try again.

Emergency Repairs (Continued)

SINK STOPS UP

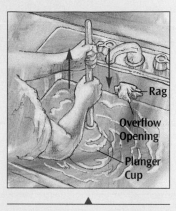

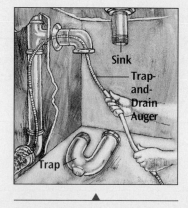

1. Bail out the sink until it's about half full of water.

2. Reach in and remove the pop-up plug (bath sinks) or the strainer (kitchen sinks). For a bathroom sink, stuff a rag tightly into the overflow opening.

3. Place the cup of a plunger over the drain and pump it at least 12 times to force the clog down or up.

4. If the clog doesn't budge, remove the trap, insert a trap-and-drain auger into the drainpipe, and crank the handle. Clean the trap and fasten it securely in its original position.

TOILET OVERFLOWS

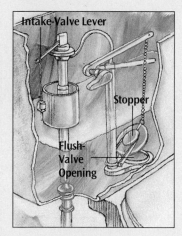

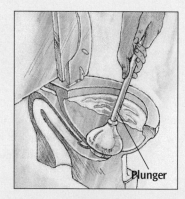

1. Turn off the water supply to the toilet. Remove the lid from the tank behind the toilet bowl. Reach inside and push the stopper closed at the bottom of the tank.

2. Put on rubber gloves. Use a small container to scoop water out of the toilet bowl and into a bucket until the toilet is half full.

3. Place the cup of the plunger over the drain trap. Pump the plunger rapidly at least 10 times and then abruptly pull it out of the bowl to release the clog.

4. If the toilet remains clogged, place the end of a closet auger into the drain trap. Very slowly turn the handle of the closet auger clockwise as you push it toward the clog. As the head of the auger works into the clog, move the auger in a back-and-forth motion until the clog breaks up.

FIGURE 27-4

A **V**ISUAL GUIDE TO...

A Basic Tool Kit

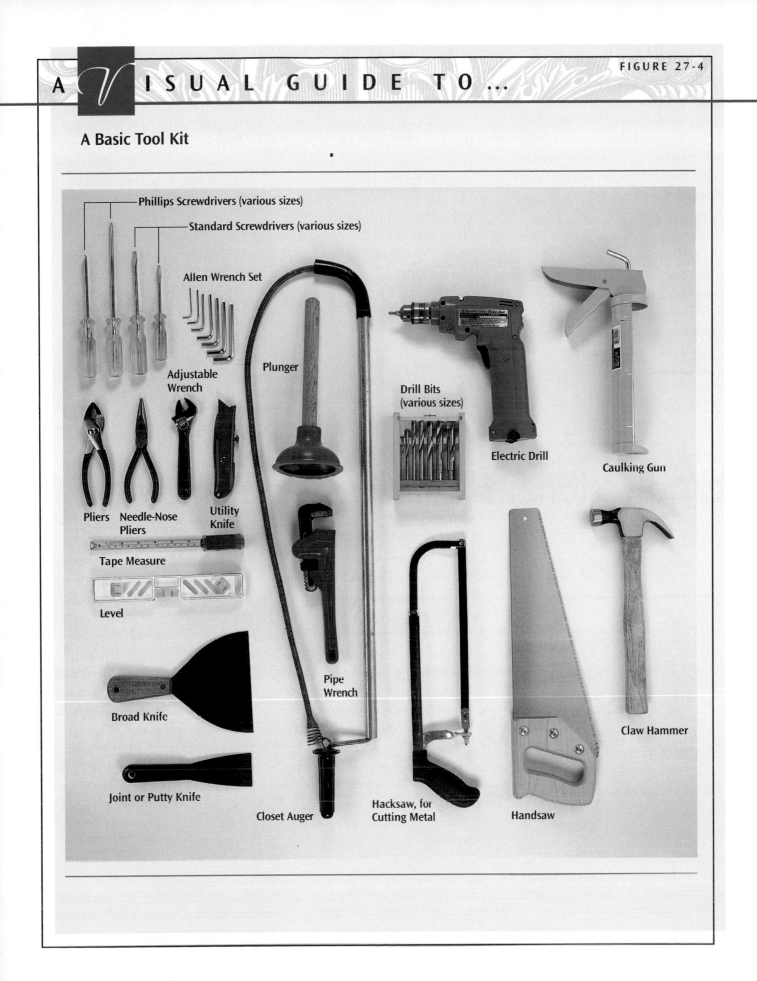

Phillips Screwdrivers (various sizes)

Standard Screwdrivers (various sizes)

Allen Wrench Set

Plunger

Adjustable Wrench

Drill Bits (various sizes)

Electric Drill

Caulking Gun

Pliers

Needle-Nose Pliers

Utility Knife

Tape Measure

Level

Broad Knife

Joint or Putty Knife

Pipe Wrench

Claw Hammer

Closet Auger

Hacksaw, for Cutting Metal

Handsaw

HOME REPAIR SAFETY

When making home repairs yourself, remember that safety is crucial. Any time you are working with tools, substances, and electricity there are potential hazards. To make sure that you make home repairs safely, follow these safety tips:

- Read and follow the directions that come with power tools and other equipment.
- Unplug power tools before making any adjustments.
- Never touch electrical tools, appliances, or outlets with wet hands or when standing on a wet surface.
- Wear safety goggles when working with power tools, even for a short job.
- Wear a breathing mask when working with materials or tools that give off toxic fumes, such as paint remover, or particles, such as sawdust.
- Use only a sturdy step stool or stepladder to reach high places. Never place the ladder or stool on an unstable surface or in front of a door that might open.
- Keep small children away from the work area.
- Don't attempt electrical repairs unless you are absolutely sure that you can do them correctly. Before working on power switches, outlets, or light fixtures, turn off the power supply to that area by switching off the circuit breaker or pulling the fuse. Post a sign on the fuse box or circuit breaker panel so no one will restore power. Use a voltage tester to make absolutely certain the power is off.
- Before attempting to repair an appliance or fixture, read and follow the manufacturer's instructions.
- Unplug electrical appliances before you work on them.

Professional Servicing of Appliances

Large appliances are another area of home repair that should generally be left to professionals. Unfortunately, service calls for appliances are always expensive even if minimum service is given. You can cut down on service calls by giving your appliances proper maintenance. Clean the appliance according to the manufacturer's recommendations. For example, vacuum refrigerator coils every few months, and empty lint screens on dryers after every load. Check electrical appliances for worn plugs and frayed cords, and replace them immediately.

Many appliances are sold with a warranty. A **warranty** is a written statement of the manufacturer's promise to replace defective parts at no charge for a certain time. Most warranties distinguish between "defect" and "damage." A **defect** is any flaw that exists in the product when it is sold, or that develops within a certain period of time. **Damage** is a problem that is the result of improper treatment by the buyer or the result of natural disasters. Defects are the manufacturer's responsibility; damage is the buyer's.

Remember—a warranty is a promise included in the purchase price of an appliance. Read warranties carefully, and keep them in a safe place. Then, if the need arises, take advantage of them.

Many manufacturers and stores offer an extended warranty, usually at an extra charge, when you purchase an appliance. These warranties extend the time limit on a warranty. Most financial advisors recommend that you not pay for an extended warranty. Statistics show that only 12 to 20 percent of the people who buy extended warranties ever need to use them.

Heating and cooling systems should be inspected periodically by technicians. You may want to purchase a **service contract**, which is an agreement purchased from a dealer or manufacturer under which regular inspections and repairs are made at no extra charge or for a small fee. Before buying a service contract, carefully evaluate whether it is a wise investment for you. One thing to consider is the age of your system and its history of problems. Older appliances are more likely to need repair than new ones. You should also weigh the cost of the contract against estimated yearly costs for individual service and repair.

Be a savvy consumer. Although most professional service companies are honest and efficient, many are not. Millions of dollars are wasted each year on needless home repair work. Never agree to expensive repair or replacement until you have checked with two other companies or independent contractors.

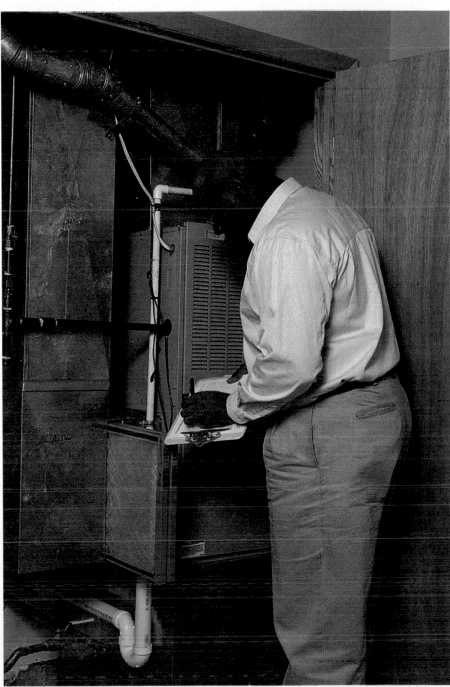

Furnaces need to be inspected and maintained on a regular basis. Would you choose to have a service contract for a furnace? Why or why not?

Home Maintenance Advice Columnist

Shireen Bloomgren

My career in the home maintenance field started with fix-up projects around the house and doing minor jobs in my father's home construction business. When he retired I took over some of the management roles. I found that I was good at solving problems that arose at building sites; so good, in fact, that people began coming to me for advice on their own home projects.

Seeing that so many people had questions about home maintenance, I approached the editor of a local newspaper and asked whether he would be interested in starting a weekly home maintenance advice column, answering questions from readers. He agreed to a trial run. Sure enough, it was quite popular with readers.

Now I'm a full-time newspaper columnist and my column runs in dozens of newspapers across the country. I receive hundreds of questions every day from readers on topics ranging from taking the squeak out of chairs to removing wallpaper that has been up for more than 30 years. My assistant and I spend a good part of every day reading those letters and sorting through them.

Another portion of my day is spent doing research. I read constantly to stay current on the latest developments in home maintenance. I keep an extensive file of newspaper and magazine articles, brochures, and manufacturer's product information and have a library of related books.

"I use my computer for online research and analyze the information from a variety of sites."

I use my computer for online research and analyze the information from a variety of sites. I often attend seminars, workshops, and conventions. Sometimes I am a presenter, but I also always learn about new items or techniques that my readers might find helpful.

Since I can't answer every letter I receive, my assistant helps me choose those that we think will interest the greatest number of readers. Only after I have completed the research do I begin writing answers for the column. I try to write clear, concise answers. A copyeditor reads each column and returns it to me with her comments and suggestions, often letting me know whether my advice is too technical. I then revise the column until it's ready to go.

Sometimes I tell myself I need to try out what I think is an answer before writing about it. It's really an excuse to get back to the hands-on work I've always loved to do.

"Only after I have completed the research do I begin writing answers for the column."

Career Profile

Home maintenance advice columnists write articles for a newspaper in response to people's questions about home maintenance and repairs. They are required to respond to questions on a wide variety of different topics, so experience in construction and home maintenance is needed. Home maintenance advice columnists spend a lot of time researching specific subjects and staying up-to-date on new products and techniques. Some give workshops to demonstrate maintenance and repairs. The information presented in the column must be accurate and easy to understand.

Education
▸ A bachelor's degree is required, preferably in English, journalism, or communications. A technical degree with courses in journalism may be substituted.
▸ Technical experience is necessary.

Skills Needed
▸ Good organizational and research skills.
▸ The ability to write well and concisely and meet deadlines.
▸ Knowledge of construction and home maintenance is needed.
▸ Experience writing for a newspaper or magazine is very helpful.

Career Outlook
▸ Employment opportunities are not expected to increase significantly.
▸ For larger newspapers, there will be difficult competition for positions.

Career Activities

1. Choose a common home repair or maintenance task. Write a question about it, then write the answer. Edit your work to make it clear and concise.
2. Search the Internet for at least ten sources of home repair and maintenance information. For the five best sites, list the web addresses and explain why each was a top pick.

Chapter Summary

➤ Although standards of cleanliness vary from person to person, there are minimum guidelines for protecting health and safety.

➤ Following a schedule for cleaning and maintenance cuts down on repairs and helps you make sure that important details are not forgotten.

➤ Efficient cleaning routines can cut the time spent doing household chores.

➤ You can take actions to reduce your cleaning time.

➤ Outdoor maintenance should be done regularly to help keep the outside of the home clean and attractive.

➤ Doing regular preventive maintenance is less expensive and less time-consuming than dealing with major repairs.

➤ There are time-tested procedures for many common household emergency repairs.

Checking Your Understanding

1. What four rules of cleanliness should never be compromised?

2. Which household cleaning chores should be done daily?

3. What are the main tasks when quick-cleaning a bedroom?

4. Name four techniques to reduce cleaning time on a regular basis.

5. What is the primary purpose of preventive maintenance? What is a secondary purpose?

6. List four areas of the home that benefit from preventive maintenance. Name one important maintenance task required for each area.

7. Describe what to do if a kitchen sink stops up.

8. Name three types of home repairs for which you should always call a professional.

Thinking Critically

1. What are the advantages of encouraging young children to help with home cleaning? What are some possible disadvantages? How might these disadvantages be avoided?

2. Why do you suppose people tend to accumulate clutter? What suggestions do you have for someone who has difficulty parting with items?

3. Rose and Jeff McCartle are buying their first washer and dryer at a total cost of $750. The appliance salesperson wants them to upgrade the one-year warranty that is included in the purchase price to a five-year warranty that would cost $49.95 per year. What are the pros and cons of purchasing the extended warranty? What advice would you give the McCartles?

Applications

1. **Designing a Cleaning Schedule.** Work with a partner to make a list of all the cleaning and maintenance chores for a shared apartment. Devise a schedule that distributes the work. Don't agree to any responsibilities that you would not actually be willing to assume. Share your schedule with the class, and discuss how you reached agreement.

2. **Alternative Cleaning Products.** Using library resources, find at least ten ways that inexpensive, environmentally friendly products (such as vinegar, lemon juice, or baking soda) can be used to solve specific cleaning problems. Make a chart or brochure of your "green" cleaning solutions.

3. **Creating a Low-Maintenance Apartment.** Plan the furnishings for an efficiency apartment, emphasizing ease of maintenance. Describe in detail the following items, what materials they are made of, and how you will care for them: sofa and chair, table for dining, walls, floor coverings, and window treatments.

4. **Maintenance Calendar.** Design a chart, poster, or calendar to help remind homeowners of preventive maintenance tasks that should be done throughout the year. Include the tasks listed in the chapter as well as others you discover through research.

5. **Filing a Complaint.** Imagine that you recently bought a home appliance, but it has stopped working. You believe the problem is the result of a defect. Write a letter to the manufacturer asking that the problem be remedied as covered in the warranty. Be specific about the nature of the problem, when and where you purchased the appliance, and what action you want the company to take. Use the correct format for a business letter.

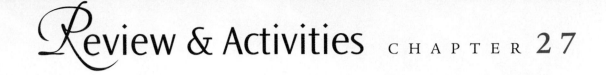

BUILDING YOUR PORTFOLIO

You've been hearing about a problem in your community concerning senior citizens who are unable to do their yard work. They can't afford to hire help, so you have decided to organize a group of volunteers to help the seniors in your town. Write a description detailing the following points:

➤ How you will recruit volunteers.

➤ How you will schedule the work.

➤ What tasks will be completed.

➤ How you will advertise your services.

➤ Other details you think are important.

Remodeling and Renovating

CHAPTER OBJECTIVES

► Identify possible reasons for remodeling a home.

► Discuss points to consider when deciding whether to move or remodel.

► Give examples of various types of remodeling projects.

► Summarize the steps in planning a remodeling project.

► Describe how to select a contractor.

► Compare professional remodeling with do-it-yourself remodeling.

TERMS TO LEARN

• bid

• contract

• conversion

• home equity loan

• performance bond

• renovation

• restoration

• setback

• variance

*D*eciding to remodel a home is a much bigger decision than deciding to redecorate. Redecorating—repainting rooms a different color, replacing drapes with blinds, or rearranging the furniture—will give the home a new look. Such changes don't, however, affect the structure of the home. Remodeling—knocking down a wall, replacing windows blocking off an entrance, adding an extra room—is much more time-consuming and costly.

*R*easons for Remodeling

Remodeling a kitchen is a major undertaking in any home, but it is one of the changes that produces the most satisfaction. What updates in this kitchen give it a more spacious appearance?

*C*hange is often both the cause of remodeling and its result. As people's lifestyles and levels of physical ability change, their housing needs also change. Families become larger or smaller, requiring adaptations in the home. Some homeowners want more storage space; others need more bedrooms or an updated kitchen. Still others want to make their home more convenient.

Remodeling often updates a home and increases its value. Installing energy-saving systems and products improve a home's energy efficiency.

Other remodeling is undertaken to make a home look more like the owners want it to. Some homeowners remodel just before putting their home on the market. Because certain features such as an updated bath or kitchen can increase the sale price, the rooms are popular choices for this type of remodeling. Keep in mind that the costs of other remodeling projects such as adding a sunroom, may not be completely recouped by a higher selling price.

Sometimes a home is sold as a "fixer-upper" and the new owners are people who enjoy tackling a variety of jobs from a fresh coat of paint to major renovation. Which remodeling tasks would you enjoy?

REMODELING VERSUS BUYING

Remodeling is one option when an existing house no longer meets its owners' needs and wants. Buying or building a new home is another possibility. There are several factors to consider when deciding whether to move or to remodel.

COSTS. The expense of remodeling should be weighed against the cost of moving. Moving costs are estimated to be at least 8 to 10 percent of a home's value. If owners can make the changes they want for around this amount, they will not save money by moving.

The length of time you plan to stay in the home should be considered. Many housing experts suggest that many remodeling projects are not a worthwhile financial investment if the owners plan to move within two years. Remodeling

kitchens and baths are usually an exception to this rule. They are likely to immediately add enough to the home's resale value to equal the costs involved. On the other hand, finishing a basement may have only a 15 percent payback over time.

Still another consideration is taxes. Property taxes are based on a home's value, which generally increases with remodeling. Therefore, the homeowner who remodels will probably face a higher yearly property tax bill. On the other hand, buying or building may also result in increased taxes. If budget is to be the deciding factor, it's important to get accurate tax estimates for all options.

CONVENIENCE. Many homeowners choose to remodel because they are pleased with the home except for its few flaws. The home may be

convenient to a school or job or be in a desirable neighborhood. It may be simpler to remodel than to go through the inconvenience of moving. With careful planning, homeowners can remodel their homes to get the new features they want without losing the features they already have.

COMMITMENT. Finally, homeowners must decide whether they are willing to put in the time and energy needed to complete a project. Remodeling can be messy and disorderly while the work is being done. It's important to anticipate the stress caused by changes in daily routines. Add in hours of research and planning, attention to such matters, and concerns about liability for injury to workers.

Types of Remodeling Projects

Remodeling a home can involve anything from replacing a plain sliding glass door with decorative French doors, to building an additional room or wing. Remodeling projects can be categorized as one of four types: changing a lived-in area, making unused space livable, adding on, and buying to remodel. Each type of project has a different cost, amount of time required for completion, and complexity of work required.

a wall might be removed between the living room and dining room to make a large open area.

Remodeling a lived-in area usually involves less complex changes than the other types of remodeling, but inconvenience is greater. Often rooms being worked on are unusable at least part of the time. Could you cope with not having a kitchen sink for awhile?

CHANGING A LIVED-IN AREA

Changing a lived-in area involves altering space that is already occupied. Most projects of this type involve kitchens and bathrooms. In a kitchen, new cabinets might be installed, appliances moved, or a door closed off to provide more wall space. In a bathroom, a skylight could be cut in the ceiling or new fixtures installed. Other lived-in areas, of course, can be remodeled. For example,

MAKING UNUSED SPACE LIVABLE

Unfinished areas of a home—such as an attic, basement, porch, or attached garage—may be remodeled. These spaces have a roof, walls, and floor but may need further structural work to make them livable. For example, the foundation under a garage or porch may not meet the requirements of the local building code.

Insulation, heating, wiring, plumbing, and lighting may also be required. Basements can be gloomy if there's no access to natural light. Even with extensive changes such as these, it is usually less expensive to remodel the spaces than to add rooms to a house.

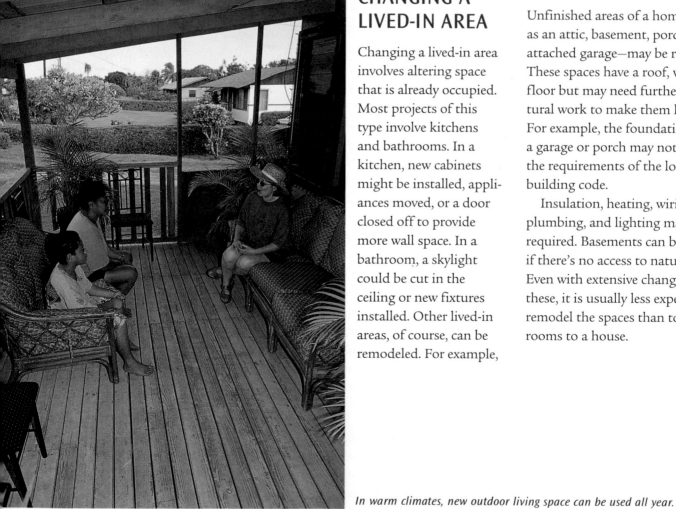

In warm climates, new outdoor living space can be used all year.

Extra space on a lot may mean room for a house addition. The first step homeowners need to take, though, is to check local zoning laws to find out if any restrictions apply.

ADDING ON

Another type of remodeling consists of adding one or more rooms to an existing house. Adding on includes enlarging a room. Early in the planning stage, the homeowner should check local zoning laws. Many contain restrictions on the size and placement of home additions. When there's not enough space on the property for a ground-level addition, a second-story addition may be the answer.

Adding on is more complex than altering space already built. To add on to a home, a foundation must usually be dug or a slab laid and exterior walls removed. Sometimes walls that are removed contain plumbing or electrical wiring that must be relocated. For a second-story addition, the roof must be removed and replaced. A stairway may also need to be constructed.

The addition must be carefully planned to blend architecturally with the existing house. If additional doors and windows are added, they should match the style of the rest of the home, to keep the exterior consistent. How the addition connects to the existing rooms should also be given some thought. Adding a bedroom adjoining a noisy family room, for instance, may not be a good choice.

Landscaping can visually tie together an addition and the existing house.

Adaptive Reuse as a Means to Historic Preservation

Have you ever walked by a magnificent old building that is in disrepair and wondered what can be done to save it? Designers have also noticed these buildings and have developed creative ways to preserve historical landmarks. Many times the building will be returned to its original historic appearance, but will be used for a different purpose. Designers refer to these projects as adaptive reuse.

What is worth saving? This is an important philosophical and practical question in any historic preservation project. Designers will first examine a building to determine if it has distinctive architectural elements and details. The old building's size, materials, colors, and architectural style are important considerations. The renovation must also be appropriate for its neighbors and surrounding area.

Understanding criteria for preserving a historic building helps designers to determine if the building is appropriate for adaptive reuse. Here are some examples of how this can work:

- *Musee D'Orsay.* Located in Paris, a museum was created in a converted railway terminal. The Orsay station was built for the 1900 International Exhibition. The structure is a striking metal structure that is highly decorated. Creating a museum required restoration and rehabilitation of the station. The interior of the museum is a very strong reminder of the turn of the century period and contains artwork dedicated to the 19th century.

- *1846 Greek Revival church.* In New York's Greenwich Village, a church was restored and turned into a multifamily housing unit. The adaptation divided the church into 15 apartments. One of the biggest challenges for the project was providing enough windows and entrances for each of the units.

- *The Bank Center.* Banks are often selected for adaptive reuse projects. One such project is the Bank Center located in Pittsburgh, Pennsylvania. Designers converted a historic bank building into a complex of small shops and a movie theatre. The exterior of the building had to be cleaned and the masonry was repaired.

However, most of the restoration occurred on the interior of the building. The original interior of the bank was retained to create interesting backgrounds for the merchandise of the shops.

You, the

Designer

Imagine you are part of a design team responsible for converting a historic courthouse into an adaptive reuse project. Decide what criteria you would use in preserving the courthouse. Give rationales for your choices.

BUYING TO REMODEL

Some people buy an older home in need of repair because they plan to repair and modernize it. The process of extensively repairing and modernizing a home is called **renovation**. When searching for a home to renovate, look for one that has a sound basic structure. A home with a sound structure, though in need of repair, can gain value that will exceed the cost of the renovation.

Restoration is a type of renovation in which an older home is returned to its original state.

Another type of major remodeling is **conversion**—buying a building for the purpose of converting it or changing its use. An example is a large single-family house converted to a duplex; another is a warehouse converted to loft apartments.

In some urban areas, old, run-down houses are sold at low cost by the government. The owners agree to make repairs within a certain period of time. In many cases, low-interest loans are made available to finance the final cost of the repairs. With such programs, old neighborhoods are rehabilitated and preserved. These programs also make it possible for people with a small or modest housing budget to afford a comfortable home.

Planning a Project

A home remodeling or renovation project is a major undertaking that can bring great satisfaction. However, it also has the potential for equally large problems. The project may be delayed when materials or workers do not arrive on time. Unexpected work may need to be done, adding to the cost of the project. Bad weather may cause delays. Even worse, the homeowner may be dissatisfied with the finished work. Problems will be greatly reduced if the remodeling project is well planned and carefully organized ahead of time.

An interior designer can help a homeowner get off to a good start with a major remodeling project. What other professionals can help with remodeling plans?

DECIDING ON DESIGN GOALS

Homeowners often begin a remodeling project without a clear idea of what they want done. As a result, they're easily swayed by the preferences of designers and contractors. These homeowners may end up with a living space that doesn't suit them. Doing some advance research can help homeowners identify their preferences.

Some good sources of ideas are home decorating and remodeling magazines. Those considering

A remodeling project has a higher satisfaction rate when the whole family participates in major decisions.

remodeling should clip pictures of materials, styles, equipment, and arrangements they like. It's also a good idea to clip things that are *not* acceptable. Put both types of information in a resource file.

Such files help people communicate their ideas to a designer or a contractor. In addition, a resource file allows members of the household to show each other how they envision the remodeled space.

Using the four-step process that follows will help further define goals for the project.

1. Examine the present home layout and identify any problems.
2. Analyze the family's habits in using the home as well as their design preferences.
3. Use the information gathered in Steps 1 and 2 to draw up a list of remodeling goals.

4. Consider all possible options for meeting the goals. Think through each potential decision before finalizing the choice of design.

These points must be established before moving forward into the next areas of project planning. Figure 28-1 on page 631 shows how one family worked through this process to establish remodeling goals.

FIGURE 28-1

A VISUAL GUIDE TO ...

Defining Kitchen Remodeling Goals

Julia and Michael Parker and their children had lived in their house for two years. They liked everything about the house except the kitchen. Last year they bought a new range, but that didn't help. The Parkers thought about moving, but because they liked the rest of the house so much, they decided to remodel instead.

Everyone had different ideas about what was wrong with the kitchen and how it should be fixed. To help organize their ideas and clarify some goals for the remodeling project, they worked their way through the following steps:

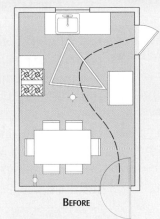

BEFORE

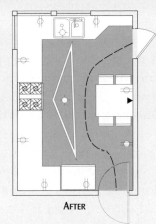

AFTER

STEP 1

EXAMINE THE PRESENT LAYOUT AND IDENTIFY PROBLEMS

The Parkers measured the kitchen and drew a floor plan to scale on a piece of graph paper. The floor plan included the dimensions of the kitchen and the location of all receptacles, switches, furniture, and permanent items such as the sink. Studying the floor plan helped the Parkers identify the following problems:

- Work triangle—refrigerator to sink to range—is interrupted by the traffic line between the two doors.
- Work space available for preparing and mixing food is on range or kitchen table.
- Not enough storage space for kitchen items.
- Not enough room to store fresh and frozen food.
- Not enough electrical receptacles.
- Sink too small.

STEP 2

ANALYZE HABITS AND PREFERENCES

By thinking about how they wanted to use the kitchen, the Parkers made the following list:

- Want to eat most meals in kitchen.
- Want to be able to look out window while working at sink.
- Want to use back door to enter and exit home.
- Want a sit-down work area.
- Want a telephone in kitchen.

STEP 3

LIST REMODELING GOALS

The Parkers used their list of problems and preferences to draw up a list of remodeling goals.

STEP 4

CONSIDER POSSIBLE OPTIONS AND MAKE DECISIONS

The Parkers made another floor plan of just the room area. They made templates to help them try out ideas. For each remodeling goal, they tried out possible options before making a final decision. Often there were special factors to consider. The result was a well-defined plan they could take to a building contractor.

REMODELING GOALS	*Considerations*	*Decisions*
EAT-IN KITCHEN	Space taken up by table and chairs needed for work triangle.	Build a low eating counter with stools between the two doors.
LARGER SINK, UNDER WINDOW	Relocating water pipes would be costly.	Buy double sink and place in current sink location.
ELIMINATE TRAFFIC FROM WORK TRIANGLE	Avoid placing appliances between the doors; three walls remain.	Change basic design of kitchen to U-shaped.
SIT-DOWN WORK AREA	Don't want to block work triangle.	Use eating counter.
ADD TELEPHONE	Would like a place to sit and write while on the phone.	Install phone beside eating counter.
ADD CABINET AND COUNTER SPACE	Putting standard-size cabinets on the wall next to the outside door would block entryway.	Have cabinets custom made to fit in that space and still leave room for people to get through.
ADD ELECTRICAL RECEPTACLES	Need for major appliances as well as small ones.	Add receptacles for every major appliance and at regular intervals.

EVALUATING THE AREA

Before beginning a complex remodeling job, homeowners should evaluate the area to be remodeled. If a new foundation is to be dug for an addition, the utility companies should mark the location of existing underground wires and pipes. A contractor, structural engineer, or architect should check the structure of the part of the home to be remodeled. The structure must be able to support the new addition or equipment.

Plumbing, heating, and wiring should also be checked. If these systems will need updating soon, it may be more convenient and less costly to do the upgrade during the remodeling process. When adding on, homeowners need to know whether the existing plumbing, heating, and electrical systems will be adequate after the job is done.

Awareness of structural and systems problems is particularly important for older homes. People who are planning to purchase an older home to remodel or renovate should make sure the foundation and structure are sound. Many prospective homeowners hire engineering inspection firms to check a home for structural problems. A professional can also advise a buyer about the age and efficiency of the home's plumbing, heating, and electrical systems. If the home isn't sound to begin with, remodeling might cost too much to make it a worthwhile investment.

CHECKING LOCAL REGULATIONS

Homeowners should know about any zoning regulations or aesthetic codes that will affect the planned remodeling job. If they proceed without proper approvals from the local government, they may have to pay a fine or even tear down an addition or make other exterior changes.

As described in Chapter 7, zoning laws and aesthetic codes in a community regulate the types of structures that may be built and the appearance of their exteriors. In some cases, zoning laws limit how much of a building lot may be occupied by a structure. They also define **setback**, or the distance any part of a building

A good contractor makes sure that a project meets all national and local regulations, thereby saving the homeowner time, money, and potential headaches.

Local building codes may require a building permit before construction begins. The permit must be displayed during the project and inspections may also be necessary. How do building codes affect the quality of homes in an area?

must be from the property line. If remodeling plans do not meet zoning requirements, the homeowner may have to apply for a variance. A **variance** is a license to waive the zoning law. It is a time-consuming process, so many people prefer to change their plans.

Homeowners should find out whether they need a building permit for their proposed job. A building permit is required for any alterations that affect the framework, size, or safety of the building. Inspections may also be necessary to ensure that the remodeling meets the building codes. As you read in Chapter 7, building codes establish minimum standards for construction in an

area. Most often, national codes— such as the Uniform Building Code, National Electrical Code, and Uniform Plumbing Code—are followed.

DECIDING ABOUT FINANCING

Some remodeling jobs are costly. A home improvement loan may be needed to meet expenses. Many people finance their remodeling projects by taking out a home equity loan. A **home equity loan** is money borrowed from a lending institution based on the current market value of a property, minus the amount owed

on the mortgage. A competitive interest rate can often be obtained with these loans. A drawback of this type of loan is that if the homeowners cannot repay the loan, the home may be taken by the bank and sold for payment of the loan.

When obtaining a loan, homeowners should shop around to find the best rate of interest. They also need to know the length of the waiting period before approval of a loan. Waiting for money can affect the building schedule. When homeowners are calculating the costs of their projects, it is often recommended that they include an additional 20 percent in the budget to cover unforeseen costs.

Contractors can minimize homeowners' frustration with building delays by keeping them informed of progress on the job and any problems that arise.

PLANNING THE SCHEDULE

Deciding when to do a remodeling project can have a great impact on its outcome. Avoid starting a large-scale remodeling job near a major holiday season or after a significant change in your life. The season of the year may be a factor as well. In a northern climate, late fall or winter is not a good time to start an addition to a house. An exposed exterior wall or roof could greatly increase heating costs and cause health problems for the residents. On the other hand, winter is a slow time for construction. Some contractors are willing to do jobs for less money just to keep busy.

It's very important that you order all materials well in advance of the starting date. Delivery of custom-made kitchen cabinets, for example, can take four to six months. If materials aren't on hand when needed, costly delays may result.

Hiring Professionals

Professional designers, architects, general contractors, and subcontractors can help with a remodeling project. Homeowners should choose these professionals carefully.

DESIGNERS

Interior designers, kitchen planners, and other design professionals translate people's ideas into concrete plans. They draw up floor plans done to scale. Designers may also suggest ways to improve a plan submitted by the homeowner. In addition to planning projects, some designers and architects supervise the entire construction process.

A good way to find a designer is to ask for referrals from friends and relatives who have had remodeling done. Listings of local designers are available from professional associations such as the American Society of Interior Designers.

Homeowners should check the designer's portfolio, which contains photographs and descriptions of completed projects. If possible, it is often informative to visit the homes of clients for whom the designer has completed projects.

CONTRACTORS

Finding an experienced, reputable contractor is crucial to the success of a remodeling project. The National Association of the Remodeling Industry offers information on selecting a professional remodeling contractor. Other sources of referrals are friends and relatives, lumberyard managers, plumbing dealers, and other suppliers. The state licensing board and Better Business Bureau are other sources of information.

QUESTIONS TO ASK. There's important legal information you should find out from contractors before hiring a specific contractor for the job. Ask such questions as:

- Does the contractor carry liability insurance? If not, and an accident takes place on your property, you are liable.
- Does the contractor carry the appropriate workers' compensation? Workers' compensation is a payment into an insurance fund which compensates, or pays, employees for injuries they suffer on the job.

Check the references of the professionals you are considering hiring for a project.

- Does the contractor have the proper credentials to work in your state? Some states require a license.
- Is a permit needed for the job? If a permit is needed, who will obtain it?

It's wise to find out whether performance bonds are required in your area. A **performance bond** is a sum of money a contractor puts up to provide insurance that a job will be completed. For example, a community might require that a contractor working on a large job post a bond; then, if that contractor fails to finish the job, the performance bond covers the cost of completion.

CHECKING REFERENCES. Asking questions of the contractor is a good start, but the contractor's references should be checked with others. Ask the contractor for business and bank references. Determine how long the contractor has been in business. In addition, it's important to visit homes at which the contractor has done work.

Request a list of previous clients for reference. Visit some of the homes your contractor has worked on. You'll probably want to ask the clients such questions as:

- Was the contractor easy to work with?
- Was concern shown for the client and property?
- Was the job completed on time?
- Were the workers easy to deal with?
- Did they do a good job?
- Were there any safety problems on the site? (OSHA regulations are meant to protect workers.)

During your visit, ask the client to point out examples of the contractor's work. Examine the quality of the work. Look at architectural elements. Is the placement of the doors and windows good? Are elements such as cabinets square and level? Look at construction details. Does the drywall or plaster have a finished look? Is the wood grain smooth? Look at the joints. Are they tightly mitered? Are the materials quality ones? Does the overall space give you a sense of a good design?

BIDS AND CONTRACTS. Contractors submit bids for projects. A **bid** is an offer from a contractor to complete a project for a certain price. The bid states the work to be done and estimates the cost of labor and materials. To make the bid, the contractor uses the homeowner's plans and any specifications from the designer or architect.

Homeowners should get three written bids on a project. The lowest bid is not always the best choice. The bids must be compared carefully to be sure nothing was omitted from any bid that would affect cost. Experienced contractors will be able to estimate the total cost of a project quite closely.

After choosing the contractor, the homeowner and the contractor should sign a contract before any work begins. The **contract** is *a legally binding agreement* that states what work the contractor will do and the amount the homeowner will pay. The contract also lists the date work is to begin and when it is expected

to end. It may also include details on the materials that will be used, including the brand and model number for appliances and fixtures. If subcontractors are to be used, their responsibilities should be clearly spelled out. The homeowner's obligation to them, should the contractor fail to pay, should also be detailed.

Once a contract has been signed, the contractor must complete the work for the specified amount, even though the finished project may actually cost more or less than this amount. If either party breaks the agreement, legal action may be taken.

Some contractors prefer to work on a time and materials basis, which means they get an hourly rate. Homeowners are at a disadvantage with this system because they're not sure at the outset what the total cost of the project will be. A better arrangement is a contract that divides the project into stages and pays the contractor a percentage of the total cost at completion of each stage. Be wary of contractors who demand large amounts of money before they begin work.

When the job begins, it's to the homeowner's advantage to establish a good working relationship with the contractor. Keeping the channels of communication open is essential. The homeowner should oversee the various steps of the project, especially when building inspections are being made. That way, there is less chance that the homeowner will be surprised or disappointed.

Doing the Work Yourself

People who do their own remodeling or renovating can save about half of what the project would cost if it were done by professionals. Also, many people take pride in being able to do the work themselves.

A disadvantage of doing the work yourself is that the project will probably take longer to finish. This means that your home and family life will be disrupted for a longer period of time. Taking care of all aspects of the project may be more complicated than you expect. The homeowner must obtain permits and schedule inspections, jobs normally done by the contractor. Buying building materials and fixtures is another task the homeowner will have to take on. Contractors often get a professional discount from wholesale distributors. Sometimes, homeowners hire professionals to do the complex work and then do the finishing work themselves.

For homeowners with the time and the skills, doing remodeling and renovating projects themselves is a great way to save money and get the results they want.

The End Result

Anyone who has remodeled can admit to experiencing at least some stress. Things do go wrong. Since most people are living in the home during the alterations, the place that is normally a haven may become a noisy, chaotic mess.

However, homeowners who plan well in advance, stay within budget, and stay involved are usually well satisfied with their new living space. The benefits—more room, updated or personalized fixtures, and increased housing value—outweigh the disadvantages.

Home Remodeling Specialist

Hector Emeralde

Who would have thought that I'd ever be running a business of my own? But that's exactly what has happened. As home remodeling specialists, my business partner and I help people make their dreams come true by turning their living space into what they really want it to be.

My home remodeling days date back to high school when I helped my family remodel our basement. We wanted to divide the unfinished area into two rooms, a family room and a laundry/utility room. We drew up plans and got a quick education in building codes. We had to hire people to check the foundation, seal the walls and floors, and put up the dry-wall. Then the hands-on work began as the whole family painted, hung wallpaper, and laid flooring. I was pretty proud of the project when it was done.

After graduating from high school, I took an entry-level position in a paint store. In that job, I added more to my remodeling experience, including the business and sales end. A contractor who came into the store all the time told me about an apprenticeship program in the area, so that's what I decided to do. After three years in a paid work-study program, I became a journey-level painter, wallpaper hanger, and drywall taper. My memories from working in the paint store, however, stayed with me, making me think that I'd like to be in business for myself someday.

A few years later, I had a family of my own, and we were busy updating an older home. Talking with construction professionals fueled my old desire to get a business going. I was ready when a friend with eight years' experience in the remodeling field suggested that we join forces and finances. With a bank loan, we found a modest location and opened our own remodeling business.

"My home remodeling days date back to high school when I helped my family remodel our basement."

At first, we took on smaller projects. When a client asked us to attach rooms to an existing home, however, my partner and I jumped at the chance. We presented a cost-effective plan for building and designing the new structure, inside and out. When our bid was accepted, we organized the work of specialists in foundation, framing, plumbing, electricity, architecture, and interior design. Safety on the job is top priority. We check to make sure all contractors follow OSHA (Occupational Safety and Health Administration) guidelines. We finished the addition under budget and on time which helped our business reputation.

By putting some of our profits back into the business, we've been able to team up with a developer who wants to turn an old, abandoned building into several independent units. We've got to assess the building's structure in order to bring it up to code. At the same time, our growing staff is working with architects and designers to create ideas for the look we want—one that combines work and living space. We think this is an exciting approach for the future. This is the kind of project that makes our work get more interesting every day.

> *"With the reputation and success of our business at stake, we finished the addition under budget and on time."*

Career Profile

A *home remodeling specialist* oversees home improvement projects for a wide variety of clients. The planning is often done in collaboration with construction trade and design professionals. Responsible for estimating costs, the specialist must also gather the appropriate materials and then work with both the homeowner and contracted labor to see that the remodeling project is brought to a successful and satisfactory completion.

Education
▸ Experience as a construction worker or completion of a related apprenticeship program is required. An advanced degree in construction is desirable since projects may require specialized knowledge and supervisory skill. Further information is available through The Remodelers Council.
▸ Training in the construction trades and blueprint reading, as well as courses in home and interior design, is helpful. Knowledge of architectural principles and CAD are a plus, as are courses in business management, accounting, and computer-related applications.

Skills Needed
▸ Knowledge of recent remodeling trends and materials, the ability to organize construction and design activities into logical steps, and a basic familiarity with building and safety codes.
▸ Entrepreneurial and supervisory skills, plus the ability to communicate with both the homeowner and related professionals throughout the remodeling process.
▸ Computer skills to evaluate various construction methods and to determine the most cost-effective plan.

Career Outlook
▸ Home remodeling specialists are in growing demand. Home improvement construction is expected to continue to grow faster than new home construction.

Career Activities

1. Check your local phone book under *home improvement, remodeling,* and *contractors* to see what types of business specialize in remodeling work. What specific types of remodeling projects are mentioned most often in the ads?
2. You have been contracted to remodel a kitchen for a client. The work to be done was specified before remodeling began. However, the client frequently changes her mind and also asks for additional work to be included. At the same time, she's complaining that the work is behind schedule. Write a letter or an explanation you would use with the client to improve the situation.

Chapter Summary

➤ People remodel their homes for a variety of reasons.

➤ When weighing the pros and cons of moving versus remodeling, consider budget, convenience, and commitment.

➤ Four basic types of remodeling are: changing a lived-in area, making unused space livable, adding on, and buying to remodel.

➤ Careful planning can eliminate many of the problems in a remodeling project.

➤ Homeowners should consider carefully before hiring professionals or deciding to do remodeling work themselves.

Checking Your Understanding

1. What are four reasons for remodeling?

2. Name three budget factors to consider when deciding whether to move or remodel.

3. In what ways might remodeling place a strain on family living?

4. Give one example of remodeling a lived-in area and one example of making unused space livable.

5. What is the difference between renovation and restoration?

6. List the basic steps involved in planning a remodeling project.

7. What is a benefit of obtaining a home equity loan for a remodeling project? What is a drawback?

8. Describe a process for selecting a good contractor.

9. What are four questions to ask a contractor you are considering for a job?

10. What are the advantages and disadvantages of doing one's own remodeling?

Thinking Critically

1. Although everyone in the Skelley family has a small bedroom, they feel crowded. There are four people in the family: Mrs. Skelley, her mother-in-law, and her two children, ages 14 and 12. There's only one bathroom in the home. Although they are planning to relocate next year, the Skelleys feel they can't deal with having one bathroom any longer. "We're not a family who deals well with disruption," explains Mrs. Skelley. Would you advise the Skelleys to remodel? Why?

2. The Downs live in an older home with an unfinished basement and attic. The basement has only one small window. They're planning to remodel to provide a family room, but can't decide whether to add on, remodel the attic, or remodel the basement. What points should they consider when making their decision?

3. What research might you do if you were planning a restoration? Briefly outline the process you might follow, and identify special sources of information you would use.

Applications

1. **Interview.** Talk to someone who has completed a home remodeling project. Identify the project, the steps involved in planning, and the materials used. Evaluate the customer's satisfaction with the final results of the project in terms of cost, time and energy used, and quality of work.

2. **Remodeling Plan.** Plan a remodeling project for your home or a fictitious home. Use design and home decorating magazines to find ideas. Cut out ideas you like and put them in your clipping file. List the professionals you would consult with and explain why each professional is relevant to the project. What regulations might you need to check? Prepare a preliminary cost estimate. Then determine how you might finance the project.

3. **Quality Checklist.** Make a checklist showing the steps you would take to ensure the quality of the work after a contractor has been hired to do a remodeling job.

4. **Preserving History.** Research a home restoration that was conducted in your area. You might call the historical society or ask the reference librarian at your local library to help you track down information. Visit the house, if possible. Report on the work that was done, how the house was changed, and the details that were preserved as a result of the restoration.

5. **Newspaper Writing.** Write an article for a newspaper about a family remodeling one or more rooms in their home. Include details of the project itself. Identify the problems, as well as the solutions to the problems. Discuss the way or ways in which the remodeling project affected the family members.

BUILDING YOUR PORTFOLIO

Assume you are the assistant to a building contractor. The contractor has assigned you to write a brief information sheet that answers common questions asked about remodeling. The title of the sheet will be "So You've Decided to Remodel." The contractor has suggested that you write it in a question-and-answer format. For example, one question might be, "How much will it cost?" You should then write an answer that will help the homeowner determine the cost of the job. Include at least eight questions and answers that cover the major aspects of most remodeling jobs. You may want to illustrate your information sheet to make it more appealing.

Glossary

A

ability. A skill a person has already developed. (Chapter 4)

accented neutral. A neutral *color scheme* that includes a small amount of bright color. Also called a neutral-plus color scheme. (Chapter 16)

active solar heating system. A system that requires mechanical devices to collect and store the sun's heat and then distribute it throughout the house when it is needed. (Chapter 14)

adaptable design. Design features that are temporary and can be easily changed. (Chapter 1)

adaptations. Furniture in the style of old designs without being an exact copy of any one piece. (Chapter 20)

adjustable rate mortgage. A home loan in which the interest rate changes depending on current rates in effect. (Chapter 11)

adobe (uh-DOH-bee). Clay formed into sun-dried bricks and used as building material. (Chapter 5)

aesthetic (es-THE-tik) **codes.** Codes that regulate the appearance of buildings in order to maintain the beauty and the desired look of an area. (Chapter 7)

alkyd (AL-ked) **paint.** A type of paint made from an oil or a synthetic resin called alkyd. (Chapter 19)

amortization. Gradual elimination of the *principal* of a mortgage. (Chapter 11)

analogous. A *color scheme* using colors that are next to each other on the color wheel. (Chapter 16)

antique. By law in the United States, a piece of furniture from an earlier period that is at least 100 years old; often used informally to mean "old." (Chapter 20)

appraisal. An estimate of the value of a property. (Chapter 11)

apprenticeship. A program that combines on-the-job training from a skilled worker and classroom instruction. (Chapter 4)

aptitude. A natural talent or a person's potential for learning a skill. (Chapter 4)

archaeologist (ahr-kee-AH-luh-jist). Scientist who studies history through the relics and remains of old civilizations. (Chapter 1)

asbestos. A flame-retardant mineral substance; was used in many building materials until it was discovered to be a health hazard. (Chapter 26)

asphyxiation. Loss of consciousness or death from lack of oxygen. (Chapter 26)

assign. To transfer a tenant's *lease* and all legal responsibility for a rental unit to someone else before the end of the lease period. (Chapter 10)

asymmetrical balance. A design effect in which elements on either side of an imaginary central line are unmatched but appear to be in balance. (Chapter 17)

automated management systems. Central computerized control units that oversee daily functions in a home, such as heating, cooling, lighting, and security. (Chapter 3)

B

baby boomers. People born in the 20-year period immediately following World War II. (Chapter 2)

bamboo. A fast-growing, woody, tropical plant used to make furniture. (Chapter 21)

barrier-free design. Living spaces designed without structures that prevent access to people with special needs. (Chapter 1)

bid. An offer from a *contractor* to complete a building or remodeling project for a certain price. (Chapter 28)

biomaterial. Organically-based building material manufactured from recycled matter. (Chapter 3)

biometric. A security system that reads the physical characteristics of a person before allowing access. (Chapter 3)

blinds. Window coverings made of a series of evenly spaced slats that may be opened or closed by a cord. (Chapter 19)

breach of contract. A legal phrase for failure to meet all terms of a *contract* or agreement. (Chapter 10)

building codes. Rules that regulate the quality of building materials and set standards of quality and safety for construction. (Chapter 7)

bungalow. A small, one-story house with an overhanging roof and a covered porch. (Chapter 6)

C

cabriole (KAB-ree-ohl) **leg.** A furniture leg that curves out at the middle and then tapers inward just above an ornamental foot. (Chapter 20)

Cape Cod house. A house with a simple rectangular design, a central chimney, and a pitched roof. (Chapter 5)

carbon monoxide. A colorless, odorless gas that is readily absorbed by red blood cells when breathed in, thus interfering with the body's oxygen supply. (Chapter 26)

case goods. Furniture pieces that are not upholstered, such as chests, desks, and tables. (Chapter 21)

caulking. Applying a sealing compound to an area where two housing surfaces meet (such as where the siding meets the foundation) in order to make the joint watertight and airtight. (Chapter 27)

cesspool. A system that collects *sewage* and lets it gradually seep into the surrounding earth; is prohibited in some areas because of a danger of contaminating nearby soil and water. (Chapter 13)

chair rail. *Molding* that runs horizontally across the wall about 3 ft. (0.9 m) from the floor. (Chapter 19)

chair table. A 17th century chair with a large back that protected the occupant from drafts and could be tipped forward to form a table. (Chapter 20)

circuit breaker. A safety device that stops the flow of electric current in an overloaded circuit. (Chapter 13)

clapboards. Exterior house siding of boards with one edge thicker than the other laid in overlapping rows to protect the walls from the elements. (Chapter 5)

clearance space. The additional space needed around furniture for ease of use. (Chapter 18)

closed plan. An interior layout in which rooms are separated and self-contained. (Chapter 7)

closed storage. A storage system in which doors or drawers conceal items. (Chapter 25)

closing. The meeting at which the legal papers are signed and money changes in hands finalizing the sale of a house. (Chapter 11)

closing costs. Fees due at the time a home purchase is finalized. (Chapter 9)

color. The effect an object produces by absorbing and reflecting light rays; hue. (Chapter 15)

color scheme. A combination of colors selected for a room design in order to create a mood or set a tone. (Chapter 16)

combustible. Capable of burning quickly. (Chapter 26)

complement. The color opposite another color on the color wheel. (Chapter 16)

complementary. A *color scheme* using two colors that are directly opposite each other on the color wheel. (Chapter 16)

computer-aided design (CAD). Software that enables designers, architects, and drafters to make construction drawings, interior designs, and other drawings using a computer. (Chapter 3)

condominium ownership. Individual ownership of a unit in a multifamily dwelling, such as an apartment or *town house*. (Chapter 9)

conduction. The transfer of heat from a body of higher temperature to one of lower temperature by direct contact. (Chapter 13)

contingency fee. An additional percentage of the total cost of a project to cover unexpected expenses. (Chapter 18)

contract. A legally binding agreement that states what work the contractor will do and the amount the homeowner will pay. (Chapter 28)

contractor. A person who oversees a construction project. (Chapter 13)

convection. The transfer of heat by means of air flow. (Chapter 13)

conventional construction. A building method in which materials are cut and assembled piece by piece at the home *site*. (Chapter 3)

conventional mortgage. A home loan in which the borrower pays a fixed interest rate for the life of the loan. (Chapter 11)

conversion. A type of major remodeling that involves buying a building for the purpose of converting it or changing its use. (Chapter 28)

cooperative ownership. A form of home ownership in which residents of a multifamily building purchase stock in a nonprofit corporation that owns the building and its grounds. (Chapter 9)

coquina (co-KEE-nuh). A soft porous limestone composed of shell and coral. (Chapter 5)

cornice (KOR-nuhs). A decorative strip at the area where the roof and the walls meet. (Chapter 6)

cornice lighting. A type of concealed light source (usually a *fluorescent light*) that is mounted near the junction of wall and ceiling and directs light downward. (Chapter 22)

cove lighting. A type of concealed light source (usually a *fluorescent light*) that is mounted near the junction of wall and ceiling and directs light upward toward the ceiling. (Chapter 22)

cross ventilation. Air flow created when air travels in one side of a home and out another. (Chapter 12)

culture. A combination of all the customs, beliefs, and ideas of a group of people. (Chapter 2)

D

damage. As defined in a *warranty*, a problem that is the result of improper treatment by the buyer or the result of natural disasters. (Chapter 27)

defect. As defined in a *warranty*, any flaw that exists in the product when it is sold, or that develops within a certain period of time. (Chapter 27)

demographics. Statistical characteristics of a population.

dormer. A structure that projects through a steeply sloping roof. The window set in this structure is called a dormer window. (Chapter 5)

down payment. A partial payment of cash made at the time of purchase. (Chapter 9)

downlight. A type of lighting that directs a beam of light from the ceiling downward. (Chapter 22)

duplex. One building that contains two separate living units. (Chapter 8)

E

earnest money. A deposit a potential buyer pays to show that he or she is serious about buying a home. (Chapter 9)

eclectic. A style of decorating that involves mixing furnishings of different styles and possibly from different periods. (Chapter 17)

efficiency apartment. A unit with one main room, a small kitchen area, and a bathroom. (Chapter 8)

elevation. A diagram that provides a side view; usually shows one wall of a room or a house exterior and displays relative heights and architectural features. (Chapter 23)

ell. An extension built at right angles to the length of the structure. (Chapter 5)

emphasis. In design, the center of interest or focal point that first catches the viewer's attention. (Chapter 17)

employability skills. Skills required to acquire and retain a job, such as responsibility, decision making, reasoning, and self-management. (Chapter 4)

energy audit. An inspection of the home to determine where heat loss may be occurring. (Chapter 14)

engineered wood product. Manufactured material formed from wood. (Chapter 3)

entrepreneur. A person who starts his or her own business. (Chapter 4)

entry-level job. A job that requires little training, although a high school diploma may be required. (Chapter 4)

equity. The difference between the market value of a piece of property and the *principal* owed on the *mortgage*. (Chapter 11)

ergonomics. An applied science concerned with designing, building, and arranging things so they are safe, comfortable, and efficient for people to use. (Chapter 25)

escrow. Money held in trust by a third party until a specified time; often pertains to payments for property taxes and insurance. (Chapter 11)

evict. A legal action that requires tenants to move out before the lease has expired. (Chapter 10)

extended family. A family that includes other relatives in addition to parents and children. (Chapter 2)

F

fanlight. A semicircular, round, or oval window with fan-shaped panes of glass. (Chapter 6)

fiber optic light. A type of light that flows through hair-like glass tubes and is focused at the other end of a tube; emits no heat and no ultraviolet rays. (Chapter 22)

flammable. Capable of burning quickly. (Chapter 26)

flashing. Strips of sheet metal placed around a chimney and other roof openings to insulate the roof from the chimney and prevent moisture leaks. (Chapter 12)

floor plan. A diagram of a home or other structure that shows the arrangement of rooms. (Chapter 7)

flue. The vertical shaft of a chimney which carries smoke and hot gases to open air. (Chapter 12)

fluorescent light. A visible light produced when chemicals inside a sealed glass tube transform ultraviolet rays into visible light. (Chapter 22)

footing. Continuous concrete base that supports the foundation walls of a house below ground level. (Chapter 12)

form. An element of design that describes the shape and structure of solid objects. (Chapter 15)

fossil fuels. Nonrenewable fuels—including oil, coal, and natural gas—that were formed in the earth from the remains of prehistoric animals or plants. (Chapter 14)

fourplex. A housing unit that is attached at the side walls to three other units. (Chapter 8)

fuse. A safety device that stops the flow of electric current in an overloaded circuit. (Chapter 13)

G

gable roof. A pitched roof with two sloped sides. (Chapter 5)

gables. Triangular end walls formed by a gable or pitched roof. (Chapter 5)

gambrel roof. A roof that has two slopes on each side, the upper slope being flatter than the lower slope, allowing interior space for full-sized upstairs rooms. (Chapter 5)

garden apartment. A unit in a low-rise building that includes landscaped grounds. (Chapter 8)

garrison house. A house with a second story that overhangs or projects from the first story. (Chapter 5)

gateleg table. A table with legs on each side that swing out to support drop leaves that are pulled up from the sides. (Chapter 20)

geothermal energy. Heat from the earth's interior. (Chapter 14)

gingerbread. Lacy-looking, cutout wood trim. (Chapter 6)

golden rectangle. A rectangle that has sides in a ratio of 2 to 3 (short sides are two-thirds the length of the long sides). (Chapter 17)

golden section. The division of a line anyplace between one-half and one-third of its total length so that the ratio of the larger segment to the smaller segment equals the ratio of the whole line to the larger segment. (Chapter 17)

gradation. A type of *rhythm* in design achieved by a gradual increase or decrease of color, size, or pattern. (Chapter 17)

graduated mortgage payment. A home loan in which the payments start out low and increase in the later years of the loan when the owners are likely to have more income. (Chapter 11)

green building. Designing, building, and operating homes to use materials, energy, and water efficiently. (Chapter 3)

ground fault circuit interrupter (GFCI). A safety device used in receptacles (outlets) near plumbing or waterthat guard people against electric shock. (Chapter 13)

ground wire. An electrical conductor that is connected to the earth, providing protection in case there is an abnormal flow of electric current. (Chapter 13)

H

half-timbered house. A style of house built by early English colonists; the wood frame of the house formed part of the outside wall. (Chapter 5)

halogen bulb. A special type of incandescent light bulb containing pressurized halogen gas. (Chapter 22)

harmonious design. A design in which every item fits well with the others. (Chapter 15)

highboy. A chest of drawers mounted on legs. (Chapter 20)

high-rise apartment. One of many separate living units in a multistory building generally equipped with elevators, most often found in cities. (Chapter 8)

hip roof. A roof with four sloped sides. (Chapter 6)

home equity loan. Money borrowed from a lending institution based on the current market value of a property, minus the amount owed on the *mortgage*. (Chapter 28)

homeowner's insurance. Insurance protection for a home and its contents. (Chapter 11)

household. All the people who live together in one housing unit. (Chapter 2)

housing. Any structure built for people to live in. (Chapter 1)

hue. The specific name of a color. (Chapter 16)

human resources. Personal qualities that people possess, including creativity, imagination, knowledge, skills, talent, time, energy, and experience. (Chapter 8)

I J K

incandescent light. Light produced by electricity passing through a tungsten filament in a glass bulb. (Chapter 22)

intensity. The brightness or dullness of a color. (Chapter 16)

interest. The money a lending company charges a buyer for a loan. (Chapter 9)

interview. A formal meeting between an employer and a job applicant. (Chapter 4)

inventory. A survey a designer uses to identify characteristics that will affect a design plan. (Chapter 18)

island. A freestanding storage and countertop unit in a kitchen; may include a cooktop. (Chapter 24)

japanning. The process of applying glossy black lacquer to furniture. (Chapter 20)

job application. A form employers use to ask questions about an applicant's skills, work experience, education, and interests. (Chapter 4)

job shadowing. Spending time with a person at work and learning by watching as he or she performs the functions of the job. (Chapter 4)

joint. The place where one piece of wood is connected to another, such as where a chair leg is joined to the seat. (Chapter 21)

L

landlord. A person who owns a property and rents it to someone else. (Chapter 9)

landscaping. The ways people use plants and objects to enhance or change the natural environment around the exterior of their homes. (Chapter 14)

latex paint. A water-based, quick-drying paint. (Chapter 19)

lease. The legal document a *tenant* signs when agreeing to rent housing for a specific period of time. (Chapter 10)

lifestyle. Way of living. (Chapter 1)

light emitting diode. A type of light made of a silicon "chip" of crystals about the size of a grain of salt; a small electrical current passing through the chip generates the light. (Chapter 22)

line. An element of design that delineates *space*, outlines *form*, and conveys a sense of movement or direction. (Chapter 15)

low-rise apartment. An apartment in a building with few floors and no elevators. (Chapter 8)

luminous ceiling panels. Consists of fluorescent tubes placed above plastic panels. (Chapter 22)

M

mansard roof. A roof that has two slopes on all sides, with the lower slope being steep and the upper slope almost flat. (Chapter 6)

manufactured home. A dwelling completely assembled at a factory and transported to the *site*. (Chapter 3)

master bath. A full bathroom that is part of the master bedroom area. (Chapter 24)

material resources. Tangible assets such as money, property, supplies, and tools. (Chapter 8)

mentor. A successful worker who shares her or his expert knowledge and demonstrates correct work behaviors with new employees or less experienced workers. (Chapter 4)

modular furniture. Furniture made from standardized pieces (modules) that can fit together in a variety of ways, like building blocks. (Chapter 20)

modular home. A *systems-built home* made up of separate boxlike sections, or modules, that are built at a factory and assembled at the *site*. (Chapter 3)

molding. Strip of shaped wood used for trim or ornamentation in a room. (Chapter 19)

monochromatic. A *color scheme* that uses tints and shades of one color on the color wheel. (Chapter 16)

mortgage. A home loan. (Chapter 9)

multipurpose furniture. Furniture pieces that serve more than one need, such as futon that serves as a couch and a bed. (Chapter 21)

multipurpose room. Room used for many things. (Chapter 18)

N

networking. Communicating with people you know or can get to know to share job and career information and advice. (Chapter 4)

nomads. People who wander from place to place in search of food for their grazing herds. (Chapter 1)

nuclear family. A family including a father, a mother, and one or more children. (Chapter 2)

O

open plan. An interior layout that has few dividing walls separating rooms. (Chapter 7)

open storage. A storage system in which stored items are visible. (Chapter 25)

opposition. When lines come together to form right angles in a design. (Chapter 17)

orientation. The position of a home on its site and the direction the home faces. (Chapter 12)

overlay. A sheet of transparent, or see-through, material that is placed over a basic drawing in order to add enhancements or special details without altering the drawing itself. (Chapter 23)

P Q

panel box. A device that controls the distribution of electricity to the home wiring system; also called a service entrance or fuse box. (Chapter 13)

particleboard. A type of board made from a combination of wood shavings, *veneer* scraps, chips, and sometimes sawdust that are all mixed with glue and pressed together under heat. (Chapter 21)

passive solar heating system. A system that makes direct use of the sun's heat without mechanical systems. (Chapter 14)

pediment (PED-uh-munt). A triangular or arched decoration over a window or doorway. (Chapter 6)

peninsula. A kitchen countertop that extends out into the room, with one end attached to a wall or a cabinet. (Chapter 24)

performance bond. A sum of money a *contractor* puts up to provide insurance that a job will be completed. (Chapter 28)

physical needs. All the things the human body needs to survive: air, sunlight, shelter, sleep, and food. (Chapter 1)

pictorial drawing. A drawing that shows the viewer several surfaces of objects in the room simultaneously. (Chapter 23)

pigment. A substance that absorbs some light rays and reflects others, affecting the color of an object. (Chapter 16)

pilaster. Decorative flattened column. (Chapter 6)

pile. The density of carpet or fabric; nap. (Chapter 19)

pitched roof. A two-sided roof with a steep angle. (Chapter 5)

plain weave. A simple weave pattern as strong in one direction as it is in the other. (Chapter 19)

plywood. A building material consisting of three, five, or seven layers of less expensive wood glued together. (Chapter 21)

points. A one-time service fee charged by lending companies to increase their yield on a *mortgage*. Each point generally equals 1 percent of the mortgage amount. (Chapter 11)

portfolio. A collection of examples of a person's best work; often used when applying for a job to show a person's abilities and accomplishments. (Chapter 4)

portico (POR-tih-koh). A tall, open porch, supported by columns, over the front entrance. (Chapter 6)

primer. A sealant that makes a surface nonporous and keeps out humidity; a base paint. (Chapter 19)

principal. The original amount of a loan (not including *interest*); also the portion of a loan payment that goes toward reducing the original amount of a loan. (Chapter 9)

prioritize. When a person rates wants and needs in order of preference and importance. (Chapter 18)

private zone. The part of the home used for sleeping, relaxing, bathing, and dressing. (Chapter 7)

proportion. The relationship in size of objects or parts of objects to one another and to the design as a whole. (Chapter 17)

psychological (sy-kuh-LAH-jih-kuhl) **needs.** Needs related to thoughts and emotions. (Chapter 1)

pueblos. Adobe houses built on top of each other into cliffs and caves and on the level ground. (Chapter 5)

R

R value. A measure of insulation's capacity to resist winter heat loss and summer heat gain. (Chapter 12)

radiation. (1) The transmission of heat by means of rays traveling in straight lines from a source. (Chapter 13) **(2)** A type of rhythm in design that occurs when lines radiate, or move outward, from a central point. (Chapter 17)

radon. A radioactive gas that occurs naturally in some types of soil and rock and can seep into homes through cracks in basement floors and walls. (Chapter 26)

recovery rate. The average amount of water that will be heated in a water heater tank in one hour. (Chapter 13)

reeding. A decorative carving consisting of vertical lines that resemble thin reeds—stems of tall grass. (Chapter 20)

references. People who will recommend a person to an employer. (Chapter 4)

rendering. A drawing in which the designer adds realistic details, such as textures, shadows, shadings, and color. (Chapter 23)

renovation. The process of extensively repairing and modernizing a home. (Chapter 28)

renter's insurance. An insurance policy that covers personal property against loss by theft, fire, or other hazards. (Chapter 9)

repetition. A type of *rhythm* in design achieved when certain colors, lines, forms, or textures are repeated. (Chapter 17)

reproduction. A furniture piece that is an accurate copy of an original design. (Chapter 20)

resilient flooring. Flooring with a semi-hard surface that returns to its original shape after stress. (Chapter 19)

resource management. The wise use of natural resources. (Chapter 14)

restoration. A type of *renovation* in which an older home is returned to its original state. (Chapter 28)

résumé. A brief summary of a person's education, skills, work experience, activities, and interests. (Chapter 4)

retrofitting. The process of making an existing home more energy-efficient. (Chapter 14)

rhythm. The design principle that suggests connected movement between different parts of a design by using colors, lines, forms, or textures; also referred to as continuity. (Chapter 17)

S

saltbox house. A two-story, pitched-roof house in which the rear portion of the roof is extended down to cover a first-floor addition. (Chapter 5)

sample board. A piece of illustration board with mounted samples of proposed wall coverings, floor coverings, upholstery, and window-treatment fabrics. (Chapter 23)

satin weave. A fabric weave pattern distinguished by long "floats," which are formed when each warp (lengthwise) thread passes over a certain number of weft (crosswise) threads at one time before passing under one. (Chapter 19)

scale. The *proportion* of an object or a space to human beings and to other objects or spaces in a design. (Chapter 17)

scale drawing. A drawing in which a given number of inches or centimeters represents a given number of feet or meters. (Chapter 18)

security deposit. A fee paid by a renter to cover the cost of any future damage that may be caused to the unit. (Chapter 9)

septic tank. A large concrete box, usually buried underground, that is used for sewage disposal. (Chapter 13)

service contract. An agreement purchased from a dealer or manufacturer under which regular inspections and repairs of a product are made at no extra charge or for a small fee. (Chapter 27)

service zone. The part of the home where most of the household work is done. (Chapter 7)

setback. The distance a building must be from the property line. (Chapter 28)

shade. A *hue* lower (darker) than its normal *value*; created by adding black to a hue. (Chapter 16)

shingles. Thin, oblong pieces of material, usually wood, that are laid in overlapping rows to cover the roof or sides of a structure. (Chapter 5)

shutters. Window coverings made of vertical sections of wood or manufactured material hinged together, much like a folding door. (Chapter 19)

single-parent family. A family that has only one parent living with one or more children. (Chapter 2)

site. The land and surrounding environment on which a home is built. (Chapter 3)

social zone. The part of the home used for activities and entertainment. (Chapter 7)

soffit lighting. A type of built-in lighting enclosed in a box-like structure that directs light downward. (Chapter 22)

space. An element of design that is the three-dimensional expanse that a designer is working with, as well as the area around or between objects within that expanse. (Chapter 15)

split-complementary. A *color scheme* that combines one color with the two colors on each side of its complement (opposite color) on the color wheel. (Chapter 16)

status. The way a person's importance in society is perceived by others. (Chapter 2)

stenciling. A type of decorative painting in which patterns are created by using a special brush to apply paint through cutout areas in a template. (Chapter 19)

strip lights. Rows of incandescent bulbs or fluorescent tubes around the tops or sides of a mirror. (Chapter 22)

stucco. A plaster material made with cement, sand, and lime. (Chapter 5)

style. The overall characteristics of a design. (Chapter 23)

subcontractor. A worker hired by a contractor or homeowner to perform a specific function in the construction of a home. (Chapter 13)

sublet. To move out of a rental unit before the *lease* is up and rent the unit to someone else while retaining legal responsibility for the original lease. (Chapter 10)

subsidized housing. Housing available at low cost to families with low incomes through programs in which the government provides assistance payments to private housing owners. (Chapter 10)

survey. A check to determine the exact boundaries of a property. (Chapter 11)

swag. A piece of fabric that is draped gracefully across the top of a window. (Chapter 19)

symmetrical balance. A design effect in which the arrangement of forms on one side of an imaginary central line is the mirror image of the arrangement of forms on the opposite side. (Chapter 17)

systems-built home. A dwelling whose parts are manufactured in a factory, with the building completed at the site. (Chapter 3)

T

technology. The practical application of knowledge. (Chapter 3)

telecommute. To work from home while keeping in touch with an employer's office via electronic devices. (Chapter 2)

templates. Cutout patterns of furniture and appliances drawn to the same scale as a floor plan. (Chapter 18)

tenant. Someone who pays rent to use or occupy property owned by someone else. (Chapter 9)

tenement. Apartment complex with minimum standards of sanitation, safety, and comfort. (Chapter 6)

texture. An element of design that is the appearance or feel of a surface. (Chapter 15)

thatch. Bundles of reeds or straw used as building material. (Chapter 5)

thermal burn. An injury caused by hot liquids, hot surfaces, or flames. (Chapter 26)

thermostat. A temperature-activated switch that turns the heating system on and off to keep the temperature of a home at a set level. (Chapter 13)

tint. A hue above (lighter) than its normal value; created by adding white to a hue. (Chapter 16)

topography. The contour, or slope, of land or a building *site.*

town house. One of several houses attached together at the side walls. (Chapter 8)

traffic patterns. The paths people take as they walk from room to room during everyday activities. (Chapter 7)

transition. The resulting effect in design when lines change direction by flowing in a curve, or when curved lines lead the eye from one object to another. (Chapter 17)

trestle table. A table with a long rectangular top and a wide vertical support at each end. (Chapter 20)

triadic. A *color scheme* that uses any three hues that are an equal distance apart on the color wheel. (Chapter 16)

triplex. A housing unit that is attached at the side walls to two other units. (Chapter 8)

trundle bed. A low bed that can be stored under a higher bed during the day. (Chapter 20)

turning. A method of adding shape to wood, such as legs and spindles, using a lathe. (Chapter 20)

twill weave. A fabric weave pattern with diagonal lines or wales. (Chapter 19)

U

U value. The measure of a window's capacity to resist winter heat loss. (Chapter 14)

unity. A principle of design that occurs when all the parts of a design are related by one idea. (Chapter 17)

universal design. A philosophy of designing interiors and products to accommodate all people with a variety of requirements, needs, and abilities. (Chapter 1)

utilities. Services such as electric power, gas, water, and telephone. (Chapter 8)

V

valance. A short length of decorative material placed across the top of a window. (Chapter 19)

valance lighting. A type of built-in lighting that consists of a light source (usually a *fluorescent light*) mounted over a window and hidden by the window valance. (Chapter 22)

value. The lightness or darkness of a color; the amount of white or black in a color. (Chapter 16)

values. The principles that you want to live by and the beliefs that are important to you. (Chapter 4)

vanity. A base cabinet in a bathroom. (Chapter 24)

vapor barrier. Materials added to walls and attic areas to help reduce drafts and prevent moisture from getting into a home. (Chapter 12)

variance. A license to waive the *zoning law*. (Chapter 28)

veneer. A thin layer of more expensive wood glued to less expensive wood furniture for a better appearance. (Chapter 20)

W

wall washer. A small recessed ceiling light that spreads light over a wall from ceiling to floor. (Chapter 22)

warping. When wood loses its straightness. (Chapter 21)

warranty. A written statement of the manufacturer's promise to replace defective parts of a product at no charge for a certain time. (Chapter 27)

wicker furniture. Furniture that is woven of thin, flexible twigs, branches, and stems, often from willow trees. (Chapter 21)

windbreak. Natural or manufactured items, such as a row of trees or a fence, that protect a housing site from strong winds. (Chapter 12)

Windsor chair. A wood chair with stick legs and a spindle back inserted into a saddle-shaped plank seat. (Chapter 20)

wing chair. An upholstered armchair with a high back and high sides (or "wings," designed to give protection from drafts. (Chapter 20)

work center. An area of a kitchen especially equipped for a particular task. (Chapter 24)

work triangle. In a kitchen, the triangle formed by drawing imaginary lines to connect the sink, range or cooktop, and refrigerator. (Chapter 24)

wrought iron. A tough, durable form of iron that can be hammered and bent into different shapes such as decorative accessories, table and chair frames, and lawn furniture. (Chapter 21)

X Y Z

Xeriscaping (ZIHR-uh-skay-ping). Landscaping to conserve water. (Chapter 14)

zoning laws. Laws that determine the type of building that may be constructed in a particular zone, or section, of a community. (Chapter 7)

Credits

Cover Photo: Roger Wade Studio

Design: Squarecrow Creative Group

A High Tech Fence and Deck/Outdoor Technologies, 64
Amana Appliances, 542
American Standard, 548
Compliments of Andersen Windows, Inc., 224, 225, 247, 390, 480, 481, 499
Ann Sacks Tile & Stone, 440, 456, 523, 528
    Photography: Baylor, Jim/Design: City Studios, 500, 501
    Photography: Graf, Todd, 378
    Photography: Seger, Miriam/Design: Glazer, Erika, 368, 369, 385
    Photography: Stickley Holly/Design: Kuleto, Pat, 414
Archive Photos, 113
    Popperfoto, 109
Aristokraft, 163
Armstrong Floors, 337, 374
Arnold & Brown, 84, 86, 444, 579, 588, 600, 603, 604, 605, 617, 633
Art MacDillos, Gary Skillestad, 134, 192, 257, 259, 260, 263, 282, 293, 371, 421, 466, 506
Bassett Furniture Industries Inc., 339, 376, 413, 439
Batemor Productions/Baker Furniture, 438, 468
Marshall Berman, 214, 261, 268, 494, 517, 609
Bradbury & Bradbury Wallpapers, Benicia, CA, 448
Bromanite Corporation, 298
Bruno Independent Living Aids, Inc. ®, 591
Butterick, 345, 360, 363, 427, 428tl, 429tr, 429bl, 433l&r
Butterick/Vogue, 340, 416, 427, 428tm, 428tr, 428bl, 428bm, 428br, 429tl, 429tm
Compliments of Calculated Industries, 80
California Redwood Assn./Karl Riek, 255, 265
The Children's Hospital of Pittsburg, 582
Corbis, 16, 17, 35, 128, 138, 151, 356
Corbis/Stock Market
    Ball, David, 375
    Barton, Paul, 6, 24, 46, 316
    Beck, Peter, 320
    Blank, James, 126
    C/B Production, 115

Chromosohm/ Sohm, Joe, 45
D' addio, James, 139
Diebold, George, 82
Disario, George, 124
Feingersh, Jon, 84, 180
Gainer, Gordon, 185
Hamilton, Chris, 6
Holbrooke, Andrew, 50
Johnson, Donald C., 111, 590
Keller, Michael, 7, 197, 232, 246
Lefkowitz, Lester, 60
Lewine, Rob, 236
Lightscapes, 248-249
Mason, Don, 194
McCarthy, Tom, 81
Miele, Jean, 310
Pelaez, Jose Luis, 565
Pierini, Javier, 36, 37, 55
Raga, Jose Fuste, 21
Roberts, John M., 170-171
Saloutos, Pete, 133, 313
Savage, Chuck, 136, 230
Skelley, Ariel, 43, 299
Smith, Grafton Marshall, 5
Stewart, Tom, 95
Thompson, Wes, 41
U-AT CSM, 72
Van Antwerp, Jack, 354
Williams, Larry, 34
Zanders, Bo, 21
Zaruba, Jeff, 317
Dal-Tile, Dallas, TX, 549, 551
Davis Caves Construction, Inc., 315
Decks Appeal Custom Redwood Decks, 323
Luis Delgado, 118, 119, 186, 187, 212, 213, 242, 273, 300, 301, 319, 380, 454, 455, 594, 595, 609, 615
Courtesy of DuPont Tyvek, 265
Photography provided by and reproduced with permission from DuPont, Corian® is a DuPont registered trademark for its solid surfaces., 10, 536
Ethan Allen Inc., 11, 353, 359, 366, 393, 397, 461, 464, 469, 473, 474, 503, 511, 560
The Eureka Company, 600

FPG
  Chapple, Ron, 26, 104-105
  French, Gerald, 254
  Gleiter, Jeri, 4
  Gridley, Peter, 127, 172, 173, 189
  Losh, Bill 598, 599, 621
  Telegraph Colour Library, 25, 124, 183, 526, 527, 557
  Tilley, Arthur, 625
  VCG, 58
Compliments of Farnsworth Group, Peoria, IL, 48, 155
Cheryl Fenton, 547, 624
Curt Fischer, 4, 8t, 23, 75, 92, 93, 192, 199, 200, 201, 209, 222, 361, 412, 461, 545, 554, 555, 564, 571, 632, 634
Fisher & Paykel, 544
David R. Frazier Photolibrary, Inc., 42, 44, 65, 66, 131, 132, 143, 181, 184, 252, 276, 309, 508, 522, 626
Tim Fuller, 9, 10, 394, 406, 407, 444, 445, 467, 505
The Futon Shop, 472
Ann Garvin, 391
Courtesy of IXL®Cabinets, Gemini ™ laminate doors style, 529
Courtesy of Gensler Architects, 487
Getty Images/Liaison Agency, 606
  McVay, Ryan, 206, 207, 223
Glencoe, 69, 89, 358, 449, 627t&b
Michelle Gray, 159, 162, 355
Habitat for Humanity, 51
Jon Haeme Construction, 62
James Hardie® Building Products, 47, 235, 325, 327
Harris-Tarkett, Inc., 350, 351, 367, 381
Hartco Quality Wood Flooring from Armstrong, 297
The Hartstone Inn, Camden, ME, 133
Heartland Appliances, Inc., Metro/Legacy Series Professional-styled Ranges & Refrigerators, 56, 57, 77
Henry Ford Museum, 446, 452mr, 452br
Compliments of Hewi Inc., 29, 552
Hoffman-Ochs, Bloomington, IL, 296, 336, 371, 384, 405
Index Stock
  Finken, Robert, 127
International Stock
  McConville, Patti, 156
  Maratea, Ronn, 628
Iridian™ Technologies, 71
Jamestown Foundation, 112
Juno® Lighting, 295, 386-387, 409, 490, 494
Ken Karp, 26, 40, 70, 71, 81, 83, 102, 583
Kitchen Aid®, 537

Knoll Archives
  The Venturi Collection, 453br
  The Saarinen Collection, 453mr
  The Breuer Collection, 453bl
Kolbe & Kolbe, 321, 334, 335, 349
Kraftmaid Cabinetry, 524, 525, 530, 538, 557, 561
Superior brand fireplace by Lennox Hearth Products, 290
Courtesy of City of Los Angeles, Dept. of Water & Power, 311
Courtesy of Randall M. MacDonald, 116
"Mahvelous" Mailboxes! Inc., 18
Joe Mallon, 581l&r
Mannington Mills Inc., 278, 279, 303, 356, 413, 419, 424, 434
Maytag, 541
Massey Maxwell, 115, 120, 136, 137
Kevin May Corporation, 27, 61, 78, 79, 103, 160, 168, 174, 175, 176, 178, 190, 191, 205, 208, 240l, 285, 352, 373, 392, 395, 399, 404, 408, 415, 425, 429bm, 429br, 462, 463, 467, 475, 478, 482, 483, 491, 495, 531, 540, 580, 582, 585, 624
Robert McNeel & Associates, 158
Herman Miller, 453tr
Ted Mishima, 49, 68, 196, 204, 217, 237
Morgan Cain/Tim Fuller, 32, 33, 52, 53, 166, 167, 202, 203, 244, 245, 328, 329, 346, 347, 364, 365, 430, 431, 476, 477, 520, 521, 572, 573, 638, 639
Museum of the City of New York, The Jacob A. Riis Collection, 130
Jon Muzzarelli Photography, 22, 54, 82, 86, 88, 90, 96, 142, 144, 145, 151, 152, 165, 178, 188, 182, 193, 198, 216, 226, 239, 240m&r, 241l&r, 280, 281, 283, 284, 286, 294, 302, 308, 357, 362, 390, 442, 491, 587, 610, 611, 637
Courtesy of L.R. Nelson Corporation, 7
North Wind Pictures, 372
Nutone, 589
Omega Cabinets, 546
Owens Corning, 11, 269, 316
Paint-Finishes/Mountain Sun Photography, Bruce Nichols, 343, 423
PeachTree® Doors and Windows, 148, 149, 169, 470
Photo Disc. Vol. 15, Family and Lifestyles, 178, 179
Photo Disc. Vol. 26, Homes & Gardens, 63, 150, 243, 266, 306, 318, 326, 330, 426, 510
Photo Disc. Vol., 35, 100, 101
Photo Disc. Vol., 55, 100

Photo Researchers, Inc.
  Belknap, Bill, 309
  Burnett, Mark C., 132, 304, 305, 331
  Gadomski, Michael P., 108, 126
  Georgia, Lowell, 157
  Hailing, George, 20
  Hemphill, Mary Ann, 146
  Hunn, Max, 112
  Hunn, Max & Bea, 117
  Koch, Paolo, 19
  Lax, Ken, 592
  Lynn, Renee, 39
  Porterfield/Chickering, 153
  Saito, Tomomi/Dunq, 38
Picture Cube
  Index Stock, Finken, Robert, 127
Plato Woodworking, 564, 566
Porcher, 550
Regency Ceiling Fans, a division of Tacony Corporation, 488, 489
Paul Rocheleau, 234, 441, 444, 447
Dolores Santoliquido, 67, 296, 324, 344, 418, 420, 446, 449, 469, 472, 484, 485, 493, 539
Jennifer Leigh Sauer, 74, 220, 221, 233, 274, 275, 382, 383, 496, 497, 507, 586, 588, 602, 608, 618, 619
Schulte Corporation, 561, 567, 569, 570, 571
Courtesy of The Sharper Image, 584
Sherman-Williams, 410, 411, 435
Smarthome/Makita, 73
Stock Boston
  Bohdan, Hrynewych, 114
Superstock, 31, 59, 76, 106, 107, 113, 121, 122, 123, 129, 135, 140, 141, 142, 147, 197, 226, 250, 251, 252, 253, 255, 256, 272, 277, 313, 342, 436, 437, 457, 553, 622, 623, 641
Randall Sutter Photography, 14-15, 218, 280, 341, 348, 370, 465, 489, 498, 538, 576, 577, 593, 597, 630, 635

Thomasville, 338, 377, 378, 379, 380, 388, 389, 399, 409, 451, 458, 459, 460, 462, 464, 471, 479
Timberline®Geodesics, Domehome, 307
Tony Stone Images, 91, 94,
Gary Torrisi, 288, 289, 312, 514, 613, 614
U.S. Environmental Protection Agency's Energy Star® Program, 314, 540
Vantage Point Imaging, Michael Berg, 144, 502
Vermont Castings, Majestic Products, 291, 322
Donald Wardlaw, Architect, ATA, 154, 262, 264, 271, 400, 506, 515, 532, 533, 631
Weathershield, 287, 504
Photo provided by Wheeling Corrugating Company, Wheeling, WV, 267
Dana White, 601
Gloria Williams, 578
Winterthur Museum, 443
  The Henry Francis du Pont, 442, 452tl, 452tr, 452ml, 453tl
Doors and Cabinetry by Woodharbor™ Doors & Cabinetry, Inc., Mason City, IA/Photography by L.A. Studios, Eden Prairie, MN, 535, 558, 559, 575, 575
Wood-Mode Inc., 332, 333, 361, 483
Ian Worpole, 210
Yorktowne® Cabinets, 562, 568

Special Thanks

B.P. Solar, Linthicum, MD, 311

J.C. Proctor Endowment Home, Peoria, IL

Two Woods Turning, Ferrum, VA
  Bill & Sue Wood, 462-463

$\mathcal{I}$ndex

A

Abbreviations, advertising, 210
Abilities, 81
Accented neutral, 359
Accent lighting, 483, 486
Accessibility designers, 32–33. *See also* Universal design
Accessories, 490–495
   choosing, 513
   in home environment inventory, 397
   for nonresidential spaces, 495
Accident prevention, 580–583, 600
Acoustical ceiling tile, 296, 426
Acrylic carpeting, 420
Acrylic fibers, 416
Active solar heating systems, 311, 312
Activity zones
   in home, 159–160
   home office, 562, 563
   kitchen. *See* Work centers
Adam, James, 128
Adam, Robert, 128, 446
Adam style, 128–129
Adaptations, 29, 450
Adaptive reuse as means to historic preservation, 628
Adding on, 627
Adjustable rate mortgage, 230
Adobe bricks, 110, 125
Advertisements
   abbreviations, housing, 210
   for furniture, 473–474, 479
   job, 88
   real estate, 236–237
   for rental housing, 209
   for roommates, 218
Advertising artist, 98
Aesthetic codes, 152–153, 541, 542
A-frame, 142
Aging stage, 27
Air conditioners. *See also* Cooling systems
   preventive maintenance for, 611
Air flow, planning effective, 256
Air pollution, 308, 578–579
Alarm systems, 588–589
Alternating pattern, 377

Aluminum, 63, 463
American Foursquare, 137, 139
American Institute of Architects (AIA), 164
American International style, 141
American Society of Interior Designers (ASID), 394, 407, 635
Americans with Disabilities Act (ADA) (1990), 152
   impact on public environments, 49
Amortization, 228
Analogous color scheme, 358
Anchor bolts, 262
Antiques, 441, 454-455
Apartments, 161, 183–184, 209. *See also* Rental housing
   efficiency, 184
   garden, 183–184
   high-rise, 42, 183
   low-rise, 183
   studio, 184
Apparent weight, 341, 377
Appearance and grooming, and jobs, 44, 90
Appliances, 69
   design of, 539-545
   electric plugs for, 283
   professional servicing of, 616–617
   shopping tips for, 539–541
   water-saving, 318–319
Application fees, 197, 198
Appraisal, 243
Appraiser, 99
Apprenticeship, 86, 112, 145, 274, 300-301, 618
Apron, of window, 271
Aptitudes, 81
Archaeologists, 18–19
Architect, landscape, 328–329
Architects, 60, 144, 632
Architectural design. *See also* Universal design
   energy efficiency in, 313–315
   fees, 401
   period styles, 124–143
   regional styles, 61, 108, 109–117, 125-126, 136-137, 255, 276, 310 316

   traditional styles of, 109–117
   unity and, 381
Architectural drawings, 256–258
Architectural symbols, 257, 258
Asbestos, 579
   inspection for, 242
Asian influences on design, 443, 444
Asphalt for flooring, 420
Asphyxiation, 578
Assessed property valuation, 235
Assessments, 235
Assign a lease, 215
Assisted living facility, 44
Asymmetrical balance, 376–377
Attitudes, cleaning, 603
Attorney's fee, 243
Auctions, 238
Automated home management systems, 71, 72, 73. *See also* Technology

B

Baby boomers, 45
Backgrounds, 411–431
   ceilings, 426
   color considerations, 413, 415
   condition of, in home environment inventory, 397
   energy-efficient, 412–413
   floor coverings, 419–422
   for hotels, 414
   in kitchen, 537
   selecting, 511–512
   textiles as, 415–418
   wall coverings, 422–425
   window coverings, 427–431
Balance, 376–377
   asymmetrical, 376–377
   symmetrical, 376
Balancing work and family, 80, 94, 220
Balloon shade, 429
Bamboo, 461
Band joists, 262
Barrier-free design, 29, 32, 50. *See also* Universal design
Basements
   building, 259–260
   inspecting, 241

Basic job skills, 86. *See also* specific careers
Basic structure, 258–262
Basic weaves, 418
Bathrooms, 548–552
  accident prevention in, 580, 581
  cabinets, 551
  cleaning routine for, 604
  fixtures, 549-550
  floor coverings for, 298
  lighting for, 489
  storage in, 569
  universal design in, 30, 100, 552
  ventilation for, 293
Bathtubs, 549
Batt insulation, 269
Bauhaus school of design, 449, 453
Beamed ceilings, 296
Bedouins, 19
Bedrooms, 22
  cleaning routine for, 604
  floor coverings for, 298
  furniture in, 470–472, 505, 569
  lighting for, 489
  storage in, 569
Beds
  construction, 470–472
  trundle, 442
  water, 472
Belter, John Henry, 448
Berber carpeting, 416, 420
Bids, project, 636
Biomaterials, 64
Biometrics, 71
Birch wood, characteristics of, 463
Blanket insulation, 268
Blinds, 429, 430–431
  horizontal, 431
  vertical, 429, 431
Blouson valance, 430
Blueprints, 256–258
Borders, wallpaper, 424–425
Box joint, 466
Box spring, 472
Bracket lighting, 486
Breach of contract, 215
Breakers, resetting electrical, 282, 613
Breuer, Marcel, 453
Bricklayers, 98
Bricks, 61
  adobe, 110, 125
  floors, 298
Bridging, 262
Broadloom carpet, 420
Budgets, 227
  in decision making, 511–512

project, 145, 167, 244, 394, 401-403, 512
  revisions, 513
Building codes, 48, 152, 258, 554
  for doors, 272
  for electric wiring, 281
  for plumbing, 284
  for toilets, 550
  water conservation and, 318
Building envelope, 317
Building laws and regulations, 151–153
Building materials, 41
  Biomaterials, 64
  recycled, 320
  wise use of, 319–320
Building permit, 633
Bungalow, 139
Burns, 582
Business, owning your own, 86–87
Butane, 308
Buyer, home furnishings, 98
Buyers
  continual costs, 199–200
  initial costs for, 198–199
Buyer's agent, 237
Buyer's market, 238
Buying. *See also* Home-buying
  to remodel, 629

C

Cabinets
  for bathrooms, 551
  for kitchen, 535
Cabriole leg, 444
CAD software, 66, 101, 144–146, 245, 258, 329, 347, 507-508, 520-521, 554, 565, 619
CAD specialist for interior design, 520-521
Café curtains, 427, 428
Calculation of materials needed, 402–403
Camelback sofa, 445
Canada, housing in, 50
Cape Cod house, 113, 381
Carbon monoxide, 578
Carbon monoxide detector, 579
Career advancement, 92–95, 96. *See also under* specific careers
Career goals, 83–85
Career paths. *See under* specific careers
Career plan, developing your, 83–86

Career preparation. *See also* Education and training; Apprenticeship, Internship, Jobs
  basic job skills, 86
  job shadowing and, 83
  researching careers, 82, 103
  and vocational counselor, 82
  work experience, 83.
Careers in housing and interiors. *See also* Jobs
  advertising artist, 98
  appraiser, 99
  archaeologist, 18, 19
  architect, 60, 144, 632
  bricklayer, 98
  buyer, 98
  carpenters, 281
  color specialist, 364–365
  computer-aided design (CAD) specialist for interior design, 520–521
  in construction and home design, 98
  construction technologist, 98
  consumer advocate, 97
  consumer science writer, 97
  contractors, 280–281, 632
  department store advertising worker, 97
  designers, 635
  drywall installers, 281
  electricians, 281
  electrician's apprentice, 300–301
  electronic home systems specialist, 74–75
  engineers, 60
  entrepreneurs 74, 86–87, 618–619
  ergonomic designer, 100–101
  floor-covering installers, 281
  furniture designer, 98
  furniture restorer, 454–455
  furniture showroom salesperson, 476–477
  heating and cooling specialists, 281
  heavy-equipment operator, 98
  in home furnishings and interior design, 98
  home maintenance advice columnist, 618–619
  in home maintenance and remodeling, 99, 638-639
  home safety inspectors, 597
  in housing and interior environments, 79–99

industrial designer, 99
interior designer, 98, 394, 406–407
kitchen planner, 554–555
land developer, 99
landscape architect, 328–329
lead abatement specialist, 594–595
lighting specialists, 496–497
maintenance worker, 99
model home designer, 244–245
mortgage loan officer, 202–203
painters, 281
pest-control worker, 99
plumbers, 281
preservationist, 118–119
professional organizer, 572–573
public relations specialist, 97
in real estate, 81, 99, 186–187
relocation specialist, 52–53
remodeling specialist, 82
researcher, 97
resident manager, 220–221
roofer, 274–275
space planner, 346–347
structural engineer, 632
subcontractors, 281
surveyor's assistant, 98
textile specialist, 432–433
urban planner, 166–167
usability engineer, 32–33
visual merchandiser, 382–383
Carpenters, 281
Carpeting, 298, 420. See also Floor coverings
calculating, 402
color and pattern, 422
cushion, 422
principal fibers for, 416–417
quality, 420
size and installation, 420
texture and construction, 420–421
Carpet tiles, 420
Carter, Jimmy, 51
Case goods, 460
caring for, 475
signs of quality in, 465
Casing, window, 271
Caulking, 316, 608–609
Cave dwellers, 18
Cedar wood, characteristics of, 463
Ceiling fans, 315
Ceilings, 426
acoustical tile, 296, 426

beam, 296
coved, 296
dropped, 296
gabled, 294
joints, 264
shed, 294
stamped metal, 296
tray, 296
vaulted, 294
Cellular shades, 430
Cement, 62–63
Center of interest, 379
Central air-conditioning systems, 292, 611. See also Cooling systems
Central Park, 156
Ceramic tile floors, 297
Cesspool, 287
CFC-free foam, 269
Chair rail, 425
Chairs, historic styles, 442, 444, 446, 452–453
Changing needs, reflection of, in housing, 157–158, 624
Chartres Cathedral, 375
Chateauesque style, 136
Cherry wood, characteristics of, 462
Chests, 442
Childproofing home, 582–583
Chimney, 136, 267–268, 584
China, housing in, 40
China plumbing fixtures, 284
Chinese-style latticework, 443
Chippendale style (1755-1780), 443, 444–445, 452
Chlorofluorocarbons (CFCs), 269
Chrysler, Walter, 60
Chrysler building, 60
Circuit breakers, 282, 283, 581
Circuits, 281
Clapboards, 112, 265
Claw-and-ball feet, 445
Cleanup center, 529
Clearance space, 398, 503
Client characteristics, assessing, 395–396
Client relationships
with furniture salesperson, 454–455
with interior designer, 393, 394, 519
with lighting specialist, 477
with mortgage loan officer, 186 187
with real estate agent, 186–187

with relocation specialist, 32
with remodeling specialist, 82
with resident manager, 202–203
with urban planner, 144-145
Closed-circuit television (CCTV), 71
Closed floor plan, 160
Closed storage, 568
Closet, organizing, 570–571, 572-573
Closing, in home buying, 243
Closing costs, 199, 227, 243
Clothes dryers, 545
Cluster homes, 153, 154
Clutter, reducing, 606
Coal, 308
Coil springs, 468
Colonial Period (1600-1780), furniture styles from, 441–445, 509
Colonial Revival style, 135
Color concept, 361
Colors, 351–363
in backgrounds, 413, 415
of carpet, 421
creating, 357
as design element, 44, 345, 356
effect of texture on, 345
energy efficiency and, 313
harmony, 361
illusions with, 354
language of, 355, 357
Munsell chart of, 365
neutral, 352, 355, 423
science of, 354
selecting, 361, 364, 510
in setting a mood, 352, 360
signature, 360
in upholstery fabric, 471
warm and cool, 353, 415, 510
Color sample board, creating, 361–362, 367
Color schemes
choosing, 510
planning, 359–361
success, 362–363
Color specialists, 364–365
Color wheel, 354 355, 355
Commercial buildings. See Nonresidential buildings; Nonresidential interiors
Commercial zoning, 151
Commission (fee), 186, 237, 394
Commons, 183
Communications, 70, 519
careers in, 97

Communication skills, 32, 33, 47, 52, 53, 86, 94, 100-101, 119, 166-167, 186-187, 202-203, 220-221, 301, 347, 365, 383, 454, 477, 595-596
Communities
　assessing services in, 181–182
　belonging to, 23–24, 51, 94
　cooperative housing, 155
　creation of diverse, 46–47
　developing, 150–156
　distinctions within, 20–21
　planned, 24, 156
　planning new, 153, 155
　resort, 153
Community planning, 166–167
Compact fluorescent lamp, 484, 490
Complaints, handling, 166-167, 220-221
Complement, 357
Complementary color scheme, 358
Composite lumber, 62
Computer-aided drafting and design (CAD), 66, 101, 144–145, 245, 258, 329, 347, 507–508, 520-521, 554, 565, 619
Computer models, 517–518
Computers. *See also* Technology
　in communication, 70
　in design, 66
　presentations, 516
　virtual tours of homes on, 237
Computer skills, 32, 33, 52, 53, 74, 75, 100-1-1, 119, 166-167, 186-187, 202-203, 245
Computer station, 563
Concrete, 62–63
　for floors, 297
Condominiums
　aesthetic codes for, 152
　buying, 195
　ownership of, 193
Conduction, heat, 287
Conflict resolution, 94, 167. *See also* Complaints; Negotiation skills
Conservation, 156. *See also* Energy conservation; Water conservation
Construction, 251–273. *See also* Exterior construction; Interior construction
　architectural drawings and, 256–258
　basic structure, 258–262
　careers in, 98

conserving energy through, 311, 313–316
　exterior, 263–273
　housing site and, 253–256
　interior, 279–299
　materials, 59, 61-65
　tools, 65-66
　types of, 66, 68
　water protection, 272–273
Construction manager, 280
Construction technologist, 98
Consumer advocate, 97
Consumer science writer, 97
Contemporary design furniture, 449–450
Contemporary style housing, 140–141
Contingency fee, 401, 633
Contingent upon financing, 238
Continuity, 377
Contract for deed agreement, 229
Contractors, 280–281, 632
　hiring for remodeling, 635–636
Contracts, 636
　offer-to-purchase, 238
　service, 617
Convection oven, 287, 289, 543
Conventional construction, 66, 258
Conventional mortgage, 229
Conventional oven, 543
Conversion of use, 629
Convoluted spring, 468
Cooking center, 529
Cooktops, shopping for, 542–543
Cool colors, 353
Cooling systems, 292, 315
　energy-efficient, 310–311
　inspection of, 617
Cooperative housing communities, 155
Cooperative ownership, 195
Copper, 64, 463
Coquina, 116
Cork for flooring, 420
Cornice, 127, 133, 429–430
Cornice lighting, 485
Corridor kitchen, 532
Costs
　buyer's, 198–200
　of housing, 45–46, 62, 68, 177, 192
　interior design, 394, 401-403, 512
　moving, 197, 199
　remodeling, 625
　real estate commissions, 186-187

renter's, 196–198
　of window treatments, 331
Cotton fibers, 417, 468
Countertops
　for bathrooms, 551
　for kitchen, 30, 536
Cove lighting, 485, 486
Coved ceilings, 296
Craftsman style, 135, 137, 139
Crawl spaces, 260–261
　vents for, 293
Creativity, 25, 33, 100, 144-145, 244-245, 329, 365, 382-383, 406-407
Credit check fees, 197, 198
Credit history, 227
Credit report, 243
Critical thinking skills. *See* Decision-making; Housing decisions
Cross ventilation, 256
Crown molding, 425
Culture, 38
　influences on housing, 38–42
　and nonresidential design, 347
Curb appeal, 235, 265
Curtains, 427, 428
Cushions for furniture, 468–469
Custom-built homes, 232

D

Dado joint, 466
Debt, 227
Decision-making, 87. *See also* Housing decisions
　and budget, 511–512
　on financing, 633
　resource management and, 307
　steps in, 174
Decorative painting, 343, 423
Decorative pillows, 495
Decorative screen, 494
Defect, 616
Delays, work, 519, 629
Demographics, 44-45
Department store advertising worker, 97
Design(s). *See also* Universal design; Architectural design
　adaptable, 29
　adapting to lay of land, 254
　Asian influences on, 443
　barrier-free, 29, 32, 50
　completing and presenting, 501–519
　computers in, 66

conserving energy through, 311, 313–316
elements of, 336
goals in remodeling, 629–631
harmonious, 342
issues for special healthcare facilities, 593
modifying and implementing, 518–519
of outdoor living space, 321–322
presenting, 513–518
principles of, 369–381
Design elements, 390
color as, 44, 345, 356
form as, 340–342
line as, 339–340
space as, 337–338
texture as, 342–344
using, 345
Designers. *See also* Interior designers
accessibility, 32–33
ergonomic, 100–101
hiring for remodeling, 635
model home, 244–245
Design plan, 389–405, 502–519
analyzing the environment, 396–400
assessing client characteristics, 395–396
choosing style and color scheme, 509–510
compiling resource file, 404
developing preliminary budget, 401–403
identifying the project, 393
modifying and implementing, 518–519
planning use of space, 502–508
presenting the design, 513–518
selecting backgrounds, furniture, lighting, and accessories, 511–513
Design presentations, 101, 145, 167, 513–518
Design principles, 369–381
applying, 381
balance, 376–377
as design tools, 390
emphasis, 379–380
proportion, 370–373
rhythm, 377–378
scale, 373–375
unity and variety, 380–381
Design resource file, 404, 630
Development homes, 231–232
Dictionary of Occupational Titles, 82

Dining area, 23
arranging space in, 504
lighting for, 488
Direct lighting, 482
Disabilities, 27, 49. *See also* Universal design
Dishwashers, 69, 318–319, 544
Disposal field, 286
Disposal units, 544
Distressing wood, 450
Divided light window, 271
Doorknobs, 29
Doors, 270, 272
Dutch, 114
locks, 588
security and, 70–71, 588
sweeps, 608
weather blocking and, 608–609
Dormers, 114, 133
Double-paned windows, 316
Dovetail joint, 466
Dowels, in joints, 466
Down, 468
Downlights, 485, 486
Down payment, 198–199, 227, 239
Downspouts, 273
preventive maintenance for, 609–610
Drain field, 286
Draperies, 427, 428, 430. *See also* Window treatments
Drawings. *See also* Computer-aided drafting and design (CAD)
architectural, 256–258
elevations, 258, 505–506
floor plans, 158, 160–163, 258, 503, 505–507, 534
pictorial, 514, 515
renderings, 515–516
scale, 398–400
types of interior design, 513–516
Dropped ceilings, 296
Dryers, clothes, 545
Drywall, 294
Drywall installers, 281
Duncan Phyfe, 452
Duplexes, 184
Dutch door, 114
Dutch settlements, 114, 125

E

Eames, Charles, 453
Early American Period (1640-1720), 110, 112–117
Early Classical Revival style, 129

Earnest money, 198, 239
Earthquake protection, 254
Earth-sheltered homes, 315
Eclectic style of decorating, 380
Economic conditions, 45–46
Education and training, 85, 96, 103
Education, continuing, 96, 244, 245, 347, 476, 521
Efficiency apartment, 184
Eighteenth-century, housing in, 125–129, 157
Electrical surge protectors, 565
Electrician's apprentice, 300–301
Electricians, 281
Electric receptacles, 29, 282
Electric shock, 581. *See also* Ground fault circuit interrupters (GFCIs)
Electric wiring, 281–283
Electrical system
in bathrooms, 551
in environment inventory, 397
in home office, 565
in kitchen, 537
Electronics, 69–73
Electronic home systems specialist, 74–75
Elevations, 258, 505–506
Elevators, 60
Ell, 113
Emergency shelter grants for homeless, 50–51
Emphasis, in design, 379–380
Empire State Building, 60
Empire style (1820-1840), 446–447, 452
Employability skills, 86
Employment. *See* Careers; Jobs
Employment agencies, 88
Employment outlook. *See* specific careers
Energy
in home environment inventory, 397
sources of, 308–310
Energy audit, 316
Energy conservation, 31, 307–317
in appliances, 69, 539–541
backgrounds and, 412–413
in commercial buildings, 317
design and construction in, 311, 313–316, 397
foam products and, 63
in heating and cooling systems, 69, 289–290, 310–311
in lighting, 69, 490

for outdoor areas, 322
    water heaters and, 285, 286
    weather blocking and, 608
    in windows, 270, 316
Energy efficiency. *See* Energy
        conservation
EnergyGuide labels, 540
Energy sources, 308–310. *See also*
        Energy conservation
Energy Star homes and products,
        307, 310, 314, 540
Engineered wood floors, 297
Engineered wood products, 62
Engineers, 60
England, housing in, 21, 41, 61, 126
English settlements, 110, 112–114,
        125, 441
Entertainment systems, 69, 395, 504
Entrepreneurship, 74, 86–87,
        454–455, 618–619
Entry-level job, 85, 92
Entryways, lighting for, 486, 488
Environment
    analyzing, 396–400
    green building, 65, 307
Environmental awareness, 46
Environment inventory, home,
        396–398
Equity-sharing loan, 229
Ergonomic designer, 100–101
Ergonomics, 100, 554, 563. *See also*
        Universal design
Escrow, 228
Ethical behavior, 93, 103, 186
Evict, 215
Expenses, monthly, 200
Extended family, 39
Exterior construction, 258-273
    doors, 270, 272
    fiber-cement siding for, 63
    insulation, 268–270
    roof, 266–268
    universal design, 29
    walls, 263–266
    water protection, 272–273
    windows, 270, 271

F

Fabrics. *See also* Fibers; Textiles
    upholstery, 469–470, 471
Fabric wall hanging, 493
Fair Housing Amendments (1988),
        49
Falls, 580, 600
Family

balancing with work and, 80, 94
    extended, 39
    inventory, 395–396
    nuclear, 39
    single-parent, 40
    structures and roles, 43
Family, Career, and Community
        Leaders of America (FCCLA)
        program, 93
Family life cycle, 26-28
Family rooms, 24
    arranging space in, 504
    lighting for, 488
    storage in, 569
Fanlight, 129
Fans
    attic, 315
    ceiling, 315
    whole house, 292, 315
Fashion and personal taste, 44
Faux finishes, 343
Federal Housing Administration
        (FHA) loan, 229
Federal Period
    furniture in, 445–446, 452
    housing in, 128–129, 446
Fees. *See* Costs
Fences, 326
Fiber-cement siding, 63
Fiberglass siding, 266
Fiber optics, 484
Fibers. *See also* Fabrics; Textiles
    natural, 417
    synthetic, 416
    in upholstery fabric, 471
Finances
    analyzing your, 200–201
    strengthening your, 201
Financial planning, 226–227
Financing
    decision making on, 633
    obtaining, 187, 239
    special arrangements, 229
Finger joint, 466
Finials, 430
Finishes for furniture, 467–468
Finish flooring, 296–298
Finish grade, 273
Finish trim, 298
Firebox, 291
Fire extinguishers, 585
Fireplaces, 290–291
Fire prevention, 584–587
Fireproof box, 565
Fire-resistant fabric for upholstered
        furniture, 471

First-time buyer programs, 229
Fixtures
    lighting, 484-485
    plumbing, 284
    water-saving, 318–319
Flagstone, 61
Flammable clothing, 582
Flammable Fabrics Act, 418
Flashing, 268
Flat roofs, 134, 267
Flax fibers, 417
Flexible design, 32. *See also* Universal
        design
Flexible insulation, 268
Floating floor, 297
Floodlights, 589
Floor-covering installers, 281
Floor coverings, 298, 419–422. *See
        also* Carpeting
    for bathrooms, 551
    contrasting, 28
    resilient, 419–420
Floor frame, 261
Floor joists, 262
Floor plans, 158, 258, 503, 505–507
    evaluating, 161, 162
    for kitchen, 506, 534
    open and closed, 160
    options, 161, 163
Floors. *See also* Floor coverings
    for exterior spaces, 322
    finish, 296-298
    inspecting, 240
Flue, 268
Fluorescent lighting, 69, 484
Foam
    as a building material, 63
    insulation, 269
    in upholstered furniture, 468
Focal point, 379, 503
Food, as a basic need, 23
Food storage center, 529
Footing, 258–259
Forced warm air system, 288
Form, 340–342
    creating effects with, 341–342
Formal balance, 376
Fossil fuels, 308
Foundation, 258–261
    inspecting, 240
Fourplex, 184
Frames, 261–263, 271
    ceiling and roof, 261, 264
    floor, 261
    furniture, 468
    wall, 261

Freezers, shopping for, 541–542
French settlements, 117
Frost line, 258–259
Fuel. *See* Energy sources
Fuel oil, 308
Full bath, 548
Fuller, R. Buckminster, 143
Functional grouping, 503
Functional room arrangement, 502
Furnaces. *See also* Heating systems
   inspecting, 241
   preventive maintenance for, 611
Furniture. *See also* Upholstered
    furniture
   advertisements for, 479
   arranging, 400, 504–505
   choosing, 476–477, 513, 606
   construction, 465–472
   design, and technology, 438, 450,
    447, 448, 563-564
   fabrics for, 471
   finishes, 467–468
   glass, 464
   in home environment inventory,
    397
   joints, 466, 467
   materials, 460
   measuring, 398–400
   metal, 461–463
   modular, 474
   multipurpose, 473
   office, 473, 563–565
   plastic, 464
   selecting, 459–475, 601, 604-605
   selling, 382-383, 476–477
   shopping for, 473–474
   in special health care facilities,
    593
   unassembled, 475
   unfinished, 474
   upholstered, 403, 468-470, 475
   used, 473
   wood, 460–461
Furniture designer, 98
Furniture restorer, 454–455
Furniture salesperson, 476–477
Furniture styles, 437–453
   Asian influence on, 443–444
   awareness of, 451
   changing, 438–439
   Chippendale style, 444–445, 452
   choosing, 509–510
   Colonial Period (1600-1780),
    441–445
   Contemporary, 449-450
   Empire style, 446–447, 452

Federal style, 445–446, 452
   International style, 449, 453
   Modern Period (1901-present),
    448–451
   Postcolonial Period (1780-1840),
    445–447
   Post-modern style, 453
   Queen Anne style (1720-1755),
    443–444
   reproductions, 450
   researching, 457
   Shaker, 447
   Victorian Period (1840-1900),
    447–448, 453
   William and Mary, 442–443, 452
Fuses, 282, 283, 581
   changing, 282, 613
Futons, 472

G

Gabled ceilings, 294
Gable roof, 113, 129, 134
Gables, 113
Gambrel roof, 113, 134
Garden apartment, 183–184
Garrison house, 114
Gateleg table, 443, 504
General contractors, 280
General home inspection, 242
General lighting, 483
Geodesic dome, 143
Georgian Period, housing in,
   126–128, 142
Geothermal energy, 310
German settlements, 114, 125
Gingerbread, 131
Girders, 262
Glass furniture, 407, 464
Glass windows, 270
Glue block joint, 466
Goals, setting, 83-85. *See also* Career
   goals
Golden rectangle, 371, 372, 373
Golden section, 371, 372, 373
Gothic Revival style, 131
Government
   checking regulations, in remodel-
    ing, 632–633
   conservation efforts of, 318
   plumbing regulations, 284
   restoration programs of, 629
   role of, in housing, 47–48, 50–51,
    151–153
Grab bars, 30, 580
Gradation, 378

Grade level, inspecting, 240
Graduated payment mortgage, 230
Great room, 113
Greek Revival style, 131, 142
Greenbelts, 151
Green building, 65, 307
Green energy, 309
Green space, 154, 156, 167
Gridiron design, 150
Grin test, 420
Gropius, Walter, 139, 449
Gross income, 200, 227
Groundcovers, 326, 327
Ground fault circuit interrupters
   (GFCIs), 283, 551, 581
Ground wire, 283
Grout, 297
Gutters, 273
   preventive maintenance for,
    609–610

H

Habitat for Humanity International,
   51
Half-bath, 548
Half-houses, 113
Half-timbered house, 112
Hallways, lighting for, 486, 488
Halogen bulbs, 484
Halogen ovens, 543
Handrails, 29, 294
Hardware, window, 430
Hardwoods, 59, 442, 460
   characteristics of various,
    462–463
Harmonious design, 342
Header, 263
Healthcare facilities, design in, 593
Health hazards, reducing, 578–579
Hearing, impaired, 592. *See also*
   Universal design
Hearth, 291
Heating, ventilating, and air condi-
   tioning (HVAC), systems, 310,
   317
Heating and cooling specialists, 281
Heating systems, 287–291
   choosing, 290
   energy-efficient, 310–311
   fireplaces, 290–291
   forced warm air, 288
   hot water, 289
   inspection of, 579, 617
   radiant, 289
   steam, 289

stoves, 290–291
 types of, 288–290
 ventilation, 292–293
 warm air gravity, 288
Heat pumps, 310–311
Heat pump water heater, 286
Heat recovery ventilators, 311
Heavy-equipment operator, 98
Hepplewhite, George, 446, 452
Highboy, 443
High-rise apartment, 42, 183
High technology, 68, 69
Hip roof, 126, 134
Historic district, 111, 152
Historic preservation, 118–119, 152,
  166-167, 628
 adaptive reuse as means to, 628
Hobby areas, arranging space in, 505
Hollow doors, 272
Home-buying process, 225–243
 agreeing to purchase, 239
 closing on, 243
 evaluating homes, 238
 financial planning, 226–227
 finding, 237–238
 inspection in, 239–242
 making an offer, 238
 mortgage, 228–231
 obtaining financing, 239
 pros and cons, 193–196
 remodeling versus, 625
 role of real estate agents, 236–237
Home cleaning, 600–606
 attitudes and routines, 603–605
 reducing time, 605
 schedule for, 601
 tools and supplies, 602–603
Home design, careers in, 98. *See also*
  Architecture
Home equity loan, 633
Home fire safety plan, 586–587
Homeless, emergency grants for,
  50–51
Home improvements. *See*
  Remodeling
Home maintenance, 599–617
Home maintenance columnist,
  618–619
Home offices, 46, 47, 560–566
 designing, 562–566
 furniture for, 473, 563–565
 lighting for, 567
 location of, 560–561
 power supply for, 566
 technology for, 565–566
 uses for, 560

Home ownership, advantages of, 194
Homeowner's insurance, 199,
  242-243
Homeowner's Warranty Plan, 233
Home-remodeling specialist, 99,
  638–639
Home safety and security, 326,
  577–593
 meeting special needs, 591–592
 preventing accidents, 580–583
 preventing fires, 584–587
 promoting, 587–590
 reducing health hazards, 578–579
Home safety inspectors, 597
Home textiles, principal fibers for,
  416–417
Horizontal-axis washing machines,
  319
Horizontal blinds, 431
Hotels, backgrounds for, 414
Households, 39-40
 allocating responsibilities, 219
Housing. *See also* Architectural design
 activity zones in, 69, 159–160
 alternatives, 183–185
 automated, 71, 73
 built on spec, 232
 challenges for tomorrow, 30–31
 childproofing, 582–583
 cost of, 45–46, 62, 68, 177, 192
 cultural influences on, 38–42,
  109-117
 defined, 18
 designing functional interiors,
  158–163
 determining budget, 200–201
 development of, 18–21
 early, 107–117
 earth-sheltered, 315
 evaluating, 238
 foundation for, 259-261
 government's role in, 47–48,
  50–51, 151–153. (*See also* Laws
  and regulations)
 influences on, 143
 inspection of, 239–242
 orientation of, 254
 public, 48, 50
 reflection of changing needs in,
  157–158
 repairs, 612–616
 resale value of, 234–236
 retrofitting, 316
 safety, 616
 sharing, 217–219
 status and, 41
 subsidized, 212

 substandard, 45–46
 technology in, 68–71, 560, 565
 trends in, 28, 42-47, 164–165, 245
 as universal need, 17–31
Housing and Urban Development,
  U.S. Department of (HUD), 50,
  68
Housing decisions. *See also* Decision-
  making
 alternatives in, 183–185
 assessing community services in,
  181–182
 assessing requirements, 208–209
 choosing location, 177–180
 condominium and cooperative
  ownership, 195
 determining budget, 200–201
 finances, 226–235
 home buying, 185, 193–196, 201,
  225–243
 influences on, 175–176
 new home versus old, 231–234
 renting, 185, 192–193, 201,
  208–215
Housing design. *See* Architectural
  design
Housing industry, trends in, 177
Housing needs, through life span,
  26–27, 624
Housing site, 66
 analyzing characteristics of,
  253–254
 choosing best view, 256
 effective use of sunlight, 255–256
 planning effective air flow, 256
 planning orientation, 254
Hue, 355
Human resources, 176
Human scale, 374
Humidity, 287
Hydroelectric and nuclear power
  plants, 308

I

Identity, 24–25
Immigrant styles, 125
Impaired mobility, 591–592. *See also*
  Universal design
Improvements, 236
Incandescent lights, 484, 490
Income, 200, 227
India, housing in, 41
Indirect lighting, 482
 for home office, 566
Individual needs, 26–30, 393,
  395–396

Indoor pollution, 290, 293
Industrial designer, 99
Industrial Designers Society of
    America, 101
Industrial Revolution, 130
Industrial zoning, 151
Infilling, 153
Informal balance, 376
Infrastructure, 167
Innovative housing designs, 142–143
Inspections
    fees, 198
    home, 238, 239–242
    for remodeling, 632
Installations, 519
Insulation, 268–270, 608
    energy efficiency and, 315
    forms of, 268–270
    inspecting, 240
    for water heaters, 285
    for windows, 270
Insurance
    homeowners', 199, 242–243
    renter's, 198
Integrated circuit, 68
Integrated electronic systems, 72
Intensity, of color, 357
Intercom systems, 589
Interest, 45, 194, 228
Interest survey, 81
Interior construction, 279–299
    cooling, 292
    designing functional, 158–163
    electric wiring, 281–283
    finishing, 294–298
    heating system, 287–291
    jobs in, 280–281
    plumbing, 284–287
    universal design in, 29
    ventilation, 292–293
    wall finishes, 295
Interior design, computer-aided
        design specialist for, 520–521
Interior designers, 98, 394, 406–407
Interior design projects
    budget for, 394, 401–403, 512
    fees for, 401
    timeline for, 519
International style, 139, 449
Internet
    in job hunting, 88
    research on, 82
Interpersonal skills. See
        Communication skills;
        Client relationships

Internship, 166, 329
Interviews, 90–91, 395
Inventories, 395
    family, 395–396
    home environment, 396–398
    nonresidential, 396
Iroquois people, 110
Island, kitchen, 531, 533
Israel, housing in, 40
Italianate style, 132

J

Jabots, 428
Jacobean furniture (1650), 441–442,
    452
Jacquard weave fibers, 417
Japan, housing in, 22
Japanning, 443, 444
Jeanneret, Charles E., 139
Jefferson, Thomas, 129
Job offer, 91
Job readiness, 80–81, 83–86
Jobs. See also Careers
    advertisements, 88
    applications, 90
    basic skills for, 86
    finding, 87–91
    leaving, 95–96
    shadowing, 83
    work experience on, 92–95
Joints
    caulking, 608–609
    furniture, 466, 467
    reinforcement of, 466
Joists, 261, 262
Journeyman, 86

K

Kacha, 41
Kibbutzim, 40
Kitchen, fires in, 584, 585
Kitchen planner, 554–555
Kitchens, 23, 24, 528–538
    appliances in, 539–545
    cabinets in, 535
    cleaning routine for, 605
    countertops in, 536
    efficient layout in, 529–534
    fire extinguishers in, 585
    floor coverings for, 298
    history of, 42–43
    lighting for, 488
    remodeling goals, 631

sinks in, 536
storage in, 569
universal design in, 30, 43,
    537–538
ventilation for, 293

L

Laminate floors, plastic, 420
Laminated plastic paneling, 425
Lamps, 486
Land developer, 99
Landlords, 192
    relationship with, 216
Landscape
    designing, 325
    manufactured elements in, 326
    natural elements in, 325–326
    plans, 323, 324
    purpose of, 323
    security and, 590
    water conservation and, 326–327
Landscape architect, 328–329
Lath, 294
Lathe, 441
Launching stage, 26
Laundry areas, 164
    planning, 546–547
    universal design and, 547
Laws and regulations. See also
        Government, Building Codes
    aesthetic codes, 152–153, 541, 542
    anti-discrimination, 49, 152
    for historic districts, 111, 152
    open space, 48
    textile, 418
    zoning, 111, 151–152, 253, 562
Layout, designing efficient, for
        kitchen, 529–534
Lead, 579
Lead abatement specialist, 594–595
Leadership, 93, 94, 166–167
Lead testing, 242
Lease, 214–215
Le Corbusier, 139, 372
Levitt, William, 155
Levittown, 155
Life cycle, housing needs through,
    26–28
Lifestyles, 25, 395
Light bulbs, 483, 484, 490
Light emitting diode (LED) bulbs,
    69, 484, 490
Lighting, 69, 482–490
    accent, 483
    for bathrooms, 551

choosing, 513
color scheme and, 360–361
decorating with, 486, 488
direct, 482
emergency repairs, 613
energy conservation and, 317
exterior, 326
fixtures, 484-485
fluorescent, 69
general, 483
in home environment inventory, 397
for home office, 566
indirect, 482
for kitchen, 537
nonstructural, 484, 486
outdoor, 326
for outdoor living space, 323
purposes of, 483
in retail stores, 487
saving energy with, 490
and security, 326
solar, 69
structural, 484, 485
task, 483, 488
Lighting controls, 29, 489
Lighting specialists, 496–497
Lights, decorating with, 486, 488
Lights of window, 271
Limestone, 61
Line, 339–340
Linen fibers, 417
Liquid petroleum (LP gas), 308
Living room, 22, 24
arranging space in, 504
cleaning routine for, 605
lighting for, 488
storage in, 569
Load-bearing walls, 261
Loans. See Mortgages; Home Equity
Locations
choosing housing, 177–182
of home office, 560–561
value of, 234–235
Locks
door, 588
window, 588
Loft, 161
Log cabins, 125
Longhouse, 110
Loose-fill insulation, 269
Louvers, 430
Love and belonging, 23–24
Low-emissivity (or low-e) glass, 270
Low-rise apartment, 183
L-shaped kitchen, 532

Lumber, treated, 322. See also Wood
Luminous ceiling panels, 485

M

Maintenance, home, 599–617
Maintenance, preventive, 607–611
air conditioners, 611
downspouts, 609–610
furnaces, 611
gutters, 609–610
joints, 608–609
water heaters, 610
Maintenance worker, 99
Mahogany wood, characteristics of, 463
Management
construction, 280
of multiple roles, 80, 94, 220
skills, 101, 144-145, 202-203, 220, 244, 406-407
of time, 52, 53, 92, 145, 407
Manager resident, 220–221
Mansard roof, 133, 134
Mansard style, 132–133
Mantel, 291
Manufactured homes, 68, 161, 185
Manufactured materials, 62–65
Manufactured paneling, 425
Manufactured siding, 265–266
Maple wood, characteristics of, 462
Marble, 61
Marketing. See also Advertisements; Purchasing; Shopping
role of lighting in, 487
Masonry siding, 266
Master bath, 548
Master planned communities, 155
Material resources, 176
Materials
calculating needed, 402–403
furniture, 460
textile, 416–417
upholstery, 469–470
Math skills, 75, 167, 186, 202, 203, 555. See also Budget; Calculation of materials; Measuring; Mortgages; Proportion; Scale
Mattresses, 470–472
Measuring
materials, 402–403
space and furniture, 398–400
Media room, 164
Mentors, 94–95
Metal furniture, 461–463

Metal roofing, 267
Metals, 63
Microwave oven, 529, 543
Mies van der Rohe, Ludwig, 139
Mission style, 136–137, 509
Mitered joint, 466
Mixing center, 530
Mobile homes, 68, 185
Mobility, 46–47
renting and, 193
Model home designer, 244–245
Models, 517–518
computer, 517–518
Modern Period (1901-Present), furniture from, 448–451, 453, 510
Modular furniture, 450, 474, 505
for home office, 564
Modular homes, 67, 68
Moldings, 298, 425. See also Trim, window
Molds, 579
Monochromatic color scheme, 358
Monticello, 129
Mood
backgrounds in setting, 412
color in setting, 352, 360
Moore, Charles, 141
Morris, William, 448
Mortgage loan officer, 202–203
Mortgages, 199, 228–231
prequalifiying for, 231
shopping for, 230
types of, 187, 229–230
Mortise and tenon joint, 466
Motion-sensitive lights, 71
Motion sensors, 490
Moving, 46–47, 52–53, 199
costs of, 197, 199
planning for, 211
Multifamily units, 161, 164, 183–184, 195
Multiple listing services, 237
Multiple roles, managing, 80, 94
Multipurpose furniture, 473, 505
Multipurpose rooms, 22, 395
Munsell color chart, 365
Musee D'Orsay (Paris), 628

N

National Association of Builders, 233
National Electrical Code, 581, 633
Native American homes, 109–110
Natural elements in landscape, 325–326

Natural fibers, 417
Natural gas, 308
Natural materials, 59, 61
   wise use of, 319–320
Needs. *See also* Universal design
   housing as universal, 17–31
   housing decision and, 175
   individual, 26–30
   physical, 22–23
   psychological, 23–26
   social, 23, 24, 35, 41–47, 55,
      157–158, 217–218
   special, 27, 100–101, 591–592
Negotiation skills, 91, 166–167
   in home buying, 187, 236, 237
Neighborhood association fees, 235
Neighborhoods, 179–180
   condition of, 180
   convenience, 180
   drawbacks, 180
   planned, 153
Neighbors, relationships with, 216
Networking in finding a job, 87
Neutral colors, 352, 355, 359, 423
New homes, 231–233
New urbanism, 155
Nigeria, housing in, 39
Nineteenth century, housing in,
   130–134, 157
Nomads, 19, 38
Nonresidential buildings
   energy conservation, 317
   impact of American with
      Disabilities Act, 49
   lighting in, 487
   scale in, 375
   skyscrapers as, 58, 60
   for special healthcare facilities,
      593
Nonresidential interiors, 396
   backgrounds for hotels, 414
   choosing accessories for, 495
   color choices in, 356
   space planning for offices, 346–
      347
Nonstructural lighting, 484, 486
Nonverbal communication, 47, 86,
   94
Nuclear family, 39
Nuclear power, 309
Nylon
   carpeting, 420
   fibers, 416

O

Oak wood, 296, 535
   characteristics of, 462
Obscure glass, 270
Occupancy sensors on lights, 490
Occupational Outlook Handbook, 82,
   103
Occupational Outlook Quarterly, 82
Occupational Health and Safety
   Administration (OSHA), 636,
   639. *See also* Safety, workplace
Offer-to-purchase contract, 238
Offices, space planning for 346–347.
   See also Home offices;
   Ergonomics
Older home, advantages of, 233
Olefin fibers, 416
Olmstead, Frederick Law, 156
On-demand water heaters, 286
One-level home, 161
One-point perspective, 514, 515
One-wall kitchen, 532
Open floor plan, 160
Open space laws, 48
Open storage, 568
Opposition, 379
Oriented strand board (OSB), 264
Origination fee, 243
Outdoor furniture, 322
Outdoor lighting, 326
Outdoor living space
   creating, 322–323
   designing, 321–322
Outdoor maintenance, 607
Outside walls, inspecting, 240
Ovens, 542–543
Overhang, 264
Overlay on drawing, 516
Owings Mills New Town, 155

P

Padding for furniture, 468–469
Painters, 281
Painting, decorative, 343, 423
Paint
   calculating amount, 402
   for exterior walls, 266
   for interior walls, 423
Panel box, 281
Paneling, 425
Panel-built homes, 67
Parapets, 136
Parenting stage, 46
Parking, 198
Parking areas, lighting for, 589

Parquet, 297
Particleboard, 461, 535
Partnership for Advanced
   Technology in Housing
   (PATH), 65
Passive solar energy, 313
Passive solar heating systems, 311,
   312
Patina, 467
Patio homes, 45
Pattern
   in fabric, 340, 471
   in rhythm, 377–378
Pecan wood, characteristics of, 462
Pedestal sink, 550
Pediment, 127
Peepholes, 588
Peninsula, 531, 533
Penn, William, 150
Perennials, 325
Performance bond, 636
Performance in appliance shopping,
   539
Performance ratings, 420
Period housing styles, 124–143
Period Revival styles, 135–137
Personality and interests, 81
Perspective drawings, 514, 515
Peru, housing in, 42
Pest-control worker, 99
PET, polyester, 420
Pet deposit, 197
Petronas towers, 60
Phyfe, Duncan, 446–447, 452
Physical needs, 22–23
Picket fence, 326
Pictorial drawings, 514, 515
Pigments, 354
Pilasters, 127
Pillows, 495
Pinch pleats, 427
Pine wood, characteristics of, 463
Pipes, 284
Pitched roof, 113
Plain weave, 418
Planned communities, 24, 156
Planned neighborhoods, 153
Planning
   bathrooms, 548–552
   financial, 226–227
   housing site, 253–256
   importance of, in good design,
      390
   kitchen, 528–538
   landscaping, 323–324
   laundry areas, 546–547

move, 211
remodeling project, 629–634
storage, 568–570
use of space, 502–508
Planning center, 530
Planning commission, 153
Plans. *See also* Drawings
home fire safety, 586–587
landscaping, 323, 324
Plants, 494
Plaster, 294
Plastic, 64
for furniture, 464
laminate flooring, 420
Pleated shades, 430
Plumbers, 281
Plumbing, 284–287
inspecting, 241
plastic in, 64
water conservation and, 318–319
Plumbing code, 284
Plywood, 461
Points, in home-buying, 230, 243
Pollution
air, 308, 578–579
indoor, 290, 293
radioactive, 309
Polyester fibers, 416, 468
Polypropylene
carpet and rugs, 420, 422
fibers, 416
Population trends, 44–45
Porcelain enamel for plumbing
fixtures, 284
Portfolio, 90
building, 35, 55, 77, 103, 121,
147, 169, 189, 205, 223, 247,
277, 303, 331, 349, 367, 385,
409, 435, 457, 479, 499, 523,
557, 575, 597, 621, 641
maintaining your, 95
Portico, 129
Postcolonial Period (1780-1840),
furniture from, 445–447
Post-modern style (Robert Venturi),
453
Post-secondary training programs,
85
Postwar modern housing styles,
140–141
Prairie style, 137
Precast concrete, 63
Precut package, 67
Prequalifiying for loan, 231
Presentation boards, 515–516
Presentations, design, 101, 145, 167,
513–518

Preservation districts, 111
Preservationist, 118–119
Prices. *See also* Costs; Resale value
of appliances, 541
of homes, 45
Primary colors, 355
Primer, 266, 423
Principal, loan, 199, 228
Priorities, housing decision and, 175
Prioritizing, 398
Privacy concerns, 40
Privately owned housing, 211
Private zone, 159
Problem solving, 32-33, 100-101,
274-275, 406-407. *See also*
Decision-making; Housing
decisions
Professional organizations, 65, 93,
101, 145, 187, 245, 365, 394,
407, 433, 476, 619, 635
Professional organizers, 572–573
Professional presentation, 518
Professionals. *See also* Careers
hiring, for remodeling, 635–636
for servicing of appliances,
616–617
Programmable heating and cooling,
69
Programmable thermostats,
289–290
Project, identifying, 393
Propane, 308
Property insurance, 242–243
Proportion, 370–373
recognizing good, 373
Psychological needs, 23–26
Public buildings, impact of
Americans with Disabilities Act
on, 49
Public housing, 48, 50, 211–212
Public relations specialist, 97
Public safety, 181
Public services, 181
Pucca, 41
Pueblo people, 20, 110
Purchase, agreeing to, 239
Purchasing. *See also* Marketing
carpeting, 420–422
interior design software, 507

Quality
in carpeting, 420
in case goods, 465
of modular furniture, 474

in upholstered furniture, 468, 469
Quarrying, 61
Queen Anne style (1720-1755), 133,
443–444, 509

R

Rabbet joint, 466
Radiant heat system, 289,
Radiation, 289, 309
in design, 378
Radon, 579
testing for, 242
Rafters, 264
Ragging, 343
Rail fence, 326
Rain leader, 273
Ramps, 29
Ranch style house, 140, 161
Ranges, shopping for, 542–543
Rapid-cook oven, 543
Rayon fibers, 416
Real estate agents, 81, 99, 186–187,
209
in home-buying process, 236–237
Real estate clerk, 99
Real estate office manager, 99
Receptacles, 283
Recovery rate, 285
Recreation, 182, 395
Recycled building materials, 64, 320
Redwood, characteristics of, 463
Reeding, 446
References, 90
checking, 636
Refinished furniture, 450
Reflective insulation, 270
Reflector bulbs, 484
Refrigerators, 69, 541–542
Regional planners, 167
Relocating. *See* Moving
Relocation specialist, 52–53
Remodeling
buying versus, 625
doing work yourself, 637
end result, 637
hiring professionals for, 635–636
low-cost updates, 553
reasons for, 624–625
Remodeling projects, 236
planning, 629–634
types of, 626–627, 629
Remodeling specialists, 82
Renaissance, 21
Renderings, 515–516
Renovation, 629

Q

Rental agreements, reviewing, 213–214
Rental housing
  accessibility of, 32–33
  assessing housing requirements, 208–209
  inspecting and comparing units, 212–213
  resident manager for, 220–221
  reviewing rental agreements, 213–214
  rights and responsibilities in, 215–216
  sharing, 217–219
Renter's insurance, 198
Renting
  advantages of, 192–193
  costs, 196–198
  disadvantages of, 193
Repetition, in design, 377
Reproductions, 441, 450
Resale value, 234–236
Research, career in, 97
Researching careers, 82, 103
Research skills, 82, 118–119, 186, 347, 364, 432, 521
Residential zoning, 151
Resident manager, 220–221
Resilient flooring, 419–420
  calculating, 402
Resort communities, 153
Resource management, 306–307
Resources, 201
  housing decisions and, 176
Restoration, 454–455, 629
Résumés, preparing, 88–89
Retail stores, lighting in, 487
Retirement housing, 27, 44–45, 153, 184
Retirement stage, 27
Retrofitting homes, 316
Revival styles, 447
Rhythm, in design, 377–379
Ridge, 264
Rights and responsibilities,
  of employees and employers, 93
  of landlords, 214–216
  of tenants, 215–216
Rigid insulation, 270
Riser, 294
Roller shades, 429, 430
Roman shade, 429, 430
Romantic Revival Period, housing in, 131–132
Roofer, 274–275

Roofs, 266–268
  drainage and, 610
  energy efficiency and, 313
  flat, 134, 267
  gable, 113, 129, 134
  gambrel, 113, 134
  hip, 126, 134
  inspecting, 240
  installing, 267–268
  mansard, 133, 134
  materials for, 266–267
  pitched, 113
  truss, 264
  vents, 293
Room air conditioner, 292, 611
Roommate
  choosing, 217–218
  getting along with, 218–219
Rosewood, 448
Row houses, 127–128, 142, 184
Rubber for flooring, 420
Rugs, 338, 402, 422
Rural Housing Service, 229
R value, 268

S

Saarinen, Eero, 453
Safety, 23. See also Security
  with electric wiring, 282–283, 300
  for fireplaces and stoves, 291
  in home environment inventory, 397
  home repair, 616
  nuclear power and, 309
  outdoor lighting and, 326
  in selecting lighting, 488
  in shopping for appliances, 539
  textile laws and, 418
  workplace, 221, 275, 300, 455, 619, 636, 639
St. Augustine (Florida), 116
Sales skills, 186–187, 237, 476–477
  of real estate agent, 186–187, 237
Saltbox house, 114
Sample board, 515–517
Sandstone, 61
Sash, window, 271
Satin weave, 418
Saudi Arabia, housing in, 38–39
Savings, 200–201, 227
Scale, in design, 373–375
Scale drawing, 398–400
Schedule, See also Timeline
  for interior construction, 281
  planning, remodeling, 634

Schools, in selecting housing location, 182
Sears Tower, 60
Seasonal Energy Efficiency Ratio (SEER), 292
Secondary colors, 355, 357
Second Empire style, 132–133
Security, 70–71. See also Safety
  deposit, 197, 216
  devices, 75, 587–589
  in special health care facilities, 593
Seller's market, 238
Septic tank, 286
  permits for, 318
Service contract, 617
Service zone, 159
Setbacks, 632
Seventeenth century furniture, 441–442
Sewage disposal, 286–287
  inspecting, 241
Shades, 357, 429, 430
  Austrian, 429
  balloon, 429
  cellular, 430
  pleated, 430
  roller, 430
  Roman, 429, 430
Shaker furniture, 447
Shakes, 267
Sheathing, 264
Shed ceilings, 294
Shed style, 141
Shelters, 22
  comfortable, 21
  natural, 18–19
  permanent, 19–20
  portable, 19
Sheraton, Thomas, 446
Shingles, 112, 267
Shopping
  for appliances, 539–541
  for furniture, 473–474
  for mortgages, 230
Showers, 549–550
  water-efficient, 319
Shutters, 429, 430
Side jambs, 271
Siding, 265–266
Signature color, 360
Silk fibers, 417
Sill plate, 262
Sill, window, 271
Single-family housing, 185
Single light, 271

Single-parent families, 40
Sinks
    bathroom, 550
    emergency repairs for, 614
    kitchen, 536
Site built, 66
Skylights, tubular, 316
Skyscrapers, 58, 60
Slab, home built on, 260–261
Slate, 61
    floors, 298
    roofs, 267
Sleep, 22
Sliding glass doors, security for, 588
Smart appliances, 69
Smart growth, 151
Smart homes, 72–73
Smoke alarms, 585
Social needs, 26–27, 35, 41, 42–47,
    55, 157, 217–218
Social zone, 159, 396
Societal trends, effect on housing,
    28, 42–47
Soffit lighting, 485
Software. See Computer-aided design
    (CAD); Computers
Softwoods, 59, 460
    characteristics of various,
    462–463
Solar heat gain coefficient (SHGC),
    316
Solar heating, 311, 312
Solar lights, 69, 326
Solar panels, 46, 111
Solar power, 309–310
Solar water heaters, 286
Solid doors, 272
Solid wood, 461
Solid wood paneling, 425
Solvent-based paint, 423
Sound, effect of backgrounds on,
    412
Space, as design element, 337–338
    arranging, 338, 503–505
    in bedrooms, 505
    in dining areas, 504
    in family rooms, 504
    in hobby areas, 505
    in home offices, 562–563
    in living rooms, 504
    making unused livable, 626
    measuring, 398–400
    planning use of, 406-407,
    502–508
    in health care facilities, 593
    storage, 567

Space planner, 346–347
Space zones, 159-160, 396-397
Space-saving laundry appliances,
    545
Spanish settlements, 116, 125
Special effects with texture, 343–344
Special healthcare facilities, design
    issues for, 593
Special needs, meeting, 27, 32–33,
    100–101, 396, 552, 591–592
Specialty stores, lighting in, 487
Spline joint, 466
Split-complementary color schemes,
    358
Split-entry home, 163
Split-level home, 141, 163
Sponging, 343
Spotlights, 326, 486
Springs
    bed, 470–472
    furniture, 468
Stainless steel, 463
    for plumbing fixtures, 284–285
Stain resistance in upholstery fabric,
    471
Stairways, 294
    lighting for, 486, 488
Stamped metal ceilings, 296
Status, housing and, 41
Steam heating system, 289
Steel, 60, 63, 65
    framing, 261
    roofs, 267
Stenciling, 423
Stick built, 66
Stock home plans, 232
Stone, 61
Stone floors, 298
Storage, 566–570. See also Closet
    arranging items in systems, 570
    choosing organizers, 569
    closed, 568
    demand for, 567
    in home environment inventory,
    397
    for home office, 563
    open, 568
    in health care facilities, 593
Storage water heater, 285
Storm doors, 272
Storm windows, 270, 313
Stoves, 290–291. See also Ranges
Strip lights, 485
Structural engineer, 632
Structural insulated panels (SIPs), 63
Structural lighting, 484, 485

Stucco, 116
Stud, 263
Studio apartment, 184
Subcontractors, 281
Subfloor, 262
Sublet, 215
Subsidized housing, 212
Substandard housing, 45–46
Suburbs, 150
Sumatra, housing in, 39
Sunlight, effective use of, 255–256
Sunroom, 165
Surge protection device (SPD), 283
Survey, of home site, 243
Surveyor's assistant, 98
Sustainability, 307
Swag, 428, 430
Swedish settlements, 115, 125
Symmetrical balance, 376
Synthetic fibers, 417
Systems, Automated home
    management, 71, 72, 73
Systems-built homes, 67, 68
Systems, security, 70–71

T

Tables, 504
    chair, 442
    gateleg, 443
    trestle, 442
Tactile texture, 342
Taj Mahal, 375
Tankless water heaters, 286
Task lighting, 483, 488
    for home office, 566
Taxes, 182, 194, 199, 235, 625
Teamwork, 92, 93, 144-145, 245, 520
Technology, 57–73
    adapting to lay of the land, 254
    automated home management
    systems, 71, 72, 73
    building materials and, 59, 61–65
    defined, 58
    framing, 262
    furniture design and, 447, 448,
    450
    in the home, 68–71, 74-75
    in home offices, 46, 565
    housing needs and, 27
    integrated systems, 72
    solar power and, 309
    tools and materials of, 65–66
    trends in, 96
Telecommuters, 46, 560, 565
Telephone line for home offices, 565

Tempered glass, 464
Templates, 399
Tenants, 192
    rights and responsibilities of,
        215–216
Tenements, 130
Tepee, 109–110
Termite guard, 260, 262
Termite inspection, 239
Tertiary colors, 355, 357
Textile Fiber Products Identification
        Act, 418
Textile laws, 418
Textiles, 415–418. *See also* Fabrics;
        Fibers
    design of, 432–433
    fibers, 417
    safety, 432
    types of, 415, 417–418
    weaves and finishes, 417–418
Textile specialists, 432–433
Texture, 342–344
    of carpet, 420–421
    effect of, on color, 345
    special effects with, 343–344
Thatch, 112
Thermal burn, 582
Thermostats, 289–290, 292
    programmable, 69, 289–290
Three-quarter bath, 548
Tieback curtains, 427, 428
Timeline of interior design project,
        519
Time management
    cleaning and, 601
    on the job, 52, 53, 92, 145, 407
    for remodeling, 634
Tint, 357
Title search, cost of, 243
Tobacco smoke, 579
Toilets, 550
    emergency repairs for, 614
    water conserving, 319
Tongue-and-groove joints, 297, 466
Tool kit, contents of, 615
Tools, construction, 65–66
Topography, 253–254
Townhouses, 127–128, 184, 235
Toxic substances, disposing of, 319
Track lighting, 486
Traditional housing styles, 109–117
Traditional influences, 142
Traffic patterns, 161, 168, 169,
        398–400, 503, 515, 554
    in environment inventory, 398
Training. *See* Education and training

Transition, 379, 439
Traverse rod, 427
Tray ceilings, 296
Tread, stair, 294
Treated lumber, 322. *See also* Wood
Trends
        housing, 28, 42–47, 164–165, 245
        societal, 28, 42–47
        in technology, 74–75, 96
Trestle table, 442
Triadic color schemes, 358
Triangle, work, 531, 532–533, 631
Trim, window, 271. *See also* Molding
Triple-paned windows, 316
Triplex, 184
Trundle bed, 442
Tubular skylights, 316
Tudor style, 136
Tufting, 421
Turning, in furniture-making, 441
Twentieth century, housing in early,
        135–137, 139–143
Twig furniture, 450
Twill weave, 418
Two-level home, 161
Two-point perspective, 514, 515

U

Unassembled furniture, 475
Underwriters Laboratories (UL), 484
Unfinished furniture, 474
Uniform Building Code (UBC), 152,
        633
Uniform Plumbing Code, 633
U.S. Capitol Building, 375
Unity, 380–381
Universal design, 28–30, 32–33, 49,
        157, 396
    and Americans with Disabilities
        Act, 49
    in bathrooms, 30, 552
    demographics and, 44
    exterior, 29
    interior, 29
    in kitchens, 30, 43, 537–538
    in laundry areas, 547
    in meeting special needs, 591–592
    usability engineer and, 32–33
Upholstered furniture
    caring for, 475
    construction, 468–469
    fabrics and materials for, 403,
        469–470
    quality in, 469, 470
Uplighting, 486

Urban homesteading, 238, 629
Urban planner, 166–167
Urban renewal, 50, 628, 629
Usability engineer, 32–33
Used furniture, 473
U-shaped kitchen, 533
Utilities, 198, 199–200
Utility services, 181
U value, 316

V

Valance, 428, 430
    lighting, 485
Values, 80, 357
    resale, 234–236
Vanity for bathrooms, 551
Vapor barriers, 268
Variance, 633
Vaulted ceilings, 294
Veneer, 266, 442, 461
Ventilation, 292–293
    for bathrooms, 551
    for kitchen, 537
Ventilators, heat recovery, 311
Venturi, Robert, 141, 453
Verbal agreement, 213–214
Versailles, Palace of, 375
Vertical blinds, 429, 431
Vestibule, 315
Veteran Affairs (VA) loan, 229
Victorian period (1840-1900), 509
    furniture in, 447–448, 453
    housing in, 132–134, 157
Village green, 150
Vinyl flooring, 420
Vinyl siding, 266
Virginia, University of, 129
Visible spectrum, 354
Vision, impaired, 592
Visual merchandiser, 382–383
Visual representations, types of,
        515–518
Visual texture, 342
Vocational counselor, 81
Volatile organic compounds (VOCs),
        266

W

Walkways, 326
    lighting for, 589
Wall arrangements, 499
Wall coverings, 422–425
    for bathrooms, 551
Wall decorations, 491–493

care of, 492–493
Wall frame, 261
Wall-hung sink, 550
Wall mirrors, 491
Wallpaper, 424
   borders, 424–425
   calculating, 402
Walls
   exterior, 263
   interior, 294
   load-bearing, 261
Wall washers, 485
Wall-washing, 486
Walnut wood, characteristics of, 462
Wants, housing decision and, 175
Warm air gravity system, 288
Warm colors, 353, 415, 510
Warp, 417, 461
Warranty, 541, 616–17
Washing machines, 544–545
   horizontal-axis, 319
Waste, 64
Water beds, 472
Water conservation, 318–319
   in landscaping, 326–327
   in showers, 319
   in toilets, 550
Water heaters, 73, 285
   emergency repairs, 613
   inspecting, 241
   preventive maintenance for, 610
Watermarks, 475
Water pipe, emergency repairs, 613
Waterproofing foundation, 259–260
Water protection, 272–273
Water-saving fixtures and appliances, 318–319
Weather blocking, 608

Weatherstripping, 316, 608
Weave, in fabric, 471
Weft, 417
Weight, apparent, 341, 377
Whole-house fan, 292, 315
Wicker furniture, 450, 461
Wigwam, 109
William and Mary style, 442–443, 452
Windbreak, 256
Windows
   coverings, 403, 427–431
   double- or triple-paned, 316
   energy-efficient, 313, 316
   frame materials, 270
   hardware, 430
   locks, 588
   parts of, 271
   seals, 608
   storm, 270, 313
   styles of, 271, 427, 435
   types of glass, 270
   weather blocking and, 608–609
Window treatments, 427–431
   calculating fabric for, 403
   factors in choosing, 427, 431
   types of, 427–430
Wind power, 310
Windsor chair, 444
Wing chair, 444
Wiring, inspecting, 240. *See also* Electrical system
Wood, 59
   distressing, 450
   as energy source, 308
   engineered products, 62
   for fireplace, 290
   for furniture, 460–461

   for outdoor space, 322
   scarcity of, 62
   types of, 462-463
Wood floors, 296–297
Wood siding, 265
Wool fibers, 417
Work centers, 43, 529–530
Work experience, 83. *See also* Apprenticeship; Internship
Work habits and attitudes. *See also under* specific careers
   in cleaning, 603–605
Workplace safety, 221, 275, 300, 455, 619, 636, 639
Work simplification
   on the job, 145
   kitchen layout and, 529-534
Work-study programs, 83
Work triangle, 531, 532–533, 631
Wright, Frank Lloyd, 137, 138, 443, 453
Written agreement, 214
Wrought iron, 462

X

Xeriscaping, 326–327

Z

Zero-lot-line homes, 153, 154
Zones, in a home, 159-160, 396-397
Zoning laws, 111, 151–152, 253, 318
   for home office, 561
   remodeling and, 627, 632–633